Microsoft® Office xp

Illustrated Second Course

Beskeen/Duffy/Friedrichsen/Reding/Wermers

APPROVED COURSEWARE

CORE
(2 of 2)

COURSE TECHNOLOGY

TM

THOMSON LEARNING

Australia • Canada • Mexico • Singapore • Spain • United Kingdom • United States

COURSE TECHNOLOGY
THOMSON LEARNING

Microsoft Office^{xp} - Illustrated Second Course
Beskeen/Duffy/Friedrichsen/Reding/Wermers

Managing Editor:
Nicole Jones Pinard

Production Editors:
Anne Valsangiacomo, Catherine DiMassa, Karen Jacot, Aimee Poirier, Jennifer Goguen

QA Manuscript Reviewers:
John Freitas, Ashlee Welz, Alex White, Harris Bierhoff, Serge Palladino, Holly Schabowski, Jeff Schwartz, Marianne Broughey

Product Manager:
Emily Heberlein

Developmental Editors:
Katherine T. Pinard, Rachel Biheller Bunin, Barbara Clemens, Pamela Conrad

Text Designer:
Joseph Lee, Black Fish Design

Associate Product Manager:
Emeline Elliott

Editorial Assistant:
Christina Kling Garrett

Composition House:
GEX Publishing Services

Contributing Author:
Marjorie Hunt

The Illustrated Series Vision

Teaching and writing about computer applications can be extremely rewarding and challenging. How do we engage students and keep their interest? How do we teach them skills that they can easily apply on the job? As we set out to write this book, our goals were to develop a textbook that:

▶ provides varied, flexible and meaningful exercises and projects to reinforce the skills

▶ serves as a reference tool

▶ makes your job as an educator easier, by providing resources above and beyond the textbook to help you teach your course

Our popular, streamlined format is based on advice from instructional designers and customers. This flexible design presents each lesson on a two-page spread, with step-by-step instructions on the left, and screen illustrations on the right. This signature style, coupled with high-caliber content, provides a comprehensive yet manageable second course in Microsoft Office XP - it is a teaching package for the instructor and a learning experience for the student.

AUTHOR ACKNOWLEDGMENTS

David Beskeen It has, once again, been a pleasure working with all the talented people at Course Technology. I would like to especially thank Katherine Pinard who has worked hard on my chapters to make them better and easier to understand. I would also like to thank my family, Karen and the three J's, for being so understanding during the long hours of writing.

Jennifer Duffy I wish to express particular thanks to Pam Conrad for her tireless help and keen editorial sensibilities. I am also deeply grateful for the support of my husband, Fred Eliot, and our daughter, Isabella, who patiently waited to be born until this book was nearly finished.

Lisa Friedrichsen The Access portion is dedicated to my students, and all who are using this book to teach and learn about Access. Thank you. Also, thank you to all of the professionals who helped me create this book.

Marjorie Hunt I would like to thank Nicole Pinard for giving me the opportunity to become an author of this book, Emily Heberlein for her masterful ability to keep us all on track, and Rachel Bunin for her thoughtful editing and constant good humor. I would also like to thank my husband Cecil, whose support, love and late night snacks gave me the strength to make (most of) my deadlines.

Elizabeth Eisner Reding Creating a book of this magnitude is a team effort: I would like to thank my husband, Michael, for putting up with my ridiculous mood swings, Emily Heberlein, the project manager, and my development editors, Barbara Clemens and Kitty Pinard, for their insightful suggestions and corrections. I would also like to thank the production and editorial staff for all their hard work that made this project a reality.

Lynn Wermers Thanks to my editor, Barbara Clemens, for her helpful suggestions and encouragement.

Thanks to all the reviewers who provided invaluable feedback and ideas to us: Diane Blaney, Anne Burchardt, Janis Cox, Stephanie Hazen, Judy Irvine, Brenda Jacobsen, Joe LaMontagne, Dr. Dominic Ligori, Glenn Rogers (Western Nevada Community College), and Rick Sheridan.

Preface

Welcome to *Microsoft Office ᵡᴾ–Illustrated Second Course.* Each lesson in this book contains elements pictured to the right.

► How is the book organized?

The book is organized into sections, by application, illustrated by the brightly colored tabs on the sides of the pages: Reviewing Office XP, Word, Excel, Access, PowerPoint, FrontPage and Publisher. Three Integration units follow the Excel, Access, and PowerPoint sections.

► What kinds of assignments are included in the book? At what level of difficulty?

The lessons use MediaLoft, a fictional chain of bookstores, as the case study. The assignments on the blue pages at the end of each unit increase in difficulty. Project files and case studies, with many international examples, provide a great variety of interesting and relevant business applications for skills. Assignments include:

• **Concepts Reviews** include multiple choice, matching, and screen identification questions.

• **Skills Reviews** provide additional hands-on, step-by-step reinforcement.

• **Independent Challenges** are case projects requiring critical thinking and application of the unit skills. The Independent Challenges increase in difficulty, with the first one in each unit being the easiest (most step-by-step with detailed instructions). Independent Challenges 2 and 3 become increasingly open-ended, requiring more independent problem solving.

• **E-Quest Independent Challenges** are case projects with a Web focus. E-Quests require the use of the World Wide Web to conduct research to complete the project.

• **Visual Workshops** show a completed file and require that the file be created without any step-by-step guidance, involving independent problem solving.

Each 2-page spread focuses on a single skill.

Concise text that introduces the basic principles in the lesson and integrates the brief case study (indicated by the paintbrush icon).

Word 2002

Illustrating a Web Page with Graphics

You can illustrate your Web pages with pictures, clip art, WordArt, text boxes, AutoShapes, and other graphic objects. When you insert a graphic on a Web page, it is inserted as an inline graphic and you must apply text wrapping to be able to move it independently of the line of text. Floating graphics align and position differently on Web pages than in Word documents, however, because browsers do not support the same graphic formatting options as Word. For example, a floating graphic with square text wrapping can only be left- or right-aligned on a Web page, whereas you can position a floating graphic anywhere in a Word document. For this reason, it's important to use Web Layout view to position graphics on a Web page. If you want to position floating graphics or text precisely on a Web page, you can create a table and then insert the text or graphics in the table cells. 🖌 Alice wants the MediaLoft logo to appear to the right of center on the Web page. She inserts the logo in the blank cell in the table, and then adjusts the table formatting to make the Web page attractive.

Steps

> **QuickTip**
> To insert a text file in a table cell, click Insert on the menu bar, click File, select the file, then click Insert.

1. Place the insertion point in the blank cell in the second column of the table, click **Insert** on the menu bar, point to **Picture**, then click **From File**
The Insert Picture dialog box opens.

2. Use the Look in list arrow to navigate to the drive and folder where your Project Files are located, click the file **mloft.jpg**, then click **Insert**
The logo is inserted in the cell as an inline graphic.

> **QuickTip**
> To resize a graphic, crop it, or change the text wrapping style, double-click the graphic to open the Format Picture dialog box.

3. Click the **logo** to select it, click the **Center button** 🔲 on the Formatting toolbar, press →, then press **[Enter]**
The graphic is centered in the table cell and a blank line is inserted under the logo.

4. Position the pointer over the border between the first and second columns until the pointer changes to ◄║►, then drag the border to approximately the 4¼" mark on the horizontal ruler
The first column widens and the second column narrows. The logo remains centered in the table cell.

5. Select **We welcome your feedback.**, click 🔲, then click in the table to deselect the text
The text is centered in the table cell, as shown in Figure G-6. In Web Layout view, text and graphics are positioned as they are in a Web browser.

6. Click the **table move handle** ⊞ to select the table, click the **Horizontal Line list arrow** on the Formatting toolbar, click the **No Border button** 🔲, deselect the table, then save your changes

TABLE G-1: Word features that are not supported by Web browsers

feature	result when viewed with a browser
Character formatting	Shadow text becomes bold, small caps become all caps, and embossed, engraved, and outline text becomes solid; character scale changes to 100%; drop caps are removed
Paragraph formatting	Indents are removed, tabs might not align correctly, and border and shading styles might change
Page layout	Margins, columns, page numbers, page borders, and headers and footers are removed; all footnotes are moved to the end of the document
Graphics	Floating graphics, including pictures, AutoShapes, text boxes, and WordArt, are left- or right-aligned
Tables	Decorative cell borders become box borders, diagonal borders are removed, vertical text is changed to horizontal

► WORD G-8 **CREATING A WEB SITE**

Hints as well as troubleshooting advice, right where you need it — next to the step itself.

Quickly accessible summaries of key terms, toolbar buttons, or keyboard alternatives connected with the lesson material. Students can refer easily to this information when working on their own projects at a later time.

Every lesson features large, full-color representations of what the screen should look like as students complete the numbered steps.

Brightly colored tabs indicate which section of the book you are in.

FIGURE G-6: Logo and text centered in the second column

Table move handle

Web Layout View button

Seattle Writers Festival 2003

October 17-19

Logo and text are centered in the table cells

FIGURE G-6: Logo and text centered in the second column

Seattle Writers Festival 2003

October 17-19

Word 2002

Adding alternate text for graphics

Graphics can take a long time to appear on a Web page, so some people turn off the display of graphics in their browsers so that they can download and view Web pages more quickly. If you don't want visitors to your Web page to see empty space where you intended that they see a graphic, you can add alternate text to appear on the Web page instead of the graphic.

Alternate text will also appear in some browsers while the graphic is loading. To add alternate text to a Web page, select the graphic, then click the Picture command on the Format menu. On the Web tab in the Format Picture dialog box, type the text you want to appear in lieu of the graphic, then click OK.

CREATING A WEB SITE WORD G-9

Clues to Use boxes provide concise information that either expands on the major lesson skill or describes an independent task that in some way relates to the major lesson skill.

The pages are numbered according to section and unit. Word indicates the section, G indicates the unit, 9 indicates the page.

▶ Is this book MOUS Certified?

When used in conjunction with *Microsoft Office XP – Illustrated Introductory*, this book covers the Core objectives for Word, Excel and Access, and the Comprehensive objectives for PowerPoint. See the inside front cover for more information on other Illustrated titles meeting MOUS certification.

The first page of each unit includes MOUS symbols to indicate which skills covered in the unit are MOUS skills. A grid in the back of the book lists all the exam objectives and cross-references them with the lessons and excercises.

▶ What distance learning options are available to accompany this book?

Visit www.course.com for more information on our Distance Learning materials to accompany Illustrated titles. Options include:

MyCourse.com

Need a quick, simple tool to help you manage your course? Try MyCourse.com, the easiest to use, most flexible syllabus and content management tool available. MyCourse.com offers you brand new content, including Topic Reviews, Extra Case Projects, and Quizzes, to accompany this book.

WebCT

Course Technology and WebCT have partnered to provide you with the highest quality online resources and Web-based tools for your class. Course Technology offers content for this book to help you create your WebCT class, such as a suggested Syllabus, Lecture Notes, Practice Test questions, and more.

Blackboard

Course Technology and Blackboard have also partnered to provide you with the highest quality online resources and Web-based tools for your class. Course Technology offers content for this book to help you create your Blackboard class, such as a suggested Syllabus, Lecture Notes, Practice Test questions, and more.

Instructor Resources

The Instructor's Resource Kit (IRK) CD is Course Technology's way of putting the resources and information needed to teach and learn effectively into your hands. All the components are available on the IRK, (pictured below), and many of the resources can be downloaded from www.course.com.

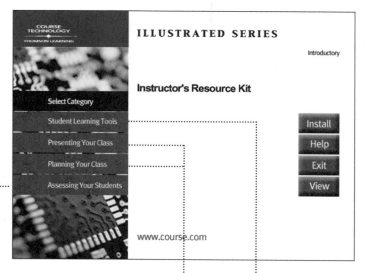

ASSESSING YOUR STUDENTS

Solution Files
Solution Files are Project Files completed with comprehensive sample answers. Use these files to evaluate your students' work. Or, distribute electronically or in hard copy so students can verify their own work.

ExamView
ExamView is a powerful testing software package that allows you to create and administer printed, computer (LAN-based), and Internet exams. ExamView includes hundreds of questions that correspond to the topics covered in this text, enabling students to generate detailed study guides that include page references for further review. The computer-based and Internet testing components allow students to take exams at their computers, and also saves you time by grading each exam automatically.

PRESENTING YOUR CLASS

Figure Files
Figure Files contain all the figures from the book in .jpg format. Use the figure files to create transparency masters or in a PowerPoint presentation.

STUDENT TOOLS

Project Files and Project Files List
To complete most of the units in this book, your students will need **Project Files**. Put them on a file server for students to copy. The Project Files are available on the Instructor's Resource Kit CD-ROM, the Review Pack, and can also be downloaded from www.course.com.

Instruct students to use the **Project Files List** at the end of the book. This list gives instructions on copying and organizing files.

PLANNING YOUR CLASS

Instructor's Manual
Available as an electronic file, the Instructor's Manual is quality-assurance tested and includes unit overviews, detailed lecture topics for each unit with teaching tips, comprehensive sample solutions to all lessons and end-of-unit material, and extra Independent Challenges. The Instructor's Manual is available on the Instructor's Resource Kit CD-ROM, or you can download it from www.course.com.

Sample Syllabus
Prepare and customize your course easily using this sample course outline (available on the Instructor's Resource Kit CD-ROM).

INTRODUCING SAM XP - Your skills-based Office assessment solution
SAM (Skills Assessment Manager) is a powerful testing and reporting tool that measures your students' proficiency in Microsoft Office XP applications through real-world, performance-based questions. (Available separately from the IRK CD).

Brief Contents

Contents

Office XP

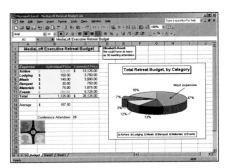

Word 2002

Contents

Illustrating Documents with Graphics WORD F-1

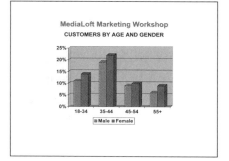

Creating a Web Site WORD G-1

Excel 2002

Contents

Managing Workbooks and Preparing Them for the Web   EXCEL F-1

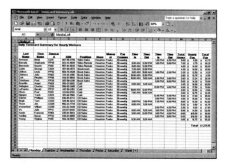

Integration

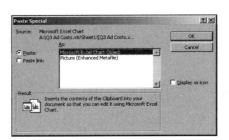

Contents

Access 2002

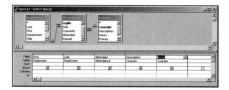

Developing Forms and Subforms

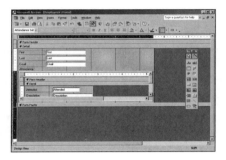

Sharing Information and Improving Reports

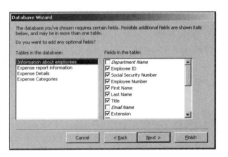

Contents

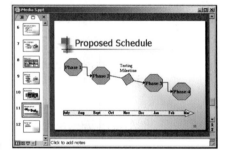
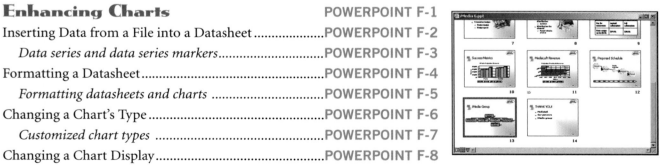

Working with Embedded and Linked Objects and Hyperlinks

Contents

FrontPage 2002

Creating a Web Site

Integration

Integrating Word, Excel, Access, and PowerPoint

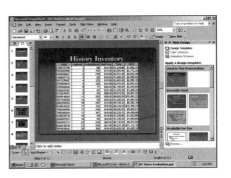

Contents

Publisher

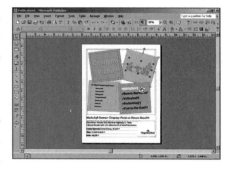

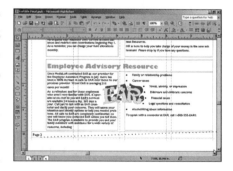

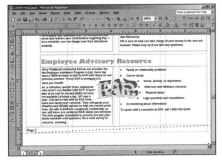

Read This Before You Begin

Software Information and Required Installation

This book was written and tested using Microsoft Office XP - Professional Edition, with a typical installation on Microsoft Windows 2000, with Internet Explorer 5.0 or higher.

Tips for Students

What are Project Files?

To complete many of the units in this book, you need to use Project Files. You use a Project File, which contains a partially completed document used in an exercise, so you don't have to type in all the information you need in the document. Your instructor will either provide you with a copy of the Project Files or ask you to make your own copy. Detailed instructions on how to organize you files, as well as a complete listing of all the files you'll need and will create, can be found in the back of the book (look for the yellow pages) in the Project Files List.

Why is my screen different from the book?

1. Your Desktop components and some dialog box options might be different if you are using an operating system other than Windows 2000

2. Depending on your computer hardware capabilities and the Windows Display settings on your computer, you may notice the following differences:
   - Your screen may look larger or smaller because of your screen resolution (the height and width of your screen)
   - The colors of the title bar in your screen may be a solid blue, and the cells in Excel may appear different from the purple and gray because of your color settings

3. Depending on your Office settings, your toolbars may display on a single row and your menus may display with a shortened list of frequently used commands. Office menus and toolbars can modify themselves to your working style by displaying only the most frequently used buttons and menu commands, as shown here:

Toolbars on one row

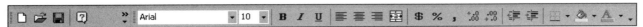

To view buttons not currently displayed, click a Toolbar Options button at the end of either the Standard or Formatting toolbar. To view the full list of menu commands, click the double arrow at the bottom of the menu.

In order to have your toolbars display on two rows, showing all buttons, and to have the full menus display, you must turn off the personalized menus and toolbars feature. Click Tools on the menu bar, click Customize, select the show Standard and Formatting toolbars on two rows and Always show full menus check boxes on the Options tab, then click Close. This book assumes you are displaying toolbars on two rows and full menus.

Toolbars on two rows

Read This Before You Begin

Important Information for Access Units if you are using floppy disks

Compact on Close?

If you are storing your Access databases on floppy disks, you should NOT use the Compact on Close option (available from the Tools menu). While the Compact on Close feature works well if your database is stored on your hard drive or on another large storage device, it can cause problems if your database is stored on a floppy when the size of your database is greater than the available free space on the floppy. Here's why: When you close a database with the Compact on Close feature turned on, the process creates a temporary file that is just as large as the original database file. In a successful compact process, this temporary file is deleted after the compact procedure is completed. But if there is not enough available space on your floppy to create this temporary file, the compact process never finishes, which means that your original database is never closed properly. And if you do not close an Access database properly before attempting to use it again, you can easily corrupt it beyond repair. *Therefore, if you use floppies to complete these exercises, please follow the guidelines on how to organize your databases on floppies in the **Project Files List** so that you do not run out of room on a floppy. Also, please **do not use the Compact on Close feature for databases stored on floppies**.*

Closing a Database Properly

It is extremely important to close your databases properly before copying, moving, e-mailing the database file, or before ejecting the Project Files floppy disk from the disk drive. Access database files are inherently multi-user, which means that multiple people can work on the same database file at the same time. To accomplish this capability, Access creates temporary files to keep track of which record you are working on while the database is open. These temporary files must be closed properly before you attempt to copy, move, or e-mail the database. They must also be closed before you eject a floppy that contains the database. If these temporary files do not get closed properly, the database can easily be corrupted beyond repair. Fortunately, Access closes these temporary files automatically when you close the Access application window. So to be sure that you have properly closed a database that is stored on a floppy, *close not only the database window, but also **close the Access application** window before copying, moving, or e-mailing a database file, as well as before ejecting a floppy that stores the database.*

2000 vs. 2002 File Format

New databases created in Access 2002 default to an Access 2000 file format. That's why "Access 2000 file format" is shown in the database window title bar for the figures in this book. This also means that Access databases now support seamless backward compatibility with the prior version of Access like other products in the Microsoft Office suite such as Word and Excel.

But while the Project Files for this book could be opened and used in Access 2000, the figures in this book present the Access 2002 application, use the Access 2002 menus and toolbars, and highlight the new features of Access 2002 including new task panes, new quick keystrokes, PivotTables, PivotCharts, and improved dynamic Web pages.

Reviewing

Microsoft Office XP

Objectives

- ► **Review Office XP programs**
- ► **Review Word: Task Reference**
- ► **Use Word: Visual Workshop**
- ► **Review Excel: Task Reference**
- ► **Use Excel: Visual Workshop**
- ► **Review Access: Task Reference**
- ► **Use Access: Visual Workshop**
- ► **Review PowerPoint: Task Reference**
- ► **Use PowerPoint: Visual Workshop**

As you know from your experience with Microsoft Office XP, the programs help you complete tasks quickly and work more efficiently. MediaLoft, a chain of café bookstores, uses Office XP programs every day in memos, worksheets, presentations, databases, publications, Web pages, and artwork. Elizabeth Reed, a MediaLoft vice president, will use Office programs to plan and prepare for an executive retreat for MediaLoft managers.

Reviewing Office XP Programs

The programs included in Microsoft Office XP provide the tools you need to complete common business tasks. Each program provides tools to meet specific needs. As you have learned, Office XP programs provide you with common tools such as task panes and the Office Clipboard to provide you with rapid access to the information you need. As you use Office, you identify which programs have the best tools for each job at hand, and how you can use them together to produce effective documents as efficiently as possible. ✎ Elizabeth Reed, a MediaLoft vice president, is planning a retreat for MediaLoft store managers. She has asked you to help her create the letter, workbook, database, and presentation she will need; the information listed on this page provides an overview of each document. The Visual Workshops that follow contain specific instructions. As you work, you can review the features you will need in the Task Reference for each program.

► Edit and format a multi-page Word document

Elizabeth wants to send a multi-page letter to managers to prepare them for the retreat. Because the document will have more than one page, you will use the header and footer feature, as well as section and column breaks. To add visual interest, you will add formatting attributes, as well as a table and a graphic, to help illustrate important points.

► Create a spreadsheet that contains sales calculations, projections, and a chart

Elizabeth wants you to use Excel tools to create a budget for the retreat. You will use the powerful Excel calculation features and include an Excel chart to display her data in an informative and engaging way.

► Query an existing database for hotel information

Elizabeth gives you an Access database containing specific information about hotels in the area. You'll use forms, queries, and reports to determine the best hotel for the retreat.

► Create a presentation for group meetings

Elizabeth wants you to create an impressive PowerPoint presentation that she will use in her main address to the managers. It will incorporate text, graphics, timing, and transitions that will both communicate information clearly and provide visual interest.

► Integrate Office documents

As you complete the Independent Challenges at the end of this unit, you will practice not only individual program skills, but also the powerful Office integration features. Integration ensures that you only have to create information once; you can then use it in documents created in other programs to save time.

Reviewing Word: Task Reference

This task reference lists the most common tasks covered in units A through D of Microsoft Word Illustrated. It is designed as a refresher to help you find the button, dialog box, or tab you can use to perform each task.

task	method
Getting Started with Word 2002	
AutoCorrect change, undo an	Click [icon], click Undo
Back, go	Click [icon]
Button, select	Click with [pointer] pointer
Button not visible, display	Click [icon]
Characters to the left, delete	Click I pointer after character, press [Backspace]
Characters to the right, delete	Click I pointer before character, press [Delete]
Document, close	Click File, Close
Document, create	Click [icon] or click Blank Document hyperlink in New Document task pane
Document, save	Click [icon]
Document, save under different name	Click File, Save As
Document, preview	Click [icon]
Document, print	Click [icon]
Folder, create	Click [icon] in Open or Save As dialog box
Folder, delete	Click [icon] in Open or Save As dialog box
Help, search	Click [icon], type question, click Search or click Type a question for help box on menu bar, type question, press [Enter]
Help, show the Office Assistant for	Click Help, Show the Office Assistant
Help questions, display list of recently asked	Click "Type a question for help" list arrow on menu bar
Hyperlink, open	Click with [pointer] pointer
Level, go up one in dialog box	Click [icon]
Line, select	Click with [pointer] pointer
New Document task pane, display	Click File, New

task	method
Normal View, change to	Click [icon] in status bar
Office Assistant, change	Right-click Office Assistant, click Assistant, Choose Assistant, click Next on Gallery tab
Office Assistant, hide	Click Help, click Hide the Office Assistant
Office Assistant, show	Click Help, show the Office Assistant
Outline View, change to	Click [icon] in status bar
Preview, close	Click [Close] on Preview toolbar
Preview, magnify	Click document preview with [icon] pointer
Preview, reduce	Click document preview with [icon] pointer
Print Layout View, change to	Click [icon] in status bar
Program, exit	Click File, Exit
Program, start	Click [Start], point to Programs, click Microsoft Word
Save location, change	In Save As dialog box, click Save in list arrow or Up One Level button [icon] to go up in folder structure; double-click folder to go down in folder structure
Smart Tag, view	Position pointer over [icon]
Toolbars, display in 1 row	Click Tools, Customize, Options tab, deselect Show Standard and Formatting toolbars on two rows
Views, change	Click [icon] in Save As dialog box
Web Layout View, change to	Click [icon] in status bar
Web, search	Click [icon] in Open or Save As dialog box
Word, start program	Click [Start], point to Programs, click Microsoft Word
Zoom, change	Click [100%]
Zoom tool, use in Print Preview	Move [icon] or [icon] pointer over document, click area

Word Task Reference (continued)

task	method
Editing Documents	
Copied selection, embed	Click Edit, Paste Special
Document, create from template	Click General Templates hyperlink in New Documents task pane
Document, open from task pane	Click More Documents hyperlink in New Documents task pane
Document, open	Click
Document, save as	Click File, Save As
Document, select all text in	Press [Ctrl][A]
Entry, undo	Click
Hyperlink, paste as	Click Edit, Paste as Hyperlink
Last action, repeat	Press [F4]
Line, select	Click ⬏ pointer to the left of the line
Nonconsecutive text blocks, select	Hold [Ctrl] while selecting each block
Office Clipboard, open	Click Edit, Office Clipboard
Paragraph, select	Triple-click paragraph
Selection, copy	Click
Selection, cut	Click
Selection, paste	Click
Sentence, select	Press [Ctrl] while clicking sentence
Special characters, Show/Hide	Click ¶
Spelling, check	Click, click Change or Ignore to accept or reject suggestions
Text, delete	Select text, press [Delete]
Text, find	Click Edit, Find
Text, replace	Click Edit, Replace
Text, select	Drag with I pointer
Text, select all in document	[Ctrl][A]
Text block, select	Click selection beginning, hold [Shift], click end of selection

task	method
Typing over characters, turn on/off	Double-click OVR in status bar (with Track Changes)
Word, select	Double-click word
Formatting Text and Paragraphs	
Bold attribute, apply	Select text, click **B**
Border, add	Select text, click
Bullets, add or remove	Select text, click
Bullet style, change	Select text, right-click list, click Bullets and Numbering
Case, change	Select text, click Format, Change Case
Character spacing, change	Select text, click Format, Font, click Character Spacing tab
First Line Indent, change	Drag ▽ on ruler
Font, change	Select text, click Arial, select font
Font color, change	Select text, click
Font size, change	Select text, click 10
Format, paint	Click in source text, click, click in target text
Formats, clear	Click Edit, Clear, Formats
Formatting task pane, show	Click Format, Reveal Formatting
Hanging indent, change	Drag △ on ruler
Indent, decrease	Click in text, click
Indent, increase	Click in text, click
Italics, apply	Select text, click *I*
Left indent, change	Click in text, drag on ruler
Line spacing, change	Select text, click
Numbering, add or remove	Click in or select text, click
Numbering style, change	Select list, right-click list, click Bullets and Numbering
Outdent, create	Click in text, drag ▽ on ruler

Word Task Reference (continued)

task	method	task	method
Outline list, create	Click Format, Bullets and Numbering, click Outlined Numbered tab	**Formatting Documents**	
Right indent, change	Click in text, drag △ on the right side of ruler	**Clip art, add**	Click Insert, Picture, Clip Art; enter search text, click desired clip
Shading, add	Click Format, Borders and Shading, click Shading tab	**Clip art, wrap text around**	Double-click image, click Layout tab
		Column break, create	Click Insert, Break
Spacing above and below paragraphs, change	Click paragraph, click Format, Paragraph, click Indents and Spacing tab	**Columns, create**	Click [icon]
		Date, insert in header/footer	Click [icon]
Style, apply character or paragraph	Select text, select style in Styles and Formatting task pane list	**Font color, change**	Select text, click [icon], click color
Styles and Formatting task pane, open	Click [icon]	**Header and Footer, insert**	Click View, Header and Footer, click [icon] to switch between header and footer
Tab, insert center	Click in paragraph, click left side of ruler to display [icon], click in ruler at tab location	**Header/Footer setup, modify**	Click [icon] on Header and Footer toolbar
Tab, insert decimal	Click in paragraph, click left side of ruler to display [icon], click in ruler at tab location	**Header/Footer, switch between**	Click [icon]
		Margins, set	Click File, Page Setup, Margins tab
Tab, insert left	Click in paragraph, click left side of ruler to display [icon], click in ruler at tab location	**Mirrored margins, create**	Click File, Page Setup, Margins tab, click Multiple pages list arrow
		Multiple pages, preview	Click [icon] on Preview toolbar
Tab, insert right	Click in paragraph, click left side of ruler to display [icon], click in ruler at tab location	**Number of pages, insert in header/footer**	Click [icon]
Tab leader, insert	Click in text, click Format, Tabs	**Page break, create**	Press [Ctrl][Enter]
Tab stops, display a paragraph's	Click in paragraph, see horizontal ruler	**Page number, insert in header/footer**	Click [icon]
Table, create	Click [icon]	**Page numbers, add**	Click Insert, Page Numbers
Text, align	Click in or select text, click [icon], [icon], [icon]	**Paper orientation, change**	Click File, Page Setup, click Margins tab
Text, center	Click in paragraph, click [icon]	**Picture file, add**	Click Insert, Picture, From File
Text, highlight	Click [icon], select color, select text	**Section break, create**	Click Insert, Break
Text, justify	Click in paragraph, click [icon]	**Symbol, insert**	Click Insert, Symbol
Underline attribute, apply	Select text, click [icon]	**Template, create document based on**	Click File, New, click General Templates hyperlink
		Time, insert in header/footer	Click [icon]
		Vertical alignment, control	Click in text, click File, Page Setup, click Layout tab

Using Word: Visual Workshop

Open the file Office B-1 from the drive and folder where your Project Files are stored, then save it as MediaLoft Update Memo. Modify the document using Figure B-1 as a guide. Replace the text "Elizabeth Reed" with your own name, save the document, then print it. As you modify the document, consider the following tasks:

- Creating bulleted text
- Adjusting line spacing and paragraph order
- Checking the spelling
- Adding formatting attributes (*Hint:* The Summary box uses a Gray-20% shading)
- Adding a graphic image (*Hint:* Search on the keyword "international.") If you don't have access to the graphic shown, use another of your choice.
- Using sections and columns
- Using Find and Replace (*Hint:* Replace "bookstores" with "stores")

- Creating a table (Select the table, then apply the Table Elegant AutoFormat style, using the AutoFormat command on the Table menu. Resize the columns using the AutoFit and AutoFit to Contents commands on the Table menu. Then choose the Table Properties command on the Table menu, click the Table tab, and center the table.)
- Adding a header and page number (*Hint:* Use a bottom border under the header, which is on the Section 1 header; there is no header or footer in the First Page Header.)

FIGURE B-1: **Word document with artwork and formatting**

MediaLoft

Memo

To:	MediaLoft Employees
From:	Elizabeth Reed, Vice President
CC:	Leilani Ho, President
Date:	6/20/2003
Re:	Progress Report for Author Retreat

Summary

The success MediaLoft is experiencing is due to your hard work. We would like to take this time to give you a progress report, and discuss some upcoming plans.

Expansion Plans

There are several new bookstores being planned (although this is still top secret) in the United States, and we plan on expanding in Europe, Canada, and Asia. Possible new locations include the following cities:

- Paris, France
- Toronto, Canada
- Beijing, China

Think about these potential locations. Are there other international locations we should consider? How should we implement such an expansion? These are topics we will be discussing at the retreat.

Employee Memo   *5/21/2003*   *Page 2*

Current Profile of Our Bookstores

MediaLoft bookstores are located in the following cities and states:

City	State	SQUARE FEET	EMPLOYEES
Boston	Massachusetts	60,000	22
Chicago	Illinois	150,000	38
Houston	Texas	75,000	23
Kansas City	Kansas	130,000	34
New York	New York	90,000	26
San Diego	California	50,000	19
San Francisco	California	80,000	34
Seattle	Washington	65,000	32

New Advertising Campaigns

As you may already know, MediaLoft has retained the award-winning public relations firm **Top Shelf**. They will provide new advertising pieces that will be distributed in our bookstores, as well as being used in print and media ads. While MediaLoft has used radio advertising, we have little experience in television media. **Top Shelf** will be guiding us through that process, and plans to saturate the market in local stations. Conservative projections estimate a 50% profit increase.

Your Contribution

We cannot underestimate your contribution. But, you may be wondering if this expansion will affect you. This expansion should not impact the everyday operations of MediaLoft, and we are counting on your feedback on the advertising pieces we see from Top Shelf. **Top Shelf** has promised to involve any employees who are interested in commenting on their progress. Periodically, you may be approached by **Top Shelf** employees who want your opinion on their work. We hope you will feel comfortable taking the time to speak with them, but please know that your involvement is not mandatory. We are counting on you to share your knowledge of our customers and our bookstores.

2

Reviewing Excel: Task Reference

This task reference lists the most common tasks covered in units A through D of Microsoft Excel Illustrated. It is designed as a refresher to help you find the button, dialog box, or tab you can use to perform each task.

task	method	task	method
Getting Started with Excel 2002		**Toolbars, display in 1 row**	Click Tools, Customize, Options tab, deselect Show Standard and Formatting toolbars on two rows
Button not visible, display	Click		
Cell, delete contents	Click Edit, Clear Contents, or press [Delete]	**Value, enter**	Click cell, type value, click ✓ or press [Enter]
Cell, select	Click the cell, or use [↑], [↓], [←], [→], or click Edit, Go To	**Window, close**	Click ✕
		Window, maximize	Click ▢
Character, delete to the left	Press [Backspace]	**Window, minimize**	Click ▬
Character, delete to the right	Press [Delete]	**Workbook, close**	Click File, Close
Entry, accept	Click ✓	**Workbook, create**	Click 🗋 or click Blank Workbook in the New Workbook task pane
Entry, cancel	Click ✕		
Folder, create	Click 📁	**Workbook, open**	Click 📂 or click workbook name or More Workbooks in the New Workbook task pane
Help, search	Click ⍰, type question, click Search or click Type a question for help box on menu bar, type question, press [Enter]		
		Workbook, open using template	Click General Templates hyperlink in the New Workbook task pane
Help, show the Office Assistant for	Click Help, Show Office Assistant	**Workbook, save**	Click 💾
Help questions, display list of recently asked	Click "Type a question for help" list arrow in menu bar	**Workbook, save with a new name**	Click File, Save As
Label, enter number as	Type apostrophe (') before number	**Worksheet, copy**	Press [Ctrl], drag sheet tab
Labels, enter	Make cell active, type label, click ✓ or press [Enter]	**Worksheet, delete**	Click sheet tab, click Edit, Delete Sheet, or right click Sheet tab, click Delete
Menu, open	Click menu name in the menu bar	**Worksheet, display next screen of**	Press [Page Up] or [Page Down]
Office Assistant, change	Right-click Office Assistant, click Choose Assistant, click Next on Gallery tab	**Worksheet, insert**	Display sheet you want to follow new sheet, click Insert, Worksheet
Office Assistant, hide	Click Help, Hide the Office Assistant	**Worksheet, move**	Drag sheet tab to new location, release mouse button when triangle pointer is correctly positioned
Preview, magnify	Click preview with 🔍 pointer		
Program, exit	Click File, Exit	**Worksheet, preview**	Click 🔍
Program, start	Click Start, point to Programs, click Microsoft Excel	**Worksheet, print using existing settings**	Click 🖨
Sheet tab, change color	Right-click sheet tab, click Tab Color	**Worksheet, rename**	Right-click sheet tab, click Rename, type a new name

Excel Task Reference (continued)

task	method
Building and Editing Worksheets	
Cells, delete	Select cells, click Edit, Delete
Cells, insert	Click Insert, Cells
Cell entry, copy	Click [icon]
Cell entry, cut	Click [icon]
Cell entry, paste	Click [icon]
Cell reference, make absolute	Highlight or click in reference in formula bar, press [F4]
Characters to the left, delete	Press [Backspace]
Characters to the right, delete	Press [Delete]
Clipboard, open	Click Edit, Office Clipboard
Clipboard entry, paste	Click item in Clipboard task pane
Drag-and-drop, copy using	Select cell(s), press and hold [Ctrl], drag with [pointer] pointer
Drag-and-drop, move using	Select cell(s), drag [pointer] pointer
Edit cell entry	Double-click cell, or press [F2]
Entry, confirm	Click [icon]
Entry, copy to right	Select entry or formula and range to right, click Edit, Fill, Right
Entry, undo	Click [icon]
Fill sequence, complete	Click Edit, point to Fill, click Series
Formula, enter	Press =, click value, press +, -, *, or /, click another value, click [icon]
Function, enter	Click [icon] f_x
Moving border, turn off	Press [Esc]
Named range, go to	Click Name box arrow, click range name
Range, name	Select range, click Name box, type name, press [Enter]
Series, fill	Select first two series cells, drag fill handle
Sum, create	Click [icon] Σ

task	method
Formatting a Worksheet	
AutoFormat, apply	Click Format, AutoFormat
Bold attribute, apply	Click **B**
Border, add	Click [icon]
Cell A1, go to	Press [Ctrl][Home]
Clip Art, insert	Click Insert, point to Picture, click Clip Art
Color, fill a cell with	Click [icon]
Column, delete	Click column heading, click Edit, Delete
Column, insert	Right-click cell in column, click Insert, select Entire column option, click OK
Column width, size to widest entry	Double-click [icon] pointer between columns
Comma format, apply	Click [icon]
Comment, add	Click Insert, Comment
Comment, edit	Click cell with comment, click Insert, Edit Comment
Comments, view	Click View, Comments
Conditional format, create	Click Format, Conditional Formatting
Conditional format, delete	Click Format, Conditional Formatting, Delete
Currency format, apply	Click [icon] $
Date format, apply	Click Format, Cells, click Number tab, click Date, select type, click OK
Decimals, decrease	Click [icon]
Decimals, increase	Click [icon]
Font, change	Click [Arial]
Font size, change	Click [10]
Font color, change	Click [icon]
Format, copy	Click [icon]
Indent, decrease	Click [icon]

Excel Task Reference (continued)

task	method
Indent, increase	Click [icon]
Italics, apply	Click *I*
Merge and Center, apply	Click [icon]
Picture, insert	Click Insert, point to Picture, click Clip Art, From File, or From Scanner or Camera
Picture, insert in header or footer	Click [icon]
Range, select contiguous	Click top-left cell, press and hold [Shift], click bottom-right cell
Row, delete	Click row heading, click Edit, Delete
Row, insert	Right-click row heading, click Insert, Cells
Row height, size to tallest entry	Double-click bottom of row heading with ┿ pointer
Spelling, check	Click [icon]
Text, center	Click [icon]
Underline, apply	Click [U]
Value to label, change	Type ' before value
Workbook, send electronically	Click [icon]

task	method
Working with Charts	
3-D chart, rotate	Click axes, drag handles
Arrow, add	Click [icon]
Chart, create	Click [icon]
Chart, delete	Click chart, press [Delete]
Chart, deselect	Click outside chart
Chart, move	Drag chart with ↔ pointer
Chart, resize	Select chart, drag corner with ↕, ↔, ⬃, or ⬈ pointer
Chart, preview	Click [icon]
Chart, print	Click [icon]
Chart, select	Click chart
Chart title, add	Select chart, click Chart, Chart Options, Titles tab
Chart type, change	Click [icon] on Chart toolbar
Data series color, edit	Double-click data series, select color on Patterns tab, click OK
Drawing toolbar, open	Click [icon]
Gridlines, add	Select chart, click Chart, Chart Options, click Gridlines tab
Paper orientation, change	Click [icon], Setup, Page tab, select orientation option
Pie slice, explode	Click pie chart, click slice, drag slice from pie

Using Excel: Visual Workshop

Open the workbook Office B-2 from the drive and folder where your Project Files are stored, then save it as **MediaLoft Retreat Budget**. Use your Excel skills to make the Project File look like Figure B-2. Enter your name in cell A30, preview the worksheet, then change the page orientation to landscape. Save and print your results. As you modify the worksheet, consider the need for the following:

- Adding, editing, and moving text and values; entering formulas
- Formatting the title and AutoFormatting the data
- Using Conditional Formatting (for prices over $200)
- Clip art (search on "meeting"). If you cannot find this clip, select another one.
- Naming and coloring the sheet tab

- Formatting chart data points (*Hint:* Change the label display to percentages by clicking Chart on the menu bar, clicking Chart Options, clicking the Data Labels tab, then clicking the Percentage check box.)
- Moving and resizing the chart legend (*Hint:* Change the legend font size to 8 point)

FIGURE B-2: Excel data and chart

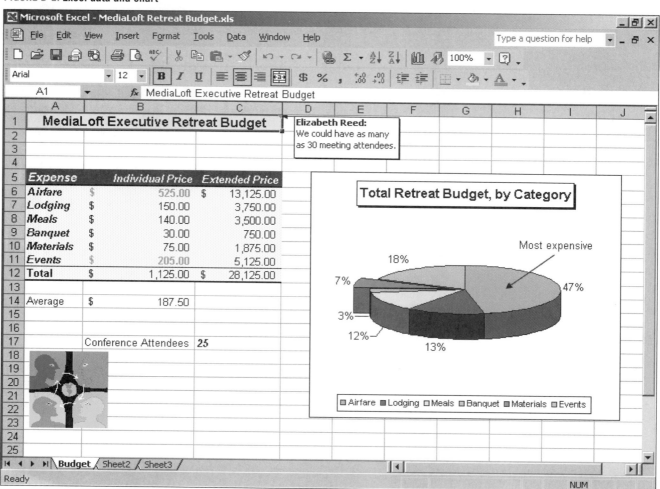

Reviewing Access: Task Reference

This task reference lists the most common tasks covered in units A through D of Microsoft Access Illustrated. It is designed as a refresher to help you find the button, dialog box, or tab you can use to perform each task.

task	method	task	method
Getting Started with Access 2002		**Field, move to current in previous record**	Press [↑]
Action, redo	Click Edit, Redo (Last Command)	**Field, move to first in current record**	Press [Home]
Action, undo	Click [↶]	**Field, move to first in first record**	Press [Ctrl][Home]
Changes to current field, undo	Press [Esc]	**Field, move to last in current record**	Press [End]
Changes to current record, undo	Press [Esc]	**Field, move to last in last record**	Press [Ctrl][End]
Character, delete to the left	Press [Backspace]	**Field, move to previous in current record**	Press [Shift][Tab]
Character, delete to the right	Press [Delete]	**Field, move to next**	Press [Tab] or [Enter]
Columns, move	Click column to be moved, then drag to new location	**Help, search**	Click [?], type question, click Search or click Ask a Question box on menu bar, type question, press [Enter]
Column, resize	Drag or double-click column header line with ↔ pointer		
Current date, insert	Press [Ctrl][;]	**Help, show the Office Assistant for**	Click Help, Show the Office Assistant
Database, close	Click File, Close		
Database, compact	Click Tools, Options, click the General Tab	**Help questions, display list of recently asked**	Click "Type a question for help" list arrow in menu bar
Database, open	Click [📂]	**Help Window, display tabs in**	Click [◀] on Help toolbar
Database, save	Click [💾]	**Menu, open**	Click menu name in the menu bar
Database object, print	Click [🖨]	**Modes, switch between**	Press [F2]
Datasheet, preview	Click [🔍]	**Navigation mode, return to**	Press [Tab] or [Enter]
Datasheet, print on close	Click [🖨]	**Object, create**	Click [▦ ▾] in Database window
Field, display	Click Format, Unhide Columns	**Office Assistant, hide**	Click Help, Hide the Office Assistant
Field, hide	Click Format, Hide Columns	**Office Assistant, change**	Right-click Office Assistant, click Choose Assistant
Field, move to current in first record	Press [Ctrl][↑]		
Field, move to current in last record	Press [Ctrl][↓]	**Pages, view two or multiple in preview**	Click [▤▤] or [▦▦]
Field, move to current in next record	Press [↓]	**Paper orientation, change**	Click File, Page Setup, Page tab
		Preview, magnify	Click Preview with [🔍] pointer

Office XP

Access Task Reference (continued)

task	method	task	method
Print Preview, close	Click Close	**First page, display in print preview**	Click
Print Preview, view	Click	**Font, change**	Click Format, Font, click font from list
Program, exit	Click File, Exit	**Formatting toolbar, display in datasheet**	Click View, Toolbars, Formatting (Datasheet)
Program, start	Click Start, point to Programs, click Microsoft Access	**Grid, clear**	Click on the Query toolbar
Record, create new	Click	**Gridlines, change color in datasheet**	Click
Record, delete	Click	**Gridlines, change display of**	Click
Record, find	Click	**Last page, display in print preview**	Click
Record, go to	Press [F5], type record number, press [Enter]	**Line/Border color, change**	Click
Spelling, check	Press [F7] or click	**Next page, display in print preview**	Click
Table, open	In Database window, click Tables, click table name, click	**Previous page, display in print preview**	Click
Toolbars, customize	Click Tools, Customize, Options tab	**Query, create**	Double-click Create query by using wizard in Database window
Value from previous record's field, insert	Press [Ctrl][']	**Records, sort ascending**	Click
Window, close	Click	**Records, sort descending**	Click
Window, maximize	Click	**Rows, delete**	In Table Design toolbar, click
Window, minimize	Click	**Rows, insert**	Click
Using Tables and Queries		**Single field, select**	Click >
Create table using Wizard	Click Tools, Options, click View tab, click New object shortcuts	**Table, create**	Double-click Create table by using wizard in Database window
Database, create	Click in Database window toolbar or Blank Database hyperlink in New section of task pane	**Task pane, display**	Click File, New
		Text, find	Click
Datasheet, view	Click	**Using Forms**	
Design, view	Click	**AutoForm, create form using**	Click on Database toolbar
Fields, select All	Click >>	**Control, resize**	Drag pointer when over handle
Filter, apply/remove	Click	**Controls, selecting multiple**	Click control, press [Shift], click additional controls, or drag selection box around controls
Filter, remove	Click		
Filter by form	Click		
Filter by selection	Click		

Access Task Reference (continued)

task	method	task	method
Fields, select all in Form Wizard	Click [>>]	**Using Reports**	
		Bold attribute, apply	Click [B]
Field List, toggle on/off	Click [▤] on Design View toolbar	**Controls, align**	Click Format, Align
Font color, change	Click [A ▾]	**Field, select single for report**	Click [>]
Font size, change	Click [10 ▾]	**Fields, select all for report**	Click [>>]
Form, create	Click [▦] in Database window	**Fill color, change**	Click [🪣 ▾]
Image, insert	Click [🖼] on Form Design toolbar	**First page, go to**	Click [◀]
Label, align text in	Click label, click [≣], [≣], or [≣]	**Fit to page, magnify**	Click [▢]
Label, modify	Click label, click [📄] on Form Design toolbar, click Format tab	**Italics, apply**	Click [I]
		Label, create	Click [Aa]
Properties, display	Select object, click [📄]	**Last page, go to**	Click [▶l]
Record, enter new	Click [▶*]	**Margins, changing**	Click File, Page Setup
Record, move to next in Form View	Click [▶]	**Next page, go to**	Click [▶]
Record, move to previous in Form View	Click [◀]	**Previous page, go to**	Click [◀]
Record, move to first in Form View	Click [l◀]	**Sorting or Grouping, create**	Click [▤]
Record, move to last in Form View	Click [▶l]	**Special effect, apply**	Click [▭ ▾]
Selection, filter by	Click [▽]	**Text, align left**	Click [≣]
Tab order, modify	Click [▨], click View, Tab Order	**Text, align right**	Click [≣]
Text box, create	Click [abl]	**Text, center**	Click [≣]
Toolbox toolbar, toggle on/off	Click [⚒] on Form Design toolbar	**Toolbox, display**	Click [⚒]

Using Access: Visual Workshop

Open the Access database Office B-3 from the drive and folder where your Project Files are stored. (*Hint:* Since there is no Save As feature in Access, you may want to make a copy of Office B-3.mdb prior to starting this project.)

- Modify the **Hotels table** using Figure B-3 and Figure B-4 as guides.
- Create the **Hotel Short List Query** using the field order shown in Figure B-5. Display all the fields in the Hotel table for accommodations having in-room data ports and more than two conference rooms. Sort the query in descending order by Zip Code, then ascending order by Hotel Name. Use the Hotel Short List Query as the data source. The results of your query should look like Figure B-5.
- Replace the hotel name for the Hilton Garden record with your own name.
- Use the Form Wizard and the Hotel Short List Query to create a columnar form that contains all the fields. Accept the default name, use the Expedition style, arrange the fields in a pleasing manner, then adjust the tab order.
- Use the Report Wizard and the Hotel Short List Query to create a columnar report that contains all the

fields. Group the report by the number of conference rooms, sorting the hotels in descending order by Hotel Name, using the Stepped layout and the Corporate style. Accept the default name, then modify the design so the full field names are displayed. Change the formatting of the Hotel Name label control to red. Change the alignment of the Zip Code field so it is centered under its label control. Add an unbound expression that calculates the average room rate for each group. Make sure the expression is italicized, formatted as currency, and aligned beneath the Room Rate data. Print this report.

- Create and print labels for participants' suitcases using the Hotel Short List Query, showing each hotel name, and the zip code. Use the label with the Avery product number C2242, use the default font and font size, place the Hotel Name field on the first line and the Zip Code field on the second line, use the default name, and sort by Hotel Name.

FIGURE B-3: Access table in Design View

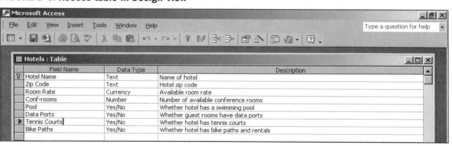

FIGURE B-4: Access table datasheet

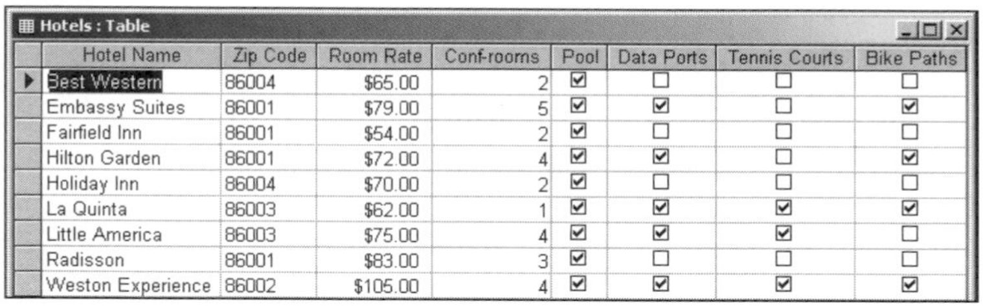

Hotel Name	Zip Code	Room Rate	Conf-rooms	Pool	Data Ports	Tennis Courts	Bike Paths
Best Western	86004	$65.00	2	☑	☐	☐	☐
Embassy Suites	86001	$79.00	5	☑	☑	☐	☑
Fairfield Inn	86001	$54.00	2	☑	☐	☐	☐
Hilton Garden	86001	$72.00	4	☑	☑	☐	☑
Holiday Inn	86004	$70.00	2	☑	☐	☐	☐
La Quinta	86003	$62.00	1	☑	☑	☑	☑
Little America	86003	$75.00	4	☑	☑	☑	☐
Radisson	86001	$83.00	3	☑	☐	☐	☐
Weston Experience	86002	$105.00	4	☑	☑	☑	☑

FIGURE B-5: Access query datasheet

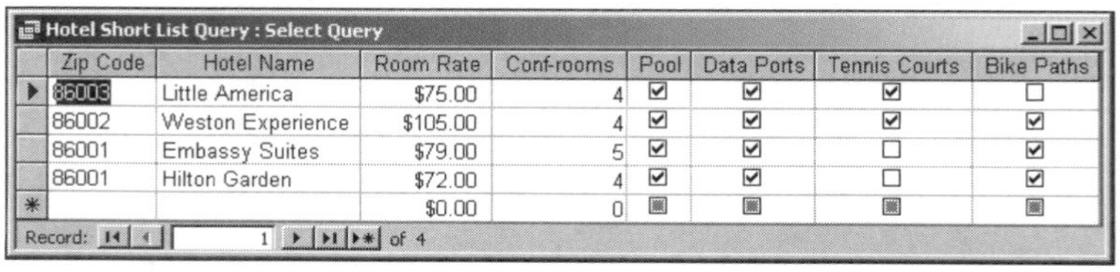

Zip Code	Hotel Name	Room Rate	Conf-rooms	Pool	Data Ports	Tennis Courts	Bike Paths
86003	Little America	$75.00	4	☑	☑	☑	☐
86002	Weston Experience	$105.00	4	☑	☑	☑	☑
86001	Embassy Suites	$79.00	5	☑	☑	☐	☑
86001	Hilton Garden	$72.00	4	☑	☑	☐	☑
*		$0.00	0	☐	☐	☐	☐

Record: 1 of 4

Reviewing PowerPoint: Task Reference

This task reference lists the most common tasks covered in units A through D of Microsoft PowerPoint Illustrated. It is designed as a refresher to help you find the button, dialog box, or tab you can use to perform each task.

task	method	task	method
Getting Started with PowerPoint 2002		**Shortcut, place program shortcut on desktop**	Click ⊞Start, point to Programs, right-click Microsoft PowerPoint, point to Send To, click Desktop (create shortcut)
Button not visible, display	Click ⏷⏷		
File, print	Click 🖨	**Slide Show, view**	Click 🖵
Fonts, save with presentation	Click File, Save As, Tools, Save Options, select Embed TrueType fonts	**Slide Sorter view, change to**	Click 🔲
Grayscale, view presentation in	Click ⬜	**Toolbars, display in 1 row**	Click Tools, Customize, Options tab, deselect Show Standard and Formatting toolbars on two rows
Help, search	Click 🔲, type question, click Search or click "Type a question for help" box on menu bar, type question, press [Enter]	**Creating a Presentation**	
Help, show the Office Assistant for	Click Help, Show the Office Assistant	**Automatic spell checking, turn off**	Click Tools, Options, Spelling and Style tab, clear Check spelling as you type option
Help questions, display list of recently asked	Click "Type a question for help" list arrow in menu bar	**Bullet, convert to new slide**	In Outline view, click in bullet, press [Shift][Tab]
Menu, open	Click menu name in the menu bar	**Bullet, move in Outline view**	Point to left of bullet, drag up or down
Normal view, change to	Click ⬜	**Bulleted list, insert**	Click 📋 in placeholder
Notes page, change to	Click View, Notes Page	**Character, delete from placeholder**	Click after character, press [Backspace]
Office Assistant, turn off	Right-click Assistant, click Options, deselect Use the Office Assistant	**Chart, insert**	Click 📊 in placeholder
		Content, insert	Click 📊 in placeholder
Overhead transparencies, print presentation for	Click File, Page Setup, click "Slides sized for" list arrow, click Overhead	**Design Template, apply**	Click Other Task Panes list arrow, click Slide Design - Design Templates, click template
Presentation, close	Click File, Close		
Presentation, create from Wizard	Click From AutoContent Wizard hyperlink in New Presentation task pane	**Diagram or Organization Chart, insert**	Click 🔲 in placeholder
Previous slide, move to	Click ⬆	**Entry, undo**	Click ↶
Presentation, preview	Click 🔍	**Graphic, insert on Notes page**	Click View, Notes Page, insert graphic using Insert Clip Art task pane
Presentation, print with current Print options	Click 🖨		
		Header and Footer, add	Click View, Header and Footer
Presentation, save	Click 💾	**Insertion point, move to next placeholder**	Press [Ctrl][Enter]
Program, exit	Click File, Exit		
Program, start	Click ⊞Start, point to Programs, click Microsoft PowerPoint	**Media Clip, insert**	Click 🎞 in placeholder

PowerPoint Task Reference (continued)

task	method	task	method
Notes, enter slide	Click in Notes pane, type text	**Color scheme, change**	Click 🖼, click Color Schemes hyperlink
Outline, display presentation	Click Outline tab in tab pane on left side of screen	**Font, change**	Click Arial ▾
Outlining toolbar, display	Click View, point to Toolbars, click Outlining	**Font color, change**	Click 🅰
Slide Show, end	Press [Esc]	**Font size, change**	Click 10 ▾
Slide text, enter	Click placeholder, type text	**Guide, add to slide**	Click existing guide, press [Ctrl], drag guide
Slide, create new	Click ⬒	**Guides, display**	Right click blank area, click Grid and Guides
Slide, create new, with specific layout	Point to layout in task pane, click layout list arrow, click Insert New Slide	**Guide, move**	Drag to new position
Spelling, check	Click ✓	**Italics, apply**	Click 𝐼
Table, insert	Click ▦ in placeholder	**Line color, add**	Click ✐
Task pane, display a different	Click Other Task Panes list arrow	**Object color, add**	Click 🖌 ▾
Template, apply to all slides	Click template list arrow in Slide Design task pane, click Apply to All slides	**Object, add or modify 3-D effect**	Click ◻
Template, apply to selected slides	Select slides, point to template list arrow in Slide Design task pane, click Apply to Selected slides	**Object, resize**	Select object, drag sizing handle
		Object, resize proportionally	Select object, press and hold [Shift], drag sizing handle
Template, create	Create desired presentation, click File, Save As, click Save as type list arrow, choose Design Template, name template, click Save	**Object, rotate**	Click object, drag rotate handle
		Objects, align or distribute	Select objects, click Draw on Drawing toolbar, point to Align or Distribute
Text, delete from slide	Select text, press [Backspace] or [Delete]	**Objects, group or ungroup**	Select objects, click Draw on Drawing toolbar, click Group or Ungroup
Text, demote in Outline view	Click ⇨ in Outlining toolbar	**Paste Options, apply**	Click 📋 next to pasted object
Modifying a Presentation		**Presentation, open**	Click 📂
AutoShape, apply shaded background to	Right-click AutoShape, click Format Autoshape	**Presentation, save as**	Click File, Save As
AutoShape, change color	Click AutoShape, click 🖌	**Presentation, search for**	Click 🔍, enter search text, click Search
AutoShapes, create	Click AutoShapes ▾ on Drawing toolbar	**Presentation, send electronically**	Click File, Send to, Mail Recipient (as Attachment)
AutoShape text, wrap	Right-click AutoShape, click Format AutoShape, click Text Box tab	**Preview, display in Open dialog box**	Click ▦ ▾, select Preview
Background, change	Click Format, Background		

PowerPoint Task Reference (continued)

task	method	task	method
Slides, import	Click Insert, Slides from Files, click Browse, locate presentation	**Next slide, advance to in Slide Show**	Press [Enter], [Spacebar], [PgDn], [N], [↓], [↑]
Text, center align	Click in text, click ▤	**Order, change object's stacking**	Click Draw ▾, point to Order
Text, import	Click Insert, Slides from Outline	**Picture, crop**	Select picture, click ▦ on Picture toolbar, drag handle
Text, left align	Click in text, click ▤	**Picture, resize and reposition**	Click ▦ on Picture toolbar, click Size and Position tabs
Text, replace	Click Edit, Replace	**Previous slide, return to**	Press [PgUp]
Text, right align	Click in text, click ▤	**Rehearse Timings, set**	Click ▦
Text box, create	Click ▤	**Screen to black, change to**	Press [B] during slide show
Text label, create non-wrapping	Click ▤, click, slide, type text	**Screen to white, change to**	Press [W] during slide show
Enhancing a Presentation		**Shadow, add**	Select object, click ▢ on Drawing toolbar
Animation effects, apply	Click Other Task Panes list arrow, Slide Design - Animation Schemes	**Slide show pointer to arrow, change**	Press [Ctrl][A]
Annotation drawing, erase	In slide show, press [E]	**Slide show pointer to pencil, change**	Press [Ctrl][P]
Bold attribute, apply	Click **B**	**Slide Show, pause**	Press [S]
Border, add	Click ▦ ▾	**Slide Show, stop**	Press [Esc]
Chart, insert	Click ▦, enter data on datasheet	**Slide Transition, add**	Click ▦ on Slide Sorter toolbar
Chart data, format	Double-click chart, close datasheet, select chart element, click formatting buttons	**Table, insert**	Click ▦
Clip Art, insert	Click ▦ on Drawing toolbar	**Text box, center vertically**	Click text block, click Format, Placeholder, click Text Box tab, click Text Anchor point list arrow
Clip Art, resize	Drag sizing handle		
Currency format, apply	Click $	**Timing, change slide show**	Click ▦, click ▦, type number in Automatically after text box
Decrease Decimal, apply	Click ▦		
First slide in Slide Show, move to	Press [Home]	**Timing, rehearse slide show**	Click ▦ on Slide Sorter toolbar, present show
Format, copy	Click in source, click ▦, click destination	**Transparent color, apply**	Click ▦
Graphic, save slide as a	Click File, Save As, click Save As type list arrow, select desired format, name file	**Underline, apply**	Click **U**
		Value to label, change	Type ' before entering value
Hidden slide, display	Press [H]		
Last slide in Slide Show, move to	Press [End]		

Using PowerPoint: Visual Workshop

Open the Project File Office B-4 from the location where your Project Files are stored, then save it as **MediaLoft Retreat Presentation**. Use Figure B-6 as a guide as you work on the modifications below. Enter your name in the footer of the master slide, save your work, then print the slides. As you create the presentation, do the following:

- Apply the Mountain Top design template.
- Change the slide order, using Figure B-7 as a guide.
- Add the AutoShape shown, then add text to the shape. (*Hint:* Use a 32 *pt* Times New Roman font.)
- Create a chart on the MediaLoft Stores, By Size slide using the data in Table B-1, then relocate the legend to the bottom of the slide.
- Copy and paste the MediaLoftLogo picture displayed in Slide 1 to the upper-left corner of the master slide.
- Add the clip art image shown in Figure B-7 (or one similar to it), create an oval shape, add Shadow Style 2 to the oval, then arrange the objects as shown.
- Add your own timing, animations, and transitions to the slides, then spell check the presentation.

TABLE B-1: **Chart data**

Location	Square Feet
Boston	60000
Chicago	150000
Houston	75000
Kansas City	130000
New York	90000
San Diego	50000
San Francisco	80000
Seattle	65000

FIGURE B-6: **PowerPoint slide in Normal View**

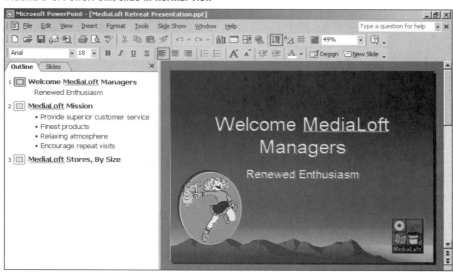

FIGURE B-7: **PowerPoint slides in Slide Sorter View**

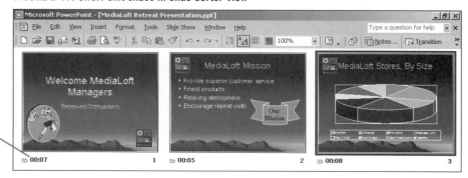

Your timing will vary

Independent Challenge 1

As the human resources director and training coordinator for Hailey Dow Attorneys-at-Law, you want to create a letter that your department can easily adapt to send to job applicants. You use Word formatting features to create a letter that is both informative and visually appealing.

a. Open the Word document Office B-5, then save it as **HD Multi-Page Letter** in the drive and folder where your Project Files are stored. Create the letter, using Figure B-8 as a guide.

b. Insert the Scales clip art file (shown in Figure B-8) at the top of the document. (*Hint:* Search clip art using the keyword "law." Substitute another piece of clip art if you do not have the image shown.) Use this artwork and the existing text to create a logo. (*Hint:* Use a blue, 48 point bold Times New Roman font with an embossed effect for the company name, and a blue, 20 point Times New Roman font with a Shadow effect for the "Attorneys-at-Law" text.)

c. Replace Elizabeth Reed with your name in the signature area of each document.

d. Spell check the document, preview it for accuracy, save, then print the document.

FIGURE B-8: Multi-page document

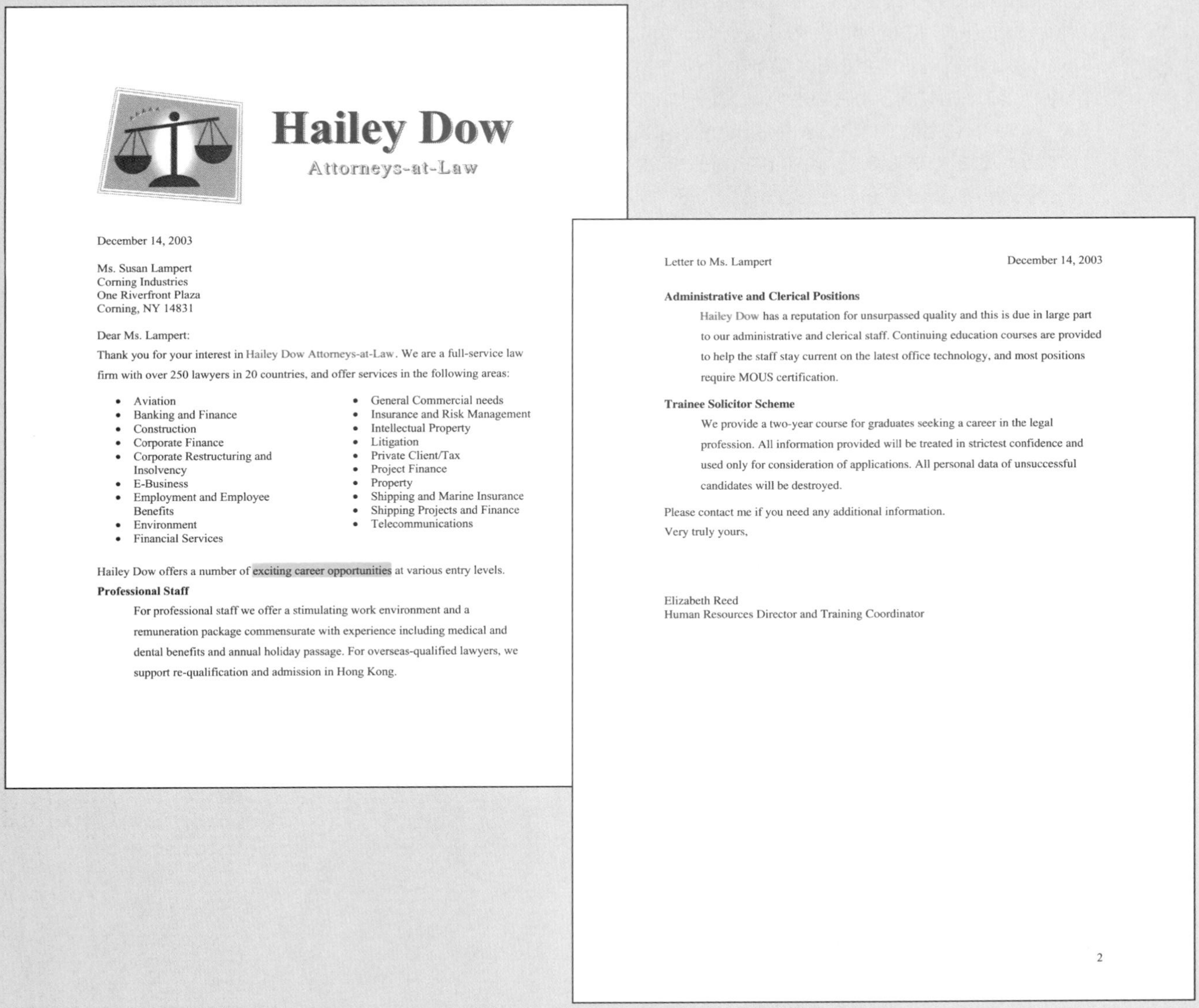

Hailey Dow
Attorneys-at-Law

December 14, 2003

Ms. Susan Lampert
Corning Industries
One Riverfront Plaza
Corning, NY 14831

Dear Ms. Lampert:

Thank you for your interest in Hailey Dow Attorneys-at-Law. We are a full-service law firm with over 250 lawyers in 20 countries, and offer services in the following areas:

- Aviation
- Banking and Finance
- Construction
- Corporate Finance
- Corporate Restructuring and Insolvency
- E-Business
- Employment and Employee Benefits
- Environment
- Financial Services
- General Commercial needs
- Insurance and Risk Management
- Intellectual Property
- Litigation
- Private Client/Tax
- Project Finance
- Property
- Shipping and Marine Insurance
- Shipping Projects and Finance
- Telecommunications

Hailey Dow offers a number of exciting career opportunities at various entry levels.

Professional Staff

For professional staff we offer a stimulating work environment and a remuneration package commensurate with experience including medical and dental benefits and annual holiday passage. For overseas-qualified lawyers, we support re-qualification and admission in Hong Kong.

Letter to Ms. Lampert December 14, 2003

Administrative and Clerical Positions

Hailey Dow has a reputation for unsurpassed quality and this is due in large part to our administrative and clerical staff. Continuing education courses are provided to help the staff stay current on the latest office technology, and most positions require MOUS certification.

Trainee Solicitor Scheme

We provide a two-year course for graduates seeking a career in the legal profession. All information provided will be treated in strictest confidence and used only for consideration of applications. All personal data of unsuccessful candidates will be destroyed.

Please contact me if you need any additional information.

Very truly yours,

Elizabeth Reed
Human Resources Director and Training Coordinator

2

Independent Challenge 2

As an assistant professor at University College, London, you have decided to examine the population of Inner London (formerly London County), and the Outer Boroughs from 1951 to 1996. Your research assistant has gathered some raw data for you, and you are ready to create worksheets that will help you analyze the data further.

a. Open the Excel workbook Office B-6 from the drive and folder where your Project Files are stored, then save it as **London Demographics**.

b. The sheet for Inner London has already been created. Copy all the data to a new sheet that will summarize data for the Outer Boroughs, then delete the data in cells D9:E14 on the new sheet. Name the sheets accordingly, then apply a different color to each of the two sheet tabs.

c. Replace the column label in cell D3 with **Outer Boroughs**, then enter the population data in Figure B-9 for the Outer Boroughs.

d. In each of the two sheets, make sure that you include the following elements:
   - Formatted labels and values, and appropriate column widths. (*Hint:* Population values should all use the comma format rounded to the nearest whole number.)
   - A formula that calculates the square mile area in cell A17 and D17 on both sheets (rounded to the nearest whole number). Apply borders and a fill color to this information.
   - Formulas that calculate the maximum, minimum, and average populations during the 1951–1996 time period in the appropriate cells for All London, Inner London, and the Outer Boroughs. (*Hint:* You can round the average to the nearest whole number.) Surround this information with borders and add a fill color.
   - Formulas that contain an absolute reference. (*Hint:* Estimate the population in the Inner and Outer Boroughs in 2010 with a 20% increase.) Place the results in the Speculation columns.
   - At least one chart for the data on each sheet using appropriate formatting
   - Formulas that contain conditional formatting
   - Formulas that determine the percentage of London's total population represented by the Inner and Outer Boroughs, place the information in the percentage columns.

e. In each sheet, delete the rows for the years 1998–2004.

f. Copy data from Sheets 1 and 2 to Sheet 3 so that you have the following information for years 1951-1996: population for all of London, population for Inner London, and population for Outer London. Name this sheet **Total Population**, and apply any color you choose to the tab.

g. Move the Total Population sheet so that it is the first sheet in the workbook.

h. Create a bar chart that displays the data for all three areas. Create your own title, make necessary formatting improvements, and position the legend appropriately.

i. Format the title of each worksheet (in cell A1) so that it is larger and a different color from the rest of the sheet, then change the row height of cell A1 (in each worksheet) to 22.

j. Insert your name in each worksheet, spell check your work, save, then print the worksheets.

k. E-mail the workbook to your instructor. (Check with your instructor to make sure this is acceptable.)

FIGURE B-9: **London demographic data**

Greater London, Inner London Population & Density History - Microsoft Internet Explorer

File   Edit   View   Favorites   Tools   Help

Back   →   ·   Search   Favorites   History

Address   http://www.demographia.com/dm-lon31.htm

Inner London & Outer London Population & Density History

Year	Population	Pop./Sq. Mi.	Inner London (Former London County)		Outer Boroughs	
			Population	Pop./Sq. Mi.	Population	Pop./Sq. Mi.
2004	7,284,000	11,716				
2002	7,244,000	11,652				
2000	7,188,000	11,562				
1998	7,187,000	11,560				
1996	7,074,300	11,379	2,707,800	22,967	4,366,500	8,667
1991	6,679,699	10,744	2,504,451	21,242	4,175,248	8,288
1981	6,696,008	10,770	2,497,978	21,187	4,198,030	8,333
1971	8,119,246	13,060	3,045,436	25,831	5,073,810	10,071
1961	8,171,902	13,144	3,195,114	27,100	4,976,788	9,878
1951	8,348,023	13,428	3,347,982	28,397	5,000,041	9,925

Independent Challenge 3

You have just taken over the management of the Competitive Edge Real Estate office. This five-year-old business specializes in residential properties. The market is booming, and since no one has ever created a database for the listings, you have decided to make this your mission.

a. Open the Access database Office B-7 from the drive and folder where your Project Files are stored. (*Hint:* Since there is no Save As feature in Access, you may want to make a copy of Office B-7.mdb prior to starting this project.)

b. Resize the fields in the Listings table so all the data is displayed, then check the spelling of the records. (*Hint:* There are easily recognizable spelling errors in the table. All the street names are spelled correctly.)

c. Format the Asking Price field as Currency, displaying no decimal places.

d. Add a new record (Property ID=10020) to the Listings table for your own street address, but use the zip code 87111. Include Radiant Floor heat and Cooling System=Yes in this record, using your own data for the remaining fields. (*Hint:* Make sure your listing has a value over 2150 for the square footage.)

e. Use all the fields in the Listings table to create a columnar form (using any layout, design, and style you choose) that can be used for data entry, called **All Listings**. Add bold formatting to the Zip Code and Asking Price fields.

f. Add any enhancing formatting. Move the fields from their original order to another logical order, then change the tab order.

g. Use the Listings table to create a query that finds all records with radiant floor heat, called **Radiant Floor Heat**. The query should display the following fields: Property ID, Address, Zip Code, Square Feet, Central Heat, and Asking Price. Print the datasheet.

h. Modify the **Radiant Floor Heat** query so it includes only those listings that are over 2500 square feet.

i. Use the Radiant Floor Heat query to create a report called **Radiant Floor Heat Listings** that includes all the fields in the query. Group the records by Zip Code. Sort the records in descending order by Asking Price.

j. Create a calculated control that determines the average price in each grouping. Use the Currency format, displaying no decimal places, and use a color of your choice. Align the control beneath the Asking Price values.

k. Modify the report so that the labels and the contents of all the fields are displayed. Center-align the data in the Property ID field.

l. Use the Listings table to create a label using Avery product number C2160. This label should use the default text attributes and contain the following information: (Line 1) Product ID / Zip Code / Asking Price, (Line 2) Address, (Line 3) Square Feet / Bedrooms / Bathrooms. Sort the labels by Zip Code, then accept the default name.

 Independent Challenge 4

As director of software training for the Quest Public Relations firm, you want to create a presentation for the first day of training that generates enthusiasm for the Microsoft Office products. You decide to focus on the benefits of using Word, Access, Excel, and PowerPoint.

a. Open the PowerPoint presentation Office B-8 from the location where your Project Files are stored, then save it as **Office XP Programs**.

b. Modify the slides for the four basic programs in the Office XP suite so that they contain text describing your favorite features of each program. Use Figure B-10 as a guide.

c. Apply the design template of your choice to all the slides. Customize the color scheme so that the title text has enough contrast with your chosen color scheme.

d. Italicize the subtitle text on the first slide.

e. Add a text box to the Word slide that contains the following text: **Word is fun to use!**

f. Include clip art on each of the four program slides, resizing and moving objects as necessary. In the Access slide, copy and paste the graphic image, scale it, then position it above the original image.

g. Apply custom animation to the Microsoft Word slide. Change the animation order of this slide to the following: Slide title, bulleted text. The title text should fly in, and the bulleted text should fly out.

h. Add three clip art images to the Excel slide, then scale, align, and group them. (*Hint:* Search on the keyword "money".)

i. Use drawing tools to create at least three shapes on the PowerPoint slide. Arrange the order of these shapes using your own judgment, then group the objects.

j. Create brief notes for each slide.

k. Insert your name in the footer of each slide, except the title slide.

l. Rehearse timings, then be prepared to present this slide show.

m. Check the spelling, save, then print the slides as handouts.

FIGURE B-10: **Sample title slide**

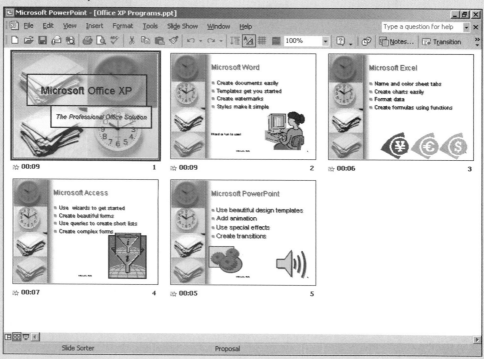

Independent Challenge 5

You are in charge of your local hospital's annual blood drive program. Since you are an experienced Office XP user, you want to use your skills to develop an exciting array of documents to promote the event.

a. Open the Word document Office B-9 from the drive and folder where your Project Files are stored, then save it as **Blood Drive Events**.

b. Replace the sender's name at the end of the document with your name, then save and print the document. Replace the date placeholder with the current date. Save and close the document, then exit Word.

c. Open the Access database Office B-10 from the drive and folder where your Project Files are stored. (*Hint:* Since there is no Save As feature in Access, you may want to make a copy of Office B-10.mdb prior to starting this project.)

d. Open the Blood Donors table, change the name and zip code in the last record of the **Blood Donors** table to your own, then modify the age and blood type to your own.

e. Open the Previous Donor Query, then merge this query with the Blood Drive Events document. In the Blood Drive Events document, replace the Address Block and Greeting Here placeholders using the Mail Merge hyperlinks and a format you feel is appropriate. Then examine the letter and insert the Blood Type field in the first paragraph of the letter.

f. Merge the document. (*Hint:* You will create multiple documents later.)

g. Open the PowerPoint presentation Office B-11 from the drive and folder where your Project Files are stored, then save it as **Blood Drive Promotion**.

h. Add a new slide after Slide 4, then add the title **Statistics From Previous Year**. Apply the Title Only slide layout.

i. Open the Excel workbook Office B-12, then save it as **Blood Donation Statistics** in the drive and folder where your Project Files are stored.

j. Copy the chart, then link it to Slide 4 in the Blood Drive Promotion presentation. Move and resize the chart so it is large enough for viewers to see clearly.

k. Link the chart to the merged Blood Drive Events document, placing it in the second empty line following the paragraph starting with "Blood donations are important. . ."

l. Tile the PowerPoint and Excel windows. Modify the June data in cell B9 of the Blood Donation Statistics workbook so it is 1347 (from 552), then save the workbook. Your screen should look similar to Figure B-11.

m. Verify that the links in the Blood Drive Events document and Slide 4 of the Blood Drive Promotion presentation have been updated, then save the updated files.

n. Print the merged letter for the last record in the Blood Drive Events document, then close the document and exit Word.

o. Print Slide 4 in the Blood Drive Promotion presentation, then close the presentation and exit PowerPoint.

p. Export the Previous Donor Query in the Office B-10 database to Excel. (*Hint:* The **Previous Donor Query.xls** workbook will be created.)

q. Enter your name in cell A35 in the Previous Donor Query, change the orientation to landscape, save and print the worksheet, then close the file and exit Excel.

r. Close the Office B-10 database, then exit Access.

FIGURE B-11: Tiled Excel and PowerPoint windows

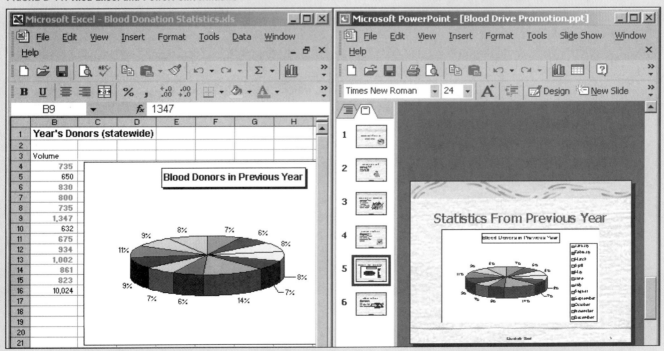

⚃ Independent Challenge 6

As coordinator of a local historical society, one of your jobs is to create documents for special events. Your club periodically investigates events and shares information with other organizations. A few members of your club have researched the well-known Roswell, New Mexico incident in which an alleged UFO landing was reported in 1947. Although the members are not convinced there was a UFO, the case remains intriguing—particularly to conspiracy buffs. The historical society members regard it as an interesting piece of history; they also want to strengthen the society's ties to the community and other historical societies. So the organization will sponsor a large-scale event on the anniversary of the "landing." You decide to use your Microsoft Office XP skills to create professional documents for the event that generate excitement within your organization. You want to prepare the preliminary documents to show other club members before proceeding further.

   a. Open the Access database Office B-13 from the drive and folder where your Project Files are stored. (*Hint:* Since there is no Save As feature for database files, you may want to make a copy of Office B-13.mdb prior to starting this project.)

   b. Modify the last record in the Preliminary Partnering Club Members table so that it contains your name, address, and telephone number.

   c. Publish the Attending Club Members query in Word. (*Hint:* The Attending Club Members.rtf document will be created.)

   d. Change the paper orientation of the Attending Club Members.rtf document to landscape, save your work, then print and close the file.

   e. Open the Word document Office B-14, then save it in the drive and folder where your Project Files are stored as **Roswell Mailing Letter**.

   f. Insert your name in the signature area of this document, then close the document and exit Word.

   g. Open the PowerPoint presentation Office B-15 from the drive and folder where your Project Files are stored, then save it as **Roswell Presentation**.

   h. Insert your name in the footer of each slide, except the title slide.

   i. Insert additional slides after Slide 4 (What Was It?) using the Slides from Outline feature and the Word document Office B-16 located in the drive and folder where your Project Files are stored.

   j. Open the Excel workbook Office B-17, then save it in the drive and folder where your Project Files are stored as **Roswell Special Event**.

   k. Link the Partnering Historical Societies data (cells A3:F24) to the last slide (Estimated Attendance). (*Hint:* Resize the linked object so it is as large as possible.)

   l. Draw a rectangle, position the shape behind the linked object, then use a fill color that makes the text in the linked object stand out.

  m. In the Excel workbook, change the data in cell B10 to 1115 (from 620), then save your work and exit Excel.

   n. Update the link in PowerPoint, save your work, print the last slide, then exit PowerPoint.

   o. Open the Attending Club Members query in the Office B-13 database, then merge this query with the Roswell Mailing Letter document.

   p. Replace the Address Block and Greeting Here placeholders in the Roswell Mailing Letter document using the Mail Merge hyperlinks and a format you feel is appropriate.

   q. Merge all records to a new document, save your work as **Merged Roswell Letters**, then print the letter for the last record.

   r. Close the document, then exit Word.

   s. Close the Office B-13 database, then exit Access.

Creating
and Formatting Tables

Objectives

- MOUS ► **Insert a table**
- MOUS ► **Insert and delete rows and columns**
- MOUS ► **Modify table rows and columns**
- MOUS ► **Sort table data**
- MOUS ► **Split and merge cells**
- MOUS ► **Perform calculations in tables**
- MOUS ► **Use Table AutoFormat**
- MOUS ► **Create a custom format for a table**

Tables are commonly used to display information for quick reference and analysis. In this unit, you learn how to create and modify a table in Word, how to sort table data and perform calculations, and how to format a table with borders and shading. You also learn how to use a table to structure the layout of a page. ◢ Alice Wegman is preparing a summary budget for an advertising campaign aimed at the Boston market. The goal of the ad campaign is to promote MediaLoft Online, the MediaLoft Web site. Alice decides to format the budget information as a table so that it is easy to read and analyze. You will work with Alice as she creates the table.

Word 2002

Inserting a Table

A **table** is a grid made up of rows and columns of cells that you can fill with text and graphics. A **cell** is the box formed by the intersection of a column and a row. The lines that divide the columns and rows and help you see the grid-like structure of a table are called **borders.** You can create a table in a document by using the Insert Table button on the Standard toolbar or the Insert command on the Table menu. Once you have created a table, you can add text and graphics to it. ✐ Alice begins by inserting a blank table into the document and then adding text to it.

Steps

1. Start **Word**, close the **New Document task pane**, click the **Print Layout View button** on the horizontal scroll bar if necessary, click the **Zoom list arrow** on the Standard toolbar, then click **Page Width**
   A blank document appears in Print Layout view.

QuickTip

To convert tabbed text to a table, select the tabbed text, click Table on the menu bar, point to Convert, then click Text to Table.

2. Click the **Insert Table button** on the Standard toolbar
   A grid opens below the button. You move the pointer across this grid to select the number of columns and rows you want the table to contain. To expand the grid, drag the lower-right corner.

3. Point to the **second box** in the fourth row to select 4 × 2 Table, then click
   A table with two columns and four rows is inserted in the document, as shown in Figure E-1. The insertion point is in the first cell in the first row.

4. Type **Location**, then press **[Tab]**
   Pressing [Tab] moves the insertion point to the next cell in the row.

5. Type **Cost**, press **[Tab]**, then type **Boston Sunday Globe**
   Pressing [Tab] at the end of a row moves the insertion point to the first cell in the next row.

6. Press **[Tab]**, type **27,600**, then type the following text in the table, pressing **[Tab]** to move from cell to cell
   | Boston.com | 25,000 |
   | Taxi tops | 18,000 |

7. Press **[Tab]**
   Pressing [Tab] at the end of the last cell of a table creates a new row at the bottom of the table, as shown in Figure E-2. The insertion point is located in the first cell in the new row.

Trouble?

If you pressed [Tab] after the last row, click the Undo button on the Standard toolbar to remove the new blank row.

8. Type the following, pressing **[Tab]** to move from cell to cell and to create new rows
Boston Herald	18,760
Townonline.com	3,250
Bus stops	12,000
Boston Magazine	12,400

9. Click the **Save button** on the Standard toolbar, then save the document with the filename **Boston Ad Budget** to the drive and folder where your Project Files are located
   The table is shown in Figure E-3.

FIGURE E-1: Blank table

Insert Table button

Column

Row

Cell

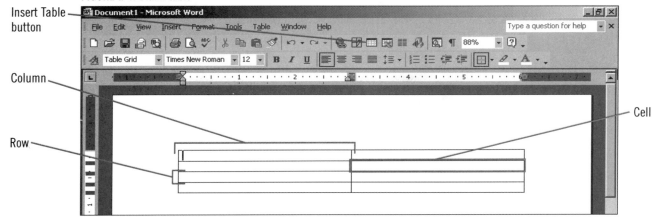

FIGURE E-2: New row in table

New row

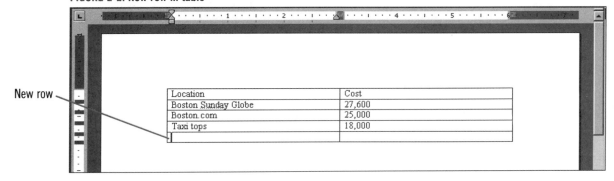

FIGURE E-3: Text in the table

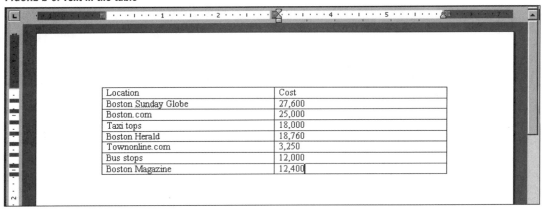

Creating a formatted blank table

When you use the Insert command on the Table menu to create a table, you have the option of formatting the table before you create it. To create a formatted blank table, point to Insert on the Table menu, then click Table to open the Insert Table dialog box. In the dialog box, first select the number of columns and rows you want your table to include. Next, in the AutoFit behavior area, choose an option for sizing the width of the columns in your table: set a specific fixed width, automatically size the columns to fit the text, or resize columns according to the width of the window. Finally, click AutoFormat to open the AutoFormat dialog box. In the AutoFormat dialog box, select a format for the table, then click OK. Click OK in the Insert Table dialog box to insert a table formatted with the options you specified.

Inserting and Deleting Rows and Columns

You can easily modify the structure of a table by adding and removing rows and columns. First, you must select an existing row or column in the table to indicate where you want to insert or delete information. You can select any element of a table using the Select command on the Table menu, but it is often easier to select rows and columns using the mouse: click in the margin to the left of a row to select the row; click the top border of a column to select the column. Alternatively, you can drag across a row or down a column to select it. To insert rows and columns, use the Insert command on the Table menu or the Insert Rows and Insert Columns button on the Standard toolbar. To delete rows and columns, use the Delete command on the Table menu. ✎ Alice adds a new row to the table and deletes an unnecessary row. She also adds new columns to the table to provide more detailed information.

Steps 1 2 3 4

1. Click the **Show/Hide/¶ button** ¶ on the Standard toolbar to display formatting marks
   An end of cell mark appears at the end of each cell and an end of row mark appears at the end of each row.

QuickTip

To insert more than one row or column, select the number of rows or columns you want to insert, then click the Insert Rows or Insert Columns button.

2. Place the pointer in the margin to the left of the **Townonline.com row** until the pointer changes to ⌐, then click
   The entire row is selected, including the end of row mark. If the end of row mark is not selected, you have selected only the text in a row, not the row itself. When a row is selected, the Insert Table button changes to the Insert Rows button.

3. Click the **Insert Rows button** 🛐 on the Standard toolbar
   A new row is inserted above the Townonline.com row, as shown in Figure E-4.

4. Click in the **first cell** of the new row, type **Boston Phoenix**, press **[Tab]**, then type **15,300**
   Clicking in a cell moves the insertion point to that cell.

QuickTip

You can also delete a row or column by using the Delete command on the Table menu or by pressing [Ctrl][X] or [Shift][Delete].

5. Select the **Boston Herald row**, right-click, then click **Delete Rows** on the shortcut menu
   The selected row is deleted. If you select a row and press [Delete], you delete only the contents of the row, not the row itself.

6. Place the pointer over the top border of the **Location column** until the pointer changes to ↓, then click
   The entire column is selected. When a column is selected, the Insert Table button changes to the Insert Columns button.

QuickTip

To select a cell, place the ◤ pointer over the left border of the cell, then click.

7. Click the **Insert Columns button** 🛐 on the Standard toolbar, then type **Type**
   A new column is inserted to the left of the Location column, as shown in Figure E-5.

8. Click in the **Location column**, click **Table** on the menu bar, point to **Insert**, click **Columns to the Right**, then type **Details** in the first cell of the new column
   A new column is added to the right of the Location column. You can also use the Insert command to add columns to the left of the active column or to insert rows above or below the active row.

9. Press **[↓]** to move the insertion point to the next cell in the Details column, enter the text shown in Figure E-6 in each cell in the Details and Type columns, click ¶ to turn off the display of formatting marks, then save your changes
   You can use the arrow keys to move the insertion point from cell to cell. Notice that text wraps to the next line in the cell as you type. Compare your table to Figure E-6.

FIGURE E-4: Inserted row

Insert Rows button

New row is inserted and selected by default

End of cell mark

End of row mark

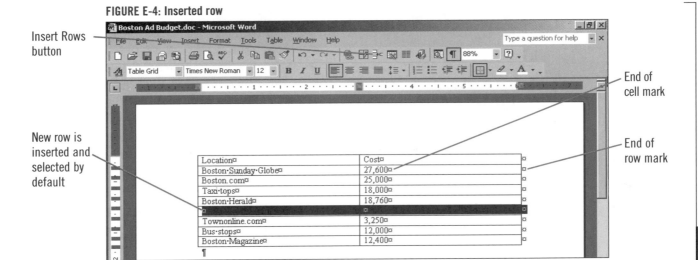

FIGURE E-5: Inserted column

New column

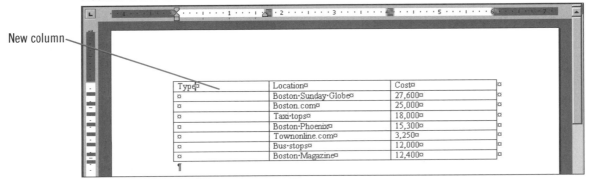

FIGURE E-6: Text in Type and Details columns

Text wraps to the next line

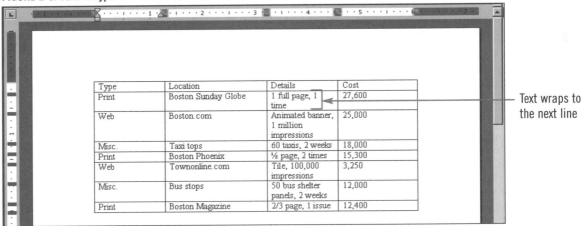

Type	Location	Details	Cost
Print	Boston Sunday Globe	1 full page, 1 time	27,600
Web	Boston.com	Animated banner, 1 million impressions	25,000
Misc.	Taxi tops	60 taxis, 2 weeks	18,000
Print	Boston Phoenix	½ page, 2 times	15,300
Web	Townonline.com	Tile, 100,000 impressions	3,250
Misc.	Bus stops	50 bus shelter panels, 2 weeks	12,000
Print	Boston Magazine	2/3 page, 1 issue	12,400

CLUES TO USE

Copying and moving rows and columns

You can copy and move rows and columns within a table in the same manner you copy and move text. Select the row or column you want to move, then use the Copy or Cut button to place the selection on the Clipboard. Place the insertion point in the location you want to insert the row or column, then click the Paste button to paste the selection. Rows are inserted above the row containing the insertion point; columns are inserted to the left of the column containing the insertion point. You can also copy or move columns and rows by selecting them and using the ▭ pointer to drag them to a new location in the table.

Word 2002

Word 2002

Modifying Table Rows and Columns

Once you create a table, you can easily adjust the size of columns and rows to make the table easier to read. You can change the size of columns and rows by dragging a border, by using the AutoFit command on the Table menu, or by setting exact measurements for column width and row height using the Table Properties dialog box. ✏ Alice adjusts the size of the columns and rows to make the table more attractive and easier to read. She also centers the text vertically in each table cell.

Steps

QuickTip

Press [Alt] as you drag a column or row border to display the column width or row height measurements on the ruler.

1. **Position the pointer over the border between the first and second columns until the pointer changes to ╋╂╋, then drag the border to approximately the ½" mark on the horizontal ruler**
   The dotted line that appears as you drag represents the border. Dragging the column border changes the width of the first and second columns: the first column is narrower and the second column is wider. When dragging a border to change the width of an entire column, make sure no cells are selected in the column. You can also drag a row border to change the width of the row above it.

2. **Position the pointer over the right border of the Location column until the pointer changes to ╋╂╋, then double-click**
   Double-clicking a column border automatically resizes the column to fit the text.

3. **Use ╋╂╋ to double-click the right border of the Details column, then use ╋╂╋ to double-click the right border of the Cost column**
   The widths of the Details and Cost columns are adjusted.

QuickTip

To move a table, drag the table move handle to a new location.

4. **Move the pointer over the table, then click the table move handle ⊞ that appears outside the upper-left corner of the table**
   Clicking the table move handle selects the entire table. You can also use the Select command on the Table menu to select an entire table.

QuickTip

Quickly resize an entire table by dragging the table resize handle to a new location.

5. **Click Table on the menu bar, point to AutoFit, click Distribute Rows Evenly, then deselect the table**
   All the rows in the table become the same height, as shown in Figure E-7. You can also use the commands on the AutoFit menu to make all the columns the same width, to make the width of the columns fit the text, and to adjust the width of the columns so the table is justified between the margins.

QuickTip

To change the margins in all the cells in a table, click Options on the Table tab, then enter new margin settings in the Table Options dialog box.

6. **Click in the Details column, click Table on the menu bar, click Table Properties, then click the Column tab in the Table Properties dialog box**
   The Column tab, shown in Figure E-8, allows you to set an exact width for columns. You can specify an exact height for rows and an exact size for cells using the Row and Cell tabs. You can also use the Table tab to set a precise size for the table, to change the alignment of the table on a page, and to wrap text around a table.

7. **Select the measurement in the Preferred width text box, type 3, then click OK**
   The width of the Details column changes to 3".

QuickTip

Quickly center a table on a page by selecting the table and clicking the Center button ▦ on the Formatting toolbar.

8. **Click ⊞ to select the table, click Table on the menu bar, click Table Properties, click the Cell tab, click the Center box in the Vertical Alignment section, click OK, deselect the table, then save your changes**
   The text is centered vertically in each table cell, as shown in Figure E-9.

FIGURE E-7: Resized columns and rows

Table move handle: click to select the table; drag to move the table

Rows are all the same height

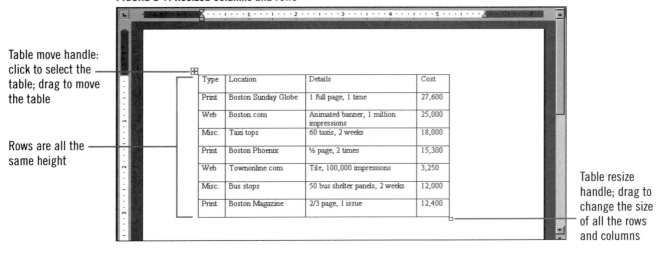

Table resize handle; drag to change the size of all the rows and columns

FIGURE E-8: Table Properties dialog box

Width of the active column (Yours might differ)

Click to change the width of the previous column

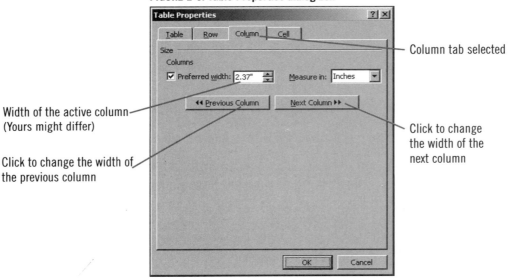

Column tab selected

Click to change the width of the next column

FIGURE E-9: Text centered vertically in cells

Text is centered vertically in the cell

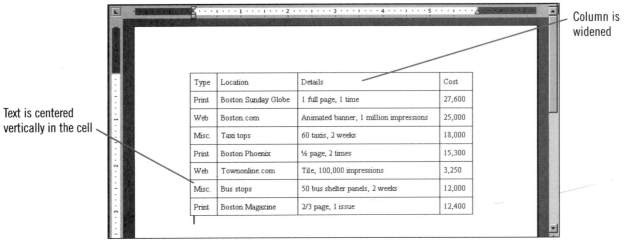

Column is widened

Word 2002

Sorting Table Data

Tables are often easier to interpret and analyze when the data is **sorted**, which means the rows are organized in alphabetical or sequential order based on the data in one or more columns. When you sort a table, Word arranges all the table data according to the criteria you set. You set sort criteria by specifying the column (or columns) by which you want to sort, and indicating the sort order—ascending or descending—you want to use. **Ascending order** lists data alphabetically or sequentially (from A to Z, 0 to 9, or earliest to latest). **Descending order** lists data in reverse alphabetical or sequential order (from Z to A, 9 to 0, or latest to earliest). You can sort using the data in one column or multiple columns. When you sort by multiple columns you must select primary, secondary, and tertiary sort criteria. You can use the Sort command on the Table menu to sort a table. Alice sorts the table so that all ads of the same type are listed together. She also adds secondary criteria so that the ads within each type are listed in descending order by cost.

1. **Place the insertion point anywhere in the table**
   To sort an entire table, you simply need to place the insertion point anywhere in the table. If you want to sort specific rows only you must select the rows you want to sort.

QuickTip

To quickly sort a table by a single column, click in the column, then click the Sort Ascending [⌵] or Sort Descending [⌵] button on the Tables and Borders toolbar. When you use these buttons, Word does not include the header row in the sort.

2. **Click Table on the menu bar, then click Sort**
   The Sort dialog box opens, as shown in Figure E-10. You use this dialog box to specify the column or columns by which you want to sort, the type of information you are sorting (text, numbers, or dates), and the sort order (ascending or descending). Column 1 is selected by default in the Sort by list box. You want to sort your table first by the information in the first column—the type of ad (Print, Web, or Misc.)—so you won't change the Sort by criteria.

3. **Click the Descending option button in the Sort by area**
   The ad type information will be sorted in descending—or reverse alphabetical—order, so that the "Web" ads will be listed first, followed by the "Print" ads, and then the "Misc." ads.

4. **In the Then by section click the Then by list arrow, click Column 4, click the Type list arrow, click Number, then click the Descending option button**
   Within the Web, Print, and Misc. groups, the rows will be sorted by the cost of the ad—the information contained in the fourth column. The data in the fourth column is numbers, not dates or text. The rows will appear in descending order within each group, with the most expensive ad listed first.

5. **Click the Header row option button in the My list has section to select it**
   The table includes a header row that you do not want included in the sort.

6. **Click OK, then deselect the table**
   The rows in the table are sorted first by the information in the Type column and second by the information in the Cost column, as shown in Figure E-11. The first row of the table, which is the Header row, is not included in the sort.

7. **Save your changes to the document**

FIGURE E-10: Sort dialog box

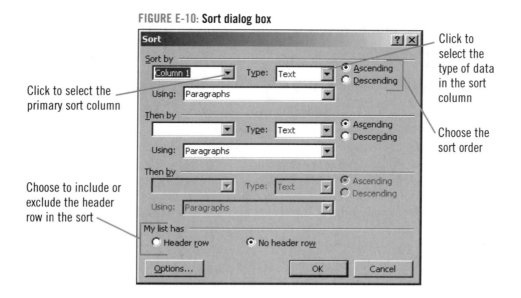

Click to select the primary sort column

Choose to include or exclude the header row in the sort

Click to select the type of data in the sort column

Choose the sort order

FIGURE E-11: Sorted table

Header row is not included in the sort

First, rows are sorted by type in descending order

Type	Location	Details	Cost
Web	Boston.com	Animated banner, 1 million impressions	25,000
Web	Townonline.com	Tile, 100,000 impressions	3,250
Print	Boston Sunday Globe	1 full page, 1 time	27,600
Print	Boston Phoenix	½ page, 2 times	15,300
Print	Boston Magazine	2/3 page, 1 issue	12,400
Misc.	Taxi tops	60 taxis, 2 weeks	18,000
Misc.	Bus stops	50 bus shelter panels, 2 weeks	12,000

Second, within each type, rows are sorted by cost in descending order

Sorting lists and paragraphs

In addition to sorting table data, you can use the Sort command on the Table menu to sort lists and paragraphs. For example, you might want to sort a list of names alphabetically. To sort lists and paragraphs, select the items you want included in the sort, click Table on the menu bar, and then click Sort. In the Sort Text dialog box, use the Sort by list arrow to select the sort by criteria (paragraphs or fields), use the Type list arrow to select the type of data (text, numbers, or dates), and then click the Ascending or Descending option button to choose a sort order.

When sorting text information in a document, "fields" refers to text or numbers that are separated by a character, such as tabs or commas. For example, if the names are listed in "Lastname, Firstname" order, the last names and first names are each considered a field, and you can choose to sort the list in alphabetical order by last name or by first name. Use the Options button in the Sort Text dialog box to specify the character that separates the fields in your lists or paragraphs, along with other sort options.

Word 2002

Splitting and Merging Cells

A convenient way to change the format and structure of a table is to merge and split the table cells. When you **merge** cells, you combine adjacent cells into a single larger cell. When you **split** a cell, you divide an existing cell into multiple cells. You can merge and split cells using the Merge Cells and Split Cells commands on the Table menu, or the Merge Cells and Split Cells buttons on the Tables and Borders toolbar. Alice merges cells in the first column to create a single cell for each ad type—Web, Print, and Misc. She also adds a new row to the bottom of the table, and splits the cells in the row to create three new rows with a different structure.

Trouble?

To move the Tables and Borders toolbar, click its title bar and drag it to a new location.

1. Click the **Tables and Borders button** ▦ on the Standard toolbar, then click the **Draw Table button** ✎ on the Tables and Borders toolbar to turn off the Draw pointer ✐ if necessary
   The Tables and Borders toolbar, which includes buttons for formatting and working with tables, opens. See Table E-1.

2. Select the two **Web cells** in the first column of the table, click the **Merge Cells button** ▦ on the Tables and Borders toolbar, then deselect the text
   The two Web cells merge to become a single cell. When you merge cells, Word converts the text in each cell into a separate paragraph in the merged cell.

3. Select the first **Web** in the cell, then press **[Delete]**

4. Select the three **Print cells** in the first column, click ▦, type **Print**, select the two **Misc. cells**, click ▦, then type **Misc.**
   The three Print cells merge to become one cell and the two Misc. cells merge to become one cell.

5. Click in the **Bus stops cell**, click the **Insert Table list arrow** ▦▾ on the Tables and Borders toolbar, then click **Insert Rows Below**
   A row is added to the bottom of the table. The Insert Table button on the Tables and Borders toolbar also changes to the Insert Rows Below button. The active buttons on the Tables and Borders toolbar reflect the most recently used commands. You can see a menu of related commands by clicking the list arrow next to a button.

QuickTip

To split a table in two, click the row you want to be the first row in the second table, click Table on the menu bar, then click Split Table.

6. Select the **first three cells** in the new last row of the table, click ▦, then deselect the cell
   The three cells in the row merge to become a single cell.

7. Click in the **first cell in the last row**, then click the **Split Cells button** ▦ on the Tables and Borders toolbar
   The Split Cells dialog box opens, as shown in Figure E-12. You use this dialog box to split the selected cell or cells into a specific number of columns and rows.

8. Type **1** in the Number of columns text box, press **[Tab]**, type **3** in the Number of rows text box, click **OK**, then deselect the cells
   The single cell is divided into three rows of equal height. When you split a cell into multiple rows and/or columns, the width of the original column does not change. If the cell you split contains text, all the text will appear in the upper left-most cell.

9. Click in the **last cell** in the Cost column, click ▦, repeat step 8, then save your changes
   The cell is split into three rows, as shown in Figure E-13. The last three rows of the table now have only two columns.

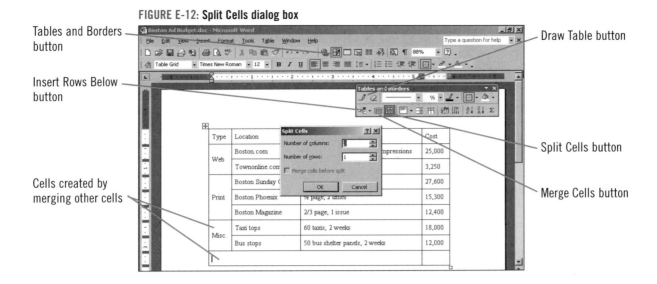

FIGURE E-12: Split Cells dialog box

Tables and Borders button

Insert Rows Below button

Cells created by merging other cells

Draw Table button

Split Cells button

Merge Cells button

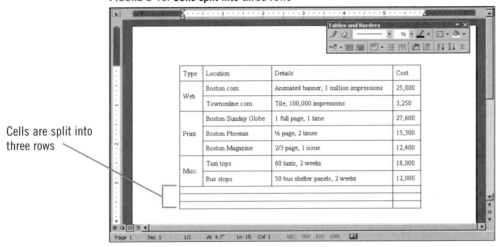

FIGURE E-13: Cells split into three rows

Cells are split into three rows

TABLE E-1: Buttons on the Tables and Borders toolbar

button	use to	button	use to
(pencil)	Draw a table or cells	(grid)	Divide a cell into multiple cells
(eraser)	Remove a border between cells	(align)	Change the alignment of text in cells
(line style)	Change border line style	(same height)	Make rows the same height
(½)	Change the thickness of borders	(same width)	Make columns the same width
(pen color)	Change the border color	(AutoFormat)	AutoFormat the table
(borders)	Add or remove individual borders	(orientation)	Change the orientation of text
(shading)	Change shading color of cells	(sort asc)	Sort rows in ascending order
(insert)	Insert rows, columns, cells, or a table, and AutoFit columns	(sort desc)	Sort rows in descending order
(merge)	Combine selected cells into a single cell	Σ	Calculate sum of values above or to the left of the active cell

Word 2002

Performing Calculations in Tables

If your table includes numerical information, you can perform simple calculations in the table. Word's AutoSum feature allows you to quickly total the numbers in a column or row. In addition, you can use the Formula command to perform other standard calculations, such as averages. When you calculate data in a table using formulas, you use cell references to refer to the cells in the table. Each cell has a unique **cell reference** composed of a letter and a number; the letter represents its column and the number represents its row. For example, the cell in the third row of the second column is cell B3. Figure E-14 shows the cell references in a simple table. ✐ Alice uses the AutoSum feature to calculate the total cost of the Boston ad campaign. She also adds information about the budgeted cost and creates a formula to calculate the difference between the actual and budgeted costs.

QuickTip

If a column or row contains blank cells, you must type a zero in any blank cell before using AutoSum.

1. Click in the **first blank cell** in column 1, type **Total Cost**, press **[Tab]**, then click the **AutoSum button** Σ on the Tables and Borders toolbar

   Word totals the numbers in the cells above the active cell and inserts the sum. You can use the AutoSum button to quickly total the numbers in a column or a row. If the cell you select is at the bottom of a column of numbers, AutoSum totals the column. If the cell is at the right end of a row of numbers, AutoSum totals the row.

2. Select **12,000** in the cell above the total, then type **13,500**

   If you change a number that is part of a calculation, you must recalculate the result.

QuickTip

When the insertion point is in the cell that contains a formula, pressing [F9] updates the calculation.

3. Press **[↓]**, then press **[F9]**

4. Press **[Tab]**, type **Budgeted**, press **[Tab]**, type **113,780**, press **[Tab]**, type **Difference**, then press **[Tab]**

   The insertion point is in the last cell of the table.

5. Click **Table** on the menu bar, then click **Formula**

   The Formula dialog box opens, as shown in Figure E-15. The SUM formula appears in the Formula text box. Word proposes to sum the numbers above the active cell, but you want to insert a formula that calculates the difference between the actual and budgeted costs.

Trouble?

Cell references are determined by the number of columns in each row, not by the number of columns in the table. Therefore, rows 9 and 10 have only two columns.

6. Select **=SUM(ABOVE)** in the Formula text box, then type **=B9-B10**

   You must type an equal sign ("=") to indicate that the text following it is a formula. You want to subtract the budgeted cost in the second column of row 10 from the actual cost in the second column of row 9; therefore, you type a formula to subtract the value in cell B10 from the value in cell B9.

7. Click **OK**, then save your changes

   The difference appears in the cell, as shown in Figure E-16.

Working with formulas

In addition to the sum function, Word includes formulas for averaging, counting, and rounding data, to name a few. To use a Word formula, click the Paste function list arrow in the Formula dialog box, select a function, then insert the cell references of the cells you want included in the calculation in parentheses after the name of the function. When entering formulas, you must separate cell references by a comma. For example, if you want to average the values in cells A1, B3, and C4, enter the formula =AVERAGE(A1,B3,C4). You must also separate cell ranges by a colon. For example, to total the values in cells A1 through A9, enter the formula =SUM(A1:A9). You can also type simple custom formulas using a plus sign (+) for addition, a minus sign (-) for subtraction, an asterisk (*) for multiplication, and a slash (/) for division. All Word formulas begin with an equal sign.

FIGURE E-14: Cell references in a table

Column B
(second column)

	A	B	C	D
1	A1	B1	C1	D1
2	A2	B2	C2	D2
3	A3	B3	C3	D3

Row 3

Cell reference indicates the cell's column and row

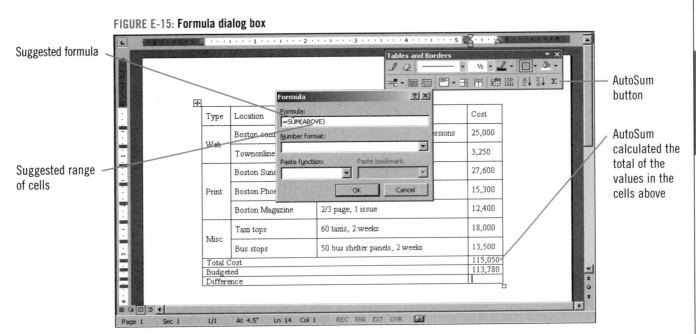

FIGURE E-15: Formula dialog box

Suggested formula

Suggested range of cells

AutoSum button

AutoSum calculated the total of the values in the cells above

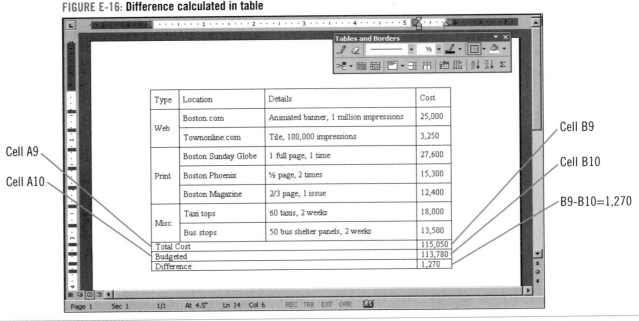

FIGURE E-16: Difference calculated in table

Cell A9

Cell A10

Cell B9

Cell B10

B9-B10=1,270

Word 2002

Using Table AutoFormat

Adding shading and other design elements to a table can help give it a polished appearance and make the data easier to read. Word's Table AutoFormat feature allows you to quickly apply a professional table design to a table. Table format styles include borders, shading, fonts, alignment, colors, and other formatting effects. You can apply a table format style to a table using the Table AutoFormat command on the Table menu or the Table AutoFormat button on the Tables and Borders toolbar. Alice wants to enhance the appearance of the table with shading, borders, and other formats. She uses the Table AutoFormat feature to quickly apply a table format style to the table.

Steps

1. Click **Table** on the menu bar, then click **Table AutoFormat**
   The Table AutoFormat dialog box opens, as shown in Figure E-17.

2. Scroll down the list of table styles, then click **Table List 7**
   A preview of the Table List 7 style appears in the Preview area.

3. Clear the **Last row** and **Last column check boxes** in the Apply special formats to area
   The Preview area shows that the formatting of the last row and column of the table now match the formatting of the other rows and columns in the table.

4. Click **Apply**
   The Table List 7 style is applied to the table, as shown in Figure E-18. Because of the structure of the table, this style neither enhances the table nor helps make the data more readable.

QuickTip

Use the Reveal Formatting task pane to view the format settings applied to tables and cells.

5. With the insertion point in the table, click the **Table AutoFormat button** on the Tables and Borders toolbar, scroll down the list of table styles in the Table AutoFormat dialog box, click **Table Professional**, then click **Apply**
   The Table Professional style is applied to the table. This style works with the structure of the table.

6. Select the **Type column**, click the **Center button** on the Formatting toolbar, select the **Cost column**, then click the **Align Right button** on the Formatting toolbar
   The data in the Type column is centered, and the data in the Cost column is right-aligned.

7. Select the **last three rows** of the table, click, then click the **Bold button** on the Formatting toolbar

8. Select the **first row** of the table, click, click the **Font Size list arrow** on the Formatting toolbar, click **16**, click, deselect the row, then save your changes
   The text in the header row is centered, enlarged, and bold, as shown in Figure E-19.

Using tables to lay out a page

Tables are often used to display information for quick reference and analysis, but you can also use tables to structure the layout of a page. You can insert any kind of information in the cell of a table—including graphics, bulleted lists, charts, and other tables (called nested tables). For example, you might use a table to lay out a resume, a newsletter, or a Web page. When you use a table to lay out a page, you generally remove the table borders to hide the table structure from the reader. When you remove a border, a gridline appears on the screen. Gridlines are light gray lines that show the edges of cells, but do not print. If your document will be viewed online—for example, if you are planning to e-mail your resume to potential employers—you should turn off the display of gridlines so that the document looks the same online as it would look if printed. To turn gridlines off or on, click the Hide Gridlines or Show Gridlines command on the Table menu.

FIGURE E-17: Table AutoFormat dialog box

List of table styles

Click to create a new table format style

Preview of the selected style

Click to modify an existing style

Options for customizing the application of style settings

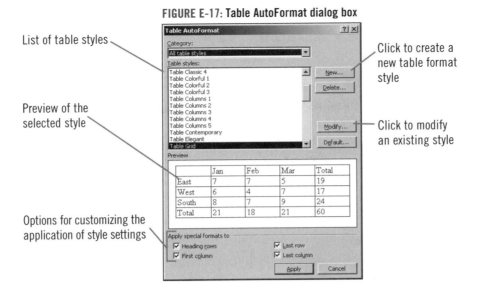

FIGURE E-18: List 7 style applied to table

The shading applied to the merged cells is confusing

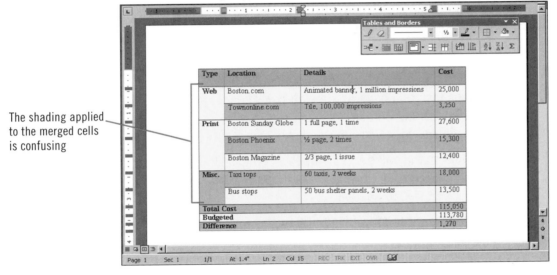

FIGURE E-19: Professional style applied to table

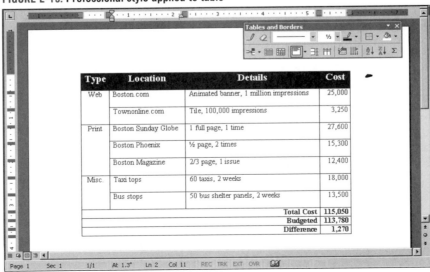

Creating a Custom Format for a Table

You can also use the buttons on the Tables and Borders toolbar to create your own table designs. For example, you can add or remove borders and shading, vary the line style, thickness, and color of borders, change the orientation of text from horizontal to vertical, and change the alignment of text in cells. ✐ Alice adjusts the text direction, shading, and borders in the table to make it easier to understand at a glance.

Steps 1234

1. Select the **Type and Location cells** in the first row, click the **Merge Cells button** 🔳 on the Tables and Borders toolbar, then type **Ad Location**

The two cells are combined into a single cell containing the text "Ad Location."

2. Select the **Web, Print, and Misc. cells** in the first column, click the **Change Text Direction button** 🔳 on the Tables and Borders toolbar twice, then deselect the cells

The text is rotated 270 degrees.

3. Position the pointer over the **right border** of the Web cell until the pointer changes to ↔, then drag the border to approximately the ¼" **mark** on the horizontal ruler

The width of the column containing the vertical text narrows.

4. Place the insertion point in the **Web cell**, then click the **Shading Color list arrow** 🔳 on the Tables and Borders toolbar

The Shading Color palette opens, as shown in Figure E-20.

5. Click **Gold** on the palette, click the **Print cell**, click 🔳, click **Aqua**, click the **Misc. cell**, click 🔳, then click **Orange**

Shading is applied to each cell.

6. Drag to select the **six white cells** in the Web rows (rows 2 and 3), click 🔳, then click **Light Yellow**

7. Repeat step 6 to apply **Light Turquoise** shading to the Print rows and **Tan** shading to the Misc. rows

Shading is applied to all the cells in rows 1-8.

8. Select the **last three rows** of the table, click the **Border list arrow** 🔳 on the Tables and Borders toolbar, click the **No Border button** 🔳 on the menu that appears, then deselect the rows

The top, bottom, left, and right borders are removed from each cell in the selected rows.

9. Select the **Total Cost row**, click the **Border list arrow** 🔳, click the **Top Border button** 🔳, click the **113,780 cell**, click **the Border list arrow** 🔳, click the **Bottom Border button** 🔳, click **Table** on the menu bar, then click **Hide Gridlines**

A top border is added to each cell in the Total Cost row, and a bottom border is added below 113,780. Hiding the gridlines allows you to see the table as it will appear when printed. The completed table is shown in Figure E-21.

10. Press **[Ctrl][Home]**, press **[Enter]**, type your name, save your changes, print a copy of the document, close the document, then exit Word

Press [Enter] at the beginning of a table to move the table down one line in a document.

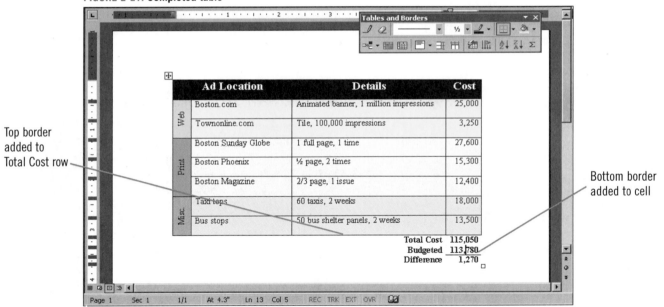

FIGURE E-20: Shading Color palette

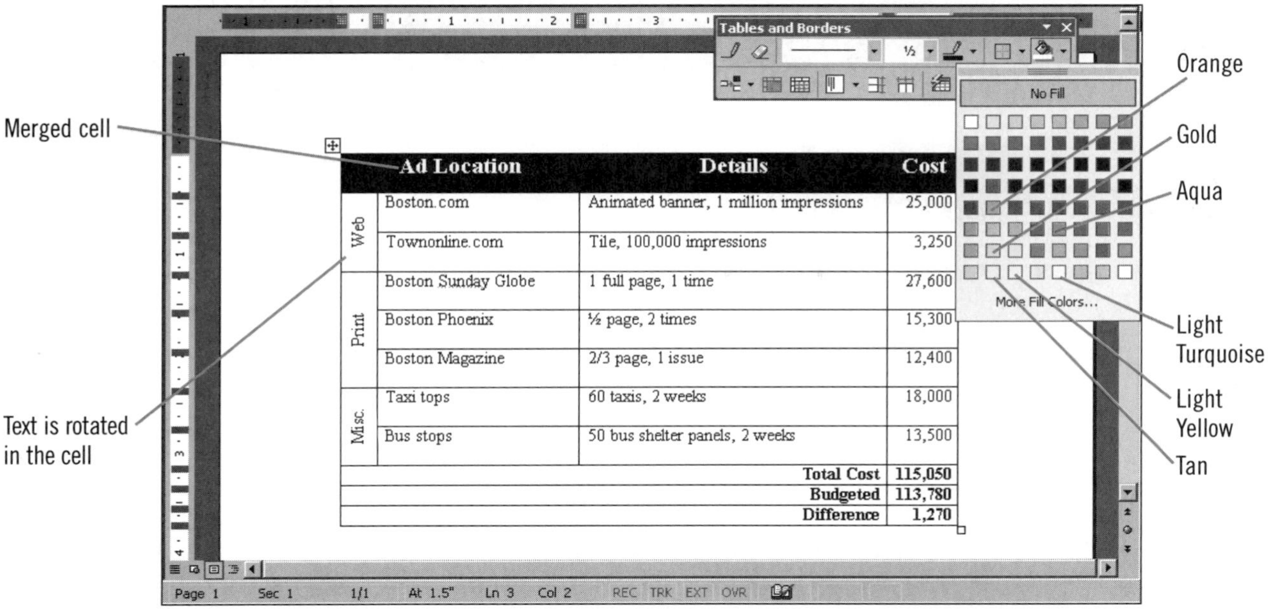

Merged cell

Text is rotated in the cell

Orange
Gold
Aqua
Light Turquoise
Light Yellow
Tan

FIGURE E-21: Completed table

Top border added to Total Cost row

Bottom border added to cell

CLUES TO USE

Drawing a table

Word's Draw Table feature allows you to draw table cells exactly where you want them. To draw a table, click the Draw Table button 📝 on the Tables and Borders toolbar to turn on the Draw pointer 🖉 , then click and drag to draw a cell. Using the same method, draw borders within the cell to create columns and rows, or draw additional cells attached to the first cell. If you want to remove a border from a table, click the Eraser button 🧽 on the Tables and Borders toolbar to activate the Eraser pointer 🖉 , then click the border you want to remove. You can use the Draw pointer and the Eraser pointer to change the structure of any table. Click the Draw Table button or the Eraser button again to turn off the draw or erase feature.

Practice

► Concepts Review

Label each element of the Tables and Borders toolbar shown in Figure E-22.

FIGURE E-22

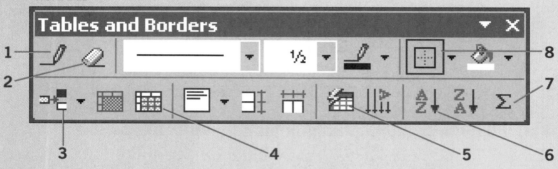

Match each term with the statement that best describes it.

9. Cell
10. Nested table
11. Ascending order
12. Descending order
13. Borders
14. Gridlines
15. Cell reference

a. An object inserted in a table cell
b. Sort order that organizes text from A to Z
c. The box formed by the intersection of a column and a row
d. Lines that show columns and rows in a table, but do not print
e. Lines that separate columns and rows in a table
f. A cell address composed of a column letter and a row number
g. Sort order that organizes text from Z to A

Select the best answer from the list of choices.

16. Which of the following is the cell reference for the third cell in the fourth column?
   a. C4
   b. 4C
   c. 3D
   d. D3

17. Which of the following is *not* a valid way to add a new row to the bottom of a table?
   a. Click in the bottom row, then click the Insert Rows button on the Standard toolbar
   b. Click in the bottom row, then click the Insert Rows Below button on the Tables and Borders toolbar
   c. Click in the bottom row, point to Insert on the Table menu, then click Rows Below
   d. Place the insertion point in the last cell of the last row, then press [Tab]

18. Which button would you use to change the orientation of text in a cell?
   a. [button]
   b. [button]
   c. [button]
   d. [button]

19. Which of the following is *not* a correct formula for adding the values in cells A1, A2, and A3?

   a. =SUM(A1~A3)   **c.** =SUM(A1:A3)

   b. =A1+A2+A3   **d.** =SUM(A1, A2, A3)

20. What happens when you double-click a column border?

   a. The columns in the table are distributed evenly.

   b. A new column is added to the right.

   c. A new column is added to the left.

   d. The column width is adjusted to fit the text.

▶ Skills Review

1. Insert a table.

   a. Start Word, open a new blank document, then save it as **Mutual Funds** to the drive and folder where your Project Files are located.

   b. Type your name, press [Enter] twice, type **Mutual Fund Performance**, then press [Enter].

   c. Insert a table that contains four columns and four rows.

   d. Type the information shown in Table E-2, pressing [Tab] to add rows as necessary.

   e. Save your changes.

TABLE E-2

Fund Name	1 Year	5 Year	10 Year
Computers	16.47	25.56	27.09
Europe	-6.15	13.89	10.61
Natural Resources	19.47	12.30	15.38
Health Care	32.45	24.26	23.25
Financial Services	22.18	21.07	24.44
500 Index	9.13	15.34	13.69

2. Insert and delete rows and columns.

   a. Insert a row above the Health Care row, then type the following text in the new row:

   Canada   **8.24**   **8.12**   **8.56**

   b. Delete the Europe row.

   c. Insert a column to the right of the 10 Year column, type **Date Purchased** in the header row, then enter a date in each cell in the column using the format MM/DD/YY (for example, 11/27/91).

   d. Move the Date Purchased column to the right of the Fund Name column, then save your changes.

3. Modify table rows and columns.

   a. Double-click the border between the first and second columns to resize the columns.

   b. Drag the border between the second and third columns to the 2¼" mark on the horizontal ruler.

   c. Double-click the right border of the 1 Year, 5 Year, and 10 Year columns, select the three columns, then distribute the columns evenly.

   d. Select rows 2-7, use the Table Properties dialog box to set the row height to exactly .3", then save your changes.

4. Sort table data.

   a. Sort the table rows in descending order by the information in the 1 Year column.

   b. Sort the rows in ascending order by date purchased.

   c. Alphabetize the table by fund name, then save your changes.

5. Split and merge cells.

   a. Insert a row above the header row.

   b. Merge the first cell in the new row with the Fund Name cell.

   c. Merge the second cell in the new row with the Date Purchased cell.

d. Merge the three remaining blank cells in the first row into a single cell, then type **Average Annual Returns** in the merged cell.

e. Add a new row to the bottom of the table.

f. Merge the first two cells in the new row, then type **Average Return** in the merged cell.

g. Select the first seven cells in the first column (from Fund Name to Natural Resources), open the Split Cells dialog box, clear the Merge cells before split check box, then split the cells into two columns.

h. Type **Trading Symbol** as the heading for the new column, then enter the following text in the remaining cells in the column: **FINX, CAND, COMP, FINS, HCRX, NARS**.

i. Double-click the right border of the first column to resize the column, double-click the right border of the last column, then save your changes.

6. Perform calculations in tables.

a. Place the insertion point in the last cell in the 1 Year column, then open the Formula dialog box.

b. Delete the text in the Formula text box, type **=average(above)**, click the Number Format list arrow, click 0.00%, then click OK.

c. Repeat step b to insert the average return in the last cell in the 5 Year and 10 Year columns.

d. Change the value of the 1-year average return for the Natural Resources fund to **10.35**.

e. Use [F9] to recalculate the average return for 1 year, then save your changes.

7. Use Table AutoFormat.

a. Open the AutoFormat dialog box, select an appropriate table style for the table, then apply the style to the table. Was the style you chose effective?

b. Using AutoFormat, apply the Table List 3 style to the table.

c. Change the font of all the text in the table to 10-point Arial.

d. Apply bold to the 1 Year, 5 Year, and 10 Year column headings, and to the bottom row of the table.

e. Center the table between the margins, center the table title **Mutual Funds Performance**, format the title in 14-point Arial bold, then save your changes.

8. Create a custom format for a table.

a. Select the entire table, then use the Align Center button on the Tables and Borders toolbar to center the text in every cell vertically and horizontally.

b. Right-align the dates and the numbers in columns 3-6.

c. Left-align the fund names and trading symbols in columns 1 and 2.

d. Right-align the text in the bottom row. Make sure the text in the header row is still centered.

e. Select all the cells in the header row, including the 1 Year, 5 Year, and 10 Year column headings, change the shading color to indigo, then change the font color to white.

f. Apply light yellow shading to the cells containing the fund names and trading symbols.

g. Apply pale blue, tan, and lavender shading to the cells containing the 1 Year, 5 Year, and 10 Year data, respectively. Do not apply shading to the bottom row of the table.

h. Remove all the borders in the table.

i. Add a ½ pt white bottom border to the Average Annual Returns cell.

j. Add a 2¼ pt black border around the outside of the table. Also add a top border to the last row of the table.

k. Examine the table, make any necessary adjustments, then save your changes.

l. Preview the table in Print Preview, print a copy, close the file, then exit Word.

▶ Independent Challenge 1

You are organizing a series of canoe races on the Murray River in southeastern Australia as part of a river festival. For each race, you need to create a flyer that describes the race for the participants. In this exercise, you will format one flyer.

a. Start Word, open the file WD E-1, then save it as **40K Relay** to the drive and folder where your Project Files are located.

b. In the second blank paragraph below the Relay Details heading, insert a table with 5 columns and 3 rows.

c. Enter the text shown in Table E-3, adding rows as necessary.

d. Resize the columns to fit the text.

e. Add a column between the Start Location and Distance columns. Type **Portages** in the header row, then enter the following information in the Portages column: **0; 0; 2 @ 300m; 1 @ 800m; 2 @ 200m each and 1 @ 500m**.

f. Resize the Portages column to fit the text, then distribute the table rows evenly.

g. Using AutoFormat, apply a table style to the table. Select a style that makes the table attractive and easy to read.

h. Center the text in each cell in the table both horizontally and vertically. (*Hint*: Use the Align Center button.)

i. Scroll up, then select the six paragraphs of tabbed text under the Race Details heading.

j. Convert the text to a 2-column table. (*Hint*: Point to Convert on the Table menu, click Text to Table, then click OK.)

k. Remove all the borders from the table, then enhance the flyer with font and paragraph formatting.

l. Press [Ctrl][End], type your name, save your changes, preview the flyer, print it, close the file, then exit Word.

TABLE E-3

Leg	Km	Check-in	Start Location	Distance
1	0	8:30	Echuca Wharf	8 km
2	8	10:00	Rosemount Homestead	8 km
3	16	11:00	Mungo Billabong	4 km
4	20	11:30	Kingfisher Park	9 km
5	29	12:30	Yarrawonga Winery	11 km

▶ Independent Challenge 2

You need new business cards with a fresh design that expresses your personality or the character of your business. In this exercise, you will create a page of business cards using a table to lay out the page. The standard size for business cards is 2"33.5". Figure E-23 shows sample business cards.

a. Start Word, open a new blank document, then save it as **Business Cards** to the drive and folder where your Project Files are located.

b. Change the top, bottom, left and right margins to .4".

c. At the top of the document, insert a table with 2 columns and 5 rows.

d. Select the table, then change the height of the rows to exactly 2" and the width of the columns to exactly 3.5".

e. Center the table on the page.

f. In one cell, enter the information you want to include on your business card. Include your name, address, phone and fax numbers, e-mail address, and Web site, if appropriate. Also include your title and the name of your

FIGURE E-23

Top End Web
Web Site Design & Hosting

Luís Vouzikas
General Manager

550 Knuckey Street, Darwin NT 0801
Phone: 08-8555-7634; Fax: 08-8555-3445
www.topendweb.com.au

 **Vouzikas Construction**
Carpentry · Construction · Remodeling

Luís Vouzikas
Owner

300 Yorkshire Street North, Guelph, Ontario NIH 5B7
Tel: 519-555-8229; vouzikas@yahoo.com

company if appropriate. (*Hint*: If Word automatically formats your e-mail or Web site address as a hyperlink, right click the underlined text, then click Remove Hyperlink.)

g. Use fonts, paragraph alignment, paragraph spacing, colors, clip art, borders, shading, symbols, and other formatting features to create an attractive design for your business card.

h. When you are satisfied with your design, double-check to make sure the row height is still 2" and the column width is still 3.5". Make any necessary adjustments.

i. Select the cell containing the business card, then copy the cell contents to each cell in the table. Once the contents are copied, check your column and row measurements again and make any necessary adjustments.

j. Remove all the table borders, save your changes, preview the business cards in Print Preview, print a copy of the document, close the file, then exit Word.

▶ Independent Challenge 3

You work in the advertising department at a magazine. Your boss has asked you to create a fact sheet on the ad dimensions for the magazine. The fact sheet should include the dimensions for each type of ad as well as a visual representation of the different ad shapes and sizes, shown in Figure E-24. You'll use tables to lay out the fact sheet, present the dimension information, and illustrate the ad shapes and sizes.

a. Start Word, open the file WD E-2 from the drive and folder where your Project Files are located, then save it as **Ad Dimensions**. Read the document to get a feel for its contents.

b. Drag the border between the first and second column to approximately the 2¾" mark on the horizontal ruler, resize the second and third columns to fit the text, then use the Table Properties dialog box to make each row in the table at least .5".

c. Change the alignment of the text in the first column to Center Left, then change the alignment of the text in the Width and Height columns to Center Right.

d. Remove all the borders from the table, then apply a 2¼ point, dark blue, dotted line, inside horizontal border to the entire table.

e. In the second blank paragraph under the table heading, insert a new table with three columns and four rows, then merge the cells in the third column of the new blank table.

f. Drag the border between the first and second columns of the new blank table to the 1¼" mark on the horizontal ruler. Drag the border between the second and third columns to the 1½" mark.

FIGURE E-24

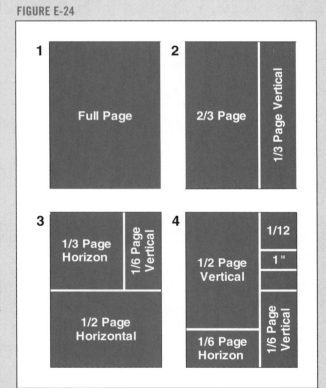

g. Select the table that contains text, cut it to the Clipboard, then paste it in the merged cell in the blank table. The table with text is now a nested table in the main table.

h. Split the nested table above the Unit Size (Bleed) row. (*Hint*: Use the Split Table command on the Table menu.)

i. Merge the cells in the first column of the main table, then merge the cells in the second column.

j. Split the first column into one column and seven rows.

k. Using the Row tab in the Table Properties dialog box, change the row height of each cell in the first column so that the rows alternate between exactly 1.8" and .25" in height. Make the height of the first, third, fifth, and seventh rows 1.8".

l. Add dark blue shading to the first, third, fifth, and seventh cells in the first column, then remove all the borders from the main table.

m. In the first blue cell, type **Full Page**, then center it vertically in the cell.

n. On the Tables and Borders toolbar, change the Line Style to a single line, change the Line Weight to 1, then change the Border Color to white.

o. Activate the Draw Table pointer, then, referring to Figure E-24, draw a vertical border that divides the second blue cell into 2/3 and 1/3. (*Hint*: You can also divide the cell using the Split Cells and Merge Cells buttons.)

p. Label the cells and align the text as shown in the figure. (*Hint*: Change the text direction and alignment before typing text. Take care not to change the size of the cells when you type. If necessary, press [Enter] to start a new line of text in a cell, or reduce the font size of the text.)

q. Referring to Figure E-24, divide the third and fourth blue cells, then label the cells as shown in the figure.

r. Hide the gridlines in the document, examine it for errors, then make any necessary adjustments.

s. Press [Ctrl][End], type your name, save your changes to the document, preview it, print a copy, close the file, then exit Word.

Independent Challenge 4

A well-written and well-formatted resume gives you a leg up on getting a job interview. In a winning resume, the content and format support your career objective and effectively present your background and qualifications. One simple way to create a resume is to lay out the page using a table. In this exercise you will research guidelines for writing and formatting resumes. You will then create your own resume using a table for its layout.

a. Use your favorite search engine to search the Web for information on writing and formatting resumes. Use the keywords resume templates. If your search does not result in links to appropriate sources, try the following Web sites: www.jobsonline.com or www.career.vt.edu.

b. Print helpful advice on writing and formatting resumes from at least two Web sites.

c. Think about the information you want to include in your resume. The header should include your name, address, telephone number, and e-mail address. The body should include your career objective and information on your education, work experience, and skills. You may want to add additional information.

d. Sketch a layout for your resume using a table as the underlying grid. Include the table rows and columns in your sketch.

e. Start Word, open a new blank document, then save it as **My Resume** to the drive and folder where your Project Files are located.

f. Set appropriate margins, then insert a table to serve as the underlying grid for your resume. Split and merge cells and adjust the size of the table columns as necessary.

g. Type your resume in the table cells. Take care to use a professional tone and keep your language to the point.

h. Format your resume with fonts, bullets, and other formatting features. Adjust the spacing between sections by resizing the table columns and rows.

i. When you are satisfied with the content and format of your resume, remove the borders from the table, then hide the gridlines.

j. Check your resume for spelling and grammar errors.

k. Save your changes, preview your resume, print a copy, close the file, then exit Word.

▶ Visual Workshop

Create the calendar shown in Figure E-25 using a table to lay out the entire page. (*Hints*: The clip art image is inserted in the table. The top and bottom margins are .5", the left and right margins are .7", the font is Century Gothic, and the clip art image uses the keyword "carnival," but you can use a different clip art image or font if necessary.) Type your name in the last table cell, save the calendar with the filename **March 2003** to the drive and folder where your Project Files are located, then print a copy.

FIGURE E-25

March 2003

Sunday	Monday	Tuesday	Wednesday	Thursday	Friday	Saturday
						1
2	3	4	5	6	7	8
9	10	11	12	13	14	15
16	17	18	19	20	21	22
23	24	25	26	27	28	29
30	31					

Illustrating
Documents with Graphics

Objectives

- MOUS ► **Add graphics**
- MOUS ► **Resize graphics**
- MOUS ► **Position graphics**
- MOUS ► **Create text boxes**
- MOUS ► **Create AutoShapes**
- MOUS ► **Use the drawing canvas**
- MOUS ► **Create WordArt**
- MOUS ► **Create charts**

Graphics can help illustrate the ideas in your documents, provide visual interest on a page, and give your documents punch and flair. In addition to clip art, you can add graphics created in other programs to a document, or you can use Word's drawing features to create your own images. In this unit, you learn how to insert, modify, and position graphics, how to draw your own images, and how to illustrate a document with WordArt and charts. ✐ Alice Wegman is preparing materials for a workshop for new MediaLoft marketing staff. She uses the graphic features of Word to illustrate three handouts on different MediaLoft marketing issues. You will work with Alice as she creates the handouts.

Word 2002

Adding Graphics

Graphic images you can insert in a document include the clip art that comes with Word, photos taken with a digital camera, scanned art, and graphics created in other graphics programs. When you first insert a graphic it is an **inline graphic**—part of the line of text in which it was inserted. You can move an inline graphic just as you would move text. To be able to move a graphic independently of text, you must apply a text wrapping style to it to make it a **floating graphic**, which can be moved anywhere on a page. You can insert clip art or another graphic file into a document using the Picture command on the Insert menu. Alice has written a handout containing tips for writing and designing ads. She wants to illustrate the handout with the MediaLoft logo, a graphic created in another graphics program. She uses the Picture, From File command to insert the logo in the document. She then wraps the text around the logo.

Steps

1. Start **Word**, open the file **WD F-1** from the drive and folder where your Project Files are located, save it as **Ad Tips**, click the **Zoom list arrow** on the Standard toolbar, click **Page Width** if necessary, then read the document to get a feel for its contents
   The document opens in Print Layout view.

QuickTip

The Drawing button is a toggle button that you can use to display and hide the Drawing toolbar.

2. Click the **Show/Hide ¶ button** ¶ on the Standard toolbar to turn on the display of formatting marks, then click the **Drawing button** on the Standard toolbar to display the Drawing toolbar if it is not already displayed
   The Drawing toolbar, located below the document window, includes buttons for inserting, creating, and modifying graphics.

3. Click before the heading **Create a simple layout**, click **Insert** on the menu bar, point to **Picture**, then click **From File**
   The Insert Picture dialog box opens. You use this dialog box to locate and insert graphic files. Most graphic files are **bitmap graphics**, which are composed of a series of small dots, called **pixels**, that define color and intensity. Bitmap graphics are often saved with a .bmp, .png, .jpg, .wmf, .tif, or .gif file extension. Use the Files of type list arrow in the Insert Picture dialog box to select the type of graphic file you want to insert. To view all the graphic files in a particular location, select All Pictures.

4. Click the **Files of type list arrow**, click **All Pictures** if necessary, use the Look in list arrow to navigate to the drive and folder where your Project Files are located, click the file **Mloft.jpg**, then click **Insert**
   The logo is inserted as an inline graphic at the location of the insertion point. Unless you want a graphic to be part of a line of text, usually the first thing you do after inserting it is to wrap text around it so it becomes a floating graphic. To be able to position a graphic anywhere on a page, you must apply a text wrapping style to it even if there is no text on the page.

Trouble?

If your Picture toolbar does not open, click View on the menu bar, point to Toolbars, then click Picture.

5. Click the **logo graphic** to select it
   Squares, called **sizing handles**, appear on the sides and corners of the graphic when it is selected, as shown in Figure F-1. The Picture toolbar also opens. The Picture toolbar includes buttons for modifying graphics.

6. Click the **Text Wrapping button** on the Picture toolbar
   A menu of text wrapping styles opens.

7. Click **Tight**
   The text wraps around the sides of the graphic, as shown in Figure F-2. Notice that the sizing handles change to circles, indicating the graphic is a floating object, and an anchor and a green rotate handle appear. The anchor indicates the floating graphic is **anchored** to the nearest paragraph, so that the graphic will move with the paragraph if the paragraph is moved. The anchor symbol appears only when formatting marks are displayed.

8. Click ¶, deselect the graphic, then click the **Save button** on the Standard toolbar to save your changes

FIGURE F-1: Inline graphic

Picture toolbar

Graphic is part of the same line of text as "Create a simple layout"

Sizing handles; square sizing handles indicate an inline graphic

Drawing toolbar

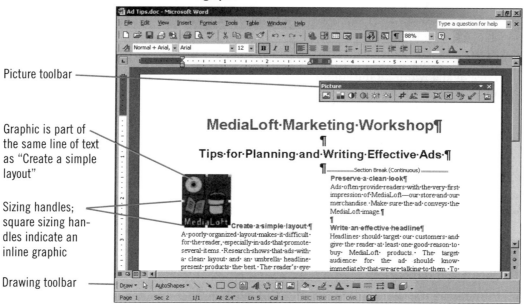

FIGURE F-2: Floating graphic

Text Wrapping button

Logo is anchored to the paragraph next to it

Rotate handle

Circular sizing handles indicate a floating graphic

Text wraps around the shape of the graphic

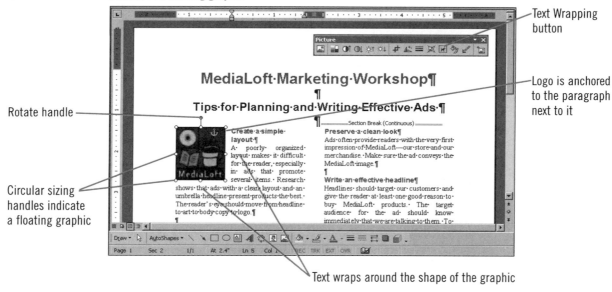

Inserting clips from the Microsoft Design Gallery Live Web site

If you have an Internet connection open when you search for clips using the Insert Clip Art task pane, your search results will automatically include clips from the Microsoft Design Gallery Live Web site, in addition to the clips stored in your Clip Organizer. You can also visit the Microsoft Design Gallery Live Web site to download clips into your Clip Organizer. To visit the Design Gallery Live Web site, click the Clips Online hyperlink in the Insert Clip Art task pane. This opens your browser and connects you to the site, where, after you have read and accepted the License Agreement, you are free to search for and download clips. You can search for clips related to a keyword, in a certain category, or of a particular file type (clip art, photos, sounds, or motion). To download a clip, click the check box under the clip to select it, then click the red arrow to the left of the check box. The clip is automatically downloaded and stored in the appropriate category in your Clip Organizer, making it available for use when you are not connected to the Internet.

Word 2002

Resizing Graphics

Once you insert a graphic into a document, you can change its shape or size by using the mouse to drag a sizing handle, or by using the Picture command on the Format menu to specify an exact height and width for the graphic. Resizing a graphic with the mouse allows you to see how the image looks as you modify it. Using the Picture command to alter a graphic's shape or size allows you to set precise measurements. ✐ Alice enlarges the MediaLoft logo.

QuickTip
Click Ruler on the View menu to display the rulers.

1. **Click the logo graphic to select it, place the pointer over the middle-right sizing handle, when the pointer changes to ↔, drag to the right until the graphic is about 1¾" wide**

   As you drag, the dotted outline indicates the size and shape of the graphic. You can refer to the ruler to gauge the measurements as you drag. When you release the mouse button, the image is stretched to be wider. Dragging a side, top, or bottom sizing handle changes only the width or height of a graphic.

QuickTip
If you enlarge a bitmap graphic too much, the dots that make up the picture become visible and the graphic is distorted.

2. **Click the Undo button** 🔄 **on the Standard toolbar, place the pointer over the upper-right sizing handle, when the pointer changes to ↗ drag up and to the right until the graphic is about 2" tall and 1¾" wide as shown in Figure F-3**

   The image is enlarged. Dragging a corner sizing handle resizes the graphic proportionally so that its width and height are reduced or enlarged by the same percentage. Table F-1 describes other ways to resize objects using the mouse.

3. **Double-click the logo graphic**

   The Format Picture dialog box opens. It includes options for changing the coloring, size, scale, text wrapping, and position of a graphic. You can double-click any graphic object or use the Picture command on the Format menu to open the Format Picture dialog box.

4. **Click the Size tab**

   The Size tab, shown in Figure F-4, allows you to enter precise height and width measurements for a graphic or to scale a graphic by entering the percentage by which you want to reduce or enlarge it. When a graphic is sized to **scale**, its height to width ratio remains the same.

Trouble?
Your height measurement might differ slightly.

5. **Change the measurement in the Width text box in the Size and rotate area to 1.5, then click the Height text box in the Size and rotate area**

   The height measurement automatically changes to 1.69". When the Lock aspect ratio check box is selected, you need only to enter a height or width measurement. Word calculates the other measurement so that the resized graphic will be proportional.

6. **Click OK, then save your changes**

   The logo is resized to be precisely 1.5" wide and approximately 1.69" tall.

TABLE F-1: Methods for resizing an object using the mouse

do this	to
Drag a corner sizing handle	Resize a clip art or bitmap graphic proportionally from a corner
Press [Shift] and drag a corner sizing handle	Resize a drawing object, such as an AutoShape or WordArt object, proportionally from a corner
Press [Ctrl] and drag a side, top, or bottom sizing handle	Resize any graphic object vertically or horizontally while keeping the center position fixed
Press [Ctrl] and drag a corner sizing handle	Resize any graphic object diagonally while keeping the center position fixed
Press [Shift][Ctrl] and drag a corner sizing handle	Resize any graphic object proportionally while keeping the center position fixed

FIGURE F-3: Dragging to resize an image

Dotted outline shows the size of the graphic as you drag

FIGURE F-4: Size tab in the Format Picture dialog box

Set specific height and width measurements (yours might differ)

Change the scale of an object

Select to keep height and width proportional

Select to make scaled measurements relative to the original size

Click to reset image to its original size

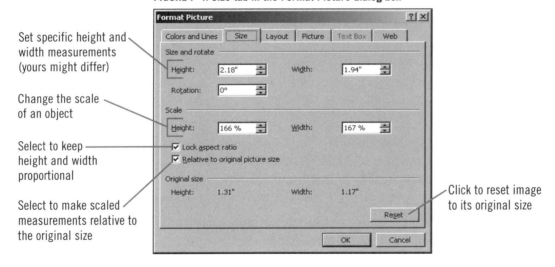

Clues to Use

Cropping graphics

If you want to use only part of a picture in a document, you can **crop** the graphic to trim the parts you don't want to use. To crop a graphic, select it, then click the Crop button ⊞ on the Picture toolbar. The pointer changes to the cropping pointer and cropping handles (solid black lines) appear on all four corners and sides of the graphic. To crop one side of a graphic, drag a side cropping handle inward to where you want to trim the graphic. To crop two sides at once, drag a corner cropping handle inward to the point where you want the corner of the cropped image to be. When you drag a cropping handle, the shape of the cropping pointer changes to correspond to the shape of the cropping handle you are dragging. When you finish adjusting the parameters of the graphic, click the Crop button again to turn off the crop feature. You can also crop a graphic by entering precise crop measurements on the Picture tab in the Format Picture dialog box.

Word 2002

Positioning Graphics

Once you insert a graphic into a document and make it a floating graphic, you can move it by dragging it with the mouse, nudging it with the arrow keys, or setting an exact location for the graphic using the Picture command on the Format menu. Dragging an object with the mouse or using the arrow keys allows you to position a graphic visually. Using the Picture command to position a graphic allows you to place an object precisely on a page. Alice experiments with different positions for the MediaLoft logo to determine which position enhances the document the most.

Steps

QuickTip

To move an object only horizontally or vertically, press [Shift] as you drag.

1. **Select** the **logo graphic** if necessary, move the pointer over the graphic, when the pointer changes to ⊹, drag the graphic down and to the right as shown in Figure F-5 so its top aligns with the top of the **Create a simple layout** heading
   As you drag, the dotted outline indicates the position of the graphic. When you release the mouse button, the graphic is moved and the text wraps around the graphic. Notice that the Create a simple layout heading is now above the graphic.

2. **With the graphic selected, press [←] four times, then press [↑] three times**
   Each time you press an arrow key the graphic is **nudged**—moved a small amount—in that direction. You can also press [Ctrl] and an arrow key to nudge an object in even smaller (one pixel) increments.

QuickTip

You can place a floating graphic anywhere on a page, including outside the margins.

3. **Double-click** the **graphic**, click the **Layout tab** in the Format Picture dialog box, then click **Advanced**
   The Advanced Layout dialog box opens. The Picture Position tab, shown in Figure F-6, allows you to specify an exact position for a graphic relative to some aspect of the document, such as a margin, column, or paragraph.

4. **Click the Picture Position tab** if necessary, click the **Alignment Option button** in the Horizontal section, click the **Alignment list arrow**, click **Centered**, click the **relative to list arrow**, then click **Margin**
   The logo will be centered horizontally between the left and right page margins.

5. **Change the measurement in the Absolute position text box in the Vertical section to 1.5**, click the **below list arrow**, then click **Margin**
   The top of the graphic will be positioned precisely 1.5" below the top margin.

6. **Click the Text Wrapping tab**
   You can use the Text Wrapping tab to change the text wrapping style, to wrap text around only one side of a graphic, and to change the distance between the edge of the graphic and the edge of the wrapped text. You want to increase the amount of white space between the sides of the graphic and the wrapped text.

7. **Select Square, select 0.13 in the Left text box, type .3, press [Tab], then type .3 in the Right text box**
   The distance between the graphic and the edge of the wrapped text will be .3" on either side.

Trouble?

If the Picture toolbar remains open after you deselect the graphic, close the toolbar.

8. **Click OK to close the Advanced Layout dialog box, click OK to close the Format Picture dialog box, deselect the graphic, then save your changes**
   The logo is centered between the margins, the top of the graphic is positioned 1.5" below the top margin, and the amount of white space between the left and right sides of the graphic and the wrapped text is increased to .3", as shown in Figure F-7.

FIGURE F-5: Dragging a graphic to move it

Top of graphic aligns with the top of the text

Dotted outline shows the position as you drag

FIGURE F-6: Picture Position tab in the Advanced Layout dialog box

Click to horizontally align a graphic relative to an aspect of the document

Click to position a graphic a precise distance from an aspect of the document

Select the aspect of the document you want to position the graphic in relationship to

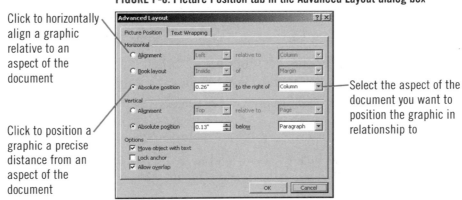

FIGURE F-7: Repositioned logo

Logo is centered and its top is 1.5" from the top margin

1.5" mark on the ruler

Space between the graphic and the text is increased

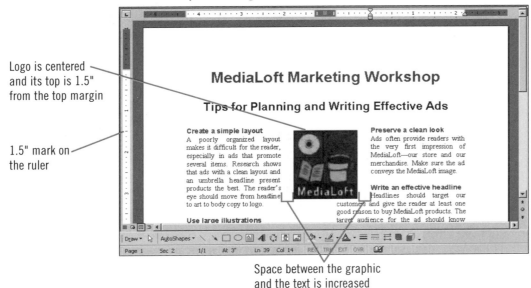

Creating Text Boxes

When you want to illustrate your documents with text, you can create a text box. A **text box** is a container that you can fill with text and graphics. Like other drawing objects, text boxes can be resized, formatted with colors, lines, and text wrapping, and positioned anywhere on a page. You can create a text box using the Text Box button on the Drawing toolbar or the Text Box command on the Insert menu. When you insert a text box or another drawing object, a drawing canvas opens in the document. A **drawing canvas** is a workspace for creating your own graphics. You can choose to draw the text box directly in the document, or to draw it in the drawing canvas. Alice wants to add a pull quote to call attention to the main point of the handout. She draws a text box, adds the pull quote text to it, formats the text, and then positions the text box on the page.

Steps

1. Scroll down, click before the **Use large illustrations** heading, then click the **Text Box button** on the Drawing toolbar

   A drawing canvas opens in the document, as shown in Figure F-8, and the pointer changes to +. You'll draw a text box outside the drawing canvas.

2. Move the + pointer directly under the lower-left corner of the MediaLoft logo, then click and drag down and to the right to draw a text box that is about 1½" wide and 2¾" tall

   When you release the mouse button, the drawing canvas disappears and the insertion point is located in the text box, as shown in Figure F-9. The Text Box toolbar also opens.

3. Type **The reader's eye should move from headline to art to body copy to logo**

4. Select the text, click the **Font list arrow** on the Formatting toolbar, click **Arial**, click the **Font size list arrow**, click **14**, click the **Bold button**, click the **Center button**, click the **Line Spacing list arrow**, click **2.0**, then click outside the text box

   The text is formatted. Notice that the text does not wrap around the text box. By default, text boxes are inserted with the In front of text wrapping style applied.

5. Click the **text box**, double-click the **text box frame**, click the **Size tab** in the Format Text Box dialog box, then change the height to **2.75"** and the width to **1.5"** in the Size and rotate section, if necessary

   When you click a text box with the I pointer, the insertion point moves inside the text box and sizing handles appear. Clicking the frame of a text box with the pointer selects the text box object itself. Double-clicking the frame opens the Format Text Box dialog box.

6. Click the **Layout tab**, click **Advanced**, click the **Picture Position tab** if necessary, click the **Alignment option button** in the Horizontal section, click the **Alignment list arrow**, click **Centered**, click the **relative to list arrow**, click **Margin**, click the **Absolute position option button** in the Vertical section if necessary, change the measurement in the Absolute position text box to **3.4**, click the **below list arrow**, then click **Margin**

   The text box will be centered between the left and right margins and its top will be precisely 3.4" below the top margin.

7. Click the **Text Wrapping tab**, click **Square**, change the Top, Bottom, Left, and Right measurements to **.3"** in the Distance from text section, click **OK** twice, then deselect the text box

   The text is wrapped in a square around the text box.

8. Click inside the text box, click the **Line Color list arrow** on the Drawing toolbar, click **No Line**, then deselect the text box

   The thin black border around the text box is removed, as shown in Figure F-10.

9. Press **[Ctrl][End]**, type your name, save your changes, print, then close the file

FIGURE F-8: Drawing canvas

Drawing canvas

Drawing Canvas toolbar (yours might be docked)

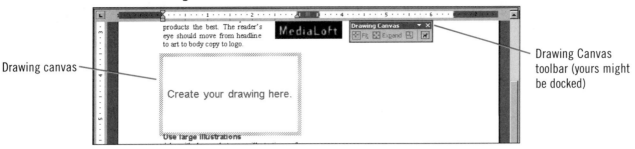

FIGURE F-9: Text box

Insertion point in text box

Text box frame

Text Box toolbar

Text Box button

Line Color list arrow

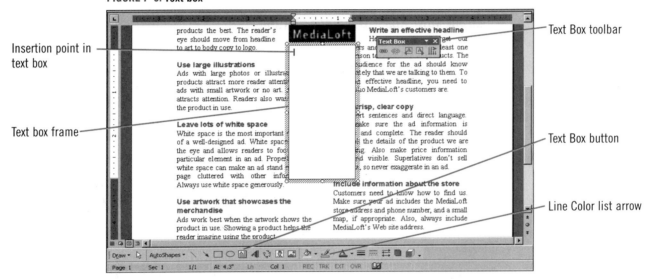

FIGURE F-10: Completed handout with text box

Text wraps around the text box

Formatted text in text box

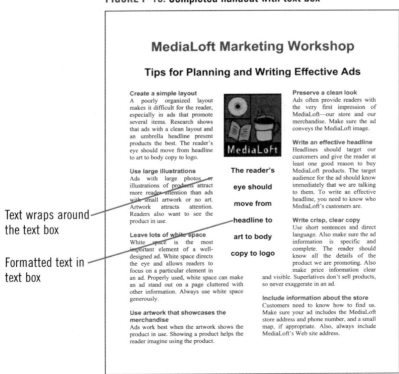

Creating AutoShapes

You can create your own graphics in Word using AutoShapes. **AutoShapes** are the rectangles, ovals, triangles, lines, block arrows, stars, banners, lightning bolts, hearts, suns, and other drawing objects you can create using the tools on the Drawing toolbar. The Drawing toolbar also includes tools for adding colors, shadows, fills, and three-dimensional effects to your images. Table F-2 describes the buttons on the Drawing toolbar. You can choose to draw a line or shape exactly where you want it in a document, or you can create a graphic in a drawing canvas. It's helpful to use a drawing canvas if your graphic includes multiple items. ✎ Alice creates a handout that illustrates MediaLoft book sales by genre. She uses AutoShapes to create a picture of a stack of books, and then adds the text, to the picture.

Steps

1. Click the **New Blank Document button** 🗋 on the Standard toolbar, then save the document as **Genre Sales** to the drive and folder where your Project Files are located

2. Click the **Rectangle button** ▢ on the Drawing toolbar
   When you click an AutoShape button, a drawing canvas opens, the Drawing Canvas toolbar appears, and the pointer changes to +. The Drawing Canvas toolbar contains buttons for sizing the graphics you create in the drawing canvas, and for wrapping text around the drawing canvas. You'll learn more about resizing and positioning the drawing canvas in the next lesson.

   QuickTip

   To draw a square, click the Rectangle button ▢, then press [Shift] while you drag the + pointer. Similarly, to draw a circle, click the Oval button ⬭, then press [Shift] while you drag the + pointer.

3. Scroll down until the entire drawing canvas is visible on your screen, place the pointer about ¾" above the lower-left corner of the drawing canvas, then drag down and to the right to create a rectangle that is about **5"** wide and **½"** tall
   You do not need to be exact in your measurements as you drag. When you release the mouse button, sizing handles appear around the rectangle to indicate it is selected. Cropping handles also appear around the edges of the drawing canvas.

4. Click **AutoShapes** on the Drawing toolbar, point to **Basic Shapes**, then click the **Sun**
   The AutoShapes menu contains categories of shapes and lines that you can draw.

5. Place the + pointer in the upper-left corner of the drawing canvas, then drag down and to the right to create a sun that is about **½"** wide
   The sun shape includes a yellow diamond-shaped adjustment handle. You can drag an **adjustment handle** to change the shape, but not the size, of many AutoShapes.

6. Position the pointer over the adjustment handle until it changes to ◺, drag the handle to the right about **¼"**, click the **Fill Color list arrow** 🎨▾ on the Drawing toolbar, click **Gold**, click the **rectangle** to select it, click 🎨▾, then click **Aqua**
   The sun shape becomes narrower and the shapes are filled with color. Notice that when you select a color, the active color changes on the Fill Color button.

   QuickTip

   You can also double-click the Oval, Line, or Arrow button to draw more than one shape or line. When you are finished drawing, click the button again.

7. Double-click ▢ to activate the rectangle tool, refer to Figure F-11 to draw three more rectangles, click ▢ to turn off the tool, then fill the rectangles with color
   After all four rectangles are drawn, use the sizing handles to resize the rectangles if necessary.

8. Press and hold **[Shift]**, click each **rectangle** to select it, click the **3-D Style button** 🔲 on the Drawing toolbar, then click **3-D Style 1** (the first style in the top row)
   The rectangles become three-dimensional, making the group look like a stack of books.

   QuickTip

   To edit text in an AutoShape, right-click it, then click Edit Text.

9. Deselect the books, right-click the **top book**, click **Add Text**, click the **Font Size list arrow** on the Formatting toolbar, click **20**, then type **Children's - 17%**
   The 3-D rectangle changes to a text box. You can convert any shape to a text box by right-clicking it and clicking Add Text.

10. Add the 20-point text as shown in Figure F-12, then save your changes

FIGURE F-11: **AutoShapes in the drawing canvas**

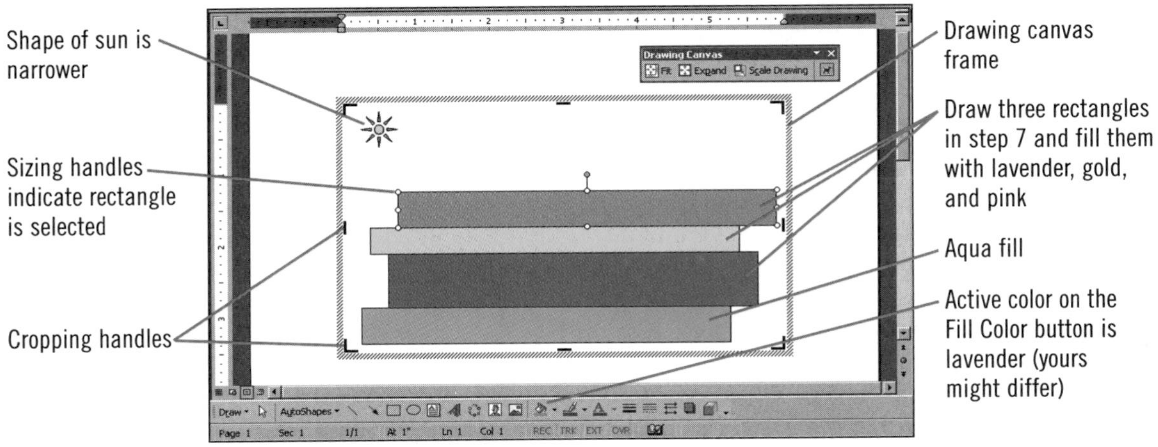

Shape of sun is narrower

Sizing handles indicate rectangle is selected

Cropping handles

Drawing canvas frame

Draw three rectangles in step 7 and fill them with lavender, gold, and pink

Aqua fill

Active color on the Fill Color button is lavender (yours might differ)

FIGURE F-12: **Text added to AutoShapes**

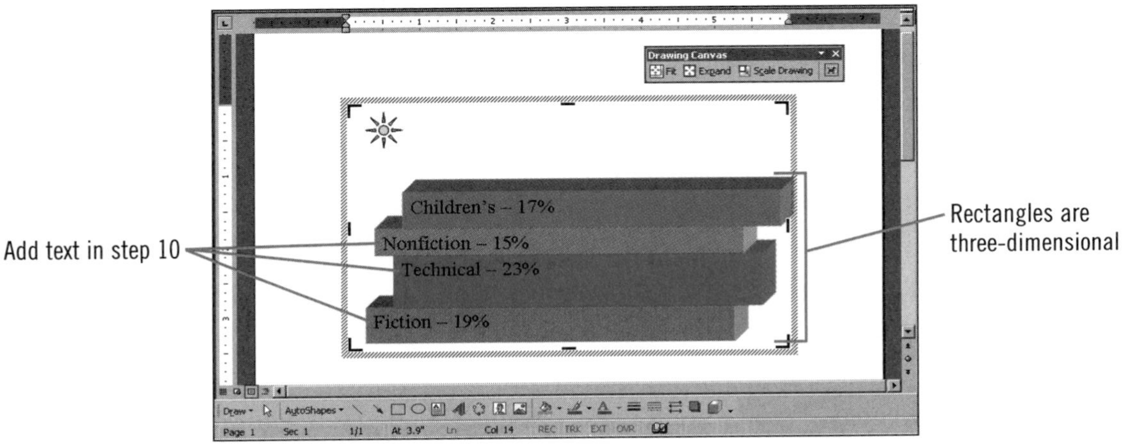

Add text in step 10

Children's – 17%
Nonfiction – 15%
Technical – 23%
Fiction – 19%

Rectangles are three-dimensional

Word 2002

TABLE F-2: **Buttons on the Drawing toolbar**

button	use to	button	use to
Draw ▾	Open a menu of commands for grouping, positioning, rotating, and wrapping text around graphics, and for changing an AutoShape to a different shape		Insert a clip art graphic
	Select graphic objects		Insert a picture from a file
AutoShapes ▾	Open a menu of drawing options for lines, shapes, and callouts	◇ ▾	Fill a shape with a color, a texture, a gradient, or a pattern
	Draw a straight line		Change the color of a line, arrow, or line around a shape
	Draw a straight line with an arrowhead	A ▾	Change the color of text
	Draw a rectangle or square		Change the style and weight of a line, arrow, or line around a shape
	Draw an oval or circle		Change the dash style of a line, arrow, or line around a shape
	Insert a text box		Change a line to an arrow; change the style of an arrow
	Insert a WordArt graphic		Add a shadow to a graphic object
	Insert a diagram or an organization chart		Make a graphic object three-dimensional

ILLUSTRATING DOCUMENTS WITH GRAPHICS WORD F-11 ◄

Using the Drawing Canvas

When multiple shapes are contained in a drawing canvas, you can resize and move them as a single graphic object. The Drawing Canvas toolbar includes buttons for sizing a drawing canvas and for wrapping text around it. Once you apply a text wrapping style to a drawing canvas, you can position it anywhere in a document. Alice wants to add another three books to the stack. She enlarges the drawing canvas, adds the shapes, sizes the drawing as a single object, and then moves it to the bottom of the page.

Steps

1. Click the **Zoom list arrow** on the Standard toolbar, click **75%**, then click the **stack of books graphic** to make the drawing canvas visible if necessary
   Cropping handles appear around the edges of the drawing canvas.

2. Place the pointer over the **top-middle cropping handle**, when the pointer changes to ⊥, drag the handle to the top of the page, then release the mouse button
   The drawing canvas is enlarged from the top, but the size of the graphic does not change. Dragging a cropping handle resizes the canvas, but not the graphic.

3. Select the **sun**, position the pointer over it until the pointer changes to ⬩, drag the **sun** on top of the right end of the Technical book, then release the mouse button
   The sun shape is moved to the spine of the book, but is hidden beneath the rectangle shape.

4. With the sun shape selected, click the **Draw button** on the Drawing toolbar, point to **Order**, then click **Bring to Front**
   The sun shape is moved on top of the rectangle shape.

5. Double-click the **Rectangle button** ▢ on the Drawing toolbar, draw three more rectangles on top of the stack of books, click ▢, then right-click each **rectangle** and add the 20-point text shown in Figure F-13

6. Select each **rectangle**, fill it with any color, then apply the **3D Style 1**

7. Click the **Fit Drawing to Contents button** ▦ on the Drawing Canvas toolbar
   The drawing canvas is automatically resized to fit the graphic within it.

8. Click the **Zoom list arrow**, click **Whole Page**, then click the **Scale Drawing button** ▦ on the Drawing Canvas toolbar
   The cropping handles on the drawing canvas change to sizing handles. You can now use the drawing canvas frame to resize the contents of the drawing canvas as a single graphic.

9. Drag the **bottom-middle sizing handle** down until the graphic is about **6"** tall
   Resizing the drawing canvas resizes all the shapes within it. Dragging a top, bottom, or side handle stretches the graphic. Dragging a corner handle resizes the graphic proportionally.

10. Click the **Text Wrapping button** ▦ on the Drawing Canvas toolbar, click **Square**, place the pointer over the **drawing canvas frame** so it changes to ⬩, drag the **canvas** down and position it so it is centered in the bottom part of the page, deselect the drawing canvas, then save your changes
    Compare your document to Figure F-14. You must wrap text around a drawing canvas to be able to position it anywhere on a page.

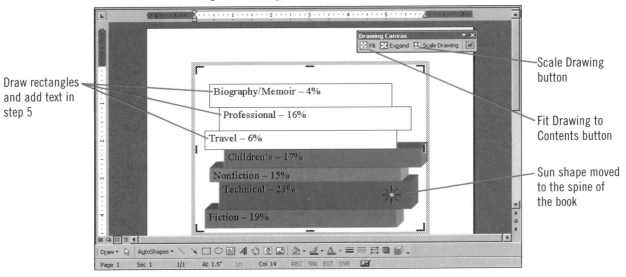

FIGURE F-13: New rectangles in drawing canvas

Draw rectangles and add text in step 5

Scale Drawing button

Fit Drawing to Contents button

Sun shape moved to the spine of the book

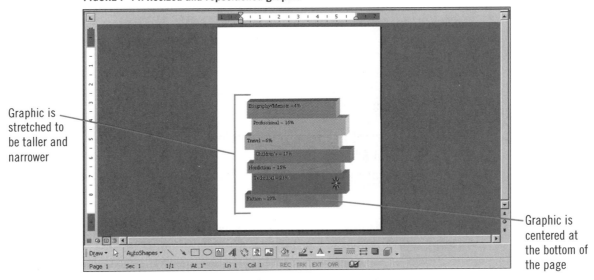

FIGURE F-14: Resized and repositioned graphic

Graphic is stretched to be taller and narrower

Graphic is centered at the bottom of the page

Drawing lines

In addition to drawing straight lines and arrows, you can use the Lines tools on the AutoShapes menu to draw curved, freeform, and scribble lines. Click AutoShapes on the Drawing toolbar, point to Lines, then select the type of line you want to draw. Choose Curve to draw an object with smooth curves, choose Freeform to draw an object with both free-hand and straight-line segments, or choose Scribble to draw a freehand object that looks like it was drawn with a pencil. The lines you draw include ver-texes—a **vertex** is either a point where two straight lines meet or the highest point in a curve. To create a curve or freeform line, click the location you want the line to begin, move the mouse, click to insert a vertex, move the mouse, and so on. Double-click to end a curve or freeform line or click near the starting point to close a shape, if that's what you have drawn. Drawing scribble lines is similar to drawing with a pen-cil: drag the pointer to draw the line, then release the mouse button when you are finished. The best way to learn about drawing curve, freeform, and scribble lines is to experiment. Once you draw a line, you can modify its shape by right-clicking it, clicking Edit Points, and then dragging a vertex to a different location.

Creating WordArt

Another way to give your documents punch and flair is to use WordArt. **WordArt** is a drawing object that contains text formatted with special shapes, patterns, and orientations. You create WordArt using either the WordArt button on the Drawing toolbar or the Picture, WordArt command on the Insert menu. ✐　　　 Alice uses WordArt to create a fun heading for her handout.

Steps 1234

1. Press **[Ctrl][Home]**, press **[Enter]**, click the **Zoom list arrow** on the Standard toolbar, click **Page Width**, then click the **Insert WordArt button** ⁴⁴ on the Drawing toolbar
The WordArt Gallery opens, as shown in Figure F-15. It includes the styles you can choose for your WordArt.

2. Click the fourth style in the fourth row, then click **OK**
The Edit WordArt Text dialog box opens. You type the text you want to format as WordArt in this dialog box and, if you wish, change the font and font size of the WordArt text.

QuickTip

You can use the Text Wrapping button on the WordArt toolbar to convert the object to a floating graphic.

3. Type **Genre Sales**, then click **OK**
The WordArt object appears at the location of the insertion point. Like other graphic objects, the WordArt object is an inline graphic until you wrap text around it.

4. Click the **WordArt object** to select it
The WordArt toolbar appears when a WordArt object is selected. It includes buttons for editing and modifying WordArt.

Trouble?

If your page goes blank, click the Undo button ↺ and repeat step 5. Take care not to make the Word Art object taller than 2".

5. Drag the **lower-right corner sizing handle** down and to the right to make the object about **2"** tall and **6"** wide
The WordArt is enlarged to span the page between the left and right margins, as shown in Figure F-16.

6. Click the **WordArt Same Letter Heights button** Aa on the WordArt toolbar, click the **WordArt Character Spacing button** ᴬᵥ on the WordArt toolbar, then click **Loose**
First, the uppercase and lowercase letters change to become the same height, and then the spacing between the characters is increased.

QuickTip

To change the color of WordArt, click the Format WordArt button ⬚ on the WordArt toolbar, then use the Colors and Lines tab in the Format WordArt dialog box.

7. Click the **WordArt Shape button** ᴬᵇᶜ on the WordArt toolbar, then click the **Curve Up** shape (the first shape in the third row)
The shape of the WordArt text changes. You can experiment with different shapes, fonts, colors, and other effects to create WordArt that has the impact you desire.

8. Click the **Zoom list arrow**, click **Whole Page**, click the **WordArt Gallery button** ⬚ on the WordArt toolbar, click the second style in the third row, click **OK**, then deselect the WordArt object
The WordArt changes to a different style. The completed handout is shown in Figure F-17.

Trouble?

Adjust the colors as necessary.

9. Press **[Ctrl][Home]**, type your name, save your changes, print the document, then close the file

FIGURE F-15: WordArt Gallery

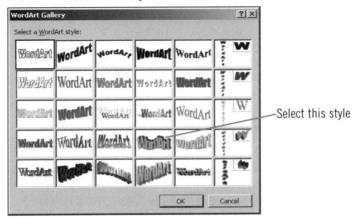

Select this style

FIGURE F-16: Resized WordArt

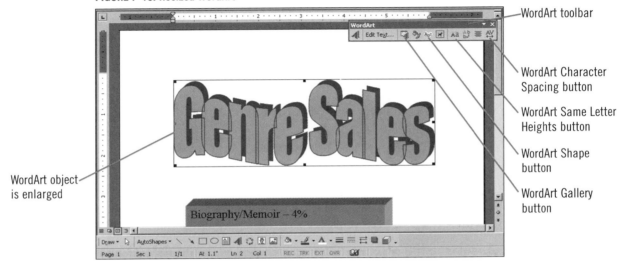

WordArt toolbar

WordArt Character Spacing button

WordArt Same Letter Heights button

WordArt Shape button

WordArt Gallery button

WordArt object is enlarged

FIGURE F-17: Completed handout with WordArt

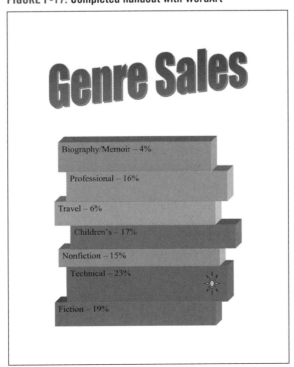

Creating Charts

Adding a chart can be an attractive way to illustrate a document that includes numerical information. A **chart** is a visual representation of numerical data and usually is used to illustrate trends, patterns, or relationships. Word's chart feature allows you to create many types of charts, including bar, column, pie, area, and line charts. You can add a chart to a document using the Picture, Chart command on the Insert menu. Alice creates a handout that includes a chart showing the distribution of MediaLoft customers by age and gender.

Steps

1. Open the file **WD F-2** from the drive and folder where your Project Files are located, save it as **Age and Gender**, then press **[Ctrl][End]**
   You will insert a chart at the location of the insertion point, which is centered under the title.

2. Click **Insert** on the menu bar, point to **Picture**, then click **Chart**
   A table opens in a datasheet window and a column chart appears in the document. The datasheet and the chart contain placeholder data that you can replace with your own data. The chart is based on the data in the datasheet. Any change you make to the data in the datasheet is made automatically to the chart. Notice that when a chart object is open, the Standard toolbar includes buttons for working with charts.

3. Click the **datasheet title bar** and drag it so that the chart is visible, then move the pointer over the **datasheet**
   The pointer changes to ✛. You use this pointer to select the cells in the datasheet.

4. Click the **East cell**, type **Male**, click the **West cell**, type **Female**, click the gray **3 cell** to select the third row, then press **[Delete]**
   When you click a cell and type, the data in the cell is replaced with the text you type. As you edit the datasheet, the changes you make are reflected in the chart.

5. Replace the remaining placeholder text with the data shown in Figure F-18, then click outside the chart to deselect it

6. Click the **chart** to select the object, press **[Ctrl]**, then drag the **lower-right corner sizing handle** down and to the right until the outline of the chart is approximately **7"** wide
   The chart is enlarged and still centered.

7. Double-click the **chart** to open it, click the **View Datasheet button** 📖 on the Standard toolbar to close the datasheet, click the **legend** to select it, then click the **Format Legend button** 🖼 on the Standard toolbar
   The name of the button is Format Legend because the legend is selected. The Format Legend dialog box opens. It includes options for modifying the legend. Select any part of a chart object and use 🖼 to open a dialog box with options for formatting that part of the chart.

8. Click the **Placement tab**, click the **Bottom option button**, then click **OK**
   The legend moves below the chart.

9. Click the **value axis** (the Y-axis), click 🖼, click the **Number tab** in the Format Axis dialog box, click **Percentage** in the Category list, click the **Decimal places down arrow** twice so **0** appears, click **OK**, then deselect the chart
   Percent signs are added to the Y-axis. The completed handout is shown in Figure F-19.

10. Type **Prepared by** followed by your name centered in the document footer, save your changes, print the handout, close the document, then exit Word

FIGURE F-18: Datasheet and chart object

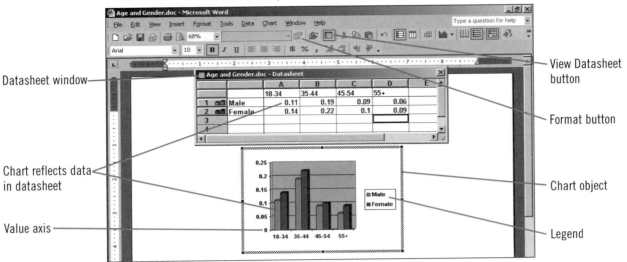

Datasheet window

Chart reflects data in datasheet

Value axis

View Datasheet button

Format button

Chart object

Legend

FIGURE F-19: Completed handout with chart

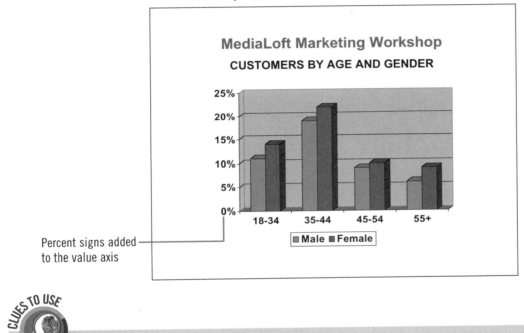

Percent signs added to the value axis

CLUES TO USE

Creating diagrams and organization charts

Diagrams are another way to illustrate concepts in your documents. Word includes a diagram feature that allows you to quickly create and format several types of diagrams, including pyramid, Venn, target, cycle, and radial diagrams, as well as organization charts. To insert a diagram or an organization chart, click the Insert Diagram button 🔲 on the Drawing toolbar or use the Diagram command on the Insert menu to open the Diagram Gallery, shown in Figure F-20. Select a diagram type in the Diagram Gallery, then click OK. The diagram appears in a drawing canvas with placeholder text, and the Diagram toolbar opens. The toolbar contains buttons for customizing and formatting the diagram, and for sizing and positioning the drawing canvas. Use the AutoFormat button on the Diagram toolbar to apply colors and shading to your diagram.

FIGURE F-20: Diagram Gallery

Diagram Gallery

Select a diagram type:

Organization Chart
Used to show hierarchical relationships

OK   Cancel

Practice

► Concepts Review

Label the elements shown in Figure F-21.

FIGURE F-21

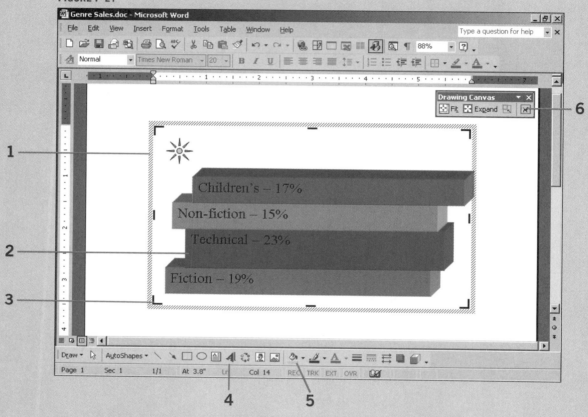

Match each term with the statement that best describes it.

7. Text box
8. Drawing canvas
9. AutoShape
10. Bitmap graphic
11. Chart
12. WordArt
13. Pixels
14. Vertex

a. A graphic object composed of specially formatted text
b. A graphic that is composed of a series of small dots
c. A graphic object that is a container for text and graphics
d. The intersection of two line sections or the highest point on a curve
e. A workspace for creating graphics
f. Dots that define color and intensity in a graphic
g. A graphic object drawn using the tools on the Drawing toolbar
h. A visual representation of numerical data

Select the best answer from the list of choices.

15. Which button can be used to create a text box?

a. 🖾   c. 🔺

b. 🔳   d. 🖾

16. What must you do to a drawing canvas before moving it to a different location?

a. Fit the drawing canvas to the contents.

b. Scale the drawing canvas.

c. Wrap text around the drawing canvas.

d. Enter a precise position for the drawing canvas in the Format Drawing Canvas dialog box.

17. What would you drag to change an AutoShape's shape, but not its size or dimensions?

a. Cropping handle   c. Sizing handle

b. Adjustment handle   d. Rotate handle

18. Which method would you use to nudge a picture?

a. Select the picture, then drag it to a new location.

b. Select the picture, then press an arrow key.

c. Select the picture, then drag a top, bottom, or side sizing handle.

d. Select the picture, then drag a corner sizing handle.

19. If you want to create an oval that contains formatted text, what kind of graphic object would you create?

a. WordArt   c. An AutoShape

b. A text box   d. A pie chart

20. What style of text wrapping is applied to a text box by default?

a. In line with text   c. Tight

b. Square   d. In front of text

▶ Skills Review

1. Add graphics.

a. Start Word, open the file **WD F-3** from the drive and folder where your Project Files are located, then save it as **Farm Flyer**.

b. Press [Ctrl][End], then insert the file **Farm.jpg** from the drive and folder where your Project Files are located.

c. Select the photo, apply the Square text wrapping style to it, then save your changes.

2. Resize graphics.

a. Scroll down so that the graphic is at the top of your screen.

b. Drag the lower-right sizing handle to enlarge the graphic proportionally so that it is about 4" wide and 3" high.

c. Click the Crop button on the Picture toolbar.

d. Drag the bottom-middle cropping handle up approximately 1", then click the Crop button again.

e. Double-click the photo, click the Size tab, then change the width of the photo to 6". (*Hint*: Make sure the Lock aspect ratio check box is selected.)

f. Save your changes.

3. Position graphics.

a. Drag the photo up so that its top is aligned with the top margin.

b. Double-click the photo, click the Layout tab, then click Advanced.

c. On the Picture Position tab, change the horizontal alignment to centered relative to the margins.

d. In the Vertical section, change the absolute position to 2" below the margin.

e. On the Text Wrapping tab, change the wrapping style to Top and bottom, change the Top measurement to 2", then change the Bottom measurement to .3".

f. Close the Advanced Layout and Format Picture dialog boxes, then save your changes.

4. Create text boxes.

a. Change the zoom level to Whole Page, then draw a 1.5" x 6" text box at the bottom of the page. (*Note*: Do not draw the text box in the drawing canvas if it opens.)

b. Change the zoom level to Page Width, type **Mountain Realty** in the text box, format the text in 20-point Arial bold, then center it in the text box.

c. Press [Enter], type **603-555-3466**, press [Enter], type **www.mountainrealty.com**, then format the text in 11-point Arial bold.

d. Resize the text box to be 1" high and 4" wide, then move it to the lower-left corner of the page, aligned with the left and bottom margin.

e. Fill the text box with Blue-Gray, change the font color of the text to White, then remove the line from around the text box.

f. With the text box selected, click Draw on the Drawing toolbar, point to Change AutoShape, point to Basic Shapes, then click the Oval. (*Note:* Adjust the text size or oval size if necessary)

g. Deselect the text box, then save your changes.

5. Create AutoShapes.

a. Click AutoShapes on the Drawing toolbar, point to Basic Shapes, then click the Isosceles Triangle shape.

b. Draw an isosceles triangle in the drawing canvas, then fill it with Violet. (*Note:* The drawing canvas appears on a new page 2. You will resize and position the drawing canvas after you finish drawing in it.)

c. Draw three more isosceles triangles in the drawing canvas, then fill them with Lavender, Blue-Gray, and Indigo.

d. Drag the triangles to position them so they overlap each other to look like mountains.

e. Draw a sun shape in the drawing canvas, fill it with Gold, then position it so it overlaps the tops of the mountains. Resize the sun if necessary.

f. Select the sun, click Draw on the Drawing toolbar, point to Order, then click Send to Back.

g. Use the Order commands to change the order of the triangles and the sun so that the shapes look like a mountain range with the sun setting behind it. Resize and reposition the shapes as necessary to create a mountain effect, then save your changes.

6. Use the drawing canvas.

a. Fit the drawing canvas to the mountain range graphic.

b. Apply the Square text wrapping style to the drawing canvas. (*Hint:* You might need to scroll the document to locate the drawing canvas after you apply text wrapping to it.)

c. Click the Scale Drawing button, then resize the drawing canvas so the graphic is approximately 1.5" wide and 1" tall. Adjust the shapes in the drawing canvas if the graphic looks awkward after resizing it.

d. Change the zoom level to Whole Page, move the drawing canvas to the lower-right corner of the page, aligned with the right and bottom margins, then deselect the drawing canvas.

e. Save your changes, then press [Ctrl][Home] to move the insertion point to the top of the document (the beginning of the text).

7. Create WordArt.

a. Insert a WordArt object, select any horizontal WordArt style, type **Farmhouse**, then click OK.

b. Apply Square text wrapping to the WordArt object, then move it above the photograph if necessary.

c. Resize the WordArt object to be 6" wide and 1.25" tall, then position it so it is 1" below the top of the page and centered between the margins.

d. Open the WordArt Gallery, then change the style to the fifth style in the second row.

e. Type **Contact** followed by your name in the document footer, center the text, then format it in 12-point Arial.

f. Save your changes to the flyer, print a copy, then close the file.

8. Create charts.

a. Open a new, blank document, then save it as **Realty Sales** to the drive and folder where your Project Files are located.

b. Click the Center button, type **Mountain Realty 2003 Sales**, then format the text in 26-point Arial bold.

c. Press [Enter] twice, then insert a chart.

d. Click the Chart Type list arrow on the Standard toolbar, then click Pie Chart.

e. Select the second and third rows in the datasheet, then press [Delete].

f. Replace the data in the datasheet with the data shown in Figure F-22, then close the datasheet.

g. Select the legend, click the Format Legend button, then change the placement of the legend to Bottom.

h. Use the Chart Objects list arrow to select the Plot Area, open the Format Plot Area dialog box, then change the Border and Area patterns to None.

i. Use the Chart Objects list arrow to select Series "Pie 1," open the Format Data Series dialog box, click the Data Labels tab, then make the data labels show the percentage.

j. Resize the chart object proportionally so it is about 5" wide.

k. Type **Prepared by** followed by your name centered in the document footer, save your changes, print the document, close the file, then exit Word.

FIGURE F-22

		A	B	C	D	E
		Houses	Land	Farms	Businesses	
1	Pie 1	11.3	4.1	4.4	6.2	
2						

Realty Sales.doc - Datasheet

▶ Independent Challenge 1

You are starting a business and need to design a letterhead. Your letterhead will include a logo, which you'll design using AutoShapes, as well as your name and contact information. Figure F-23 shows a sample letterhead.

a. Start Word, open a new blank document, then save it as **Letterhead** to the drive and folder where your Project Files are located.

b. Identify the nature of your business, then examine the shapes available on the AutoShapes menus and decide what kind of logo to create.

c. Using pencil and paper, sketch a design for your letterhead. Determine the positions for your logo, name, address, and any other design elements you want to include. You will create and organize all the elements of your letterhead in a drawing canvas.

d. Using AutoShapes, create your logo in a drawing canvas. Use the buttons on the Drawing toolbar to enhance the logo with color, text, lines, shadows, and other effects.

e. Resize the logo and position it in the drawing canvas.

FIGURE F-23

Georgia J. McQueeney
Architect/Planner
54 Erie Street _ Syracuse, NY 13219 _ 315-555-3288 _ gjmcq@earthlink.net

f. In the drawing canvas, create a text box that includes your name, address, and other important contact information. Format the text and the text box using the buttons on the Formatting and Drawing toolbars.

g. Resize the text box as necessary and position it in the drawing canvas.

h. Add to the drawing canvas any other design elements you want to include.

i. When you are satisfied with the layout of your letterhead in the drawing canvas, fit the drawing canvas to its contents, then resize the drawing canvas as necessary.

j. Wrap text around the drawing canvas, then position it on the page.

k. Save your changes, preview the letterhead, print a copy, close the file, then exit Word.

▶ Independent Challenge 2

You design ads for GoTroppo.com, a company that specializes in discounted travel to tropical destinations. Your next assignment is to design a full-page ad for a travel magazine. Your ad will contain a photograph of a vacation scene, shown in Figure F-24, the text "Your vacation begins here and now," and the Web address "www.gotroppo.com."

a. Start Word, open a new, blank document, then save it as **GoTroppo Ad** to the drive and folder where your Project Files are located.

b. Change all four page margins to .7".

FIGURE F-24

c. Insert the file **Vacation.jpg** from the drive and folder where your Project Files are located, then examine the photo. Think about how you can use this photo effectively in your ad.

d. Using pencil and paper, sketch the layout for your ad. You can use AutoShapes, lines, text boxes, WordArt, and any other design elements in your ad to make it powerful and eye-catching.

e. Apply a text wrapping style to the photograph to make it a floating graphic, then format the photograph as you planned. You can crop it, resize it, move it, and combine it with other design elements.

f. Using text boxes or WordArt, add the text **Your vacation begins here and now** and the Web address **www.gotroppo.com** to the ad.

g. Use the buttons on the Drawing and Formatting toolbars to format the graphic objects.

h. Adjust the layout and design of the ad: adjust the colors, add or remove design elements, and resize and reposition the objects if necessary.

i. When you are satisfied with your ad, type your name in the document header, save your changes, print a copy, close the document, then exit Word.

Independent Challenge 3

You are a graphic designer. The public library has hired you to design a bookmark for Literacy Week. Their only request is that the bookmark includes the words Literacy Week. You'll create three different bookmarks for the library.

a. Start Word, open a new, blank document, then save it as **Bookmarks** to the drive and folder where your Project Files are located.

b. Change the page orientation to landscape, change all four page margins to .7", and change the zoom level to Whole Page.

c. Draw three rectangles in a drawing canvas. Resize the rectangles to be 2.5" x 6.5" and move them so they do not overlap. Each rectangle will become a bookmark.

d. In the first rectangle, design a bookmark using AutoShapes.

e. In the second rectangle, design a bookmark using WordArt.

f. In the third rectangle, design a bookmark using clip art.

g. Use the buttons on the Drawing toolbar to format the bookmarks with fills, colors, lines, and other effects. Be sure to add the words Literacy Week to each bookmark.

h. Type your name in the document header, save your changes, print, close the document, then exit Word.

 # Independent Challenge 4

One way to find graphic images to use in your documents is to download them from the Web. Many Web sites feature images that are in the public domain, which means they have no copyright restrictions. You are free to download these images and use them in your documents, although often you must acknowledge the artist or identify the source. Other Web sites include images that are copyrighted and require written permission, and often payment, to use. Before downloading and using graphics from the Web, it's important to research and establish their copyright status and permission requirements. In this exercise you will download photographs from the Web and research their copyright restrictions.

a. Start Word, open the file WD F-4 from the drive and folder where your Project Files are located, then save it as **Copyright Info**. This document contains a table that you will fill with the photos you find on the Web and the copyright restrictions for those photos.

b. Use your favorite search engine to search the Web for photographs. Use the keywords **photo archives** to conduct your search. If your search does not result in appropriate links, try looking at the following Web sites: http://pictures.fws.gov, http://gimp-savvy.com, http://www-pao.ksc.nasa.gov, or http://vulcan.wr.usgs.gov.

c. Find at least three Web sites that contain photos you could use in a document. Save a photo from each Web site to your computer, and note the URL and copyright restrictions. To save an image from a Web page, right-click the image, then click the appropriate command on the shortcut menu.

d. Insert the photos you saved from the Web in the Photo column of the table. Resize the photos proportionally so that they are no more than 1.5" tall or 1.5" wide. Wrap text around the photos and center them in the table cells.

e. For each photo, enter the URL and the copyright restrictions for the photo in the table. In the Copyright Restrictions column, indicate if the photo is copyright or in the public domain, and note the requirements for using that photo in a document.

f. Type your name in the document header, save your changes, print a copy, close the file, then exit Word.

► Visual Workshop

Using WD F-5.doc and Surfing.jpg (found in the drive and folder where your Project Files are located), create the flyer shown in Figure F-25. Type your name in the header, save the flyer as **Surf Safe**, then print a copy.

FIGURE F-25

surf safe

NEVER
SURF
ALONE

Follow the rules

All beginning surfers need to follow basic safety rules before heading into the waves. The key to safe surfing is caution and awareness.

Wear sunscreen

Sunscreen helps prevent skin cancer and aging of the skin. 30+ SPF broad spectrum sunscreen screens out both UVA and UVB rays and provides more than 30 times your natural sunburn protection. Apply sunscreen at least 15 minutes before exposing yourself to the sun, and reapply it every two hours or after swimming, drying with a towel, or excessive perspiration. Zinc cream also helps prevent sunburn and guards against harmful UV rays.

Dress appropriately

Wear a wet suit or a rash vest. Choose a wet suit that is appropriate for the water temperature. Rash vests help protect against UV rays.

Use a safe surfboard

A safe surfboard is a surfboard that suits your ability. Beginners need a big, thick surfboard for stability.

Learn how to escape rips

A rip current is a volume of water moving out to sea: the bigger the surf, the stronger the rips associated with it. Indicators of rips include:

- Brown water caused by stirred up sand
- Foam on the surface of the water that trails past the break
- Waves breaking on both sides of a rip current
- A rippled appearance between calm water
- Debris floating out to sea

If you are dragged out by a rip, don't panic! Stay calm and examine the rip conditions before trying to escape the current. Poor swimmers should ride the rip out from the beach and then swim parallel to the shore for 30 or 40 meters. Once you have escaped the rip, swim toward the shore where the waves are breaking. You can also probe with your feet to see if a sand bar has formed near the edge of the rip. Strong swimmers should swim at a 45 degree angle across the rip.

Study the surf

Always study the surf before going in. Select a safe beach with waves under 1 meter, and pick waves that are suitable for your ability.

Creating
a Web Site

Objectives

- [MOUS] ► **Plan a Web site**
- [MOUS] ► **Create a Web page**
- [MOUS] ► **Format a Web page with themes**
- [MOUS] ► **Illustrate a Web page with graphics**
- [MOUS] ► **Save a document as a Web page**
- [MOUS] ► **Add hyperlinks**
- [MOUS] ► **Modify hyperlinks**
- [MOUS] ► **Preview a Web page in a browser**

Creating a Web site and posting it on the Internet or an intranet is a powerful way to share information with other people. The Web page formatting features of Word allow you to easily create professional-looking Web pages from scratch or to save an existing document in HTML format so it can be viewed using a browser. In this unit, you learn how to create a new Web page and how to save an existing document as a Web page. You also learn how to edit and format Web pages, create and modify hyperlinks, and preview a Web page in a browser. ◄►— MediaLoft is sponsoring the Seattle Writers Festival, a major public event featuring prominent writers from around the world. Alice Wegman needs to create a Web site that she will post on the World Wide Web to promote the event and provide information to the public. You will work with Alice as she creates the Seattle Writers Festival Web site.

Word 2002

Planning a Web Site

A **Web page** is a document that can be stored on a computer called a Web server and viewed on the World Wide Web or on an intranet using a **browser**, a software program used to access and display Web pages. A **Web site** is a group of associated Web pages that are linked together with hyperlinks. Before creating a Web page or a Web site, it's important to plan its content and organization. The **home page** is the main page of a Web site, and is the first Web page viewers see when they open a site. Usually, it is the first page you plan and create. The Seattle Writers Festival Web site will include a home page that serves both as an introduction to the festival and as a table of contents for the other Web pages in the site. Before creating the home page, Alice identifies the content she wants to include, plans the organization of the Web site, and sketches the design for each Web page.

Details

► ### Identify the goal of the Web site
A successful Web site has a clear purpose. For example, it might promote a product, communicate information, or facilitate a transaction. Alice's Web site will communicate information about the Seattle Writers Festival to the public.

QuickTip

Take care to limit the text and graphics on each Web page to those that help you meet your specific goal.

► ### Sketch the Web site
Identify the information you want to include on each Web page, sketch the layout and design of each Web page, and map the links between the pages in the Web site. A well-designed Web site is visually interesting and easy for viewers to use. Figure G-1 shows the sketch of Alice's Web site.

► ### Create each Web page and save it in HTML format
You can create a Web page from scratch in Word, use a Word template to create a standard type of Web page, or convert an existing document to a Web page. When you create a Web page in Word, you save it in HTML format. **HTML** (Hypertext Markup Language) is the programming language used to describe how each element of a Web page should appear when viewed with a browser. Alice will use a blank Web page template to create her home page. She will create the Program of Events Web page by saving an existing document in HTML format. Files saved in HTML format can be recognized by their .htm or .html file extension.

QuickTip

If you intend to publish to the Web, filenames should use all lower-case letters and include no special characters or blank spaces. Valid characters include letters, numbers, and the underscore character.

► ### Determine the filenaming convention to use
Different operating systems place various restrictions on Web site filenames. It's safest to name Web pages using the standard eight-dot-three filenaming convention, which specifies that a filename have a maximum of eight letters followed by a period and a three-letter file extension—mypage.htm or chap_1.htm, for example. Alice will use the eight-dot-three naming convention for her Web pages.

► ### Format each Web page
You can use the standard Word formatting features to enhance Web pages with fonts, backgrounds, graphics, lines, tables, and other format effects. Word also includes visual themes that you can apply to Web pages to format them quickly. The look of a Web page impacts the viewer as much as its content, so it's important to select fonts, colors, and graphics that complement the goal of your Web site. Alice will apply a theme that expresses the spirit of the writers festival to each Web page. A consistent look between Web pages is an important factor in Web site design.

► ### Create the hyperlinks between Web pages
Hyperlinks are text or graphics that viewers can click to open a file, another Web page, or an e-mail message, or click to jump to a specific location in the same file. Hyperlinks are commonly used to link the pages of a Web site to each other. Alice will add hyperlinks that link the home page to other Web pages in her Web site. She will also add links from the home page to other Web sites on the Internet and to an e-mail message to MediaLoft.

► ### View the Web site using a browser
Before publishing your Web site to the Web or an intranet, it's important to view your Web pages in a browser to make sure they look and work as you intended. Alice will use the Web Page Preview feature to check the formatting of each Web page in her browser and to test the hyperlinks.

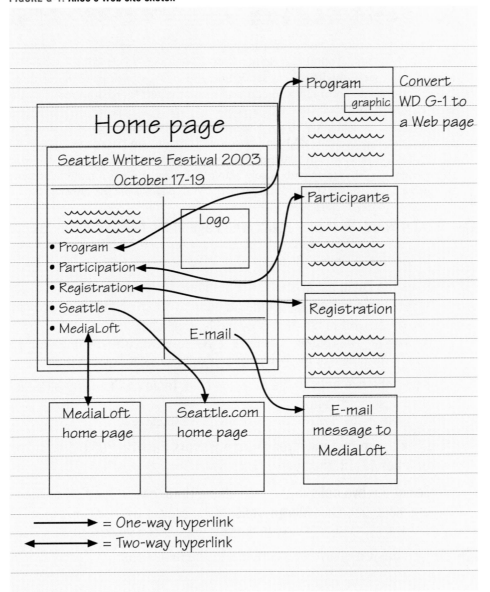

Creating a Web site with the Web Page Wizard

Once you have determined the content and organization of a Web site, one quick way to create it is to use the Web Page Wizard. Through a series of dialog boxes, the Wizard prompts you to: enter a title and save as location for your Web site; choose between using a frame or a separate Web page for the hyperlinks between pages; select the files or templates to include as Web pages; organize and name the Web pages and hyperlinks; and select a common visual theme to apply to each page. When you are finished tailoring your selection, Word creates the Web site for you and the first Web page appears in the document window. You can then use Word's formatting features to customize each page in the Web site. To start the Web Page Wizard, click the General Templates hyperlink in the New Document task pane, click the Web Pages tab in the Templates dialog box, click the Web Page Wizard icon, then click OK to open the Web Page Wizard. Click Next to begin, then answer the questions and choose from the options in each Wizard dialog box, clicking Next to move to the next dialog box. When you are satisfied with your selections, click Finish.

Creating a Web Page

Creating a Web page involves creating a document that uses HTML formatting. HTML places codes, called **tags**, around the elements of a Web page to describe how each element should appear when viewed with a browser. When you create a Web page in Word, you use the usual Word buttons and commands to edit and format it and Word automatically inserts the HTML tags for you. A quick way to create a new Web page is to start with a template. Word includes a template for a new blank Web page, as well as templates for many standard types of Web pages. Because text and graphics align and position differently on Web pages than in Word documents, it's helpful to use a table to structure the layout of a Web page. Alice begins by creating the home page. She starts with a new blank Web page, inserts a table to structure the layout of the home page, adds text, and then saves the Web page in HTML format.

Steps

1. Start **Word**, then click **Blank Web Page** in the New Document task pane
A blank Web page opens in the document window in Web Layout view, which shows a Web page as it will appear when viewed in a Web browser.

2. Click the **Zoom list arrow** on the Standard toolbar, click **100%** if necessary, click the **Insert Table button** on the Standard toolbar, point to the second box in the third row of the grid to create a 3 x 2 Table, then click
A table with two columns and three rows is inserted. After you finish using the table to help lay out the design of the Web page, you will remove the table borders.

3. Select the **two cells** in the first row, click **Table** on the menu bar, click **Merge Cells**, then deselect the row
Two cells in the first row merge to become a single cell.

4. Click in the first row, type **Seattle Writers Festival 2003**, press **[Enter]** twice, type **October 17-19**, then press **[Enter]**

5. Select the **two cells** in the second and third rows of the first column, click **Table** on the menu bar, click **Merge Cells**, then deselect the cell
The two cells in the first column merge to become a single cell.

6. Type the text shown in Figure G-2 in the table cells

7. Click the **Save button** on the Standard toolbar
The Save As dialog box opens. Word assigns a default page title and filename for the Web page and indicates Web Page (*.htm; *html) as the Save as type. Web pages are automatically saved in HTML format.

8. Click **Change Title**, type **Seattle Writers Festival - Home (Your Name)** in the Set Page Title dialog box, then click **OK**
The page title appears in the title bar when the Web page is viewed with a browser. It's important to assign a page title that describes the Web page for visitors.

9. Drag to select **Seattle Writers Festival 2003.htm** in the File name text box, type **swfhome**, then use the Save in list arrow to navigate to the drive and folder where your Project Files are located
The filename appears in the title bar when the Web page is viewed in Word. Compare your Save As dialog box with Figure G-3. Word automatically assigns the .htm file extension when Web Page (*.htm; *.html) is selected as the Save as type, so you do not need to type it.

10. Click **Save**
The filename swfhome appears in the title bar. Depending on your Windows settings, the filename extension may or may not appear after the filename.

FIGURE G-2: Web page in Web Layout view

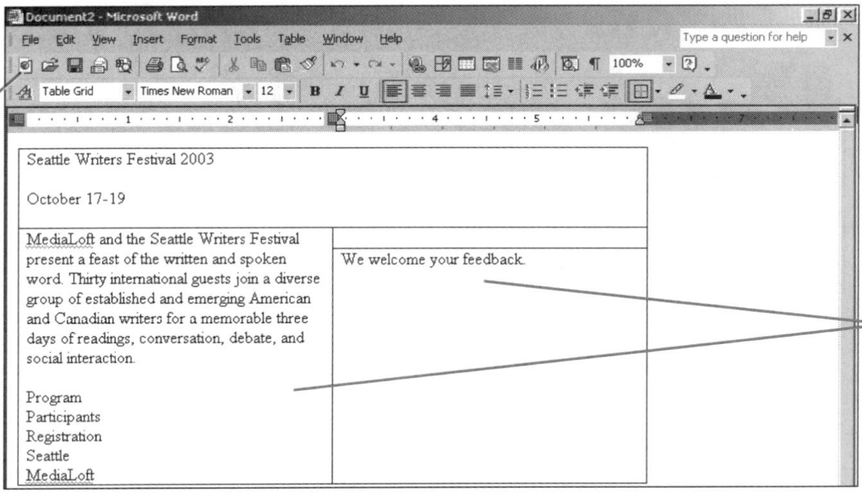

New Web Page button

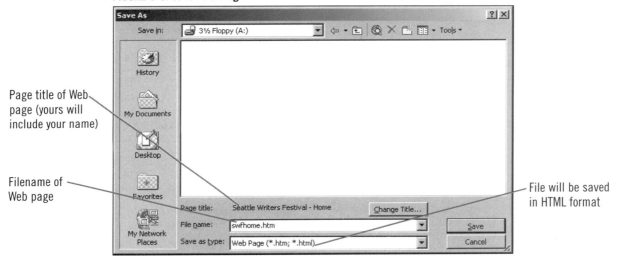

Type the text in these table cells in your table

FIGURE G-3: Save As dialog box

Page title of Web page (yours will include your name)

Filename of Web page

File will be saved in HTML format

CLUES TO USE

Adding frames to a Web page

Many Web pages you visit on the Internet include frames for displaying fixed information. A frame is a section of a Web page window in which a separate Web page can be displayed. Frames commonly contain hyperlinks and other navigation elements that help visitors browse a Web site. A header that remains at the top of the screen while visitors browse a Web site is one example of a frame; a left column that contains hyperlinks to each page in the Web site and stays on the screen while readers visit different pages is another example. You can add a frame to a Web page by pointing to Frames on the Format menu, and then clicking the type of frame you want to add. Click New Frames Page to open the Frames toolbar, which you can use to select a location (left, right, above, or below) for a new, empty frame. Alternately, if you have applied heading styles to text in the current Web page, you can click Table of Contents in Frame to create a frame that includes hyperlinks to each heading in the Web page.

Formatting a Web Page with Themes

Word includes a multitude of themes that you can apply to Web pages to quickly give them an attractive and consistent look. A **theme** is a set of complementary design elements that you can apply to Web pages, e-mail messages, and other documents that are viewed on-screen. Themes include Web page backgrounds, styles for headings and hyperlinks, picture bullets, horizontal lines, table borders, and other specially designed formats that work well together. You can apply a theme to a Web page using the Theme command on the Format menu. ✐ Alice applies a theme to the Web page, formats the text using the theme styles, and adds a horizontal line and bullets. She then experiments with alternate themes to find a design that more closely matches the character of the Writers Festival.

Steps

1. Click **Format** on the menu bar, click **Theme**, scroll down the Choose a Theme list box, then click **Refined**

   A preview of the Refined theme appears in the Theme dialog box, as shown in Figure G-4. The theme includes a background and styles for text, hyperlinks, bullet characters, and horizontal lines.

2. Click **OK**

   The theme background is added to the Web page and the Normal style that comes with the theme is applied to the text.

3. Select **Seattle Writers Festival 2003**, click the **Style list arrow** on the Formatting toolbar, click **Heading 1** in the Style list, then deselect the text

   The Heading 1 style—24-point Times New Roman white—is applied to the heading text.

4. Select **October 17-19**, click the Style list arrow, click **Heading 2**, then deselect the text

   The Heading 2 style—18-point Times New Roman white—is applied to the date text.

5. Select the **heading** and the **date**, click the **Center button** ▤ on the Formatting toolbar, move the pointer over the table, click the **table move handle** ⊞ to select the table, then click ▤

   The heading, date, and table are centered on the Web page.

6. Place the insertion point in the blank line between the heading and the date, click the **Outside Border list arrow** ▣ on the Formatting toolbar, then click the **Horizontal Line button** ▤

   A horizontal line formatted in the theme design is added below the heading.

7. Select the five-line list at the bottom of the first column, then click the **Bullets button** ☰ on the Formatting toolbar

   The list is formatted using bullets from the theme design.

8. Click **Format** on the menu bar, click **Theme**, scroll down the Choose a Theme list box, select **Sumi Painting**, then click **OK**

   The background and the text, line, and bullet styles applied to the Web page change to the designs used in the Sumi Painting theme. You do not need to reapply the styles to a Web page when you change its theme.

9. Select **Seattle Writers Festival 2003**, click the **Bold button** ▣ on the Formatting toolbar, deselect the text, then save your changes

   The heading is formatted in bold. Once you have applied styles to text you can customize the format to suit your purpose. Compare your Web page with Figure G-5.

FIGURE G-4: Refined theme in the Theme dialog box

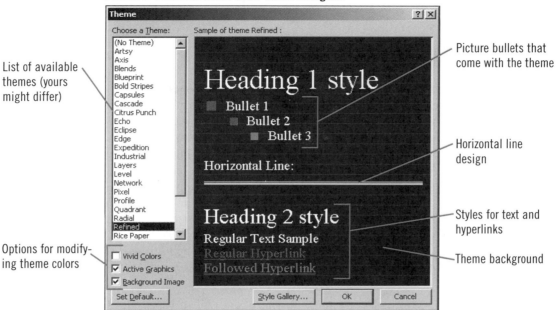

List of available themes (yours might differ)

Options for modifying theme colors

Picture bullets that come with the theme

Horizontal line design

Styles for text and hyperlinks

Theme background

FIGURE G-5: Sumi Painting theme applied to the Web page

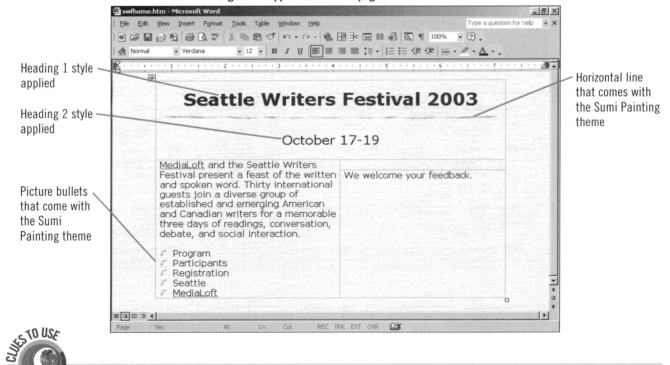

Heading 1 style applied

Heading 2 style applied

Picture bullets that come with the Sumi Painting theme

Horizontal line that comes with the Sumi Painting theme

CLUES TO USE

Managing Web page files

When you save a document as a Web page, Word automatically creates a supporting folder in the same location as the .htm file. This folder has the same name as the .htm file plus the suffix _files. It houses the supporting files associated with the Web page. For example, when you create a new Web page or save an existing document as an .htm file, each graphic—including the bullets, background textures, horizontal lines, and other graphics included on the Web page—is automatically converted to a GIF or JPEG format file and saved in the supporting folder. Be aware that if you copy or move a Web page to a different location, it's important that you copy or move the supporting folder (and all the files in it) along with the .htm file, otherwise the links between the .htm file and the supporting files may be broken. If a browser cannot locate the graphic files associated with a Web page, the browser will display a placeholder (often a red X) instead of a graphic.

Word 2002

Illustrating a Web Page with Graphics

You can illustrate your Web pages with pictures, clip art, WordArt, text boxes, AutoShapes, and other graphic objects. When you insert a graphic on a Web page, it is inserted as an inline graphic and you must apply text wrapping to be able to move it independently of the line of text. Floating graphics align and position differently on Web pages than in Word documents, however, because browsers do not support the same graphic formatting options as Word. For example, a floating graphic with square text wrapping can only be left- or right-aligned on a Web page, whereas you can position a floating graphic anywhere in a Word document. For this reason, it's important to use Web Layout view to position graphics on a Web page. If you want to position floating graphics or text precisely on a Web page, you can create a table and then insert the text or graphics in the table cells.   Alice wants the MediaLoft logo to appear to the right of center on the Web page. She inserts the logo in the blank cell in the table, and then adjusts the table formatting to make the Web page attractive.

QuickTip

To insert a text file in a table cell, click Insert on the menu bar, click File, select the file, then click Insert.

1. Place the insertion point in the blank cell in the second column of the table, click **Insert** on the menu bar, point to **Picture**, then click **From File**
   The Insert Picture dialog box opens.

2. Use the Look in list arrow to navigate to the drive and folder where your Project Files are located, click the file **mloft.jpg**, then click **Insert**
   The logo is inserted in the cell as an inline graphic.

QuickTip

To resize a graphic, crop it, or change the text wrapping style, double-click the graphic to open the Format Picture dialog box.

3. Click the **logo** to select it, click the **Center button** ▤ on the Formatting toolbar, press [→], then press [**Enter**]
   The graphic is centered in the table cell and a blank line is inserted under the logo.

4. Position the pointer over the border between the first and second columns until the pointer changes to ◄║►, then drag the border to approximately the **4¼" mark** on the horizontal ruler
   The first column widens and the second column narrows. The logo remains centered in the table cell.

5. Select **We welcome your feedback.**, click ▤, then click in the table to deselect the text
   The text is centered in the table cell, as shown in Figure G-6. In Web Layout view, text and graphics are positioned as they are in a Web browser.

Trouble?

If gridlines appear on your Web page after you remove the borders, click Table on the menu bar, then click Hide Gridlines.

6. Click the **table move handle** ⊞ to select the table, click the **Horizontal Line list arrow** ▬▾ on the Formatting toolbar, click the **No Border button** ▦, deselect the table, then save your changes
   Removing the table borders masks that the underlying structure of the Web page is a table, as shown in Figure G-7. The text on the left is now a wide column and the logo and text under the logo are positioned to the right of center. By inserting text and graphics in a table, you can position them exactly where you want.

FIGURE G-6: Logo and text centered in the second column

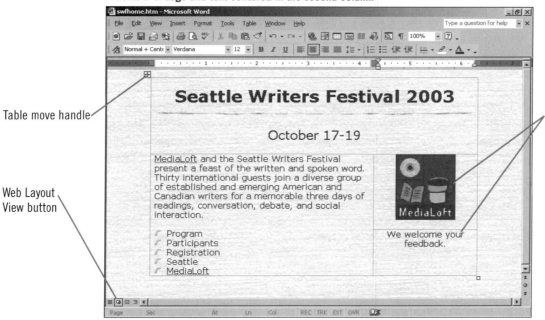

Table move handle

Web Layout View button

Logo and text are centered in the table cells

FIGURE G-7: Web page with table borders removed

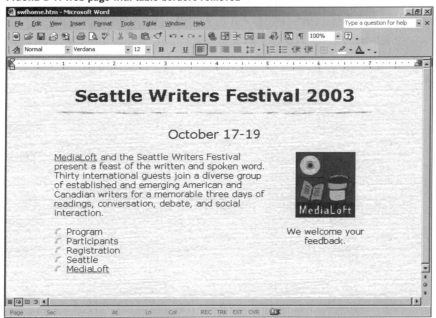

Adding alternate text for graphics

Graphics can take a long time to appear on a Web page, so some people turn off the display of graphics in their browsers so that they can download and view Web pages more quickly. If you don't want visitors to your Web page to see empty space where you intended that they see a graphic, you can add alternate text to appear on the Web page instead of the graphic.

Alternate text will also appear in some browsers while the graphic is loading. To add alternate text to a Web page, select the graphic, then click the Picture command on the Format menu. On the Web tab in the Format Picture dialog box, type the text you want to appear in lieu of the graphic, then click OK.

Saving a Document as a Web Page

When you save an existing document as a Web page, Word converts the content and formatting of the Word file to HTML and displays the Web page as it will appear in a browser. Any formatting that is not supported by Web browsers is either converted to similar supported formatting or removed from the Web page. For example, if you save a document that contains a floating graphic in HTML format, the graphic will be left- or right-aligned on the Web page. Table G-1 describes several common formatting elements that are not supported by Web browsers. You can save a document as a Web page using the Save as Web Page command on the File menu. Alice wants to add a Web page that includes the festival program of events to her Web site. Rather than create the Web page from scratch, she converts an existing document to HTML format. She then adjusts the formatting of the new Web page and applies the Sumi Painting theme.

Steps

1. Open the file **WD G-1** from the drive and folder where your Project Files are located, click the **Zoom list arrow** on the Standard toolbar, then click **Two Pages**

   The document opens in Print Layout view, as shown in Figure G-8. Notice that the document is two pages long, the text is formatted in three columns, and the graphic on the first page is centered.

2. Click **File** on the menu bar, click **Save as Web Page**, click **Change Title**, type **Seattle Writers Festival – Program of Events (Your Name)** in the Set Page Title dialog box, click **OK**, select **WD G-1.htm** in the Filename text box, type **swfevent**, then click **Save**

   A dialog box opens and informs you that browsers do not support some of the formatting features of the document. It says the floating graphic will be left- or right-aligned in the Web page. You can click Tell Me More in the dialog box to learn more about features not supported by Web browsers.

3. Click **Continue**

   A copy of the document is saved in HTML format with the filename "swfevent" and the page title "Seattle Writers Festival – Events (Your Name)." The Web page appears in Web Layout view. Notice that the graphic is now left-aligned on the Web page.

4. Click the **Zoom list arrow** on the Standard toolbar, click **100%** if necessary, then scroll to the bottom of the Web page

   The text is now formatted in a single column, there are no margins on the Web page, and the document is one long page.

5. Press **[Ctrl][Home]**, double-click the **graphic** to open the Format Picture dialog box, click the **Size tab**, select **3.76** in the Height text box, type **2**, then click **OK**

   The size of the graphic is reduced.

6. Drag the **graphic** to the upper-right corner of the Web page, then deselect the graphic

   The graphic jumps into place in the upper-right corner when you release the mouse button.

7. Click **Format** on the menu bar, click **Theme**, click **Sumi Painting** in the Choose a Theme list box, click **OK**, then save your changes

   The Sumi Painting theme is applied to the Web page, giving it a look that is consistent with the home page. Notice that the bullet characters change to the picture bullets included with the theme. The font of the body text also changes to the Normal style font used in the theme (12-point Verdana). Compare your Web page with Figure G-9.

FIGURE G-8: Word document in Print Layout view

Floating graphic is centered

Document is two pages long

Text is formatted in columns

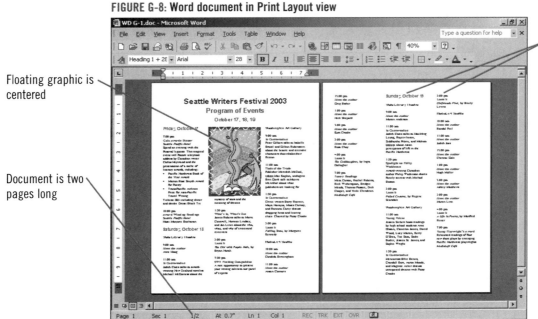

FIGURE G-9: Web page in Web Layout view

Body text changes to Sumi Painting theme Normal style

Bullets change to Sumi Painting theme picture bullets

Graphic is moved to the upper-right corner

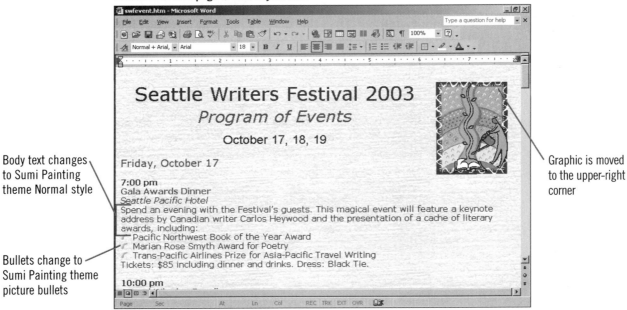

TABLE G-1: Word features that are not supported by Web browsers

feature	result when viewed with a browser
Character formatting	Shadow text becomes bold, small caps become all caps, and embossed, engraved, and outline text becomes solid; character scale changes to 100%; drop caps are removed
Paragraph formatting	Indents are removed, tabs might not align correctly, and border and shading styles might change
Page layout	Margins, columns, page numbers, page borders, and headers and footers are removed; all footnotes are moved to the end of the document
Graphics	Floating graphics, including pictures, AutoShapes, text boxes, and WordArt, are left- or right-aligned
Tables	Decorative cell borders become box borders, diagonal borders are removed, vertical text is changed to horizontal

Adding Hyperlinks

Hyperlinks allow readers to link to (or "jump") to a Web page, e-mail address, file, or a specific location in a document. When you create a hyperlink in a document, you select the text or graphic you want to use as a hyperlink and then specify the location you want to jump to when the hyperlink is clicked. You create hyperlinks using the Insert Hyperlink button on the Standard toolbar. Text that is formatted as a hyperlink appears as colored, underlined text. To make navigating the Events Web page easier, Alice creates hyperlinks that jump from the dates in the third line of the Web page to the schedule for those dates farther down the Web page. She then inserts several hyperlinks on her home page: one to link to the Events Web page, one to link to the Seattle.com Web site on the Internet, and one to link to an e-mail message to MediaLoft.

Steps 123 4

1. Select **19** in the third line of the Events Web page, then click the **Insert Hyperlink button** on the Standard toolbar

   The Insert Hyperlink dialog box opens. You use this dialog box to specify the location of the Web page, file, e-mail address, or position in the current document you want to jump to when the hyperlink—in this case, the text "19"—is clicked.

2. Click **Place in This Document** in the Link to section

   All the headings in the Web page are displayed in the dialog box, as shown in Figure G-10. In this context, "heading" is any text to which a heading style has been applied.

3. Click **Sunday, October 19** in the Select a place in this document section, then click **OK**

   The selected text, "19", is formatted in bright blue and underlined, the hyperlink style when the Sumi Painting theme is applied. When the Web page is viewed in a browser, clicking the 19 hyperlink will jump the viewer to the heading "Sunday, October 19" farther down the Web page.

4. Select **18**, click , click **Saturday, October 18** in the Insert Hyperlink dialog box, click **OK**, select **17**, click , click **Friday, October 17**, click **OK**, save your changes, then close the file

   The numbers 18 and 17 are formatted as hyperlinks to the headings for those dates in the Web page. After you save and close the file, the home page appears in the document window.

5. Select **Program** in the bulleted list, click , click **Existing File or Web Page** in the Link to section, use the Look in list arrow to navigate to the drive and folder where your Project Files are located, then click **swfevent.htm**

   The filename swfevent.htm appears in the Address text box, as shown in Figure G-11.

6. Click **OK**

   "Program" is formatted as a hyperlink to the Program of Events Web page. If you point to a hyperlink in Word, the address of the file or Web page it links to appears in a ScreenTip.

7. Select **Seattle** in the list, click , type **www.seattle.com** in the Address text box in the Insert Hyperlink dialog box, then click **OK**

   As you type the Web address, Word automatically adds "http://" in front of "www". A Web address is also called a **URL**, which stands for Uniform Resource Locator. "Seattle" is formatted as a hyperlink to the Seattle.com Web site on the Internet.

8. Select **feedback** under the logo, click , then click **E-mail Address** in the Link to section of the Insert Hyperlink dialog box

   The Insert Hyperlink dialog box changes so you can create a link to an e-mail message.

9. Type **swf@medialoft.com** in the E-mail address text box, type **Seattle Writers Festival** in the Subject text box, click **OK**, then save your changes

   "Feedback" is formatted as a hyperlink, as shown in Figure G-12.

FIGURE G-10: Creating a hyperlink to a heading

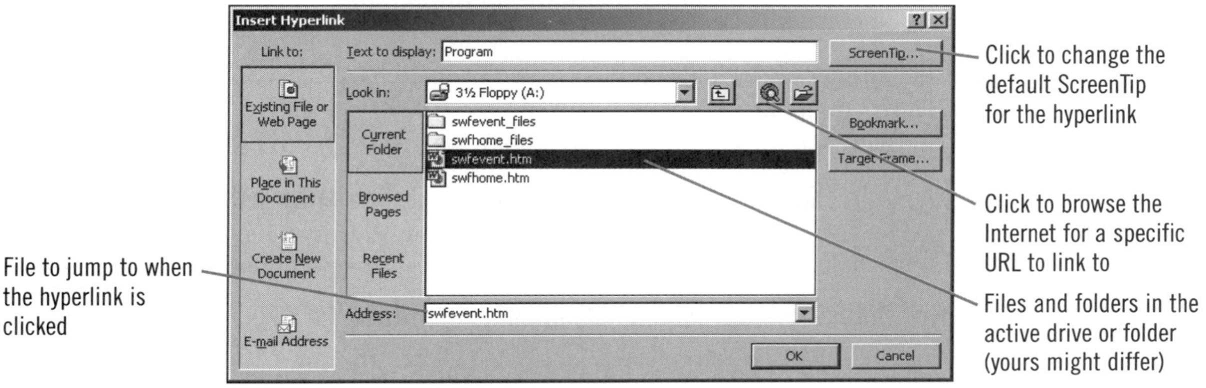

Creates a hyperlink to a Web page or file

Creates a hyperlink to a location in the current file

Creates a hyperlink to a new blank document

Creates a hyperlink to an e-mail address

Text selected to be formatted as a hyperlink

These headings in the document are formatted with heading styles

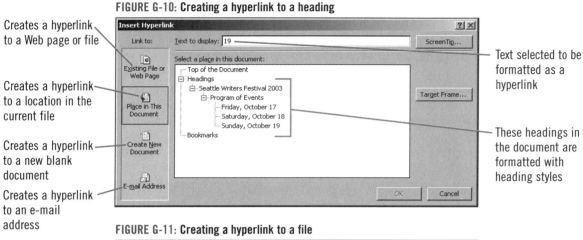

FIGURE G-11: Creating a hyperlink to a file

File to jump to when the hyperlink is clicked

Click to change the default ScreenTip for the hyperlink

Click to browse the Internet for a specific URL to link to

Files and folders in the active drive or folder (yours might differ)

FIGURE G-12: Hyperlinks in the Web page

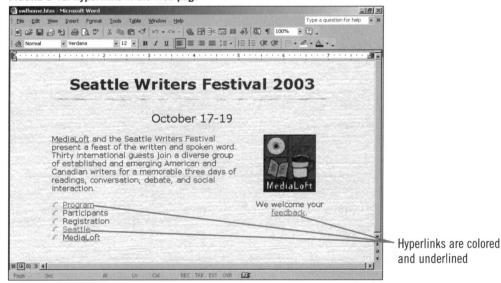

Hyperlinks are colored and underlined

Word 2002

CLUES TO USE

Pasting text as a hyperlink

You can quickly create a hyperlink to a specific location in any document by copying text from the destination location and pasting it as a hyperlink. To copy and paste text as a hyperlink, select the text you want to jump to, copy it to the Clipboard, place the insertion point in the location you want to insert the hyperlink, click Edit on the menu bar, then click Paste as Hyperlink. The text you copied is pasted and formatted as a hyperlink.

Modifying Hyperlinks

Over time, you might need to edit the hyperlinks on your Web pages with new information or remove them altogether. When you edit a hyperlink, you can change the hyperlink destination, the hyperlink text, or the ScreenTip that displays when a viewer points to the hyperlink. You can easily update or remove a hyperlink by right-clicking it and selecting the Edit Hyperlink or Remove Hyperlink command on the shortcut menu. Alice changes the hyperlink text for the Program and Seattle hyperlinks to make them more descriptive. She also adds a ScreenTip to the Seattle hyperlink so that visitors to the home page will better understand what the link offers.

Steps

1. Right-click **Program**, then click **Edit Hyperlink** on the shortcut menu
   The Edit Hyperlink dialog box opens.

2. Click after **Program** in the Text to display text box, press **[Spacebar]**, type **of Festival Events**, then click **OK**
   The hyperlink text changes to "Program of Festival Events" on the Web page.

3. Right-click **Seattle**, click **Edit Hyperlink**, then click **ScreenTip** in the Edit Hyperlink dialog box
   The Set Hyperlink ScreenTip dialog box opens, as shown in Figure G-14. Any text you type in this dialog box will appear as a ScreenTip when a viewer points to the hyperlink.

4. Type **Hotels, dining, and entertainment in Seattle** in the ScreenTip text box, then click **OK**

5. Click in front of **Seattle** in the Text to display text box in the Edit Hyperlink dialog box, type **Visiting**, press **[Spacebar]**, click **OK**, then save your changes
   The hyperlink text changes to "Visiting Seattle."

6. Point to **Visiting Seattle**
   The ScreenTip you added appears, as shown in Figure G-15.

Adding comments to Web pages and documents

A comment is an embedded note that you add to a document or a Web page. Comments appear in a balloon in the right margin of a document in Print Layout or Web Layout view, as shown in Figure G-13, and are generally used to facilitate collaboration when two or more people are working on the same document or Web page.

To insert a comment in a document, select the text you want to comment upon, click Insert on the menu bar, click Comment, type your comment in the comment balloon that appears, then click outside the balloon. To respond to a comment, click in the comment balloon, click Comment on the Insert menu, then type a response in the new comment balloon that opens. To delete a comment, right-click it, then click Delete Comment on the shortcut menu. Note that comments also appear on a Web page when it is viewed in a browser. Comments appear as ScreenTips in a browser when a reader points to a comment mark (usually the author's initials in brackets).

Before you publish Web pages be sure to remove any comments you don't want others to see.

FIGURE G-13: Comment in a document

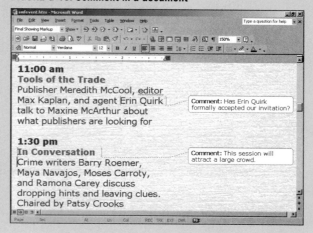

FIGURE G-14: Set Hyperlink ScreenTip dialog box

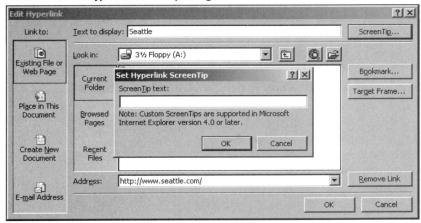

FIGURE G-15: ScreenTip and edited hyperlinks

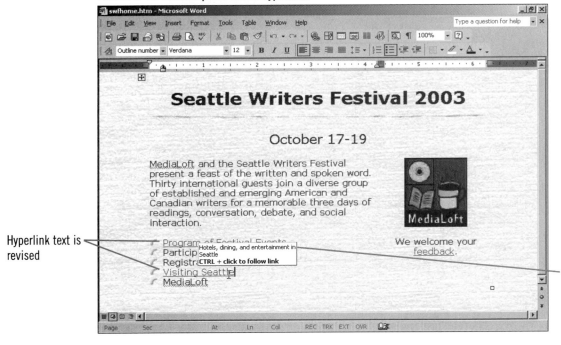

Hyperlink text is revised

ScreenTip for the Visiting Seattle hyperlink

Word 2002

E-mailing a document from Word

Another way to share information online is to e-mail a Word document to others. To e-mail a document directly from Word, open the document, then click the E-mail button on the Standard toolbar. An e-mail message header opens in the program window. Type the e-mail address(es) of the recipient(s) in the To and Cc text boxes in the message header, separating multiple addresses with a comma or a semicolon. When you are ready to send the file, click Send a Copy on the e-mail header toolbar. Your default e-mail program sends a copy of the document to each recipient.

Preview a Web Page in a Browser

Before you publish Web pages to the Web or an intranet, it's important to preview the pages in a browser to make sure they look as you intended. You can use the Web Page Preview command on the Edit menu to open a copy of a Web page in your default browser. When previewing a Web page, you should check for formatting errors and test each hyperlink. Alice previews the Web site in her browser and tests the hyperlinks. After viewing the Program Web page, she uses Word to adjust its formatting.

Steps

1. Click **File** on the menu bar, click **Web Page Preview**, then click the Maximize button on the browser title bar if necessary
   The browser opens and the home page is displayed in the browser window, as shown in Figure G-16. Notice that the page title—Seattle Writers Festival - Home—appears in the browser title bar. Your page title will also include your name.

2. Click the **Program of Festival Events hyperlink**
   The Seattle Writers Festival – Program of Events Web page opens in the browser window.

3. Click the **19 hyperlink**
   The browser jumps down the page and displays the program for Sunday, October 19 in the browser window.

4. Click the **Back button** ⟵ Back on the browser toolbar
   The top of the Program of Events Web page is displayed in the browser window. The browser toolbar includes buttons for navigating between Web pages, searching the Internet, and printing and editing the current Web page.

5. Click the **Edit with Microsoft Word button** 🔳 on the browser toolbar
   The Program of Events Web page appears in a Word document window.

6. Click the **Zoom list arrow** on the Standard toolbar, click **100%** if necessary, select **Tickets** under the bulleted list, press and hold **[Ctrl]**, select **Dress**, release **[Ctrl]**, click the **Bold button** 🅱 on the Formatting toolbar, save your changes, then close the file
   The home page appears in the Word document window. You want to check that your changes to the Program of Events Web page will preview correctly in the browser.

7. Click **File** on the menu bar, click **Web Page Preview**, then click the **Program of Festival Events** hyperlink
   The revised Program of Events Web page appears in the browser, as shown in Figure G-17.

8. Click the **Print button** 🖨 on the browser toolbar to print a copy of the swfevent Web page, click ⟵ Back, then point to the **Visiting Seattle hyperlink**
   The ScreenTip you created for the hyperlink appears. The URL of the Seattle.com Web site also appears in the status bar. If you are connected to the Internet you can click the Visiting Seattle hyperlink to open the Seattle.com Web site in your browser window. Click the Back button on the browser toolbar to return to the Seattle Writers Festival home page when you are finished.

9. Click the **feedback hyperlink**
   An e-mail message that is automatically addressed to swf@medialoft.com with the subject "Seattle Writers Festival" opens in your default e-mail program.

10. Close the e-mail message, click 🖨 to print the swfhome Web page, exit your browser, then exit Word

FIGURE G-16: Home page in Internet Explorer

Page title (yours will include your name)

Edit with Microsoft Word button

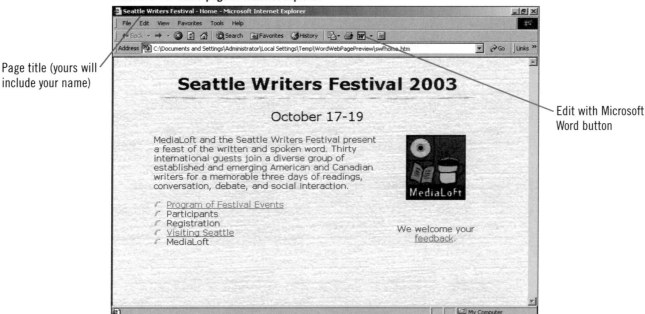

FIGURE G-17: Program of Events page in Internet Explorer

Print button

Text is bold

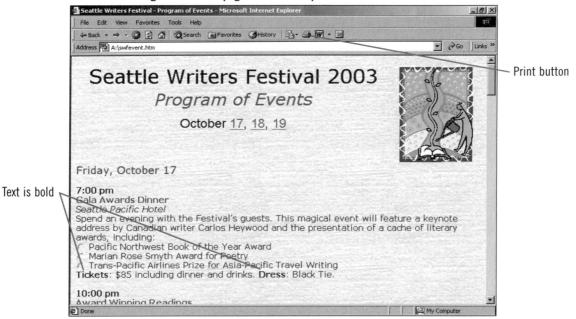

Posting a Web site to the Web or an intranet

To make your Web site available to others, you must post (or publish) it to the Web or to a local intranet. Publishing a Web site involves copying the HTML files and the supporting folders and files to a Web server—either your Internet Service Provider's (ISP) server, if you want to publish it to the Internet, or the server for your local intranet. Check with your ISP or your network administrator for instructions on how to post your Web pages to the correct server.

Practice

► Concepts Review

Label each element shown in Figure G-18.

FIGURE G-18

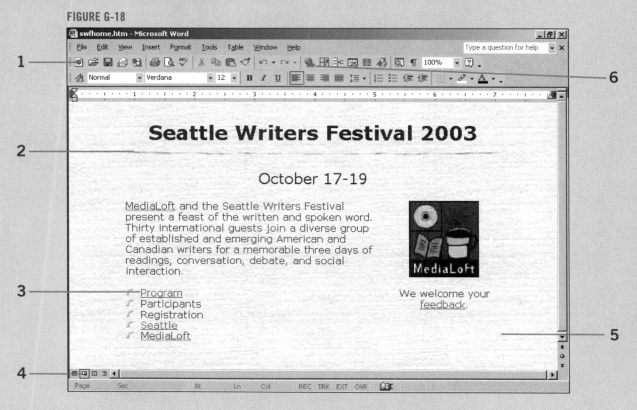

Match each term with the statement that best describes it.

7. **Hyperlink**
8. **Web page**
9. **Home page**
10. **HTML**
11. **Theme**
12. **Web site**
13. **Browser**
14. **URL**

a. The main page of a Web site
b. A software program used to access and display Web pages
c. A document that can be viewed using a browser
d. A group of associated Web pages
e. The address of a Web page on the World Wide Web
f. A programming language used to create Web pages
g. Text or graphic that jumps the viewer to a different location when clicked
h. A set of common design elements that can be applied to a Web page

Select the best answer from the list of choices.

15. Which of the following is *not* a design element included in a theme?
   a. Web page background
   b. Horizontal line style
   c. Font effects
   d. Picture bullets

16. Which of the following *cannot* be opened using a hyperlink?
a. Support folders
b. Web pages
c. E-mail messages
d. Files

17. Which of the following formats is supported by Web browsers?
a. Headers and footers
b. Page numbers
c. Columns of text
d. Inline graphics

18. What does using the Save as Web Page command accomplish?
a. Opens the active file in a browser
b. Converts the active file to HTML format
c. Applies a Web theme to the active file
d. Converts floating graphics to inline graphics

19. Where does the page title of a Web page appear?
a. On the home page
b. In the Word title bar
c. In the name of the supporting folder
d. In the browser title bar

20. Which of the following statements is false?
a. The supporting folder for a Web page holds GIF and JPEG files.
b. When you save a document as a Web page, Word adds HTML tags to the file.
c. You can use the Center button to center a floating graphic in Web Layout view.
d. Hyperlink text is underlined.

▶ Skills Review

1. Create a Web page.
a. Study the sketch for the Web site devoted to literacy issues shown in Figure G-19.
b. Start Word and create a blank Web page.
c. Create a table with two columns and three rows, select the table, then AutoFit the table to fit the window. (*Hint:* Click Table on the menu bar, point to AutoFit, click AutoFit to window.)
d. Merge the two cells in the first row of the table, then type **Literacy Facts** in the first row.
e. Merge the cells in rows 2 and 3 in the second column, click Insert on the menu bar, click File, navigate to the drive and folder where your Project Files are located, select WD G-2, then click Insert.
f. In the last cell of the first column, type the following three-item list: **What you can do, Literacy Volunteers of America, Contact us**.
g. Save the file as a Web page to the drive and folder where your Project Files are located with the page title **Literacy Facts – Home** and the filename **literacy**.

2. Format a Web page with themes.
a. Apply the Poetic or Network theme to the Web page. (*Note:* Select a different theme if neither of these themes is available to you.)
b. Format Literacy Facts in the Heading 1 style, center the text, then press [Enter].
c. Insert a horizontal line below the heading.
d. Apply bullets to the list in the last cell of the first column, then save your changes.

3. Illustrate a Web page with graphics.
a. In the blank cell in the first column, insert the graphic file reader.gif from the drive and folder where your Project Files are located.
b. Center the graphic in the cell, press [Enter], type **Literacy is not just reading and writing; the ability to perform basic math and solve problems is also important.**, press [Enter], then change the font size of the text to 10.
c. Drag the border between the first and second columns to approximately the 2¼" mark on the horizontal ruler.
d. Click Format on the menu bar, point to Background, click Fill Effects, click the Gradient tab, select the Two Colors Option button in the Colors section, click the Color 1 list arrow, click Lavender, click the Color 2 list arrow, click Light Yellow, then click OK.

e. Select the table, remove the table borders, then save your changes.

4. Save a document as a Web page.

a. Open the file WD G-3 from the drive and folder where your Project Files are located.

b. Examine the document, then save it as a Web page with the page title **Literacy – what you can do** and the filename **whattodo**.

c. Read the message about formatting changes, then click Continue.

d. Apply the theme you used with the Literacy page to the Web page, then apply the Heading 1 style to the heading.

e. Double-click the graphic, click the Layout tab, change its text wrapping style to In line with text, then move it before Literacy in the heading.

f. Change the background to a lavender and light yellow gradient. (*Hint*: See Step 3d).

g. Save your changes, then close the file.

5. Add hyperlinks.

a. In the Literacy Facts file, select What you can do, then format it as a hyperlink to the whattodo.htm file.

b. Format Literacy Volunteers of America as a hyperlink to the Web address **www.literacyvolunteers.com**.

c. Format Contact us as a hyperlink to your e-mail address with the message subject **Literacy information**. (*Note:* If you do not have an e-mail address, skip this step.)

d. Save your changes.

6. Modify hyperlinks.

a. Right-click the Contact us hyperlink, click Edit Hyperlink, then change the Text to display to **For more information on literacy, contact** followed by your name.

b. Edit the Literacy Volunteers of America hyperlink so that the ScreenTip says **Information on LVA and links to literacy Web sites**.

c. Edit the What you can do hyperlink so that the ScreenTip says **Simple actions you can take to help eliminate illiteracy**.

d. Save your changes.

7. Preview a Web page in a browser.

a. Preview the Literacy Facts Web page in your browser, test all the hyperlinks, then print a copy of the Literacy Facts Web page.

b. Open the whattodo.htm file in Word.

c. Press [Ctrl][End], press [Enter], type **For more information, contact** followed by your name, format your name as a hyperlink to your e-mail address, then save your changes.

d. Preview the Literacy - what you can do Web page in your browser, test the hyperlink, then print the page.

e. Close the browser, close all open Word files, then exit Word.

FIGURE G-19

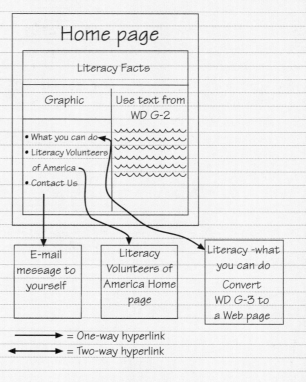

▶ Independent Challenge 1

You have written a story about a recent hiking expedition you took and want to share it and some photos with your family and friends. You decide to create a Web page. Figure G-20 shows how you will arrange the photos.

FIGURE G-20

Rising Wolf Mountain (elev. 9513 feet)

Jackson enjoying the view

a. Start Word, open a blank Web page, save the Web page with the page title **A long walk with Jackson** and the filename **longwalk** to the drive and folder where your Project Files are located, then change the zoom level to 100% if necessary.

b. Insert a table with two columns and four rows, merge the two cells in the first row, merge the three cells in the second column, select the table, then AutoFit the table to fit the window.

c. Type **A long walk with Jackson** in the first row of the table, then press [Enter].

d. Click in the second column, then insert the file WD G-4 from the drive and folder where your Project Files are located. (*Hint*: Use the File command on the Insert menu.)

e. Click in the first blank cell in the first column, then insert the graphic file **rwolf.jpg** from the drive and folder where your Project Files are located.

f. Press [Enter], then type **Rising Wolf Mountain (elev. 9513 feet)**.

g. In the last blank cell in the first column, insert the graphic file jackson.jpg from the drive and folder where your Project Files are located, then resize the photo proportionally to be the same width as the Rising Wolf Mountain photo.

h. Press [Enter], then type **Jackson enjoying the view**.

i. Drag the border between the first and second columns left to approximately the 3¼" mark.

j. Apply a theme, then format the Web page using theme elements and other formatting features.

k. Select Glacier National Park in the first paragraph in the second column, format it as a hyperlink to the URL **www.nps.gov/glac/home.htm** with the ScreenTip **Glacier National Park Website Visitor Center**.

l. Press [Ctrl][End], press [Enter], type **E-mail** followed by your name, center the text, then format your name as a hyperlink to your e-mail address, if you have one.

m. Resize the table rows and columns as necessary to make the Web page attractive, remove the borders from the table, save your changes, preview the Web page in your browser, then test the hyperlinks.

n. Switch to Word, make any necessary adjustments, save your changes, preview the Web page in your browser, print a copy, close the browser, close the file in Word, then exit Word.

▶ Independent Challenge 2

You and your partner have just started a mail-order business called Monet's Garden. You create a small Web site that includes a home page and a list of your products and prices.

a. Start Word, open the Templates dialog box, double-click Web Page Wizard on the Web pages tab, then click Next.

b. Name the Web site **Monet's Garden**, click Browse, navigate to the drive and folder where your Project Files are located, click Open, then click Next.

c. Click Separate Page, then click Next.

d. Click Remove Page three times to remove each Web page, click Add Template Page, select Right-aligned Column, click OK, click Add Existing File, navigate to the drive and folder where your Project Files are located, click WD G-5, click Open, then click Next.

e. Select Right-aligned Column in the list, click Rename, type **Monet's Garden Home**, click OK, click WD G-5, click Rename, type **Products and Prices**, click OK, then click Next.

f. Click Browse Themes, select the Nature theme (or another theme), click OK, click Next, then click Finish.

g. After the wizard creates the Web site, the default contents page of the Web site opens in Word. It has the filename default.htm. This page provides links to the other pages in the Web site.

h. Select the table on the default.htm page, remove the borders, then save your changes.

i. Press [Ctrl], click the Monet's Garden Home hyperlink on the default.htm page to open the home page in your browser, then open the Monet's Garden Home page in Word.

j. At the top of the home page, type **Order** in the blank table cell, format Order as a hyperlink to the e-mail address **monetsgarden@monad.net**, then remove the table borders.

k. Replace the main heading placeholder with **Monet's Garden,** replace the first section heading placeholder with **Professionally Designed Perennial Gardens!,** then replace the first body paragraph with the following: **If you've admired perennial gardens but thought it would be too complicated or expensive to create your own, here's great news. Our fail-proof garden packages will get you off to a sure-fire start and guarantee you glorious blooms for years to come.**

l. Delete the remaining placeholder text in the first column, delete the caption placeholder in the second column, then replace the graphic with an appropriate clip art image.

m. Adjust the formatting of the Web page to make it attractive, press [Ctrl][End], type **For more information, contact** followed by your name, make your name a hyperlink to your e-mail address, then save your changes.

n. Open the Products and Prices page in Word.

o. At the top of the Products and Prices page, type **Order** in the blank table cell, right-align Order, format it as a hyperlink to the e-mail address **monetsgarden@monad.net**, then remove the table borders.

p. Scroll down the Web page, read the comment, change 60 to 30 in the Web page text, then delete the comment. (*Hint*: Right-click the comment, then click Delete comment.)

q. Apply styles and other formatting to the Web page to make it attractive and give it a look consistent with the Monet's Garden Home page, press [Ctrl][End], type **For more information, contact** followed by your name, make your name a hyperlink to your e-mail address, then save your changes.

r. Preview the Web site in your browser, test the hyperlinks, print a copy of the home page and the Products and Prices page, exit your browser, close all open files, then exit Word.

► Independent Challenge 3

You are in charge of publicity for the Sydney Triathlon 2003 World Cup. One of your responsibilities is to create a Web site to provide details of the event. You have created the content for the Web pages as Word documents, and now need to save and format them as Web pages. Your Web site will include a home page and three other Web pages. One of the Web pages is shown in Figure G-21.

FIGURE G-21

a. Start Word, open the file WD G-6 from the drive and folder where your Project Files are located, then save it as a Web page with the page title **Sydney Triathlon 2003 World Cup - Home** and the filename **tri_home**.

b. Apply the Geared Up Factory or Cascade theme, but first remove the check from the Background Image check box in the Theme dialog box. (*Note*: Use a different theme if neither of these themes is available to you.)

c. Press [Ctrl][A], then change the font size to 10.

d. Apply the Heading 1 style to the heading Sydney Triathlon 2003 World Cup in the first row of the table, right-align the text, apply italic, select Sydney Triathlon 2003 in the heading, apply bold, select Triathlon 2003, then change the font color to a different color.

e. Apply the Heading 4 style to Welcome to the Sydney Triathlon 2003 World Cup! in the upper-left cell of the table, apply bold, then center the text.

f. Read the remaining text on the Web page, then format it with heading styles, fonts, font colors, and other formatting effects to make it look attractive. Preview the Web page in your browser.

g. Remove the table borders from the Web page, press [Ctrl][End], type your name, save your changes, then close the file.

h. Open the files listed in the table from the drive and folder where your Project Files are located, then save them as Web pages with the page titles and filenames listed in the table.

Project File	Page Title	Filename
WD G-7	Sydney Triathlon 2003 World Cup – Best Views	tri_view
WD G-8	Sydney Triathlon 2003 World Cup – Getting There	tri_get
WD G-9	Sydney Triathlon 2003 World Cup – The Athletes	tri_athl

i. In Word, open the tri_home.htm file, then change the zoom level to 100% if necessary.

j. Select Best Views, then format it as a hyperlink to the tri_view.htm file. Format Getting There and The Athletes as hyperlinks to the tri_get.htm and tri_athl.htm files, then save your changes.

k. Open each of the remaining three files—tri_view.htm, tri_get.htm, and tri_athl.htm—and format the text in the left column of each Web page as a hyperlink to the appropriate file. Save your changes, then close each Web page.

l. Preview the home page in your browser. Test each hyperlink on the home page and on the other Web pages.

m. Examine each Web page in your browser, make any necessary formatting adjustments in Word, print a copy of each Web page from your browser, then close your browser, close all open files, and exit Word.

Independent Challenge 4

In this independent challenge you will use the Personal Web page template to create a Web page that provides information about you and your interests. Your Web page will include hyperlinks to Web sites that you think will be useful to people who share your passions.

a. Start Word, open the Templates dialog box, then create a new Web page based on the Personal Web page template.

b. Save the Web page with the filename **my_page** to the drive and folder where your Project Files are located. Use your name for the page title.

c. Under Contents, delete the Work Information and Current Projects items, then scroll down and delete the placeholders in the Work Information and Current projects sections of the Web page. (*Note:* Delete from the heading for each section to the "Back to top" hyperlink.)

d. Use your favorite search engine to search for Web sites related to your interests. Write down the page titles and URLs of at least three Web sites that you think are worth visiting.

e. Replace the placeholder text in the Favorite Links section with the names of the three Web sites you liked. Format each name as a hyperlink to the Web site, and create a ScreenTip that explains why you think it's a good Web site.

f. Replace the remaining placeholder text in the Web page with information about yourself.

g. Format your e-mail and Web addresses as hyperlinks to those addresses. Edit each Back to top hyperlink so that it jumps to the main heading at the top of the page rather than to the top of the document.

h. Illustrate the Web page with a clip art graphic. Create a table to position the graphic if necessary.

i. Format the Web page with a background, heading styles, lines, bullets, fonts, colors, and any other formatting features.

j. Save your changes, preview the Web page in your browser, test each hyperlink, then make any necessary adjustments.

k. Save your changes, preview the Web page in your browser again, print a copy, close the browser, close the file, then exit Word.

► Visual Workshop

Create the Web pages shown in Figure G-22 using the graphic files rest.jpg, bridge.jpg, and studlamp.jpg, found on the drive and folder where your Project Files are located. Save the home page with the page title **Gallery Azul Home (Your Name)** and the filename **azulhome**. Save the exhibit page with the page title **Gallery Azul Exhibit (Your Name)** and the filename **azulexhb**. On the home page, create a hyperlink to the exhibit page and a hyperlink to the e-mail address **GalleryAzul@ptown.net**. On the Exhibit page, create a hyperlink to the home page. View the Web pages in your browser, then print a copy of each Web page.

FIGURE G-22

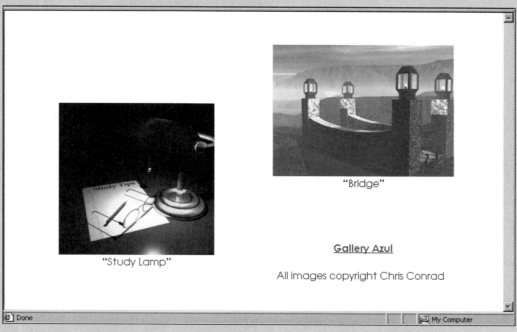

Merging
Word Documents

Objectives

- MOUS ► **Understand mail merge**
- MOUS ► **Create a main document**
- MOUS ► **Design a data source**
- MOUS ► **Enter and edit records**
- MOUS ► **Add merge fields**
- MOUS ► **Merge data**
- MOUS ► **Create labels**
- MOUS ► **Sort and filter records**

A mail merge operation combines a standard document, such as a form letter, with customized data, such as a set of names and addresses, to create a set of personalized documents. You can perform a mail merge to create documents used in mass mailings, such as letters and labels. You also can use mail merge to create documents that include customized information, such as business cards. In this unit you learn how to use the Mail Merge Wizard to set up and perform a mail merge. ✐ Alice Wegman needs to send a welcome letter to the new members of the MediaLoft Coffee Club, a program designed to attract customers to the MediaLoft Café. She also needs to send a brochure to all the members of the club. She uses mail merge to create a personalized form letter and mailing labels for the brochures.

Understanding Mail Merge

When you perform a mail merge, you merge a standard document with a file that contains customized information for many individuals or items. The document with the standard text is called the **main document**. The file with the unique data for individual people or items is called the **data source**. Merging the main document with a data source results in a merged document that contains customized versions of the main document, as shown in Figure H-1. The Mail Merge Wizard steps you through the process of setting up and performing a mail merge. Alice uses the Mail Merge Wizard to create her form letters and mailing labels. Before beginning, she explores the steps involved in performing a mail merge.

► **Create the main document**

The main document contains the text—often called **boilerplate text**—that appears in every version of the merged document. The main document also includes the merge fields, which indicate where the customized information will be inserted when you perform the merge. You insert the merge fields in the main document after you have created or selected the data source.

► **Create a data source or select an existing data source**

The data source is a file that contains the unique information for each individual or item. It provides the information that varies in every version of the merged document. A data source is composed of data fields and data records. A **data field** is a category of information, such as last name, first name, street address, city, or postal code. A **data record** is a complete set of related information for an individual or an item, such as one person's name and address. It is easiest to think of a data source file as a table: the header row contains the names of the data fields (the **field names**), and each row in the table is an individual data record. You can use the Mail Merge Wizard to create a new data source, or you can merge a main document with an existing data source, such as a data source created in Word, an Outlook Contact List, or an Access database.

► **Identify the fields to include in the data source and enter the records**

When you create a new data source, you must first identify the fields to include. It's important to think of and include all the fields before you begin to enter data. For example, if you are creating a data source that will include addresses, you might need to include fields for a person's middle name, title, department name, or country, even though every address in the data source will not include that information. Once you have identified the fields and set up your data source, you are ready to enter the data for each record.

► **Add merge fields to the main document**

A **merge field** is a placeholder that you insert in the main document to indicate where the data from each record should be inserted when you perform the merge. For example, in the location you want to insert a zip code, you insert a zip code merge field. The merge fields in a main document must correspond with the field names in the associated data source. Merge fields must be inserted, not typed, in the main document. The Mail Merge Wizard provides access to the dialog boxes you use to insert merge fields.

► **Merge the data from the data source into the main document**

Once you have established your data source and inserted the merge fields in the main document, you are ready to perform the merge. You can merge to a new file, which will contain a customized version of the main document for each record in the data source, or you can merge directly to a printer, fax, or e-mail message.

FIGURE H-1: Mail merge process

Data source document

Field name

Store	Title	First Name	Last Name	Address Line 1	City	State	Zip Code	Country
Seattle	Ms.	Linda	Barker	62 Cloud St.	Bellevue	WA	83459	US
Boston	Mr.	Bob	Cruz	23 Plum St.	Boston	MA	02483	US
Chicago	Ms.	Joan	Yatco	456 Elm St.	Chicago	IL	60603	US
Seattle	Ms.	Anne	Butler	48 East Ave.	Vancouver	BC	V6F 1AH	CANADA
Boston	Mr.	Fred	Silver	56 Pearl St.	Cambridge	MA	02139	US

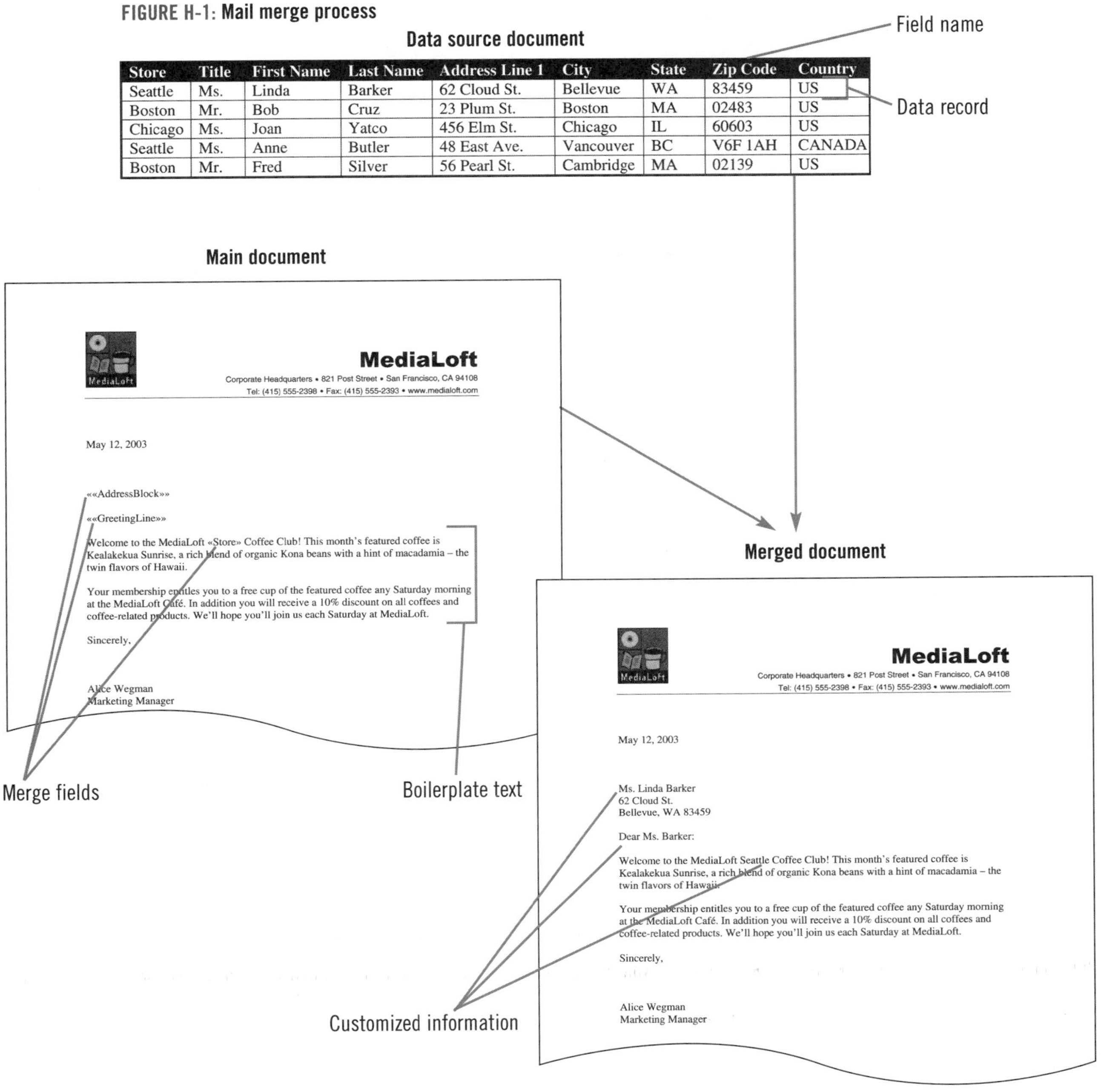

Data record

Main document

MediaLoft
Corporate Headquarters • 821 Post Street • San Francisco, CA 94108
Tel: (415) 555-2398 • Fax: (415) 555-2393 • www.medialoft.com

May 12, 2003

««AddressBlock»»

««GreetingLine»»

Welcome to the MediaLoft «Store» Coffee Club! This month's featured coffee is Kealakekua Sunrise, a rich blend of organic Kona beans with a hint of macadamia – the twin flavors of Hawaii.

Your membership entitles you to a free cup of the featured coffee any Saturday morning at the MediaLoft Café. In addition you will receive a 10% discount on all coffees and coffee-related products. We'll hope you'll join us each Saturday at MediaLoft.

Sincerely,

Alice Wegman
Marketing Manager

Merge fields

Boilerplate text

Merged document

MediaLoft
Corporate Headquarters • 821 Post Street • San Francisco, CA 94108
Tel: (415) 555-2398 • Fax: (415) 555-2393 • www.medialoft.com

May 12, 2003

Ms. Linda Barker
62 Cloud St.
Bellevue, WA 83459

Dear Ms. Barker:

Welcome to the MediaLoft Seattle Coffee Club! This month's featured coffee is Kealakekua Sunrise, a rich blend of organic Kona beans with a hint of macadamia – the twin flavors of Hawaii.

Your membership entitles you to a free cup of the featured coffee any Saturday morning at the MediaLoft Café. In addition you will receive a 10% discount on all coffees and coffee-related products. We'll hope you'll join us each Saturday at MediaLoft.

Sincerely,

Alice Wegman
Marketing Manager

Customized information

Understanding compare and merge

The Word compare and merge feature is different from mail merge. Mail merge combines a main document with a file containing customized information to create a set of unique documents. Compare and merge is used to compare any two documents—usually an original document and an edited copy of the original—to create a third document that shows the differences between the two. To compare and merge two documents, open the edited copy of the document, click Tools on the menu bar, then click Compare and Merge Documents. In the Compare and Merge dialog box, select the original document, click the Merge button list arrow, then click Merge into new document. A new merge document showing the differences between the edited document and the original document opens. The differences between the two documents are shown as tracked changes (colored and underlined text). You can then examine the merged document, edit it, and save it with a new filename.

Creating a Main Document

Word 2002

The first step in performing a mail merge is to create the main document—the file that contains the boilerplate text. You can create a main document from scratch, save an existing document as a main document, or use a mail merge template to create a main document. The Mail Merge Wizard walks you through the process of selecting the type of main document to create. ✒️ Alice uses an existing form letter for her main document. She begins by starting the Mail Merge Wizard.

> **QuickTip**
>
> You can click an option button in the task pane to read a description of each type of merge document.

1. Start **Word**, click **Tools** on the menu bar, point to **Letters and Mailings**, then click **Mail Merge Wizard**
   The Mail Merge task pane opens, as shown in Figure H-2, and displays information for the first step in the mail merge process: selecting the type of merge document to create.

2. Make sure the **Letters option button** is selected, then click **Next: Starting document** to continue with the next wizard step
   The task pane displays the options for the second step: selecting the main document. You can use the current document, start with a mail merge template, or use an existing file.

> **QuickTip**
>
> If you choose "Use the current document" and the current document is blank, you can create a main document from scratch. Either type the boilerplate text at this wizard step, or wait until the wizard prompts you to do so.

3. Select the **Start from existing document option button**, select **More files** in the Start from existing list box if necessary, then click **Open**
   The Open dialog box opens.

4. Use the Look in list arrow to navigate to the drive and folder where your Project Files are located, select the file **WD H-1**, then click **Open**
   The letter that opens contains the boilerplate text for the main document. Notice the filename in the title bar is Document1. When you create a main document that is based on an existing document, Word gives the main document a default temporary filename.

5. Click the **Save button** 💾 on the Standard toolbar, then save the main document with the filename **Coffee Letter Main** to the drive and folder where your Project Files are located
   It's a good idea to include "main" in the filename so that you can easily recognize the file as a main document.

6. Click the **Zoom list arrow** on the Standard toolbar, click **Text Width**, select **April 9, 2003** in the letter, type today's date, scroll down, select **Alice Wegman**, type your name, press **[Ctrl][Home]**, then save your changes
   The edited main document is shown in Figure H-3.

7. Click **Next: Select recipients** to continue with the next wizard step
   You will continue with Step 3 of 6 in the next lesson.

Working with smart tags

Smart tags are labels applied to data (text) that Word recognizes as a date, address, place, name, or other type of data. Text that is labeled with a smart tag is marked with a dotted purple underline. Smart tags allow you to use Word to perform tasks that you would normally need to do in another Office program. For example, in Word you can click a smart tag labeling a person's name to add the person's name and address to one of your contact lists in Outlook, without having to open Outlook first. To find out the kinds of actions you can take with a smart tag, point to the smart tag, click the Smart Tag Actions button that appears, then select from the menu of options.

FIGURE H-2: Step 1 of 6 Mail Merge task pane

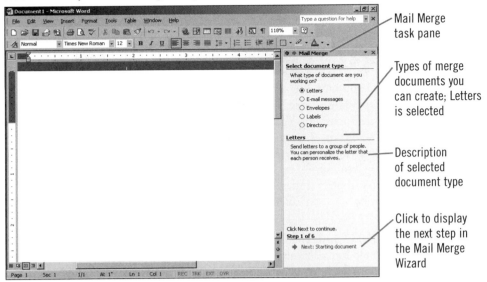

Mail Merge task pane

Types of merge documents you can create; Letters is selected

Description of selected document type

Click to display the next step in the Mail Merge Wizard

FIGURE H-3: Main document with the Step 2 of 6 Mail Merge task pane

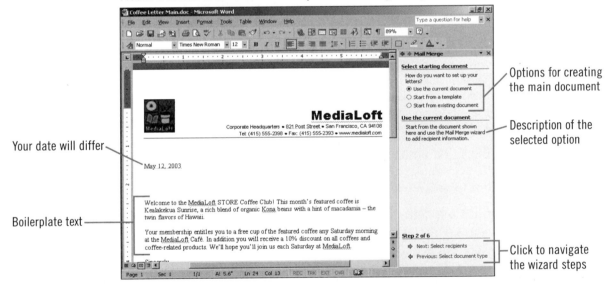

Your date will differ

Boilerplate text

Options for creating the main document

Description of the selected option

Click to navigate the wizard steps

Word 2002

CLUES TO USE

Using a mail merge template

If you are creating a letter, fax, or directory, you can use a mail merge template to start your main document. Each template includes boilerplate text, which you can customize, and merge fields, which you can match to the field names in your data source. To create a main document that is based on a mail merge template, click the Start from a template option button in the Step 2 of 6 Mail Merge task pane, then click Select template. In the Templates dialog box that opens, select a template on the Mail Merge tab, then click OK to create the document. Once you have created the main document, you can customize it

with your own information: edit the boilerplate text, change the document format, or add, remove, or modify the merge fields. Before performing the merge, make sure to match the names of the address merge fields used in the template with the field names used in your data source. To match the field names, click the Match Fields button on the Mail Merge toolbar, then use the list arrows in the Match fields dialog box to select the field name in your data source that corresponds to each address field component in the main document.

Designing a Data Source

Once you have identified the main document, the next step in the mail merge process is to identify the data source, the file that contains the information that will differ in each version of the merge document. You can use an existing data source that already contains the records you want to include in your merge, or you can create a new data source. When you create a new data source you must determine the fields to include—the categories of information, such as a first name, last name, city, or a zip code—and then add the records. Alice creates a new data source that includes fields for the name, address, and MediaLoft store location of each new member of the Coffee Club.

Steps

1. **Make sure the Mail Merge task pane displays Step 3 of 6 at the bottom**
   Step 3 of 6 involves selecting a data source to use for the merge. You can use an existing data source, a list of contacts created in Microsoft Outlook, or a new data source.

2. **Select the Type a new list option button, then click Create**
   The New Address List dialog box opens, as shown in Figure H-4. You use this dialog box both to design your data source and to enter records. The Enter Address information section of the dialog box includes fields that are commonly used in form letters, but you can customize your data source by adding and removing fields from this list. A data source can be merged with more than one main document, so it's important to design a data source to be flexible. The more fields you include in a data source, the more flexible it is. For example, if you include separate fields for a person's title, first name, middle name, and last name, you can use the same data source to create an envelope addressed to "Mr. John Montgomery Smith" and a form letter addressed to "Dear John."

3. **Click Customize**
   The Customize Address List dialog box opens, as shown in Figure H-5. You use this dialog box to add, delete, rename, and reorder the fields in the data source.

4. **Click Company Name in the list of field names, click Delete, then click Yes in the warning dialog box that opens**
   Company Name is removed from the list of field names. The Company Name field will not be part of the data source.

5. **Repeat step 4 to delete the Address Line 2, Home Phone, Work Phone and E-mail Address fields**
   The fields are removed from the data source.

6. **Click Add, type Store in the Add Field dialog box, then click OK**
   A field called "Store," which you will use to indicate the location of the MediaLoft store where the customer joined the Coffee Club, is added to the data source.

7. **Select Store in the list of field names if necessary, then click Move Up eight times**
   The field name "Store" is moved to the top of the list. Although the order of field names does not matter in a data source, it's convenient to arrange the field names logically to make it easier to enter and edit records.

8. **Click OK**
   The New Address List dialog box shows the customized list of fields, with the Store field first in the list. The next step is to enter each record you want to include in the data source. You will add records to the data source in the next lesson.

FIGURE H-4: New Address List dialog box

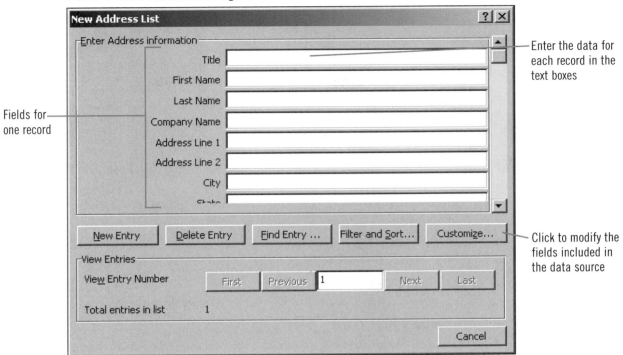

Fields for one record

Enter the data for each record in the text boxes

Click to modify the fields included in the data source

FIGURE H-5: Customize Address List dialog box

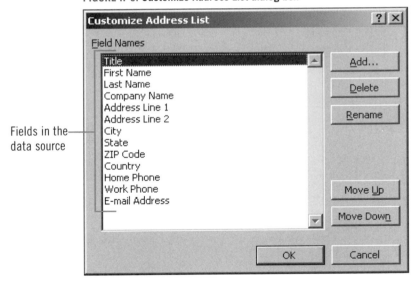

Fields in the data source

Merging with an Outlook data source

If you maintain lists of contacts in Microsoft Outlook, you can use one of your Outlook contact lists as a data source for a merge. To merge with an Outlook data source, click the Select from Outlook contacts option button in the Step 3 of 6 Mail Merge task pane, then click Choose Contacts Folder to open the Select Contact List folder dialog box. In this dialog box, select the contact list you want to use as the data source, then click OK. All the contacts included in the selected folder appear in the Mail Merge Recipients dialog box. Here you can refine the list of recipients to include in the merge by sorting and filtering the records. When you are satisfied, click OK in the Mail Merge Recipients dialog box.

Entering and Editing Records

Once you have established the structure of a data source, the next step is to enter the records. Each record includes the complete set of information for each individual or item you include in the data source. ◢▬▬ Alice creates a record for each new member of the Coffee Club.

Steps

1. Place the insertion point in the Store text box in the New Address List dialog box, type **Seattle**, then press **[Tab]**

"Seattle" appears in the Store field and the insertion point moves to the next field in the list, the Title field.

2. Type **Ms.**, press **[Tab]**, type **Linda**, press **[Tab]**, type **Barker**, press **[Tab]**, type **62 Cloud St.**, press **[Tab]**, type **Bellevue**, press **[Tab]**, type **WA**, press **[Tab]**, type **83459**, press **[Tab]**, then type **US**

Compare your New Address List dialog box with Figure H-6.

3. Click **New Entry**

The record for Linda Barker is added to the data source and the dialog box displays empty fields for the next record, record 2.

4. Enter the following four records, pressing **[Tab]** to move from field to field, and clicking **New Entry** at the end of each record except the last:

Store	Title	First Name	Last Name	Address Line 1	City	State	ZIP Code	Country
Boston	Mr.	Bob	Cruz	23 Plum St.	Boston	MA	02483	US
Chicago	Ms.	Joan	Yatco	456 Elm St.	Chicago	IL	60603	US
Seattle	Ms.	Anne	Butler	48 East Ave.	Vancouver	BC	V6F 1AH	CANADA
Boston	Mr.	Fred	Silver	56 Pearl St.	Cambridge	MA	02139	US

5. Click **Close**

The Save Address List dialog box opens. Data sources are saved by default in the My Data Sources folder so that you can easily locate them to use in other merge operations. Data sources you create in Word are saved in Microsoft Office Address Lists (*.mdb) format.

6. Type **New Coffee Club Data** in the File name text box, use the Save in list arrow to navigate to the drive and folder where your Project Files are located, then click **Save**

The data source is saved, and the Mail Merge Recipients dialog box opens, as shown in Figure H-7. The dialog box shows the records in the data source in table format. You can use the dialog box to edit, sort, and filter records, and to select the recipients to include in the mail merge. You will learn more about sorting and filtering in a later lesson. The check marks in the first column indicate the records that will be included in the merge.

7. Click the **Joan Yatco record**, click **Edit**, select **Ms.** in the Title text box in the New Coffee Club Data.mdb dialog box, type **Dr.**, then click **Close**

The data in the Title field for Joan Yatco changes from "Ms." to "Dr." and the New Coffee Club Data.mdb dialog box closes.

8. Click **OK** in the Mail Merge Recipients dialog box

The dialog box closes. The file type and filename of the data source attached to the main document now appear under Use an existing list in the Mail Merge task pane, as shown in Figure H-8. The Mail Merge toolbar also appears in the program window when you close the data source. You'll learn more about the Mail Merge toolbar in later lessons.

FIGURE H-6: Record in New Address List dialog box

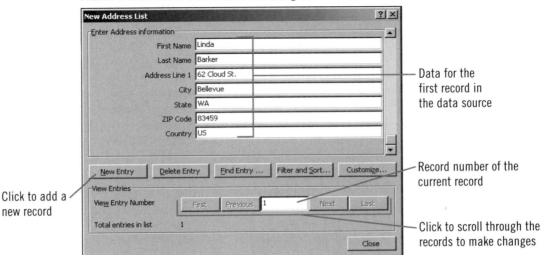

Click to add a new record

Data for the first record in the data source

Record number of the current record

Click to scroll through the records to make changes

FIGURE H-7: Mail Merge Recipients dialog box

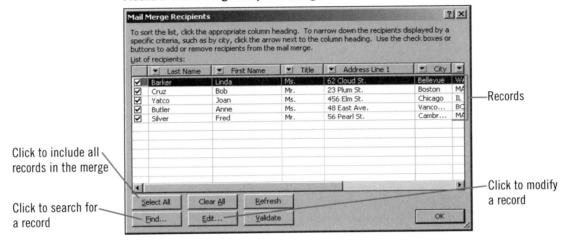

Click to include all records in the merge

Click to search for a record

Records

Click to modify a record

FIGURE H-8: Data source attached to the main document

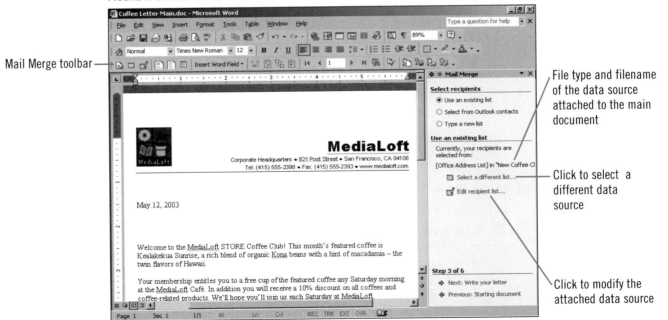

Mail Merge toolbar

File type and filename of the data source attached to the main document

Click to select a different data source

Click to modify the attached data source

Adding Merge Fields

After you have created and identified the data source, the next step is to insert the merge fields in the main document. Merge fields serve as placeholders for text that will be inserted when the main document and the data source are merged. The names of merge fields correspond to the field names in the data source. You can insert merge fields using the Mail Merge task pane or the Insert Merge Field button on the Mail Merge toolbar. You cannot type merge fields into the main document.

Alice uses the Mail Merge task pane to insert merge fields for the inside address and greeting of her letter. She also inserts a merge field for the store location in the body of the letter.

1. Click the Show/Hide ¶ button ¶ on the Standard toolbar to display formatting marks, then click Next: Write your letter in the Mail Merge task pane

The Mail Merge task pane shows the options for Step 4 of 6: writing the letter and inserting the merge fields in the main document. Since your form letter is already written, you are ready to add the merge fields to it.

2. Place the insertion point in the blank line above the first body paragraph, then click Address block in the Mail Merge task pane

The Insert Address Block dialog box opens, as shown in Figure H-9. You use this dialog box to specify the fields you want to include in an address block. In this merge, the address block is the inside address of the form letter. An address block automatically includes fields for the street, city, state, and postal code, but you can select the format for the recipient's name and indicate whether to include a company name or country in the address.

3. Scroll the list of formats for a recipient's name to get a feel for the kinds of formats you can use, then click Mr. Joshua Randall Jr. if necessary

The selected format uses the recipient's title, first name, and last name.

4. Click the Only include the country/region if different than: option button, then type US in the text box

You only need to include the country in the address block if the country is different from the United States, so you indicate that all entries in the Country field except "US" should be included in the printed address.

5. Click OK, then press [Enter] twice

The merge field AddressBlock is added to the main document. Chevrons (<< and >>) surround a merge field to distinguish it from the boilerplate text.

6. Click Greeting line in the Mail Merge task pane

The Greeting Line dialog box opens. You want to use the format "Dear Mr. Randall:" (the recipient's title and last name, followed by a colon) for a greeting. The default format uses a comma, so you have to change the comma to a colon.

7. Click the , list arrow, click :, click OK, then press [Enter]

The merge field GreetingLine is added to the main document.

8. In the body of the letter select STORE, then click More items in the Mail Merge task pane

The Insert Merge Field dialog box opens and displays the list of field names included in the data source.

9. Select Store if necessary, click Insert, click Close, press [Spacebar] to add a space between the merge field and Coffee if necessary, save your changes, then click ¶ to turn off the display of formatting marks

The merge field Store is inserted in the main document, as shown in Figure H-10. You must type spaces and punctuation between merge fields if you want spaces and punctuation to appear between the data in the merged documents. You will preview the merged data and perform the merge in the next lesson.

FIGURE H-9: Address Block dialog box

Formats for the recipient's name →

Click to match the default address field names to the field names used in your data source →

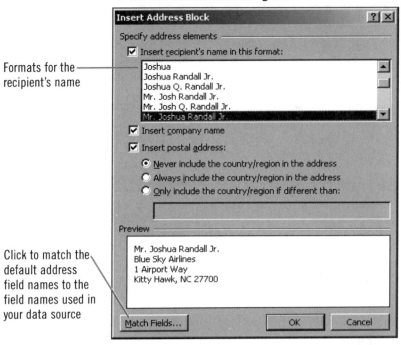

FIGURE H-10: Merge fields in the main document

Merge fields →

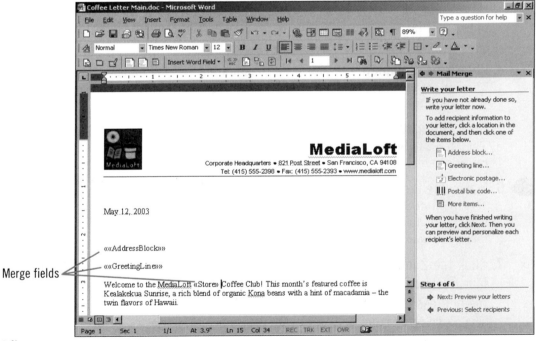

Matching fields

The merge fields you insert in a main document must correspond with the field names in the associated data source. If you are using the Address Block merge field, you must make sure that the default address field names correspond with the field names used in your data source. If the default address field names do not match the field names in your data source, click Match Field in the Insert Address Block dialog box, then use the list arrows in the Match Fields dialog box to select the field name in the data source that corresponds to each default address field name.

Merging Data

Once you have added records to your data source and inserted merge fields in the main document, you are ready to perform the merge. Before merging, it's a good idea to preview the merged data to make sure the printed documents will appear as you want them to. You can preview the merge using the wizard or the View Merged Data button on the Mail Merge toolbar. When you merge the main document with the data source, you must choose between merging to a new file or directly to a printer. Before merging the form letter with the data source, Alice previews the merge to make sure each customized letter looks as she intended. She then merges the two files to a new document.

Steps

1. **Click Next: Preview your letters in the Mail Merge task pane**
   The data from the first record in the data source appears in place of the merge fields in the main document, as shown in Figure H-11. Always check the preview document to make sure the merge fields, punctuation, page breaks, and spacing all appear as you intend before you perform the merge.

2. **Click the Next Recipient button** ⟩⟩ **in the Mail Merge task pane**
   The data from the second record in the data source appears in place of the merge fields.

3. **Click in the Go to Record text box on the Mail Merge toolbar, press [Backspace], type 4, then press [Enter]**
   The data for the fourth record appears in the document window. The non-US country name, in this case Canada, is included in the address block, just as you specified. You can also use the First Record ⟨◀, Previous Record ◀, Next Record ▶, and Last Record ▶⟩ buttons on the Mail Merge toolbar to preview the merged data. Table H-1 describes other buttons on the Mail Merge toolbar.

4. **Click Next: Complete the Merge in the Mail Merge task pane**
   The options for Step 6 of 6 appear in the Mail Merge task pane. Merging to a new file allows you to edit the individual letters.

5. **Click Edit individual letters to merge the data to a new document**
   The Merge to New Document dialog box opens. You can use this dialog box to specify the records to include in the merge.

6. **Make sure the All option button is selected, then click OK**
   The main document and the data source are merged to a new document called Letters1, which contains a customized form letter for each record in the data source. You can now further personalize the letters without affecting the main document or the data source.

7. **Click the Zoom list arrow on the Standard toolbar, click Page Width, scroll to the fourth letter (addressed to Ms. Anne Butler), place the insertion point before V6F in the address block, then press [Enter]**
   The postal code is now consistent with the proper format for a Canadian address.

8. **Click the Save button 🖫 on the Standard toolbar to open the Save As dialog box, then save the merge document as Coffee Letter Merge to the drive and folder where your Project Files are located**
   You may decide not to save a merged file if your data source is large. Once you have created the main document and the data source, you can create the letters by performing the merge again.

9. **Click File on the menu bar, click Print, click the Current Page option button in the Page Range section of the Print dialog box, click OK, then close all open Word files, saving changes if prompted**
   The letter to Anne Butler prints.

FIGURE H-11: Preview of merged data

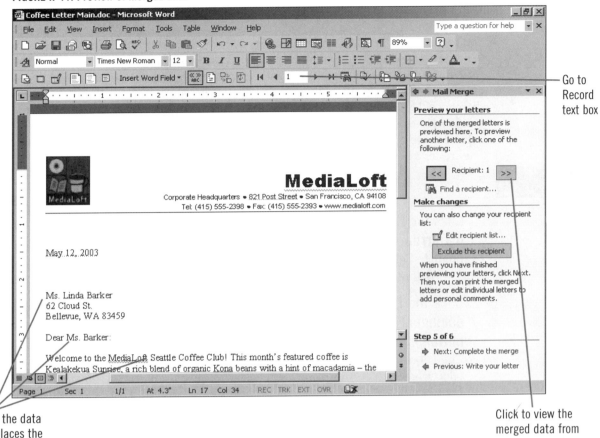

Go to Record text box

Data from the data source replaces the merge fields

Click to view the merged data from the next record

TABLE H-1: Buttons on the Mail Merge toolbar

button	use to
	Change the main document to a different type, or convert it to a normal Word document
	Select an existing data source
	Edit, sort, or filter the associated data source
	Insert an Address Block merge field
	Insert a Greeting Line merge field
	Insert a merge field from the data source
	Switch between viewing the main document with merge fields and with merged data
	Highlight the merge fields in the main document
	Match address fields with the field names used in the data source
	Search for a record in the merged documents
	Check for errors in the merged documents
	Merge the data to a new document and display it on screen
	Print the merged documents without first reviewing them on screen

Word 2002

Creating Labels

You can also use the Mail Merge Wizard to create mailing labels or print envelopes for a mailing. When you create labels or envelopes, you must select a standard label or envelope size to use as the main document, select a data source, and then insert the merge fields in the main document before performing the merge. In addition to mailing labels, you can use mail merge to create labels for diskettes, CDs, videos, and other items, and to create documents that are based on standard or custom label sizes, such as business cards, nametags, and postcards. ✐━━ Alice uses the Mail Merge Wizard to create mailing labels for a brochure she needs to send to all members of the Coffee Club. She creates a new label main document and attaches an existing data source.

Steps

1. Click the **New Blank Document button** ▫ on the Standard toolbar, click the **Zoom list arrow** on the Standard toolbar, click **Page Width**, click **Tools** on the menu bar, point to **Letters and Mailings**, then click **Mail Merge Wizard**

The Mail Merge task pane opens.

2. Click the **Labels option button** in the Mail Merge task pane, click **Next: Starting document** to move to step 2 of 6, make sure the **Change document layout option button** is selected, then click **Label options**

The Label Options dialog box opens, as shown in Figure H-12. You use this dialog box to select a label size for your labels and to specify the type of printer you plan to use. The default brand name Avery standard appears in the Label products list box. You can use the Label products list arrow to select other label products or a custom label. The many standard types of Avery labels for mailings, file folders, diskettes, post cards, and other types of labels are listed in the Product number list box. The type, height, width, and paper size for the selected product is displayed in the Label information section.

> **Trouble?**
>
> If your dialog box does not show Avery standard, click the Label products list arrow, then click Avery standard.

> **Trouble?**
>
> If your gridlines are not visible, click Table on the menu bar, then click Show Gridlines.

3. Scroll down the Product number list, click **5161 – Address**, then click **OK**

A table with gridlines appears in the main document, as shown in Figure H-13. Each table cell is the size of a label for the label product you selected.

4. Save the label main document with the filename **Coffee Labels Main** to the drive and folder where your Project Files are located

Next you need to select a data source for the labels.

5. Click **Next: Select recipients** to move to Step 3 of 6, click the **Use an existing list option button** if necessary, then click **Browse**

The Select Data Source dialog box opens.

6. Use the Look in list arrow to navigate to the drive and folder where your Project Files are located, then open the file **WD H-2.mdb**

The Mail Merge Recipients dialog box opens and displays all the records in the data source. In the next lesson you will sort and filter the records before performing the mail merge.

FIGURE H-12: Label Options dialog box

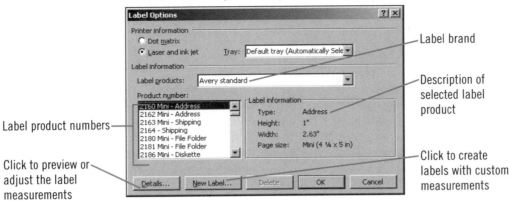

Label brand

Description of
selected label
product

Label product numbers

Click to preview or
adjust the label
measurements

Click to create
labels with custom
measurements

FIGURE H-13: Label main document

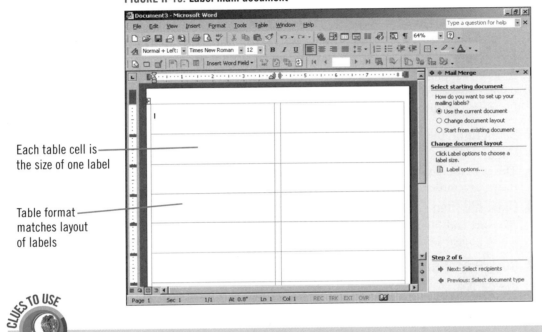

Each table cell is
the size of one label

Table format
matches layout
of labels

CLUES TO USE

Printing individual envelopes and labels

The Mail Merge Wizard allows you to easily print envelopes and labels for mass mailings, but you can also quickly format and print individual envelopes and labels using the Envelopes and Labels dialog box. To open the Envelopes and Labels dialog box, point to Letters and Mailings on the Tools menu, then click Envelopes and Labels. On the Envelopes tab, shown in Figure H-14, type the recipient's address in the Delivery address box and the return address in the Return address box. Click Options to open the Envelope Options dialog box, which you can use to select the envelope size, change the font and font size of the delivery and return addresses, and change the printing options. When you are ready to print the envelope, click Print in the Envelopes and Labels dialog box. The procedure for printing an individual label is similar to printing an individual envelope:

Enter the recipient's address on the Labels tab, click Options to select a label product number, click OK, then click Print.

FIGURE H-14: Envelopes tab in the Envelopes and Labels dialog box

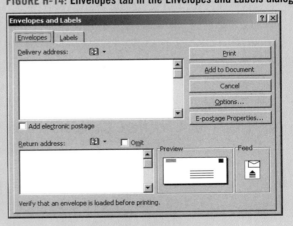

Word 2002

Sorting and Filtering Records

If you are using a large data source, you might want to sort and/or filter the records before performing a merge. **Sorting** the records determines the order in which the records are merged. For example, you might want to sort an address data source so that records are merged alphabetically by last name or in zip code order. **Filtering** the records pulls out the records that meet specific criteria and includes only those records in the merge. For instance, you might want to filter a data source to send a mailing only to people who live in the state of New York. You can use the Mail Merge Recipients dialog box both to sort and to filter a data source. Alice applies a filter to the data source so that only United States addresses are included in the merge. She then sorts those records so that they merge in zip code order.

1. In the Mail Merge Recipients dialog box, scroll right to display the Country field, click the **Country column heading list arrow**, then click **US** on the menu that opens
   A filter is applied to the data source so that only the records with "US" in the Country field will be merged. You can filter a data source by as many criteria as you like. To remove a filter, click a column heading list arrow, then click "All."

QuickTip

For more advanced sort and filter options, click Filter and Sort in the New Address List dialog box when you create or edit the data source.

QuickTip

You can click a column heading again to reverse the sort order.

2. Scroll right, click the **ZIP Code column heading**, then scroll right again to see the ZIP Code column
   The Mail Merge Recipients dialog box now displays only the records with a US address sorted in zip code order, as shown in Figure H-15.

3. Click **OK**, then click **Next: Arrange your labels** in the Mail Merge task pane
   The sort and filter criteria you set are saved for the current merge, and the options for Step 4 of 6 appear in the task pane.

QuickTip

You use the Insert Postal Bar Code dialog box to select the field names for the zip code and street address in your data source. Postal bar codes can be inserted only for U.S. addresses.

4. Click **Postal Bar Code** in the task pane, then click **OK** in the Insert Postal Bar Code dialog box
   A merge field for a U.S. postal bar code is inserted in the first label in the main document. When the main document is merged with the data source, a customized postal bar code determined by the recipient's zip code and street address will appear on every label.

5. Press [→], press [Enter], click **Address Block** in the task pane, then click **OK** in the Insert Address Block dialog box
   The Address Block merge field is added to the first label.

6. Point to the **down arrow** at the bottom of the task pane to scroll down, then click **Update all labels** in the task pane
   The merge fields are copied from the first label to every label in the main document.

QuickTip

To change the font or paragraph formatting of merged data, format the merge fields before performing a merge.

7. Click **Next: Preview your labels** in the task pane
   A preview of the merged label data appears in the main document. Only U.S. addresses are included, and the labels are organized in zip code order.

8. Click **Next: Complete the merge** in the task pane, click **Edit individual labels**, then click **OK** in the Merge to New Document dialog box
   The merged labels document is shown in Figure H-16.

9. In the first label replace **Ms. Clarissa Landfair** with your name, save the document with the filename **US Coffee Labels Zip Code Merge** to the drive and folder where your Project Files are located, print the labels, save and close all open files, then exit Word

► WORD H-16 **MERGING WORD DOCUMENTS**

FIGURE H-15: US records sorted in zip code order

Click the column heading to sort the records

All records with a US address are sorted by zip code in ascending order

Click the list arrow to filter the records

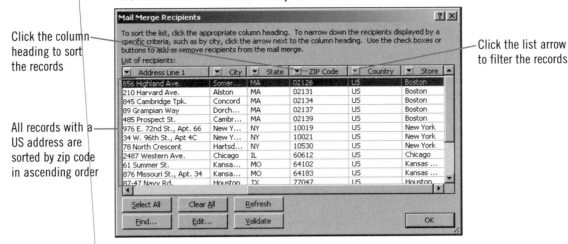

FIGURE H-16: Merged labels

Postal bar code

Labels are sorted by zip code

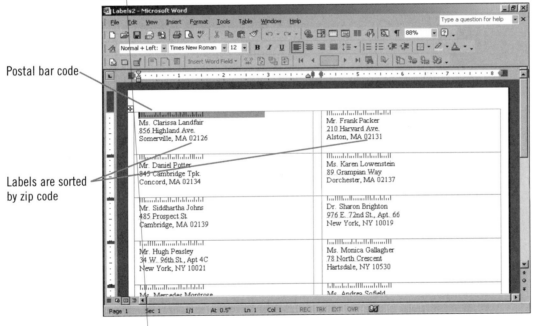

CLUES TO USE

Inserting individual merge fields

You must include proper punctuation, spacing, and blank lines between the merge fields in a main document if you want punctuation, spaces, and blank lines to appear between the data in the merge documents. For example, to create an address line with a city, state, and zip code, you would insert the City merge field, type a comma and a space, insert the State merge field, type a space, and then insert the Zip Code merge field: <<City>>, <<State>> <<Zip Code>>.

You can insert an individual merge field by selecting the field name in the Insert Merge Fields dialog box, clicking Insert, and then clicking Close. You can also insert several merge fields at once by clicking a field name in the Insert Merge Field dialog box, clicking Insert, clicking another field name, clicking Insert, and so on. When you have finished inserting the merge fields, click Close. You can then add spaces, punctuation, and lines between the merge fields you inserted in the main document.

Practice

► Concepts Review

Label each toolbar button shown in **Figure H-17**.

FIGURE H-17

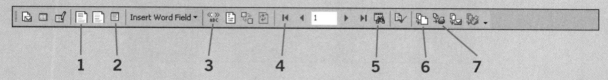

```
1   2        3        4          5   6    7
```

Match each term with the statement that best describes it.

8. **Main document**	**a.** The standard text that appears in every version of a merged document
9. **Merge field**	**b.** A complete set of information for one item or individual
10. **Data field**	**c.** To organize records in a sequence
11. **Boilerplate text**	**d.** A file that contains boilerplate text and merge fields
12. **Data source**	**e.** A file that contains customized information for each item or individual
13. **Data record**	**f.** To pull out records that meet certain criteria
14. **Filter**	**g.** A placeholder for merged data in the main document
15. **Sort**	**h.** A category of information in a data source

Select the best answer from the list of choices.

16. **In a mail merge, which type of file contains the information that varies for each individual or item?**
    a. Main document
    b. Data source
    c. Merge document
    d. Label document

17. **Which of the following buttons can be used to insert a merge field for an inside address?**
    a.
    b.
    c.
    d.

18. **Which of the following buttons can be used to preview the merged data in the main document?**
    a.
    b.
    c.
    d.

19. **Which command is used to merge two documents to create a third document that shows the difference between the two?**
    a. AutoSummarize
    b. Mail Merge Wizard
    c. Track Changes
    d. Compare and Merge Documents

20. **Which of the following is included in a data source?**
    a. Boilerplate text
    b. Records
    c. Merge fields
    d. Labels

▶ Skills Review

1. Create a main document.

a. Start Word, then open the Mail Merge task pane.

b. Use the Mail Merge Wizard to create a letter main document, click Next, then select the current (blank) document.

c. At the top of the blank document, press [Enter] four times, type today's date, press [Enter] five times, then type **We are delighted to receive your generous contribution of AMOUNT to the New England Humanities Council (NEHC).**

d. Press [Enter] twice, then type **Whether we are helping adult new readers learn to read or bringing humanities programs into our public schools, senior centers, and prisons, NEHC depends upon private contributions to ensure that free public humanities programs continue to flourish in CITY and throughout the REGION region. I hope we will see you at a humanities event soon.**

e. Press [Enter] twice, type **Sincerely**, press [Enter] four times, type your name, press [Enter], then type **Executive Director.**

f. Save the main document as **Donor Thank You Main** to the drive and folder where your Project Files are located.

2. Design a data source.

a. Click Next; in the Step 3 of 6 Mail Merge task pane, select the Type a new list option button, then click Create.

b. Click Customize in the New Address List dialog box, then remove the fields from the data source: Company Name, Address Line 2, Country, Home Phone, Work Phone, and E-mail Address.

c. Add an **Amount** field and a **Region** field to the data source. Be sure these fields follow the Zip Code field.

d. Rename the Address Line 1 field **Street**, then click OK to close the Customize Address List dialog box.

3. Enter and edit records.

a. Add the following records to the data source:

Title	First Name	Last Name	Street	City	State	Zip Code	Amount	Region
Mr.	John	Conlin	34 Mill St.	Exeter	NH	03833	$250	Seacoast
Mr.	Bill	Webster	289 Sugar Hill Rd.	Franconia	NH	03632	$1000	Seacoast
Ms.	Susan	Janak	742 Main St.	Derby	VT	04634	$25	North Country
Mr.	Derek	Gray	987 Ocean Rd.	Portsmouth	NH	03828	$50	Seacoast
Ms.	Rita	Murphy	73 Bay Rd.	Durham	NH	03814	$500	Seacoast
Ms.	Amy	Hunt	67 Apple St.	Northfield	MA	01360	$75	Pioneer Valley
Ms.	Eliza	Perkins	287 Mountain Rd.	Dublin	NH	03436	$100	Pioneer Valley

b. Save the data source as **Donor Data** to the drive and folder where your Project Files are located.

c. Change the region for record 2 (Bill Webster) from Seacoast to **White Mountain**.

d. Click OK to close the Mail Merge Recipients dialog box.

4. Add merge fields.

a. Click Next, then in the blank line above the first body paragraph, insert an Address Block merge field.

b. In the Insert Address Block dialog box, click Match Fields.

c. Click the list arrow next to Address 1 in the Match Fields dialog box, click Street, click OK, then click OK in the Insert Address Block dialog box to accept the default address block format.

d. Press [Enter] twice, insert a Greeting Line merge field using the default greeting line format, then press [Enter].

e. In the first body paragraph, replace AMOUNT with the Amount merge field.

f. In the second body paragraph, replace CITY with the City merge field and REGION with the Region merge field. (*Note*: Make sure to insert a space before or after each merge field as needed.)

g. Save your changes to the main document.

5. Merge data.

  a. Click Next to preview the merged data, then scroll through each letter.

  b. Click the View Merged Data button on the Mail Merge toolbar, then make any necessary adjustments.

  c. Place the insertion point before "I hope" in the second sentence of the second body paragraph, then press [Enter] twice to create a new paragraph.

  d. Combine the first and second body paragraphs into a single paragraph, then save your changes.

  e. Click Next, click Edit individual letters, then merge all the records to a new file.

  f. Save the merged document as **Donor Thank You Merge** to the drive and folder where your Project Files are located, print a copy of the first letter, then save and close all open files.

6. Create labels.

  a. Open a new blank document, then start the Mail Merge Wizard.

  b. Create a label main document, click Next, then select Change the document layout if necessary in the Step 2 of 6 Mail Merge task pane.

  c. Open the Label Options dialog box, select Avery 5162 – Address labels, then click OK, save the label main document as **Donor Labels Main** to the drive and folder where your Project Files are located, then click Next.

  d. Use an existing list, click Browse, then open the Donor Data.mdb file you created.

7. Sort and filter records.

  a. Filter the records so that only the records with NH in the State field are included in the merge.

  b. Sort the records in zip code order, then click OK.

  c. Click Next, insert a Postal Bar Code merge field using the default settings, press [→], then press [Enter].

  d. Insert an Address Block merge field using the default settings, then click the View Merged Data button.

  e. Click the View Merged Data button again, click the Address Block merge field in the upper-left table cell to select it if necessary, then click Address Block in the Mail Merge task pane.

  f. Click Match Fields in the Insert Address Block dialog box, click the list arrow next to Address 1, click Street, click OK, then click OK again.

  g. Click the View Merged Data button to preview the merged data, click Update All Labels in the Mail Merge task pane, then click Next to move to Step 5 of the Mail Merge Wizard.

  h. Preview the merged data, then click Next to move to Step 6 of the Mail Merge Wizard.

  i. Click Edit individual labels, merge all the records, then save the merged file as **NH Donor Labels Merge** to the drive and folder where your Project Files are located.

  j. In the first label, change Ms. Eliza Perkins to your name, save the document, then print it.

  k. Save and close all open Word files, then exit Word.

► Independent Challenge 1

You are the director of the Emerson Arts Center (EAC). The EAC is hosting an exhibit of ceramic art in the city of Cambridge, MA, and you want to send a letter advertising the exhibit to all EAC members with a Cambridge address. You'll use Mail Merge to create the letter. If you are able to print envelopes on your printer, you will also use Word to print an envelope for one letter that you need to separate from the mass mailing.

  a. Start Word, then use the Mail Merge Wizard to create a letter main document using the file WD H-3, found on the drive and folder where your Project Files are located.

  b. Replace Your Name with your name in the signature block, then save the main document as **Member Letter Main** to the drive and folder where your Project Files are located.

  c. Use the file WD H-4, found on the drive and folder where your Project Files are located, as the data source. Alternatively, if you maintain a list of contacts in Outlook, use your Outlook contact list as the data source.

  d. Sort the data source by last name, then filter the data so that only records with Cambridge as the city are included in the merge. (*Note:* If you are using an Outlook data source, select different filter criteria.)

e. Insert an address block and a greeting line merge field in the main document, preview the merged letters, then make any necessary adjustments. (*Note*: If you are using an Outlook data source, you might need to match the fields.)

f. Merge all the records to a new document, then save it as **Member Letter Merge** to the drive and folder where your Project Files are located. (*Note*: If you are using an Outlook data source, merge only the first four records.)

g. Print the first letter. If you can print envelopes on your printer, continue with the next step. If you cannot print envelopes, close all open Word files, saving changes, and then exit Word.

h. If you can print envelopes, select the inside address in the first merge letter, click Tools on the menu bar, point to Letters and Mailings, then click Envelopes and Labels.

i. On the Envelopes tab, type your name in the Return address text box, type **60 Crandall Street, Concord, MA 01742**, click Options, make sure the Envelope size is set to Size 10, then change the font of the Delivery address and the Return address to 12-point Times New Roman.

j. On the Printing Options tab, select the appropriate Feed method for your printer, then click OK.

k. Click Print, then click No to save the return address as the default.

l. Save the merge document, close it, save the main document, close it, then exit Word.

► Independent Challenge 2

One of your responsibilities at DSI Enterprises, a growing computer software company, is to create business cards for the staff. You use mail merge to create the cards so that you can easily produce standard business cards for future employees.

a. Start Word, then use the Mail Merge Wizard to create labels using the current blank document as the main document.

b. Select Avery standard 3612 – Business Card labels.

c. Create a new data source that includes the following fields: Title, First Name, Last Name, Phone, Fax, E-mail, and Hire Date. Add the following records to the data source:

Title	First Name	Last Name	Phone	Fax	E-mail	Hire Date
President	Sandra	Bryson	(312) 555-3982	(312) 555-6654	sbryson@dsi.com	1/12/01
Vice President	Philip	Holm	(312) 555-2323	(312) 555-4956	pholm@dsi.com	1/12/01

d. Add six more records to the data source, including one with your name as the Administrative Assistant.

e. Save the data source with the filename **Employee Data** to the drive and folder where your Project Files are located, then sort the data by Title.

f. In the first table cell, create the DSI Enterprises business card. Figure H-18 shows a sample DSI business card, but you should create your own design. Include the company name, a street address, and the Web site address www.dsi.com. Also include a First Name, Last Name, Title, Phone, Fax, and E-mail merge field. (*Hint*: If your design includes a graphic, insert the graphic before inserting the merge fields. Use the Insert Merge Field dialog box to insert each merge field, adjusting the spacing between merge fields as necessary.)

g. Format the business card with fonts, colors, and other formatting features. (*Note*: Use the Other Task Panes list arrow to reopen the Mail Merge task pane if necessary.)

FIGURE H-18

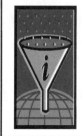

h. Update all the labels, preview the data, make any necessary adjustments, then merge all the records to a new document.

i. Save the merge document with the filename **Business Cards Merge** to the drive and folder where your Project Files are located, print a copy, then close the file.

j. Save the main document with the filename **Business Cards Main** to the drive and folder where your Project Files are located, close the file, then exit Word.

Word 2002

Independent Challenge 3

You need to create a team roster for the children's softball team you coach. You use mail merge to create both the team roster and mailing labels.

a. Start Word, then use the Mail Merge Wizard to create a directory using the current blank document.

b. Create a new data source that includes the following fields: First Name, Last Name, Age, Position, Parent First Name, Parent Last Name, Address, City, State, Zip Code, and Home Phone.

c. Enter the following records in the data source:

First Name	Last Name	Age	Position	Parent First Name	Parent Last Name	Address	City	State	Zip Code	Home Phone
Sophie	Wright	8	Shortstop	Kerry	Wright	58 Main St.	Camillus	NY	13031	555-2345
Will	Jacob	7	Catcher	Bob	Jacob	32 North Way	Camillus	NY	13031	555-9827
Brett	Eliot	8	First base	Olivia	Eliot	289 Sylvan Way	Marcellus	NY	13032	555-9724
Abby	Herman	7	Pitcher	Sarah	Thomas	438 Lariat St.	Marcellus	NY	13032	555-8347

d. Add five additional records to the data source using the following last names and positions: O'Keefe, Second base; George, Third base; Goleman, Left field; Siebert, Center field; Choy, Right field. Make up the remaining information for the records.

e. Save the data source as **Softball Team Data** to the drive and folder where your Project Files are located.

f. Sort the records by last name, then click Next in the Mail Merge task pane.

g. Insert a table that includes five columns and one row in the main document.

h. In the first table cell, insert the First Name and Last Name merge fields, separated by a space.

i. In the second cell, insert the Position merge field.

j. In the third cell, insert the Address and City merge fields, separated by a comma and a space.

k. In the fourth cell, insert the Home Phone merge field.

l. In the fifth cell, insert the Parent First Name and Parent Last Name merge fields, separated by a space.

m. Preview the merged data and make any necessary adjustments. (*Hint*: Only the first record will display when you preview the data.)

n. Merge all the records to a new document, then save the document with the filename **Softball Roster Merge** to the drive and folder where your Project Files are located.

o. Press [Ctrl][Home], press [Enter], type **Tigers Team Roster** at the top of the document, press [Enter], type **Coach:**, followed by your name, then press [Enter] twice.

p. Insert a new row at the top of the table, then type the following column headings in the new row: **Name, Position, Address, Phone, Parent Name**.

q. Format the roster to make it attractive and readable, save your changes, print a copy, then close the file.

r. Close the main document without saving changes.

s. Open a new blank document, then use the Mail Merge Wizard to create mailing labels using Avery 5162 – Address labels.

t. Use the Softball Team data source you created, and sort the records in zip code order.

u. In the first table cell, create your own address block using the Parent First Name, Parent Last Name, Address, City, State, and Zip Code merge fields. Be sure to include proper spacing and punctuation.

v. Update all the labels, preview the merged data, merge all the records to a new document, then type your name centered in the document header.

w. Save the document with the filename **Softball Labels Merge** to the drive and folder where your Project Files are located, print a copy, close the file, close the main document without saving changes, then exit Word.

Independent Challenge 4

Your boss has given you the task of purchasing mailing labels for a mass mailing of your company's annual report. Your company plans to use Avery standard 5160 white labels for a laser printer, or their equivalent, for the mailing. The annual report will be sent to 55,000 people. In this independent challenge, you will search for Web sites that sell Avery labels, compare the costs, and then write a memo to your boss detailing your purchasing recommendations.

a. Use your favorite search engine to search for Web sites that sell Avery labels. Use the keywords **Avery labels** to conduct your search. If your search does not result in appropriate links, try looking at the following Web sites: www.staples.com, www.officeworld.com, www.worldlabel.com.

b. Find at least three Web sites that sell Avery 5160 white labels for a laser printer, or their equivalent. Note the URL of the Web sites and the price and quantity of the labels. You need to purchase enough labels for a mailing of 55,000, plus enough extras in case you make mistakes.

c. Start Word, then use the Professional Memo template to create a memo to your boss. Save the memo as **5160 Labels Memo** to the drive and folder where your Project Files are located.

d. In the memo, make up information to replace the placeholder text in the memo header, then type the body of your memo.

e. In the body, include a table that shows the URL of each Web site, the product name, the unit cost, the number of labels in each unit, the number of units you need to purchase, and the total cost of purchasing the labels. Also make a brief recommendation to your boss.

f. Format the memo so it is attractive and readable, save your changes, print a copy, close the file, then exit Word.

► Visual Workshop

Using the Mail Merge Wizard, create the post cards shown in Figure H-19. Use Avery standard 3611–Post Card labels for the main document and create a data source that contains at least four records. Save the data source as **Party Data**, save the main document as **Party Card Main**, and save the merge document as **Party Card Merge**, all to the drive and folder where your Project Files are located. (*Hint:* Use a table to lay out the postcard; the clip art graphic uses the keyword "party;" and the font is Comic Sans MS.) Print a copy of the postcards.

FIGURE H-19

You're invited to a surprise party!

Grace Pappas
186 Buena Vista Terrace
Apt. 5C
San Francisco, CA 94117

For: Claudette Summer
When: August 3rd, 7:00 p.m.
Where: The Wharf Grill
Given by: Your Name

You're invited to a surprise party!

Mika Takeda
456 Parker Ave.
San Francisco, CA 94118

For: Claudette Summer
When: August 3rd, 7:00 p.m.
Where: The Wharf Grill
Given by: Your Name

Working

with Formulas and Functions

Objectives

- MOUS ▶ **Create a formula with several operators**
- MOUS ▶ **Use names in a formula**
- ▶ **Generate multiple totals with AutoSum**
- MOUS ▶ **Use dates in calculations**
- MOUS ▶ **Build a conditional formula with the IF function**
- MOUS ▶ **Use statistical functions**
- MOUS ▶ **Calculate payments with the PMT function**
- MOUS ▶ **Display and print formula contents**

Without formulas, Excel would simply be an electronic grid with text and numbers. Used with formulas, Excel becomes a powerful data analysis software tool. As you learn how to analyze data using different types of formulas, including those that call for functions, you will discover more ways to use Excel. In this unit, you will gain a further understanding of Excel formulas and learn how to build several Excel functions. Top management at MediaLoft has asked Jim Fernandez to analyze various company data. To do this, Jim creates several worksheets that require the use of formulas and functions. Because management is considering raising salaries for store managers, Jim has asked you to create a report that compares the payroll deductions and net pay for store managers before and after a proposed raise.

Creating a Formula with Several Operators

You can create formulas that contain a combination of cell references (for example, Z100 and B2), operators (for example, * [multiplication] and - [subtraction]), and values (for example, 99 or 1.56). Formulas can also contain functions. You have used AutoSum to insert the Sum function into a cell. You can also create a single formula that performs several calculations. If you enter a formula with more than one operator, Excel performs the calculations in a particular sequence based on algebraic rules, called the order of precedence (also called the order of operations); that is, Excel performs the operation(s) within the parentheses first, then performs the other calculations in a specific order. See Table E-1. ▰▰▰ Jim has been given the gross pay and payroll deductions for the monthly payroll and needs to complete his analysis. He has also preformatted, with the Comma style, any cells that are to contain values. He asks you to enter a formula for net pay that subtracts the payroll deductions from gross pay.

Steps

1. **Start Excel if necessary, open the Project File EX E-1 from the drive and folder where your Project Files are stored, then save it as Company Data**
   The first part of the net pay formula will go in cell B11.

2. **Click Edit on the menu bar, click Go To, type B11 in the Reference box, then click OK**
   Cell B11 is now the active cell. The Go To command is especially useful when you want to select a cell in a large worksheet.

Trouble?

If you make a mistake while building a formula, press [Esc] and begin again.

3. **Type =, click cell B6, type -, then click the Insert Function button 𝑓ₓ on the formula bar to open the Insert Function dialog box**
   You type the equal sign (=) to tell Excel that a formula follows. B6 references the cell containing the gross pay, and the minus sign (-) indicates that the next entry, a sum, will be subtracted from cell B6. The Function Wizard begins by displaying the Insert Function dialog box, which allows you to choose from a list of available functions or search for a specific function. See Figure E-1.

4. **Type Sum in the Search for a function text box, click Go, make sure Sum is selected in the Select a function list, then click OK**
   B6:B10 appears in the Number1 text box. You want to sum the range B7:B10.

5. **With the Number1 argument selected in the Function Arguments dialog box, click the Number1 Collapse Dialog box button ▦, select the range B7:B10 in the worksheet, click the Redisplay Dialog Box button ▦, then click OK**
   Collapsing the dialog box allows you to select the worksheet range. The net pay for Payroll Period 1 appears in cell B11.

6. **Copy the formula in cell B11 into cells C11:F11, then return to cell A1**
   The formula in cell B11 is copied to the range C11:F11 to complete row 11. See Figure E-2.

7. **Save the workbook**

FIGURE E-1: Insert Function dialog box

Type a function description

Click to start a function search

Your function listing may be different

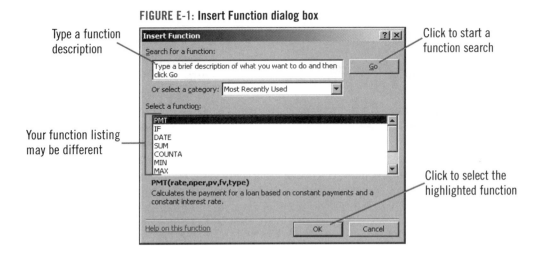

Click to select the highlighted function

FIGURE E-2: Worksheet with copied formulas

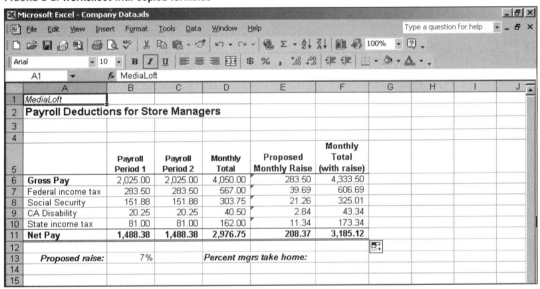

TABLE E-1: Sample formulas using parentheses and several operators

formula	order of precedence	calculated result
=10-20/10-5	Divide 20 by 10; subtract the result from 10, then subtarct 5	3
=(10-20)/10-5	Subtract 20 from 10; divide that by 10; then subtract 5	-6
=(10*2)*(10+2)	Multiply 10 by 2; add 10 to 2; then multiply the results	240

CLUES TO USE

Using Paste Special to paste formulas and values and to perform calculations

You can use the Paste Special command to quickly enter formulas and values or even to perform quick calculations. Click the cell(s) containing the formula or value you want to copy, click the Copy button 🗐 on the Standard toolbar, then right-click the cell where you want the result to appear. In the pop-up menu, choose Paste Special, choose the feature you want to paste, then click OK.

Excel 2002

Using Names in a Formula

To reduce errors and make your worksheet easier to follow, you can assign names to cells and ranges. You can also use names in formulas to make formulas easier to build. For example, the formula Revenue-Cost is much easier to understand than the formula A2-D3. When used in formulas, names become absolute cell references by default. Names can use uppercase or lowercase letters as well as digits. After you name a cell or range, you can use the name on any sheet in the workbook. If you move a named cell or range, its name moves with it. ✎ Jim wants to include a formula that calculates the percentage of monthly gross pay the managers would actually take home (their net pay) if they received a 7% raise. He asks you to name the cells you'll use in the calculation.

Steps

QuickTip

You can also assign names to ranges of cells. Select the range, click the name box, then type in the range name. You can also name a range by pointing to Name on the Insert menu then choosing Define to provide the name.

1. **Click cell F6, click the name box on the formula bar to select the active cell reference, type Gross_with_Raise, then press [Enter]**
   The name assigned to cell F6, Gross_with_Raise, appears in the name box. Note that you must type underscores instead of spaces between words. Cell F6 is now named Gross_with_Raise to refer to the monthly gross pay amount that includes the 7% raise. The name box displays as much of the name as fits (Gross_with_...). The net pay cell needs a name.

2. **Click cell F11, click the name box, type Net_with_Raise, then press [Enter]**
   The new formula will use names instead of cell references.

QuickTip

You can use the Label Ranges dialog box (Insert menu, Name submenu, Label command) to designate existing column or row headings as labels. Then instead of using cell references for the column or row in formulas, you can use the labels. (If this feature is not turned on, go to Tools/Options/Calculation tab/Accept labels in formulas.)

3. **Click cell F13, type =Net_with_Raise/Gross_with_Raise, then click the Enter button ☑ on the formula bar (make sure you begin the formula with an equal sign)**
   Notice that as you finish typing each name, the name changes color to match the outline around the cell reference. The formula bar now shows the new formula, and the result, 0.735, appears in the cell. You can also insert names in a formula by clicking Insert on the menu bar, pointing to Name, then clicking Paste. If you want to replace existing formula references with the corresponding names you have added, click Insert on the menu bar, point to Name, click Apply, click the name or names, then click OK. Cell F13 needs to be formatted in Percent style.

4. **Select cell F13 if necessary, click Format on the menu bar, click Style, click the Style name list arrow, click Percent, then click OK**
   The result shown in cell F13, 74%, is rounded to the nearest whole percent, as shown in Figure E-3. A **style** is a combination of formatting characteristics, such as bold, italic, and underlined. You can use the Style dialog box instead of the Formatting toolbar to apply styles. You can also use it to remove styles: select the cell that has a style and select Normal in the Style name list. To define your own style (such as bold, italic, and 14 point), select a cell, format it using the Formatting toolbar, open the Style dialog box and type a name for your style, then click Add. Later, you can apply all those formatting characteristics by applying your new style from the dialog box.

QuickTip

To delete a cell or range name, click Insert on the menu bar, point to Name, then click Define. Select the name, click Delete, then click OK.

5. Add your name to cell A20, save the workbook, then preview and print the worksheet

FIGURE E-3: Worksheet formula that includes cell names

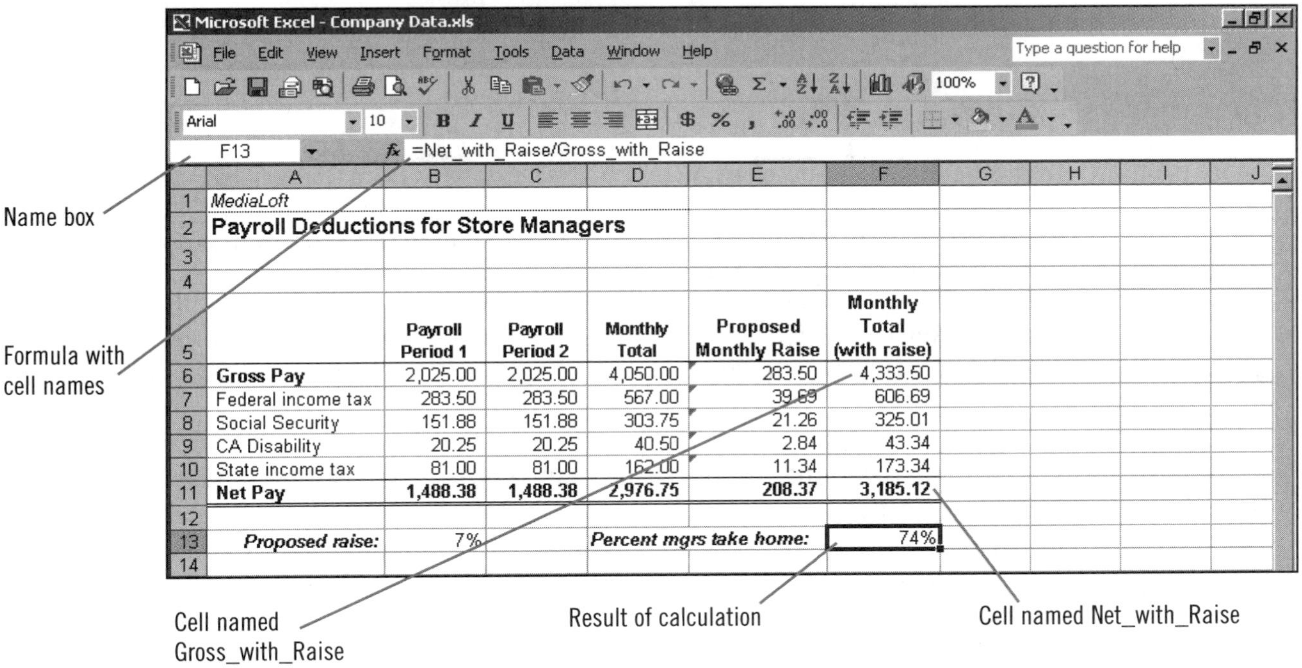

Name box

Formula with cell names

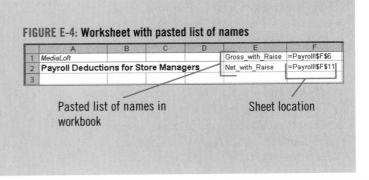

Cell named Gross_with_Raise

Result of calculation

Cell named Net_with_Raise

Producing a list of names

You might want to verify the names you have in a workbook and the cells they reference. To paste a list of names in a workbook, select a blank cell that has several blank cells beside and beneath it. Click Insert on the menu bar, point to Name, then click Paste. In the Paste Name dialog box, click Paste List. Excel produces a list of names that includes the sheet name and the cell or range the name identifies. See Figure E-4.

FIGURE E-4: Worksheet with pasted list of names

	A	B	C	D	E	F
1	MediaLoft				Gross_with_Raise	=Payroll!$F$6
2	Payroll Deductions for Store Managers				Net_with_Raise	=Payroll!$F$11
3						

Pasted list of names in workbook

Sheet location

Generating Multiple Totals with AutoSum

In most cases, the result of a function is a value derived from a single calculation. You have used AutoSum to produce a total of a single range of numbers; you can also use it to total multiple ranges. If you include blank cells to the right or at the bottom of a selected range, AutoSum will generate several totals and enter the results in the blank cells. You can have Excel generate grand totals of worksheet subtotals by selecting a range of cells and using the AutoSum function. ✎ Maria Abbott, MediaLoft's general sales manager, has given Jim a worksheet summarizing store sales. He asks you to complete the worksheet totals.

Trouble?

If you select the wrong combination of cells, click on a single cell and begin again.

1. **Make the Sales sheet active, select range B5:E9, press and hold [Ctrl], then select range B11:E15**
   To select nonadjacent cells, you must press and hold [Ctrl] while selecting the additional cells. Compare your selections with Figure E-6. The totals will appear in the last line of each selection.

2. **Click the AutoSum button Σ on the Standard toolbar**
   When the selected range you want to sum (B5:E9 and B11:E15, in this example) includes a blank cell with data values above it, AutoSum enters the total in the blank cell.

3. **Select the range B5:F17, then click Σ**
   Whenever the selected range you want to sum includes a blank cell in the bottom row or right column, AutoSum enters the total in the blank cell. In this case, Excel ignores the data values and totals only the sums. Although Excel generates totals when you click the AutoSum button, it is a good idea to check the results.

4. **Click cell B17**
   The formula bar reads =SUM(B15,B9). See Figure E-7. When generating grand totals, Excel references the cells contained in SUM functions with a comma separator between cell references. Excel uses commas to separate multiple arguments in all functions, not just in SUM.

5. **Enter your name into cell A20, save the workbook, then preview and print the worksheet**

Quick calculations with AutoCalculate

To view a total quickly without entering a formula, just select the range you want to sum, and the answer appears in the status bar next to SUM=. You also can perform other quick calculations, such as averaging or finding the minimum value in a selection. To do this, right-click the AutoCalculate area in the status bar and select from the list of options. The option you select remains in effect and in the status bar until you make another selection. See Figure E-5.

FIGURE E-5: Using AutoCalculate

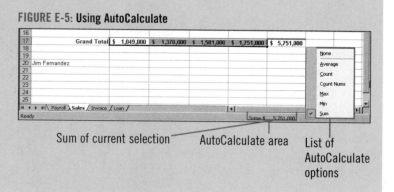

Sum of current selection   AutoCalculate area   List of AutoCalculate options

FIGURE E-6: Selecting nonadjacent ranges using [Ctrl]

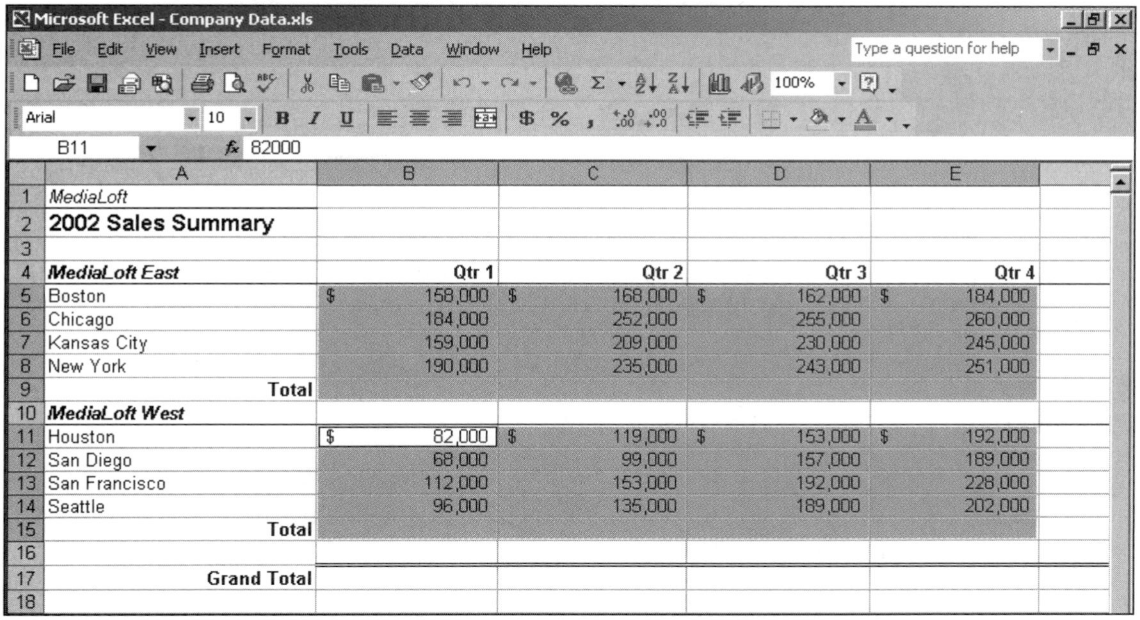

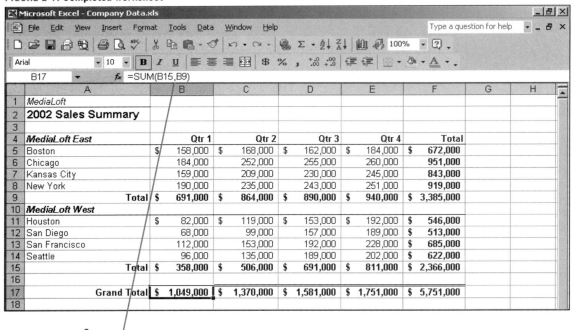

FIGURE E-7: Completed worksheet

Comma
separates
multiple
arguments

Using Dates in Calculations

Excel 2002

If you enter dates in a worksheet in a format that Excel recognizes as a date, you can sort them and perform date calculations. When you enter an Excel date format, Excel converts it to a serial number so it can be used in calculations. A date's serial number is the number of days it is from January 1, 1900. Excel assigns the serial number of "1" to January 1, 1900 and counts up from there; the serial number of January 1, 2003, for example, is 37,622. Jim's next task is to calculate the due date and age of each invoice on the worksheet. He reminds you to enter the worksheet dates in a format that Excel recognizes, so he can use date calculations.

Steps

1. **Make the Invoice sheet active, click cell C4, click the Insert Function button 𝑓ₓ on the formula bar, type Date in the Search for a function text box, click Go, click Date in the Select a function list, then click OK**
   The calculations will be based on a current date of 4/1/03, the date that Jim is revising his worksheet.

Trouble?

If the year appears with four digits instead of two, your system administrator may have set a four-digit year display. You can continue with the lesson.

2. **Enter 2003 in the Year text box, enter 4 in the month text box, enter 1 in the Day text box, then click OK**
   The date appears in cell C4 as 4/1/03. The Date function uses the format DATE(year, month, day). You want to enter a formula that calculates the invoice due date, which is 30 days from the invoice date. The formula adds 30 days to the invoice date.

3. **Click cell E7, type =, click cell B7, type +30, then click the Enter button ✓ on the formula bar**
   Excel calculates the result by converting the 3/1/03 invoice date to a serial date number, adding 30 to it, then automatically formatting the result as the date 3/31/03, as shown in Figure E-8. You can use the same formula to calculate the due dates of the other invoices.

QuickTip

You can also perform time calculations in Excel. For example, you can enter an employee's starting and ending time, then calculate how long he or she worked. You must enter time in an Excel time format.

4. **Drag the fill handle to copy the formula in cell E7 into cells E8:E13**
   Relative cell referencing adjusts the copied formula to contain the appropriate cell references. Now you are ready to enter the formula that calculates the age of each invoice. You do this by subtracting the invoice date from the current date. Because each invoice age formula must refer to the current date, you must make cell C4, the current date cell, an absolute reference in the formula.

5. **Click cell F7, type =, click cell C4, press [F4] to add the absolute reference symbols ($), type -, click B7, then click ✓**
   The formula bar displays the formula $C$4-B7. The numerical result, 31, appears in cell F7 because there are 31 days between 3/1/03 and 4/1/03. You can use the same formula to calculate the age of the remaining invoices.

QuickTip

You can also insert the current date into a worksheet by using the TODAY() function. The NOW() function inserts the current date and time into a cell.

6. **Drag the fill handle to copy the formula in F7 to the range F8:F13, then return to cell A1**
   The age of each invoice appears in column F, as shown in Figure E-9.

7. **Save the workbook**

FIGURE E-8: Worksheet with formula for invoice due date

Formula is invoice date +30

Formula result automatically calculated as date

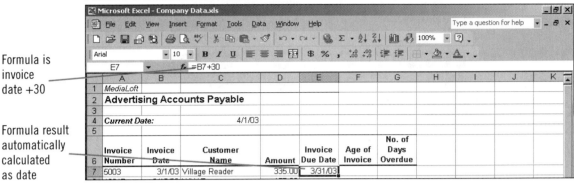

FIGURE E-9: Worksheet with copied formulas

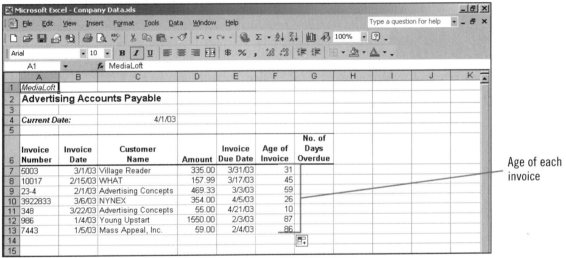

Age of each invoice

Clues to Use

Custom number and date formats

When you use numbers and dates in worksheets or calculations, you can use built-in Excel formats or create your own. For example, 9/1/03 uses the Excel format m/d/yy, but you could change it to the format d-mmm, or 1-Sep. The value $3,789 uses the number format $#,### where # represents positive numbers. To apply number formats, click Format on the menu bar, click Cells, then click the Number tab. In the category list, click a category, then specify the exact format in the list or scroll box to the right. To create a custom format, click Custom in the category list, then click a format that resembles the one you want. In the Type box, edit the symbols until they represent the format you want, then click OK. See Figure E-10.

FIGURE E-10: Custom formats on the Number tab in the Format Cells dialog box

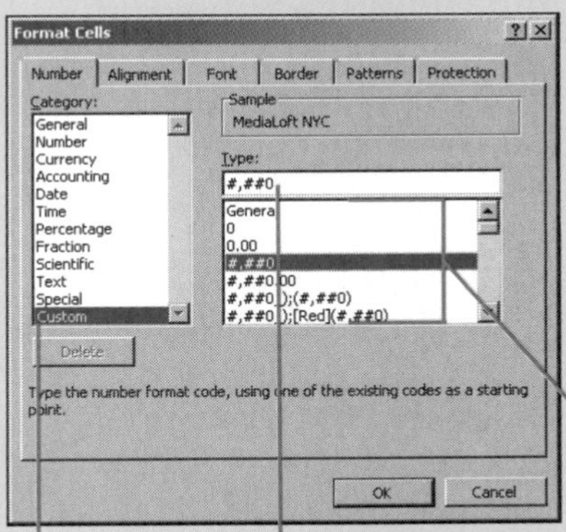

Custom formats category

Edit these symbols to customize this format

Custom formats

Building a Conditional Formula with the IF Function

You can build a conditional formula using an IF function. A **conditional formula** is one that makes calculations based on stated conditions. For example, you can build a formula to calculate bonuses based on a person's performance rating. If a person is rated a 5 (the stated condition) on a scale of 1 to 5, with 5 being the highest rating, he or she receives 10% of his or her salary as a bonus; otherwise, there is no bonus. A condition that can be answered with a true or false response is called a **logical test**. The IF function has three parts, separated by commas: a condition or logical test, an action to take if the logical test or condition is true, then an action to take if the logical test or condition is false. Another way of expressing this is: IF(test_cond,do_this,else_this). Translated into an Excel IF function, the formula to calculate bonuses would look something like this: IF(Rating=5,Salary*0.10,0). The translation would be: If the rating equals 5, multiply the salary by 0.10 (the decimal equivalent of 10%), then place the result in the selected cell; if the rating does not equal 5, place a 0 in the cell. When entering the logical test portion of an IF statement, you typically use some combination of the comparison operators listed in Table E-2. You are almost finished with the invoice worksheet. To complete it, you need to use an IF function that calculates the number of days each invoice is overdue.

Steps

1. **Click cell G7, click the Insert Function button 𝑓x on the formula bar, enter Conditional in the Search for a function text box, click Go, click IF in the Select a function list, then click OK**

   You want the function to calculate the number of days overdue as follows: If the age of the invoice is greater than 30, calculate the days overdue (Age of Invoice - 30), and place the result in cell G7; otherwise, place a 0 (zero) in the cell.

2. **Enter F7>30 in the Logical_test text box**

   The symbol (>) represents "greater than". So far, the formula reads: If Age of Invoice is greater than 30 (in other words, if the invoice is overdue). The next part of the function tells Excel the action to take if the invoice is over 30 days old.

3. **Enter F7-30 in the Value_if_true text box**

   This part of the formula is what you want Excel to do if the logical test is true (that is, if the age of the invoice is over 30). Continuing the translation of the formula, this part means: Take the Age of Invoice value and subtract 30. The last part of the formula tells Excel the action to take if the logical test is false (that is, if the age of the invoice is 30 days or less).

4. **Enter 0 in the Value_if_false text box, then click OK**

   The function is complete, and the result, 1 (the number of days overdue), appears in cell G7. See Figure E-11.

5. **Copy the formula in cell G7 into cells G8:G13 and return to cell A1**

   Compare your results with Figure E-12.

6. **Save the workbook**

FIGURE E-11: Worksheet with IF function

Logical test

Action taken if test is
true

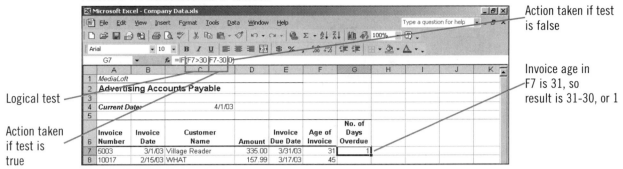

Action taken if test
is false

Invoice age in
F7 is 31, so
result is 31-30, or 1

FIGURE E-12: Completed worksheet

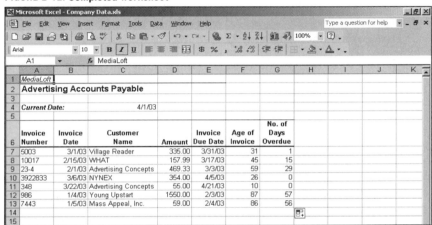

TABLE E-2: Comparison operators

operator	function	operator	function
<	Less than	<=	Less than or equal to
>	Greater than	>=	Greater than or equal to
=	Equal to	<>	Not equal to

Correcting circular references

A cell with a circular reference contains a formula that refers to its own cell location. If you accidentally enter a formula with a circular reference, a warning box will open alerting you to the problem. Click OK to display the Circular Reference toolbar or HELP to open a Help window explaining how to find the circular reference. In simple formulas, a circular reference is easy to spot. To correct it, edit the formula to remove any reference to the cell where the formula is located.

Using Statistical Functions

Excel offers several hundred worksheet functions. A small group of these functions calculates statistics such as averages, minimum values, and maximum values. See Table E-3 for a brief description of these commonly used functions. Now that you have experience using the Function Wizard, you'll type in a few of the more common functions. ✎ Jim wants to present summary information about open accounts payable. To do this, he asks you to add some statistical functions to the worksheet. You begin by using the MAX function to calculate the maximum value in a range.

Steps 1234

1. Click cell **D19**, type **=MAX(** , select range **G7:G13**, then press **[Enter]**

Excel automatically adds the closing parenthesis. The age of the oldest invoice (or maximum value in range G7:G13) is 57 days, as shown in cell D19. Jim needs to know the largest dollar amount among the outstanding invoices.

2. In cell D20, type **=MAX(** , select range **D7:D13**, then press **[Enter]**

The largest outstanding invoice, of 1550.00, is shown in cell D20. The MIN function finds the smallest dollar amount and the age of the newest invoice.

3. In cell D21, type **=MIN(** , select range **D7:D13**, then press **[Enter]**; in cell D22, type **=MIN(** , select range **F7:F13**, then press **[Enter]**

The smallest dollar amount owed is 55.00, as shown in cell D21, and the newest invoice is 10 days old. The COUNT function calculates the number of invoices by counting the number of entries in column A.

4. In cell D23, click the **Insert Function button** *fx* on the formula bar to open the Insert Function dialog box

5. Click the Select a category list arrow, choose **Statistical**, then in the Select a function box, click **COUNT**

After selecting the function name, notice that the description of the COUNT function reads, "Counts the number of cells that contain numbers…" Because the invoice numbers are formatted in General rather than in the Number format, they are considered text entries, not numerical entries, so the COUNT function will not work. There is another function, COUNTA, that counts the number of cells that are not empty and therefore can be used to count the number of invoice number entries.

6. Under Select a function, click **COUNTA**, then click **OK**

The Function Arguments dialog box opens and automatically references the range above the active cell as the first argument (in this case, range D19:D22, which is not the range you want to count). See Figure E-13. You need to select the correct range of invoice numbers.

7. With the Value1 argument selected in the Function Arguments dialog box, click the Value1 **Collapse Dialog Box button** 🔳, select range **A7:A13** in the worksheet, click the **Redisplay Dialog Box button** 🔳, click **OK**, then return to cell A1

Cell D23 confirms that there are seven invoices. Compare your worksheet with Figure E-14.

8. Enter your name in cell A26, save the workbook, then print the worksheet

Trouble?

If your results do not match those shown here, check your formulas and make sure you did not type a comma following each open parenthesis. The formula in cell D20, for example, should be =MAX(D7:D13).

QuickTip

If you don't see the desired function in the Function name list, scroll to display more function names.

QuickTip

Instead of using the Collaspe dialog box button, you can click the desired worksheet cell to insert a cell address.

FIGURE E-13: Formula Palette showing COUNTA function

Click to pick a different function

Default range is incorrect

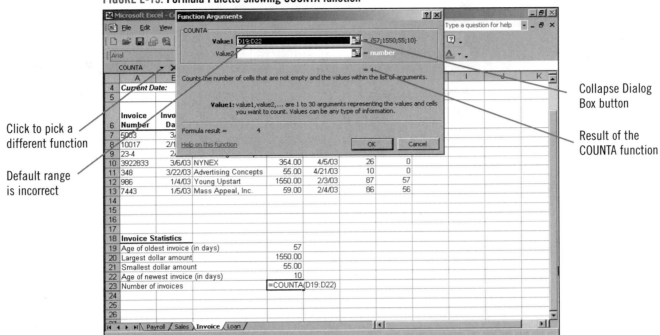

Collapse Dialog Box button

Result of the COUNTA function

FIGURE E-14: Worksheet with invoice statistics

Number of invoices in A7:A13

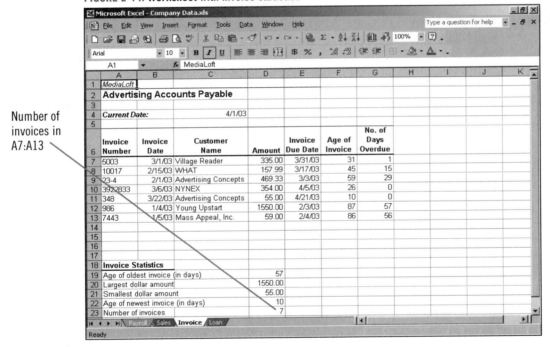

TABLE E-3: Commonly used statistical functions

function	worksheet action	function	worksheet action
AVERAGE	Calculates an average value	MAX	Finds the largest value
COUNT	Counts the number of values	MIN	Finds the smallest value
COUNTA	Counts the number of nonblank entries	MEDIAN	Finds the middle value

Calculating Payments with the PMT Function

PMT is a financial function that calculates the periodic payment amount for money borrowed. For example, if you want to borrow money to buy a car, the PMT function can calculate your monthly payment on the loan. Let's say you want to borrow $15,000 at 8.5% interest and pay the loan off in five years. The Excel PMT function can tell you that your monthly payment will be $311.38. The parts of the PMT function are: PMT(rate, nper, pv, fv, type). See Figure E-15 for an illustration of a PMT function that calculates the monthly payment in the car loan example. ✒️ For several months, MediaLoft management has been discussing the expansion of the San Diego store. Jim has obtained quotes from three different lenders on borrowing $27,000 to begin the expansion. He obtained loan quotes from a commercial bank, a venture capitalist, and an investment banker. He wants you to summarize the information, using the Excel PMT function.

Steps

1. Make the Loan sheet active, click cell **E5**, click the **Insert Function button** 𝑓ₓ on the formula bar, enter **PMT** in the Search for a function text box, click **Go**, click **PMT** in the Select a function list if necessary, then click **OK**

2. Move the Function Arguments dialog box to display row 5 of the worksheet; with the cursor in the Rate text box, click cell **C5** on the worksheet, type **/12**, then press **[Tab]**

3. With the cursor in the Nper text box, click cell **D5**; click the PV text box, click cell **B5**, then click **OK**

   You must divide the annual interest by 12 because you are calculating monthly, not annual, payments. The FV and Type are optional arguments. Note that the payment of ($587.05) in cell E5 appears in red, indicating that it is a negative amount. Excel displays the result of a PMT function as a negative value to reflect the negative cash flow the loan represents to the borrower. To show the monthly payment as a positive number, you place a minus sign in front of the PV cell reference in the function.

4. Edit cell E5 so it reads **=PMT(C5/12,D5,-B5)**, then click ✔️

   A positive value of $587.05 now appears in cell E5. See Figure E-16. You can use the same formula to generate the monthly payments for the other loans.

5. With cell **E5** selected, drag the fill handle to fill the range **E6:E7**

   A monthly payment of $883.95 for the venture capitalist loan appears in cell E6. A monthly payment of $1,270.98 for the investment banker loan appears in cell E7. The loans with shorter terms have much higher payments. You will not know the entire financial picture until you calculate the total payments and total interest for each lender.

6. Click cell **F5**, type **=E5*D5**, then press **[Tab]**; in cell G5, type **=F5-B5**, then click ✔️

7. Copy the formulas in cells F5:G5 into the range **F6:G7**, then return to cell **A1**

   You can experiment with different interest rates, loan amounts, or terms for any one of the lenders; the PMT function generates a new set of values automatically. Compare your results with those in Figure E-17.

8. Enter your name in cell A13, save the workbook, then preview and print the worksheet

FIGURE E-15: Example of PMT function for car loan

$$PMT(.085/12,60,15000) = \$311.38$$

Interest rate per period (rate) — Number of payments (nper) — Present value of loan amount (pv) — Monthly payment calculated

FIGURE E-16: PMT function calculating monthly loan payment

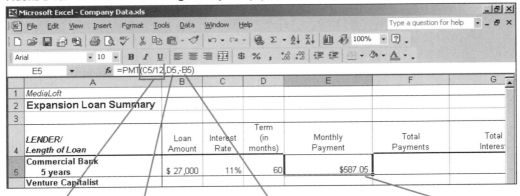

Annual interest rate ÷ 12 months — Loan term — Loan amount (preceded by a minus sign) — Monthly payment calculated

FIGURE E-17: Completed worksheet

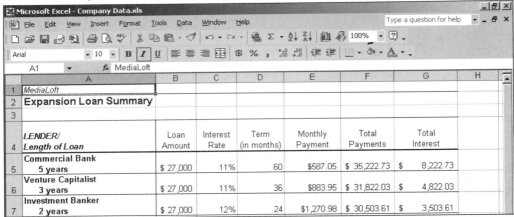

Calculating future value with the FV function

You can use the FV (Future Value) function to determine the amount of money a given monthly investment will amount to, at a given interest rate after a given number of payment periods. The syntax is similar to that of the PMT function: FV(rate,nper,pmt,pv,type). For example, suppose you want to invest $1,000 every month for the next 12 months into an account that pays 12% a year, and you want to know how much you will have at the end of 12 months (that is, its future value). You would enter the function FV(.01,12,-1000), and Excel would return the value $12,682.50 as the future value of your investment. As with the PMT function, the units for the rate and nper must be consistent. If you made monthly payments on a three-year loan at 6% annual interest, you would use the rate .06/12 and 36 periods (12*3). The arguments pv and type are optional; pv is the present value, or the total amount the series of payments is worth now. If you omit it, Excel assumes the pv is 0. The "type" argument indicates when the payments are made; 0 is the end of the period, and 1 is the beginning of the period.

Displaying and Printing Formula Contents

Excel usually displays the result of formula calculations in the worksheet area and displays formula contents for the active cell in the formula bar. However, you can instruct Excel to display the formulas directly in the worksheet cells in which they were entered. You can document worksheet formulas by first displaying the formulas, then printing them. These formula printouts are valuable paper-based worksheet documentation. Because formulas are often longer than their corresponding values, landscape orientation is the best choice for printing formulas. ✎ Jim wants you to produce a formula printout to submit with the worksheet.

Steps 1 2 3 4

1. **Click Tools on the menu bar, click Options, then click the View tab**
   The View tab of the Options dialog box appears, as shown in Figure E-18.

2. **Under Window options, click the Formulas check box to select it, then click OK**
   The columns widen and retain their original formats.

   > **QuickTip**
   > Move the Formula Auditing toolbar if necessary.

3. **Scroll horizontally to bring columns E through G into view**
   Instead of displaying formula results in the cells, Excel shows the actual formulas and automatically adjusts the column widths to accommodate them.

4. **Click the Print Preview button 🔍 on the Standard toolbar**
   The status bar reads Preview: Page 1 of 2, indicating that the worksheet will print on two pages. You want to print it on one page and include the row number and column letter headings.

   > **QuickTip**
   > All Page Setup options—such as Landscape orientation, Fit to scaling—apply to the active worksheet and are saved with the workbook.

5. **Click Setup in the Print Preview window, then click the Page tab**

6. **Under Orientation, click the Landscape option button; then under Scaling, click the Fit to option button and note that the wide and tall check boxes contain the number "1".**
   Selecting Landscape instructs Excel to print the worksheet sideways on the page. The Fit to option ensures that the document is printed on a single page.

   > **QuickTip**
   > To print row and column labels on every page of a multiple-page worksheet, click the Sheet tab, and fill in the Rows to repeat at top and the Columns to repeat at left in the Print titles section.

7. **Click the Sheet tab, under Print click the Row and column headings check box to select it, click OK, then position the Zoom pointer 🔍 over column A and click**
   The worksheet formulas now appear on a single page, in landscape orientation, with row (number) and column (letter) headings. See Figure E-19.

8. **Click Print in the Print Preview window, then click OK**
   After you retrieve the printout, you want to return the worksheet to displaying formula results. You can do this easily by using a key combination.

9. **Press [Ctrl][`] to redisplay formula results**
   [Ctrl][`] (grave accent mark) toggles between displaying formula results and displaying formula contents.

10. **Save the workbook, then close it and exit Excel**
    The completed figure for the payroll worksheet is displayed in Figure E-3; the completed sales worksheet is displayed in Figure E-7; and the completed invoice worksheet is shown in Figure E-14.

FIGURE E-18: **View tab of the Options dialog box**

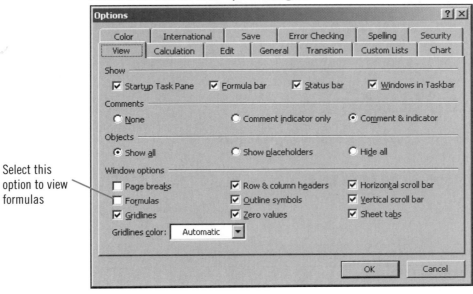

Select this option to view formulas

FIGURE E-19: **Print Preview window**

Column headings

Row headings

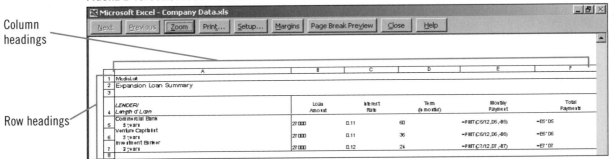

CLUES TO USE

Setting margins and alignment when printing part of a worksheet

You can set custom margins to print smaller sections of a worksheet. Select the range you want to print, click File on the menu bar, click Print, under Print what click Selection, then click Preview. In the Print Preview window, click Setup, then click the Margins tab. See Figure E-20. Double-click the margin numbers and type new ones. Use the Center on page check boxes to center the range horizontally or vertically. If you plan to print the range again, save the view after you print: Click View on the menu bar, click Custom Views, click Add, then type a view name and click OK.

FIGURE E-20: **Margins tab in the Page Setup dialog box**

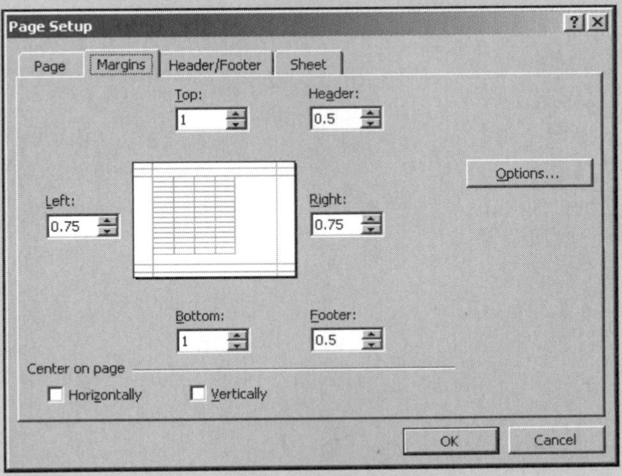

Practice

► Concepts Review

Label each element of the Excel screen shown in Figure E-21.

FIGURE E-21

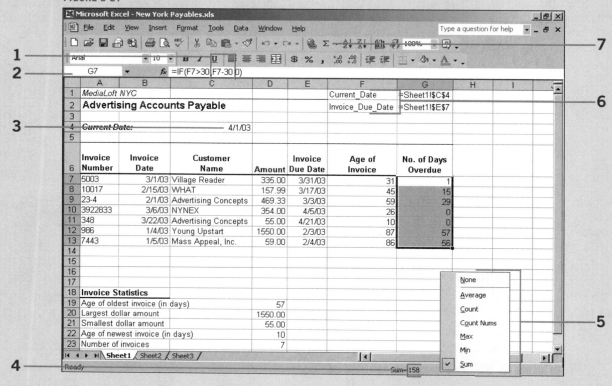

Match each term with the statement that best describes its function.

8. Style
9. COUNTA
10. test_cond
11. COUNT
12. pv

a. Part of the IF function in which the conditions are stated
b. Function used to count the number of numerical entries
c. Part of the PMT function that represents the loan amount
d. Function used to count the number of nonblank entries
e. A combination of formatting characteristics

Select the best answer from the list of choices.

13. To generate a positive payment value when using the PMT function, you must:
   a. Enter the function arguments as positive values.
   b. Enter the function arguments as negative values.
   c. Enter the amount being borrowed as a negative value.
   d. Enter the interest rate divisor as a negative value.

14. When you enter the rate and nper arguments in a PMT function, you must:
   a. Multiply both units by 12.
   b. Be consistent in the units used.
   c. Divide both values by 12.
   d. Use monthly units instead of annual units.

15. To express conditions such as less than or equal to, you can use a(n):
   a. IF function.
   b. Comparison operator.
   c. AutoCalculate formula.
   d. PMT function.

16. Which of the following statements is false?
   a. $#,### is an Excel number format.
   b. You can create custom number and date formats in Excel.
   c. You can use only existing number and date formats in Excel.
   d. m/d/yy is an Excel date format.

▶ Skills Review

1. Create a formula with several operators.
   a. Start Excel, open the Project File EX E-2 from the drive and folder where your Project Files are stored, then save the workbook as **Manager Bonuses**.
   b. On the Bonuses worksheet, select cell **C15** using the Go To command.
   c. Enter the formula **C13+(C14*7)**.
   d. Use the Paste Special command to paste the values and formats in B4:B10 to G4:G10, then save your work.

2. Use names in a formula.
   a. Name cell C13 **Dept_Bonus**.
   b. Name cell C14 **Project_Bonus**.
   c. Select the range **C4:C10** and name it **Base_Pay**.
   d. In cell E4, enter the formula **Dept_Bonus*D4+Project_Bonus**.
   e. Copy the formula in cell E4 into the range E5:E10.
   f. Format range E4:E10 with the Comma style, using the Style dialog box.
   g. Select the range **E4:E10** and name it **Bonus_Total**.
   h. In cell F4, enter a formula that sums Base_Pay and Bonus_Total.
   i. Copy the formula in cell F4 into the range F5:F10.
   j. Format range F4:F10 with the Comma style, using the Style dialog box.
   k. Save your work.

3. **Generate multiple totals with AutoSum.**
   a. Select range **E4:F11**.
   b. Enter the totals using AutoSum.
   c. Format range E11:F11 with the Currency style, using the Style dialog box.
   d. Enter your name in cell A18, save your work, then preview and print this worksheet.

4. **Use dates in calculations.**
   a. Make the Merit Pay sheet active.
   b. In cell D6, enter the formula **B6+183**.
   c. Copy the formula in cell D6 into the range D7:D14.
   d. Use the NOW function to insert the date and time in cell A3, widening the column as necessary.
   e. In cell E18, enter the text **Next Pay Date**, and, in cell G18, use the Date function to enter the date **10/1/03**. (*Hint*: You must enter the year as 2003. You can format it as a two-digit year using the Modify button on the Style dialog box and choosing Date in the Category list on the Number tab.)
   f. Save your work.

5. **Build a conditional formula with the IF function.**
   a. In cell F6, use the Function Wizard to enter the formula **IF(C6=5,E6*0.05,0)**.
   b. Copy the formula in cell F6 into the range F7:F14.
   c. Apply the comma format with no decimal places to F6:F14.
   d. Select the range **A4:G4** and delete the cells, using the Delete command on the Edit menu. Shift the remaining cells up.
   e. Repeat the procedure to delete the cells A15:G15.
   f. Use the Cells command on the Insert menu to insert a cell between Department Statistics and Average Salary, moving the remaining cells down.
   g. Check your formulas to make sure the cell references have been updated.
   h. Save your work.

6. **Use statistical functions.**
   a. In cell C18, enter a function to calculate the average salary in the range E5:E13 with no decimal places. Use dragging to select the cells.
   b. In cell C19, enter a function to calculate the largest bonus in the range F5:F13.
   c. In cell C20, enter a function to calculate the lowest performance rating in the range C5:C13.
   d. In cell C21, enter a function to calculate the number of entries in range A5:A13.
   e. Enter your name into cell A28, then save, preview, and print the worksheet.

7. **Calculate payments with the PMT function.**
   a. Make the Loan sheet active.
   b. In cell B9, use the Function Wizard to enter the formula **PMT(B5/12,B6,-B4)**.
   c. In cell B10, enter the formula **B9*B6**.
   d. AutoFit column B, if necessary.
   e. In cell B11, enter the formula **B10-B4**.
   f. Enter your name in cell A15, then save, preview, and print the worksheet.

8. **Display and print formula contents.**
   a. Use the View tab in the Options dialog box to display formulas.
   b. Adjust the column widths as necessary.
   c. Save, preview, and print this worksheet in landscape orientation with the row and column headings.
   d. Redisplay the formula results in the worksheet.
   e. Close the workbook, then exit Excel.

▶ Independent Challenge 1

As manager of Mike's Ice Cream Parlor, you have been asked to create a worksheet that totals the monthly sales of all store products. Your monthly report should include the following:

- Sales totals for the current month for each product
- Sales totals for the last month for each product
- The percent change in sales from last month to this month

To document the report further, you decide to include a printout of the worksheet formulas.

a. Start Excel, open the Project File EX E-3 from the drive and folder where your Project Files are stored, then save it as **Mike's Sales**.
b. Use the TODAY function to enter today's date in cell A3. Create and apply a custom format for the date entry.
c. Complete the headings for weeks 2 through 4. Enter totals for each week, and current month totals for each product. Calculate the percent change in sales from last month to this month. (*Hint*: The formula in words would be (Current Month-Last Month)/Last Month.)
d. After you enter the percent change formula for regular ice cream, copy the formula down the column and format the column with the Percent style.
e. Apply a comma format with no decimal places to all numbers and totals.
f. Enter your name into cell A15, then save, preview, and print the worksheet on a single page. If necessary, print in landscape orientation. If you make any page setup changes, save the worksheet again.
g. Display and print the worksheet formulas, then print the formulas on one page with row and column headings.
h. Close the workbook without saving the changes for displaying formulas, then exit Excel.

▶ Independent Challenge 2

You are an auditor with a certified public accounting firm. Fly Away, a manufacturer of skating products, has contacted you to audit its financial records. The management at Fly Away is considering opening a branch in Great Britain and needs its records audited to prepare the business plan. The managers at Fly Away have asked you to assist them in preparing their year-end sales summary as part of this audit. Specifically, they want to add expenses and show the percent of annual expenses that each expense category represents. They also want to show what percent of annual sales each expense category represents. You should include a formula calculating the difference between sales and expenses and another formula calculating expenses divided by sales. The expense categories and their respective dollar amounts are as follows: Building Lease $46,000; Equipment $208,000; Office $25,000; Salary $355,000; Taxes $310,000. Use these expense amounts to prepare the year-end sales and expenses summary for Fly Away.

a. Start Excel, open the Project File EX E-4 from the drive and folder where your Project Files are stored, then save the workbook as **Fly Away Sales**.
b. Name the cell containing the formula for total annual expenses **Annual_Expenses**. Use the name Annual_Expenses in cell C12 to create a formula calculating percent of annual expenses. Copy this formula as appropriate and apply the Percent style. Make sure to include a formula that sums all the values for percent of annual expenses, which should equal 100%.

c. Enter a formula calculating the percent of annual sales each expense category represents. Use the name **Annual_Sales** in the formula and format it appropriately. Copy this formula as appropriate and apply the Percent style. Make sure to include a formula that sums all the values for percent of annual sales.

d. Enter the formula calculating Net Profit, using the names Annual_Sales and Annual_Expenses.

e. Enter the formula for Expenses as a percent of sales, using the names Annual_Sales and Annual_Expenses.

f. Format the cells using the Currency, Percent, or Comma style as appropriate. Widen the columns as necessary to display cell contents.

g. Set the top and bottom margins at 4 inches and center the worksheet horizontally so the worksheet will print on two pages. *(Hint:* Use the Margins tab on the Page Setup dialog box.)

h. Print the first row containing the company name on each page. (*Hint*: Use the Sheet tab on the Page Setup dialog box and specify row 1 to repeat at the top.)

i. Enter your name into cell A22, then save, preview, and print the worksheet. Save any page setup changes you make.

j. Close the workbook then exit Excel.

► Independent Challenge 3

As the owner of Custom Fit, a general contracting firm specializing in home-storage projects, you are facing yet another business challenge at your firm. Because jobs are taking longer than expected, you decide to take out a loan to purchase some new power tools. According to your estimates, you need a $7,000 loan to purchase the tools. You check three loan sources: the Small Business Administration (SBA), your local bank, and a consortium of investors. The SBA will lend you the money at 8% interest, but you have to pay it off in three years. The local bank offers you the loan at 8.75% interest over four years. The consortium offers you a 7.75% loan, but they require you to pay it back in two years. To analyze all three loan options, you decide to build a tool loan summary worksheet. Using the loan terms provided, build a worksheet summarizing your options.

a. Start Excel, open a new workbook, then save it as **Custom Fit Loan Options** in the drive and folder where your Project Files are stored.

b. Enter today's date in cell A3, using the TODAY function.

c. Enter labels and worksheet data. You need headings for the loan source, loan amount, interest rate, term or number of payments, monthly payment, total payments, and total interest. Fill in the data provided for the three loan sources.

d. Enter formulas as appropriate: a PMT formula for the monthly payment, a formula calculating the total payments based on the monthly payment and term values, and a formula for total interest based on the total payments and the loan amount.

e. Format the worksheet as desired.

f. Enter your name in cell A14, then save, preview, and print the worksheet on a single page using landscape orientation. Print the worksheet formulas showing row and column headings. Do not save the worksheet with the formula settings.

g. Close the workbook then exit Excel.

Independent Challenge 4

The MediaLoft management wants to start IRAs for its employees. The company plans to deposit $2,000 in the employees' accounts at the beginning of each year. You have been asked to research current rates at financial institutions. You will use the Web to find this information.

a. Go to the Alta Vista search engine at www.altavista.com and enter "IRA rates" in the Search box. You can also use Yahoo, Excite, Infoseek or another search engine of your choice. Find IRA rates offered by three institutions for a $2,000 deposit, then write down the institution name, the rate, and the minimum deposit in the table below.

b. Start Excel, open a new workbook, then save it as **IRA Rates** in the drive and folder where your Project Files are stored.

c. Enter the column headings, row headings, and, research results from the table below into your IRA Rates workbook.

IRA WORKSHEET

Institution	Rate	Minimum Deposit	Number of Years	Amount Deposited (Yearly)	Future Value
			35	2000	
			35	2000	
			35	2000	
Highest Rate					
Average Rate					
Highest Future Value					

d. Use the FV function to calculate the future value of a $2,000 yearly deposit over 35 years for each institution, making sure it displays as a positive number. Assume that the payments are made at the beginning of the period, so the Type argument equals 1.

e. Use Excel functions to enter the highest rate, the average rate, and the highest future value into the workbook.

f. Enter your name in cell A15, then save, preview, and print the worksheet on a single page.

g. Display and print the formulas for the worksheet on a single page using landscape orientation. Do not save the worksheet with the formulas displayed.

h. Close the workbook then exit Excel.

Excel 2002

► Visual Workshop

Create the worksheet shown in Figure E-22. (Hint: Enter the items in range C9:C11 as labels by typing an apostrophe before each formula.) Enter your name in row 15, and save the workbook as **Car Payment Calculator**. Preview, then print, the worksheet.

FIGURE E-22

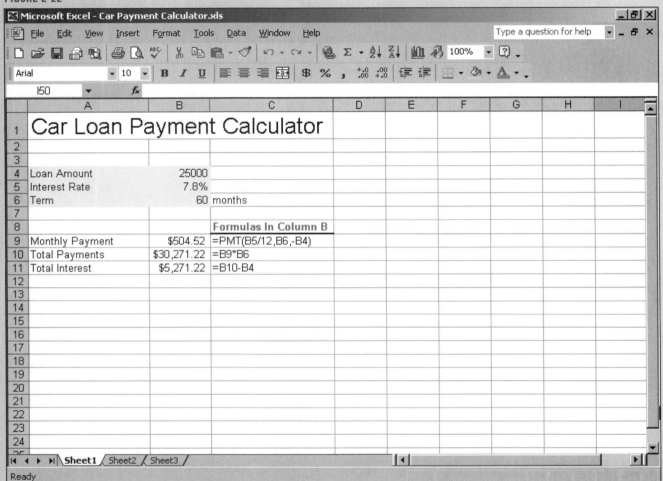

Excel 2002

Unit F

Managing

Workbooks and Preparing Them for the Web

Objectives

- [MOUS] ► **Freeze columns and rows**
- [MOUS] ► **Insert and delete worksheets**
- [MOUS] ► **Consolidate data with 3-D references**
- [MOUS] ► **Hide and protect worksheet areas**
- [MOUS] ► **Save custom views of a worksheet**
- ► **Control page breaks and page numbering**
- [MOUS] ► **Create a hyperlink between Excel files**
- [MOUS] ► **Save an Excel file as a Web page**

In this unit you will learn several Excel features to help you manage and print workbook data. You will also learn how to prepare workbooks for publication on the World Wide Web. ✎ MediaLoft's accounting department asks Jim Fernandez to design a timecard summary worksheet to track salary costs for hourly workers. He asks you to design a worksheet using some employees from the MediaLoft Houston store. When the worksheet is complete, the accounting department will add the rest of the employees and place it on the MediaLoft intranet site for review by store managers. Jim wants you to save the worksheet in HTML format for viewing on the site.

Excel 2002

Freezing Columns and Rows

As rows and columns fill up with data, you might need to scroll through the worksheet to add, delete, modify, and view information. Looking at information without row or column labels can be confusing. In Excel, you can temporarily freeze columns and rows, which enables you to view separate areas of your worksheets at the same time. **Panes** are the columns and rows that **freeze**, or remain in place, while you scroll through your worksheet. Freezing rows and columns is especially useful when you're dealing with large worksheets. ✎━━ Jim needs to verify the total hours worked, hourly pay rate, and total pay for salespeople Paul Cristifano and Virginia Young. Because the worksheet is becoming more difficult to read as its size increases, Jim wants you to freeze the column and row labels.

Steps 1234

1. Start Excel if necessary, open the Project File **EX F-1** from the drive and folder where your Project Files are stored, then save it as **Timecard Summary**

2. Scroll through the Monday worksheet to view the data, then click cell **D6**
   You move to cell D6 because Excel freezes the columns to the left and the rows above the cell pointer. You want to freeze columns A, B, and C as well as rows 1 through 5. By doing so, you will be able to see each employee's last name, first name, and timecard number on the screen when you scroll to the right, and you will also be able to read the labels in rows 1 through 5.

3. Click **Window** on the menu bar, then click **Freeze Panes**
   A thin line appears along the column border to the left of the active cell, and another line appears along the row above the active cell, indicating that columns A through C and rows 1 through 5 are frozen.

4. Scroll to the right until columns **A** through **C** and **L** through **O** are visible
   Because columns A, B, and C are frozen, they remain on the screen; columns D through K are temporarily hidden from view. Notice that the information you are looking for in row 13 (last name, total hours, hourly pay rate, and total pay for Paul Cristifano) is readily available. Paul's data appears to be correct, but you still need to verify Virginia Young's information.

5. Scroll down until **row 26** is visible
   In addition to columns A through C, rows 1 through 5 remain on the screen. See Figure F-1. Jim jots down the information for Virginia Young. Even though a pane is frozen, you can click in the frozen area of the worksheet and edit the contents of the cells there, if necessary.

6. Press **[Ctrl][Home]**
   Because the panes are frozen, the cell pointer moves to cell D6, not A1.

7. Click **Window** on the menu bar, then click **Unfreeze Panes**
   The panes are unfrozen.

8. Return to cell A1, then save the workbook

FIGURE F-1: Scrolled worksheet with frozen rows and columns

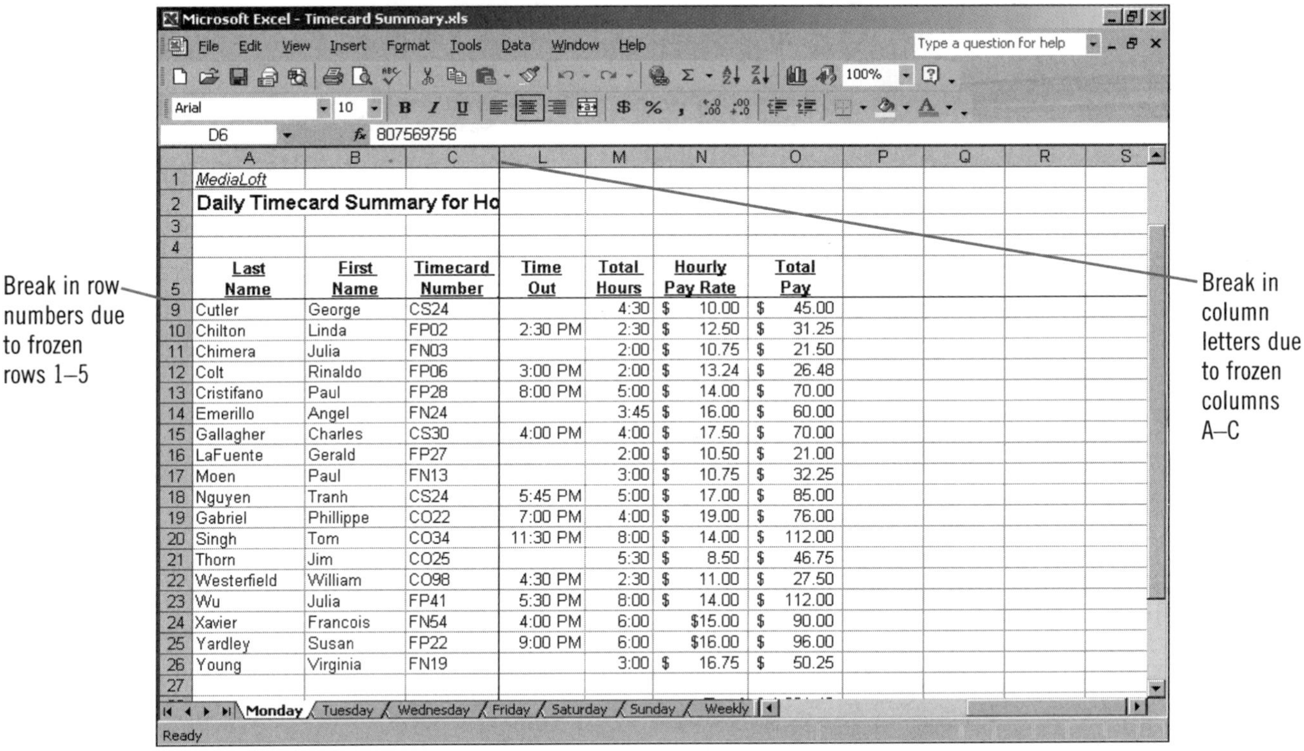

Break in row numbers due to frozen rows 1–5

Break in column letters due to frozen columns A–C

Splitting the worksheet into multiple panes

Excel provides a way to split the worksheet area into vertical and/or horizontal panes, so that you can click inside any one pane and scroll to locate information in that pane while the other panes remain in place. See Figure F-2. To split a worksheet area into multiple panes, drag the split box (the small box at the top of the vertical scroll bar or at the right end of the horizontal scroll bar) in the direction you want the split to appear. To remove the split, move the mouse over the split until the pointer changes to a double pointed arrow, then double-click.

FIGURE F-2: Worksheet split into two horizontal panes

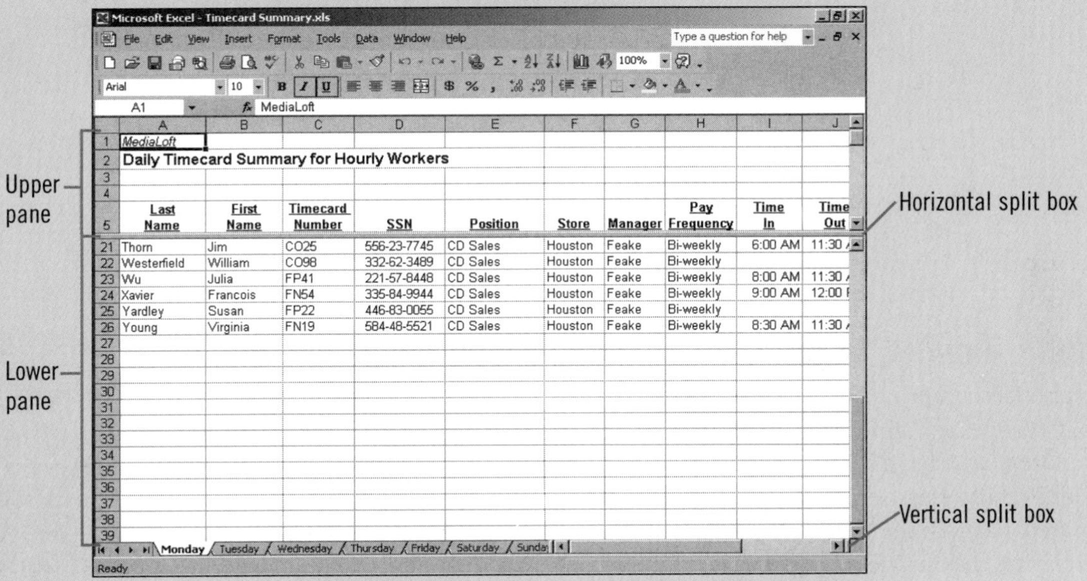

Upper pane

Lower pane

Horizontal split box

Vertical split box

Inserting and Deleting Worksheets

Excel 2002

You can insert and delete worksheets in a workbook at any time. For example, because new workbooks open with only three sheets available (Sheet1, Sheet2, and Sheet3), you need to insert at least one more sheet if you want to have four quarterly worksheets in an annual financial budget workbook. You can do this by using commands on the menu bar or shortcut menu. ✎ Jim was in a hurry when he added the sheet tabs to the Timecard Summary workbook. He wants you to insert a sheet for Thursday and delete the sheet for Sunday because Houston workers do not work on Sundays.

Steps

QuickTip
You can copy a selected worksheet by clicking Edit on the menu bar, then clicking Move or Copy Sheet. Choose the sheet the copy will precede, then select the Create a copy check box.

1. Click the **Friday sheet tab**, click **Insert** on the menu bar, then click **Worksheet**
Excel inserts a new sheet tab labeled Sheet1 to the left of the Friday sheet.

2. Double-click the Sheet1 tab and rename it **Thursday**
Now the tabs read Monday, Tuesday, Wednesday, Thursday, Friday, and Saturday. The tab for the Weekly Summary is not visible. You still need to delete the Sunday worksheet.

3. Right-click the **Sunday sheet tab**, then click **Delete** on the shortcut menu shown in Figure F-3
The shortcut menu allows you to insert, delete, rename, move, or copy sheets; select all the sheets; change tab color; and view any Visual Basic programming code in a worksheet.

4. Move the mouse pointer over any tab scrolling button, then right-click
Excel opens a menu of the worksheets in the active workbook. Compare your list with Figure F-4.

QuickTip
You can scroll several tabs at once by pressing [Shift] while clicking one of the middle tab scrolling buttons.

5. Return to the Monday sheet, then save the workbook

Previewing and printing multiple worksheets

To preview and print multiple worksheets, press and hold down [Ctrl] and click the tabs for the sheets you want to print, then click the Preview or Print button. In Print Preview, the multiple worksheets will appear as separate pages in the Preview window, which you can display by clicking Next and Previous. To preview and print an entire workbook, click File on the menu bar, click Print, click to select the Entire Workbook option button, then click Preview. In the Preview window, you can page through the entire workbook. (Blank worksheets will not appear as pages in Print Preview.) When you click Print, the entire workbook will print.

FIGURE F-3: Worksheet shortcut menu

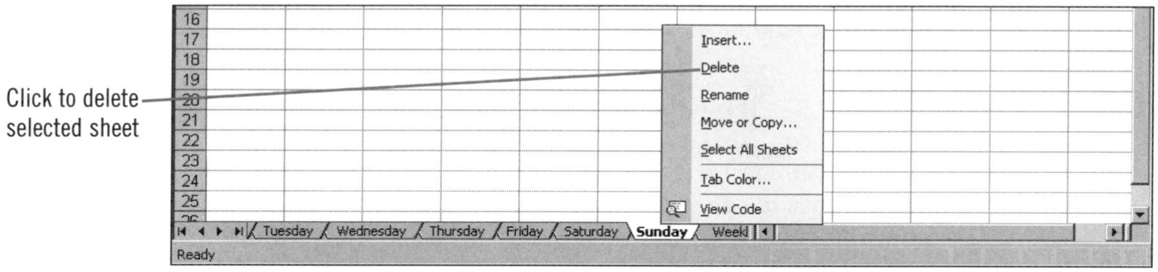

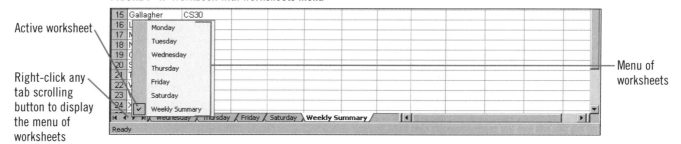

Click to delete selected sheet

FIGURE F-4: Workbook with worksheets menu

Active worksheet

Right-click any tab scrolling button to display the menu of worksheets

Menu of worksheets

Specifying headers and footers

As you prepare a workbook for others to view, it is helpful to provide as much data as possible about the worksheets such as the number of pages, who created it, and when. You can do this easily in a header or footer, information that prints at the top or bottom of each printed page. Headers and footers are visible on the screen only in Print Preview. To add a header, for example, click View on the menu bar, click Header and Footer, then click Custom Header. You will see a dialog box similar to that in Figure F-5. Both the header and the footer are divided into three sections, and you can enter information in any or all of them. You can type

information, such as your name, and click the icons to enter the page number 🔢, total pages 📄, date 📅, time 🕐, file path 📁, filename 📄 or sheet name 🗔. You can insert a picture by clicking the Insert Picture icon 🖼️, and you can format the picture by clicking the Format picture icon 🔧 and selecting formatting options. When you click an icon, Excel inserts a symbol in the footer section containing an ampersand (&) and the element name in brackets. When you are finished, click OK, click the Print Preview button on the Header/Footer tab to see your header and footer, then click Close.

FIGURE F-5: Header dialog box

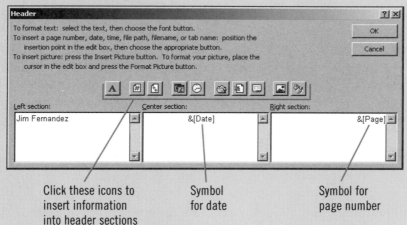

Click these icons to insert information into header sections

Symbol for date

Symbol for page number

Excel 2002

Excel 2002

Consolidating Data with 3-D References

When you want to summarize similar data that exists in different sheets or workbooks, you can combine and display it in one sheet. For example, you might have departmental sales figures on four different store sheets that you want to consolidate on one summary sheet showing total departmental sales for all stores. The best way to consolidate data is to use cell references to the various sheets on a consolidation, or summary, sheet. Because they reference other sheets that are usually behind the summary sheet, such references effectively create another dimension in the workbook and are called **3-D references.** You can reference data in other sheets and in other workbooks. Referencing cells is a better method than retyping calculated results because the data values on which calculated totals depend might change. If you reference the values instead, any changes to the original values are automatically reflected in the consolidation sheet. ✎ Although Jim does not have timecard data for the remaining days of the week, he wants you to test the Weekly Summary sheet that will consolidate the timesheet data. He asks you to do this by creating a reference from the total pay data in the Monday sheet to the Weekly Summary sheet. You will freeze panes to improve the view of the worksheet before initiating the reference between them.

Steps

1. On the Monday sheet, click cell **D6**, click **Window** on the menu bar, click **Freeze Panes,** then scroll horizontally to bring columns L through O into view

2. Right-click a **tab scrolling button**, then click **Weekly Summary**
   Because the Weekly Summary sheet (which is the consolidation sheet) will contain the reference, the cell pointer must reside there when you initiate the reference. A **simple reference** displays the contents of another cell.

QuickTip

If you have difficulty referencing cells between sheets, press [Esc] and begin again.

3. While in the Weekly Summary sheet, click cell **C6**, type **=**, activate the Monday sheet, click cell **O6**, then click the **Enter button** ☑ on the formula bar
   The Weekly Summary sheet becomes active, and formula bar reads =Monday!O6. See Figure F-6. *Monday* references the Monday sheet. The ! (exclamation point) is an **external reference indicator,** meaning that the cell referenced is outside the active sheet; O6 is the actual cell reference in the external sheet. The result, $34.20, appears in cell C6 of the Weekly Summary sheet, showing the reference to the value in cell O6 of the Monday sheet.

4. In the Weekly Summary sheet, copy cell **C6** into cells **C7:C26**
   Excel copies the contents of cell C6 with its relative reference to the Monday sheet data. You can test a reference by changing one cell value on which the reference is based and seeing if the reference changes.

5. Activate the Monday sheet, edit cell L6 to read **6:30 PM**, then activate the Weekly Summary sheet
   Cell C6 now shows $42.75. Changing Beryl Arenson's "time out" from 5:30 to 6:30 increased her pay from $34.20 to $42.75. This makes sense because Beryl's hours went from four to five, and her hourly salary is $8.55. The reference to Monday's total pay was automatically updated in the Weekly Summary sheet. See Figure F-7.

6. Enter your name in the left section of the footer, preview the worksheet, then print it

7. Activate the Monday sheet, unfreeze the panes, then save the workbook

FIGURE F-6: Worksheet showing referenced cell

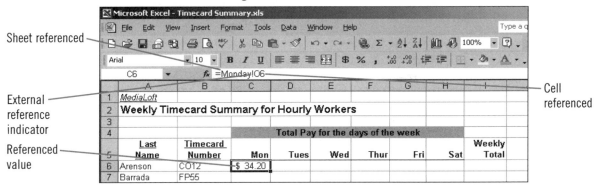

Sheet referenced

External reference indicator

Referenced value

Cell referenced

FIGURE F-7: Weekly Summary worksheet with updated reference

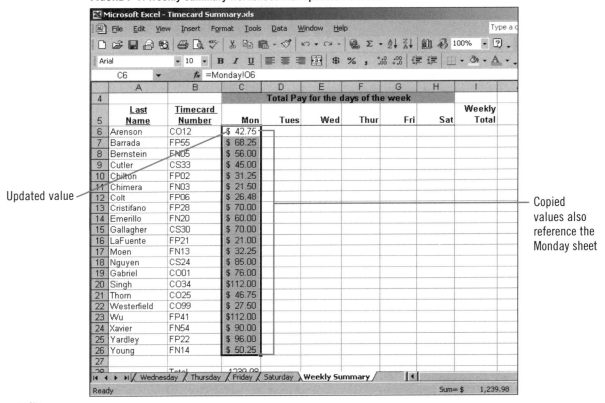

Updated value

Copied values also reference the Monday sheet

Linking data between workbooks

Just as you can reference data between cells in a worksheet and between sheets, you can reference data between workbooks dynamically so that changes made in referenced cells in one workbook are reflected in the consolidation sheet in the other workbook. This dynamic referencing is called **linking**. To link a single cell between workbooks, open both workbooks, select the cell to receive the linked data, type = (the equal sign), select the cell in the other workbook containing the data to be linked, then press [Enter]. Excel automatically inserts the name of the referenced workbook in the cell reference. For example if the linked data is contained in cell C7 of worksheet New in the Products workbook, the cell entry will read ='[Product.xls]New'!$C$7. To perform calculations, enter formulas on the consolidation sheet using cells in the supporting sheets. If you are linking more than one cell, you can copy the linked data to the Clipboard, select the upper-left cell in the workbook to receive the link, click Edit on the menu bar, click Paste Special, then click Paste Link.

Hiding and Protecting Worksheet Areas

Worksheets can contain sensitive information that you don't want others to view or alter. To protect such information, Excel gives you two options. You can **hide** the formulas in selected cells (or rows, columns, or entire sheets), and you can **lock** selected cells, in which case other people will be able to view the data (values, numbers, labels, formulas, etc.) in those cells but not to change it. See Table F-1 for a list of options you can use to protect a worksheet. You set the lock and hide options in the Format Cells dialog box. Excel locks all cells by default but this protection is not in effect until you activate the Excel protection feature via the Tools menu. A common worksheet protection strategy is to unlock cells in which data will be changed, sometimes referred to as the **data entry area**, and to lock cells in which the data should not be changed. Then, when you protect the worksheet, the unlocked areas can still be changed. ✐⟶ Because Jim will assign someone to enter the sensitive timecard information into the worksheet, he wants you to hide and lock selected areas of the worksheet.

1. On the Monday sheet, select the range **I6:L27**, click **Format** on the menu bar, click **Cells**, then click the **Protection tab**
   You include row 27, even though it does not contain data, in the event that new data is added to the row later. Notice that the Locked box in the Protection tab is already checked, as shown in Figure F-8. The Locked check box is selected by default, meaning that all the cells in a new workbook start out locked. (Note, however, that cell locking is not applied unless the protection feature is also activated. The protection feature is inactive by default.)

2. Click the **Locked check box** to deselect it, then click **OK**
   Excel stores time as a fraction of a 24-hour day. In the formula for total pay, hours must be multiplied by 24. This concept might be confusing to the data entry person, so you hide the formulas.

3. Select range **O6:O26**, click **Format** on the menu bar, click **Cells**, click the **Protection tab**, click the **Hidden check box** to select it, then click **OK**
   The data remains the same (unhidden and unlocked) until you set the protection in the next step.

4. Click **Tools** on the menu bar, point to **Protection**, then click **Protect Sheet**
   The Protect Sheet dialog box opens. The default options allow you to protect the worksheet while allowing users to select locked or unlocked cells only. You choose not to use a password.

5. Click **OK**
   You are ready to test the new worksheet protection.

6. Click cell **O6**
   The formula bar is empty because of the hidden formula setting.

7. In cell **O6**, type **T** to confirm that locked cells cannot be changed, then click **OK**
   When you attempt to change a locked cell, a message box reminds you of the protected cell's read-only status. See Figure F-9.

8. Click cell **I6**, type **9**, and notice that Excel allows you to begin the entry, press **[Esc]** to cancel the entry, then save the workbook
   Because you unlocked the cells in columns I through L before you protected the worksheet, you can make changes to these cells. Jim is satisfied that the Time In and Time Out data can be changed as necessary.

QuickTip

To turn off worksheet protection, click Tools on the menu bar, point to Protection, then click Unprotect Sheet. If prompted for a password, type the password, then click OK.

FIGURE F-8: Protection tab in Format Cells dialog box

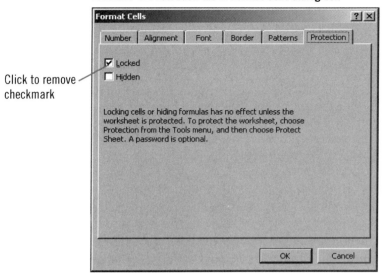

Click to remove
checkmark

FIGURE F-9: Reminder of protected cell's read-only status

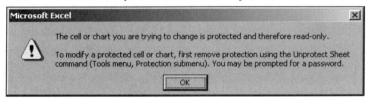

TABLE F-1: Options for hiding and protecting worksheet elements

task	menu commands
Hide/Unhide a column	Format, Column, Hide or Unhide
Hide/Unhide a formula	Format, Cells, Protection tab, select/deselect Hidden check box
Hide/Unhide a row	Format, Row, Hide or Unhide
Hide/Unhide a sheet	Format, Sheet, Hide or Unhide
Protect workbook	Tools, Protection, Protect Workbook, assign optional password
Protect worksheet	Tools, Protection, Protect Sheet, assign optional password
Unlock/Relock cells	Format, Cells, Protection tab, deselect/select Locked check box

Note: Some of the hide and protect options do not take effect until protection is enabled.

Changing workbook properties

You can also password-protect an entire workbook from being opened or modified by changing its file properties. Click File on the menu bar, click Save As, click Tools, then click General Options. Specify the password(s) for opening or modifying the workbook. To remove a workbook password, you can double-click the asterisks in the Password to open or Password to modify text boxes and press [Delete]. You can also use this dialog text box to offer users an option to open the workbook in read-only format so that users can open but not change it. Another way to make an entire workbook read-only is to right-click Start on the Taskbar, then click Explore (or Explore All Users). Locate and right-click the filename, click Properties, click the General tab, then, in the Attributes section, select the Read-only check box.

Excel 2002

Saving Custom Views of a Worksheet

A **view** is a set of display and/or print settings that you can name and save, then access at a later time. By using the Excel Custom Views feature, you can create several different views of a worksheet without having to create separate sheets. For example, if you often switch between portrait and landscape orientations when printing different parts of a worksheet, you can create two views with the appropriate print settings for each view. You set the display and/or print settings first, then name the view. Because Jim will generate several reports from his data, he asks you to save the current print and display settings as a custom view. To better view the data, he wants you to use the Zoom box to display the entire worksheet on one screen.

Steps

1. With the Monday sheet active, select range **A1:O28**, click the **Zoom list arrow** on the Standard toolbar, click **Selection**, then press **[Ctrl][Home]** to return to cell A1
   Excel adjusts the display magnification so that the data selected fits on one screen. See Figure F-10. After selecting the **Zoom box**, you can also pick a magnification percentage from the list or type the desired percentage.

2. Click **View** on the menu bar, then click **Custom Views**
   The Custom Views dialog box opens. Any previously defined views for the active worksheet appear in the Views box. In this case, Jim had created a custom view named Generic containing default print and display settings. See Figure F-11.

QuickTip

To delete views from the active worksheet, select the view in the Views list box, then click Delete.

3. Click **Add**
   The Add View dialog box opens, as shown in Figure F-12. Here, you enter a name for the view and decide whether to include print settings and hidden rows, columns, and filter settings. You want to include the selected options.

4. In the Name box, type **Complete Daily Worksheet**, then click **OK**
   After creating a custom view of the worksheet, you return to the worksheet area. You are ready to test the two custom views. In case the views require a change to the worksheet, it's a good idea to turn off worksheet protection.

5. Click **Tools** on the menu bar, point to **Protection**, then click **Unprotect Sheet**

6. Click **View** on the menu bar, then click **Custom Views**
   The Custom Views dialog box opens, listing both the Complete Daily Worksheet and Generic views.

Trouble?

If you receive the message "Some view settings could not be applied," repeat Step 5 to ensure that worksheet protection is turned off.

7. Click **Generic** in the Views list box, click **Show**, preview the worksheet, then close the Preview window
   The Generic custom view returns the worksheet to the Excel default print and display settings. Now you are ready to test the new custom view.

8. Click **View** on the menu bar, click **Custom Views**, click **Complete Daily Worksheet** in the Views list box, then click **Show**
   The entire worksheet fits on the screen.

9. Return to the Generic view, then save your work

FIGURE F-10: Selected data fitted to one screen

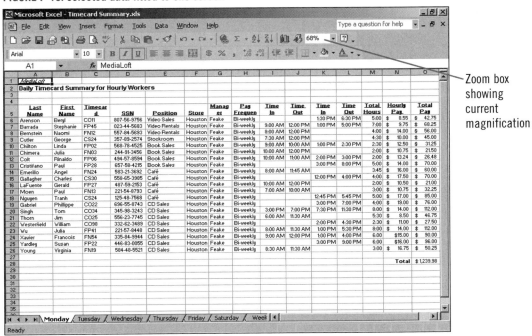

Zoom box
showing
current
magnification

FIGURE F-11: Custom Views dialog box

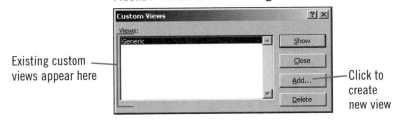

Existing custom
views appear here

Click to
create
new view

FIGURE F-12: Add View dialog box

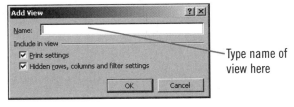

Type name of
view here

Creating a workspace

If you work with several workbooks at a time, you can group them so you can open them in one step by creating a **workspace**, a file with an .xlw extension. Then, instead of opening each workbook individually, you can open the workspace. To create a workspace, open the workbooks you wish to group and locate and size them as you would like them to appear. Click File on the menu bar, click Save Workspace, type a name for the workspace file, then click Save. Remember, however, that the workspace file does not contain the workbooks themselves, so you still have to save any changes you make to the original workbook files. To open the workbooks in the workspace automatically when you start Excel, place the workspace file in your XLStart folder (C:\Program Files\Microsoft Office\Office\XLStart).

Controlling Page Breaks and Page Numbering

The vertical and horizontal dashed lines in worksheets indicate page breaks. Excel automatically inserts a page break when your worksheet data doesn't fit on one page. These page breaks are **dynamic**, which means they adjust automatically when you insert or delete rows and columns and when you change column widths or row heights. Everything to the left of the first vertical dashed line and above the first horizontal dashed line is printed on the first page. You can override the automatic breaks by choosing the Page Break command on the Insert menu. Table F-2 describes the different types of page breaks you can use. Jim wants another report displaying no more than half the hourly workers on each page. To accomplish this, he asks you to insert a manual page break.

Steps

1. Click cell **A16**, click **Insert** on the menu bar, then click **Page Break**
   A dashed line appears between rows 15 and 16, indicating a horizontal page break. See Figure F-13. After you set page breaks, it's a good idea to preview each page.

2. Preview the worksheet, then click **Zoom**
   Notice that the status bar reads "Page 1 of 4" and that the data for the employees up through Charles Gallagher appears on the first page. Jim decides to place the date in the footer.

3. While in the Print Preview window, click **Setup**, click the **Header/Footer tab**, click **Custom Footer**, click the **Right section box**, click the **Date button**

4. Click the **Left section box**, type your name, then click **OK**
   Your name, the page number, and the date appear in the Footer preview area.

5. In the Page Setup dialog box, click **OK**, and while still in Print Preview, check to make sure that all the pages show your name, the page numbers, and the date, click **Close**, save the workbook, then print the worksheet

6. Click **View** on the menu bar, click **Custom Views**, click **Add**, type **Half and Half**, then click **OK**
   Your new custom view has the page breaks and all current print settings.

7. Make sure cell A16 is selected, then click **Insert** on the menu bar and click **Remove Page Break**
   Excel removes the manual page break above or to the left of the active cell.

8. Save the workbook

TABLE F-2: Page break options

type of page break	where to position cell pointer
Both horizontal and vertical page breaks	Select the cell below and to the right of the gridline where you want the breaks to occur
Only a horizontal page break	Select the cell in column A that is directly below the gridline where you want the page to break
Only a vertical page break	Select a cell in row 1 that is to the right of the gridline where you want the page to break

FIGURE F-13: Worksheet with horizontal page break

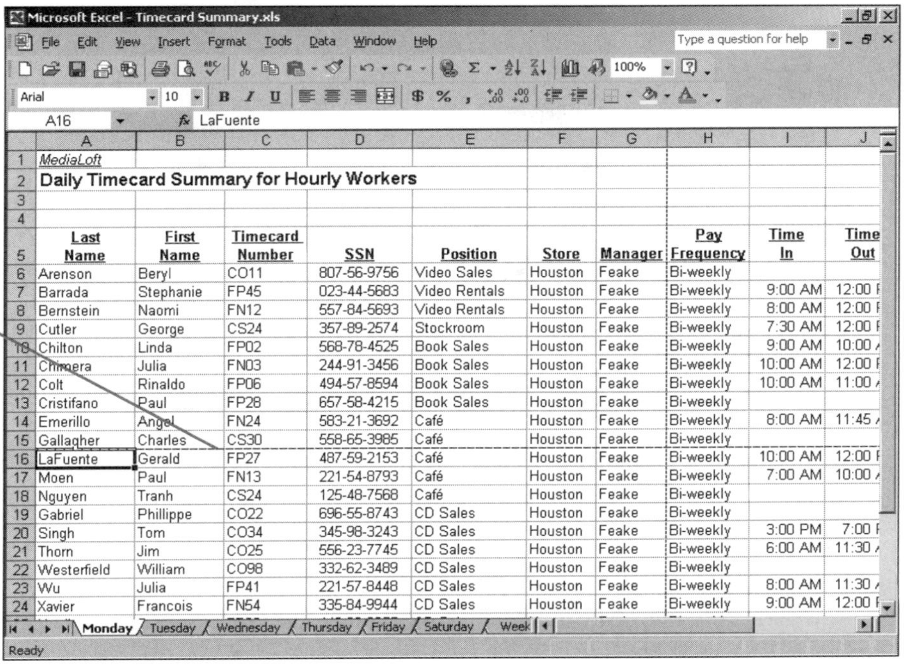

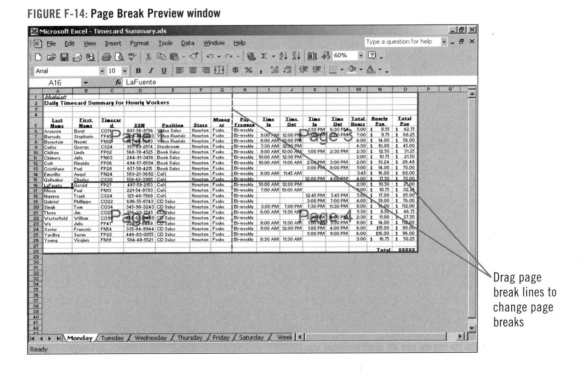

Dashed line indicates horizontal break after row 15

FIGURE F-14: Page Break Preview window

Drag page break lines to change page breaks

Using Page Break Preview

You can view and change page breaks manually by clicking View on the menu bar, then clicking Page Break Preview, or clicking Page Break Preview in the Print Preview window. (If you see a Welcome to Page Break Preview dialog box, click OK to close it.) Drag the page break lines to the desired location. See Figure F-14. To exit Page Break Preview, click View on the menu bar, then click Normal.

Excel 2002

Creating a Hyperlink Between Excel Files

As you manage the content and appearance of your workbooks, you may want the workbook user to view information in another workbook. It might be nonessential information or data that is too detailed to place in the workbook itself. In these cases, you can create a **hyperlink**, an object (a filename, a word, a phrase, or a graphic) in a worksheet that, when you click it, will display, or "jump to," another worksheet, called the **target**. The target can also be a document or a site on the World Wide Web. Hyperlinks are navigational tools between worksheets and are not used to exchange information. For example, in a worksheet that lists customer invoices, at each customer's name, you might create a hyperlink to an Excel file containing payment terms for each customer. Jim wants managers who view the Timecard Summary workbook to be able to view the pay categories for MediaLoft store employees. He asks you to create a hyperlink at the Hourly Pay Rate column heading. Users will click the hyperlink to view the Pay Rate worksheet.

1. Display the Monday worksheet

2. Click **Edit**, click **Go To**, type **N5** (the cell containing the text Hourly Pay Rate), then click **OK**

QuickTip

To remove a hyperlink or change its target, right-click it, point to Hyperlink, then click Remove Hyperlink or Edit Hyperlink.

3. Click the **Insert Hyperlink button** on the Standard toolbar, then click **Existing File or Web Page**, if it is not already selected
   The Insert Hyperlink dialog box opens. See Figure F-15. The icons under "Link to" on the left side of the dialog box let you specify the type of location you want the link to jump to: an existing file or Web page, a place in the same document, a new document, or an e-mail address. Because Jim wants users to display a document he has created, the first icon, Existing File or Web Page, is correct.

4. Click the **Look in list arrow** to navigate to the location where your Project Files are stored, then click **Pay Rate Classifications** in the file list
   The filename you selected appears in the Address text box. This is the document users will see when they click this hyperlink. You can also specify the ScreenTip that users will see when they hold the pointer over the hyperlink.

5. Click **ScreenTip**, type **Click here to see MediaLoft pay rate classifications**, click **OK**, then click **OK** again
   Cell N5 now contains underlined blue text, indicating that it is a hyperlink. After you create a hyperlink, you should check it to make sure that it jumps to the correct destination.

QuickTip

If you link to a Web page you must open a connection to the Internet to test the link.

6. Move the pointer over the **Hourly Pay Rate text**, view the ScreenTip, then click once
   Notice that when you move the pointer over the text, the pointer changes to 🖑, indicating that it is a hyperlink, and the ScreenTip appears. After you click, the Pay Rate Classifications worksheet appears. See Figure F-16. The Web toolbar appears beneath the Standard and Formatting toolbars.

7. Click the **Back button** on the Web toolbar, save the workbook, then print the worksheet

Using hyperlinks to navigate large worksheets

Hyperlinks are useful in navigating large worksheets or workbooks. You can create a hyperlink from a cell to another cell in the same worksheet, a cell in another worksheet, or a defined name anywhere in the workbook. Under "Link to" in the Insert Hyperlink dialog box, click Place in This Document. Then type the cell reference and indicate the sheet, or select a named location.

FIGURE F-15: Insert Hyperlink dialog box

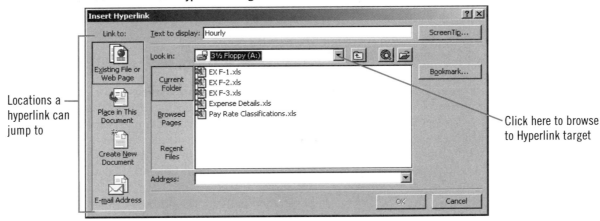

Locations a hyperlink can jump to

Click here to browse to Hyperlink target

FIGURE F-16: Target document

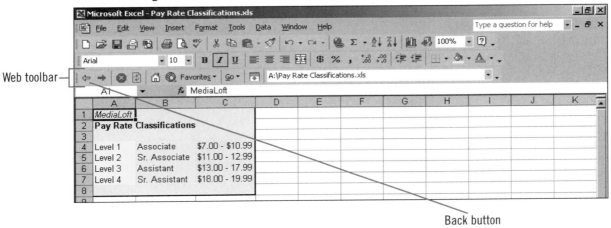

Web toolbar

Back button

Finding and replacing data and formats

You can easily change worksheet data by using the find-and-replace feature in Excel. Click Edit on the menu bar, click Replace, enter the text you want to find, press [Tab], then enter the text you want to replace it with. Use the Find Next, Find All, Replace, and Replace All buttons to find and replace any or all occurrences of the specified text. You can specify a data format for your search criteria by clicking the Options button, clicking the Format list arrow, and selecting a format.

Saving an Excel File as a Web Page

One way to share Excel data is to place, or **publish**, it over a network or on the Web so that others can access it using their Web browsers. The network can be an **intranet**, which is an internal network site used by a particular group of people who work together. If you post an entire workbook, users can click worksheet tabs to view each sheet. You can make the workbook interactive, meaning that users can enter, format, and calculate data. To publish an Excel document to an intranet or the Web, you must first save it as an **HTML (Hypertext Markup Language)** document, so it can be interpreted by a Web browser. ✐ Jim asks you to save the entire Timecard Summary workbook in HTML format so he can publish it on the MediaLoft intranet for managers to use.

Steps

1. **Click File on the menu bar, then click Save as Web Page**
   The Save As dialog box opens. By default, the Entire Workbook option button is selected, which is what Jim wants. However, he wants the title bar of the Web page to be more descriptive than the filename.

2. **Click Change Title**
   The Set Page Title dialog box opens.

3. **Type MediaLoft Houston Timecard Summary, then click OK**
   The new title appears in the Page title area. The Save as type list box indicates that the workbook will be saved as a Web page, which is in HTML format. See Figure F-17.

4. **Change the filename to timesum, then click the Save in list arrow to navigate to the drive and folder where your Project Files are stored**

5. **Click Save**
   A dialog box appears, indicating that the custom views you saved earlier will not be part of the HTML file.

6. **Click Yes**
   Excel saves the workbook as an HTML file in the folder location you specified in the Save As dialog box, and in the same place creates a folder in which it places associated files, such as a file for each worksheet. To make the workbook available to others, you would publish all these files on an intranet or Web server. When the save process is complete, the original XLS file closes and the HTML file opens on your screen.

7. **Click File on the menu bar, click Web Page Preview, then maximize the browser window**
   The workbook opens in your default Web browser, which could be Internet Explorer or Netscape, showing you what it would look like if you opened it on an intranet or on the Web. See Figure F-18. The Monday worksheet appears as it would if it were on a Web site or intranet, with tabs at the bottom of the screen for each sheet.

8. **Click the Weekly Summary Sheet tab then print the worksheet using your browser**

9. **Close the Web browser window, then close the timesum workbook and the Pay Rate Classifications workbook**

FIGURE F-17: Save As dialog box

New title
appears here

Indicates that
saved file will be
in HTML format

Click here to
modify the title of
the Web page

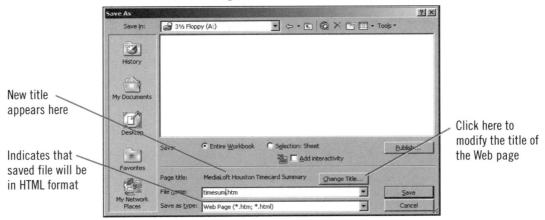

FIGURE F-18: Workbook in Web page preview

Your screen will
differ if you are
using a different
browser

New title
appears in
the title bar

Sheet tabs
allow users
to view other
sheets in
their browser

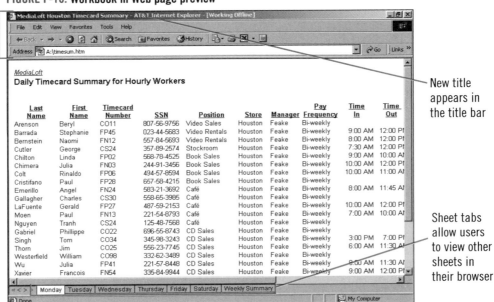

Holding Web discussions

You can attach a discussion comment to an Excel worksheet that you will save as an HTML document. This allows people viewing your worksheet on the Web to review and reply to your comments. To insert a discussion comment in Excel, click Tools on the menu bar, point to Online Collaboration, then click Web Discussions. This will display the Web Discussions Toolbar. See Figure F-19. You can add comments that others can view on the Web by clicking the Insert Discussion about the Workbook button 🗐 on the Web

Discussions Toolbar. Your comments, which are stored on a discussion server, will appear with the worksheet when it is saved and published as a Web document. People viewing your worksheet on the Web can reply by clicking the Discuss button 🗐 on the Standard Buttons toolbar in Internet Explorer to display the Discussions Toolbar. Then they can click the Insert Discussion in the Document button 🗐. *Note*: You must specify a discussion server to use this feature.

FIGURE F-19: Web Discussion toolbar

Web Discussion
Toolbar

| ⏮ ◀ ▶ ⏭ | **Monday** ╱ Tuesday ╱ Wednesday ╱ Thursday ╱ Friday ╱ Saturday ╱ Week ◀ |

| Discussions ▾ | 🗐 | Subscribe... | 🗐 | 📤 Close ▾ |

Ready

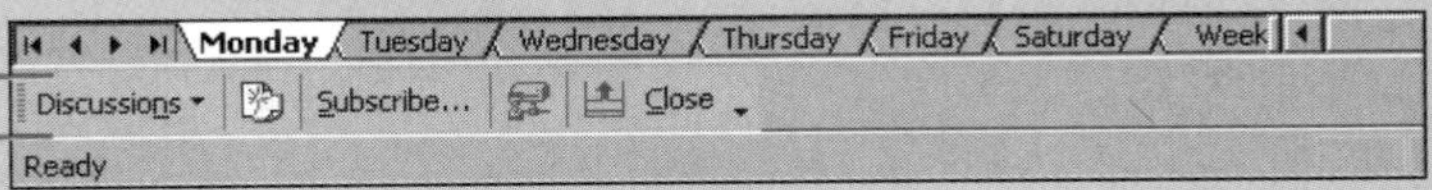

Practice

► Concepts Review

Label each element of the Excel screen shown in Figure F-20.

FIGURE F-20

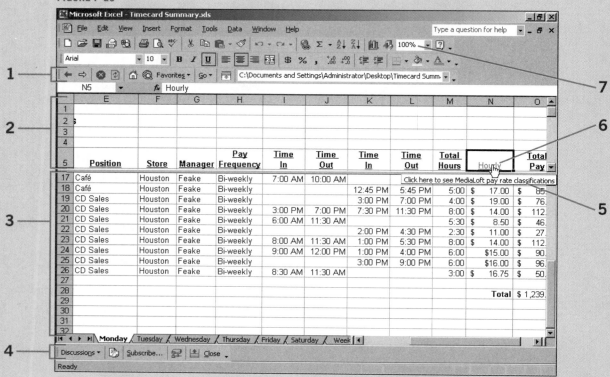

Match each of the terms with the statement that describes its function.

8. Dashed line
9. Hyperlink
10. 3-D reference
11.
12. 🖼

a. Inserts a picture into header or footer.
b. Uses values from different worksheets or workbooks
c. Indicates a page break
d. Inserts a code to print the sheet name in a header or footer
e. A navigational tool for use between worksheets or workbooks

Select the best answer from the list of choices.

13. You can save frequently used display and print settings by using the _____ feature.

   a. HTML
   b. View menu

   c. Custom Views
   d. Save command

14. You can group several workbooks in a _____ so they can be opened together rather than individually.

   a. Workgroup
   b. Workspace

   c. Consolidated workbook
   d. Work unit

15. You can specify data formats in the Find and Replace dialog box by clicking the _____ button.

   a. Format
   b. Options >>

   c. Data
   d. Tools

▶ Skills Review

1. Freeze columns and rows.

   a. Start Excel, open the Project File EX F-2 from the drive and folder where your Project Files are stored, then save it as **San Francisco Budget**.

   b. Activate the 2003 sheet, then freeze columns A and B and rows 1 through 3 for improved viewing. (*Hint*: Click cell C4 prior to issuing the Freeze Panes command.)

   c. Scroll until columns A and B and F through H are visible.

   d. Press **[Ctrl][Home]** to return to cell C4.

   e. Unfreeze the panes.

2. Insert and delete worksheets.

   a. With the 2003 sheet active, use the sheet shortcut menu to insert a new sheet to its left.

   b. Delete the 2002 sheet, rename the new sheet 2005 and move it after the 2004 sheet.

   c. Add a custom footer to the 2003 sheet with your name on the left side and the page number on the right side.

   d. Add a custom header with the worksheet name on the left side.

   e. Save and preview the worksheet, compare your results to Figure F-21, then print it.

3. Consolidate data with 3-D references.

   a. In cell C22, enter a reference to cell G7.

   b. In cell C23, enter a reference to cell G18.

   c. Activate the 2004 worksheet.

   d. In cell C4, enter a reference to cell C4 on the 2003 worksheet.

FIGURE F-21

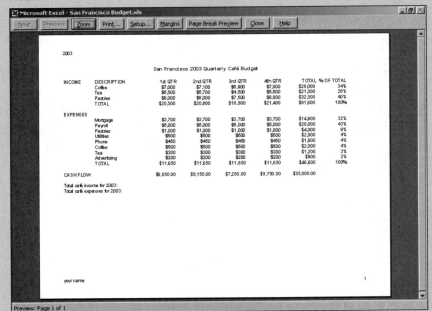

e. In the 2004 worksheet, copy the contents of cell C4 into cells C5:C6.

f. Preview the 2004 worksheet, then use the Setup button to add your name to the footer.

g. Print the 2004 worksheet, then save your work.

4. **Hide and protect worksheet areas.**

   a. On the 2003 sheet, unlock the expense data in the range C10:F17.

   b. On the 2003 sheet, hide the percent of total formulas in column H and the cash flow formulas in row 20.

   c. Protect the sheet without using a password.

   d. To make sure the other cells are locked, attempt to make an entry in cell D4. You should see the error message displayed in Figure F-22.

   e. Change the first quarter mortgage expense to $3,900.

   f. Verify the formulas in column H and row 20 are hidden.

   g. Unprotect the worksheet.

   h. Save the workbook.

FIGURE F-22

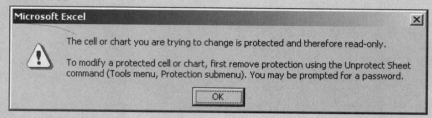

5. **Save custom views of a worksheet.**

   a. Set the zoom on the 2003 worksheet so that all the data fits on your screen.

   b. Make this a new view called **Entire 2003 Budget**.

   c. Use the Custom Views dialog box to return to Generic view. (*Note*: Using custom views may affect your headers, footers, and page orientation.)

   d. Save the workbook.

6. **Control page breaks and page numbering.**

   a. Insert a page break above cell A10.

   b. Save the view as **Halves**.

   c. Save the workbook.

7. **Create a hyperlink between Excel files.**

   a. On the 2003 worksheet, make cell A9 a hyperlink to the file **Expense Details**.

   b. Test the link, then print the Expense Details worksheet.

   c. Edit the hyperlink in cell A9, adding a ScreenTip that reads **Click here to see expense assumptions**.

   d. Return to the San Francisco Budget worksheet by using the Web toolbar.

   e. On the 2004 worksheet, enter the text **Based on 2003 budget** in cell A2.

   f. Make the text in cell A2 a hyperlink to cell A1 in the 2003 worksheet. (*Hint*: Use the Place in This Document button and note the cell reference in the Type the cell reference text box.)

   g. Test the hyperlink.

   h. Save the workbook and protect it with the password **pass**.

   i. Close and reopen the workbook to test the password.

   j. Remove the password and save the workbook again.

8. **Save an Excel file as a Web page.**

   a. If you have access to a Web discussion server, attach a discussion comment to the 2003 worksheet with your name and the date you reviewed the budget. (If you don't have access to discussion server, proceed to step b.)

b. Save the entire budget workbook as a Web page with a title bar that reads **Our Budget** and the file named **sfbudget**.

c. Preview the Web page in your browser. If your browser doesn't open automatically, check your taskbar.

d. Test the worksheet tabs in the browser to make sure they work.

e. Print the 2003 worksheet from your browser.

f. Close your browser.

g. Return to Excel, close the HTML document and the Expense Details workbook, then exit Excel.

▶ Independent Challenge 1

As a new employee at SoftSales, a computer software retailer, you are responsible for tracking the sales of different product lines and determining which computer operating system generates the most software sales each month. Although sales figures vary from month to month, the format in which data is entered does not. You decide to create a worksheet tracking sales across platforms by month. Use a separate worksheet for each month and create data for three months. Use your own data for the number of software packages sold in the Windows and Macintosh columns for each product.

a. Start Excel, create a new workbook, then save it as **Software Sales Summary** in the drive and folder where your Project Files are stored.

b. Create three worksheets to hold software sales information for the months of January, February, and March. Use Table F-3 as a guide to enter row and column labels, your own data, and formulas for the totals.

c. Create a summary sheet that totals the information in all three sheets.

d. Add headers to all four worksheets that includes your name, the sheet name, and the date.

e. Format the worksheet appropriately.

f. Save the workbook, preview and print the four worksheets, then exit Excel.

TABLE F-3

	Windows	Macintosh	Total
Games Software			
Combat Flight Simulator			
Safari			
NASCAR Racing			
Total			
Business Software			
Word Processing			
Spreadsheet			
Presentation			
Graphics			
Page Layout			
Total			
Utilities			
Antivirus			
File Recovery			
Total			

Excel 2002

Independent Challenge 2

You own PC Assist, a software training company located in Montreal, Canada. You have added several new entries to the August check register and are ready to enter September's check activity. Because the sheet for August will include much of the same information you need for September, you decide to copy it. Then you will edit the new sheet to fit your needs for the September check activity. You will use sheet referencing to enter the beginning balance and beginning check number. Using your own data, you will complete five checks for the September register.

   a. Start Excel, open the Project File EX F-3 from the drive and folder where your Project Files are stored, then save it as **Update to Check Register**. The expense amounts in the worksheet include the Goods and Services tax (GST)/(TPS), the Harmonized Sales Tax (HST)/(TVH), and the Quebec sales tax (TVQ).

   b. Delete Sheet 2 and Sheet 3, then create a worksheet for September by copying the August sheet and renaming it.

   c. With the September sheet active, delete the data in range A6:E24.

   d. To update the balance at the beginning of the month, use sheet referencing from the last balance entry in the August sheet.

   e. Generate the first check number. (*Hint*: Use a formula that references the last check number in August and adds one.)

   f. Enter data for five checks using September 2003 dates. For the check number, use the number above it and add 1.

   g. Add a footer to both sheets that includes your name on the left side of the printout and the system date on the right side. Add a header for the worksheets that displays the sheet name centered on the printout. (*Hint*: Select both sheets using the Shift key, then apply the header and footer)

   h. Save the workbook.

   i. Use the Find and Replace dialog box to change the beginning balance for August from **20000** to **25000**, formatted as a number with two decimal places. (*Hint*: The Options >> button will allow you to change the data format)

   j. Select both worksheets, preview the entire workbook, then close the Preview window.

   k. Print the September worksheet in landscape orientation on a single page.

   l. Save and close the workbook, then exit Excel.

 # Independent Challenge 3

You are a college student with two roommates. Each month you receive your long-distance telephone bill. Because no one wants to figure out who owes what, you split the bill three ways. You are sure that one of your roommates makes most of the long-distance calls. To make the situation more equitable, you decide to create a spreadsheet to track the long-distance phone calls each month. You will create a workbook with a separate sheet for each roommate and track the following information for each month's long-distance calls: date of call, time of call (AM or PM), call minutes, location called, state called, area code, phone number, and call charge. Then you will total the charges for each roommate and create a summary sheet of all three roommates' charges for the month. Since your roommate is working with an older version of Excel, you'll also save the workbook in a format he can open.

   a. Start Excel, create a new workbook, then save it as **Monthly Long Distance** in the drive and folder where your Project Files are stored.

   b. Enter column headings and row labels to track each call.

   c. Use your own data, entering at least three long-distance calls for each roommate.

   d. Create totals for minutes and charges on each roommate's sheet.

   e. Create a summary sheet that shows each name and uses cell references to display the total minutes and total charges for each person.

   f. On the summary sheet, create a hyperlink from each person's name to cell A1 of their respective worksheet. Enter your name on all worksheet footers, then save the workbook.

   g. Create a workbook with the same type of information for the two people in the apartment next door. Save it as **Next Door**.

h. Use linking to create a 3-D reference that displays the neighbors' totals on your summary sheet so your room-mates can compare their expenses with the neighbors'.

i. Create a workspace that groups the workbooks Monthly Long Distance and Next Door. Name the workspace **Phonebill**. (*Hint*: Save Workspace is an option on the File menu.)

j. Change the workbook properties of the Next Door workbook to Read-only.

k. Save the Monthly Long Distance Excel file again in Microsoft Excel 5.0 worksheet format. Name the workbook **Monthly Long Distance-5**. (*Hint*: Use the Save As command on the file menu.) Notice that the links don't work in Excel 5.0.

l. Close your browser then close any open files and exit Excel.

 # Independent Challenge 4

Lynne Watson, the creative director at WebProductions, a web design company, is considering purchasing digital cameras for the New York and Montreal offices. You have been asked to research this purchase by comparing features and current prices in US and Canadian currencies. Lynne would like you to prepare a worksheet containing the following information about each camera: Product Description, Manufacturer, Platform (MacOS, Windows), Max Resolution, Image Capacity, and Price in both US and Canadian currencies. You decide to investigate online vendors for this information. You will also use an online currency converter to display the price information in Canadian currency.

a. Find features and pricing for five digital cameras that you think would be appropriate for commercial images. Go to the Alta Vista search engine at www.altavista.com or Yahoo at www.yahoo.com and use their shopping directories. You can also use Excite, Hotbot, Infoseek, or another search engine of your choice. Use your search engine to find a currency converter site, then convert the prices you found from the online vendors into Canadian currency.

b. Start Excel, create a new workbook, then save it as **Camera Research** in the drive and folder where your Project Files are stored.

c. Enter the information you found on the Web in the table below. The image capacity and price information may include ranges of values.

Description	Manufacturer	Platform	Max Resolution	Image Capacity	Price $USD	Price $CAD

d. Enter the information from the table into your Camera Research workbook. Name the worksheet **Online Vendors**.

e. Add a custom header that displays the sheet name centered on the printout.

f. Add a custom footer that includes your name on the left side of the printout.

g. Make the cells in the Manufacturer column hyperlinks to the manufacturer's Web site. Save the workbook.

h. Save the workbook with the name **camera** in HTML format for management's use and preview it in your Web browser.

i. Print the worksheet from your browser.

j. Exit your browser then close any open files and exit Excel.

► Visual Workshop

Create the worksheet shown in Figure F-23, then save it as **Martinez.xls**. Enter your name in the footer, save the workbook and print the worksheet. Then save the workbook as a Web page using the name **martinez.htm**. Preview the worksheet in your Web browser, then print the sheet from the browser. Notice that the text in cell A1 is a hyperlink to the Our History worksheet; the graphic is from the Clip Gallery. If you don't have this graphic, substitute the graphic of your choice.

FIGURE F-23

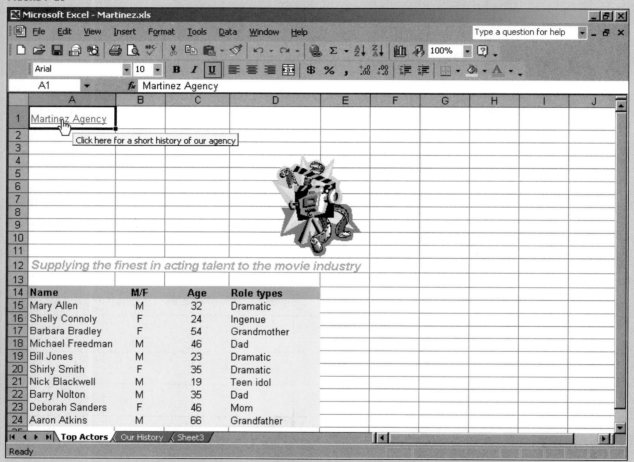

Automating
Worksheet Tasks

Objectives

[MOUS] ► **Plan a macro**

[MOUS] ► **Record a macro**

[MOUS] ► **Run a macro**

[MOUS] ► **Edit a macro**

► **Use shortcut keys with macros**

► **Use the Personal Macro Workbook**

[MOUS] ► **Add a macro as a menu item**

[MOUS] ► **Create a toolbar for macros**

A **macro** is a set of instructions that performs tasks in the order you specify. You create macros to automate frequently performed Excel tasks that require a series of steps. For example, if you usually enter your name and date in a worksheet footer, you can record the keystrokes in an Excel macro that enters the text and inserts the current date automatically. In this unit, you will plan and design a simple macro, then record and run it. Then you will edit the macro. You will also assign shortcut keys to a macro, store a macro in the Personal Macro Workbook, add a macro option to the Tools menu, and create a new toolbar for macros. ◢◣ Jim wants you to create a macro for the Accounting Department. The macro will automatically insert text that will identify the worksheet as an Accounting Department document.

Planning a Macro

You create macros for tasks that you perform on a regular basis. For example, you can create a macro to enter and format text or to save and print a worksheet. To create a macro, you record the series of actions or write the instructions in a special programming language. Because the sequence of actions is important, you need to plan the macro carefully before you record it. You use the Macro command on the Tools menu to record, run, and modify macros. ✐ Jim wants you to create a macro for the Accounting Department that inserts the text "Accounting Department" in the upper-left corner of any worksheet. You work with him to plan the macro using the following guidelines:

Details

▶ **Assign the macro a descriptive name**

The first character of a macro name must be a letter; the remaining characters can be letters, numbers, or underscores. Spaces are not allowed in macro names; use underscores in place of spaces. (Press [Shift][-] to enter an underscore character.) Jim wants you to name the macro "DeptStamp". See Table G-1 for a list of macros Jim might create to automate other tasks.

▶ **Write out the steps the macro will perform**

This planning helps eliminate careless errors. Jim writes a description of the macro he wants, as shown in Figure G-1.

▶ **Decide how you will perform the actions you want to record**

You can use the mouse, the keyboard, or a combination of the two. Jim wants you to use both the mouse and the keyboard.

▶ **Practice the steps you want Excel to record, and write them down**

Jim wrote down the sequence of actions he wants you to include in the macro.

▶ **Decide where to locate the description of the macro and the macro itself**

Macros can be stored in an unused area of the active workbook, in a new workbook, or in the Personal Macro Workbook, a special workbook used only for macro storage. Jim wants you to store the macro in a new workbook.

TABLE G-1: Possible macros and their descriptive names

description of macro	descriptive name
Enter a frequently used proper name, such as Jim Fernandez	JimFernandez
Enter a frequently used company name, such as MediaLoft	CompanyName
Print the active worksheet on a single page, in landscape orientation	FitToLand
Turn off the header and footer in the active worksheet	HeadFootOff
Show a frequently used custom view, such as a generic view of the worksheet, setting the print and display settings back to the Excel defaults	GenericView

Macro to create stamp with the department name

Name:	DeptStamp
Description:	Adds a stamp to the top left of the worksheet, identifying it as an Accounting Department worksheet
Steps:	1. Position the cell pointer in cell A1.
	2. Type Accounting Department, then click the Enter button.
	3. Click Format on the menu bar, then click Cells.
	4. Click Font tab, under Font style click Bold, under Underline click Single, and under Color click Red, then click OK.

CLUES TO USE

Macros and viruses

When you open an Excel workbook that has macros, you will see a message asking you if you want to enable or disable macros. This is because macros can contain viruses, destructive software programs that can damage your computer files. If you know your workbook came from a trusted source, click Enable macros. If you are not sure of the workbook's source, click Disable macros. If you disable the macros in a workbook, you will not be able to use them. For more information about macro security and security levels type "About macro security" in the Type a question for help text box.

Recording a Macro

The easiest way to create a macro is to record it using the Excel Macro Recorder. You turn the Macro Recorder on, name the macro, enter the keystrokes and select the commands you want the macro to perform, then stop the recorder. As you record the macro, each action is translated into program code you can later view and modify. You can take as long as you want to record the macro; a recorded macro contains only your actions, not the amount of time you took to record it. ✎ Jim wants you to create a macro that enters a department stamp in cell A1 of the active worksheet. You create this macro by recording your actions.

Steps

Trouble?

If the task pane is not visible, click View on the menu bar, then click Task Pane. You can also open a blank workbook by clicking the New button on the Standard toolbar.

1. Start Excel, click the **Blank Workbook button** 🗋 on the New Workbook task pane, save the blank workbook as **My Excel Macros** in the drive and folder where your Project Files are stored, then close the task pane.
   You are ready to start recording the macro.

2. Click **Tools** on the menu bar, point to **Macro**, then click **Record New Macro**
   The Record Macro dialog box opens. See Figure G-2. The default name Macro1 is selected. You can either assign this name or enter a new name. This dialog box also allows you to assign a shortcut key for running the macro and assign a storage location for the macro.

3. Type **DeptStamp** in the Macro name text box

4. If the "Store macro" in list box does not display "This Workbook", click the **list arrow** and select **This Workbook**

Trouble?

If the Stop Recording toolbar is not displayed, click View, point to Toolbars, then click Stop Recording.

5. If the Description text box does not contain your name, select the existing name, type your own name, then click **OK**
   The dialog box closes. A small Stop Recording toolbar appears containing the Stop Recording button 🔲, and the word "Recording" appears on the status bar. Take your time performing the steps below. Excel records every keystroke, menu selection, and mouse action that you make.

6. Press **[Ctrl][Home]**
   When you begin an Excel session, macros record absolute cell references. By beginning the recording in cell A1, you ensure that the macro includes the instruction to select cell A1 as the first step, even if cell A1 is already selected.

7. Type **Accounting Department** in cell A1, then click the **Enter button** ✅ on the formula bar

8. Click **Format** on the menu bar, then click **Cells**

9. Click the **Font tab**, in the Font style list box click **Bold**, click the **Underline list arrow** and click **Single**, then click the **Color list arrow** and click **red** (third row, first color on left)
   See Figure G-3.

Trouble?

If your results differ from Figure G-4, clear the contents of cell A1, then slowly and carefully repeat Steps 2 through 10. When prompted to replace the existing macro at the end of Step 5, click Yes.

10. Click **OK**, click the **Stop Recording button** 🔲 on the Stop Recording toolbar, click **cell D1** to deselect cell A1, then save the workbook
    Compare your results with Figure G-4.

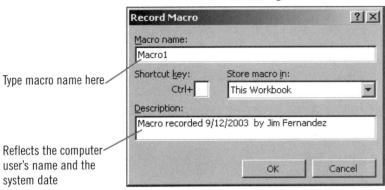

FIGURE G-2: Record Macro dialog box

Type macro name here

Reflects the computer user's name and the system date

FIGURE G-3: Font tab of the Format Cells dialog box

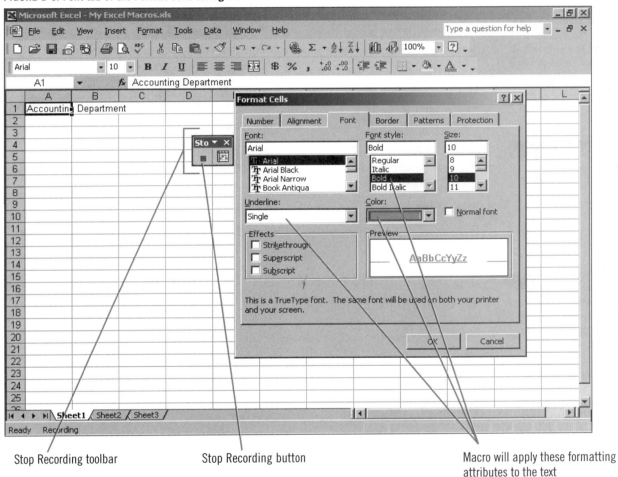

Stop Recording toolbar

Stop Recording button

Macro will apply these formatting attributes to the text

FIGURE G-4: Accounting Department stamp

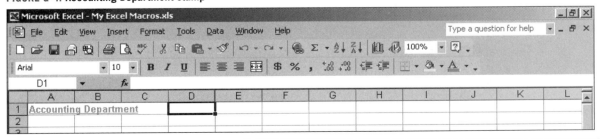

Excel 2002

Running a Macro

Once you record a macro, you should test it to make sure that the actions it performs are correct. To test a macro, you **run**, or execute, it. One way to run a macro is to select the macro in the Macros dialog box, then click Run. ✐━━ Jim asks you to clear the contents of cell A1 then test the DeptStamp macro. After you run the macro in the My Excel Macros workbook, he asks you to test the macro once more from a newly opened workbook.

Steps

1. Click **cell A1**, click **Edit** on the menu bar, point to **Clear**, click **All**, then click any other cell to deselect cell A1

When you delete only the contents of a cell, any formatting still remains in the cell. By using the Clear All option on the Edit menu, you can be sure that the cell is free of contents and formatting.

QuickTip
To delete a macro, select the macro name in the Macro dialog box, click Delete, then click Yes to confirm the action.

2. Click **Tools** on the menu bar, point to **Macro**, then click **Macros**

The Macro dialog box, shown in Figure G-5, lists all the macros contained in the open workbooks. If other people have used your computer, other macros may be listed.

3. Make sure **DeptStamp** is selected, click **Run**, then deselect cell A1

Watch your screen as the macro quickly plays back the steps you recorded in the previous lesson. When the macro is finished, your screen should look like Figure G-6. As long as the workbook containing the macro remains open, you can run the macro in any open workbook.

QuickTip
To stop a macro while it is running, press [Esc] then click End.

4. Click the **New button** 🗋 on the Standard toolbar

Because the new workbook automatically fills the screen, it is difficult to be sure that the My Excel Macros workbook is still open.

5. Click **Window** on the menu bar

A list of open workbooks appears underneath the menu options. The active workbook name (in this case, Book2) appears with a check mark to its left. The My Excel Macros workbook appears on the menu, so you know it's open. See Figure G-7.

Trouble?
If you get a security error message when attempting to run your macro, the security level may be set too high in the workbook. You can enable macros for the workbook by clicking the Macro option on the Tools menu and selecting Security. Set the security level to Medium or Low, then close and reopen the workbook.

6. Deselect cell A1, click **Tools** on the menu bar, point to **Macro**, click **Macros**, make sure **'My Excel Macros.xls'!DeptStamp** is selected, click **Run**, then deselect cell A1

When multiple workbooks are open, the macro name in the Macro dialog box includes the workbook name between single quotation marks, followed by an exclamation point, indicating that the macro is outside the active workbook. Because you only used this workbook to test the macro, you don't need to save it.

7. Close Book2 without saving changes

The My Excel Macros workbook reappears.

FIGURE G-5: Macro dialog box

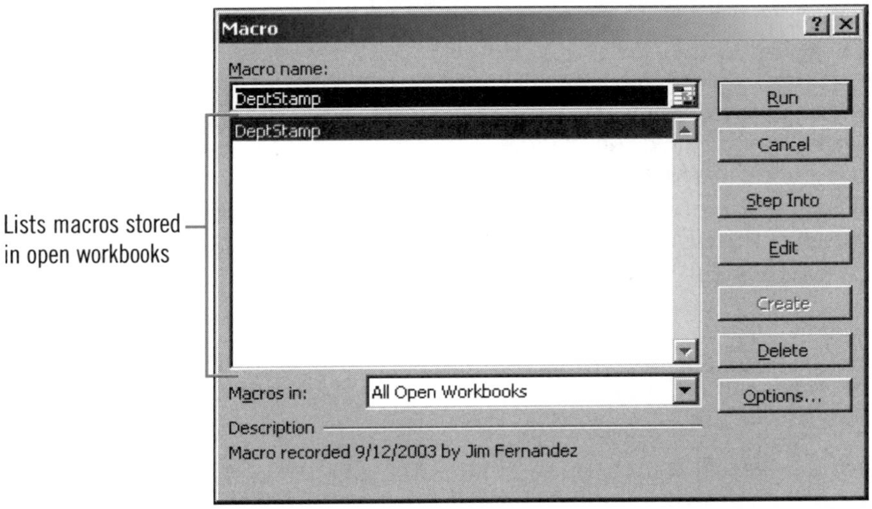

Lists macros stored in open workbooks

FIGURE G-6: Result of running DeptStamp macro

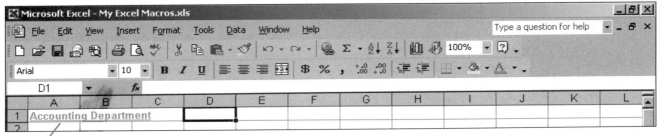

DeptStamp macro inserts formatted text in cell A1

FIGURE G-7: Window menu showing the list of open workbooks

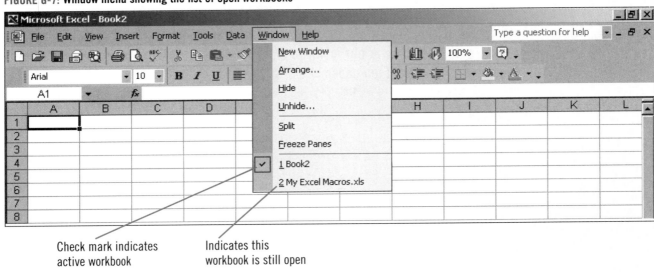

Check mark indicates active workbook

Indicates this workbook is still open

Unit G

Excel 2002

Editing a Macro

When you use the Macro Recorder to create a macro, the program instructions, called **program code**, are recorded automatically in the Visual Basic for Applications (VBA) programming language. Each macro is stored as a **module**, or program code container, attached to the workbook. After you record a macro, you might need to change it. If you have a lot of changes to make, it might be best to rerecord the macro. If you need to make only minor adjustments, you can edit the macro code directly using the Visual Basic Editor. ✐ Jim wants you to modify his macro to change the point size of the department stamp to 12.

Steps

QuickTip

Another way to start the Visual Basic Editor is to click Tools on the menu bar, point to Macro, then click Visual Basic Editor, or press [Alt][F11].

1. Make sure the My Excel Macros workbook is open, click **Tools** on the menu bar, point to **Macro**, click **Macros**, make sure **DeptStamp** is selected, then click **Edit**
The Visual Basic Editor starts, showing the DeptStamp macro steps in a numbered module window (in this case, Module1).

2. If necessary, maximize the window titled **My Excel Macros.xls – [Module1(Code)]**, then examine the steps in the macro
The name of the macro and the date it was recorded appear at the top of the module window. Below that, Excel has translated your keystrokes and commands into macro code. When you open and make selections in a dialog box during macro recording, Excel automatically stores all the dialog box settings in the macro code. For example, the line .FontStyle = "Bold" was generated when you clicked Bold in the Format Cells dialog box. You also see lines of code that you didn't generate directly while recording the DeptStamp macro; for example, .Name = "Arial".

3. In the line .Size = 10, double-click **10** to select it, then type **12**
See Figure G-8. Because Module1 is attached to the workbook and not stored as a separate file, any changes to the module are saved automatically when you save the workbook.

4. In the Visual Basic Editor, click **File** on the menu bar, click **Print**, click **OK** to print the module, then review the printout

QuickTip

You can return to Excel without closing the module by clicking the View Microsoft Excel button [icon] on the standard toolbar.

5. Click **File** on the menu bar, then click **Close and Return to Microsoft Excel**
You want to rerun the DeptStamp macro to make sure the macro reflects the change you made using the Visual Basic Editor.

6. Click cell **A1**, click **Edit** on the menu bar, point to **Clear**, click **All**, deselect cell **A1**, click **Tools** on the menu bar, point to **Macro**, click **Macros**, make sure **DeptStamp** is selected, click **Run**, then deselect cell **A1**
Compare your results to Figure G-9. The department stamp is now in 12-point type.

7. Save the workbook

FIGURE G-8: Visual Basic Editor showing Module1

Name of macro

Project Explorer with open module selected

Properties window showing properties for selected objects

Macro program code

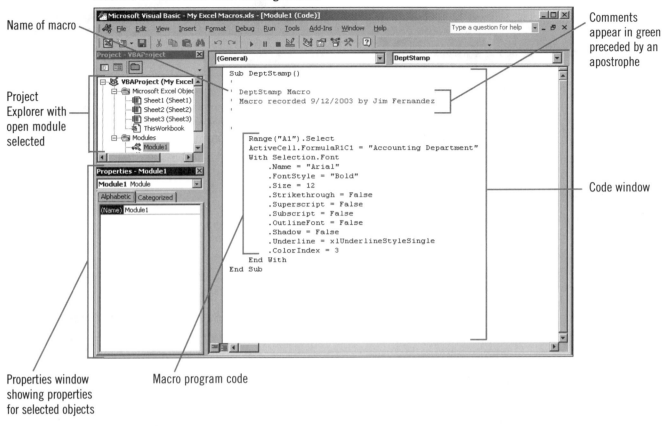

Comments appear in green preceded by an apostrophe

Code window

```
Sub DeptStamp()
'
' DeptStamp Macro
' Macro recorded 9/12/2003 by Jim Fernandez


    Range("A1").Select
    ActiveCell.FormulaR1C1 = "Accounting Department"
    With Selection.Font
        .Name = "Arial"
        .FontStyle = "Bold"
        .Size = 12
        .Strikethrough = False
        .Superscript = False
        .Subscript = False
        .OutlineFont = False
        .Shadow = False
        .Underline = xlUnderlineStyleSingle
        .ColorIndex = 3
    End With
End Sub
```

FIGURE G-9: Result of running edited DeptStamp macro

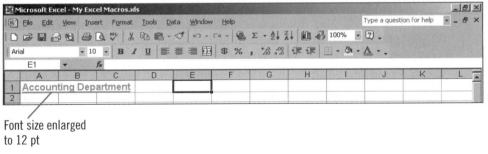

Font size enlarged to 12 pt

Adding comments to Visual Basic code

With practice, you will be able to interpret the lines of code within your macro. Others who use your macro, however, might want to know the function of a particular line. You can explain the code by adding comments to the macro. Comments are explanatory text added to the lines of code. When you enter a comment, you must type an apostrophe (') before the comment text. Otherwise, the program will try to interpret it as a command. On the screen, comments appear in green after you press [Enter]. See Figure G-8. You also can insert blank lines as comments in the macro code to make the code more readable. To do this, type an apostrophe, then press [Enter].

Using Shortcut Keys with Macros

In addition to running a macro from the Macro dialog box, you can run a macro by assigning a shortcut key combination to it. Using shortcut keys to run macros reduces the number of actions required to begin macro playback. You assign shortcut key combinations in the Record Macro dialog box. ◣━━━ Jim also wants you to create a macro called CompanyName to enter the company name into a worksheet. You will assign a shortcut key combination to run the macro.

1. **Click cell B2**
   You will record the macro in cell B2. You want the macro to enter the company name anywhere in a worksheet. Therefore, you will not begin the macro with an instruction to position the cell pointer, as you did in the DeptStamp macro.

2. **Click Tools on the menu bar, point to Macro, then click Record New Macro**
   The Record Macro dialog box opens. Notice the option Shortcut key: Ctrl+ followed by a blank box. You can type a letter (A–Z) in the Shortcut key text box to assign the key combination of [Ctrl] plus that letter to run the macro. You use the key combination [Ctrl][Shift] plus a letter to avoid overriding any of the Excel [Ctrl] [letter] shortcut keys, such as [Ctrl][C] for Copy.

3. **With the default macro name selected, type CompanyName, click the Shortcut key text box, press and hold [Shift], type C, then, if necessary, replace the name in the Description box with your name**
   Compare your screen with Figure G-10. You are ready to record the CompanyName macro.

4. **Click OK to close the dialog box**
   By default, Excel records absolute cell references in macros. Beginning the macro in cell B2 causes the macro code to begin with a statement to select cell B2. Because you want to be able to run this macro in any active cell, you need to instruct Excel to record relative cell references while recording the macro.

5. **Click the Relative Reference button 🏛 on the Stop Recording toolbar**
   The Relative Reference button is now selected. See Figure G-11. This button is a toggle and retains the relative reference setting until you click it again to turn it off or you exit Excel.

6. **Type MediaLoft in cell B2, click the Enter button ☑ on the formula bar, press [Ctrl][I] to italicize the text, click the Stop Recording button ■ on the Stop Recording toolbar, then deselect cell B2**
   MediaLoft appears in italics in cell B2. You are ready to run the macro in cell A5 using the shortcut key combination.

7. **Click cell A5, press and hold [Ctrl][Shift], type C, then deselect the cell**
   The company name appears in cell A5. See Figure G-12. Because the macro played back in the selected cell (A5) instead of the cell where it was recorded (B2), you know that the macro recorded relative cell references.

8. **Save the workbook**

FIGURE G-10: Record Macro dialog box with shortcut key assigned

Shortcut to run macro

FIGURE G-11: **Stop Recording toolbar with Relative Reference button selected**

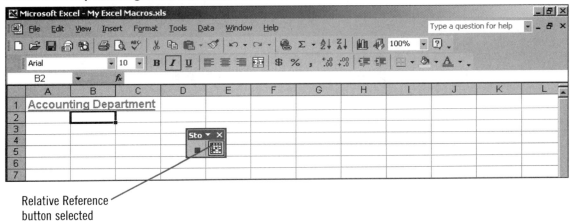

Relative Reference button selected

FIGURE G-12: **Result of running the CompanyName macro**

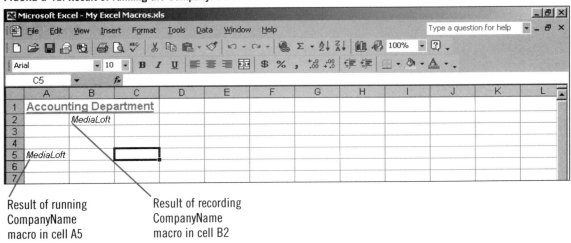

Result of running CompanyName macro in cell A5

Result of recording CompanyName macro in cell B2

Excel 2002

Using the Personal Macro Workbook

You can store commonly used macros in a **Personal Macro Workbook**. The Personal Macro Workbook is always available, unless you specify otherwise, and gives you access to all the macros it contains, regardless of which workbooks are open. The Personal Macro Workbook file is created automatically the first time you choose to store a macro in it. You can add additional macros to the Personal Macro Workbook by saving them there. ✐ Jim often likes to add a footer to his worksheets identifying his department, the workbook name, the worksheet name, his name, and the current date. He wants you to create a macro that automatically inserts this footer. Because he wants to use this macro in future worksheets, he asks you to store this macro in the Personal Macro Workbook.

Steps

1. From any cell in the active worksheet, click **Tools** on the menu bar, point to **Macro**, then click **Record New Macro**
   The Record Macro dialog box opens.

2. Type **FooterStamp** in the Macro name text box, click the **Shortcut key text box**, press and hold **[Shift]**, type **F**, then click the **Store macro in list arrow**
   You have named the macro FooterStamp and assigned it the shortcut combination [Ctrl][Shift][F]. Notice that This Workbook is selected by default, indicating that Excel automatically stores macros in the active workbook. See Figure G-13. You also can choose to store the macro in a new workbook or in the Personal Macro Workbook.

   QuickTip

   If you see a message saying that the Personal Macro Workbook needs to be opened, open it, then begin again from Step 1. The Personal Macro Workbook file is usually stored in the Documents and Settings/Administrator/Application Data/Microsoft/Excel/XLSTART folder under the name "Personal.xls" and opens when you open Excel.

3. Click **Personal Macro Workbook**, replace the existing name in the Description text box with your own name, if necessary, then click **OK**
   The recorder is on, and you are ready to record the macro keystrokes. If you are prompted to replace an existing macro named FooterStamp, click Yes.

4. Click **File** on the menu bar, click **Page Setup**, click the **Header/Footer tab** (make sure to do this even if it is already active), click **Custom Footer**, in the Left section box, type **Accounting**; click the **Center section box**, click the **File Name button** 🔲, press **[Spacebar]**, type **/**, press **[Spacebar]**, click the **Tab Name button** 🔲 to insert the sheet name; click the **Right section box**, type your name followed by a comma, press **[Spacebar]**, click the **Date button** 🔲, click **OK** to return to the Header/Footer tab
   The footer stamp is set up, as shown in Figure G-14.

   QuickTip

   You can copy or move macros stored in other workbooks to the Personal Macro Workbook by using the Visual Basic Editor.

5. Click **OK** to return to the worksheet, then click the **Stop Recording button** 🔲 on the Stop Recording toolbar
   You want to ensure that the macro will set the footer stamp in any active worksheet.

6. Activate Sheet2, in cell A1 type **Testing the FooterStamp macro**, press **[Enter]**, press and hold **[Ctrl][Shift]**, then type **F**
   The FooterStamp macro plays back the sequence of commands.

7. Preview the worksheet to verify that the new footer was inserted, then close the Preview window

8. Save the workbook, then print the worksheet
   Jim is satisfied that the FooterStamp macro works in any active worksheet.

FIGURE G-13: Record Macro dialog box showing macro storage options

Click to store in new blank workbook

Stores macro in active workbook

Click to store in Personal Macro Workbook

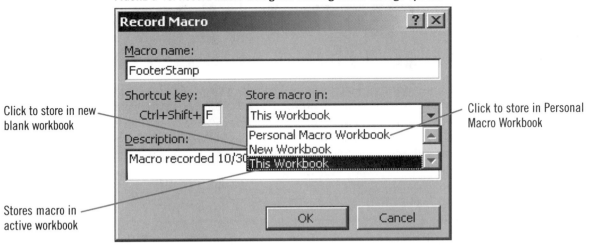

FIGURE G-14: Header/Footer tab showing custom footer settings

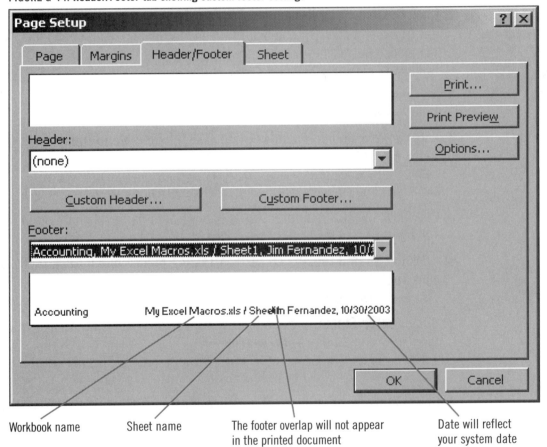

Workbook name

Sheet name

The footer overlap will not appear in the printed document

Date will reflect your system date

CLUES TO USE

Working with the Personal Macro Workbook

Once you use the Personal Macro Workbook, it opens automatically each time you start Excel so you can add macros to it. By default, the Personal Macro Workbook is hidden as a precautionary measure so you don't accidentally delete anything from it. If you need to delete a macro from the Personal Macro Workbook, click Unhide on the Window menu, click Personal.xls, then click OK.

Adding a Macro as a Menu Item

Excel 2002

In addition to storing macros in the Personal Macro Workbook so that they are always available, you can add macros as items on the Excel Worksheet menu bar. The **Worksheet menu bar** is the toolbar at the top of the Excel screen. To increase the availability of the FooterStamp macro, Jim decides to add it as an item on the Tools menu. He wants you to add a custom menu item to the Tools menu, then assign the macro to that menu item.

Steps

1. With Sheet2 active, click **Tools** on the menu bar, click **Customize**, click the **Commands tab**, then under Categories, click **Macros**
   See Figure G-15.

   QuickTip
   You may need to reposition the Customize dialog box to make the Tools option on the Worksheet menu bar visible.

2. Click **Custom Menu Item** under Commands, drag the selection to **Tools** on the menu bar (the menu opens), then point just under the last menu option, but do not release the mouse button
   Compare your screen to Figure G-16.

3. Release the mouse button
   Now, Custom Menu Item is the last item on the Tools menu.

4. With the Tools menu still open, right-click **Custom Menu Item**, select the text in the Name box (&Custom Menu Item), type **Footer Stamp**, then click **Assign Macro**
   Unlike a macro name, the name of a custom menu item can have spaces between words like all standard menu items. The Assign Macro dialog box opens.

5. Click **PERSONAL.XLS!FooterStamp** under Macro name, click **OK**, then click **Close**
   You have assigned the FooterStamp macro to the new menu command.

6. Click the **Sheet3 tab**, in cell A1 type **Testing macro menu item**, press **[Enter]**, then click **Tools** on the menu bar
   The Tools menu appears with the new menu option at the bottom. See Figure G-17.

7. Click **Footer Stamp**, preview the worksheet to verify that the footer was inserted, then close the Print Preview window
   The Print Preview window appears with the footer stamp. Because others using your computer might be confused by the macro on the menu, it's a good idea to remove it.

8. Click **Tools** on the menu bar, click **Customize**, click the **Toolbars tab**, click **Worksheet Menu Bar** to highlight it, click **Reset**, click **OK** to confirm, click **Close**, click **Tools** on the menu bar to make sure that the custom item has been deleted, then save the workbook

Adding a custom menu

You can create a custom menu on an existing toolbar and assign macros to it. To do this, click Tools on the menu bar, click Customize, click the Commands tab, click New Menu in the Categories list, then drag the New Menu from the Commands box to the toolbar. To name the new menu, right-click, then enter a name in the Name box.

FIGURE G-15: Commands tab of the Customize dialog box

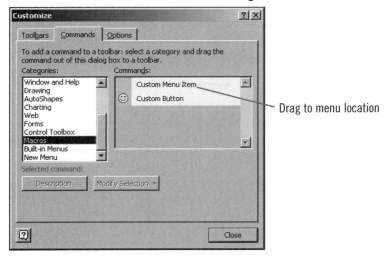

Drag to menu location

FIGURE G-16: Tools menu showing placement of the Custom Menu Item

Pointer and line showing location at which to drop menu item

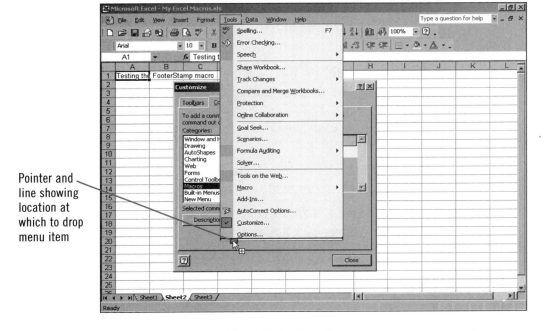

FIGURE G-17: Tools menu with new Footer Stamp item

Added menu item

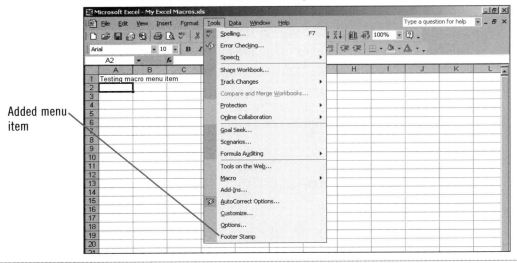

Excel 2002

Creating a Toolbar for Macros

Toolbars contain buttons that allow you to access commonly used commands. You can create your own custom toolbars to organize commands so that you can find and use them quickly. Once you create a toolbar, you can add buttons to access Excel commands such as macros. Jim asks you to create a custom toolbar called Macros that will contain buttons to run two of his macros.

Steps

QuickTip

Toolbars you create or customize are available to all workbooks on your computer. You can ensure that a custom toolbar is visible in a specific workbook by attaching the toolbar to the workbook using the Toolbars tab in the Customize dialog box.

1. With Sheet3 active, click **Tools** on the menu bar, click **Customize**, click the **Toolbars tab**, then click **New**
   The New Toolbar dialog box opens, as shown in Figure G-18. Under Toolbar name, a default name of Custom1 is selected.

2. Type **Macros**, then click **OK**
   Excel adds the new toolbar named Macros to the bottom of the Toolbars list, and a small, empty toolbar named Macros opens. See Figure G-19. You cannot see the entire toolbar name. A toolbar starts out small and expands to fit the buttons you assign to it.

3. Click the **Commands tab** in the Customize dialog box, click **Macros** under Categories, then drag the **Custom button** ☺ over the new Macros toolbar and release the mouse button
   The Macros toolbar contains one button. You want the toolbar to contain two macros, so you need to add one more button.

4. Drag the **Custom button** ☺ over the Macros toolbar again
   With the two buttons in place, you are ready to customize the buttons and assign macros to them.

5. Right-click the left button ☺ on the Macros toolbar, select **&Custom Button** in the Name box, type **Department Stamp**, click **Assign Macro**, click **DeptStamp**, then click **OK**
   With the first toolbar button customized, you are ready to customize the second button.

6. With the Customize dialog box open, right-click the right button ☺ on the Macros toolbar, edit the name to read **Company Name**, click **Change Button Image**, click ▮ (seventh row, first column), right-click ▮, click **Assign Macro**, click **CompanyName** to select it, click **OK**, then close the Customize dialog box
   The Macros toolbar appears with the two customized macro buttons.

7. Move the mouse pointer over ☺ on the Macros toolbar to display the macro name (Department Stamp), then click to run the macro; click **cell B2**, move the mouse pointer over ▮ on the Macros toolbar to display the macro name (Company Name), then click to run that macro; deselect the cell
   Compare your screen with Figure G-20. The DeptStamp macro automatically replaces the contents of cell A1. Because others using your computer might be confused by the new toolbar, it's a good idea to remove it.

8. Click **Tools** on the menu bar, click **Customize**, click the **Toolbars tab** if necessary, in the Toolbars window click **Macros** to highlight it, click **Delete**, click **OK** to confirm the deletion, then click **Close**

9. Save the workbook, print Sheet 3, then close the document and exit Excel
   The completed figure for Sheet1 is shown in Figure G-12.

FIGURE G-18: New Toolbar dialog box

Type toolbar name here

FIGURE G-19: Customize dialog box with new Macros toolbar

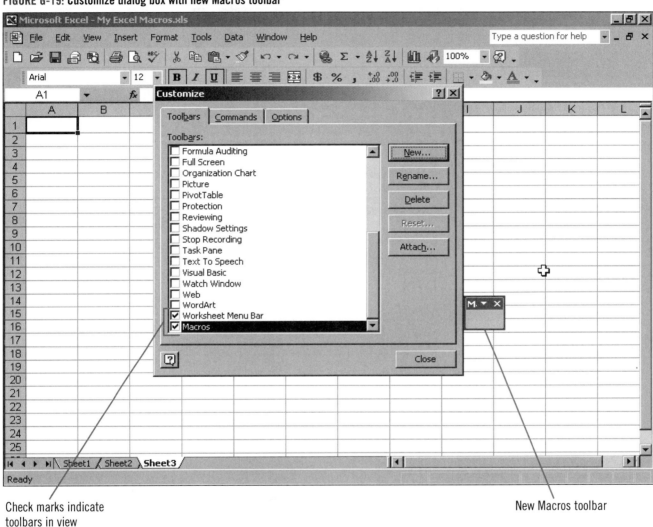

Check marks indicate toolbars in view

New Macros toolbar

FIGURE G-20: Worksheet showing Macros toolbar with two customized buttons

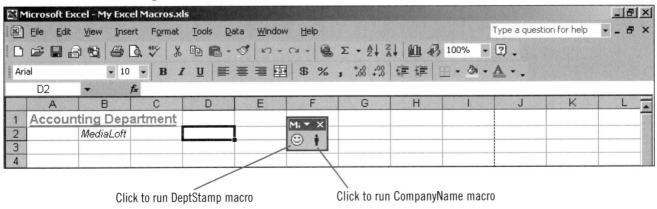

Click to run DeptStamp macro

Click to run CompanyName macro

Practice

▶ Concepts Review

Label each element of the Excel screen shown in Figure G-21.

FIGURE G-21

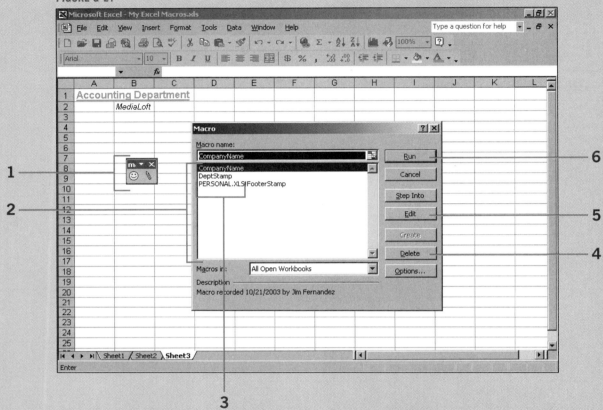

Match each term or button with the statement that describes it.

7. **Visual Basic Editor**
8. **Macro comments**
9. **Personal Macro Workbook**
10. 🖼
11. 😊

a. Statements that appear in green explaining macro code
b. Used to store commonly used macros
c. Used to make changes to macro code
d. Used to record relative cell references
e. Used to add a custom button on a macros toolbar

Select the best answer from the list of choices.

12. Which of the following is the best candidate for a macro?
   a. One-button or one-keystroke commands.
   b. Often-used sequences of commands or actions.
   c. Seldom-used commands or tasks.
   d. Nonsequential tasks.

13. When you are recording a macro, you can execute commands by using:
   a. Only the keyboard.
   b. Only the mouse.
   c. Any combination of the keyboard and the mouse.
   d. Only menu commands.

14. Commonly used macros should be stored in:
   a. The Common Macro Workbook.
   b. The Master Macro Workbook.
   c. The Personal Macro Workbook.
   d. The Custom Macro Workbook.

15. Which of the following is *not* true about editing a macro?
   a. You edit macros using the Visual Basic Editor.
   b. A macro cannot be edited and must be recorded again.
   c. You can type changes directly in the existing program code.
   d. You can make more than one editing change in a macro.

16. Why is it important to plan a macro?
   a. Macros won't be stored if they contain errors.
   b. Planning helps prevent careless errors from being introduced into the macro.
   c. It is impossible to edit a macro.
   d. Macros can't be deleted.

17. Macros are recorded with relative references:
   a. Only if the Relative Reference button is selected.
   b. In all cases.
   c. Only if relative references are chosen while recording the macro.
   d. Only if the Absolute Reference button is not selected.

18. You can run macros:
   a. From the Macro dialog box.
   b. From shortcut key combinations.
   c. As items on menus.
   d. Using all of the above.

Skills Review

1. Record a macro.
a. Start Excel, open a new workbook, then save it as **Macros** in the drive and folder where your Project Files are stored. You will record a macro titled **MyAddress** that enters and formats your name, address, and telephone number in a worksheet.

b. Store the macro in the current workbook.

c. Record the macro, entering your name in cell A1, your street address in cell A2, your city, state, and ZIP code in cell A3, and your telephone number in cell A4.

d. Format the information in 12-point Arial bold.

e. Add a border and make the text red.

f. Stop the recorder and save the workbook.

2. Run a macro.
a. Clear cell entries and formats in the range affected by the macro.

b. Run the MyAddress macro in cell A1.

c. On the worksheet, clear all the cell entries and formats generated by running the MyAddress macro.

d. Save the workbook.

3. Edit a macro.
a. Open the MyAddress macro in the Visual Basic Editor.

b. Locate the line of code that defines the font size, then change the size to 16 point.

c. Edit the Range in the fifth line of macro to A1:D4 to accommodate the increased label size.

d. Add a comment line that describes this macro.

e. Save and print the module, then return to Excel.

f. Test the macro in Sheet1.

g. Save the workbook.

4. Use shortcut keys with macros.
a. Record a macro called **MyName** in the current workbook that enters your full name in boldface in the selected cell of a worksheet. (*Hint*: You will need to record a relative cell reference).

b. Assign your macro the shortcut key combination [Ctrl][Shift][Q] and store it in the current workbook.

c. After you record the macro, clear the cell containing your name that you used to record the macro.

d. Use the shortcut key combination to run the MyName macro.

e. Save the workbook.

5. Use the Personal Macro Workbook.
a. Record a new macro called **FitToLand** that sets print orientation to landscape, with content scaled to fit on one page.

b. Store the macro in the Personal Macro Workbook. If you are prompted to replace the existing FitToLand macro, click Yes.

c. After you record the macro, activate Sheet2, and enter some test data in row 1 that exceeds one page width.

d. In the Page Setup dialog box, make sure the orientation is set to portrait and the scaling is 100 percent of normal size.

e. Run the macro.

f. Preview Sheet2 and verify that it's in landscape view and fits on one page.

g. Save the workbook.

6. Add a macro as a menu item.

a. On the Commands tab in the Customize dialog box, specify that you want to create a Custom Menu Item for macros.

b. Place the Custom Menu Item at the bottom of the Tools menu.

c. Rename the Custom Menu Item **Fit to Landscape**.

d. Assign the macro PERSONAL.XLS!FitToLand to the command.

e. Go to Sheet3 and make sure the orientation is set to portrait, then enter some test data in column A.

f. Run the Fit to Landscape macro from the Tools menu.

g. Preview the worksheet and verify that it is in landscape view.

h. Reset the Worksheet Menu bar.

i. Verify that the Fit to Landscape command has been removed from the Tools menu.

j. Save the workbook.

7. Create a toolbar for macros.

a. With the Macros workbook still open, you will create a new custom toolbar, titled My Info.

b. Display the Macros command category in the customize dialog box, then drag the Custom Button to the My Info toolbar.

c. Drag the Custom Button to the My Info toolbar a second time to create another button.

d. Rename the first button **My Address**, and assign the MyAddress macro to it.

e. Rename the second button **My Name**, and assign the MyName macro to it.

f. Change the second button image to one of your choice.

g. On Sheet3, clear the existing cell data, then test both macro buttons on the My Info toolbar.

h. Use the Toolbars tab of the Customize dialog box to delete the toolbar named My Info.

i. Save the workbook, print the worksheet, close the workbook, then exit Excel.

► Independent Challenge 1

As a computer-support employee of Boston Accounting Solutions, you need to develop ways to help your fellow employees work more efficiently. Employees have asked for Excel macros that will do the following:

- Delete the current row and insert a blank row
- Delete the current column and insert a blank column
- Place the department name of Accounting in a 14-point red font in cell A1 (The width of A1 should be increased if necessary)

a. Plan and write the steps necessary for each macro.

b. Start Excel, create a new workbook, then save it as **Excel Utility Macros** in the drive and folder where your Project Files are stored.

c. Create a new toolbar called **Helpers**.

d. Create a macro for each employee request described above, name them DeleteRow, DeleteColumn, and DepartmentName, then save them in the Excel Utility Macros workbook.

e. Add comment lines to each module, describing the function of the macro and your name, then return to Excel.

f. Add each macro to the Tools menu.

g. On the Helpers toolbar, install buttons to run the macros.

h. Test each macro by using the Run command, the menu command, and the new buttons.

i. Delete the new toolbar, then reset the Worksheet menu bar.

j. Save the workbook, print the module containing the program code for all three macros, then close the workbook and exit Excel.

 # Independent Challenge 2

You are an analyst in the Loan Department of Atlantic Bank. Every quarter, you produce a number of single-page quarterly budget worksheets. Your manager has informed you that certain worksheets need to contain a footer stamp indicating that the worksheet was produced in the Loan Department. The footer should also show the current page number out of the total number of pages, (for example, 1 of 5) and the workbook filename. It's tedious to add the footer stamp to the numerous worksheets you produce. You will record a macro to do this.

a. Plan and write the steps to create the macro.

b. Start Excel, create a new workbook, then save it as **Header and Footer Stamp** in the drive and folder where your Project Files are stored.

c. Create the macro described above, name it footerstamp, assign it the shortcut key combination [Ctrl][Shift][F], and store it in the current workbook. Make sure it adds the footer with the department name and the other required information.

d. Add a descriptive comment line to the macro code with your name.

e. Add the macro to the Tools menu.

f. Create a toolbar titled **Stamp**, then add a button to the toolbar to run the macro.

g. Enter the text **Footer Test** in cell A1. Test the macro using the shortcut key combination, the menu command, and the new button.

h. Delete the new toolbar, then reset the Worksheet menu bar.

i. Save the workbook, print the module for the macro, close the module and the workbook, then exit Excel.

 # Independent Challenge 3

You are an administrative assistant at the Sydney, Australia, branch of Computers Inc. A major part of your job is to create spreadsheets that project sales results in different markets. It seems that you are constantly changing the print settings so that workbooks print in landscape orientation and are scaled to fit on one page. You have decided that it's time to create a macro to streamline this process.

a. Plan and write the steps necessary to create the macro.

b. Start Excel, create a new workbook, then save it as **Computers Inc Macro** in the drive and folder where your Project Files are stored.

c. Create a macro that changes the page orientation to landscape and scales the worksheet to fit on one page.

d. Name the macro **Landscape**, assign it the shortcut key combination [Ctrl][Shift][L], and store it in the current workbook.

e. Add the macro to the Tools menu.

f. Enter the text **Macro test** in cell A1 and add your name. Test the macro using the new menu command.

g. Reset the Worksheet menu bar and change the page orientation back to portrait.

h. Edit the macro to include the company name, Computers Inc, in the center footer and add your name as a comment. Test the macro using the shortcut key combination, making sure the footer was added.

i. Add a custom menu to the standard toolbar and name it **Macros**. Add a custom menu item to the new Macros menu, name the menu option **Page Orientation**, and assign the landscape macro to it.

j. Delete the footer and change the page orientation to portrait, then test the macro using the new menu.

k. Reset the standard toolbar.

l. Save the workbook, print the module for the macro; close the workbook, then exit Excel.

 # Independent Challenge 4

PC Assist, a software training company, has decided to begin purchasing its branch office supplies through online vendors. One of the products the company needs to purchase is toner for the Hewlett-Packard LaserJet 2100 printers in the offices. You have been asked to research vendors and prices on the Web. You will create a workbook to hold office supply vendor information that you can use for various products. You will add a macro to this workbook to find the lowest price of the product, format the information, and add a descriptive footer to the worksheet.

Go to the AltaVista search engine at www.altavista.com and enter **Office Supplies** in the Search box. You can also use Yahoo!, Excite, Infoseek, or another search engine of your choice. You may want to use the shopping directories on the search engines as another source of information. Find three online suppliers of toner for the company's printers and note their prices.

a. Start Excel, open the Project File EX G-1 from the drive and folder where your Project Files are stored, enter your name into cell A15, then save the workbook as **Office Supplies**.

b. Complete the table below with three online suppliers of office products you found in your search.

Office Product	
Vendor	Price
Lowest Price	

c. Enter three vendors and their prices from your table into the Excel worksheet. Enter the Product name **Toner** in the cell next to Office Product.

d. Create a macro named **Toner** in the Office Supplies workbook that can be activated by the [Ctrl][Shift][T] key combination. The macro should do the following:
   • Find the lowest price for the office product and insert it to the right of the Lowest Price label.
   • Boldface the Lowest Price text and the cell to its right that will contain the lowest value.
   • Place a thick box border around all the information.
   • Fill the information area with a light turquoise color.
   • Add a footer with the company name **PC Assist** on the left and the workbook name on the right.
   • Include your name in a comment line.

e. Clear all the formatting, the footer, and the lowest price from the worksheet.

f. Test the macro using the key combination [Ctrl][Shift][T].

g. Save your workbook, print the results of the macro, then open the macro in the Visual Basic Editor and print the macro code.

h. Return to Excel, close the workbook, then exit Excel.

▶ Visual Workshop

Create the macro shown in Figure G-22. (*Hint*: Save a blank workbook as **File Utility Macros**, then create a macro in the current workbook called **SaveClose** that saves a previously named workbook. Finally, include the line **ActiveWorkbook.Close** in the module, as shown in the figure.) Print the module. Test the macro. If the "Macro recorded" comment doesn't contain your name, edit it accordingly.

FIGURE G-22

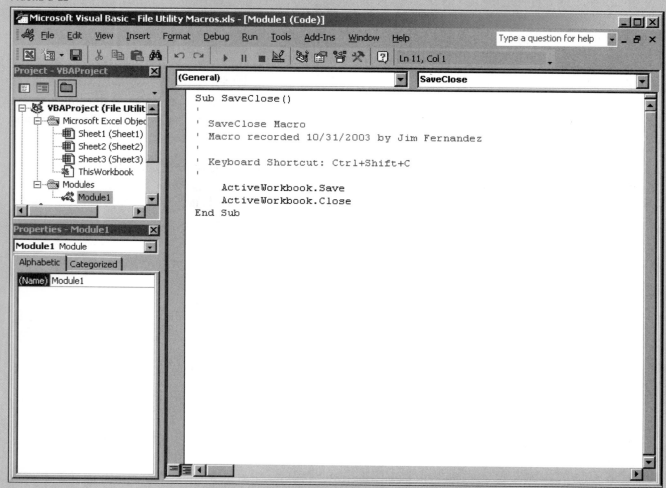

Using

Lists

Objectives

- ► **Plan a list**
- MOUS ► **Create a list**
- ► **Add records with the data form**
- ► **Find records**
- ► **Delete records**
- ► **Sort a list on one field**
- ► **Sort a list on multiple fields**
- MOUS ► **Print a list**

A **database** is an organized collection of related information. Examples of databases include a telephone book, a card catalog, and a roster of company employees. Excel refers to a database as a **list**. Using an Excel list, you can organize and manage worksheet information so that you can quickly find data for projects, reports, and charts. In this unit, you'll learn how to plan and create a list; add, change, find, and delete information in a list; and then sort and print list.

MediaLoft uses lists to analyze new customer information. Jim Fernandez has asked you to help him build and manage a list of new customers as part of the ongoing strategy to focus on the expenditure of the company's advertising dollars.

Planning a List

When planning a list, consider what information the list will contain and how you will work with the data now and in the future. Lists are organized into records. A **record** contains data about an object or person. Records are rows in the list and are comprised of fields. **Fields** are columns in the list; each field describes a characteristic about the record, such as a customer's last name or street address. Each field has a **field name**, a column label that describes the field. See Table H-1 for additional planning guidelines. ✐ Jim has asked you to compile a list of new customers. Before entering the data into an Excel worksheet, you will plan the list using the following guidelines:

Details

► **Identify the purpose of the list**
Determine the kind of information the list should contain. Jim will use the list to identify areas of the country in which new customers live.

► **Plan the structure of the list**
Determine the fields that make up a record. Jim has customer cards that contain information about each new customer. Figure H-1 shows a typical card. Each customer in the list will have a record. The fields in the record correspond to the information on the cards.

► **Write down the names of the fields**
Field names can be up to 255 characters long (the maximum column width), although shorter names are easier to see in the cells. Field names appear in the first row of a list. Jim writes down field names that describe each piece of information shown in Figure H-1.

► **Determine any special number formatting required in the list**
Most lists contain both text and numbers. When planning a list, consider whether any fields require specific number formatting or prefixes. Jim notes that some ZIP codes begin with zero. Because Excel automatically drops a leading zero, Jim must type an apostrophe (') when he enters a ZIP code that begins with 0 (zero). The apostrophe tells Excel that the cell contains a label rather than a value. If a column contains a combination of numbers and text, you should format the field as text. Otherwise, the numbers are sorted first, and the numbers that contain text characters are sorted after that; for example, 11542, 60614, 87105, '01810, '02115. To instruct Excel to sort the ZIP codes properly, Jim enters all ZIP codes with a leading apostrophe and formats the field as text.

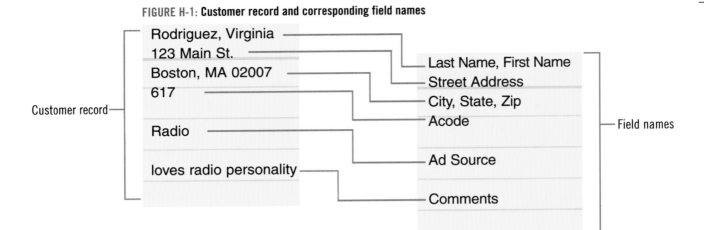

FIGURE H-1: **Customer record and corresponding field names**

Customer record

Rodriguez, Virginia — Last Name, First Name
123 Main St. — Street Address
Boston, MA 02007 — City, State, Zip
617 — Acode

Radio — Ad Source

loves radio personality — Comments

Field names

TABLE H-1: **Guidelines for planning a list**

size and location guidelines	row and column content guidelines
Devote an entire worksheet to your list and list summary information because some list management features can be used on only one list at a time.	Plan and design your list so that all rows have similar items in the same column.
Leave at least one blank column and one blank row between your list and list summary data. Doing this helps Excel select your list when it performs list management tasks such as sorting.	Do not insert extra spaces at the beginning of a cell because that can affect sorting and searching.
Avoid placing critical data to the left or right of the list.	Use the same format for all cells in a column.
	Instead of blank rows or columns between your labels and your data, use formatting to make column labels stand out from the data.

CLUES TO USE

Using lists versus databases

If your list contains more records than can fit on one worksheet (that is, more than 65,536), you should consider using database software rather than spreadsheet software.

Creating a List

Excel 2002

Once you have planned the list structure, the sequence of fields, and any appropriate formatting, you need to create field names. Table H-2 provides guidelines for naming fields. You are ready to create the list using the field names you wrote down earlier.

Steps

1. Start Excel if necessary, open the Project File **EX H-1** from the drive and folder where your Project Files are stored, then save it as **New Customer List**

2. Rename Sheet1 **Practice**, then if necessary maximize the Excel window
   It is a good idea to devote an entire worksheet to your list.

QuickTip

If the field name you plan to use is wider than the data in the column, you can turn on Wrap Text on the Alignment tab in the Format Cells dialog box to stack the heading in the cell. You can also press [Alt][Enter] to force a line break while entering field names.

3. Beginning in cell A1 and moving horizontally, enter each field name in a separate cell, as shown in Figure H-2
   Always put field names in the first row of the list. Don't worry if your field names are wider than the cells; you will fix this later.

4. Select the field headings in range **A1:I1**, then click the **Bold button** on the Formatting toolbar; with range A1:I1 still selected, click the **Borders list arrow**, then click the **Thick Bottom Border** (second column, second row)

Trouble?

Cells F2:F4 may have a green error indicator in the upper-left corner of the cell, and an error button may appear. This warning is a result of storing the ZIP code numbers as text. To remove the warnings and prevent similar ones in the future, select Options from the Tools menu, click the Error Checking tab, and remove the check next to Number stored as text.

5. Enter the information from Figure H-3 in the rows immediately below the field names, using a leading apostrophe (') for all ZIP codes; do not leave any blank rows
   If you don't type an apostrophe, Excel deletes the leading zero (0) in the ZIP code. The data appears in columns organized by field name.

6. Select the range **A1:I4**, click **Format** on the menu bar, point to **Column**, click **AutoFit Selection**, click anywhere in the worksheet to deselect the range, then save the workbook
   Resizing the column widths this way is faster than double-clicking the column divider lines between each pair of columns. Compare your screen with Figure H-4.

TABLE H-2: Guidelines for naming fields

guideline	explanation
Use labels to name fields	Numbers can be interpreted as parts of formulas
Do not use duplicate field names	Duplicate field names can cause information to be incorrectly entered and sorted
Format the field names to stand out from the list data	Use a font, alignment, format, pattern, border, or capitalization style for the column labels that are different from the format of your list data
Use descriptive names	Avoid names that might be confused with cell addresses, such as Q4

FIGURE H-2: Field names entered and formatted in row 1

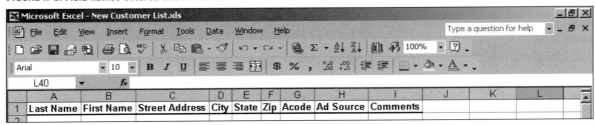

FIGURE H-3: Cards with customer information

Rodriguez, Virginia	Wong, Sam	Frei, Carol
123 Main St.	2120 Central NE.	123 Elm St.
Boston, MA 02007	San Francisco, CA 93772	Salem, MA 01970
617	415	978
Radio	Newspaper	Newspaper
loves radio personality	graphics caught eye	no comments

FIGURE H-4: List with three records

Leading apostrophe

New records

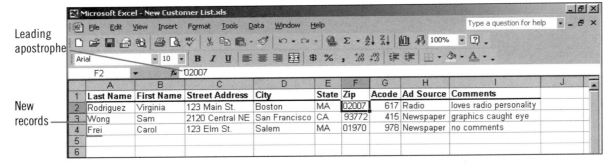

Filtering lists using AutoFilter

You can filter a list to show only the rows that meet specific criteria. For example, you might want to display only the records of customers in a certain ZIP code, or only residents of California. (A filter is different from a sort, which rearranges list records.) The AutoFilter feature is the easiest way to apply a filter.

To use AutoFilter, click Data on the menu bar, point to Filter, then click AutoFilter. List arrows will appear next to the field names, allowing you to select criteria for a field. For example, if you specify MA as the criteria in a State field, Excel displays only the records where MA is entered as the state.

Excel 2002

Adding Records with the Data Form

You can add records to a list by typing data directly into the cells within the list range. Once the field names are created, you can also use the data form as a quick, easy method of data entry. A **data form** is a dialog box that displays one record at a time. You have entered all the customer records Jim had on his cards, but he receives the names of two additional customers. You decide to use the Excel data form to add the new customer information.

Steps 1 2 3 4

1. Make sure the New Customer List file is open, then activate **Sheet2** and rename it **Working List**

   Working List contains the nearly completed customer list.

2. Select any cell in the customer list, click **Data** on the menu bar, then click **Form**

   A data form containing the first record appears, as shown in Figure H-5.

3. Click **New**

   A blank data form appears with the insertion point in the first field.

4. Type **Chavez** in the Last Name box, then press **[Tab]** to move the insertion point to the next field

Trouble?

If you accidentally press [▲] or [▼] while in a data form and find that you displayed the wrong record, press [▲] or [▼] until you return to the desired record.

5. Enter the rest of the information for Jeffrey Chavez, as shown in Figure H-6

   Press [Tab] to move the insertion point to the next field, or click in the next field box to move the insertion point there.

6. Click **New** to add Jeffrey Chavez's record and open another blank data form, enter the record for Cathy Relman as shown in Figure H-6, then click **Close**

   The records that you added with the data form are placed at the end of the list and are formatted in the same way as the previous records.

QuickTip

Excel automatically extends formatting and formulas in lists.

7. If necessary, scroll down the worksheet to bring rows 46 and 47 into view, check both new records, return to cell A1, then save the workbook

FIGURE H-5: Data form showing first record in the list

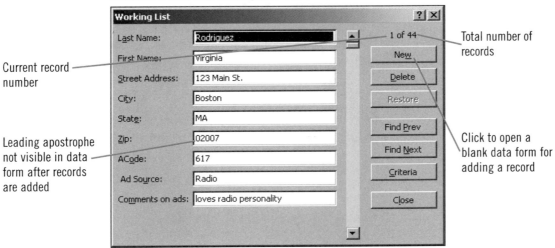

Current record number → Current record

Leading apostrophe not visible in data form after records are added

Total number of records

Click to open a blank data form for adding a record

FIGURE H-6: Two data forms with information for two new records

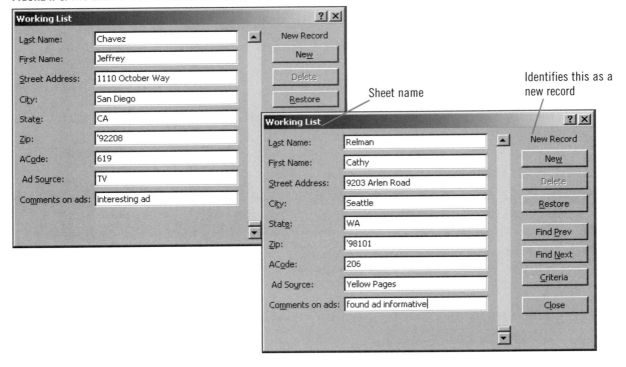

Sheet name

Identifies this as a new record

Excel 2002

Finding Records

From time to time, you need to locate specific records in your list. You can use the Excel Find command on the Edit menu or the data form to search your list. You can also use the Replace command on the Edit menu to locate and replace existing entries or portions of entries with specified information. Jim wants to be more specific about the radio ad source, so he asks you to replace "Radio" with "KWIN Radio." He also wants to know how many of the new customers originated from the company's TV ads. You begin by searching for those records with the ad source "TV".

Trouble?

If you receive the message "No list found," select any cell within the list, then repeat Step 1.

1. Click any cell within the list, click Data on the menu bar, click Form, then click Criteria

The data form changes so that all fields are blank and "Criteria" appears in the upper-right corner. See Figure H-7. You want to search for records whose Ad Source field contains the label "TV".

2. Click in the Ad Source text box, type TV, then click Find Next

Excel displays the first record for a customer who learned about the company through its TV ads. See Figure H-8.

QuickTip

You can also use comparison operators when performing a search using the data form. For example, you could specify >50,000 in a Salary field box to return those records in the Salary field with a value greater than $50,000.

3. Click Find Next until there are no more matching records, then click Close

There are six customers whose ad source is TV.

4. Return to cell A1, click Edit on the menu bar, then click Replace

The Find and Replace dialog box opens with the Replace tab selected and the insertion point in the Find what box. See Figure H-9.

5. Type Radio in the Find what text box, then click the Replace with text box

Jim wants you to search for entries containing "Radio" and replace them with "KWIN Radio".

6. Type KWIN Radio in the Replace with text box

Because you notice that there are other list entries containing the word "radio" with a lowercase "r" (in the Comments column), you need to make sure that only capitalized instances of the word are replaced.

QuickTip

Be sure to clear this option for future searches, where you may not want to use it.

7. Click Options >>, click the Match case check box to select it, click Options <<, then click Find Next

Excel moves the cell pointer to the first occurrence of "Radio".

8. Click Replace All, click OK, then click Close

The dialog box closes. Note that in the Comments column, each instance of the word "radio" remains unchanged.

9. Make sure there are no entries in the Ad Source column that read "Radio", then save the workbook

Using wildcards to fine-tune your search

You can use special symbols called **wildcards** when defining search criteria in the data form or Replace dialog box. The question mark (?) wildcard stands for any single character. For example, if you do not know whether a customer's last name is Paulsen or Paulson, you can specify Pauls?n as the search criteria to locate both options. The asterisk (*) wildcard stands for any group of characters. For example, if you specify Jan* as the search criteria in the First Name field, Excel locates all records with first names beginning with Jan (for instance, Jan, Janet, Janice).

FIGURE H-7: Criteria data form

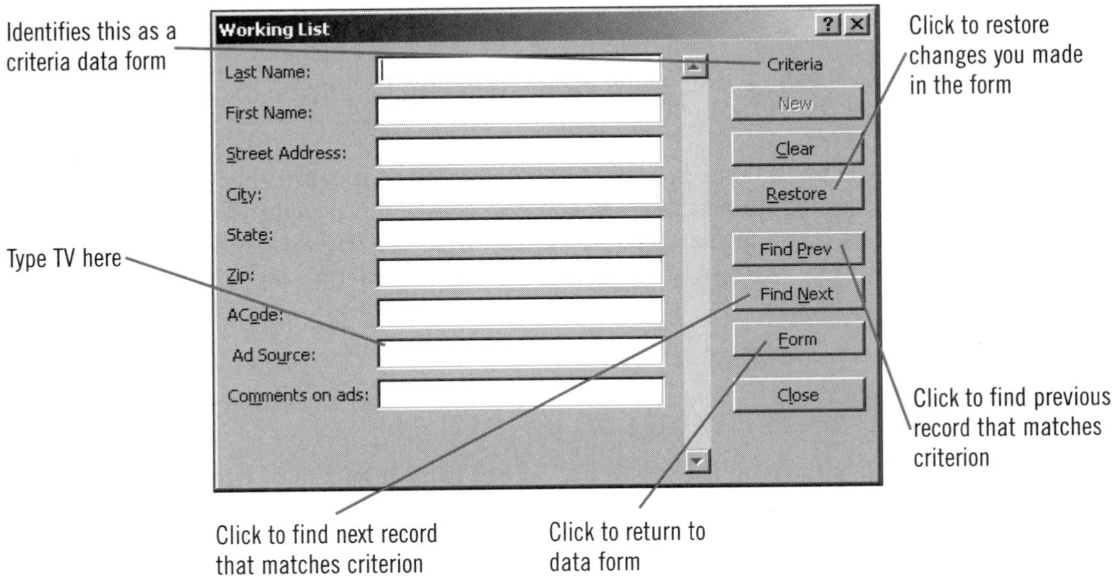

Identifies this as a criteria data form
Working List
Last Name:
First Name:
Street Address:
City:
State:
Zip:
ACode:
Ad Source:
Comments on ads:
Criteria
New
Clear
Restore
Find Prev
Find Next
Form
Close
Click to restore changes you made in the form
Type TV here
Click to find previous record that matches criterion
Click to find next record that matches criterion
Click to return to data form

FIGURE H-8: Finding a record using the data form

Working List
Last Name: Ryland
First Name: Susan
Street Address: 4257 Avenida San Juan
City: San Diego
State: CA
Zip: 92108
ACode: 619
Ad Source: TV
Comments on ads: liked ad
4 of 46
New
Delete
Restore
Find Prev
Find Next
Criteria
Close
Record number of the displayed record

FIGURE H-9: Find and Replace dialog box

Type Radio here
Type KWIN Radio here
Click to replace all occurrences of the item in the Find what text box
Find and Replace
Find
Replace
Find what:
Replace with:
Options >>
Replace All
Replace
Find All
Find Next
Close
Click here to set the Match case option
Click to find next occurrence of item in Find what text box
Click to replace current item that matches Find what text box

Excel 2002

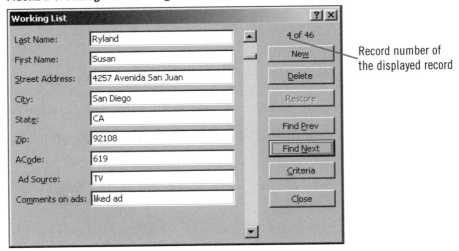

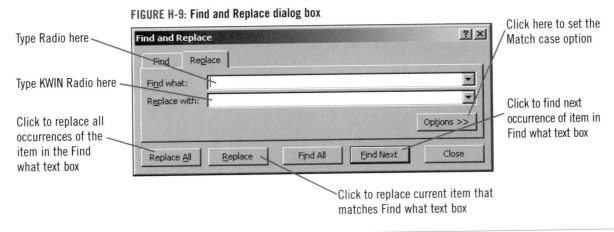

Deleting Records

You need to keep your list up to date by removing obsolete records. One way to remove records is to use the Delete button on the data form. You can also delete all records that share something in common—that is, records that meet certain criteria. For example, you can specify a criterion for Excel to find the next record containing ZIP code 01879, then remove the record by using the Delete button. If specifying one criterion does not meet your needs, you can set multiple criteria. Jim notices two entries for Carolyn Smith, and wants you to check the list for additional duplicate entries. You will use the data form to delete the duplicate record.

Steps

1. **Click Data on the menu bar, click Form, then click Criteria**
   The Criteria data form opens.

QuickTip

You can use the data form to edit records as well as to add, search for, and delete them. Just find the desired record and edit the data directly in the appropriate box.

2. **Type Smith in the Last Name text box, press Tab to move the insertion point to the First Name text box, type Carolyn, then click Find Next**
   Excel displays the first record for a customer whose name is Carolyn Smith. You decide to leave the initial entry for Carolyn Smith (record 5 of 46) and delete the second one, once you confirm that it is a duplicate.

3. **Click Find Next**
   The duplicate record for Carolyn Smith, number 40, appears as shown in Figure H-10. You are ready to delete the duplicate entry.

QuickTip

Clicking Restore on the data form will undo your changes when you are adding a new record, as long as you click it before you press Enter or click Close. Restore will not restore deleted record(s).

4. **Click Delete, then click OK to confirm the deletion**
   The duplicate record for Carolyn Smith is deleted, and all the other records move up one row. The data form now shows the record for Julio Manuel.

5. **Click Close to return to the worksheet, scroll down until rows 41–46 are visible, then read the entry in row 41**
   Notice that the duplicate entry for Carolyn Smith is gone and that Manuel Julio moved up a row and is now in row 41. You also notice a record for K. C. Splint in row 43, which is a duplicate entry.

6. **Return to cell A1, and read the record information for K. C. Splint in row 8**
   After confirming the duplicate entry, you decide to delete the row.

7. **Click cell A8, click Edit on the menu bar, then click Delete**
   The Delete dialog box opens, as shown in Figure H-11.

8. **Click the Entire row option button, then click OK**
   You have deleted the entire row. The duplicate record for K. C. Splint is deleted and the other records move up to fill in the gap.

9. **Save the workbook**

FIGURE H-10: Data form showing duplicate record for Carolyn Smith

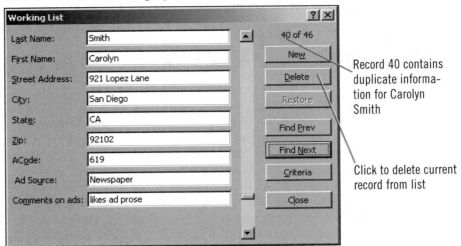

Record 40 contains duplicate informa-tion for Carolyn Smith

Click to delete current record from list

FIGURE H-11: Delete dialog box

Click to shift remaining cells to fill gap created by deleting cells

Click to delete current row

Click to delete current column

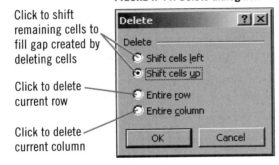

CLUES TO USE

Deleting records using the worksheet

When you delete a record using the data form, you cannot undo your deletion. When you delete a record by deleting its row in the worksheet, however, you can immediately retrieve it; use the Undo command on the Edit menu, click the Undo button, or press [Ctrl][Z].

Sorting a List on One Field

Usually, you enter records in the order in which they are received, rather than in alphabetical or numerical order. When you add records to a list using the data form, the records are added to the end of the list. Using the Excel sorting feature, you can rearrange the order of the records. You can use the sort buttons on the Standard toolbar to sort records by one field, or you can use the Sort command on the Data menu to perform more advanced sorts. Alternately, you can sort an entire list or any portion of a list, and you can arrange sorted information in ascending or descending order. In ascending order, the lowest value (the beginning of the alphabet, for instance, or the earliest date) appears at the top of the list. In a field containing labels and numbers, numbers come first. In descending order, the highest value (the end of the alphabet or the latest date) appears at the top of the list. In a field containing labels and numbers, labels come first. Table H-3 provides examples of ascending and descending sorts. ✍ Because Jim wants to be able to return the records to their original order following any sorts, he wants you to create a new field called Entry Order. You will then perform several single field sorts on the list.

Steps

QuickTip

Before you sort records, it is a good idea to make a backup copy of your list or create a field that numbers the records so you can return them to their original order, if necessary.

1. In cell **J1**, enter the column heading and format as shown in Figure H-12, then AutoFit column J

2. Type **1** in cell J2, press **[Enter]**, type **2** in cell J3, press **[Enter]**, select cells **J2:J3**, drag the fill handle to cell **J45**
   You are now ready to sort the list in ascending order by last name. You must position the cell pointer within the column you want to sort prior to issuing the sort command.

3. Return to cell A1, then click the **Sort Ascending button** 🔲 on the Standard toolbar
   Excel rearranges the records in ascending order by last name, as shown in Figure H-13. You can also sort the list in descending order by any field.

Trouble?

If your sort does not perform as intended, press [Ctrl][Z] immediately to undo the sort.

4. Click cell **G1**, then click the **Sort Descending button** 🔲 on the Standard toolbar
   Excel sorts the list, placing those records with higher-digit area codes at the top. You are now ready to return the list to original entry order.

5. Click cell **J1**, click the **Sort Ascending button** 🔲 on the Standard toolbar, then save the workbook
   The list is back to its original order, and the workbook is saved.

FIGURE H-12: List with Entry Order field added

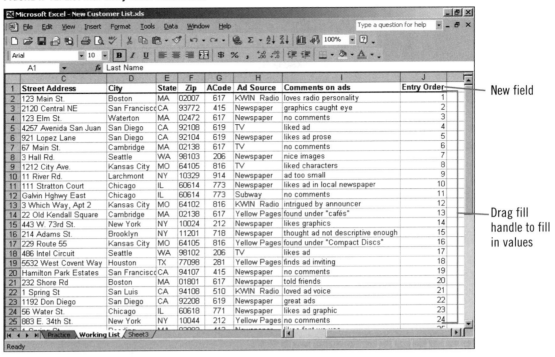

New field

Drag fill
handle to fill
in values

FIGURE H-13: List sorted alphabetically by Last Name

List sorted in
ascending order
by Last Name

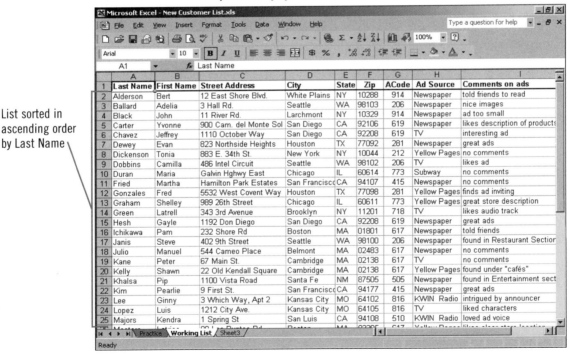

TABLE H-3: Sort order options and examples

option	alphabetic	numeric	date	alphanumeric
Ascending	A, B, C	7, 8, 9	1/1, 2/1, 3/1	12A, 99B, DX8, QT7
Descending	C, B, A	9, 8, 7	3/1, 2/1, 1/1	QT7, DX8, 99B, 12A

Excel 2002

Sorting a List on Multiple Fields

You can sort lists by as many as three fields by specifying **sort keys**, the criteria on which the sort is based. Up to three column headings can be entered in the Sort dialog box to specify the sort criteria. Jim wants you to sort the records alphabetically by state first, then within the state by ZIP code.

Steps

QuickTip

You can specify a capitalization sort by clicking Options in the Sort dialog box, then selecting the Case sensitive box. When you choose this option, lowercase entries precede uppercase entries.

1. **Click Data on the menu bar, then click Sort**
   The Sort dialog box opens, as shown in Figure H-14. You want to sort the list by state and then by ZIP code.

2. **Click the Sort by list arrow, click State, then click the Ascending option button to select it, if necessary**
   The list will be sorted alphabetically in ascending order (A–Z) by the State field. A second sort criterion will sort the entries within each state grouping.

3. **Click the top Then by list arrow, click Zip, then click the Descending option button**
   You could also sort by a third key by selecting a field in the bottom Then by list box.

QuickTip

The Sort warning dialog box will appear if you are sorting a list on a field containing numbers that are formatted as text.

4. **Click OK to perform the sort, click OK on the Sort Warning dialog box, press [Ctrl][Home], then scroll through the list to see the result of the sort**
   The list is sorted alphabetically by state in ascending order, then within each state by ZIP code in descending order. Compare your results with Figure H-15.

5. **Save the workbook**

FIGURE H-14: Sort dialog box

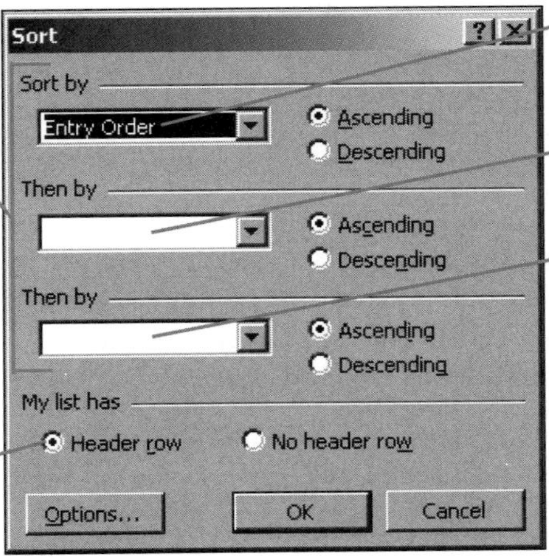

First sort field

Fields on which the sort will be based

Second sort field

Third sort field

Indicates that field name labels will not be included in sort

FIGURE H-15: List sorted by multiple fields

First sort by state

Second sort by ZIP code within state

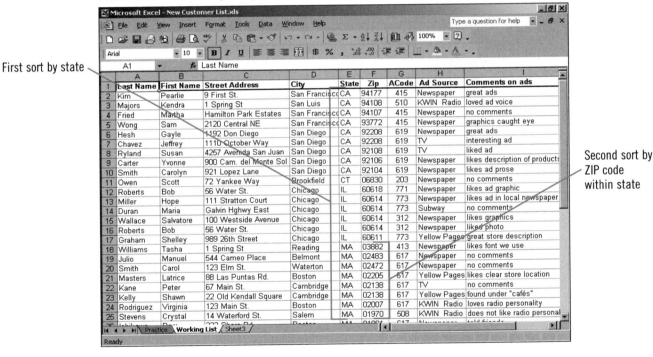

Specifying a custom sort order

You can identify a custom sort order for the field selected in the Sort by box. To do this, click Options in the Sort dialog box, click the First key sort order list arrow, then click the desired custom order.

Commonly used custom sort orders are days of the week (Sun, Mon, Tues, Wed, etc.) and months (Jan, Feb, Mar, etc.); alphabetic sorts do not sort these items properly.

Printing a List

If a list is small enough to fit on one page, you can print it as you would any other Excel worksheet. If you have more columns than can fit on a portrait-oriented page, try setting the page orientation to landscape. Because lists often have more rows than can fit on a page, you can define the first row of the list (containing the field names) as the **print title**, which prints at the top of every page. Most lists do not have any descriptive information above the field names on the worksheet. To augment the information contained in the field names, you can use headers and footers to add identifying text, such as the list title or report date. If you want to exclude any fields from your list report, you can hide the selected columns from view so that they do not print. Jim has finished updating his list and would like you to print it. You begin by previewing the list.

Steps

1. **Click the Print Preview button on the Standard toolbar**
   The status bar reads Preview: Page 1 of 2. You want all the fields in the list to fit on a single page, but you'll need two pages to fit all the data.

2. **From the Print Preview window, click Setup, click the Page tab, click the Landscape option button under Orientation, click the Fit to option button under Scaling, double-click the tall box and type 2, click OK**
   The list still does not fit on a single page. Because the records on page 2 appear without column headings, you want to set up the first row of the list, which contains the field names, as a repeating print title.

3. **Click Close to exit the Print Preview window, click File on the menu bar, click Page Setup, click the Sheet tab, click the Rows to repeat at top text box under Print titles, click any cell in row 1, compare your screen to Figure H-16, then click OK**
   When you select row 1 as a print title, Excel automatically inserts an absolute reference to a beginning row to repeat at the top of each page—in this case, the print title to repeat beginning and ending with row 1.

4. **Click the Print Preview button , click Next to view the second page, then click Zoom**
   Setting up a print title to repeat row 1 causes the field names to appear at the top of each printed page. You can save these print settings by creating a custom view.

5. **Click Close, click View on the menu bar, click Custom Views, click Add, enter Print-Title in the Name text box, then click OK**
   This creates a custom view named Print-Title that you can use at any time. You can use the worksheet header to provide information about the list.

6. **Click , click Setup, click the Header/Footer tab, click Custom Header, click the Left section box and enter your name, then click the Center section box and enter MediaLoft -, press [Spacebar], then click the Filename button**

7. **Select the header information in the Center section box, click the Font button , change the font size to 14 and the style to Bold, click OK, click OK again to return to the Header/Footer tab, click OK to preview the list, then click Close**

8. **Save the workbook, print the worksheet, then close the workbook**
   Compare your printed worksheet with Figure H-17.

FIGURE H-16: Sheet tab of the Page Setup dialog box

Indicates that row 1 will appear at top of each printed page

Indicates which columns will appear at the left of each printed page

Turns gridline display on or off

Specifies high or draft quality printing

Displays row and column headings on printout

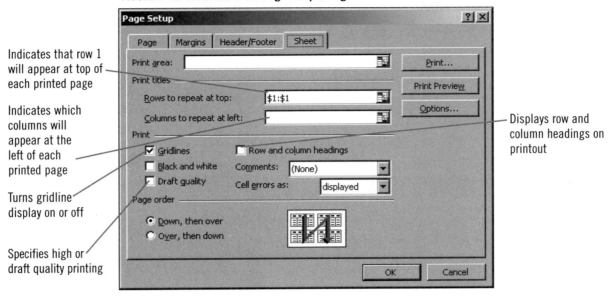

FIGURE H-17: Completed list

Setting a print area

There are times when you want to print only part of a worksheet. You can do this in the Print dialog box by choosing Selection under Print what. If you want to print a selected area repeatedly, it's best to define a print area, which will print when you click the Print button on the Standard toolbar. To set a print area, click View on the menu bar, then click Page Break Preview. In the preview window, select the area you want to print. Right-click the area, then select Set Print Area. The print area becomes outlined in a blue border. You can drag the border to extend the print area or add nonadjacent cells to it by selecting them, right-clicking them, then selecting Add to Print Area. To clear a print area, click File on the menu bar, point to Print Area, then click Clear Print Area.

Practice

► Concepts Review

Label each of the elements of the Excel screen shown in Figure H-18.

FIGURE H-18

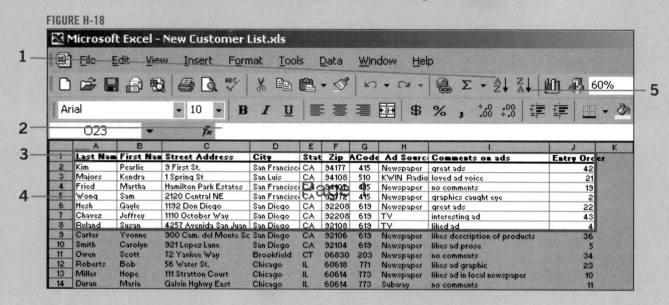

Match each term with the statement that best describes it.

6. List   **a.** Arrange records in a particular sequence

7. Record   **b.** Organized collection of related information in Excel

8. Database   **c.** Row in an Excel list

9. Sort   **d.** Type of software used for lists containing more than 65,536 records

10. Field name   **e.** Label positioned at the top of the column identifying data

Select the best answer from the list of choices.

11. **Which of the following Excel sorting options do you use to sort a list of employee names in A-to-Z order?**
    a. Ascending
    b. Absolute
    c. Alphabetic
    d. Descending

12. **Which of the following series is in descending order?**
    a. 4, 5, 6, A, B, C
    b. C, B, A, 6, 5, 4
    c. 8, 7, 6, 5, 6, 7
    d. 8, 6, 4, C, B, A

13. **To prevent field name labels from being included in a sort, you need to make sure _____ is selected in the Sort dialog box.**
    a. Field row
    b. No field row
    c. No header row
    d. Header row

14. **When printing a list on multiple pages, you can define a print title containing repeating row(s) to:**
    a. Include appropriate fields in the printout.
    b. Include field names at the top of each printed page.
    c. Include the header in list reports.
    d. Exclude from the printout all rows under the first row.

► ## Skills Review

1. **Create a list.**
   a. Create a new workbook, then save it as **MediaLoft New York Employee List** in the drive and folder where your Project files are stored.
   b. In cell A1, enter the title **MediaLoft New York Employees**.
   c. Enter the field names and records, using the information in the following table.

Last Name	First Name	Years	Position	Full/Part Time	Training?
Long	Sarah	3	CD Sales	F	Y
Marino	Donato	2	CD Sales	P	N
Khederian	Jay	4	Video Sales	F	Y
Johnson	Carol	1	Video Sales	F	N
Rabinowicz	Miriam	2	Café Sales	P	Y

   d. Apply bold formatting to the field names.
   e. Center the entries in the Years, Full/Part Time, and Training? fields.
   f. Adjust the column widths to make the data readable.
   g. Enter your name in the footer, save, then print the list.

Excel 2002

2. **Add records with the data form.**
   a. Click any record in the list.
   b. Open the data form and add a new record for **David Gitano**, a one-year employee in Book Sales. David is full time and has not completed training.
   c. Add a new record for **George Worley**, the café manager. George is full time, has worked there two years, and has completed training.
   d. Save the file.

3. **Find and delete records.**
   a. Use the Find command to find the record for **Carol Johnson**.
   b. Delete the record.
   c. Save the file.

4. **Sort a list by one field.**
   a. Sort the list alphabetically in ascending order by last name.
   b. Save the file.

5. **Sort a list by multiple fields.**
   a. Sort the list alphabetically in ascending order, first by whether or not the employees have completed training and then by last name.
   b. Save the file.

6. **Print a list.**
   a. Add a header that reads **Employee Information** in the center; format the header in bold.
   b. Set the print area to include the range A1:F8.
   c. Save the workbook, print the print area, then close the workbook.
   d. Exit Excel.

► Independent Challenge 1

You own Personalize IT, an advertising firm located in Australia. The firm sells specialty items imprinted with the customer's name and/or logo such as hats, pens, mugs, and T-shirts. Plan and build a list of order information with a minimum of 10 records using the items sold. Your list should contain at least five different customers. (Some customers may place more than one order.) Each record should contain the following fields:

Customer last: Customer last name
Customer first: Customer first name
Item: Item description
Quantity: The number of items purchased
Cost: The item's price

a. Prepare a list plan that states your goal, outlines the data you'll need, and identifies the list elements.
b. Sketch a sample list on a piece of paper, indicating how the list should be built. Which of the data fields will be formatted as labels? As values?
c. Start Excel, create a new workbook, then save it as **Personalize IT** in the drive and folder where your Project Files are stored. Build the list by first entering **Personalize IT** as the worksheet title in cell A1, then enter the following field names in the designated cells:

Cell	Field name
A2	**Customer last**
B2	**Customer first**
C2	**Item**
D2	**Quantity**
E2	**Cost**

d. Enter 8 data records using your own data.

e. Add a new record to your list using the data form.

f. Enter **Subtotal** in cell F2, **Total** in cell G2, **Tax** in cell H2, and **.1** in cell I2 (the 10% sales tax).

g. Enter formulas to calculate the subtotal (Quantity*Cost) in cell F3 and the total (including tax) in cell G3. Copy the formulas down the columns.

h. Format the Cost, Subtotal, and Total columns as currency. Adjust the column widths as necessary.

i. Sort the list in ascending order by Item, then by Customer last.

j. Enter your name in the worksheet footer, then save the workbook.

k. Preview the worksheet, print the worksheet on one page, close the workbook, then exit Excel.

► Independent Challenge 2

You are taking a class titled Television Shows: Past and Present at a local community college. The instructor has provided you with an Excel list of television programs from the '60s and '70s. She has included fields tracking the following information: the number of years the show was a favorite, favorite character, the show's length in minutes, least favorite character, and comments about the show. The instructor has included data for each show in the list. She has asked you to add a field (column label) and one record (show of your choosing) to the list. Because the list should cover only 30-minute shows, you need to delete any records for shows longer than 30 minutes. Also, your instructor wants you to sort the list by television show and format the list as needed prior to printing. Feel free to change any of the list data to suit your tastes and opinions.

FIGURE H-19

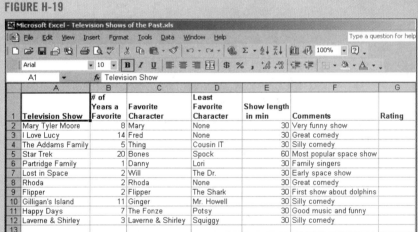

a. Start Excel, open the Project File EX H-2 from the drive and folder where your Project Files are stored, then save it as **Television Shows of the Past**.

b. Add a field called **Rating** in column G. Your worksheet should look like Figure H-19. Complete the Rating field for each record with a value of 1–5 that reflects the rating you would give the television show.

c. Use the data form to add one record to the list. Make sure to enter information in every field.

d. Delete any records having show lengths other than 30. (*Hint*: Use the comparison operator <> in the Show length field to find records not equal to 30.)

e. Make any formatting changes to the list as needed and save the list.

f. Sort the list in ascending order by show name.

g. Enter your name in the worksheet footer, save the workbook, then print the nonadjacent columns Television Show and Rating.

h. Sort the list again, this time in descending order by number of years the show was a favorite.

i. Add a centered header that reads **Television Shows of the Past: '60s and '70s.**

j. Save the workbook, then preview the list and print it on a single page modifying its orientation if necessary.

k. Close the workbook and exit Excel.

▶ Independent Challenge 3

You are the assistant manager at Nite Owl Video in Brisbane, Australia. You have assembled an Excel list of the most popular Australian films your store rents, along with information about the Australian Film Institute (AFI) award they won, the release dates, and the film genres. Your customers have suggested that you prepare an in-store handout listing the films with the information sorted in different ways.

a. Start Excel, open the Project File EX H-3 from the drive and folder where your Project Files are stored, then save it as **Best Films.**

b. Format the list using Figure H-20 as a guide.

c. Sort the list in ascending order by Genre. Sort the list again in ascending order by Film Name.

d. Sort the list again using two fields, this time in descending order by the Genre, then in ascending order by Release Year.

FIGURE H-20

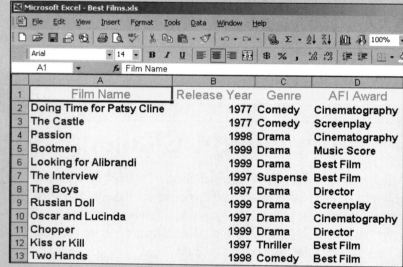

e. Enter your name in the worksheet footer, save your work, then print the worksheet.

f. Use the data form to add a record to the list with the following information: Film name: In a Savage Land; Release year: 1998; Genre: Drama; AFI Award: Sound.

g. Use the data form to find and delete the record for the film "Passion."

h. Activate AutoFilter, use it to display only dramas, then print the list.

i. Redisplay all films, then set a print area that includes the range A1:C13.

j. Clear the print area and print the worksheet.

k. Close the workbook and exit Excel.

Independent Challenge 4

The Local newspaper you work for has decided to start publishing the top selling MP3 titles. They would like to list the best-selling titles in the genres of Pop and Rock, Jazz, and Latin music. You have been asked to research the best-selling MP3 music along with price information. You will create a workbook to hold the information about the top three titles for each genre. You will add an AutoFilter to the Genre field to make it easier to view titles by the type of music.

a. Go to the AltaVista search engine at www.altavista.com and enter " MP3" in the Search box, then click the direct link to the MP3 site. You can also use Yahoo!, Excite, Infoseek, or another search engine of your choice. (If you prefer, you can enter the URL www.mp3.com directly in your browser.)

b. Complete the table below with the MP3 title information you found in your search.

Title	Artist	Genre	Price

c. Start Excel, open a new workbook enter your name in the worksheet footer, then save the workbook as **MP3 Titles**.

d. Use your table to enter the top three titles for the three music categories along with the Artist and price information into your Excel worksheet. Save the workbook.

e. Add an AutoFilter to the Genre column then use the filter to display only the Jazz records. (*Hint*: To apply a filter to only one column, select the column before applying the AutoFilter.)

f. Print only the records for the Jazz genre, then use the AutoFilter to display all the records.

g. Save the workbook again, set a print area to print only the Title and Artist columns, then print the print area.

h. Clear the print area, save the worksheet, close the workbook, then exit Excel.

Excel 2002

► Visual Workshop

Create the worksheet shown in Figure H-21. Save the workbook as **Famous Jazz Performers** in the drive and folder where your Project Files are stored. Once you've entered the field names and records, sort the list using two fields. The first sort should be in ascending order by Contribution to Jazz, and the second sort should be in ascending order by Last Name. Change the page setup so that the list is centered on the page horizontally and the header reads "Famous Jazz Performers". Enter your name in the worksheet footer. Preview and print the list, then save the workbook.

FIGURE H-21

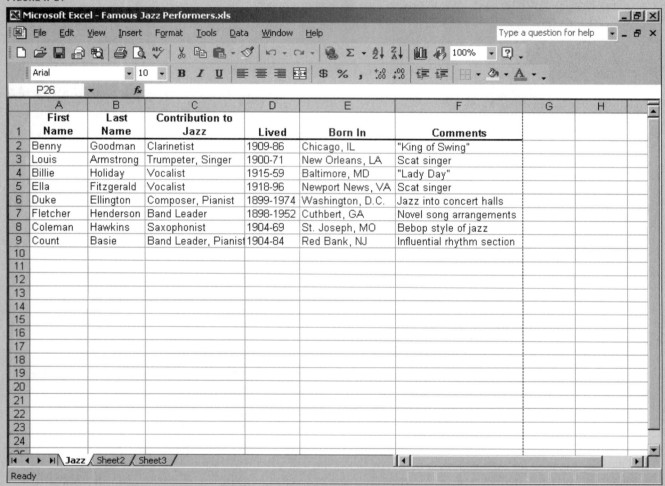

Integrating

Word and Excel

Objectives

► **Link an Excel chart to a Word document**
► **Embed an Excel worksheet in a Word document**
► **Insert a hyperlink to an Excel file in a Word document**

Sometimes the information you want to include in a Word document is stored in a file that was created in Excel. One way to include Excel data in a Word document is to insert the information into the document as a linked or embedded object. An **object** is an item that can be manipulated and shared among programs, for example, graphics, spreadsheets, charts, or sound and video clips. You can also create a hyperlink from the Word document to the Excel file. Alice Wegman, marketing manager at MediaLoft, is preparing a brief report on MediaLoft San Francisco's quarterly advertising expenditures. She created the report using Word, and she wants to enhance it by adding a worksheet and a chart that she created in Excel. She also wants to insert a hyperlink in the Word document to link it to an Excel file that details all quarterly advertising activity.

Linking an Excel chart to a Word document

When you insert an Excel object in a Word document, you have the option to create a linked object. A **link** is a connection between the source and destination files; changes you make to the source file are automatically updated in the linked object in the destination file. You can link objects using the Object command on the Insert menu or the Paste Special command on the Edit menu. ◢◣ Alice uses the Paste Special command to insert an Excel chart into her marketing report as a linked object.

Steps

1. Start Word, open the file **INT E-1.doc** from the drive and location where your Project Files are located, save it as **Advertising Report**, then click the **Show/Hide ¶ button** ¶ on the Standard toolbar to display formatting marks, if necessary
   The report opens in Print Layout view.

2. Start Excel, open the file **INT E-2.xls** from the drive and location where your Project Files are located, then save it as **Q3 Ad Costs**
   The Excel file contains the chart you want to insert in the advertising report.

QuickTip

You cannot use the Paste Special command to paste items from the Office Clipboard.

3. Select the **chart**, then click the **Copy button** 📋 on the Standard toolbar
   The chart is copied to the Clipboard.

4. Click the **Word program button** on the taskbar, scroll down until the Advertising Expenditures heading is at the top of your screen, then place the insertion point in the **second blank paragraph** under the Advertising Expenditures heading

5. Click **Edit** on the menu bar, then click **Paste Special**
   The Paste Special dialog box opens, as shown in Figure E-1. You use this dialog box to choose between embedding and linking an object, and to select the format you want the pasted object to have.

QuickTip

To create an embedded object in the destination file, select the Paste option button in the Paste Special dialog box instead of the Paste link option button.

6. Click the **Paste link option button** to select it, make sure **Microsoft Excel Chart Object** is selected in the As list box, then click **OK**
   The Excel data is inserted in the document as a linked Microsoft Excel chart object, as shown in Figure E-2.

7. Double-click the **chart object**
   The **Q3 Ad Costs** file opens in the Excel program window. You need to update the worksheet.

8. Click cell **B4**, type **45770**, then press **[Enter]**, watching the Print (purple) segment of the pie chart as you do
   The chart is adjusted to reflect the change to the data.

Trouble?

If the chart object is not updated, right-click it, then click Update Link on the shortcut menu.

9. Save your changes to the Excel file, then exit Excel
   Excel closes and you return to the Word program window. The change you made to the chart in the Excel source file is reflected in the linked chart in the Word document.

10. With the chart object still selected, click the **Center button** 📄 on the Standard toolbar, click outside the object to deselect it, then save your changes
    When an object is selected, you can format it using Word commands. The centered object appears as shown in Figure E-3.

FIGURE E-1: Paste Special dialog box

Select to embed the data from the Clipboard

Select to create a link to the source file

List of format options for inserting the data stored on the Clipboard

Describes result of selected settings

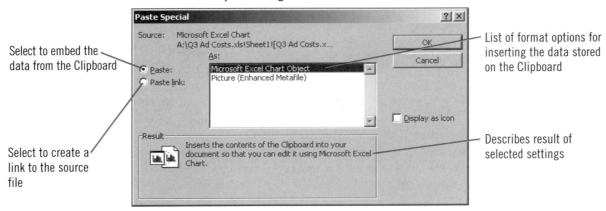

FIGURE E-2: Linked Excel object

Linked Excel chart object

Click the Paste Options button to change the paste format of the pasted object

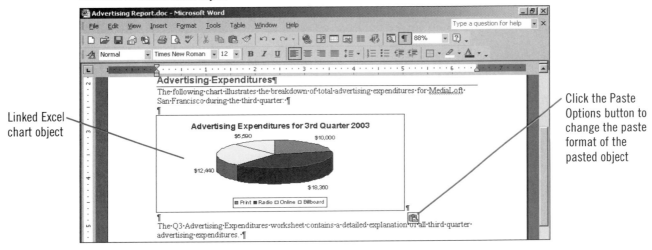

FIGURE E-3: Revised chart in document

Chart object is centered

Change to the data in Excel is reflected in the linked object in Word

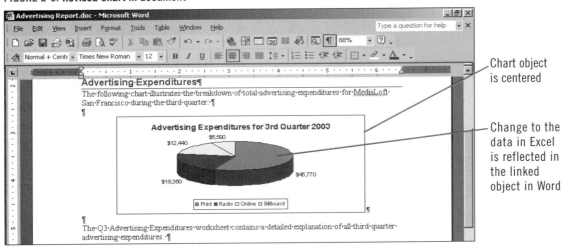

Integration

Embedding an Excel worksheet into a Word document

If you do not need to maintain a link between the source and target file, you can embed an object. When you **embed** an object, the object is stored only in the destination file. You can edit the embedded object by double-clicking it to open the source program without ever leaving the destination file. Any change you make to an embedded object is saved only within the destination file. As with linking, you can embed an Excel object in Word by using the Object command on the Insert menu or the Paste Special command on the Edit menu. ✐ Alice uses the Object command to embed an Excel worksheet detailing MediaLoft San Francisco's print advertising expenses into her report.

Steps 1234

QuickTip
Click the Insert Microsoft Excel Worksheet button 📊 on the Standard toolbar to embed a blank worksheet in a document.

1. Scroll until the Print Advertising heading is near the top of your screen, then place the insertion point in the **second blank paragraph** under the Print Advertising heading
You want to embed the Excel object at the location of the insertion point.

2. Click **Insert** on the menu bar, click **Object**, then click the **Create from File tab**, if necessary
The Object dialog box opens, similar to Figure E-4. You can use the Create New tab in this dialog box to create a new object in your Word document using another program, or you can use the Create from File tab to insert an object from an existing file.

3. Click **Browse**
The Browse dialog box opens.

QuickTip
To create a linked object in the destination file, select the Link to file check box.

4. Navigate to the drive and location where your Project Files are located, select the Excel file **Int E-3.xls**, then click **Insert**
The Excel file Int E-3.xls contains the worksheet you want to embed in the advertising report. Compare your screen to Figure E-4.

5. Click **OK**
The Excel data is inserted in the document as an embedded Microsoft Excel worksheet object. You want to change the formatting of the embedded object to better match the memo formatting.

6. Double-click the **worksheet object**
The worksheet opens in an Excel object window, and the menus and toolbars change to Excel menus and toolbars, as shown in Figure E-5.

7. Select the range **A2:F11**, click **Format** on the menu bar, click **AutoFormat**, select the **Classic 2 style** in the AutoFormat dialog box, click **Options** in the dialog box, clear the **Font** and **Alignment check boxes** in the Formats to apply area, then click **OK**
The Classic 2 AutoFormat is applied to the embedded worksheet.

8. Click outside the object to close the Excel object window
When you close the object window, the menus and toolbars return to Word menus toolbars.

9. Click the **object** once to select it, click the **Center button** 🖺 on the Formatting toolbar, deselect the object, then save your changes
The centered object appears as shown in Figure E-6. The changes you made to the embedded Excel worksheet object are not made to the source file in Excel.

FIGURE E-4: Object dialog box

Use this tab to create a new object

File to be inserted

Describes the result of the selected settings

Click to select the file to insert

Select to create a link to the source file

Select to insert an icon that represents the contents of the source file

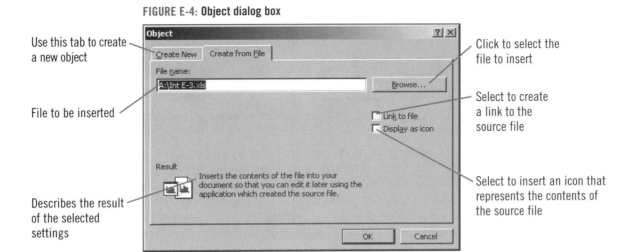

FIGURE E-5: Embedded Excel object

Title bar indicates Word is the active program

Menus and toolbars change to Excel menus and toolbars

Worksheet in Excel object window

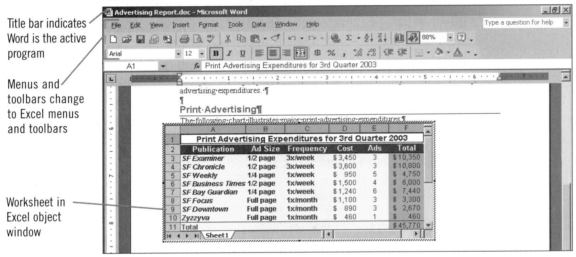

FIGURE E-6: Formatted object in document

Menus and toolbars return to Word menus and toolbars

Object is centered

Formatting changes are saved in Word only

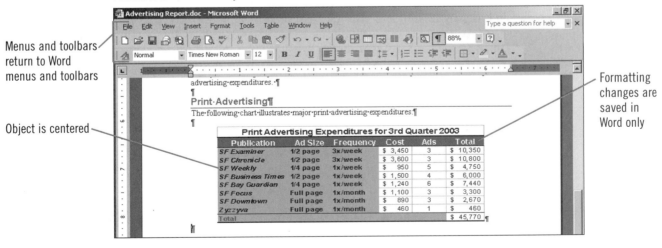

Integration

Inserting a hyperlink to an Excel file in a Word document

Another way to include information stored in a different file in a Word document is to insert a hyperlink to the file into the document. A **hyperlink** is text or an object that when clicked opens (or jumps to) another location in the current document, another file, or a Web page. Hyperlinks can also link to an e-mail address. When you create a hyperlink, you specify where you want to jump when the hyperlink is clicked. ⟍⟍⟍ Alice wants to include the third quarter advertising expenditures in her report. She realizes that not everyone who reads her report will be interested in this level of detail, so instead of inserting this information directly into the report, she creates a hyperlink to an Excel file that contains the detailed information. Anyone who is interested can click the hyperlink to open the worksheet and review the data.

1. Scroll until the Advertising Expenditures heading is at the top of your screen, then select **Q3 Advertising Expenditures worksheet** in the sentence under the chart object
This text will be the hyperlink to the Q3 Advertising Expenditures worksheet file.

QuickTip

Click 🔗 on the Excel Standard toolbar to insert a hyperlink in a worksheet.

2. Click the **Insert Hyperlink button** 🔗 on the Standard toolbar
The Insert Hyperlink dialog box opens, similar to Figure E-7. You use this dialog box to specify the location you want to jump to when the hyperlink is clicked.

3. Click **Existing File or Web Page** in the Link to area if necessary, use the **Look in list arrow** to navigate to the drive and location where your Project Files are stored, select the file **Q3 Advertising Expenditures.xls**, then click **OK**
The Insert Hyperlink dialog box closes, and the text in the document is formatted as a hyperlink—colored blue and underlined.

QuickTip

To edit, select, open, copy, or remove a hyperlink, right-click the hyperlink, then click the appropriate command on the shortcut menu.

4. Position the pointer over the hyperlink
When you point to the hyperlink, a ScreenTip showing the path and filename of the linked file appears.

5. Press and hold **[Ctrl]**
When you press [Ctrl] while pointing to a link, the pointer changes to 👆.

QuickTip

If you link to another file, the person clicking the link must have access to both files.

6. Click the **hyperlink** with the 👆 pointer
The Q3 Advertising Expenditures worksheet opens in the Excel program window. The Web toolbar opens below the Standard and Formatting toolbars. You can use the buttons on the Web toolbar to navigate between hyperlinked files and Web pages.

7. Click the **Back button** ⇐ on the Web toolbar
The Advertising Report document appears in the Word document window. Notice that the hyperlink color has changed to purple, indicating that the hyperlink has been followed.

8. Press **[Ctrl][End]**, press **[Enter]**, click the **Align Right button** ▤ on the Formatting toolbar, type **Prepared** by, then type your name
The completed report is shown in Figure E-8.

9. Save your changes to the Word document, print a copy, close the file, exit Word, then exit Excel

FIGURE E-7: Insert Hyperlink dialog box

Current drive or folder (yours might differ)

Your list of files might be different

Text selected in the document to be formatted as a hyperlink

Filename or Web address of hyperlinked file or Web page will appear here

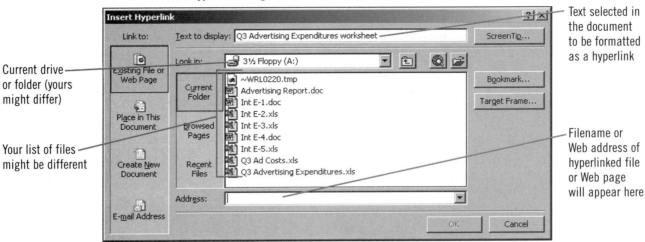

FIGURE E-8: Competed report

Linked chart object

Hyperlink

Embedded worksheet object

Your name will appear here

MediaLoft San Francisco Advertising Report
Third Quarter 2003

Summary

This report details the regional advertising activities of the MediaLoft San Francisco store during the third quarter of 2003. MediaLoft San Francisco engaged in print, online, radio, and billboard advertising during this quarter, with the majority of expenditures devoted to print advertising.

Advertising Expenditures

The following chart illustrates the breakdown of total advertising expenditures for MediaLoft San Francisco during the third quarter:

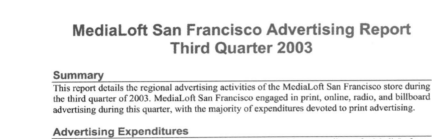

Advertising Expenditures for 3rd Quarter 2003

$5,590
$12,440
$45,770
$18,360

■ Print ■ Radio □ Online □ Billboard

The Q3 Advertising Expenditures worksheet contains a detailed explanation of all third quarter advertising expenditures.

Print Advertising

The following chart illustrates major print advertising expenditures:

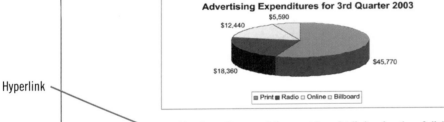

Print Advertising Expenditures for 3rd Quarter 2003					
Publication	Ad Size	Frequency	Cost	Ads	Total
SF Examiner	1/2 page	3x/week	$ 3,450	3	$ 10,350
SF Chronicle	1/2 page	3x/week	$ 3,600	3	$ 10,800
SF Weekly	1/4 page	1x/week	$ 950	5	$ 4,750
SF Business Times	1/2 page	1x/week	$ 1,500	4	$ 6,000
SF Bay Guardian	1/4 page	1x/week	$ 1,240	6	$ 7,440
SF Focus	Full page	1x/month	$ 1,100	3	$ 3,300
SF Downtown	Full page	1x/month	$ 890	3	$ 2,670
Zyzzyva	Full page	1x/month	$ 460	1	$ 460
Total					$ 45,770

Prepared by Your Name

Independent Challenge 1

As secretary of the Budget Committee for the town of Lysander, it's your job to send the first draft of the budget to the town council. You have prepared a worksheet that summarizes the draft budget for 2004. You'll use the data to create several charts that illustrate the draft budget, and then insert the charts in a memo to the town council.

  a. Start Word, open the file INT E-4.doc from the drive and location where your Project Files are stored, then save it as **Lysander Budget Memo**. Enter your name in the memo header, then read the memo to get a feel for its content.

  b. Start Excel, open the file INT E-5.xls from the drive and location where your Project Files are stored. Enter your name in cell A20, then save it as **Lysander Budget**.

  c. Using the data in the worksheet, create a column chart that compares the budgeted expenditures for 2003 with the actual expenditures. Create the chart on a new chart sheet named **2003**.

  d. Create a pie chart showing the distribution of the 2004 budget among departments. Create the chart on a new chart sheet named **2004**. Format the chart so it is useful, attractive, and readable.

  e. Save your changes to the workbook, then switch to the memo in Word.

  f. Embed the column chart in the memo. Use Excel's formatting features to modify the format of the chart so it is useful, attractive, and readable.

  g. Insert the pie chart in the memo and establish a link to the source file.

  h. Select the text **Lysander Budget.xls** in the second paragraph, and create a hyperlink to the Excel file Lysander Budget.xls (located in the drive and folder where your Project Files are stored.). Test the hyperlink.

  i. In the Excel file Lysander Budget, change the budgeted value for the Water Department to 700,000. Switch back to the Word document and verify that the charts changed to reflect the new data (update the links, if necessary).

  j. Save your changes to the workbook, then close the file and exit Excel.

  k. In the memo, make any necessary formatting changes to the memo.

  l. Save your changes to the memo, print a copy, close the file, then exit Word.

 Independent Challenge 2

Your boss has given you a $10,000 budget to buy computer equipment for your department. Before releasing the funds, she would like you to research and prepare a proposal on how you intend to best spend the money. You decide to research computer equipment online.

  a. Determine the type of equipment your department most needs (i.e., computers, printers, scanners, monitors, etc.).

  b. Use your favorite search engine to search the Web for computer price information. Use the keywords **computer equipment**. If your search does not result in links to information on buying computers, try looking at the following Web sites: www.dell.com, www.hp.com, and www.gateway.com.

  c. Start Excel, open a new workbook, then save it as **Computer Budget** to the drive and location where your Project Files are stored.

  d. Create a worksheet that compares prices for similar equipment from at least two different companies. Spend as close to $10,000 as possible. Save your changes.

  e. Start Word, open a new document, then save it as **Computer Memo** to the location where your Project Files are stored.

  f. Type a memo to your boss explaining your recommendations for purchasing computer equipment. Include your name in the memo header.

  g. Embed the worksheet you created in your memo. Format the worksheet so it is attractive and readable.

  h. Insert hyperlinks to the Web pages you consulted into your memo. (*Hint*: Type the URL for the Web page in the document, then press [Spacebar]. Right-click the link, then click Edit Hyperlink to see that the URL appears in the Text to display and Address text boxes in the Insert Hyperlink dialog box.)

  i. Save your changes to the memo, print a copy, close the document, exit Word, then close the workbook and exit Excel.

Modifying
a Database Structure

Objectives

- ▶ **Examine relational databases**
- ▶ **Plan related tables and lookups**
- ▶ **Create related tables**
- ▶ **Define Text fields**
- ▶ **Define Number and Currency fields**
- ▶ **Define Date/Time and Yes/No fields**
- ▶ **Define field validation properties**
- ▶ **Create one-to-many relationships**
- ▶ **Create lookups**

In this unit, you will add new tables to an existing database and link them in one-to-many relationships to create a relational database. You will also modify several field properties to format and validate data. Fred Ames, the new coordinator of training at MediaLoft, has created an Access database to track the courses attended by MediaLoft employees. Courses include hands-on computer classes, business seminars, and self-improvement workshops. The database consists of multiple tables. Fred will link them together to create a relational database.

Examining Relational Databases

Access 2002

A **relational database** is a collection of related tables that share information. The purpose of a relational database is to satisfy dynamic information management needs and to eliminate duplicate data entry wherever possible. ✒ MediaLoft employees have tried to track course attendance using a single Access table called Attendance Log, as shown in Figure E-1. Fred sees a data redundancy problem because there are multiple occurrences of the same employee and same course information. He knows that redundant data in one table is a major clue that the database needs to be redesigned. Therefore, Fred studies the principles of relational database design.

Details

▶ **A relational database is based on multiple tables of data, and each table should be based on only one subject**

Right now the Attendance Log table in the Training database contains three subjects: courses, attendance, and employees. Therefore, you have to duplicate several fields of information such as the employee's name every time an employee attends a course. Redundant data in one table causes extra data entry work, a higher rate of data inconsistencies and errors, and larger physical storage requirements. Moreover, it limits the user's ability to search for, analyze, and report on the data. These problems can be minimized or eliminated by implementing a properly designed relational database.

▶ **Each record in a table should be uniquely identified with a primary key field or key field combination**

A **primary key field** is a field that contains unique information for each record. An Employee Identification or Social Security Number field often serves this purpose in an Employees table. Although using the employee's last name as the primary key field might accommodate a small database, it is a poor choice because it does not accommodate the situation in which two employees have the same last name. The primary key field is also often called the **key field**.

▶ **Tables in the same database should be related, or linked, through a common field in a one-to-many relationship**

To tie the information from one table to another, a field must be common to each table. This common field will be the primary key field in one of the tables, creating the "one" side of the relationship and the **foreign key field** in the other table creating the "many" side of the relationship. The primary key field contains a unique entry for each record, but the foreign key field contains the same value "many" times to create a **one-to-many relationship** between the tables. Table E-1 shows common examples of one-to-many relationships between two database tables.

TABLE E-1: One-to-many relationships

table on "one" side of relationship	table on "many" side of relationship	linking field	description
Products	Sales	ProductID	A ProductID field must have a unique entry in a Products table, but will be listed many times in a Sales table as multiple copies of that item are sold
Customers	Sales	CustomerID	A CustomerID field must have a unique entry in a Customers table, but will be listed many times in a Sales table as multiple sales are recorded for the same customer
Employees	Promotions	EmployeeID	An EmployeeID field must have a unique entry in an Employees table, but will be listed many times in a Promotions table as the employee is promoted over time

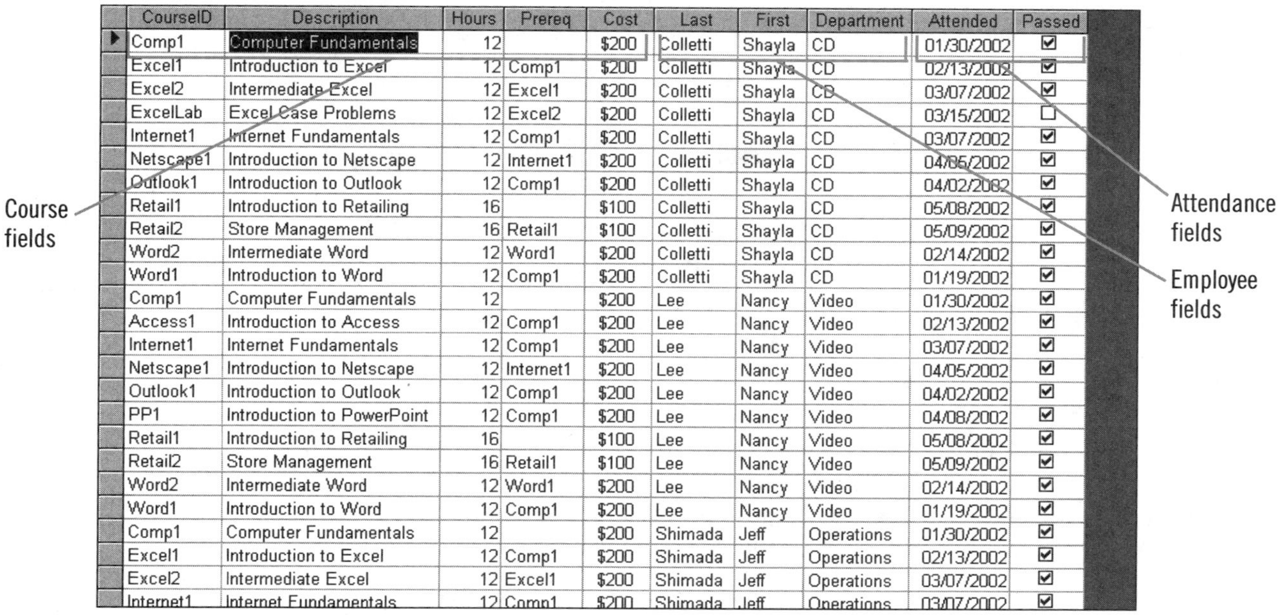

CourseID	Description	Hours	Prereq	Cost	Last	First	Department	Attended	Passed
Comp1	Computer Fundamentals	12		$200	Colletti	Shayla	CD	01/30/2002	☑
Excel1	Introduction to Excel	12	Comp1	$200	Colletti	Shayla	CD	02/13/2002	☑
Excel2	Intermediate Excel	12	Excel1	$200	Colletti	Shayla	CD	03/07/2002	☑
ExcelLab	Excel Case Problems	12	Excel2	$200	Colletti	Shayla	CD	03/15/2002	☐
Internet1	Internet Fundamentals	12	Comp1	$200	Colletti	Shayla	CD	03/07/2002	☑
Netscape1	Introduction to Netscape	12	Internet1	$200	Colletti	Shayla	CD	04/05/2002	☑
Outlook1	Introduction to Outlook	12	Comp1	$200	Colletti	Shayla	CD	04/02/2002	☑
Retail1	Introduction to Retailing	16		$100	Colletti	Shayla	CD	05/08/2002	☑
Retail2	Store Management	16	Retail1	$100	Colletti	Shayla	CD	05/09/2002	☑
Word2	Intermediate Word	12	Word1	$200	Colletti	Shayla	CD	02/14/2002	☑
Word1	Introduction to Word	12	Comp1	$200	Colletti	Shayla	CD	01/19/2002	☑
Comp1	Computer Fundamentals	12		$200	Lee	Nancy	Video	01/30/2002	☑
Access1	Introduction to Access	12	Comp1	$200	Lee	Nancy	Video	02/13/2002	☑
Internet1	Internet Fundamentals	12	Comp1	$200	Lee	Nancy	Video	03/07/2002	☑
Netscape1	Introduction to Netscape	12	Internet1	$200	Lee	Nancy	Video	04/05/2002	☑
Outlook1	Introduction to Outlook	12	Comp1	$200	Lee	Nancy	Video	04/02/2002	☑
PP1	Introduction to PowerPoint	12	Comp1	$200	Lee	Nancy	Video	04/08/2002	☑
Retail1	Introduction to Retailing	16		$100	Lee	Nancy	Video	05/08/2002	☑
Retail2	Store Management	16	Retail1	$100	Lee	Nancy	Video	05/09/2002	☑
Word2	Intermediate Word	12	Word1	$200	Lee	Nancy	Video	02/14/2002	☑
Word1	Introduction to Word	12	Comp1	$200	Lee	Nancy	Video	01/19/2002	☑
Comp1	Computer Fundamentals	12		$200	Shimada	Jeff	Operations	01/30/2002	☑
Excel1	Introduction to Excel	12	Comp1	$200	Shimada	Jeff	Operations	02/13/2002	☑
Excel2	Intermediate Excel	12	Excel1	$200	Shimada	Jeff	Operations	03/07/2002	☑
Internet1	Internet Fundamentals	12	Comp1	$200	Shimada	Jeff	Operations	03/07/2002	☑

Course fields

Attendance fields

Employee fields

Many-to-many relationships

As you are designing your database, you may find that two tables have a many-to-many relationship. To join them, you must establish a third table called a junction table, which creates separate one-to-many relationships with the two original tables. For example, the Customers and Products tables usually have a many-to-many relationship. One customer can purchase many products and one product can be sold to many customers. To implement a connection between the Customers and Products tables in an Access database, you would build a junction table between them, perhaps called the Sales table. Using the Sales table, you would establish one-to-many relationships with the original two tables. Figure E-2 shows how the Sales table would connect the original Customers and Products tables.

FIGURE E-2: Using a junction table

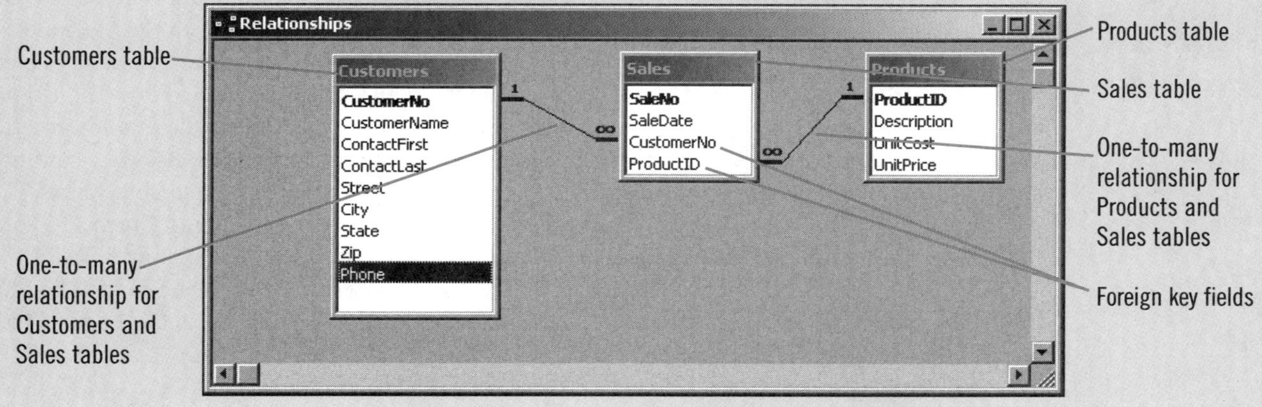

Customers table

Products table

Sales table

One-to-many relationship for Products and Sales tables

Foreign key fields

One-to-many relationship for Customers and Sales tables

Relationships

Customers
- **CustomerNo**
- CustomerName
- ContactFirst
- ContactLast
- Street
- City
- State
- Zip
- Phone

Sales
- **SaleNo**
- SaleDate
- CustomerNo
- ProductID

Products
- **ProductID**
- Description
- UnitCost
- UnitPrice

Planning Related Tables and Lookups

Careful planning is crucial to successful relational database design. When a database is not planned carefully before it is created, several common database problems occur. These problems range from simple issues such as confusing field names, to complex issues such as improper table structures that limit the flexibility and reliability of information in the database. The most common symptom of an inappropriately designed database is the existence of excessively duplicated data, such as the same customer's name entered in multiple records in the Customers table. Duplicated data is not only prone to error and inefficient to enter, but also limits the query and reporting capabilities of the overall database. A well-designed database minimizes redundant data. 🖉 After studying the concepts of relational database design, Fred is ready to redesign MediaLoft's Training database. He follows these steps to move from a single table of data to the powerful relational database capabilities provided by Access.

▶ **List all of the fields of data that need to be tracked**

Typically, these fields are already present in existing tables or paper reports. Still, it is a good idea to document each field in order to examine all fields at the same time.

▶ **Group fields together in subject matter tables**

The new MediaLoft training database will track courses attended by employees. It will contain three core tables: Courses, Employees, and Attendance. It will also contain one lookup table: Departments.

▶ **Identify primary key fields that exist in tables**

Each table should include a key field or key field combination in order to uniquely identify each record. Fred will create a SSN field in the Employees table, a CourseID field in the Courses table, and an automatically incrementing (AutoNumber data type) LogID field in the Attendance table to handle this requirement. DeptNo is the primary key field for the Departments table.

▶ **Link the tables with a one-to-many relationship via a common field**

By adding an SSN field to the Attendance table, Fred creates a common field in both the Employees and Attendance tables that can serve as the link between them. Similarly, by adding a CourseID field to the Attendance table, Fred creates a common field in both the Attendance and Courses tables that can serve as the link. For a valid one-to-many relationship, the linking field must be designated as the primary key field in the "one" side of the one-to-many relationship.

▶ **Create lookups**

Lookups are reference tables or lists that are used to populate the values of a field. Lookups are established by adding Lookup properties to the field for which you want the lookup behavior to occur. Foreign key fields are good lookup candidates because the data that they contain would often be easier to understand if accompanied by descriptive text. For example, in the MediaLoft-E database the Employees table contains the foreign key field DeptNo that stores numeric department codes. Fred decides to apply Lookup properties to the DeptNo field to look up and display the descriptive DeptName values from the Departments table rather than the less informative departmental numeric code which is physically stored in the DeptNo field. Another common application for Lookup properties exists when a field has a limited set of possible values. The ParkingLot field in the Employees table has only three valid entries: Red, Blue, and Green. Fred uses the Lookup properties of the ParkingLot field to create a value list to store these choices. Fields that contain Lookup properties are called **lookup fields**. Table E-2 summarizes the fields with Lookup properties for the MediaLoft database. The final relationships, fields, and tables for Fred's redesigned relational database are shown in Figure E-3.

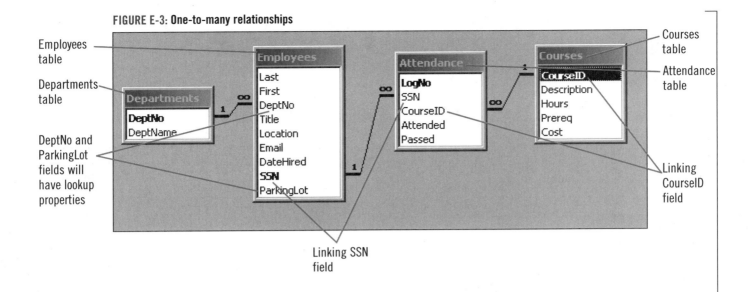

FIGURE E-3: One-to-many relationships

Employees table

Departments table

DeptNo and ParkingLot fields will have lookup properties

Linking SSN field

Courses table

Attendance table

Linking CourseID field

TABLE E-2: Lookup fields

lookup field	table that contains the lookup field	values displayed by the lookup field	where values displayed by the lookup field are stored
DeptNo	Employees	Accounting, Human Resources, Information Systems, Marketing, Operations, Shipping, Training, Book, Café, CD, Video	In the DeptName field of the Departments table
ParkingLot	Employees	Red, Green, Blue	In the Row Source lookup property of the ParkingLot field

Identifying key field combinations

Identifying a single primary key field may be difficult in some tables. Consider, for instance, a table that records employee promotions over time and contains the three fields of EmployeeNumber, Date, and PayRate. None of the fields could individually serve as a valid key field because none are restricted to unique data. The values in the EmployeeNumber and Date fields considered together, however, could serve as a valid key field combination because an employee can only be promoted once on any given date.

Access 2002

Creating Related Tables

Once you have developed a valid relational database design on paper, you are ready to define the tables in Access. All characteristics of a table including field names, data types, field descriptions, field properties, lookup properties, and primary key field designations are defined in **Table Design View.** Using the new database design, Fred creates the Attendance table.

Steps

1. **Start Access, then open the Training-E database from the drive and folder where your Project Files are located**
   The Courses, Employees, and Departments tables already exist in the database.

2. **Click Tables on the Objects Bar (if it is not already selected), then click the New Table button in the Training-E database window**
   The New Table dialog box opens. You define fields for a new table in Table Design View.

3. **Click Design View in the New Table dialog box, then click OK**
   Field names should be as short as possible, but long enough to be descriptive. The field name entered in Table Design View is used as the default name for the field in all later queries, forms, reports, and Web pages.

QuickTip

When specifying field data types, you can type the first letter of the data type; for example, type a for AutoNumber, d for Date/Time, or c for Currency.

4. **Type LogNo, press [Enter], click the Data Type list arrow, click AutoNumber, then press [Enter] twice to move to the next row**
   The LogNo field will contain a unique number used to identify each record in the Attendance table (each occurrence of an employee taking a course). The AutoNumber data type, which automatically sequences each new record with the next available integer, works well for this field.

5. **Type the other field names, data types, and descriptions as shown in Figure E-4**
   Field descriptions entered in Table Design View are optional. In Table Datasheet View, the description entry appears in the status bar, and therefore provides further clarification about the data. The descriptions for SSN and CourseID fields are used to clarify the role of these foreign key fields. You are not required to use the same field name for the primary and foreign key fields, but doing so makes it easier to understand the one-to-many relationship.

6. **Click LogNo in the Field Name column, then click the Primary Key button on the Table Design toolbar**
   A **key symbol** appears to the left of LogNo to indicate that this field is defined as the primary key field for this table.

7. **Click the Save button on the Table Design toolbar, type Attendance in the Table Name text box, click OK, then close the table**
   The Attendance table is now displayed as a table object in the Training-E database window.

Primary Key button

LogNo will be the primary key field

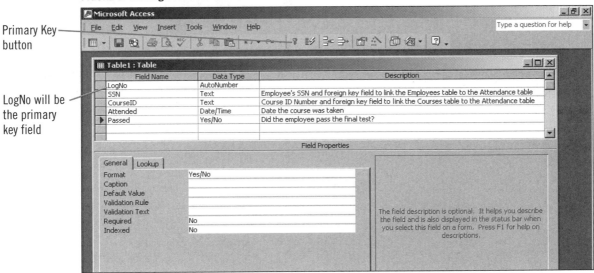

Comparing linked to imported tables

The data in a linked table is stored in a file that is separate from the open database. For example, you may want to create a linked table to connect an Excel workbook to an Access database. Even though the data is physically stored in the Excel workbook, you can still add, delete, and edit records from within Access. Because the data presented by a linked table is stored in an external file, you cannot change the structure (add, modify, or delete fields) of a linked table from within Access. An imported table is a copy of data from an external file. An imported table works exactly the same as a table originally created in Access. There are no restrictions on modifying the data or the structure of a table that was created through an import process.

Access 2002

Defining Text Fields

Field properties are the characteristics that apply to each field in a table, such as Field Size, Default Value, or Caption. These properties help ensure database accuracy and clarity because they can be used to restrict the way data is entered and displayed. Field properties are modified in Table Design View. See Table E-3 for more information on Text field properties. ✏ Fred decides to make field property changes to several Text fields in the Employees table.

Steps 1 2 3 4

1. **If not already selected, click Tables on the Objects bar, right-click the Employees table, then click Design View from the shortcut menu**
   The Employees table opens in Design View. The field properties appear in the lower half of the Table Design View window and display the properties of the selected field. Field properties change depending on the field's data type. For example, when a field with a Text data type is selected, the Field Size property is visible. However, when a field with a Date/Time data type is selected, Access controls the Field Size property, so that property is not displayed. Most field properties are optional, but if they require an entry, Access provides a default value.

2. **Click the SSN field name, look at the field properties, then click each of the field names while viewing the field properties**
   A small black triangle in the **field selector button** to the left of the field indicates which field is currently selected.

3. **Click the Last field name, double-click 50 in the Field Size property text box, then type 30**
   Fifty is the default value for the Field Size property for a Text field, but you do not anticipate last name field values to be greater than 30.

4. **Change the Field Size property to 30 for the following field names: First, Title, Location, and Email**
   Changing the Field Size property to 30 for each of these text fields in this table will accommodate the longest entry for each field. The **Input Mask** property provides a visual guide for users as they enter data. It also helps determine what types of values can be entered into a field.

5. **Click the SSN field name, click the Input Mask property text box, click the Build button [...], click Yes if prompted to save the table, click Yes when alerted that some data may be lost (because you changed the field size of several fields from 50 to 30 in the previous step), click Social Security Number in the Input Mask list, click Next, click Next to accept the default input mask, click Next to accept the option to store the data without the symbols in the mask, then click Finish**
   The Design View of the Employees table should look like Figure E-5. Notice that the SSN field is selected, and the new Input Mask property is entered. The SSN field is also the primary key field for the Employees table as evidenced by the key symbol beside the field name.

6. **Click the Save button [💾] on the Table Design toolbar, click the Datasheet View button [▦] on the Table Design toolbar, maximize the datasheet, press [Tab] enough times to move to the SSN field for the first record, then type 115774444**
   The SSN Input Mask property creates an easy-to-use visual guide to facilitate accurate data entry.

7. **Close the Employees table**

FIGURE E-5: Changing Text field properties

Employees table
SSN field is selected
Input Mask property

Build button
Short description of selected property

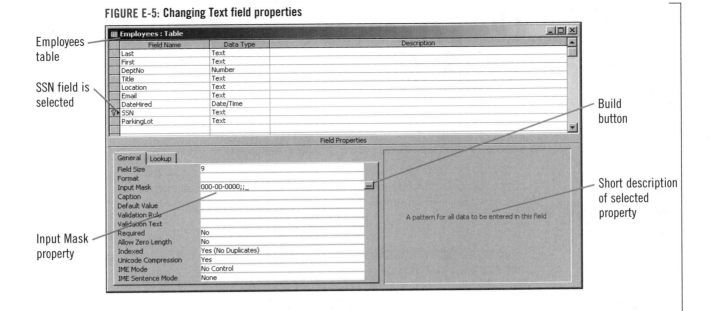

TABLE E-3: Common Text field properties

property	description	sample field name	sample property entry
Field Size	Controls how many characters can be entered into the field.	State	2
Format	Controls how information will be displayed and printed. < forces all characters to display lowercase even though the data is stored in the same way it was entered. > forces all characters to display uppercase even though the data is stored in the same way it was entered.	PartNo State	< >
Input Mask	Provides a pattern for data to be entered and contains three parts separated by semicolons. The first part controls what type of data can be entered and how it will be displayed: **9** represents an optional number; **0** represents a required number; **?** represents an optional letter; **L** represents a required letter. The second part determines whether all displayed characters (such as dashes in the SSN field) are stored in the field, or just the entry; the **0** (zero) entry stores all characters; the **1** (one) entry stores only the entered characters. The third part determines which character Access will display for the space where a character is typed in the input mask. Common entries are the asterisk (*), underscore (_), or pound sign (#).	Phone PartNo SSN ZIP Date	(999") "000-0000;1;_ LOL 0L0;0;* 000-00-0000;1;_ 00000-9999;1;# 99/99/0000;0;_
Caption	A label used to describe the field. When a Caption property isn't entered, the field name is used to label the field.	Emp#	Employee Number
Default Value	Value that is automatically entered in the given field for new records.	City	Kansas City
Required	Determines if an entry is required for this field.	LastName	Yes

Access 2002

Access 2002

Defining Number and Currency Fields

Even though some of the properties for Number and Currency fields are the same as for Text fields, each data type has its own specific list of valid properties. Numeric and Currency fields have very similar properties because they both contain numbers. One important difference, however, is that a Currency field limits the user's control over the field size. A Currency field is accurate to fifteen digits to the left of the decimal point and four digits to the right. The Courses table contains both a Number field (Hours), and a Currency field (Cost). Fred modifies the properties of these two fields.

Steps 1 2 3 4

1. **Click the Courses table, click the Design button** 📝 **in the Training-E database window, then click the Hours field name**
   The Field Size property for a Number field defaults to Long Integer. See Table E-4 for more information on common Number field properties.

2. **Click the Field Size property text box, click the Field Size list arrow, then click Byte**
   Choosing Byte and Integer Field Size property values for a Number field lowers possible values and the storage requirements for that field. The Byte Field Size property value allows entries only from 0 to 255.

3. **Click the Cost field name, click the Decimal Places property text box, click the Decimal Places list arrow, then click 0**
   Your screen should look like Figure E-6. Because all of MediaLoft's courses are priced at a round dollar value, there is no need to display cents in each field entry.

4. **Click the Save button** 💾 **on the Table Design toolbar, click Yes** when prompted that some data may be lost (because you entered a more restrictive Field Size property for the Hours field in a previous step), then click the **Datasheet View button** 🔳 on the Table Design toolbar
   Since none of the entries in the Hours field were greater than 255, the maximum value allowed by a Number field with a Byte Field Size, you won't lose any data. You want to test the new property changes.

5. **Press [Tab] twice to move to the Hours field for the first record, type 1000, then press [Tab]**
   Because 1,000 is larger than the Byte Field Size property will allow, you are cautioned with an Access error message indicating that the value isn't valid for this field.

QuickTip

Pressing [Esc] once removes edits from the current field. Pressing [Esc] twice removes edits from all fields of the current record.

6. **Click OK, press [Esc] to remove the inappropriate entry in the Hours field, then press [Tab] twice to move to the Cost field**
   The Cost field displays zero digits after the decimal point.

7. **Type 199.75 in the Cost field of the first record, press [Enter], then click 200 in the Access1 record's Cost field**
   Even though the Decimal Places property for the Cost field dictates that entries in the field are formatted to display zero digits after the decimal point, 199.75 is the actual value stored in the field. Formatting properties such as Decimal Places do not change the actual data, but only the way it is displayed.

8. **Close the Courses table**

FIGURE E-6: **Changing Currency and Number field properties**

Courses table

Cost field is selected

Decimal Places property

Currency fields have no Field Size property

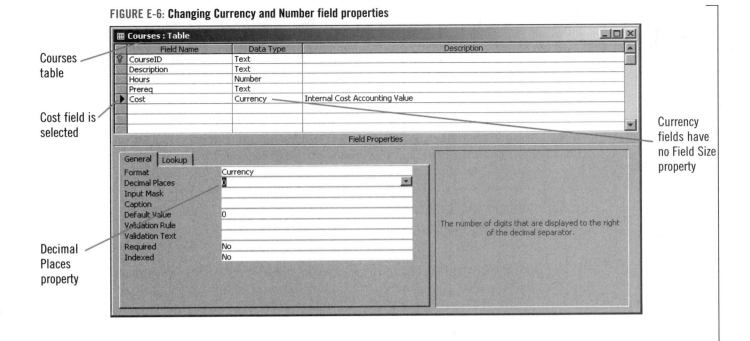

TABLE E-4: **Common Number and Currency field properties**

property	description
Field Size (for a Number field)	Determines the largest number that can be entered in the field, as well as the type of data (e.g., integer or fraction)
	Byte stores numbers from 0 to 255 (no fractions)
	Integer stores numbers from −32,768 to 32,767 (no fractions)
	Long Integer stores numbers from −2,147,483,648 to 2,147,483,647 (no fractions)
	Single stores numbers (including fractions with six digits to the right of the decimal point) times 10 to the −38th to +38th power
	Double stores numbers (including fractions with over 10 digits to the right of the decimal point) in the range of 10 to the −324th to +324th power
Decimal Places	The number of digits displayed to the right of the decimal point

Access 2002

Defining Date/Time and Yes/No Fields

A Date/Time field's **Format** property helps you format dates in many ways such as January 5, 2003; 05-Jan-03; or 1/5/2003. Many of a Date/Time field's other properties such as Input Mask, Caption, and Default Value are very similar to fields with a Text or Number data type. ✏ Fred wants to change the format of Date/Time fields in the database. He also wants to make sure that the Yes/No field is displayed as a check box rather than a text entry of "Yes" or "No."

Steps

1. **Right-click the Attended table, click Design View on the shortcut menu, then click the Attended field name**
   You want the dates of attendance to display as 01/07/2002 instead of as 1/7/2002.

2. **Click the Format text box in the Field Properties, then click the Format list arrow**
   Although several predefined Date/Time formats are available, none matches the format you want. To define a custom format, enter symbols that represent how you want the date to appear.

3. **Type mm/dd/yyyy**
   The updated Format property for the Attended field shown in Figure E-7 forces the date to appear with two digits for the month, two digits for the day, and four digits for the year. The parts of the date will be separated by forward slashes. The **Display Control** property that determines how a Yes/No field appears is on the Lookup tab and you want to examine this property for the Passed field.

4. **Click the Passed field name, then click the Lookup properties tab**
   A Yes/No field may appear as a check box in which checked equals "yes" and unchecked equals "no," as a text box that displays "yes" or "no," or as a combo box that displays "yes" and "no" in the drop-down list. By default, Yes/No fields appear as check boxes. The SSN field in this table would be improved if it contained the same Input Mask property as previously defined for the SSN field in the Employees table.

5. **Click the SSN field, click the General properties tab, click the Input Mask text box, then type 000-00-0000;;_**
   While some properties provide helpful wizards such as the Input Mask Wizard, you can always directly enter a property if you know what it should be.

6. **Click the Save button 🖫 on the Table Design toolbar**
   Access automatically added backslash (\) characters to the Input Mask property when you saved the table. A backslash in the Input Mask property causes the next character to be displayed as a literal character. Access provides default entries for many properties as well as syntax support throughout the program. **Syntax** refers to the technical rules that govern a language or program.

7. **Click the Datasheet View button 🖽 on the Table Design toolbar, press [Tab] to move to the SSN field, type 115774444, press [Tab], type Comp1, press [Tab], type 1/25/02, press [Tab], then press [Spacebar]**
   Your screen should look like Figure E-8. Double-check that the SSN and Attended fields are formatted correctly, too.

8. **Press [Enter], press [Tab] to move through the LogNo field, type 222334400, press [Tab], type Comp1, press [Tab], type 1/25/02, press [Tab], then press [Spacebar]**
   Two records are entered in the Attendance table.

FIGURE E-7: Changing Date/Time field properties

Attendance table

Attended field is selected

General properties tab

Lookup properties tab

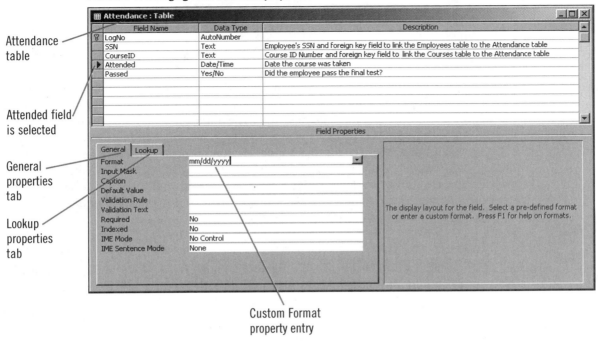

Custom Format property entry

FIGURE E-8: Testing field property changes

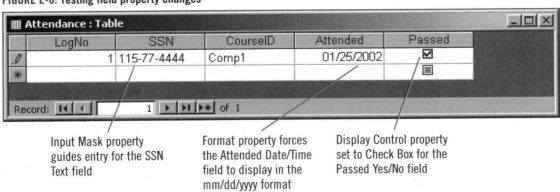

Input Mask property guides entry for the SSN Text field

Format property forces the Attended Date/Time field to display in the mm/dd/yyyy format

Display Control property set to Check Box for the Passed Yes/No field

Unit E

Access 2002

Defining Field Validation Properties

The **Validation Rule** and Validation Text field properties can help you eliminate unreasonable entries by establishing criteria for an entry before it is accepted into the database. For example, the Validation Rule property of a Gender field might be modified to allow only two entries: male or female. The **Validation Text** property is used to display an explanatory message when a user tries to enter data that doesn't pass the Validation Rule property for that field. Without a Validation Rule entry, the Validation Text property is meaningless. MediaLoft started providing in-house courses on January 17, 2002. Therefore, it wouldn't make sense to enter a date before that time. Fred modifies the validation properties of the Date field in the Attendance table to help prevent users from entering incorrect dates.

Steps

1. **Click the Design View button ▨ on the Table Datasheet toolbar, click the Attended field, click the Validation Rule property text box, then type >=1/17/2002**
   This property forces all dates in the Attended field to be greater than or equal to 1/17/2002. See Table E-5 for more examples of Validation Rule expressions.

2. **Click the Validation Text text box, then type Date must be on or after 1/17/2002**
   The Validation Text property provides a helpful message to the user in the event that he or she attempts to make an entry in that field that doesn't pass the criteria entered in the Validation Rule property. The Design View of the Attendance table should now look like Figure E-9. Once again, Access modified a property to include additional syntax by changing the entry in the Validation Rule property to >=#1/17/2002#. Pound signs (#) are used to surround date criteria.

3. **Click the Save button ▤ on the Table Design toolbar, then click Yes when asked to test the existing data with new data integrity rules**
   Because all dates in the Attended field are more recent than 1/17/2002, there are no date errors in the current data, and the table is saved. You should test the Validation Rule and Validation Text properties in the datasheet.

QuickTip
Access assumes that years entered with two digits in the range 30 to 99 refer to the years 1930 through 1999, whereas digits in the range 00 to 29 refer to the years 2000 through 2029. If you wish to indicate a year outside these ranges, you must enter all four digits of the year.

4. **Click the Datasheet View button ▦ on the Table Design toolbar, press [Tab] three times to move to Attended field, type 1/1/99, then press [Tab]**
   Because you tried to enter a date that was not true for the Validation Rule property for the Attended field, a dialog box opens and displays the Validation Text entry as shown in Figure E-10.

5. **Click OK to close the Validation Rule dialog box**
   You know that the Validation Rule and Validation Text properties work properly.

6. **Press [Esc] to reject the invalid date entry in the Attended field**

7. **Close the Attendance table**

FIGURE E-9: Using the validation properties

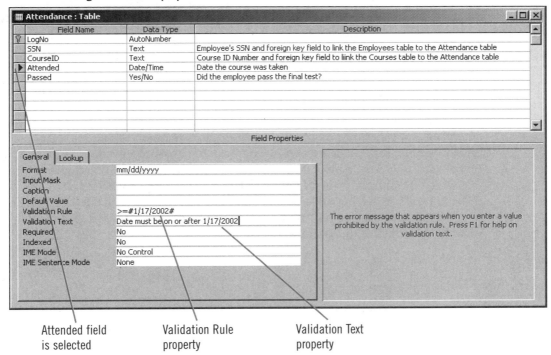

Attended field
is selected

Validation Rule
property

Validation Text
property

FIGURE E-10: Validation Text message

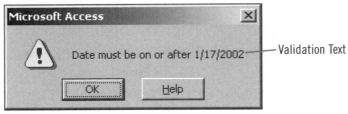

Validation Text

TABLE E-5: Validation Rule expressions

data type	validation rule expression	description
Number or Currency	>0	The number must be positive
Number or Currency	>10 And <100	The number must be between 10 and 100
Number or Currency	10 Or 20 Or 30	The number must be 10, 20, or 30
Text	"IA" Or "NE" Or "MO"	The entry must be IA, NE, or MO
Date/Time	>=#1/1/93#	The date must be on or after 1/1/1993
Date/Time	>#1/1/80# And <#1/1/90#	The date must be between 1/1/1980 and 1/1/1990

Access 2002

Creating One-to-Many Relationships

Once the initial database design and table design phase have been completed, you must link the tables together in appropriate one-to-many relationships. Some field properties that do not affect how the data is stored (such as the Format property) can be changed after the tables are linked, but other properties (such as the Field Size property) are more difficult to change once tables are linked. Therefore, it is best to complete all of the table and field design activities before linking the tables. Once the tables are linked, you can design queries, reports, and forms with fields from multiple tables. Fred's initial database sketch revealed that the SSN field will link the Employee table to the Attendance table, and that the CourseID field will link the Courses table to the Attendance table. Fred defines the one-to-many relationships between the tables of the Training-E database.

Trouble?

If the three tables do not appear in the Relationships window, click the Show Table button on the Relationships toolbar to add them.

1. Click the **Relationships button** on the Database toolbar
   The Employees, Attendance, and Courses table field lists appear in the Relationships window. The primary key fields are bold.

2. Click **SSN** in the Employees table field list, then drag it to the **SSN** field in the Attendance table field list
   Dragging a field from one table to another in the Relationships window links the two tables with the selected fields and opens the Edit Relationships dialog box as shown in Figure E-11. Referential integrity helps ensure data accuracy.

QuickTip

To display all of a table's field names, drag the bottom border of the field list until all fields are visible. Drag the table's title bar to move the field list.

3. Click the **Enforce Referential Integrity check box** in the Edit Relationships dialog box, then click **Create**
   The **one-to-many line** shows the linkage between the SSN field of the Employees table and the Attendance table. The "one" side of the relationship is the unique SSN for each record in the Employees table. The "many" side of the relationship is identified by an infinity symbol pointing to the SSN field in the Attendance table. The CourseID field will link the Courses table to the Attendance table.

Trouble?

To delete a relationship from the Relationships window, click the relationship line then press [Delete].

4. Click **CourseID** in the Courses table field list, drag it to **CourseID** in the Attendance table field list, click the **Enforce Referential Integrity check box**, then click **Create**
   The finished Relationships window should look like Figure E-12.

5. Click **File** on the menu bar, click **Print Relationships**, click the **Print button** on the Print Preview toolbar, close the Relationships report without saving it, then close the Relationships window
   A printout of the Relationships window, called the Relationships report, shows structural information including table names, field names, key fields, and relationships between tables.

6. Double-click the **Courses table** to open the datasheet, then click the **Comp1 expand button** ⊞
   Your screen should look like Figure E-13. When a table is related to another, its datasheet will show an **expand button** ⊞ to the left of the record. Click the expand button to show related records in the "many" table as a **subdatasheet**. When the related records appear, the expand button becomes a **collapse button** ⊟. Click the collapse button to close the subdatasheet.

7. Close the Courses table

FIGURE E-11: **Edit Relationships dialog box**

"One" table —
"Many" table

Linking field

Enforce Referential Integrity check box

One-to-many relationship

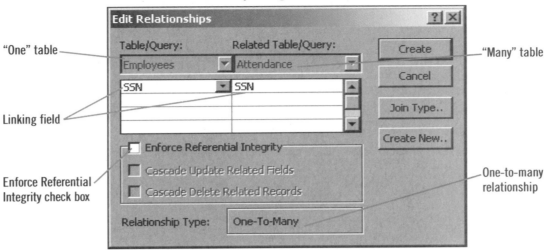

FIGURE E-12: **Final Relationships window**

"Many" side of one-to-many relationship

"One" side of one-to-many relationship

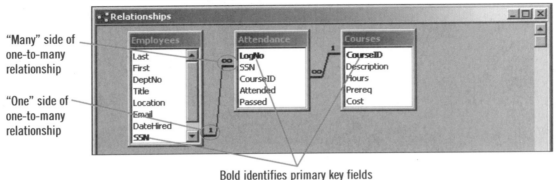

Bold identifies primary key fields

FIGURE E-13: **A subdatasheet allows you to view related records**

Expand button

Collapse button

One record in the Courses table is related to two records in the Attendance table

Subdatasheet

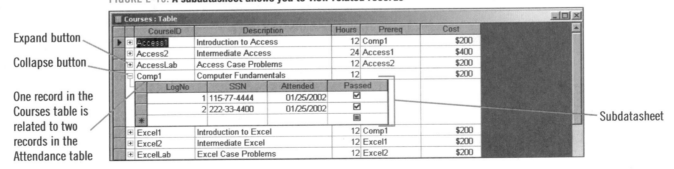

CLUES TO USE

Enforcing referential integrity

Referential integrity is a set of rules that help ensure that no orphan records are entered or created in the database. An orphan record is a record in the "many" table that doesn't have a matching entry in the linking field of the "one" table. (In this case, an orphan record would be a record in the Attendance table that contains an SSN entry that is not present in the Employees table, or a CourseID entry that is not present in the Courses table.) Referential integrity also prevents the user from deleting a record from the "one" table if a matching entry exists in the linking field of the "many" table. You should enforce referential integrity on all one-to-many relationships if possible. Unfortunately, if you are working with a database that already contains orphan records, you will not be able to enforce this powerful set of rules.

Access 2002

Creating Lookups

A Lookup field may display values stored in a related table or you may enter a lookup list in the **Row Source** Lookup property of the field itself. The **Lookup Wizard** can also be used to set Lookup properties. Fred wants the ParkingLot and the DeptNo fields in the Employees table to behave as Lookup fields. The ParkingLot field will lookup a list of values stored in the field's Row Source property, and the DeptNo field will lookup the DeptName field values from the Departments table.

Steps

1. Right-click the **Employees table**, then click **Design View**
   The Lookup Wizard is the last entry in the Data Type list.

2. Click the **ParkingLot Text** data type, click the **Data Type list arrow**, then click **Lookup Wizard**
   The Lookup Wizard starts and prompts you for information about where the lookup column will get its values.

3. Click the **I will type in the values that I want option button**, click **Next**, click the first **cell** in the Col1 column, type **Red**, press **[Tab]**, type **Blue**, press **[Tab]**, then type **Green** as shown in Figure E-14
   These values will populate the lookup value list for the ParkingLot field.

4. Click **Next**, then click **Finish** to accept the default label of ParkingLot and to complete the wizard
   Note that the data type for the ParkingLot field is still Text. The Lookup Wizard is a process for setting Lookup property values for a field, and is not a data type itself.

5. Click the **DeptNo Number** data type, click the **Data Type list arrow**, then click **Lookup Wizard**
   In this case, you want the Lookup field to lookup department name values in another table. Department names are stored in the DeptName field in the Departments table.

6. Click **Next**, click **Table: Departments**, click **Next**, double-click **DeptName** to move it to the Selected Fields list, click **Next**, click **Next** to accept the column width, click **Finish**, then click **Yes** to save the table
   Now the DeptNo field in the Employees table will lookup and present department names from the Departments table.

7. Click the **Lookup properties tab** to observe the new Lookup properties for the DeptNo field, then click the **ParkingLot field name** to observe the new Lookup properties, as shown in Figure E-15
   The Lookup Wizard helped you enter the correct Lookup properties for these fields.

8. Click the **Datasheet button** 🔲 on the Table Design toolbar, press **[Tab]** twice to move to the DeptNo field, click the **DeptNo list arrow**, click **Book**, press **[Tab]** six times to move to the ParkingLot field, click the **ParkingLot list arrow** as shown in Figure E-16, then click **Blue**
   Both the ParkingLot and DeptNo fields now present lookup values. The DeptNo field looks up actual department names from the DeptName field of the Departments table instead of showing the DeptNo number. The ParkingLot field looks up a list of values that you entered via the Lookup Wizard, which are stored in its Row Source Lookup property.

9. Close the Employees datasheet, close the Training-E database, then exit Access

FIGURE E-14: **Entering a Lookup list of values**

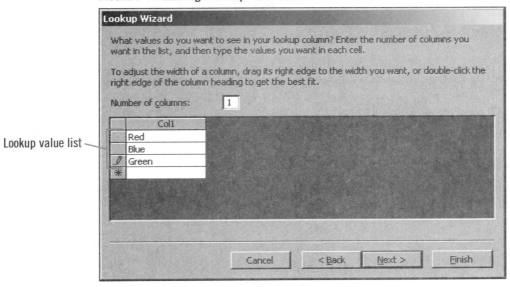

Lookup value list

FIGURE E-15: **Viewing Lookup properties**

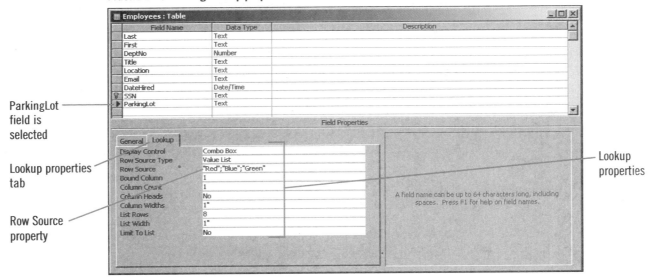

ParkingLot field is selected

Lookup properties tab

Row Source property

Lookup properties

FIGURE E-16: **Using a Lookup field in a datasheet**

		Location	Email	DateHired	SSN	ParkingLot	
✐	+	New York	scolletti@medialoft.com	2/15/1998	115-77-4444	▼	
	+	San Francisco	nlee@medialoft.com	3/22/1998	134-70-3883	Red	
	+	Corporate	jshimada@medialoft.com	8/20/1998	173-48-5873	Blue	
	+	Corporate	lalber@medialoft.com	8/6/1998	222-33-4400	Green	
	+	Boston	mrath@medialoft.com	1/3/1997	234-56-7800		
	+	Corporate	jfernandez@medialoft.com	7/1/1998	321-00-8888		
	+	Corporate	ddumont@medialoft.com	1/1/1999	333-33-8887		
	+	Seattle	jhayashi@medialoft.com	9/23/1998	333-44-0099		
	+	Kansas City	mrollo@medialoft.com	4/6/1999	345-88-0098		

Record: ◄◄ ◄ 1 ► ►► ►* of 20

List of values for the ParkingLot Lookup field

Practice

▶ Concepts Review

Identify each element of the Table Design View shown in Figure E-17.

FIGURE E-17

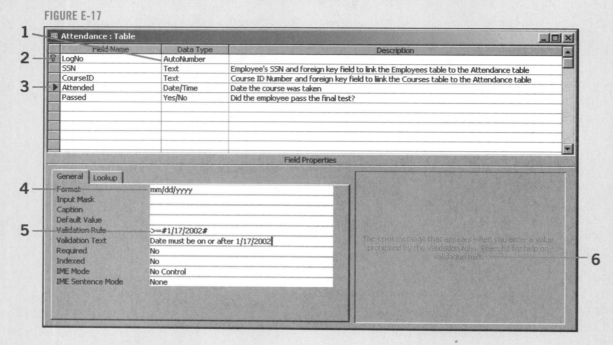

Match each term with the statement that describes its function.

7. **Primary key**
8. **Properties**
9. **Table Design View**
10. **Validation Rule**
11. **Relational database**

a. Several tables linked together in one-to-many relationships

b. A field that holds unique information for each record in the table

c. Where all characteristics of a table, including the field names, the primary key field, and all field properties are defined

d. Characteristics that apply to the fields of a table, such as Field Size, Default Value, or Format

e. Helps eliminate unreasonable entries by establishing criteria for the entry

Select the best answer from the list of choices.

12. Which of the following problems most clearly indicates that you need to redesign your database?

a. There is duplicated data in many fields and records of a table.

b. Referential integrity is enforced on table relationships.

c. Not all fields have Validation Rule properties.

d. The Input Mask Wizard has not been used.

13. Which of the following is NOT defined in Table Design View?

a. The primary key field

b. Duplicate data

c. Field Size properties

d. Field data types

▶ Skills Review

1. **Examine relational databases.**
   a. Examine your address book.
   b. Write down the fields you will need if you were to enter this information into an Access relational database.
   c. Identify those fields that contain duplicate values if all of the fields were to be stored in one table.

2. **Plan related tables and lookups.**
   a. Group the fields that you identified into subject matter tables, then identify the primary key field for each table.
   b. Your database will contain two tables: Names and Zips. If you did not identify these two tables earlier, regroup the fields within these two table names, then identify how the tables will be related.
   c. Identify potential lookups.

3. **Create related tables.**
   a. Start Access, then click the Blank Database link in the New section of the New File task pane.
   b. Type **Membership-E** as the filename, then save the database where your Project Files are located.
   c. Create a new table using Table Design View with the following field names and data types: **First**, Text; **Last**, Text; **Street**, Text; **Zip**, Text; **Birthday**, Date/Time; **Dues**, Currency; **MemberNo**, Text; **MemberType**, Text; **CharterMember**, Yes/No.
   d. Identify MemberNo as the primary key field, save the table as **Names**, then close it.
   e. Create a new table using Table Design View with the following field names and data types: **Zip**, Text; **City**, Text; **State**, Text.
   f. Identify Zip as the primary key field, save the table as **Zips**, then close it.
   g. Create a new table using Table Design View with the following field names and data types: **MemberNo**, Text; **ActivityDate**, Date/Time; **Hours**, Number.
   h. Save the table without a primary key field, name it **Activities**, then close it.

4. **Define Text fields.**
   a. Open the Zips table in Design View.
   b. Change the Field Size property of the State field to 2 and the Field Size property of the Zip field to 9, then save the table.
   c. Use the Input Mask Wizard to create the Input Mask property for the Zip field. Choose the Zip Code Input Mask. Accept the other default options provided by the Input Mask Wizard, then click Finish.
   d. Save the changes, then close the Zips table. Open the Names table in Design View.
   e. Change the Field Size property of the First, Last, and Street fields to 30, the MemberNo field to 5, and the Zip field to 9. Save the changes to the table.
   f. Use the Input Mask Wizard to create the Input Mask property for the Zip field. Choose the Zip Code input mask. Accept the other default options provided by the Input Mask Wizard. If the Input Mask Wizard is not installed on your computer, type **00000\-9999;;_** for the Input Mask property for the Zip field.
   g. Save the changes, then close Names table. Open the Activities table in Design View.
   h. Change the Field Size property of the MemberNo field to 5, save the change, then close the Activities table.

5. **Define Number and Currency fields.**
   a. Open the Names table in Design View.
   b. Change the Decimal Places property of the Dues field to 0. Save the change then close the Names table.
   c. Open the Activities table in Design View.
   d. Change the Field Size property of the Hours field to Byte. Save the change, then close the Activities table.

6. **Define Date/Time and Yes/No fields.**
   a. Open the Names table in Design View.
   b. Change the Format property of the Birthday field to **mm/dd/yyyy**.

   c. Check to ensure that the Display Control property (on the Lookup tab of the Field Properties) of the CharterMember field is set to **Check Box**.

   d. Save the changes, then close the Names table.

   e. Open the Activities table in Design View.

   f. Change the Format property of the ActivityDate field to **mm/dd/yyyy**.

   g. Save the change, then close the Activities table.

7. Define field validation properties.

   a. Open the Zips table in Design View.

   b. Click the State field name, click the Validation Rule text box, then type **=IA OR KS OR MO**

   c. Click the Validation Text text box, then type **State must be IA, KS, or MO**. Note the quotation marks, the additional syntax, that Access automatically added to the Validation Rule property.

   d. Save the changes then open the Zips table in Datasheet View.

   e. Test the Validation Text and Validation Rule properties by entering a new record with the Zip value of **661112222**, a City value of **Blue Valley**, and a State value of **MN**. Click OK when prompted with the Validation Text message, edit the State value to be **IA**, then close the Zips table.

8. Create one-to-many relationships.

   a. Open the Relationships window, double-click Activities, double-click Names, then double-click Zips to add all three tables to the Relationships window. Close the Show Table dialog box.

   b. Drag the Zip field from the Zips table to the Zip field in the Names table to create a one-to-many relationship between the Zips table and Names table using the common Zip field.

   c. Enforce referential integrity for this relationship.

   d. Drag the MemberNo field from the Names table to the MemberNo field in the Activities table to create a one-to-many relationship between the Names and the Activities table using the common MemberNo field.

   e. Enforce referential integrity for this relationship.

   f. Resize all of the field lists by dragging the borders of the lists so that all fields are visible.

   g. Click File on the menu bar, click Print Relationships to create a report of the Relationships window, add your name as a label to the Report Header section if desired, then print the report.

   h. Close the Relationships report without saving the report, then close the Relationships window. Save the changes to the Relationships window if prompted.

9. Create lookups.

   a. Open the Names table in Design View, then start the Lookup Wizard for the MemberType field.

   b. Select the option that allows you to enter your own values, use [Tab] to enter **Senior**, **Active**, and **Inactive** as the values for the lookup column, then accept the rest of the Lookup Wizard defaults.

   c. In Datasheet View, enter a new record using your name and the Zip value of **661112222** to test the Lookup properties for the MemberType field, then print, save, and close the Names datasheet.

   d. Close the Membership-E database then exit Access.

▶ Independent Challenge 1

As the manager of a music store's instrument rental program, you have decided to create a database to track instrument rentals to schoolchildren. The fields you need to track can be organized with four tables: Instruments, Rentals, Customers, and Schools.

   a. Start Access, then create a new blank database called **Music Store-E**, where your Project Files are located.

   b. Use Design View to create the four tables in the Music Store-E database using the following information. Note that the primary key fields are bold in the table.

c. Enter >=#1/1/02# as the Validation Rule property to the Date field of the Rentals table. This change will only allow dates of 1/1/02 or later to be entered into this field.

d. Enter **Dates must be on or later than 1/1/2002** as the Validation Text property to the Date field of the Rentals table.

e. Open the Relationships window, add all four tables to the window in the arrangement shown in Figure E-18, then create one-to-many relationships as shown.

f. Preview the Relationships report, then print the report making sure that all fields of each table are visible. (If you need your name on the printout, add your name as a label to the Report Header.)

g Close the Relationships report without saving it. Close the Relationships window, then save the layout if prompted.

h. Close the Music Store-E database, then exit Access.

table	field name	data type
Customers	FirstName	Text
	LastName	Text
	Street	Text
	City	Text
	State	Text
	Zip	Text
	CustNo	AutoNumber
	SchoolNo	Number
Instruments	Description	Text
	SerialNo	Text
	MonthlyFee	Currency
Schools	SchoolName	Text
	SchoolNo	AutoNumber
Rentals	**RentalNo**	AutoNumber
	CustNo	Number
	SerialNo	Text
	Date	Date/Time

FIGURE E-18

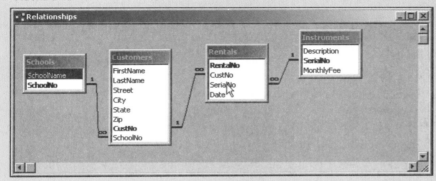

▶ Independent Challenge 2

You want to document the books you've read by creating and storing the information in a relational database. You will design the database on paper including the tables, field names, data types, and relationships.

a. On paper, create three balanced columns by drawing two vertical lines from the top to the bottom of the paper. At the top of the first column write **Table**. At the top of the second column write **Field Name**, and at the top of the third column write **Data Type**.

b. In the middle column, list all of the fields that need to be tracked to record information about the books you've read. You'll want to track such information as the book title, category (such as Biography, Mystery, or Science Fiction), rating (a numeric value from 1–10 that indicates how satisfied you were with the book), date you read the book, author's first name, and author's last name.

c. In the first column, identify the table where this field would be found. (Hint: You should identify two tables of information for this listing of fields.)

d. Identify the primary key fields found in the tables by circling the field name. If you do not find any fields that are good candidates for key fields, you may have to create additional fields. (*Hint:* Each book has an ISBN—International Standard Book Number—that is a unique number assigned to every book. To uniquely identify each author, you will have to create a new field. Don't use the author's last name as the primary key field as that precludes you from entering two authors with the same last name.)

e. In a third column, identify the appropriate data type for each field.

f. On a new piece of paper, sketch the fields as they would appear in the Relationships window of Access.

▶ Independent Challenge 3

You want to create a database that documents blood donations by employees. You will design the database on paper including the tables, field names, data types, and relationships. You'll want to track information such as employee name, employee Social Security number (SSN), employee department, employee blood type, date of donation, and hospital the donation was given to. Also, you'll want to track basic hospital information, such as the hospital name and address.

    a. Complete Steps a. through f. as described in Independant Challenge 2 using the new case information. You should identify three tables for this case.

 Independent Challenge 4

You are on the staff of an economic development team whose goal is to encourage tourism in the Baltic Sea region. You have created an Access database called Baltic-E to track important fields of information for the countries in that region, and will use the Internet to find information about the area and enter it into existing forms.

    a. Start Access, then open the **Baltic-E** database from the drive and folder where your Project Files are located.

    b. Connect to the Internet, and then go to www.google.com, www.lycos.com, or any general search engine to conduct research for your database. Your goal is to find three upcoming events for Munich, Germany, and to print that Web page.

    c. Open the Cities form, find the Munich record, and enter three more events for Munich into the Events fields. EventID is an AutoNumber field, so it will automatically increment as you enter the EventName and EventDate information.

    d. Open the Cities table in Design View, then add a field called **MemberStatus** with a Text data type and a Field Size property of 11 to document the city's status with your economic development team.

    e. Use the Lookup Wizard to provide the values **Charter**, **Active**, **Inactive**, and **No Interest** for the Lookup list.

    f. Using the Report Wizard, create a report based on the Baltic Area Festivals query. Use all of the fields. View the data by Cities, do not add any more grouping levels, then sort the records by EventDate.

    g. Use a Stepped layout, a Portrait orientation, and a Corporate style.

    h. Title the report **Baltic Area Events**, then apply additional formatting embellishments as desired.

    i. Add your name as a label to the Report Header section. Save, print, then close the report.

    j. Close the Baltic-E database, then exit Access.

FIGURE E-19

▶ Visual Workshop

Open the Training-E database, create a new table called Vendors using the Table Design View shown in Figure E-19 to determine field names and data types. Additional property changes include changing the Field Size property of the VState field to 2, the VZip field to 9, the VendorID and VPhone fields to 10, and all other text fields to 30. Be sure to specify that the VendorID field is the primary key field. Enter one record into the datasheet with your name in the VendorName field, then print the datasheet.

Vendors : Table

Field Name	Data Type
VendorID	Text
VendorName	Text
VStreet	Text
VCity	Text
VState	Text
VZip	Text
VPhone	Text

General	Lookup
Field Size	10
Format	
Input Mask	
Caption	
Default Value	
Validation Rule	
Validation Text	
Required	No
Allow Zero Length	Yes
Indexed	Yes (No Duplicates)
Unicode Compression	Yes
IME Mode	No Control
IME Sentence Mode	None

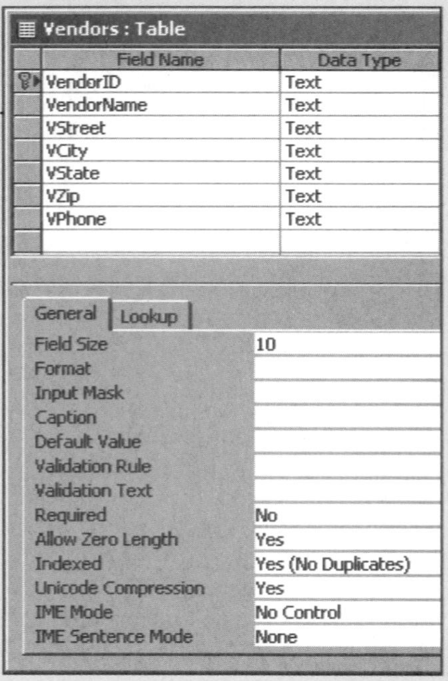

Creating
Multiple Table Queries

Objectives

MOUS ► **Create select queries**

MOUS ► **Sort a query on multiple fields**

MOUS ► **Develop AND queries**

MOUS ► **Develop OR queries**

MOUS ► **Create calculated fields**

MOUS ► **Build summary queries**

MOUS ► **Create crosstab queries**

MOUS ► **Create PivotTables and PivotCharts**

Queries are database objects that answer questions about the data by pulling fields and records that match specific criteria into a single datasheet. A **select query**, the most common type of query, retrieves data from one or more linked tables and displays the results in a datasheet. In addition, queries can sort records, calculate new fields of data, or develop summary calculations such as the sum or average of the values in a field. **Crosstab queries** present information in a cross-tabular report, similar to PivotTables in Microsoft Excel. ►►► The MediaLoft Training database has been updated so that it contains information concerning which employees are taking which classes. Fred Ames, coordinator of training, creates select queries and crosstab queries to analyze the data in the database.

Creating Select Queries

You create queries by using the **Query Wizard** or by directly specifying requested fields and query criteria in **Query Design View**. The resulting query datasheet is not a duplication of the data that resides in the original table's datasheet; it is simply a logical *view* of the data. If you change or enter data in a query's datasheet, the data in the underlying table (and any other logical view) is automatically updated. Queries are often used to present and sort a subset of fields from multiple tables. Fred creates a query to answer the question, "Who is taking what courses?" He pulls fields from several tables into a query object to display a single datasheet that answers this question.

1. Start Access, then open the **Training-F** database from the drive and folder where your Project Files are stored

2. Click **Queries** on the Objects bar, then double-click **Create query in Design view**
The Show Table dialog box opens and lists all the tables in the database. You use the Show Table dialog box to add the tables that contain the fields you want to view in the final query datasheet.

Trouble?
If you add a table to Query Design View twice by mistake, click the title bar of the extra field list, then press [Delete].

3. Click **Employees**, click **Add**, double-click **Attendance**, double-click **Courses**, then click **Close**
The upper part of Query Design View displays **field lists** for the three tables. Each table's name is in the field list title bar. Drag the title bar of a field list to move it. Drag the edge of a field list to resize it. Key fields are bold, and serve as the "one" side of the one-to-many relationship between two tables. Relationships are displayed with **one-to-many join lines** between the linking fields, as shown in Figure F-1. The fields you want displayed in the datasheet must be added to the columns in the lower part of Query Design View. The lower pane of the Query Design View window is called the **query design grid**, or simply the **design grid**.

QuickTip
When you drag a field to the query design grid, the existing fields move to the right to accommodate the new field.

4. Click the **First field** in the Employees table field list, then drag the **First field** to the Field cell in the first column of the query design grid
The order in which the fields are placed in the query design grid is the order they appear in the datasheet.

Trouble?
If you add the wrong field, click the Field cell list arrow in the query design grid, then choose another field from the list. Choose a field from another table by clicking the Table cell list arrow in the query design grid, and choosing another table.

5. Double-click the **Last field** in the Employees field list, double-click the **Attended field** in the Attendance field list, double-click the **Description field** in the Courses field list, then double-click the **Hours field** in the Courses field list
Your Query Design View should look like Figure F-2. You may delete a field from the query design grid by clicking the field selector above the field name and pressing [Delete]. Deleting a field from the query design grid removes it from the logical view of this query's datasheet, but does not delete the field from the database. A field is defined and the field's contents are stored in a table object only.

6. Click the **Hours field selector**, press [Delete] to remove the field from the query design grid, then click the **Datasheet View button** on the Query Design toolbar
The resulting datasheet looks like Figure F-3. The datasheet shows the four fields selected in Query Design View and displays 153 records. The records represent the 153 different times a MediaLoft employee attended a class. Shayla Colletti appears in 11 records because she attended 11 classes.

FIGURE F-1: Query Design View with multiple tables

Table names for field lists

Fields in the Employees table

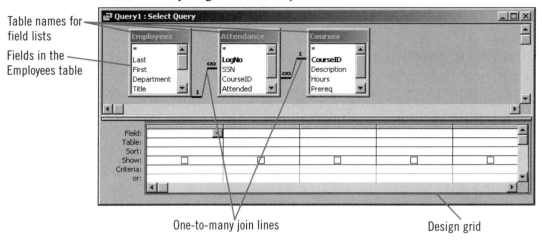

One-to-many join lines

Design grid

FIGURE F-2: Query Design View with five fields in the query design grid

Scroll bars indicate that not all fields are currently visible

Resize bar

Field selector

Drag border of field list to resize it

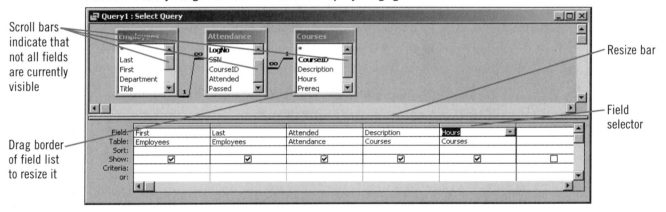

FIGURE F-3: Query datasheet showing related information from three tables

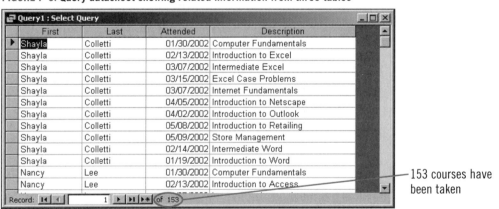

153 courses have been taken

CLUES TO USE

Resizing Query Design View

Drag the **resize bar** up or down to provide more room for the upper (field lists) or lower (query design grid) panes of Query Design View. By dragging the resize bar down, you may have enough room to enlarge each field list so that you can see all of the field names for each table.

Sorting a Query on Multiple Fields

Sorting refers to reorganizing the records in either ascending or descending order based on the values in a field. Queries allow you to specify more than one sort field in Query Design View. Queries evaluate the sort fields from left to right. The sort field farthest to the left is the primary sort field. Sort orders defined in Query Design View are saved with the query object. Fred wants to put the records in alphabetical order based on the employee's last name. If more than one record exists for an employee (if the employee attended more than one class), Fred further sorts the records by the date the course was attended.

Steps

1. **Click the Design View button on the Query Datasheet toolbar**
   To sort the records according to Fred's plan, the Last field must be the primary sort field, and the Attended field the secondary sort field.

2. **Click the Last field Sort cell in the query design grid, click the Sort list arrow, click Ascending, click the Attended field Sort cell in the query design grid, click the Sort list arrow, then click Ascending**
   The resulting query design grid should look like Figure F-4.

3. **Click the Datasheet View button on the Query Design toolbar**
   The records of the datasheet are now listed alphabetically by the entry in the Last field, then in chronological order by the entry in the Attended field, as shown in Figure F-5. Maria Abbott attended six classes, but you notice that her name has been incorrectly entered in the database as "Marie." Fix this error in the query datasheet.

4. **Type Maria, then press [↓]**
   This update shows that you are using a properly designed relational database because changing any occurrence of an employee's name should cause all other occurrences of that name to be automatically updated. The employee name is physically stored only once in the Employees table, although it is displayed in this datasheet once for every time the employee has attended a course. Similarly, the values in the Description field are physically stored only once in the Courses table, but appear many times in this datasheet because many employees have taken the same course.

5. **Double-click Fundamentals in the Description field of the third record, type Concepts, press [↓], then observe the automatic change to record 8**
   All occurrences of Computer Fundamentals have now been updated to Computer Concepts. Changes made to data through a query, form, or page object actually update data that is stored in the table object. Table data populates every other view of the information. A query object creates a set of **Structured Query Language (SQL)** statements that retrieves the data from the tables in the arrangement defined in Query Design View.

6. **Click the View button list arrow on the Query Datasheet toolbar, then click SQL View**
   The three SQL statements determine what fields are selected, how the tables are joined, and how the resulting records will be sorted. When you save a query, you are saving SQL statements. Fortunately, you do not have to be able to write or even understand SQL code to use Access. The easy-to-use Query Design View gives you a way to select and sort data from underlying tables without being an SQL programmer.

7. **Close the SQL window, click Yes when prompted to save the changes, type Employee Progress Query in the Query Name text box, then click OK**
   The query is now saved and listed as a query object in the Training-F database window.

FIGURE F-4: Specifying multiple sort orders in Query Design View

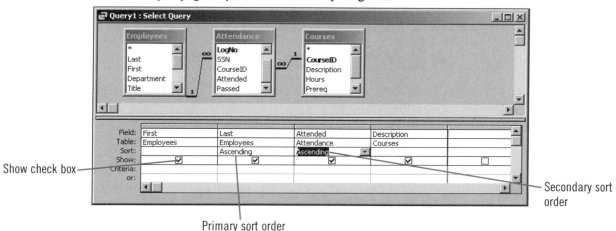

Show check box

Primary sort order

Secondary sort order

FIGURE F-5: Records sorted by Last, then Attended

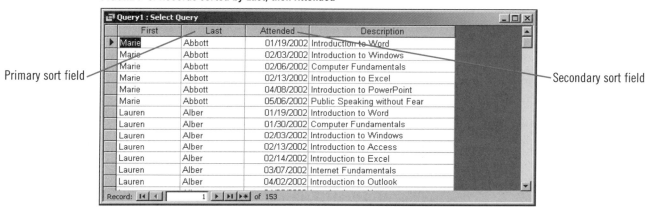

Primary sort field

Secondary sort field

Specifying a sort order different from the field order in the datasheet

You cannot modify the left-to-right sort order hierarchy in Query Design View. However, if you wish to have the fields in the datasheet appear in an order different than the order by which they are sorted, there is a simple solution, as shown in Figure F-6. By adding a field to the query design grid twice and by unchecking the Show check box for the sort fields, the resulting datasheet can be sorted in one order (Department then Last) yet display data in another order (Last then Department).

FIGURE F-6: Query grid for sorting out of order

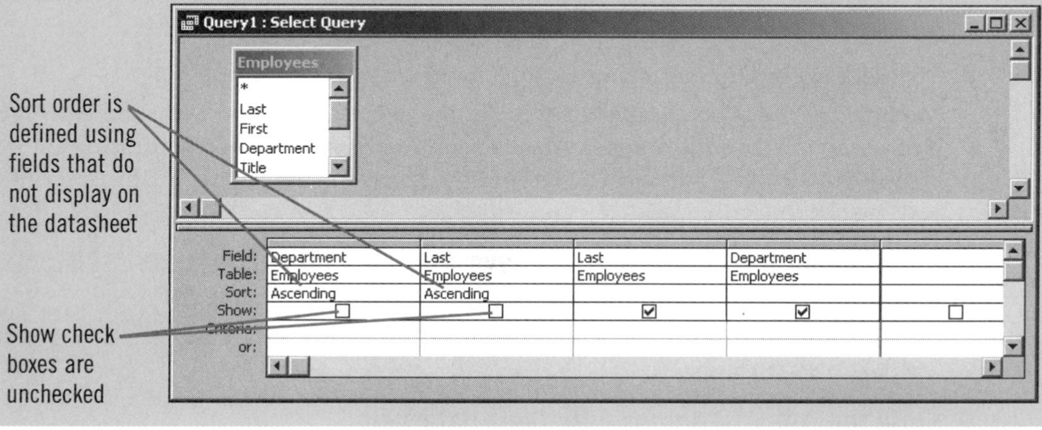

Sort order is defined using fields that do not display on the datasheet

Show check boxes are unchecked

Developing AND Queries

Often, you'll want to limit the number of records that display on the resulting datasheet. **Criteria** are tests, or limiting conditions, for which the record must be true to be selected for a datasheet. To create an **AND query** in which two or more criteria are present, enter the criteria for the fields on the same Criteria row of the query design grid. If two AND criteria are entered for the *same* field, the AND operator separates the criteria in the Criteria cell for that field. Fred is looking for a person to assist the Access teacher in the classroom. In order to compile a list of potential candidates, he creates an AND query to find all employees who have taken MediaLoft's Access courses and passed the exams.

Steps

1. **Right-click the Employee Progress Query, click Design View from the shortcut menu, click the View button list arrow** ⊞▾ **on the Query Design toolbar, then click Design View**
   Instead of creating a new query from scratch to find potential Access teachers, you decide to modify the Employee Progress Query as this query already contains most of the data you need. The only additional field you have to add to the query is the Passed field.

2. **Double-click the Passed field in the Attendance field list to add it to the fifth column in the query design grid**
   MediaLoft offers several Access courses, so the criteria must specify all the records that contain the word "Access" anywhere in the Description field. You use the asterisk (∗), a **wildcard character** that represents any combination of characters, to create this criterion.

3. **Click the Description field Criteria cell, type *access*, then click the Datasheet View button** ⊞ **on the Query Design toolbar**
   The resulting datasheet, as shown in Figure F-7, shows thirteen records that match the criteria. The resulting records all contain the word "access" in some part of the Description field, but because of the placement of the asterisks, it didn't matter *where* (beginning, middle, or end) the word was found.

4. **Click the Design View button** ⊠ **on the Query Datasheet toolbar, click the Passed field Criteria cell, then type yes**
   You added the criteria to display only those records where the Passed field equals Yes. The resulting query design grid is shown in Figure F-8. Access assists you with **criteria syntax**, rules by which criteria need to be entered. Access automatically adds quotation marks to surround text criteria in Text fields, and pound signs (#) to surround date criteria in Date/Time fields. The criteria in Number, Currency, and Yes/No fields are not surrounded by any characters. Notice that Access entered quotation marks around "∗access∗" in the Description field, and added the **Like operator**. See Table F-1 for more information on common Access comparison operators.

5. **Click** ⊞ **on the Query Design toolbar to view the resulting records**
   Multiple criteria added to the same line of the query design grid (AND criteria) must *each* be true for the record to appear in the resulting datasheet, thereby causing the resulting datasheet to display *fewer* records. Only nine records contain "access" in the Description field and "yes" in the Passed field.

6. **Click File on the menu bar, click Save As, type Potential Access Assistants in the Save Query 'Employee Progress Query' To: text box, then click OK**
   The query is saved with the new name, Potential Access Assistants, as a new object in the MediaLoft-F database.

7. **Close the Potential Access Assistants datasheet**

FIGURE F-7: Datasheet for Access records

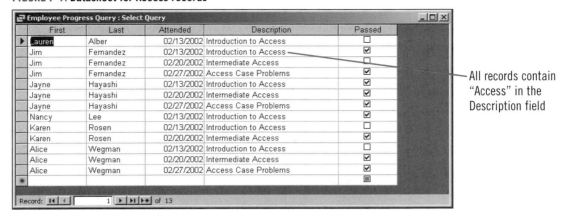

All records contain "Access" in the Description field

FIGURE F-8: AND criteria

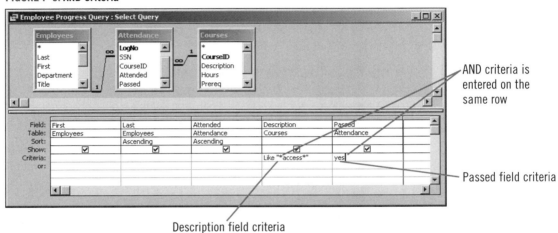

AND criteria is entered on the same row

Passed field criteria

Description field criteria

TABLE F-1: Common comparison operators

operator	description	example	result
>	greater than	>50	Value exceeds 50
>=	greater than or equal to	>=50	Value is 50 or greater
<	less than	<50	Value is less than 50
<=	less than or equal to	<=50	Value is 50 or less
<>	not equal to	<>50	Value is any number other than 50
Between...And	finds values between two numbers or dates	Between #2/2/01# And #2/2/03#	Dates between 2/2/2001 and 2/2/2003, inclusive
In	finds a value that is one of a list	In("IA","KS","NE")	Value equals IA or KS or NE
Null	finds records that have no entry in a particular field	Null	No value has been entered in a field
Is Not Null	finds records that have any entry in a particular field	Is Not Null	Any value has been entered in a field
Like	finds records that match the criteria	Like "A*"	Value starts with A
Not	finds records that do not match the criteria	Not 2	Numbers other than 2

Developing OR Queries

AND queries *narrow* the number of records in the resulting datasheet by requiring that a record be true for multiple criteria in one criteria row. **OR queries** *expand* the number of records that will appear in the datasheet because a record needs to be true *for only one* of the criteria rows. OR criteria are entered in the query design grid on different lines (criteria rows). Each criteria row of the query design grid is evaluated separately, adding the records that are true for that row to the resulting datasheet. ✎ Fred is looking for an assistant for the Excel courses. He modifies the Potential Access Assistants query to expand the number of records to include those who have passed Excel courses.

Steps 1 2 3 4

1. Click the **Potential Access Assistants** query, then click the **Design button** 📐 in the Training-F database window
   To add OR criteria, you have to enter criteria in the "or" row of the query design grid. You want to find all Excel courses.

2. Click the **or Description criteria cell** below Like "*access*", then type ***excel***

3. Click the **or Passed criteria cell** below Yes, then type **yes**, as shown in Figure F-9
   As soon as you clicked elsewhere in the design grid, Access added the appropriate criteria syntax. If a record matches *either criteria* row of the criteria grid, it is included in the query's datasheet. Each row is evaluated separately, which is why it was necessary to put the Yes criteria for the Passed field in both rows of the query design grid. Otherwise, the second row would pull all records where "excel" is in the description regardless of whether the test was passed or not.

4. Click the **Datasheet View button** 🔲 on the Query Design toolbar
   The resulting datasheet displays 28 records, as shown in Figure F-10. All of the records contain course Descriptions that contain the word Access or Excel as well as Yes in the Passed field. Also, notice that the sort order (Last, then Attended) is still in effect.

5. Click **File** on the menu bar, click **Save As**, click between **Access and Assistants**, type **or Excel**, press **[Spacebar]**, then click **OK**
   The Potential Access or Excel Assistants query is saved as a separate database object.

6. Close the Potential Access or Excel Assistants query
   The Training-F database displays the three queries you created in addition to the two queries that were already in the database.

FIGURE F-9: **OR criteria**

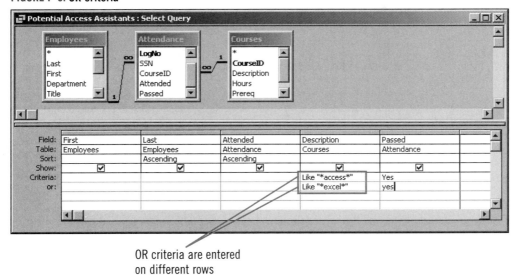

OR criteria are entered
on different rows

FIGURE F-10: **OR criteria adds more records to the datasheet**

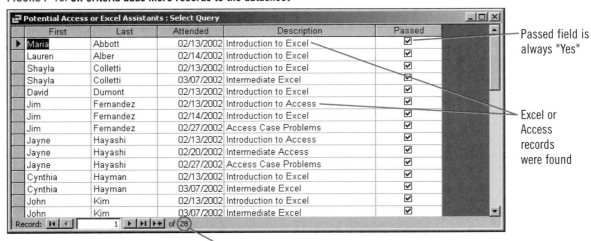

Passed field is
always "Yes"

Excel or
Access
records
were found

28 records found

Using wildcard characters in query criteria

To search for a pattern, a wildcard character is used to represent any character in the criteria entry. Use a ? (question mark) to search for any single character and an * (asterisk) to search for any number of characters.

Wildcard characters are often used with the Like operator. For example, the criterion Like "10/*/03" would find all dates in October of 2003, and the criterion Like "F*" would find all entries that start with the letter F.

Creating
Calculated Fields

If you can calculate a new field of information based on existing fields in a database, never define it as a separate field in Table Design View. Rather, use a query object to create the new **calculated field** to guarantee that the new field always contains accurate, up-to-date information. **Arithmetic operators** and functions shown in Table F-2 and Table F-3 are used to create expressions within Access. An expression determines the value for a calculated field. **Functions** are special shortcut formulas that help you calculate common values such as counts and subtotals on groups of records, a loan payment (if working with financial data), or the current date. Fred has been asked to report on the hourly cost of each course. The data to calculate this answer already exists in the Cost (the cost of the course) and Hours (the number of contact hours per course) fields of the Courses table.

1. Click **Queries** on the Objects bar, double-click **Create query in Design View**, click **Courses** in the Show Table dialog box, click **Add**, then click **Close** in the Show Table dialog box
   The Courses field list is in the upper pane of the query design window.

2. Double-click the **Description field**, double-click the **Hours field**, then double-click the **Cost field**
   A **calculated field** is created by entering a new descriptive field name followed by a colon in the Field cell of the design grid followed by an expression. An **expression** is a combination of **operators** such as + (add), – (subtract), * (multiply), or / (divide); raw values (such as numbers or dates), functions; and fields that produce a result. Field names used in an expression are surrounded by square brackets.

QuickTip

If an expression becomes too long to fit completely in a cell of the query design grid, you can right-click the cell, then click Zoom to use the Zoom dialog box for long entries.

3. Click the blank **Field cell** of the fourth column, type **HourlyRate:[Cost]/[Hours]**, then drag ✛ on the right edge of the fourth column selector to the right to display the entire entry, as shown in Figure F-11

4. Click the **Datasheet View button** 🖩 on the Query Design toolbar
   It is not necessary to show the fields used in the calculated expression in the datasheet (in this case, Hours and Cost), but viewing these fields next to the new calculated field helps confirm that your new calculated field is working properly. The HourlyRate field appears to be accurate, but the data is not formatted in a useful way.

5. Click the **Design View button** 🖺 on the Query Datasheet toolbar, right-click the **HourlyRate field** in the query design grid, then click **Properties** on the shortcut menu
   The Field Properties dialog box opens. The HourlyRate field represents dollars per hour.

6. Click the **Format text box**, click the **Format list arrow**, click **Currency**, close the property sheet, then click 🖩 to display the records
   The data shown in the HourlyRate field displays as currency with dollar signs and is rounded to the nearest cent.

7. Press **[Tab]** twice, type **300** in the Introduction to Access Cost field, then press **[Enter]**
   The resulting datasheet is shown in Figure F-12. The HourlyRate field was recalculated as soon as the Cost field was updated. This is why it is extremely important to create calculated fields in queries rather than define them as fields in Table Design View. When created as calculated fields, they always display current data.

8. Click the **Save button** 🖫 on the Query Datasheet toolbar, type **Hourly Rate** in the Save As dialog box, click **OK**, then close the datasheet
   The query is saved as an object in the database.

FIGURE F-11: Entering a calculated field in Query Design View

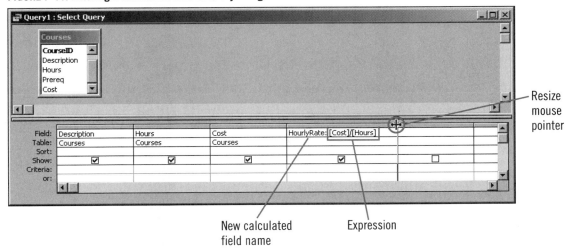

New calculated
field name

Expression

Resize
mouse
pointer

FIGURE F-12: **Formatting and testing the calculated field**

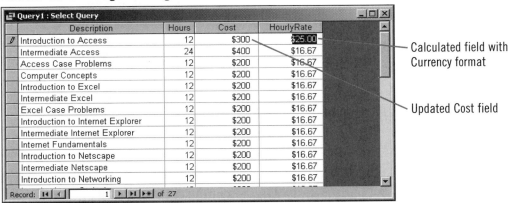

Calculated field with
Currency format

Updated Cost field

TABLE F-2: **Arithmetic operators**

operator	description
+	Addition
−	Subtraction
*	Multiplication
/	Division
^	Exponentiation

TABLE F-3: **Common functions**

function	sample expression and description
DATE	DATE()-[BirthDate] Calculates the number of days between today and the date in the BirthDate field
PMT	PMT([Rate],[Term],[Loan]) Calculates the monthly payment on a loan where the Rate field contains the monthly interest rate, the Term field contains the number of monthly payments, and the Loan field contains the total amount financed
LEFT	LEFT([Lastname],2) Returns the first two characters of the entry in the Lastname field
RIGHT	RIGHT([Partno],3) Returns the last three characters of the entry in the Partno field
LEN	LEN([Description]) Returns the number of characters in the Description field

Building Summary Queries

As your database grows, you will probably be less interested in viewing individual records and more interested in analyzing information about groups of records. A **summary query** can be used to calculate information about a group of records by adding appropriate **aggregate functions** to the Total row of the query design grid. Aggregate functions calculate information about a *group of records* rather than a new field of information for *each record*. Aggregate functions are summarized in Table F-4. Some aggregate functions such as Sum can be used only on fields with Number or Currency data types, but others such as Min, Max, or Count can be used on Text fields, too. ✎ The Accounting Department has asked Fred for a report on costs by department showing how many classes employees of each department have attended as well as the summarized costs for these courses. He builds a summary query to provide this information.

Steps 1 2 3 4

1. Click **Queries** on the Objects bar, then double-click **Create query in Design View**

2. Double-click **Courses**, double-click **Attendance**, double-click **Employees**, then click **Close** in the Show Table dialog box
   Even though you won't explicitly use fields from the Attendance table, you need this table in your query to tie the fields from the Courses and Employees tables together.

3. Double-click the **Department field** in the Employees table, double-click the **Cost field** in the Courses table, then double-click the **Cost field** in the Courses table again
   You added the Cost field to the query grid twice because you wish to compute two different summary statistics (subtotal and count) on the data in this field.

4. Click the **Totals button** ∑ on the Query Design toolbar
   The **Total row** is added to the query grid below the Table row. Use the Total row to specify how you want the resulting datasheet grouped and summarized.

5. Click the **Cost field Total cell** in the second column, click the **Group By list arrow**, click **Sum**, click the **Cost field Total cell** in the third column, click the **Group By list arrow**, then click **Count**
   The query groups the records by the Department field, then sums (adds) and counts the data in the Cost field. Your Query Design View should look like Figure F-13.

6. Click the **Datasheet View button** 🖽 on the Query Design toolbar
   The Accounting Department had $3,700 of internal charges for the 16 classes its employees attended, as shown in Figure F-14. By counting the Cost field in addition to summing it, you know how many records were combined to reach the total figure of $3,700. You can sort and filter summary queries, but you cannot enter or edit data in a summary query because each record represents the summarization of several records.

QuickTip
The query name is automatically placed in the header of the datasheet printout. So to uniquely identify your printout, include your name or initials in the query name.

7. Click the **Save button** 🖫 on the Query Datasheet toolbar, type **Internal Costs - Your Initials**, click **OK**, click the **Print button** 🖨, then close the datasheet

FIGURE F-13: Summary Query Design View

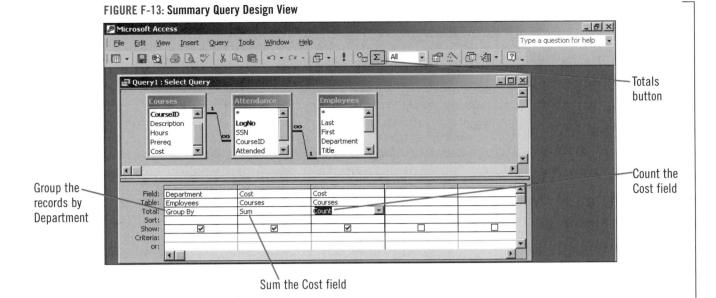

Group the records by Department

Sum the Cost field

Count the Cost field

Totals button

FIGURE F-14: Summarized records

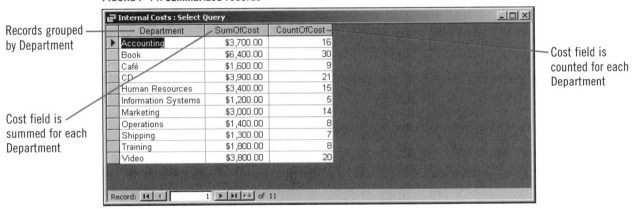

Records grouped by Department

Cost field is summed for each Department

Cost field is counted for each Department

TABLE F-4: Aggregate functions

aggregate function	used to find the
Sum	Total of values in a field
Avg	Average of values in a field
Min	Minimum value in the field
Max	Maximum value in the field
Count	Number of values in a field (not counting null values)
StDev	Standard deviation of values in a field
Var	Variance of values in a field
First	Field value from the first record in a table or query
Last	Field value from the last record in a table or query

Access 2002

Creating Crosstab Queries

Crosstab queries provide another way to summarize information about groups of records. Crosstab queries calculate a statistic such as sum or average by grouping records according to a field that serves as a row heading as well as a field that serves as a column heading. You can use the **Crosstab Query Wizard** to identify how the datasheet will be organized or build the crosstab query directly within Query Design View. ✎ Fred needs to summarize the total cost within each department by the course description. A crosstab query can be used to find this information because Fred is summarizing information by two fields, one that will serve as the row heading (Description), and one that will serve as the column heading (Department).

Steps

Trouble?

The Create query by using wizard option in the database window creates a select query. You must click the New button to use the other query wizards.

1. Click the **New button** 🔲 on the database window toolbar, click **Crosstab Query Wizard** in the New Query dialog box, then click **OK**
   The Crosstab Query Wizard dialog box opens. The first question asks you which table or query contains the fields for the crosstab query. The fields for this crosstab query were previously saved in the Crosstab Fields query.

2. Click the **Queries option button** in the View section, click **Crosstab Fields** in the list of available queries, then click **Next**
   The answers to the next questions in the Crosstab Query Wizard organize how the fields are displayed in the datasheet.

3. Double-click **Description** to select it as the row heading, click **Next**, click **Department** for the column heading, click **Next**, then click **Sum** in the Functions list
   The Sample portion of the Crosstab Query Wizard dialog box presents the Description field as the row heading, the Department field as the column heading, and the summarized Cost field within the body of the crosstab query, as shown in Figure F-15.

4. Click **Next**, type **Costs by Department and Course - Your Initials** in the query name text box, then click **Finish** to display the crosstab query, as shown in Figure F-16
   You can modify a crosstab query to change the row heading field, the column heading field, or the calculation statistic in Query Design View.

QuickTip

Click the Query Type button list arrow 🔲 ▾ on the Query Design toolbar, then click Crosstab Query to change any select query into a crosstab query.

5. Click the **Design View button** 🔲 on the Query Datasheet toolbar
   The Query Type button 🔲 ▾ on the Query Design toolbar displays the crosstab icon indicating that the resulting datasheet will organize the records in a crosstab arrangement. The Total row shows that the datasheet is grouped by both the Description and the Department fields. The **Crosstab row** specifies that the Description field will be used as a Row Heading, and that the Department field will be used as a Column Heading.

6. Click the **Total Of Cost: Cost field Total cell**, click the **Sum list arrow**, then click **Count**, as shown in Figure F-17
   The Total Of Cost: Cost field creates the second column on the datasheet, and will now count the number of times each course was taken, rather than sum the costs for each row.

7. Click the **Datasheet View button** 🔲 on the Query Design toolbar, then click the **Print button** 🖨

8. Click the **Save button** 💾, then close the crosstab query
   Crosstab queries appear with a crosstab icon to the left of the query name in the Database window.

FIGURE F-15: Crosstab Query Wizard

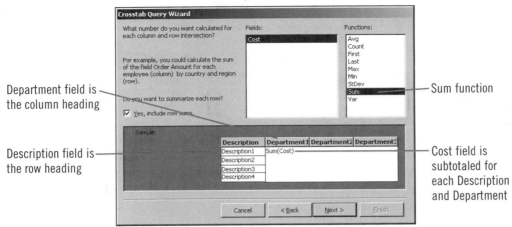

Department field is the column heading

Description field is the row heading

Sum function

Cost field is subtotaled for each Description and Department

FIGURE F-16: Crosstab Query datasheet

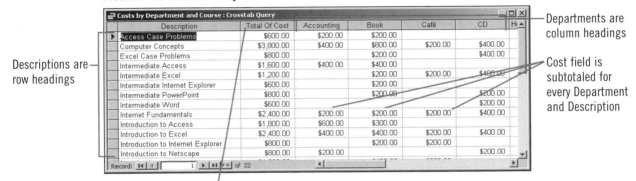

Descriptions are row headings

Departments are column headings

Cost field is subtotaled for every Department and Description

Total Of Cost column summarizes the costs for every row

FIGURE F-17: Query Design View of a crosstab query

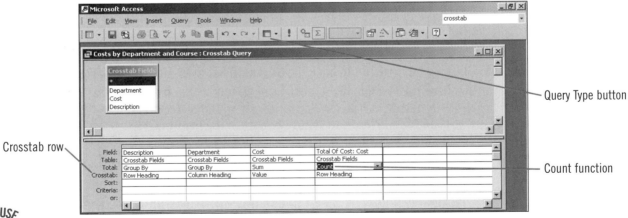

Query Type button

Crosstab row

Count function

Query Wizards

The **Simple Query Wizard** is an alternative way to create a select query, rather than going directly into Query Design View. The **Find Duplicates Query Wizard** is used to determine whether a table contains duplicate values in one or more fields. The **Find Unmatched Query Wizard** is used to find records in one table that don't have related records in another table. To start the Find Duplicates, Find Unmatched, or Crosstab Query Wizards, you must click the New button 📇 when viewing the query objects within the Database window.

Access 2002

Creating PivotTables and PivotCharts

Summarized data can be presented using a PivotTable and PivotChart. Similar to a crosstab query, a **PivotTable** calculates a statistic such as sum or average, by grouping records according to a field that serves as a row heading as well as a field that serves as a column heading. A **PivotChart** is a graphical presentation of the data in the PivotTable. You build a PivotTable using **PivotTable View**. Similarly, you work with PivotCharts in **PivotChart View**. The PivotChart and PivotTable Views are bound to one another so that when a change is made in one view, the other is automatically updated as well. ➤ Fred uses PivotChart View to summarize data in the Training database.

1. Double-click the **PivotTable Fields query**

   The PivotTable Fields query datasheet opens. You can build a PivotTable and PivotChart based on the fields of an existing table, query, or form.

Trouble?

If the Chart Field List does not appear, click the Field List button 📋 to toggle it on.

2. Click the **Design View button list arrow** 📉▾, then click **PivotChart View**

   The PivotChart View and Chart Field List appear, as shown in Figure F-18. In PivotChart View, you drag a field from the Chart Field List to a **drop area,** a position on the chart where you want the field to appear. The fields in the **Chart Field List** are the fields in the underlying object, in this case, the PivotTable Fields query. The relationship between drop areas on a PivotChart, PivotTable, and crosstab query are summarized in Table F-5.

Trouble?

If you drop a field to an incorrect area, drag it off the chart, then try again.

3. Drag **Department** from the Chart Field List to the Drop Category Fields Here drop area

   When you drag a field to a drop area, the drop area will display a blue border. Department field values now appear on the x-axis, also called the **category axis**.

Trouble?

Drag the title bar of the Chart Field List if you cannot see the Series drop area.

4. Drag **Cost** from the Chart Field List to the Drop Data Fields Here drop area, drag **Last** to the Drop Filter Fields Here drop area, then drag **CourseID** to the Drop Series Fields Here drop area, as shown in Figure F-19

   Cost field values are now displayed as bars on the chart, and are measured by the numbers displayed on the y-axis, also called the **value axis**. The CourseID field is in the legend, also called the **series**, position for the chart. The Last field is in the filter position for the chart. PivotChart and PivotTable Views are used to design a presentation of data as well as to analyze data. For example, PivotChart fields can be used to filter for only those records you wish to analyze.

5. Click 📋 to toggle it off, click the **CourseID list arrow**, click the **(All) check box** to remove all checkmarks, click the **Access1 check box**, then click **OK** in the CourseID filter list

   Now the PivotChart is filtered to display only the records for the Access1 CourseID. All PivotTable and PivotChart fields (except for the field summarized in the Data area) can be used to filter information.

QuickTip

If the data is filtered by that field, the field's list arrow will change from black to blue.

6. Click the **CourseID list arrow**, click **(All)** to add all checkmarks, click **OK** in the CourseID filter list, click the **Last list arrow**, click the **(All) check box** to remove all checkmarks, click the **Abbot check box**, then click **OK** in the Last filter list

   The resulting PivotChart shows you that Abbot is in the Marketing department, and has attended six classes. In order to see which classes Abbot attended, however, you need the CourseID values, which can be viewed in PivotTable View.

7. Click 📉▾ on the Formatting (PivotTable/PivotChart) toolbar, then click **PivotTable View**

   The PivotTable appears as shown in Figure F-20. The six CourseIDs are identified as column headings, and a grand total for each column and row is shown. You may also filter, reorganize, and analyze data in PivotTable View.

8. Click the **Save button** 💾, print and close the PivotTable, close the Training-F database, then exit Access

FIGURE F-18: PivotChart drop areas

Data field area

Filter field area

Numeric increments vary based on size of window

Category field area

Field List button

Chart Field List

Series field area

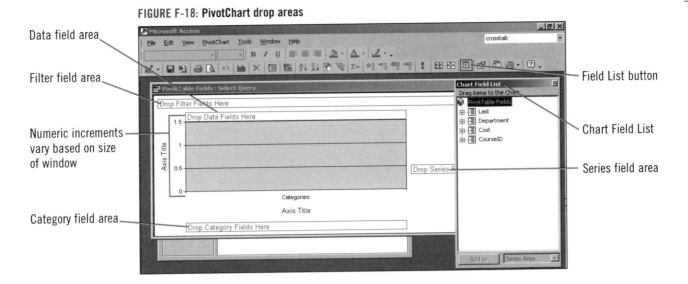

FIGURE F-19: PivotChart View

Last field in Filter area

Cost field in Data area

Value axis, y-axis

Department field in Category area

CourseID field in Series area, legend

Category axis, x-axis

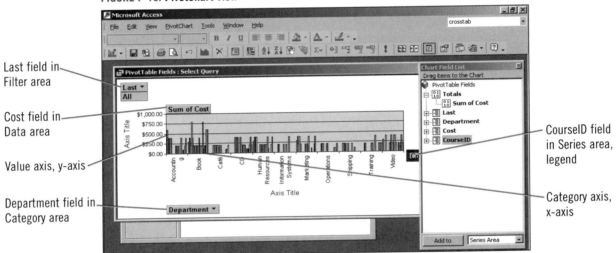

FIGURE F-20: PivotTable View

Field list arrows

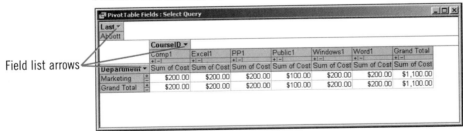

TABLE F-5: PivotTable and PivotChart drop areas

drop area on PivotTable	drop area on PivotChart	crosstab query field position
Filter Field	Filter Field	(NA)
Row Field	Category Field	Row Heading
Column Field	Series Field	Column Heading
Totals or Detail Field	Data Field	Value

Practice

► Concepts Review

Identify each element of Query Design View shown in Figure F-21.

FIGURE F-21

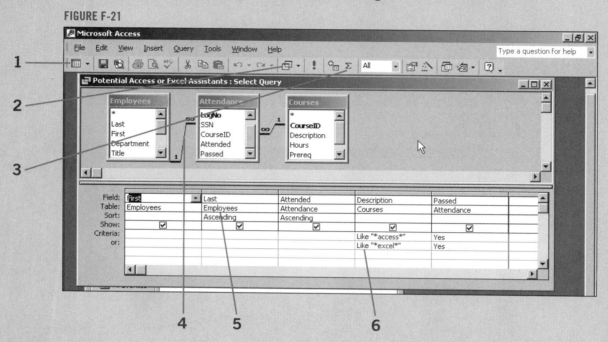

1
2
3
4   5   6

Match each term with the statement that describes its function.

7. **Query**
8. **Arithmetic operators**
9. **AND criteria**
10. **Sorting**
11. **OR Criteria**

a. Placing the records of a datasheet in a certain order
b. Used within mathematical calculations
c. A database object that answers questions about the data
d. Entered on more than one row of the query design grid
e. Entered on one row of the query design grid

Select the best answer from the list of choices.

12. **The query datasheet can best be described as a:**
    a. Duplication of the data in the underlying table's datasheet.
    b. Logical view of the selected data from an underlying table's datasheet.
    c. Separate file of data.
    d. Second copy of the data in the underlying tables.

13. **Queries are often used to:**
    a. Create copies of database files.
    b. Eliminate the need to build multiple tables.
    c. Create option boxes and list boxes from which to choose field values.
    d. Present a subset of fields from multiple tables.

14. **When you update data in a table that is displayed in a query:**
    a. You must also update the query.
    b. You must relink the query to the table.
    c. The data is automatically updated in the query.
    d. You have the choice whether or not you want to update the data in the query.

15. **To assemble several fields from different tables on one datasheet, use a(n):**
    a. Select query.
    b. Update query.
    c. Delete query.
    d. Append query.

16. **The order in which records are sorted is determined by:**
    a. The order in which the fields are defined in the underlying table.
    b. The alphabetic order of the field names.
    c. The left-to-right position of the fields in the query design grid that contain a sort order choice.
    d. The ascending fields are sorted first in the query design grid, then the descending fields are sorted second.

17. **Crosstab queries are used to:**
    a. Summarize information based on fields in the column and row headings areas.
    b. Update several records at the same time.
    c. Show a graphical representation of data.
    d. Calculate price increases on numeric fields.

18. **The PivotTable View is *not* available for which database object?**
    a. Tables
    b. Queries
    c. Forms
    d. Reports

19. **In Query Design View, which button identifies the type of query that is currently selected?**
    a. Query View
    b. Save
    c. Properties
    d. Query Type

20. **In a crosstab query, which field is the most likely candidate for the Value position?**
    a. FName
    b. Cost
    c. State
    d. Department

► Skills Review

1. **Create select queries.**
   a. Start Access and open the **Membership-F** database from the drive and folder where your Project Files are stored.
   b. Create a new select query in Design View using the Names and Zips tables.
   c. Add the following fields to the query design grid in this order:
      First, Last, and Street from the Names table
      City, State, and Zip from the Zips table
   d. In Datasheet View, replace the current Last name with your last name in the Last field of the first record.
   e. Save the query as **Basic Address List**, print the datasheet, then close the query.

2. **Sort a query on multiple fields.**
   a. Open the Basic Address List query in Design View.
   b. Drag the First field from the Names field list to the right of the Last field in the query design grid to make the first three fields in the query design grid First, Last, and First.
   c. Add the ascending sort criteria to the second and third fields in the query design grid, and uncheck the Show check box in the third column. The query is sorted in ascending order by Last, then by First, but the order of the fields in the resulting datasheet is First, Last.
   d. Use Save As to save the query as **Sorted Address List**, view the datasheet, print the datasheet, then close the query.

3. **Develop AND queries.**
   a. Open the Basic Address List in Design View.
   b. Type **M*** (the asterisk is a wildcard) in the Last field criteria row to choose all people whose last name starts with M. Access assists you with the syntax for this type of criterion and enters Like "M*" in the cell when you click elsewhere in the query design grid.
   c. Enter **KS** as the criterion for the State field. Be sure to enter the criteria on the same line in the query design grid as the Like "M*" criteria.
   d. View the datasheet that selects only those people from Kansas with a last name that starts with the letter M.
   e. Enter a new value in the City field of the first record to uniquely identify the printout.
   f. Use Save As to save the query as **Kansas M Names**, print, then close the datasheet.

4. **Develop OR queries.**
   a. Open the Kansas M Names query in Design View.
   b. Enter **C*** in the second criteria row (the or row) of the Last field.
   c. Enter **KS** as the criterion in the second criteria row (the or row) of the State field so that only those people from KS with a last name that starts with either the letters M or C are selected.
   d. Use Save As to save the query as **Kansas C or M Names**, view and print the datasheet, then close the query.

5. **Create calculated fields.**
   a. Create a new select query using Design View using only the Names table.
   b. Add the following fields to the query design grid in this order: First, Last, Birthday.
   c. Create a calculated field called DaysOld in the fourth column of the query design grid by entering the expression: **DaysOld:Date()-[Birthday]** to determine the number of days old each person is based on the information in the Birthday field.
   d. Sort the query in descending order on the calculated DaysOld field, then view the datasheet.
   e. Return to Query Design View, open the Property sheet for the DaysOld field, then format the DaysOld field with a Standard format and **0** in the Decimal Places property text box.
   f. Save the query with the name **Age**, view the datasheet, print the datasheet, then close the query.

6. **Build summary queries.**

   a. Create a new select query in Design View using the Names and Activities tables.

   b. Add the following fields: First and Last from the Names table, Hours from the Activities table.

   c. Add the Total row to the query design grid, then change the function for the Hours field from Group By to Sum.

   d. Sort in descending order by Hours.

   e. Save the query as **Total Hours-Your Initials**, view the datasheet, print the datasheet, then close the query.

7. **Create crosstab queries.**

   a. Create a select query with the City and State fields from the Zips table, and the Dues field from the Names table. Save the query as **Crosstab Fields**, then close the query.

   b. Click the New button in the database window, click Crosstab Query Wizard in the New Query dialog box, click OK, then base the crosstab query on the Crosstab Fields query you just created.

   c. Select City as the row heading, State as the column heading, and sum the Dues field within the crosstab datasheet.

   d. Name the query **Crosstab of Dues by City and State-Your Initials**, then click Finish.

   e. View, print, then close the datasheet.

8. **Create PivotTables and PivotCharts.**

   a. Create a select query with the State field from the Zips table, and the CharterMember and Dues fields from the Names table. Save it as **Dues Analysis-Your Initials**.

   b. Switch to PivotChart View, open the Chart Field List if it is not already visible, then drag the State field to the Drop Category Fields Here drop area, the CharterMember field to the Drop Series Fields Here drop area, and the Dues field to the Drop Data Fields Here drop area.

   c. Use the CharterMember field to display only the data for the records where the CharterMember value is Yes, as shown in Figure F-22.

   FIGURE F-22

   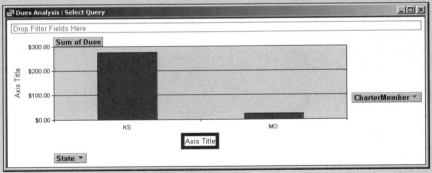

   d. Switch to PivotTable View, then print it.

   e. Save the changes to the Dues Analysis-Your Initials query, close it, close the Membership-F database, then exit Access.

▶ Independent Challenge 1

As the manager of a music store's instrument rental program, you have created a database to track instrument rentals to schoolchildren. Now that several rentals have been made, you want to query the database for several different datasheet printouts to analyze school information.

   a. Start Access and open the **Music Store-F** database from the drive and folder where your Project Files are stored.

   b. In Query Design View create a select query with the SchoolName field from the Schools table, the Date field from the Rentals table, and the Description field from the Instruments table. (*Hint:* You will need to add the Customers table to this query to make the connection between the Schools table and the Rentals table even though you don't need any Customers fields in this query's datasheet.)

   c. Sort ascending by SchoolName, then ascending by Date.

   d. Save the query as **School Rentals**, replace the current entry in the first record with your elementary school name, then print the datasheet.

Access 2002

e. Modify the School Rentals query by deleting the Description field. Then, use the Totals button to group the records by SchoolName and to Count the Date field. Print the datasheet and save the query as **School Count**. Close the datasheet.

f. Use the Crosstab Query Wizard to create a crosstab query based on the School Rentals query. Use Description as the row heading and SchoolName as the column heading. Count the Date field.

g. Save the query as **School Crosstab**, then view, print, and close it.

h. Modify the School Rentals query so that only those schools with the word Elementary in the SchoolName field are displayed. (*Hint:* You will have to use wildcard characters in the criteria.)

i. Save the query as **Elementary Rentals**, then view, print, and close the datasheet.

j. Close the Music Store-F database, then exit Access.

▶ Independent Challenge 2

As the manager of a music store's instrument rental program, you have created a database to track instrument rentals to schoolchildren. The database has already been used to answer several basic questions, and now that you've shown how easy it is to get the answers using queries, more and more questions are being asked. You will use queries to analyze customer and rental information.

a. Start Access and open the **Music Store-F** database from the drive and folder where your Project Files are stored.

b. In Query Design View, create a select query with the Description and MonthlyFee fields from Instruments table, and the Zip and City fields from the Customers table. (*Hint:* You will need to add the Rentals table to this query to make the connection between the Customers table and the Instruments table even though you don't need any fields from the Rentals table in this query's datasheet.)

c. Add the Zip field to the first column of the query grid and specify an Ascending sort order for this field. Uncheck the Show check box for the first Zip field so that it will not display in the datasheet.

d. Specify an Ascending sort order for the Description field.

e. Save the query as **Zip Analysis**.

f. View the datasheet, replace Des Moines with a unique city entry in the first record's City field, then print and close the datasheet.

g. Modify the Zip Analysis query by adding criteria to find the records where the Description is equal to **viola**.

h. Save this query as **Violas**. How many records are in the datasheet?

i. Modify the Violas query with AND criteria that further specifies that the City must be **Des Moines**.

j. Save this query as **Violas in Des Moines**. How many records are in the datasheet?

k. Modify the Violas query with OR criteria that finds all violas or violins, regardless of where they are located.

l. Save this query as **Violas or Violins**. How many records are in the datasheet?

m. Using the Crosstab Query Wizard, create a crosstab query based on the School Analysis query that uses the Description field for the row headings, the SchoolName field for the column headings, and that Counts the RentalNo field.

n. Save the crosstab query as **Crosstab School and Instrument-Your Initials**, preview the datasheet, then print the datasheet in landscape orientation so that it fits on one page.

o. Close the **Music Store-F** database then exit Access.

▶ Independent Challenge 3

As the manager of a music store's instrument rental program, you have created a database to track instrument rentals to schoolchildren. Now that several rentals have been made, you wish to query the database to analyze customer and rental information.

a. Start Access and open the **Music Store-F** database from the drive and folder where your Project Files are stored.

b. In Query Design View, create a query that uses the following fields in the following order:
   FirstName and LastName from the Customers Table
   Description and MonthlyFee from the Instruments Table
   (*Hint:* You will need to add the Rentals table to this query to make the connection between the Customers table and the Instruments table even though you don't need any fields from the Rentals table in this query's datasheet.)

c. Sort the records in ascending order by the LastName field.

d. Save the query as **Customer Rentals-Your Initials**, view the datasheet, enter your own last name in the first record's LastName field, then print the datasheet.

e. In Query Design View, modify the Customer Rentals query by deleting the FirstName and LastName fields. Then, click the Totals button to group the records by Description and to Sum the MonthlyFee field.

f. Add another MonthlyFee field as a third column to the query design grid, and use the Count function to find the total number of rentals within that group.

g. Sort the records in ascending order by the Description field.

h. Save the query as **Monthly Instrument Income-Your Initials**.

i. View, print, then close the datasheet.

FIGURE F-23

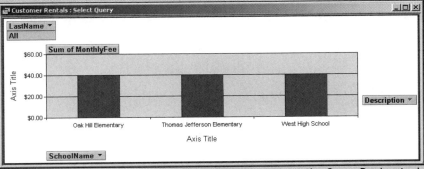

j. Open the Customer Rentals-Your Initials query in Design View, click the Show Table button on the Query Design toolbar to add the Schools table to the query, then add the SchoolName field as the fifth field in the query design grid.

k. Display PivotChart View, then create the PivotChart shown in Figure F-23. The Description field has been used as a filter to show only the cello records.

l. Print the PivotTable view, save and close the Customer Rentals-Your Initials query, close the **Music Store-F** database, then exit Access.

Independent Challenge 4

You are on the staff of an economic development team whose goal is to encourage tourism in the Baltic Sea region. You have created an Access database called Baltic-F to track important fields of information for the countries in that region, and are using the Internet to find information about the area that you then enter into existing forms.

a. Start Access and open the **Baltic-F** database from the drive and folder where your Project Files are stored.

b. Connect to the Internet, then go to www.hotbot.com, www.go.com or any general search engine to conduct some research for your database. Your goal is to find three upcoming events for Stockholm, Sweden, then print the Web page.

c. Open the Cities table datasheet, expand the Stockholm record, and enter three events for Stockholm into the subdatasheet. EventID is an AutoNumber field, so it will automatically increment as you enter the EventName and EventDate information.

d. Using Query Design View, create a select query with the following fields: Country and City from the Cities table and EventName and EventDate from the Events table.

e. Save the query with the name **Event Info**, then close it.

f. Use the Crosstab Query Wizard to create a query based on the Event Info query. City should be the row heading, Country the column heading, and the EventDate field should be Counted within the body of the crosstab query.

g. Title the query **Country Crosstab-Your Initials**, view, then print the datasheet.

h. Close the **Baltic-F** database, then exit Access.

▶ Visual Workshop

Open the **Training-F** database from the drive and folder where your Project Files are located. In Query Design View create a new select query with the Department field from the Employees table, and the Cost and CourseID fields from the Courses table. Add the Attendance table to the query to connect the Employees table to the Courses table in the query. Display the query in PivotChart View, save it with the name **Accounting – Access - Your Initials**, then filter the records to show only the Access1, Access2, and AccessLab CourseIDs for the Accounting Department, as shown in Figure F-24. Print the PivotTable View of the Accounting – Access - Your Initials query.

FIGURE F-24

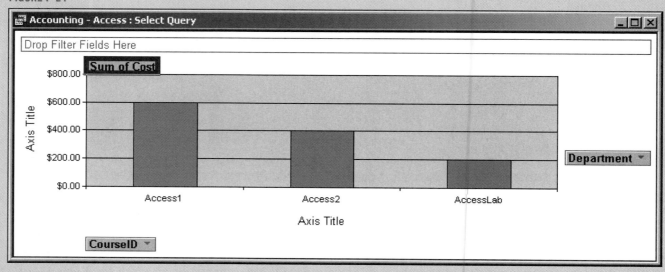

Unit
G

Developing
Forms and Subforms

Objectives

MOUS ► **Understand the form/subform relationship**

MOUS ► **Create subforms using the Form Wizard**

MOUS ► **Create subforms using queries**

MOUS ► **Modify subforms**

MOUS ► **Add combo boxes**

MOUS ► **Add option groups**

MOUS ► **Add command buttons**

MOUS ► **Add ActiveX controls**

Finding, entering, and editing data in a database must be easy and straightforward for all database users. A **form** can be designed to present data in any logical screen arrangement. It serves as the primary interface for most database users. Forms contain **controls** such as labels, text boxes, combo boxes, and command buttons to help identify and enter data. A form with a **subform** allows you to show a record and its related records from another object (table or query) at the same time. For example, you could display one customer and all of the orders placed by that customer at the same time. ✒️ Fred Ames wants to improve the usability of several forms in the MediaLoft database by using subform controls. He also wants to improve several forms by adding various controls such as combo boxes, option groups, command buttons, and ActiveX controls.

Understanding the Form/Subform Relationship

A **subform** control is actually a form within a form. The primary form is called the **main form,** and it contains the subform control. The subform shows related records that are linked to the single record currently displayed in the main form. The relationship between the main form and subform is often called a **parent/child relationship,** because the "parent" record in the main form is linked to many "children" records displayed in the subform. The link between the main form and subform is established through a linking field common to both, the same way a one-to-many relationship is created between underlying tables in the database. Well-designed form/subforms encourage fast, accurate data entry, and shield the data entry person from the complexity of underlying tables, queries, and datasheets.  Creating forms with subforms requires careful planning, so Fred studies form/subform planning guidelines before he attempts to create the forms in Access.

▶ **Sketch the layout of the form/subform on paper, identifying which fields belong in the main form and which belong in the subform**

Fred sketched two forms with subforms that he wants to create. Figure G-1 displays employee information in the main form and attendance information in the subform. Figure G-2 displays course information in the main form and employee information in the subform.

▶ **Determine whether you are going to create separate queries upon which the main form and subform will be based, or if you are going to use the Form Wizard to collect fields from multiple tables to create the form and subform objects**

This decision may have important consequences later because it determines the form's recordset. The **recordset** defines the fields and records that will appear on the form. To modify the recordset of forms created solely through the Form Wizard, you have to modify the form's **Record Source property,** where the recordset is defined. When the form is based on an intermediate query, changing the query object automatically updates the Record Source property for the form, because the query object name *is* the Record Source property entry for that form.

If you use the Form Wizard to create a form with fields from multiple tables without an intermediary query object, the Record Source property of the form often displays an **SQL (Structured Query Language) statement.** This SQL statement can be modified to change the recordset, but requires some knowledge of SQL.

Create the form and subform objects based on the appropriate intermediary queries.
▶ **If intermediary queries were not created, use the Form Wizard to gather the fields for both the form and subform**

Fred uses the Form Wizard technique as well as the intermediary query technique so that he can compare the two.

FIGURE G-1: Employees Main Form with Attendance Subform

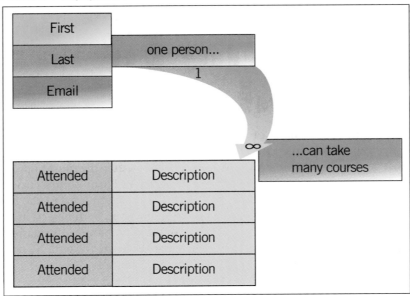

FIGURE G-2: Courses Main Form with Employee Subform

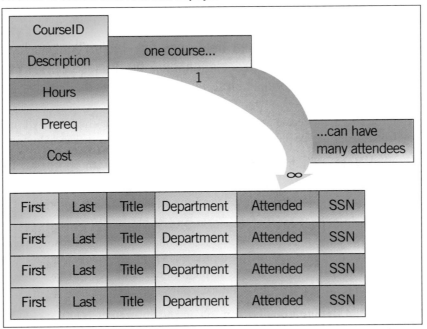

Creating Subforms Using the Form Wizard

A form displays the fields of a table or query in an arrangement that you design, based on one of five general **layouts**: Columnar, Tabular, Datasheet, Chart, and PivotTable. **Columnar** is the most popular layout for a main form, and **Datasheet** is the most popular layout for a subform. See Table G-1 for more information on the different Form Wizard layouts. Once the main form is created, the subform control is added in Form Design View of the main form. If you create the form/subform through the Form Wizard, however, both objects are created in one process. Fred creates a form and subform showing employee information in the main form and course information in the subform. By using the Form Wizard, he creates the form/subform objects without first creating intermediary query objects.

Steps

1. Start Access, then open the **Training-G** database from the drive and folder where your Project Files are stored
   The Training-G database opens. The database has three tables.

2. Click **Forms** on the Objects bar, then double-click **Create form by using wizard** in the Training-G Database window
   The **Form Wizard** appears and prompts you to select the fields of the form. You need five fields that are stored in three different tables for the final form/subform.

3. Double-click the **Attended field**, click the **Tables/Queries list arrow**, click **Table: Courses**, double-click **Description**, click the **Tables/Queries list arrow**, click **Table: Employees**, double-click **First**, double-click **Last**, then double-click **Email**, as shown in Figure G-3
   Next, you must decide how to view the data. Arranging the form by Employees places the fields from the Employees table in the main form, and the Attended and Description fields in a subform.

QuickTip
Use the Standard style when saving a database to a floppy disk. The other styles contain graphics that increase the storage requirements of the form.

4. Click **Next**, click **by Employees**, click the **Form with subform(s) option button** (if not already selected), click **Next**, click the **Datasheet option button** (if not already selected), click **Next**, click **Standard** (if not already selected), click **Next**, then click **Finish** to accept the default form and subform names
   The final Employees main form and Attendance Subform is shown in Figure G-4. Two sets of Navigation buttons appear, one for the main form and one for the subform. The Navigation buttons show that 20 employees are in the recordset and that the first employee attended 11 courses. You can resize the form and subform control to display more information.

Trouble?
If the subform control appears as a white box in Form Design View, click the Form View button ⊞, then click the Design View button ⊠ to refresh the window.

5. Click the **Design View button** ⊠ on the Form View toolbar, click the **Employees Form Maximize button** ☐, click the **subform control** so that sizing handles appear, then drag the bottom middle sizing handle of the subform control to the bottom of the screen using the ↕ pointer, as shown in Figure G-5
   The controls on the Attendance Subform appear within the subform control, and can be modified, just like controls in the main form. To select the subform control, click its edge.

6. Click the **Form View button** ⊞ on the Form Design toolbar to view the resized subform, click the **Save button** 🖫 on the Form View toolbar, then close the Employees form
   The Employees form and the Attendance Subform appear with other form objects in the Training-G Database window.

FIGURE G-3: Form Wizard

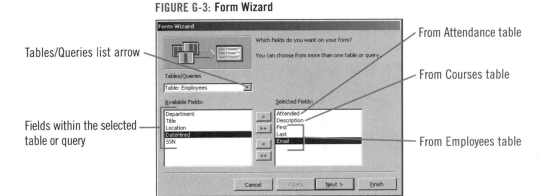

Tables/Queries list arrow

Fields within the selected table or query

From Attendance table

From Courses table

From Employees table

FIGURE G-4: Employees Main Form with Attendance Subform

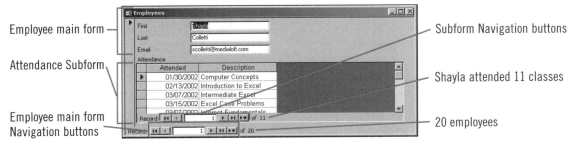

Employee main form

Attendance Subform

Employee main form Navigation buttons

Subform Navigation buttons

Shayla attended 11 classes

20 employees

FIGURE G-5: Resizing the Attendance Subform

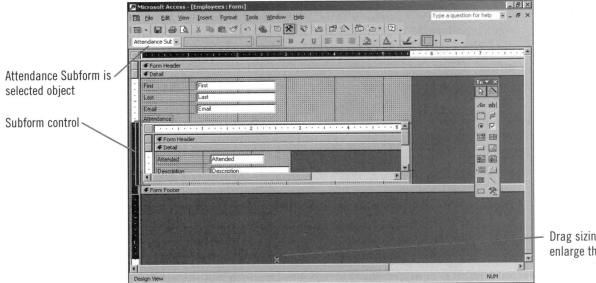

Attendance Subform is selected object

Subform control

Drag sizing handle to enlarge the subform

TABLE G-1: Form Wizard layouts

layout	description
Columnar	Each field appears on a separate line with a label to its left. The form displays one record at a time.
Tabular	Each field appears as a column heading and each record as a row. Multiple records appear just as they do in a Datasheet layout.
Datasheet	Each field appears as a column heading and each record as a row. The Datasheet layout shows multiple records at a time and emulates the datasheet of a table or query object. Formatting options are limited to the formats that you can apply to a datasheet. To display the data in the same general arrangement but preserve form design and formatting features, use the Tabular layout.
Justified	Each field name appears as a column heading with as much column width as needed to display field values. Unlike a Datasheet or Tabular layout, if all of the fields do not fit on one row, remaining fields will wrap to the second, third, etc., rows so that you can view all of the fields for the recordset on a form at the same time. The form displays one record at a time.

Creating Subforms Using Queries

Another way to create a form with a subform is to create both forms separately, basing them on either table or query objects, then linking the two forms together in a form/subform relationship. Although creating the forms by building them on separate query objects takes more work than building the form/subform using the Form Wizard, the advantage is your ability to quickly change the recordset of the form by modifying the underlying query. ✎ Fred creates a form and subform showing course information in the main form and employee information in the subform using query objects that he has already created.

Steps

Trouble?

If the property sheet doesn't show the word "Form" in the title bar, click the Form Selector button.

1. **Double-click Create form in Design view**, click the **Properties button** 🖼 on the Form Design toolbar to display the form's property sheet, click the **Data tab**, click the **Record Source list arrow**, then click **Employee Info**
   The field list for the Employee Info query opens to display the fields available to this form. The **Default View** property determines the initial layout of the form. The Datasheet Default View is a popular style for subforms because it arranges the fields horizontally.

2. Click the **Format tab**, click the **Default View list arrow**, click **Datasheet**, then click 🖼 to toggle off the property sheet
   With the Record Source and Default View specified, you are ready to add the fields to the form.

Trouble?

If you incorrectly drag and position the fields on the form, click Undo 🔙, then try again.

3. Double-click the **Employee Info field list title bar** to select all fields in the list, then drag the **selected fields** to the form as shown in Figure G-6.
   You have added all of the fields from the Employee Info query to the form.

4. Click the **Field List button** to toggle off the field list, then click the **Datasheet View button** 🔲 on the Form Design toolbar
   All forms can be viewed as datasheets, but in this case, the Datasheet View button appears on the Form Design toolbar because the Default View property was set to Datasheet.

5. Click the **Save button** 💾 on the Form View toolbar to open the Save As dialog box, type **Employee Info Subform** in the Form Name text box, click **OK**, then close the form
   The Employee Info Subform will be added later as a subform control to the Courses form, which will serve as the main form in this form/subform relationship.

6. Right-click **Courses**, then click **Design View** from the shortcut menu
   The Courses form displays fields from the Courses table in the upper portion of the form. It displays information on one course at a time. The Employee Info Subform will be related to the Courses form through the common CourseID field.

Trouble?

If the SubForm Wizard does not appear, delete the subform control, make sure that the Control Wizards button 🔳 on the Toolbox toolbar is selected, then repeat Step 7.

7. Click the **Toolbox button** 🛠 on the Form Design toolbar to display the Toolbox toolbar (if not already displayed), click the **Subform/Subreport button** 🔲 on the Toolbox toolbar, then drag ⁺🔲 to create a rectangle, as shown in Figure G-7
   If you drag a control beyond the edges of an existing form, the form will automatically enlarge to accept the control. The SubForm Wizard appears.

8. Click **Employee Info Subform** in the Use an existing form list, click **Next**, click the **Show Employee Info for each record in Courses using CourseID** (if not already selected), click **Next**, click **Finish** to accept the default name for the new subform control, then click the **Form View button** 🔲 on the Form Design toolbar
   The final form/subform is shown in Figure G-8. The first of 27 courses, Access1, is displayed in the main form. The six employees who completed that course are displayed in the subform. The number of fields displayed in the subform is dependent on the width of the subform control in Form Design View.

FIGURE G-6: Creating the Employee Info Subform

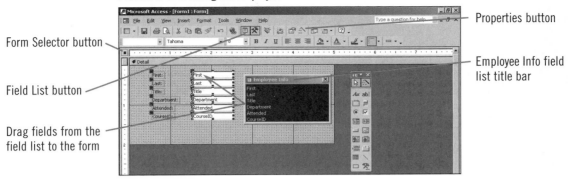

Form Selector button

Field List button

Drag fields from the field list to the form

Properties button

Employee Info field list title bar

FIGURE G-7: Adding a subform control

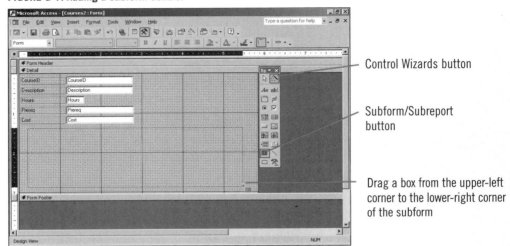

Control Wizards button

Subform/Subreport button

Drag a box from the upper-left corner to the lower-right corner of the subform

FIGURE G-8: Courses main form with Employee Info Subform

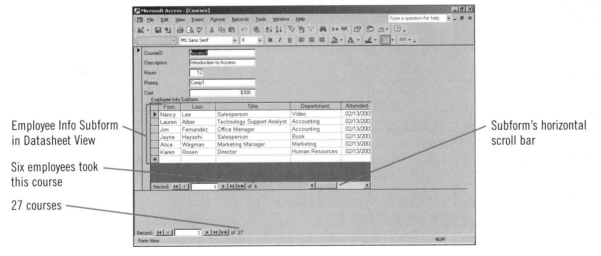

Employee Info Subform in Datasheet View

Six employees took this course

27 courses

Subform's horizontal scroll bar

Linking the form and subform

If the form and subform do not appear to be correctly linked, examine the subform's property sheet, paying special attention to the **Link Child Fields** and **Link Master Fields** properties on the Data tab. These properties tell you which field serves as the link between the main form and subform. The field specified for this property should be present in the queries that underlie the main form and subform, and is the same field that creates a one-to-many relationship between tables.

Access 2002

Modifying Subforms

Because the form/subform arrangement packs so much information on one screen, it is important to modify and format the form/subform to present the data clearly. In Form View, you can resize, hide, or move the columns of the subform as well as change the font, grid color, or background color of the subform. To modify other aspects of either the form or subform, you need to work in Form Design View. You can modify the controls of both the main form and the subform when working in Design View of the main form. ____ Fred likes the form/subform arrangement that displays each course in the main form and each employee who has taken that course in the subform, but he will improve upon the subform's design to display the employee subform information more clearly.

Steps

Trouble?

If sizing handles do not appear around the entire subform control or if the subform name is not in the Object box on the Formatting Form/Report toolbar, click outside the control, then click the subform control again to select it.

1. Click the **Design View button** on the Form View toolbar, click the edge of the **subform control** to select it (if it is not already selected), then drag the **middle right sizing handle** to the 7" mark on the horizontal ruler, as shown in Figure G-9

   Widening the subform control allows you to display more fields at the same time. Even though the fields of the subform appear to be in a vertical arrangement in the subform control, the Datasheet Default View property forces them to display horizontally, like a datasheet. Other options for a subform's Default View property are shown in Table G-2.

2. Click the **Form View button** on the Form Design toolbar to view the widened subform

   The appearance of a horizontal scroll bar on the subform tells you that not all of the fields are visible on the datasheet of the subform. You can resize the columns of the datasheet directly in Form View.

Trouble?

You do not see ↔ when pointing within the datasheet itself. It appears only when you point to the edge of the field selector (between field names at the top of the datasheet).

3. Point to the **column separator** between the First and Last fields, double-click with ↔ to automatically adjust the column to accommodate the widest entry, double-click each **column separator** in the subform, then click the **Save button** on the Form View toolbar

   Your screen should look like Figure G-10. Notice that the horizontal scroll bar disappears when all fields within the subform are visible. You can always sort, filter, and find records directly on a form or subform, but filters are not saved with the form object. By basing form objects on queries, you can easily modify the form's recordset by modifying the underlying query. MediaLoft's Accounting Department wants to use this form to display the subform data for the employees in their own department.

4. Close the Courses form, click **Queries** on the Objects bar, right-click **Employee Info**, then click **Design View**

   The Design View of the Employee Info query, upon which the Employee Info Subform is based, opens. Modifying this query will automatically modify the recordset displayed by the Employee Info Subform.

5. Click the **Department field Criteria cell**, type **Accounting**, then click the **Datasheet View button**

   The query now displays only the sixteen records that have a Department value equal to Accounting.

6. Click , then close the Employee Info query

7. Click **Forms** on the Objects bar, then double-click **Courses** to open it

   The Employee Info Subform that is based on the Employee Info query displays only those two employees from the Accounting department, as shown in Figure G-11.

8. Press **[Page Down]** several times to observe the data in the subform

FIGURE G-9: Widening a subform

Employee Info Subform is selected

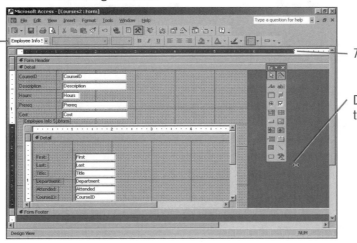

7" mark on horizontal ruler

Drag subform's sizing handle to 7" mark

FIGURE G-10: Resizing columns of a subform

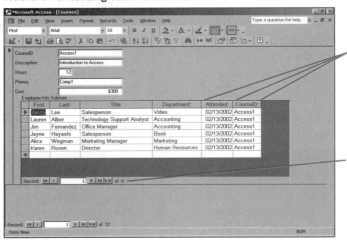

Double-click the right edge of the field name to resize the column

Subform does not have a horizontal scroll bar when all fields are displayed

FIGURE G-11: The final form/subform

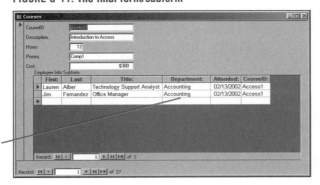

Department equals Accounting

TABLE G-2: Default View property options for subforms

default view property	description
Single Form	Displays one record at a time. Gives the user full ability to format the controls.
Continuous Form	Displays multiple records at a time, and is often used as the Default View property for subforms. Gives the user the ability to format the controls in Design View.
Datasheet	Displays multiple records at the same time in a datasheet arrangement regardless of how they are formatted in Design View. This is the most common Default View property choice for subforms.

Adding Combo Boxes

By default, most fields are added to a form as text boxes, but sometimes other types of controls such as list boxes, combo boxes, or options buttons would work better for a particular field. Both the **list box** and **combo box** controls provide a list of values from which the user can choose an entry. A combo box also allows the user to make an entry from the keyboard; therefore, it is a "combination" of the list box and text box controls. You can create a combo box by using the Combo Box Wizard to guide your actions, or you can change an existing text box or list box into a combo box. ➡ Fred changes the Prereq text box (which specifies if a prerequisite course is required) from a text box into a combo box to give users a list of existing courses offered at MediaLoft when entering data into the Prereq field.

Steps

1. Click the **Design View button** 📐, click the **Prereq text box** in the Detail section of the form, then press **[Delete]**
   Although you deleted the control, you can add the Prereq field back to the form as a combo box using the Combo Box Wizard.

2. Click the **Field List button** 📋 to toggle it on (if it is not already visible), click the **Combo Box button** 📰 on the Toolbox toolbar, then drag the **Prereq** field from the field list to the space between the Hours and Cost text boxes
   The Combo Box Wizard appears. You want the Prereq combo box to display the CourseID and Description field values from the Courses table.

3. Click the **I want the combo box to look up the values in a table or query option button** (if not already selected), click **Next**, click **Table: Courses**, click **Next**, double-click **CourseID**, double-click **Description**, click **Next** three times to move through the Combo Box Wizard and to accept column and value default options, type **Prereq** when prompted to enter a label for the combo box, then click **Finish**
   The new combo box control, bound to the Prereq field, is added to the form.

QuickTip

Press and hold [Ctrl], then press the arrow keys to move the control one pixel at a time.

4. Move and resize the Prereq combo box so that the form looks similar to Figure G-12
   Your final step will be to change the Cost text box into a combo box as well. MediaLoft has only four internal charges for its classes, $100, $200, $300, and $400. You want to display these values in the combo box.

5. Right-click the **Cost text box**, point to **Change To** on the shortcut menu, then click **Combo Box**
   This action changed the control from a text box to a combo box. You need to use the combo box's property sheet to specify where this combo box will get its values since a wizard did not prompt you for this information.

6. Click the **Properties button** 📄, click the **Data tab** (if not already selected), click the **Row Source Type text box**, click the **Row Source Type list arrow**, then click **Value List**
   This property choice indicates that the combo box will get its values from the list entered in the Row Source property.

Trouble?

Be sure to enter semicolons between the values in the Row Source property.

7. Click the **Row Source property text box**, type **$100; $200; $300; $400**, press **[Enter]**, click the **Limit to List property list arrow**, click **Yes**, then click 📄 to close the property sheet
   The entries in the **Row Source** property list become the values for the combo box's list. By changing the **Limit to List** property to "Yes," the user cannot enter a new entry from the keyboard.

8. Click the **Save button** 💾, click the **Form View button** 📰, click the **Cost combo box list arrow**, click **$400**, then click the **Restore Window button** 🗗 to restore the form window
   The updated form with two combo boxes should look like Figure G-13.

FIGURE G-12: Adding the Prereq combo box

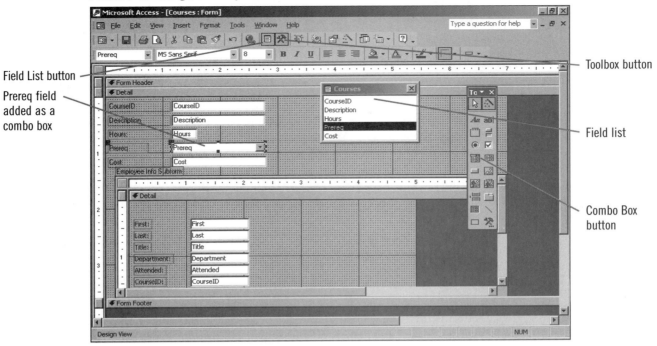

Field List button

Prereq field
added as a
combo box

Toolbox button

Field list

Combo Box
button

FIGURE G-13: Two new combo boxes

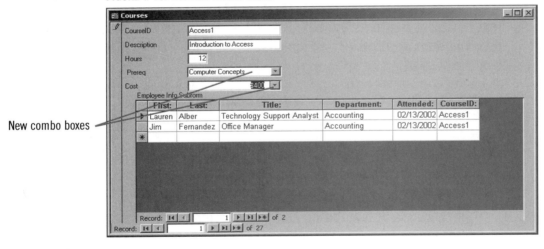

New combo boxes

Choosing between a combo box and a list box

The list box and combo box controls are very similar, but the combo box is more popular for at least two reasons. While both provide a list of values from which the user can choose to make an entry in a field, the combo box also allows the user to make a unique entry from the keyboard. More importantly, however, most users like the drop-down behavior of the combo box. A list box simply provides a list of values from which the user scrolls and selects a choice (the list box has no drop-down action). That's also why users often refer to the combo box as a drop-down list.

Access 2002

Adding Option Groups

An **option group** is a special type of bound control that is often used when a limited number of values are available for a field. You place **option button** controls within the option group to determine the value that is placed in the field. One option button exists for each possible entry. When the user clicks an option button, the numeric value associated with that option button is entered into the field bound to the option group. Option buttons within an option group are mutually exclusive, which means that only one can be chosen at a time. MediaLoft's classes are offered in 6-, 8-, 12-, and 16-hour formats. Because this represents a limited number of options, Fred uses an option group control for the Hours field to further simplify the Courses form.

Steps

1. Click the **Design View button** , click the **Hours text box**, then press **[Delete]**
   You can add the Hours field back to the form as an option group.

2. Click the **Option Group button** on the Toolbox, then drag the **Hours** field from the field list to the top of the right side of the form
   The **Option Group Wizard** helps guide the process of developing an option group. The first question asks about label names for the option buttons.

3. Type **6 hrs**, press **[Tab]**, type **8 hrs**, press **[Tab]**, type **12 hrs**, press **[Tab]**, type **16 hrs**, click **Next**, click the **No, I don't want a default option button**, then click **Next**
   The next question prompts you for the actual values associated with each option button.

4. Type **6**, press **[Tab]**, type **8**, press **[Tab]**, type **12**, press **[Tab]**, type **16**, click **Next**, click **Next** to accept **Hours** as the field that the value is stored in, click **Next** to accept **Option buttons controls** in an **Etched style**, type **Classroom Hours** as the caption, then click **Finish**
   An option group can contain option buttons, check boxes, or toggle button controls. The most common choice, however, are option buttons in an etched style. The **Control Source property** of the option group identifies the field it will update. The **Option Value property** of each option button identifies what value will be placed in the field when that option button is clicked. The new option group and option button controls are shown in Figure G-14.

5. Click the **Form View button** , then click the **16 hrs option button**
   Your screen should look like Figure G-15. You changed the Access1 course from 12 to 16 hrs.

QuickTip

The option group control will darken while you are adding an option button to it.

6. Click , click the **Option Button button** on the Toolbox toolbar, then click below the **16 hrs option button** in the option group
   Your screen should look similar to Figure G-16. This option button in the group will represent the new 24-hour classes that were just announced.

7. Double-click the **label** of the new option button, then type **24 hrs**
   You changed the new option button's label. The Option Value property for the new option button must be changed to reflect the value that you want entered into the Hours field if this option button is clicked.

8. Double-click the new **option button** to open its property sheet, click the **Data tab**, double-click **5** in the Option Value property text box to select it, type **24**, close the property sheet, move the **24 hrs option button** as necessary to align it with the other option buttons, click the **Save button** , then click to observe the new option button in Form View

FIGURE G-14: Adding an option group with option buttons

Four option buttons

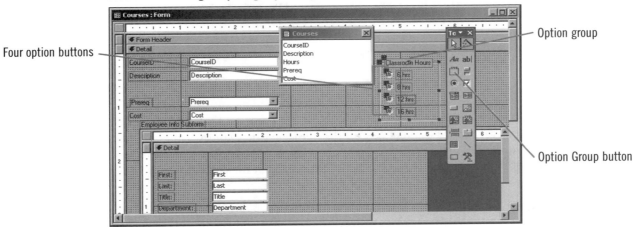

Option group

Option Group button

FIGURE G-15: Using an option group

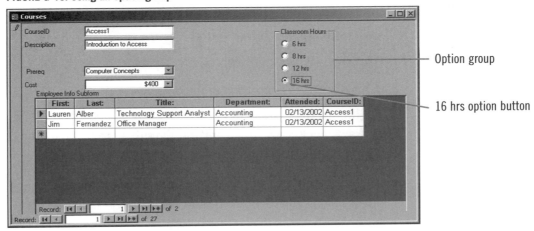

Option group

16 hrs option button

FIGURE G-16: Adding another option button

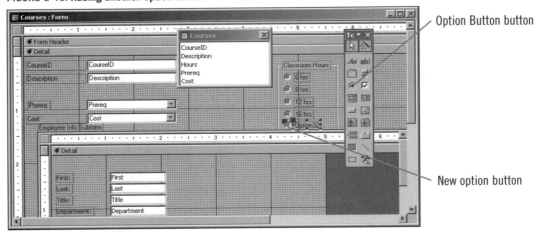

Option Button button

New option button

CLUES TO USE

Protecting data

You may not want all the data that appears on a form to be able to be changed by all users who view that form. You can design forms to limit access to certain fields by changing the enabled and locked properties of a control. The **Enabled** property specifies whether a control can have the focus in Form View. The **Locked** property specifies whether you can edit data in a control in Form View.

Unit G
Access 2002

Adding Command Buttons

A **command button** is a powerful unbound control used to initiate a common action in Form View such as printing the current record, opening another form, or closing the current form. Command buttons are added in Form Design View. They are often added to the **form header** or **form footer** sections. **Sections** determine where controls appear and print. See Table G-3 for more information on form sections. ✎ Fred adds a command button to the header section of the Courses form to help the users print the current record.

Steps 1 2 3 4

If the Form Header section is not visible, click View on the menu bar, then click Form Header/Footer.

1. **Click the Form Design View button** 🗏, point to the horizontal line that separates the Form Header and Detail section so that the pointer changes to ✛, then drag down to increase the size of the Form Header section about 0.5"
   Now that the Form Header is expanded, you can place controls in that section.

2. **Click the Command Button button** ▢ on the Toolbox toolbar, then click ⁺▭ on the right side of the Form Header
   The Command Button Wizard opens, listing over 30 of the most popular actions for the command button, organized within six categories.

3. **Click Record Operations in the Categories list, click Print Record in the Actions list, click Next, click Next to accept the default button appearance, type Print Current Record as the button name, then click Finish**
   Your screen should look similar to Figure G-17. By default, the Print button 🖨 on the Standard toolbar prints the entire recordset displayed by the form. Therefore, adding a command button to print only the current record is very useful.

4. **Click the Form View button** 🗗 to view the new command button, double-click **Alber** in the first record of the subform, type your last name, click the **Print Record command button** in the Form Header section, save, then close the form
   The printout required two pages. You can adjust the left and right margins so that the printout fits neatly on one page.

Double-click the menu bar to immediately display all options for that menu.

5. **Click File on the menu bar, click Page Setup, click the Margins tab** (if not already selected), press **[Tab]** three times to select **1** in the Left text box, type **0.5**, press **[Tab]** once to select **1** in the Right text box, type **0.5**, then click **OK**
   You can also choose to not print controls in certain form sections. The **Display When** property of the Form Header determines when the controls in that section display and print.

6. **Click** 🗏, double-click the **Form Header section** to open its property sheet, click the **Format tab**, click the **Display When list arrow**, click **Screen Only**, then click the **Properties button** 🗐
   The **Display When** property determines whether that control will appear only on the screen, only when printed, or at all times.

If your printout is still too wide for one sheet of paper, drag the right edge of the form to the left in Form Design View to narrow it.

7. **Click the Save button** 🖫, click 🗗, then click the **Print Record command button**
   Your final Courses Main Form should look like Figure G-18, and your printout should fit on one page, without displaying the form header.

8. **Close the Courses form**

FIGURE G-17: Adding a command button

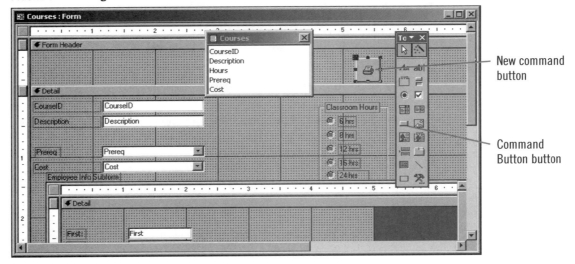

New command button

Command Button button

FIGURE G-18: The final Courses main form

Your last name will appear here

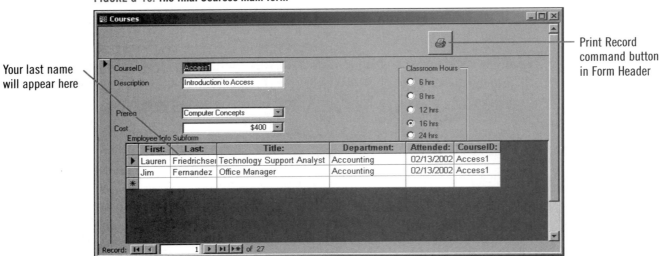

Print Record command button in Form Header

TABLE G-3: Form Sections

section	description
Detail	Appears once for every individual record
Form Header	Appears at the top of the form and often contains command buttons or a label with the title of the form
Form Footer	Appears at the bottom of the form and often contains command buttons or a label with instructions on how to use the form
Page Header	Appears at the top of a printed form with information such as page numbers or dates; the Page Header and Page Footer sections can be added to the form by clicking View on the menu bar, then clicking Page Header/Footer
Page Footer	Appears at the bottom of a printed form with information such as page numbers or dates

Adding ActiveX Controls

An **ActiveX Control** is a control that follows ActiveX standards. **ActiveX standards** are programming standards that were developed by Microsoft to allow developers to more easily share software components and functionality across multiple applications. For example, the same ActiveX control can be used in an Access form, in an Excel workbook, and on a Web page opened in Internet Explorer. The functionality of ActiveX controls range from multimedia players to charting programs to encryption software. Users of the Attendance form have asked Fred if there is a way to easily calculate the number of days between two dates. Fred uses a Calendar and Spreadsheet ActiveX control to give the users the functionality they have requested.

Steps

1. Right-click **Attendance**, then click **Design View** on the shortcut menu
Right now, the form lists six fields in a horizontal arrangement. The ActiveX controls will be placed just below the text boxes in the Detail section.

QuickTip

ActiveX controls are also available by clicking the More Controls button on the Toolbox toolbar.

2. Click **Insert** on the menu bar, then click **ActiveX Control**
The Insert ActiveX Control dialog box opens as shown in Figure G-19. All of the ActiveX controls available on your computer are listed alphabetically in the dialog box. The number and type of ActiveX controls will depend on the other programs loaded on your computer.

3. Press **C** to move to the ActiveX Controls that start with the letter "C", click **Calendar Control 10.0**, then click **OK**

4. Click **Insert** on the menu bar, click **ActiveX Control**, press **M,** click **Microsoft Office Spreadsheet 10.0**, click **OK** in the Insert ActiveX Control dialog box, then move and resize both new controls below the text boxes, as shown in Figure G-20
The **Calendar control** appears with the current date chosen. You can use the Calendar control to find or display a date. The **Spreadsheet control** provides similar functionality to that of an Excel spreadsheet, such as calculating the number of days between two dates.

5. Click the **Form View button** , click the **Month list arrow**, click **January**, click the **Year list arrow**, then click **2002**
Using the Calendar control, you can quickly find out what day of the week a particular class started on. In this case, you determine that the class for Shayla Colletti started on a Wednesday.

6. Click cell **A1** of the spreadsheet control, type **=today()**, then press **[Enter]**
This formula returns today's date, which is stored in the battery of your computer.

7. Type **1/30/2002** in cell A2, click cell **A3**, type **=A1-A2**, then press **[Enter]**
The formula in cell A3 determined the number of days between the two dates and presents it as the number of days since Shayla finished her Computer Concepts class. Right now, however, it is formatted as a date instead of as a whole number.

8. Right-click cell **A3**, click **Commands and Options** from the shortcut menu, click the **Number Format list arrow**, then click **General** as shown in Figure G-21
Using ActiveX technology, programmers can build small programs such as the Calendar and Spreadsheet control, and reuse them in many different ways in different programs.

9. Close the Commands and Options dialog box, click cell **C1**, type **your name**, click the **Save button** , click **File** on the menu bar, click **Print**, click the **Selected Record Option** button, then click **OK**

10. Close the Attendance form, close the **Training-G** database, then exit Access

FIGURE G-19: Insert ActiveX Control dialog box

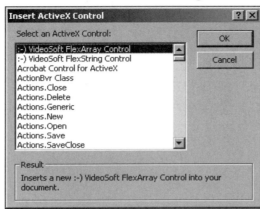

FIGURE G-20: ActiveX Controls in Form Design View

Calendar control

Spreadsheet control

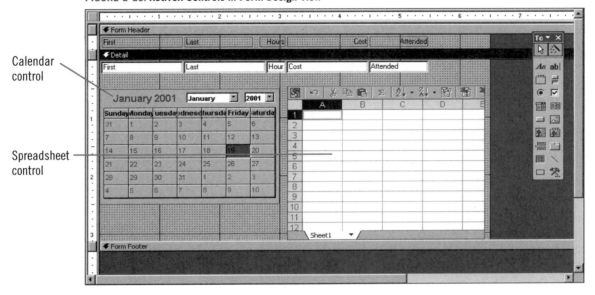

FIGURE G-21: Using ActiveX Controls

Month list arrow

Year list arrow

General Number Format

Formula calculates the number of days between two dates

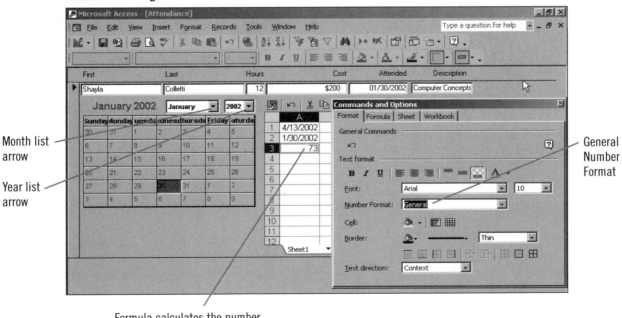

Practice

► Concepts Review

Identify each element of the Form Design View shown in Figure G-22.

FIGURE G-22

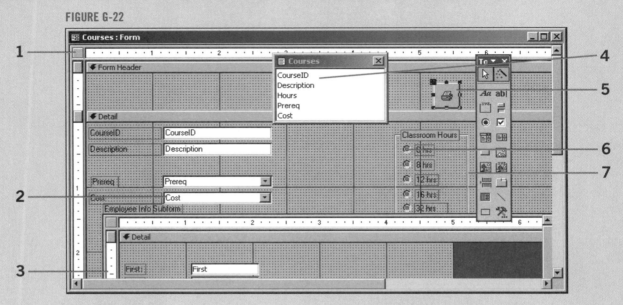

Match each term with the statement that describes its function.

8. **Option group**
9. **Controls**
10. **Command button**
11. **Subform**
12. **Combo box**

a. Elements you add to a form such as labels, text boxes, and list boxes
b. A control that shows records that are related to one record shown in the main form
c. An unbound control that executes an action when it is clicked
d. A bound control that is really both a list box and a text box
e. A bound control that displays a few mutually exclusive entries for a field

Select the best answer from the list of choices.

13. **Which control would work best to display two choices for a field?**
    a. Text box
    b. Label
    c. Option group
    d. Command button
14. **Which control would you use to initiate a print action?**
    a. Option group
    b. List box
    c. Text box
    d. Command button

15. **Which control would you use to display a drop-down list of 50 states?**
    a. Check box
    b. Field label
    c. List box
    d. Combo box

16. **To view linked records within a form use a:**
    a. Subform.
    b. List box.
    c. Design template.
    d. Link control.

17. **Which of the following defines what fields and records display on a form?**
    a. Recordset
    b. Toolbox
    c. Property sheet
    d. ActiveX control

18. **Which is a popular layout for a main form?**
    a. Datasheet
    b. PivotTable
    c. Columnar
    d. Global

19. **Which is a popular layout for a subform?**
    a. Datasheet
    b. PivotTable
    c. Columnar
    d. Global

20. **Which of the following is true of ActiveX controls?**
    a. They always display data from the recordset.
    b. They can be used in many applications.
    c. They are quite limited in scope and functionality.
    d. They are added to a form in Form View.

▶ Skills Review

1. **Understand the form/subform relationship.**
   a. Start Access and open the **Membership-G** database from the drive and folder where your Project Files are stored.
   b. Click the Relationships button on the Database toolbar.
   c. Double-click File on the menu bar, then click Print Relationships.
   d. The Relationships for Membership-G will appear as a previewed report. Click the Design View button, type your name as a label in the Report Header section, then print the report.
   e. Close the preview window without saving the report, and then close the Relationships window.
   f. Based on the one-to-many relationships defined in the Membership-G database, sketch two form/subform combinations that you could create.

2. **Create subforms using the Form Wizard.**
   a. Click Forms on the Objects bar in the Membership-G database window.
   b. Double-click Create form by using wizard.
   c. Select all of the fields from both the Activities and the Names tables.
   d. View the data by Names, then verify that the Form with subform(s) option button is selected.

e. Accept a Datasheet layout for the subform, a Standard style, and the default titles. Click Finish to view the Names form with the Activities subform.

f. Find the record for Lois Goode (record number 3) and change Lois's first and last name to your first and last name.

g. Resize the columns of the datasheet in the subform so that all of the data is clearly visible.

h. Click File on the menu bar, then click Print. Click the Selected records option button in the Print dialog box to print only the data for your name.

i. Save, then close the Names form.

3. Create subforms using queries.

a. Open the Zips in IA or MO query in Design View, then add the criteria to find only those records from IA or MO in the State field. View the datasheet, then save and close the query.

b. Using either the Form Wizard or Form Design View, build a columnar form based on the Zips in IA or MO query using all three fields in the query. Name the form **Zips in IA or MO.**

c. Open the Zips in IA or MO form in Design View, and add a subform control about 5" wide by about 3" high below the three text boxes in the Detail section of the form.

d. Use the Subform Wizard to specify that the subform will use an existing query, then select all of the fields in the Dues query for the subform.

e. Allow the wizard to link the form and subform so that they show Dues for each record in Zips in IA or MO using Zip.

f. Accept Dues Subform as the subform's name.

g. Maximize the form, expand the size of the subform, move the subform as necessary, and display it in Form View.

h. Resize the datasheet column widths so that all of the information in the subform is clearly visible. When all fields are visible, the horizontal scroll bar does not display in Form View and text from the subform doesn't overlap the main form.

i. Find the record for Zip 64105, enter your last name in the Last field of the first record, and print only that record.

j. Click File on the menu bar, click Save As, name the main form **Zips**, then save and close the form and subform.

4. Modify subforms.

a. Click the Queries button in the Objects bar and open the Zips in IA or MO query in Design View.

b. Delete the criteria that specifies that only the records with State values of IA or MO appear in the recordset.

c. Use Save As to save the modified query as **All Zips**, then close the query.

d. Click the Forms button on the Objects bar and open the Zips form in Design View.

e. Open the property sheet for the form by double-clicking the Form Selector button in the upper-left corner at the intersection of the rulers. Click the Data tab, then change the Record Source property from Zips in IA or MO to **All Zips**.

f. Close the property sheet, save the form, view the form in Form View, then navigate to record number 13, which displays Zip 64145 for Shawnee, Kansas.

g. Change the city to the name of your hometown, print only this record, then close the Zips form.

5. Add combo boxes.

a. Open the Names form in Design View, then delete the Zip text box.

b. Use the Combo Box Wizard to add the Zip field back to the same location as a combo box.

c. The Combo Box Wizard should look up values in a table or query.

d. Choose the Zips table and the Zip field as the column values.

e. Store the value in the Zip field, then label the Combo Box **ZipCode**.

f. Reposition the new ZipCode label and combo box as necessary, save the form, then display it in Form View.

g. Navigate to the third record, then change the Zip to **50266** using the new combo box.

6. Add option groups.

a. Open the Names form in Design View, then delete the Dues text box.

b. Add the Dues field back to the form below the CharterMember check box control using an Option Group control with the Option Group Wizard.

c. Enter **$25** and **$50** as the label names, then accept **$25** as the default choice.

d. Change the values to **25** and **50** to correspond with the labels.

e. Store the value in the Dues field, choose Option buttons with an Etched style, type the caption **Annual Dues**, then click Finish.

f. Save the form, display it in Form View, find the record with your address, then change the Annual Dues to **$25**.

g. Save the form.

7. Add command buttons.

a. Open the Names form in Design View.

b. Open the Form Header to display about 0.5" of space, then add a command button to the upper-right corner using the Command Button Wizard.

c. Choose the Print Record action from the Record Operations category.

d. Display the text **Print Current Record** on the button, then name the button **Print**.

e. Save the form and display it in Form View. The final form should look similar to Figure G-23.

f. Navigate to the record with your own name, change the month and day of the Birthday entry to your own, then print the record using the new Print Current Record command button.

g. Save, then close the Names form.

8. Add ActiveX Controls.

a. Open the Names form in Design View, then add a Microsoft Office Spreadsheet 10.0 ActiveX control to the Detail section of the main form.

FIGURE G-23

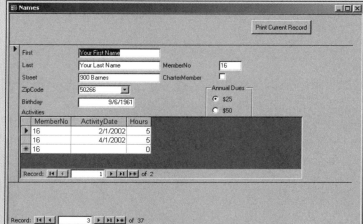

b. Resize the spreadsheet control so that about three columns and four rows are visible, then move it to the upper right corner of the Detail section of the main form.

c. Save the form, then view it in Form View. The spreadsheet ActiveX control will be used to calculate the value of time donated to various activities.

d. Navigate to the record with your name. In cell A1 of the spreadsheet, type **10**, the total number of hours you have contributed based on the information in the subform.

e. In Cell A2 of the spreadsheet, type **12**, the value of one hour of work for the purposes of determining contribution to this club.

f. In Cell A3 of the spreadsheet, type **=A1*A2**, then press [Enter] to calculate the total value of the hours of time you have donated.

g. Click the Print Current Record button to print this record.

h. Save and close the Names form, close the Membership-G database, then exit Access.

► Independent Challenge 1

As the manager of a music store's instrument rental program, you have created a database to track instrument rentals to schoolchildren. Now that several rentals have been made, you wish to create a form/subform to facilitate the user's ability to enter a new rental record.

a. Start Access then open the database **Music Store-G** from the drive and folder where your Project Files are stored.

b. Using the Form Wizard, create a new form based on all of the fields in the Customers and Rentals tables.

c. View the data by Customers, choose a Datasheet layout for the subform and a Standard style, then accept the default form titles of Customers for the main form and Rentals Subform for the subform.

d. Add another record to the rental subform by pressing [Tab] through both the RentalNo and CustNo fields, then typing **888335** as the SerialNo entry and **5/1/03** as the Date entry.

e. Close the Customers form.

f. You want to add the Description field to the subform information. To do this, click the Queries button on the Objects bar, then double-click Create query in Design view. This query will include the Description field, and will serve as the record source for the subform.

g. Add the Rentals and Instruments tables, then close the Show Table dialog box.

h. Add all of the fields from the Rentals table and the Description field from the Instruments table to the query, save the query with the name **Rental Description**, view the query datasheet, then close it.

i. Open the Rentals Subform in Design View, then change the Record Source property of the form from Rentals to **Rental Description**.

j. Open the subform's field list (if it is not already open), then drag the Description field to just below the Date text box in the Detail section. The field may not line up perfectly with the others and the Description label may seem to be on top of other controls. Because the Default View of this form is set to Datasheet, this form will appear as a datasheet regardless of the organization of the controls in Design View.

k. Close the property sheet, save, then close the Rentals Subform.

l. Open the Customers form. It now contains a new Description field in the subform. Enter your first and last name in the first record of the main form, then print it.

m. Close the Customers form, close the Music Store-G database, then exit Access.

► Independent Challenge 2

As the manager of a music store's instrument rental program, you have created a database to track instrument rentals to schoolchildren. You add command buttons to a form to make it easier to use.

a. Start Access then open the database **Music Store-G** from the drive and folder where your Project Files are stored.

b. Using the Form Wizard, create a form/subform using all the fields of both the Customers and Schools tables.

c. View the data by Schools, use a Datasheet layout for the subform, then choose a Standard style.

d. Accept the default names of **Schools** for the main form and **Customers Subform** for the subform.

e. Maximize the main form then resize the columns of the subform so that as many fields as possible can be displayed. Save the form.

f. In Form Design View, widen the subform to the 6.5" mark on the horizontal ruler, then open the Form Header section by 0.5".

g. In Form Design View, add a command button in the Form Header using the Command Button Wizard. The action should print the current record and display the text **Print School Record**. Name the button **Print**.

h. Add a second command button to the Form Header section using the Command Button Wizard. The action should add a new record and display the text **Add New School**. Name the button **Add**.

i. Open the property sheet for the Form Header and give the Display When property the **Screen Only** value. Close the property sheet, then save the Schools form.

j. Display the form in Form View, resize the columns of the datasheet to display all fields, edit the first record in the subform datasheet to display your name and your address, then use the Print School Record button to print that record.

k. Click the Add New School button, then add the name of your elementary school to the SchoolName field, allow the SchoolNo to increment automatically, then add the name of a friend as the first record within the subform.

l. Use the Print School Record button to print this new school record.

m. Close the Schools form, save any changes, close the Music Store-G database, then exit Access.

▶ Independent Challenge 3

As the manager of a music store's instrument rental program, you have created a database to track instrument rentals to schoolchildren. Now that the users are becoming accustomed to forms, you add a combo box and option group to make the forms easier to use.

a. Start Access, then open the database **Music Store-G**.

b. Using the Form Wizard, create a form/subform using all the fields of both the Instruments and Rentals tables.

c. View the data by Instruments, use a Datasheet layout for the subform, and choose a Standard style.

d. Enter the name **Instruments Main Form** for the main form and **Rental Information** for the subform.

e. In Form Design View, delete the Condition text box and label in the main form.

f. Using the field list and the Toolbox toolbar, add the Condition field as a combo box under the MonthlyFee text box using the Combo Box Wizard. Choose the I will type in the values that I want option, then enter **Poor**, **Fair**, **Good**, and **Excellent** as the values for the first and only column.

g. Store the value in the Condition field, and label the new combo box as **Condition**.

h. Move, then resize the new combo box as necessary so that it is aligned with the three text boxes above it.

i. Delete the MonthlyFee textbox and associated label.

j. Using the field list and the Toolbox toolbar, add the MonthlyFee field as an option group to the right side of the main form using the Option Group Wizard.

k. Enter the Label Names as **$35**, **$40**, **$45**, and **$50**. Do not specify a default option. The corresponding values for the option buttons should be **35**, **40**, **45**, and **50**.

l. Store the value in the MonthlyFee field. Use Option buttons with an Etched style.

m. Caption the option group **Monthly Fee**, save the form, then view it in Form View.

n. Navigate to the second record for the cello, Serial Number 1234568, change the Monthly Fee to **$45**, choose **Excellent** for the Condition, then change the Description field to include your name.

o. Print only that record by clicking File on the menu bar, clicking Print, then choosing the Selected Records option button before clicking OK in the Print dialog box.

p. Save, then close the Instruments Main Form, close the Music Store-G database, and then exit Access.

Independent Challenge 4

You are in the process of organizing your family's photo library. After reviewing the general template sample databases, but not finding any good matches to use for your project, you decide to browse the template gallery featured at the Microsoft Web site to determine if there is a sample database that you can download and use or modify for this purpose.

a. Connect to the Internet, start Access, then click the Templates on Microsoft.com link in the New from template section of the New File task pane.

b. Click the category link for Personal Interests, Community, and Politics, then click the Personal Use link

c. Click the Photograph database link, click the Accept button at the bottom of the End-User License Agreement for Templates page, then click the Edit in Microsoft Access link.

d. A database is downloaded to your computer, which automatically opens a switchboard form that helps you navigate the sample Picture Library database. Click the Enter/View Rolls of Film link, scroll through the main form to view information about the five sample vacations that are presented in the main form, then view the sample photo information for each vacation in the subform.

e. Return to the first vacation record in the main form (the Paris Vacation), edit the Subject Name field entry in the first photo record of the subform to your name, then print the selected main form record.

f. Close the Rolls of Film form, then explore the rest of the sample Picture Library database.

g. Click the Exit This Database link on the Main Switchboard form to close the Photograph library database, then exit Access.

► Visual Workshop

Open the **Training-G** database. Use the Form Wizard to create a new form, as shown in Figure G-24. The First, Last, and Department fields are from the Employees table, the Description field is from the Courses table, and the Attended and Passed fields are from the Attendance table. View the form by Employees, choose a Datasheet layout for the sub-form, and choose a Standard style. Name the form **Employee Basics**, then name the subform **Test Results**. The Department combo box contains the following entries: **Accounting, Book, Cafe, CD, Human Resources, Marketing, Operations, Shipping, Training,** and **Video.** Use the command buttons in the Form Header to print the current record then close the form. Add your name as a label to the Form Header section, then print the first record.

FIGURE G-24

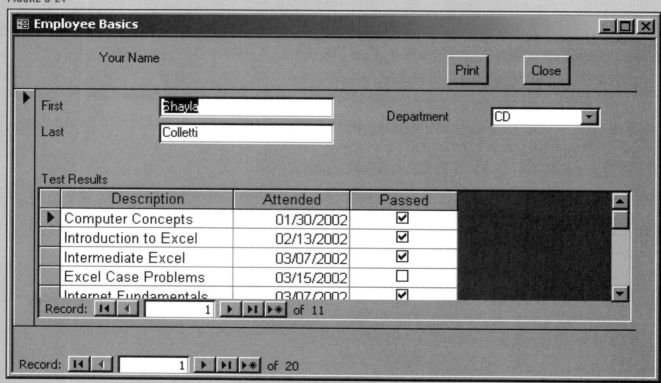

Sharing
Information and Improving Reports

Objectives

- ► **Use the Database Wizard**
- ► **Import data**
- ► **Apply advanced formatting**
- ► **Add lines**
- ► **Use the Format Painter and AutoFormats**
- ► **Create a Web page**
- ► **Export data**
- ► **Compact and repair a database**

Although you can print data in forms and datasheets, **reports** give you more control over how data is printed and greater flexibility in presenting summary information. To create a report, you add bound controls such as text boxes that display values from underlying fields, and unbound controls such as lines, graphics, or labels to clarify or enhance the information. Using the export and Web page features of Access you can electronically share information with other people. Fred Ames, coordinator of training at Medialoft, will use the Access import and export features to share data between the Training-H database and other file formats such as Excel workbooks and Web pages. He will also use advanced reporting and formatting features such as conditional formatting, colors, and lines to improve his reports.

Using the Database Wizard

The **Database Wizard** is a powerful Access tool that creates a sample database file for a general purpose such as inventory control, event tracking, or expenses. These sample databases include several sample objects (tables, forms, reports, and others) that you can use or modify. The Accounting department tracks a training budget to determine how various departments are using MediaLoft's in-house classes, and has requested a quarterly update of this data, currently stored in the Training-H database. In addition, the Accounting department wants this information in an electronic format so that they can further analyze it on their own. Fred decides to create a separate Access database for the Accounting department into which he will regularly import quarterly information on course attendance and costs from the Training-H database.

Steps

Trouble?

If the task pane is not visible, click the New button on the Database toolbar.

1. **Start Access, click the General Templates... link in the New from template section of the New File task pane, then click the Databases tab in the Templates dialog box**
   The Databases tab of the Templates dialog box is shown in Figure H-1. **Templates** are sample databases that you can use and modify for your own purposes. Some templates invoke the Database Wizard, which prompt you with further questions about how to create the database and the type of information it will store.

2. **Double-click Expenses in the Templates dialog box**
   When you create a new database, you must first name the database file, regardless of whether it is created by a wizard or from scratch.

3. **Type Accounting in the File name text box, click the Save in list arrow, navigate to the drive and folder where your Project Files are stored, then click Create**
   The Database Wizard starts and provides information about what type of data the database will store.

4. **Click Next**
   The sample database will include the four tables, as shown in Figure H-2. The fields for the selected table appear in the second list. You can select or unselect suggested fields for the chosen table by clicking the check boxes to the left of the field names.

5. **Click Expense report information in the Tables list to view the fields in this table, then click Next to accept the default field choices for all four tables**

6. **Click Standard, click Next, click Corporate, click Next, type Accounting as the database title, click Next, make sure that the Yes, start the database check box is checked, then click Finish**
   It takes several seconds for Access to build all of the objects for the Accounting database and then open the Main Switchboard form, as shown in Figure H-3. When you use the Database Wizard, Access creates a **switchboard**, a special Access form with command buttons used to navigate through the database. You decide to directly explore the database rather than work with the Switchboard.

Trouble?

The Accounting database window is minimized in the Access window.

7. **Click the Main Switchboard Close button ⊠, click the Accounting database Maximize button ▣, review the available forms, click Reports on the Objects bar, click Queries on the Objects bar, then click Tables on the Objects bar**
   The form, report, and table objects that were created by the wizard can be used, modified, or deleted just like any user-created object. The wizard did not create any query, page, or macro objects for this database. Not only did the Expenses Database Wizard create the four tables identified in the initial dialog box, a fifth table called Switchboard Items was also created to store information used in the Main Switchboard form.

FIGURE H-1: Database wizards

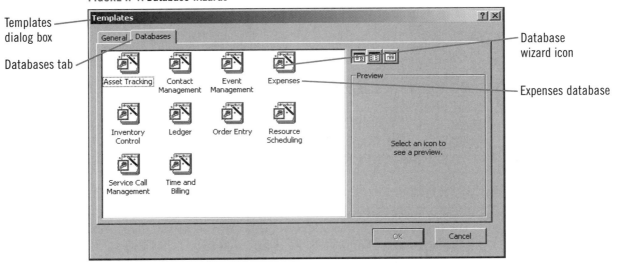

Templates dialog box
Databases tab

Database wizard icon
Expenses database

FIGURE H-2: Tables and fields within the Expenses Database Wizard

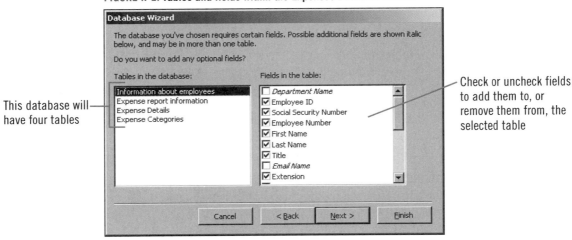

This database will have four tables

Check or uncheck fields to add them to, or remove them from, the selected table

FIGURE H-3: Main Switchboard form for the Accounting database

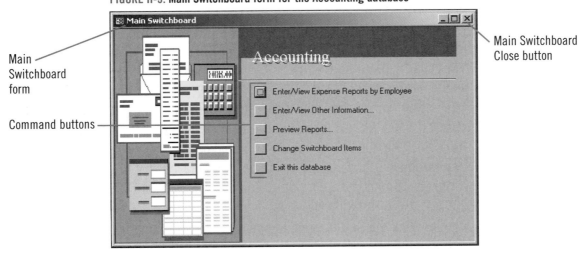

Main Switchboard form

Command buttons

Main Switchboard Close button

Importing Data

Importing is a process to quickly convert data from an external file, such as an Excel workbook or other database format, and bring it into an Access database. The Access import process copies the data from the original source and pastes the data in the Access database. Therefore, if you update data in either the original source or in the imported copy in Access, the other copy is not updated. See Table H-1 for more information on the types of data that Access can import. Now that the Accounting database has been created, Fred imports historical cost and attendance information from the Training-H database so that the Accounting department can analyze and manipulate this data without disturbing Fred's original Training-H database.

Steps

1. Click **File** on the menu bar, point to **Get External Data**, click **Import**, navigate to the drive and folder where your Project Files are stored, click **Training-H**, then click **Import**
   The Import Objects dialog box opens, as shown in Figure H-4. Any object in the Training-H database can be imported into the Accounting database.

2. Click the **Tables tab** (if not already selected), click **1QTR-2002**, click **Courses**, click the **Queries tab**, click **Accounting Query**, click the **Reports tab**, click **Accounting Report**, then click **OK**
   The four selected objects are imported from the Training-H database into the Accounting database.

3. Click **Tables** on the Objects bar, then click the **Details button** 📰 in the Database window
   The Created and Modified dates of both the 1QTR-2002 and the Courses tables should be today's date. If you update these tables in the future, the Modified date will change. The Created date always displays the original date and time that the object was first created. By default, objects in the database window are sorted in ascending order by name, but clicking on the column headings allows you to sort the objects by that column.

4. Click the **Modified column heading** to sort the Table objects in ascending order by the date and time they were last modified, then click the **Name column heading**
   The database window should look like Figure H-5. In this case, sorting by the Modified column doesn't provide much value because all of the tables were created on the same date, and none have been modified since that time. But you will find this technique very helpful when trying to find objects that were recently modified. Clicking the column heading a second time sorts the objects in descending order by that column. The MediaLoft Accounting department stores department codes in an Excel workbook that also needs to be imported into this database.

5. Click **File** on the menu bar, point to **Get External Data**, click **Import**, click the **Files of type list arrow**, click **Microsoft Excel**, then double-click **Deptcodes**
   The Import Spreadsheet Wizard presents the data that you are trying to import, and then guides you through the rest of the import process.

6. Click **Next**, make sure the **First Row Contains Column Headings** check box is checked, click **Next**, make sure the **In a New Table option button** is selected, click **Next**, click **Next** to accept the default field options, click the **Choose my own primary key option button**, make sure **Code** is displayed in the primary key list box, click **Next**, type **Codes** in the Import to Table text box, click **Finish**, then click **OK**
   The Deptcodes spreadsheet is now a table named Codes in the Accounting database.

7. Double-click the **Codes** table to open it
   The Accounting department has more work to do before they can use their new database, but using the Database Wizard and Access importing features helped them get off to a quick start.

8. Close the Codes datasheet, then close the Accounting database

FIGURE H-4: Import Objects dialog box

Tables tab is
selected

Table objects in
Training-H database

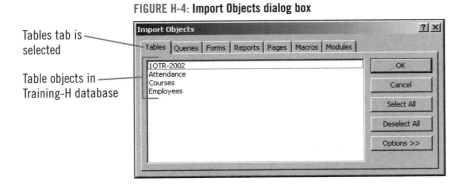

FIGURE H-5: Database window showing object details

Name column
heading

Resize column
pointer

Details button

Created date
column heading

Modified date
column heading

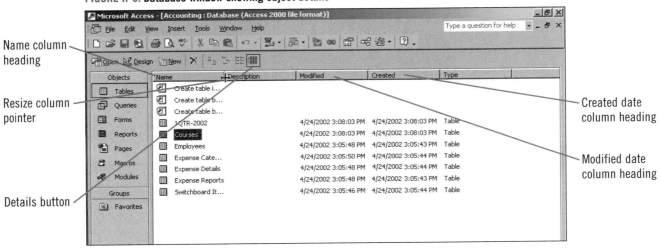

TABLE H-1: Data sources Microsoft Access can import

data source	version or format supported	data source	version or format supported
Microsoft Access database	2.0, 7.0/95, 8.0/97, 9.0/2000, and 10.0/2002	**Microsoft Exchange**	All versions
Microsoft Access project	9.0/2000, 10.0/2002	**Delimited text files**	All character sets
dBASE	III, IV, 5, 7	**Fixed-width text files**	All character sets
Paradox, Paradox for Windows	3.x, 4.x, 5.0, 8.0	**HTML**	1.0 (if a list) 2.0, 3.x (if a table or list)
Microsoft Excel	3.0, 4.0, 5.0, 7.0/95, 8.0/97, 9.0/2000, 10.0/2002	**XML Documents**	All versions
Lotus 1-2-3	.wks, .wk1, .wk3, .wk4	**SQL tables, Microsoft Visual FoxPro, and other data sources that support ODBC protocol**	**ODBC** (Open Database Connectivity) is a protocol for accessing data in **SQL** (Structured Query Language) database servers

Applying Advanced Formatting

Conditional formatting allows you to change the appearance of a control based on criteria you specify. **Grouping controls** allows you to identify several controls as a group in order to quickly apply the same formatting properties to them. Other report embellishments such as hiding duplicate values and adding Group Footer calculations also improve a report. ✏ Fred wants to improve the Attendance by Department report by applying conditional formatting. He explores other report techniques such as hiding duplicate values and grouping controls.

Steps

QuickTip

Click the Sorting and Grouping button ▣ on the Report Design toolbar to view the order of the grouping and sorting fields used for the report.

1. Open the **Training-H** database, click **Reports** on the Objects bar, right-click **Attendance by Department**, then click **Design View**

   The Attendance by Department report opens in Design View, as shown in Figure H-6. The report uses the Department field to group the records. The Department Footer section subtotals the Hours (of in-class training) for that department using a text box that contains the =Sum([Hours]) expression.

2. Click the **Last text box** in the Detail section, press and hold **[Shift]**, click the **First text box** in the Detail section, click the **Title text box**, release **[Shift]**, click **Format** on the menu bar, then click **Group**

   Group selection handles surround the group of three text boxes, so when you click on *any* control in a group, you select *every* control in the group. Clicking a control within a *selected group* still selects just that single control.

QuickTip

The title bar of the property sheet indicates that multiple controls have been selected.

3. Click the **Properties button** ▣, click the **Format tab**, click the **Hide Duplicates text box**, click the **Hide Duplicates list arrow**, click **Yes**, then click ▣

   With the **Hide Duplicates** property set to Yes, the First, Last, and Title values will print only once per employee rather than once for each record in the Detail section. It is common to copy and paste calculated controls from a Group Footer section to the Report Footer section in order to quickly create the same calculations for the entire report.

4. Right-click the **=Sum([Hours]) text box** in the Department Footer, click **Copy** on the shortcut menu, right-click the **Report Footer section**, then click **Paste**

   The text box containing the =Sum([Hours]) calculation has been pasted at the left edge of the Report Footer section.

5. Use the 🖑 pointer to drag the **=Sum([Hours]) text box** in the Report Footer section to the right edge of that section

   You cannot group controls in different sections, but you can select multiple controls in different sections in order to apply the same formatting commands to all selected controls.

QuickTip

You can add up to three conditional formats for any combination of selected controls.

6. Press **[Shift]**, click the **=Sum([Hours]) text box** in the Department Footer section to add it to the current selection, click **Format** on the menu bar, click **Conditional Formatting**, click the **between list arrow**, click **greater than**, click the **text box**, type **200**, click the **Bold button** ▣ for Condition 1, then click the red **Font/Fore Color button** ▣ for Condition 1

   The Conditional Formatting dialog box should look like Figure H-7.

7. Click **OK** in the Conditional Formatting dialog box, click the **Save button** ▣ on the Report Design toolbar, click the **Print Preview button** ▣, then zoom and position the report, as shown in Figure H-8

8. Click the **Design View button** ▣, click the **Label button** ▣ on the Toolbox toolbar, click the right side of the Report Header section, then type your name

9. Save, print, then close the Attendance by Department report

FIGURE H-6: Attendance by Department report in Report Design View

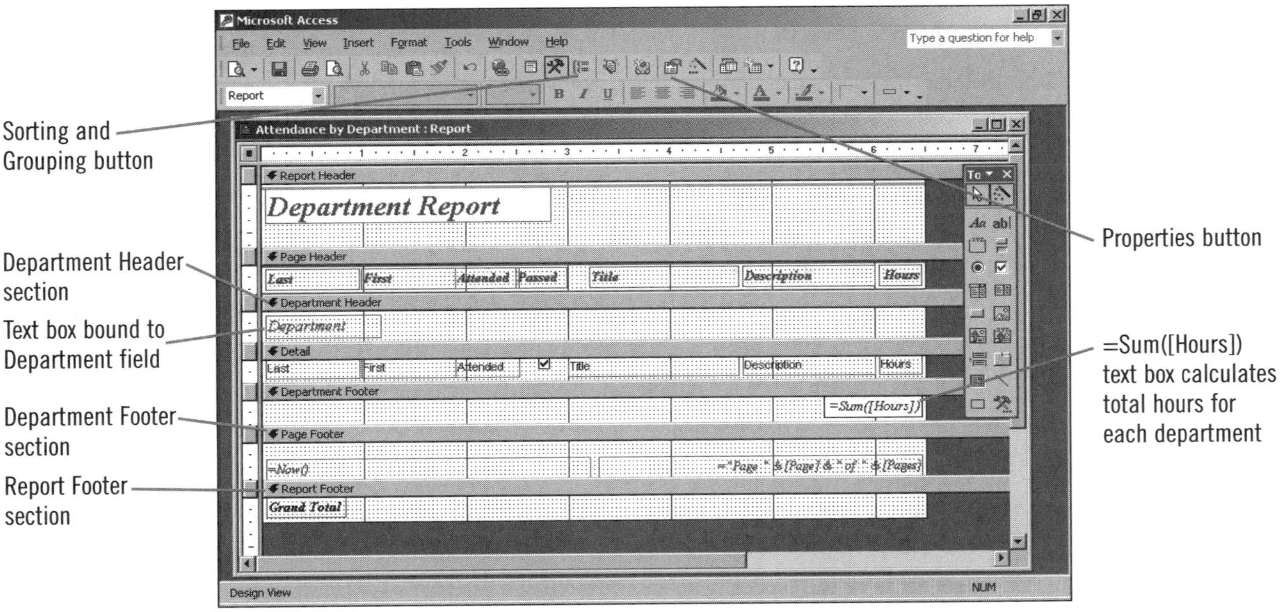

Sorting and Grouping button
Department Header section
Text box bound to Department field
Department Footer section
Report Footer section
Properties button
=Sum([Hours]) text box calculates total hours for each department
Attendance by Department : Report
Department Report
Grand Total

FIGURE H-7: Conditional Formatting dialog box

Default formatting if condition is not true
Comparison operator
Conditional formatting if Condition 1 is true
200 is the criteria
Font/Fore Color button for Condition 1
Bold button for Condition 1
Conditional Formatting
Default Formatting
This format will be used if no conditions are met:
Condition 1
Field Value Is
greater than
200
Preview of format to use when condition is true:
Add >>
Delete...
OK
Cancel

FIGURE H-8: Final Attendance by Department report for the Book department

Duplicate values are hidden
Hours are subtotaled for each department, with conditional formatting applied to values greater than 200
Microsoft Access - [Department Report]
Accounting
228

Access 2002

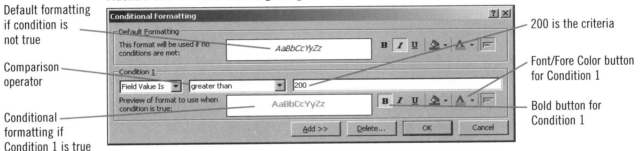

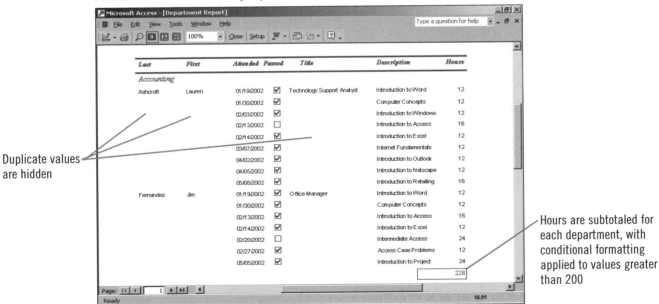

Access 2002

Adding Lines

Unbound controls such as labels, lines, and rectangles enhance the clarity of a report. The Report Wizard often creates line controls at the bottom of the Report Header, Page Header, or Group Header sections that visually separate the parts of a report. Lines can be formatted in many ways. ✐ The Personnel department has asked Fred to create a report that lists all of the Medialoft courses and to subtotal the courses by hours and costs. Fred uses line controls to enhance the appearance of this report.

Steps

1. Double-click **Create report by using wizard**, click the **Tables/Queries list arrow**, click **Query: Course Summary Query**, click the **Select All Fields button**, click **Next**, click **by Attendance**, click **Next**, double-click **Department**, then click **Next**
   After determining the grouping field(s), the wizard prompts for the sort field(s).

2. Click the **first sort field list arrow**, click **Attended** to sort the detail records by the date the classes were attended, then click the **Summary Options button**
   The Summary Options dialog box allows you to include the sum, average, minimum, or maximum value of fields to various sections of the report.

Trouble?

If your report title doesn't display the entire title, widen the label that displays this text in Report Design View.

3. Click the **Hours Sum check box**, click the **Cost Sum check box**, click **OK**, click **Next**, click the **Outline 2 Layout option button**, click the **Landscape Orientation option button**, click **Next**, click the **Formal** Style, click **Next**, type **Course Summary Report** as the report title, click **Finish**, then click the **Zoom Out pointer** 🔍 on the report
   The wizard created several line and rectangle controls identified in Figure H-9.

Trouble?

The easiest place to select the line control in the Detail section is between the Passed check box and Description text box.

4. Click the **Design View button** 🖉 on the Print Preview toolbar, click the **line control** near the top of the Detail section, then press **[Delete]**

5. Click the **Line button** ╲ on the Toolbox toolbar, press and hold **[Shift]**, drag a line from the bottom-left edge of the =Sum([Hours]) text box to the bottom-right edge of the =Sum([Cost]) text box in the Report Footer section, then release **[Shift]**
   Copying and pasting lines creates an exact duplicate of the line.

Trouble?

Be sure to add the lines to the Report Footer section, and not the Department Footer section.

6. Click the **Copy button** 📄 on the Formatting (Form/Report) toolbar, click the **Paste button** 📄, then press ▲
   Design View of the report should look like Figure H-10. Short double lines under the calculations in the Report Footer section indicate grand totals. Moving a control with the arrow keys while pressing [Ctrl] moves the control one **pixel** (picture element) at a time.

7. Click the **Print Preview button** 🔍 on the Formatting (Form/Report) toolbar, then click the **Last Page Navigation button** ▶|
   The last page of the report should look like Figure H-11. The two lines under the final values indicate that they are grand totals.

Line troubles

As you work with your report in Report Design View, it is easy to accidentally widen a line beyond the physical limits of the page, thus creating extra pages in your printout showing the portion of the line that extends off the right edge of the paper. The solution to this problem is to narrow the lines and the right edge of the report in Report Design View to within the margins set for a physical page. Remember, though, that lines are sometimes difficult to find in Report Design View because they are often hidden by the edge of a section. Also, remember to hold [Shift] down while resizing a line. This will keep the line perfectly horizontal as you resize it.

FIGURE H-9: First page of Course Summary Report

Line in Report Header

Rectangle in Department Header

Line in Detail section

Line in Department Footer

Line in Page Footer

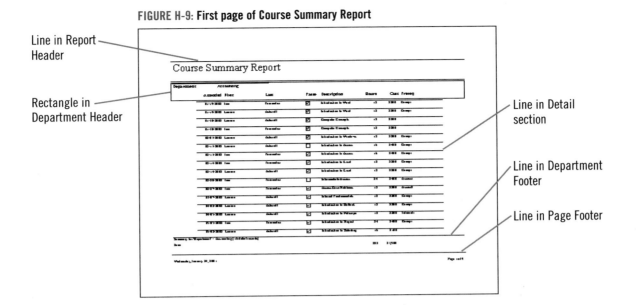

FIGURE H-10: Course Summary Report in Design View

Line control deleted in the Detail section

Line button

Double lines

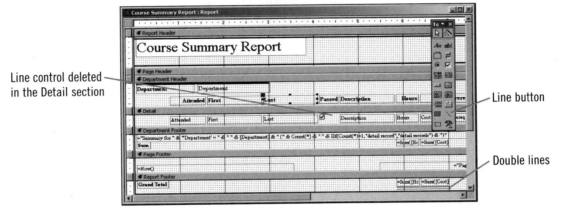

FIGURE H-11: Last page of modified Course Summary Report

Department Footer line

Page Footer line

Double lines indicate grand totals

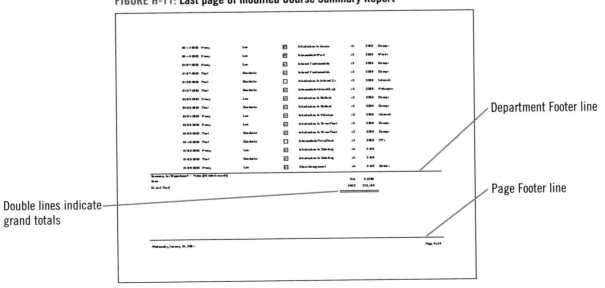

Using the Format Painter and AutoFormats

The **Format Painter** is a handy tool used to copy formatting properties from one control to another. **AutoFormats** are predefined formats that you can apply to a form or report to determine the background pictures, font, color, and alignment choices applied to the report. You can modify the existing AutoFormats or create your own. The report AutoFormats are available every time you use the Report Wizard. ✎ Fred uses the Format Painter to change the characteristics of selected lines, then saves the report's formatting scheme as a new AutoFormat so that he can apply it to other reports.

Steps

1. Click the **Design View button** 🖳, click the **Attended label** in the Department Header section, click the **Font/Fore Color button list arrow** 🔺, click the **blue** box in the second row, click the **Fill/Back Color button list arrow** 🖌, click the **yellow** box in the fourth row, then click the **Align Left button** ▤
   Some of the buttons on the Formatting (Form/Report) toolbar such as the **Bold button** 🅱 and the **Align Left button** ▤ display with a blue square to indicate that they are applied to the selected control. Others, such as the **Font/Fore Color button** 🔺 and **Fill/Back Color button** 🖌, display the last color that was used for this report. The Format Painter can help you apply these formats to other controls very quickly.

2. Double-click the **Format Painter button** 🖌 on the Formatting (Form/Report) toolbar, then click all of the **labels** in the Department Header section
   The Format Painter copied the color and other formatting properties from the Attended label, and pasted those formats to the other labels in the Department Header section, as shown in Figure H-12. You can save this set of formatting embellishments as an AutoFormat so that you can quickly apply them to another report.

QuickTip
Press [Esc] to release the Format Painter.

3. Click 🖌 to release it, click the **AutoFormat button** 🖼 on the Report Design toolbar, click **Customize**, click the **Create a new AutoFormat based on the Report 'Course Summary Report' option button**, click **OK**, type **Yellow-Blue-YourFirstName**, then click **OK**
   The AutoFormat dialog box should look similar to Figure H-13.

4. Click **OK** to close the AutoFormat dialog box, save, then close the Course Summary Report

5. Double-click the **Employee Detail Report** to view the current formatting, click 🖳, click 🖼, click **Yellow-Blue-YourFirstName** in the Report AutoFormats list, click **OK**, then click the **Print Preview button** 🔍
   Your screen should look like Figure H-14. The AutoFormat you applied changed the formatting properties of labels in the Department Header section.

6. Click 🖳, then click the **Save button** 🖫
   You should delete AutoFormats that you will no longer use.

7. Click 🖼, click **Yellow-Blue-YourFirstName**, click **Customize**, click the **Delete 'Yellow-Blue-YourFirstName' option button**, click **OK**, then click **Close**

8. Click the **Label button** 🄰 on the Toolbox toolbar, click the right side of the Report Header section, type **your name**, print, then save and close the Employee Detail Report

FIGURE H-12: Using the Format Painter

Format Painter button

AutoFormat button

Attended label

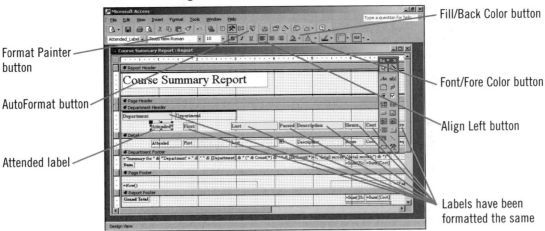

Fill/Back Color button

Font/Fore Color button

Align Left button

Labels have been formatted the same

FIGURE H-13: The AutoFormat dialog box

New AutoFormat

Other AutoFormats may be listed

Sample of new AutoFormat

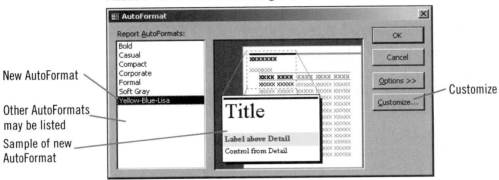

Customize

FIGURE H-14: Applying a custom AutoFormat to a different report

Label formatting changed

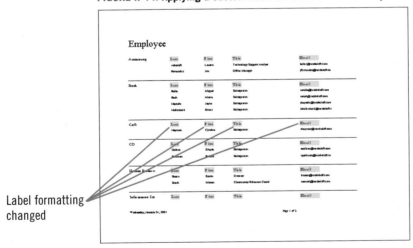

CLUES TO USE

Creating summary reports

Sometimes you may not want to show all the details of a report, but rather only the summary information that is calculated in the Group Footer section. You can accomplish this by deleting all controls in the Detail section. Calculated controls in a Group Footer section will still calculate properly even if the individual records used within the calculation are not displayed on the report.

Creating a Web Page

A **Web page** is a file that is viewed using **browser** software such as Microsoft Internet Explorer. You can use the export capabilities of Access to create **static** Web pages that show data as of the moment the Web page was created. These Web pages do not change when the database is updated. You can also use Access to create **dynamic** Web pages that are automatically updated with the latest changes to the database and therefore show current data. The page object creates **data access pages,** Web pages that are dynamically connected to the database. The benefit of converting Access data into any type of Web page is that it makes the information more accessible to a larger audience. ✎ Fred uses the page object to create a dynamic Web page to report employee information.

Steps

1. Click **Pages** on the Objects bar, then double-click **Create data access page by using wizard**
   The Page Wizard opens with an interface similar to the Form and Report Wizards. First, you need to determine what fields you want the Web page to display.

2. Click the **Tables/Queries list arrow**, click **Table: Employees**, click the **Select All button** ⟫, then click **Next**
   Web pages, like reports, can be used to group and sort records.

3. Double-click **Department** to specify it as a grouping field, click **Next**, click the **first sort order list arrow**, click **Last**, then click **Next**

Trouble?

If the Web page opens in Design View, click the Page View button 🔳 to switch to Page View.

4. Type **Employees Info Web Page** for the title, click the **Open the page option button**, then click **Finish**
   The Web page opens in **Page View,** a special view within Access that allows you to see how your Web page will appear when opened in Internet Explorer. You modify the structure of a data access page in **Page Design View.**

5. Click the **Expand button** ⊞ to the left of the Department label to show the fields within that group
   Your page should look like Figure H-15. On a data access page, the **Navigation bars** not only allow you to move from record to record, they contain buttons to edit, sort, and filter the data. Page View shows you how the Web page will appear from within Internet Explorer (IE).

6. Click the **Save button** 🔳 on the Page View toolbar, type **einfo** as the File name, navigate to the drive and folder where your Project Files are stored, click **Save**, click **OK** when prompted with information about the path between the Web page and the database, then close the page

7. Click the **Start button** ⊞Start on the taskbar, point to **Programs**, click **Internet Explorer**, click **File** on the menu bar, click **Open**, click **Browse**, navigate to the drive and folder where you saved the Web page, double-click **einfo.htm**, then click **OK**
   Internet Explorer loads and presents the Web page.

Trouble?

Web pages created through the page object in Access require Internet Explorer version 5.0 or later to support dynamic connectivity with the database.

8. Click the **Next button** ▶ on the Employees-Department navigation toolbar, click ⊞ to the left of the Department label, then click the **Sort Descending button** 🔳 on the Employees Navigation bar
   The Web page should look like Figure H-16. The address of the Web page displays the drive and folder where you saved the file.

9. Close Internet Explorer

FIGURE H-15: Web page in Page View

Grouping field

Collapse button

Sorting field

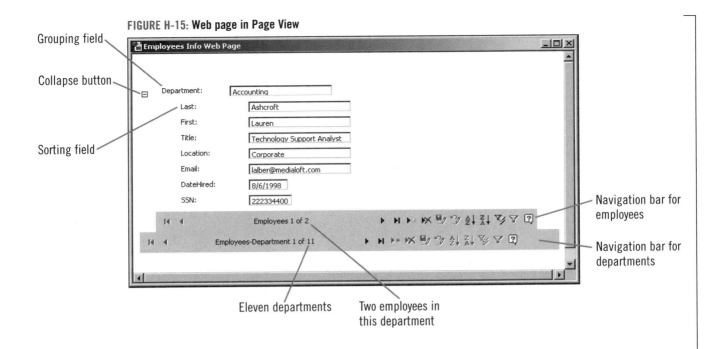

Navigation bar for
employees

Navigation bar for
departments

Eleven departments

Two employees in
this department

FIGURE H-16: einfo Web page in Internet Explorer

Internet
Explorer

Web page
address

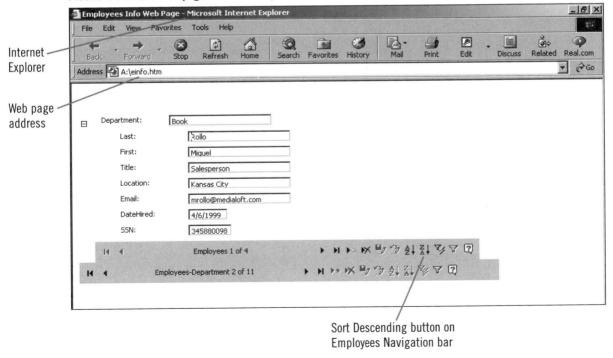

Sort Descending button on
Employees Navigation bar

Exporting Data

Exporting is a process to quickly convert data from Access to another file format such as an Excel workbook, a Word document, or a static Web page. Importing is a process used to copy and paste data *into* an Access database, whereas exporting is a process used to copy and paste data *out of* the database. Since there is no dynamic link between the original Access database and an exported copy of the data, changes made to the information in the database will *not* affect the exported copy. See Table H-2 for more information on the types of data that Access can export. Fred received a request from the Human Resources department to copy the data in the Employees table to an Excel workbook. Fred uses the export features to send this data to an Excel workbook. He also experiments with exporting data as a Web page.

Steps

1. Click **Tables** on the Objects bar, click **Employees**, click **File** on the menu bar, click **Export**, type **EmployeeData** as the file name, click the **Save as type list arrow**, click **Microsoft Excel 97-2002**, navigate to the drive and folder where your Project Files are stored, then click **Export**

   The export process creates the EmployeeData.xls Excel workbook that contains the Employees data.

2. Click the **Start button** [Start] on the taskbar, point to **Programs**, click **Microsoft Excel**, click the **Open button** on the Excel Standard toolbar, navigate to the drive and folder where you exported the Employees table, then double-click **EmployeeData**

   The Excel workbook appears, as shown in Figure H-17. All of the data has been successfully exported, but some of it is hidden because the columns are narrow.

3. Click the **Select All button**, point between column heading A and column heading B so that the pointer becomes ✛, then double-click

   With all columns selected, you can adjust the width of all of them at the same time so that you can clearly see that all Access data was successfully exported.

4. Click the **Save button**, click **File** on the menu bar, then click **Exit**

   You closed the EmployeeData workbook and exited Excel. Exporting Access data to other file formats, including Web pages, is a similar process.

QuickTip

If you want to create a *dynamic* Web page that automatically updates as the information is modified in the database, use the page object rather than the Export option.

5. Click **File** on the Access Training-H Database menu bar, click **Export**, type **edata** as the file name, click the **Save as type list arrow**, click **HTML Documents**, navigate to the drive and folder where your Project Files are stored, then click **Export**

   The Employees table is saved as an HTML file. **HTML** is short for **HyperText Markup Language**, a set of codes inserted into a text file that browser software such as Internet Explorer use to determine the way text, hyperlinks, images, and other elements should appear on a Web page. Web pages created using the export feature are *static*, and will not change after they are created.

6. Click the **Start button** [Start] on the taskbar, point to **Programs**, click **Internet Explorer**, click **File** on the Internet Explorer menu bar, click **Open**, click **Browse**, navigate to the drive and folder where you saved the Web page, double-click **edata.html**, then click **OK**

   The Web page with the information from the Employees table appears, as shown in Figure H-18. Static Web pages created through the export process can be viewed using either Microsoft Internet Explorer or Netscape Navigator.

7. Close **Internet Explorer**

FIGURE H-17: EmployeeData workbook

Excel

EmployeeData.xls

Select All button

Field names

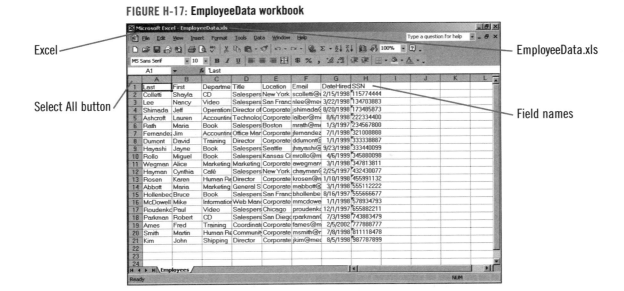

FIGURE H-18: edata Web page

Internet Explorer

Web page address

TABLE H-2: Data formats Microsoft Access can export

application	version or format supported	application	version or format supported
Microsoft Access database	2.0, 7.0/95, 8.0/97, 9.0/2000, 10.0/2002	Lotus 1-2-3	.wk2, .wk1, and .wk3
Microsoft Access project	9.0/2000, 10.0/2002	Delimited text files	All character sets
dBASE	III, IV, 5, and 7	Fixed-width text files	All character sets
Paradox, Paradox for Windows	3.x, 4.x, 5.0, and 8.0	HTML	1.0 (if a list), 2.0, 3.x, 4.x (if a table or list)
Microsoft Excel	3.0, 4.0, 5.0, 7.0/95, 8.0/97, 9.0/2000, 10.0/2002	SQL tables, Microsoft Visual FoxPro, and other data sources that support ODBC protocol	Visual FoxPro 3.0, 5.0, and 6.x
Microsoft Active Server Pages	All	XML Documents	All

Access 2002

Access 2002

Compacting and Repairing a Database

When you delete data and objects in an Access database, the database can become fragmented and use disk space inefficiently. **Compacting** the database rearranges the data and objects to improve performance by reusing the space formerly occupied by the deleted objects. The compacting process also repairs damaged databases. A good time to back up a database is right after it has been compacted. If hardware is stolen or destroyed, a recent **backup**, an up-to-date copy of the data files, can minimize the impact of that loss to the business. Use Windows Explorer to copy individual database files and floppy disks, or use back-up software such as Microsoft Backup to create back-up schedules to automate the process. ⬛⬛⬛ Fred needs to secure the Training-H database. He explores the Compact and Repair feature, then uses Windows Explorer to make a backup copy of the database.

1. Click **Tools** on the menu bar, click **Options**, then point to **Database Utilities**

   The **Compact and Repair Database** option on the Database Utilities menu allows you to compact and repair an open database, but *if you are working on a floppy disk, do not compact the database*. The compaction process creates a temporary file that is just as large as the database itself. If the floppy disk does not have the needed space to build the temporary file, it will not be able to finish the compaction process or close your database, and you may corrupt your database beyond repair. If you are working on a hard drive, though, it's a good practice to use the **Compact on Close** feature, which compacts and repairs the database every time it is closed.

2. Click **Tools** on the menu bar, click **Options**, then click the **General tab** of the Options dialog box

   The Options dialog box with the Compact on Close option is shown in Figure H-19. By default, the Compact on Close option is not checked for new databases.

QuickTip

Make sure that you have a blank floppy disk ready to complete the following steps.

3. Click **Cancel** in the Options dialog box, close the **Training-H** database, exit **Access**, right-click the **Start button** 🔲**Start** on the taskbar, click **Explore**, then click **3½ Floppy (A:)** in the Folders list to display the files stored on your floppy disk

   Windows Explorer should look similar to Figure H-20. You may see more files depending on how your Project Files are organized. You may see fewer details on each file depending on the current view of Windows Explorer. You will, of course, see different folders and drives that describe your own unique computer.

4. Right-click **3½ Floppy (A:)** in the Folders list, then click **Copy Disk**

   The Copy Disk dialog box opens, as shown in Figure H-21. This command allows you to copy an entire floppy disk from one disk to another without first copying the contents to the computer's C: drive.

5. Click **Start**

   Windows Explorer will start copying your original Project Disk, the **source disk**, and will prompt you to insert a blank disk, the **destination disk**, where the files will be pasted.

6. Insert the destination disk when prompted, then click **OK**

   Explorer was able to copy all of the files from the Project Disk to the blank disk with one process. Sometimes you are prompted to reinsert the source disk and then the destination disk because all of the files cannot be copied in one process.

7. Click **Close** in the Copy Disk dialog box, then close **Windows Explorer**

8. Remove the disk from the disk drive, then label the disk

FIGURE H-19: **Options dialog box**

General tab

Compact on Close

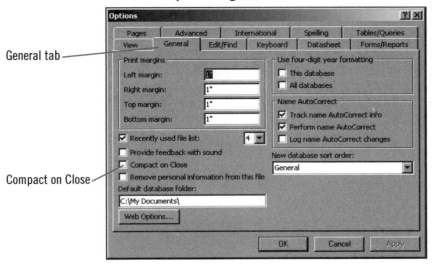

FIGURE H-20: **Windows Explorer**

3½ Floppy (A:)

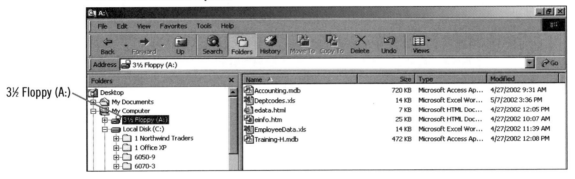

FIGURE H-21: **Copy Disk dialog box**

3½ Floppy (A:) is chosen in both locations

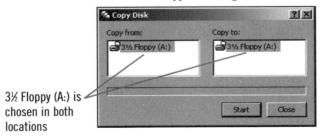

Backing up Project Files stored on your hard drive

If your Project Files are on the hard drive, the backup process is very similar. First, locate the folder that stores your Project Files in the Folders list within Windows Explorer. Right-click the folder, click Send To on the shortcut menu, then click 3½ Floppy (A:). Insert a blank floppy disk into the A: drive when prompted. If all of the copied files will not fit on one floppy disk, you will be prompted to insert another one. One file, however, cannot be larger than a single floppy disk for

this backup method to work. If one file is larger than the storage space of a floppy disk, approximately 1.44 MB, you must use backup software such as Microsoft Backup or compression software such as WinZip to compress the files before copying them to a floppy. Or, you can copy them to a larger storage device such as a Zip, Jazz, or network drive or a Web site that allows you to upload and store files such as www.xdrive.com.

Access 2002

Practice

► Concepts Review

Identify each element of the Report Design View shown in Figure H-22.

FIGURE-H-22

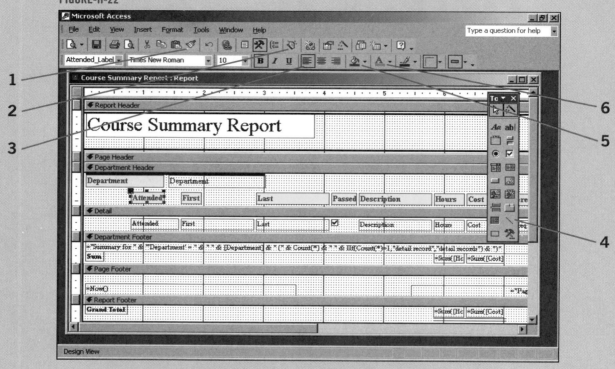

1

2

3

6

5

4

Match each term with the statement that describes its function.

7. Exporting
8. Compacting
9. Backup
10. Format Painter
11. Importing

a. A process to quickly copy data from an external source into an Access database

b. A process that rearranges the data and objects of a database to improve performance and to decrease storage requirements

c. An up-to-date copy of Project Files

d. Used to copy formatting properties from one control to another

e. A process to quickly copy data from an Access database to an external file

Select the best answer from the list of choices.

12. What Access tool creates a sample database file for a general purpose such as inventory control, event tracking, or expenses?
    a. Database Wizard
    b. Object Wizard
    c. Relationships Wizard
    d. AutoData Wizard

13. Which control would you use to visually separate groups of records on a report?
    a. Option group
    b. Image
    c. Bound Object Frame
    d. Line

14. Which wizard would you use to create a dynamic Web page?
    a. Page Wizard
    b. Table Wizard
    c. HTML Wizard
    d. Lookup Wizard

15. What feature allows you to apply the formatting characteristics of one report to another?
    a. AutoContent Wizard
    b. AutoFormat
    c. Report Layout Wizard
    d. PivotTables

16. Which of the following file types cannot be imported into Access?
    a. Excel
    b. Lotus 1-2-3
    c. Lotus Notes
    d. HTML

17. Sample databases that you can use and modify for your own purposes are called:
    a. MicroSamples.
    b. Templates.
    c. Controls.
    d. Datasets.

18. Which feature compacts and repairs the database every time it is closed?
    a. Compact on Close
    b. Conversion Wizard
    c. Backup Wizard
    d. Repair Wizard

19. Which Access feature would you use to create a static Web page?
    a. Web page Wizard
    b. Export
    c. Mailto: HTML
    d. Conversion Wizard

20. What feature allows you to change the appearance of a control on a form or report based on criteria you specify?
    a. Autoformat
    b. Behavioral formatting
    c. Event-driven formatting
    d. Conditional formatting

Skills Review

1. Use the Database Wizard.

a. Start Access, click the General Templates link in the New from template section of the task pane, then click the Databases tab.

b. Double-click the Contact Management Wizard, then create the new database with the name **Contacts**. If working on floppies, be sure to create the database on the floppy disk that contains the other Skills Review Project Files for this unit.

c. Respond to the prompts in the Database Wizard by accepting all of the default field suggestions. Use the Standard style for screen displays and the Soft Gray style for printed reports. Accept the name **Contact Management** as the title of the database.

d. After all of the objects are created, close the Main Switchboard form, then maximize the Contacts Database window.

2. Import data.

a. Click File on the menu bar, point to Get External Data, then click Import.

b. In the Import dialog box, click the Files of type list arrow, click Microsoft Excel, navigate to the drive and folder where your Project Files are stored, then double-click **Prospects**.

c. In the Import Spreadsheet Wizard, make sure that the Show Worksheets option button is selected, click Next, check the First Row Contains Column Headings check box, click Next, click the In a New Table option button, click Next, click Next to accept the default field options, click the Choose my own primary key option button, verify that ContactID is the primary key field, click Next, type **Prospects** in the Import to Table text box, then click Finish.

d. Click OK when prompted that the import was successful, then open the Prospects table.

e. Add your personal information as a new record using **10** as the entry for the ContactID field.

f. Print the datasheet in landscape orientation, close the datasheet, then close the Contacts database.

3. Apply advanced formatting.

a. Open the **Membership-H** database from the drive and folder where your Project Files are stored.

b. Using the Report Wizard, create a report based on the Member Activity Log using all of the fields in that query.

c. View the data by Names, do not add any additional grouping levels, sort ascending by ActivityDate, then Sum the Hours field.

d. Use the Outline 2 Layout, Portrait Orientation, Compact style, type **Member Activity Log** as the report title, then open the report in Design View.

e. Select the =Sum([Hours]) calculated field in the MemberNo Footer section.

f. Use Conditional Formatting to change the Font/Fore color to blue and text formatted with italics if the field value is greater than or equal to **10**.

g. Add a label to the Report Footer section with the text **Created by Your Name**.

h. Group all of the controls in the Report Footer section, then apply italics to the group.

i. Save, then print the last page of the report.

4. Add lines.

a. Open the Member Activity Log report in Design View, then delete the line at the top of the MemberNo Header section. Delete the line at the top of the Detail section. (*Hint*: Click between the ActivityDate and Hours text boxes.)

b. Delete the text box with the ="Summary for ..." calculation and the line at the top of the MemberNo Footer section.

c. Add a short horizontal line just above the =Sum([Hours]) calculation in the MemberNo Footer section. (*Hint*: Press and hold [Shift] while creating the line for it to be perfectly horizontal.)

d. Copy and paste the line into the Report Footer section, then move the line directly under the =Sum([Hours]) control in that section.

e. Copy and paste the line in the Report Footer section, then move the two lines under the =Sum([Hours]) control to indicate a grand total.

f. Save the report, then print the last page.

5. Use the Format Painter and AutoFormats.

a. Open the Member Activity Log report in Design View.

b. Format the MemberNo label in the MemberNo Header section with a bold Tahoma 12pt font.

c. Use the Format Painter to copy that format to the five other labels in the MemberNo Header section (First, Last, Dues, ActivityDate, and Hours). Also, be careful to format the labels rather than the text boxes in the MemberNo Header section.

d. Change the color of the two lines in the Report Header section to red.

e. Create a new AutoFormat named **Red Lines-Your Name** based on the Member Activity Log report.

f. Add a label with your name to the Report Header section, print the first page of the Member Activity Log report, then save it.

g. In Design View, apply the Corporate AutoFormat. (*Hint*: Click the report selector button in the upper left corner of the report to select the entire report before applying an AutoFormat. If an individual section or control is selected when you apply an AutoFormat, it will be applied to only that section or control.)

h. Use the Customize button in the AutoFormat dialog box to delete the Red Lines-Your Name style.

i. Preview, then print the first page of the Member Activity Log report. Save, then close the report.

6. Create a Web page.

a. Use the Page Wizard to create a Web page based on all of the fields in the Names table.

b. Group the information by Zip, do not add any sorting orders, title the page **Zip Code Groups**, then open it in Page View.

c. Navigate to the 50266 zip code, then navigate to the record for the name Kristen Larson. Enter your first and last name into the page, as shown in Figure H-23, then save and print that page.

d. Save the data access page with the name **zip** to the drive and folder where your Project Files are stored, then click OK when prompted about the connection string.

e. Close the zip Web page.

FIGURE-H-23

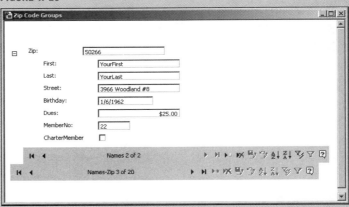

7. Export data.

a. Export the Names table as an HTML Document with the name **list-yourinitials** (e.g., list-ab or list-kf) to the drive and folder where your Project Files are stored.

b. Start Internet Explorer, click the File menu bar, click Open, then click Browse. Find and then double-click the **list-yourinitials** Web page, click OK to view it in Internet Explorer, then click Print on the Standard Buttons toolbar to print that page.

c. Close Internet Explorer, then return to the Membership-H database window.

8. Compact and repair a database.

a. If working on a hard drive, click Tools on the menu bar, point to Database Utilities, then click Compact and Repair Database. (*Note*: You can also complete this step on a floppy disk if your disk has enough space [in this case, about 400 KB of disk storage] to create the temporary file used during the compacting process.)

b. Close the Membership-H database, then exit Access.

c. Start Explorer, right-click 3½ Floppy (A:) in the Folder's list, then click Copy Disk. Follow the prompts to make a back-up copy of your Project Files to a blank floppy disk, then exit Windows Explorer. If your Project Files are located on the hard drive or other storage device, locate and right-click the folder that contains your Project Files in the Folders list, then click Copy. Right-click 3½ Floppy (A:) in the Folders list, click Paste, then exit Windows Explorer.

 # Independent Challenge 1

As the manager of a music store's instrument rental program, you created a database to track instrument rentals to schoolchildren. Now that several instruments have been purchased, you often need to print a report listing instruments in inventory. You create a single instrument inventory report based on a parameter query that prompts the user for the type of instrument to be displayed on the report. You conditionally format the report to highlight instruments in poor condition.

a. Start Access, then open the database **Music Store-H**.
b. Use the Report Wizard to create a report based on the Instruments by Type query. Select all of the fields, group by the Description field, sort in ascending order by the SerialNo field, do not specify any summary options, use a Stepped Layout, use a Portrait Orientation, apply a Corporate style, then title the report **Instruments in Inventory**.
c. Type **Cello** when prompted for the type of instrument.
d. Open the report in Design View, then add a label with your name to the Report Header.
e. Select the Condition text box in the Detail section, then use conditional formatting so that when the field value is equal to **Poor**, the Font/Fore Color is italic and red.
f. Save, then preview the report. Enter **Violin** when prompted for the type of instrument.
g. Print the report, then close the Instruments in Inventory report.
h. Close the Music Store-H database, then exit Access.

Independent Challenge 2

As the manager of a music store's instrument rental program, you have created a database to track instrument rentals to schoolchildren. Now that several instruments have been rented, you need to create a conditionally formatted report that lists which schools have a large number of rentals.

a. Start Access, then open the database **Music Store-H**.
b. Use the Report Wizard to create a report with the following fields from the following tables:
  Schools: SchoolName
  Instruments: Description, MonthlyFee
  Rentals: Date
c. View the data by Schools, do not add any additional grouping levels, sort in ascending order by Date, then Sum the MonthlyFee field.
d. Use an Outline 1 Layout, Portrait Orientation, and Casual style.
e. Title the report **School Summary Report**.
f. Open the report in Design View, then click the =Sum([MonthlyFee]) control in the SchoolNo Footer section.
g. Use Conditional Formatting to specify that the field be Bold and have a bright yellow Fill/Back Color if the sum is greater than or equal to 200.
h. Add a label to the Report Header section with your name, then save the report.
i. Print the first page of the report.
j. Close the School Summary Report, close the Music Store-H database, then exit Access.

► Independent Challenge 3

As the manager of a music store's instrument rental program, you have created a database to track instrument rentals to schoolchildren. You need to build both static and dynamic Web pages for this database.

a. Start Access, then open the database **Music Store-H**.

b. Use the Page Wizard to create a data access page with the SchoolName field from the Schools table, the Date from the Rentals table, and all of the fields in the Instruments table.

c. Group the records by SchoolName, sort them in ascending order by Date, title the page **School Rentals**, then display it in Page View.

d. In Design View, click in the Click here and type title text prompt, then type your name.

e. Save the page as **school** in the folder where your Project Files are located, then open the school.htm file in Internet Explorer.

f. Find the record for the Thomas Jefferson Elementary school, then click the Expand button.

g. Double-click Excellent in the Condition field for the first record within this school, then click the Filter by Selection button in the upper Navigation bar to find all instruments rented to this school with that criteria.

h. Navigate to the third instrument with an Excellent condition for the Thomas Jefferson Elementary school, then print that page.

i. Close Internet Explorer, close the Music-H database, then exit Access.

 # Independent Challenge 4

As the manager of a Human Resources Department for a company that specializes in developing trade partners in Southeast Asia, you have developed an Access database to track personnel benefits. Eventually, you want to convert some of the existing Access reports and forms to Web pages, which would be accessible to employees across the world. You already have offices in both Singapore and Hong Kong, and are excited to use the World Wide Web to establish global communication. You decide to go to Microsoft's Web site to find some information about how Access can be used to create Web pages.

a. Connect to the Internet, then go to www.microsoft.com/access (which will redirect you to the homepage for Microsoft Access).

b. The Microsoft Web site is extremely large, and, depending on whether you are looking for tips, downloads, introductory articles, or specific technical support, there are many places where you could go to find good information. Explore the Web site at your own pace. Your goal is to find and read articles that discuss how Access 2002 can be used to create Web pages, then print the first page of one of the articles. (Note: Some articles are quite long. Click File on the menu bar, then click Print to open the Print dialog box to specify a print range.)

c. Web sites change often, but after searching on your own, try to find articles with these titles:
  • Upgrading to Access 2002 (includes a section on Web pages)
  • Choosing a Web browser for multilingual Web pages
  • Comparing the Three Types of Web Pages
  • Data Access Pages
  • Deploying Data Access Pages on the Internet or Your Intranet (from the Microsoft Developers Network, MSDN, Library)

d. Access 2002 offers many improvements to Web page development over Access 2000. Search the Microsoft site for What's New? or What's Improved? in Access 2002, then print that article. Highlight the sections on what is new in regard to Web pages and Web page development.

e. On the back of one of your printouts, write a paragraph about what you learned from the research you conducted. Write a second paragraph about what questions you still have about how to use Access to create Web pages.

Visual Workshop

Open the **Training-H** database and use the Report Wizard to create the report shown in Figure H-24. Select the First, Last, and Department fields from the Employees table, and the Description and Hours fields from the Courses table. View the data by Employees, do not add any more grouping levels, sort in ascending order by Description, and Sum the Hours. Use the Outline 1, Landscape, and Corporate style Report Wizard options. Title the report **Employee Education Report**. Enter your name as a label in the Report Header to uniquely identify your printout. In Report Design View, make the necessary changes so that your report matches the figure as shown. You'll need to move and resize some controls. You'll also have to delete the long, calculated control that counts the records, and work with line controls in the SSN Footer section. Print the first page of the report.

FIGURE H-24

Employee Education Report   *Your Name*

First	Shayla	Department	CD
Last	Colletti		

Description	Hours
Computer Concepts	12
Excel Case Problems	12
Intermediate Excel	12
Intermediate Word	12
Internet Fundamentals	12
Introduction to Excel	12
Introduction to Netscape	12
Introduction to Outlook	12
Introduction to Retailing	16
Introduction to Word	12
Store Management	16
Sum	*140*

First	Nancy	Department	Video
Last	Lee		

Integrating

Word, Excel, and Access

Objectives

► **Copy an Access datasheet into a Word document**
► **Copying an Access datasheet to Excel**
► **Embed an Excel chart into a Word document**

Using data from different Office programs to complete a single document is an efficient way to take advantage of existing files. The analytical features of Excel and Access provide valuable ways to integrate information easily and effectively. In this unit, Maria Abbott, the regional sales manager at MediaLoft, is considering reducing the stock of historical books at the Kansas City store, based on the numbers in stock at the end of the fiscal year. She has asked Andrew Fleming, the store manager in Kansas City, to send her information on the stock of history books in his store.

Copying an Access Datasheet into a Word Document

The more files you create using Office programs, the more important it is to be able to merge information together to create documents. Access data can be sent to a new Word document by using the OfficeLinks button on the Standard toolbar or by copying the data from Access and pasting it into Word. The easiest way to merge data from an Access table with an existing Word document is to copy and paste the data from Access to Word. Maria asks Andrew to send her the current History stock list for the Kansas City store, sorted by author.

Steps

1. Start Access, open the **KC StockList-IF.mdb** database from the drive and location where your Project Files are stored, click **Tables** on the Objects bar if necessary, then open **Stock Table** and **Author Table**

   Note that the Stock Table identifies the history books in stock at the Kansas City store. Each book in the table is identified by its ISBN number, title, and an author ID field. The Author Table lists all the history authors' first and last names and each author's Author ID number. The AuthorID field corresponds to the field with the same name in the Stock Table.

2. Create a query named **History Stock** that displays the fields in the following order: **ISBN**, **LastName**, **FirstName**, **BookTitle**, and **Units in Stock**, sorted alphabetically by **LastName**

3. Open the query in Datasheet view

   Compare your query results with those shown in Figure F-1.

4. Start Word, open the file **INT F-1.doc** from the drive and location where your Project Files are stored, then save it as **KC Store Memo.doc**

   You'll copy the Access table into this document.

5. Click the **Zoom button list arrow** [100%] on the Standard toolbar, then click **75%**

   Decreasing the zoom setting allows you to see more of the document at one time.

6. Click the **History Stock query Access program button** on the Windows taskbar, select all of the columns in the History Stock query, then click the **Copy button** on the Access Standard toolbar

   The table is copied to the Clipboard.

7. Click the **Word program button** on the Window taskbar, click I to position the insertion point below the heading **History Stock (KC store)**, click the **Paste button** on the Standard toolbar, then scroll the document to view the entire table

   The data from the Access query is pasted into the Word document. The table does not all fit on the first page of the document, so Word creates a second page.

8. Add your name as a footer in the document, save your changes, print and close the document, then minimize the Word program window

   You are returned to the Access program window.

9. Click the **Close button** [X] in the History Stock query datasheet window, then click **No** in the dialog box that asks if you want to save the data stored on the clipboard

10. Close the **Author Table** and **Stock Table** datasheet windows

FIGURE F-1: Query results

Modified query showing units in ascending order

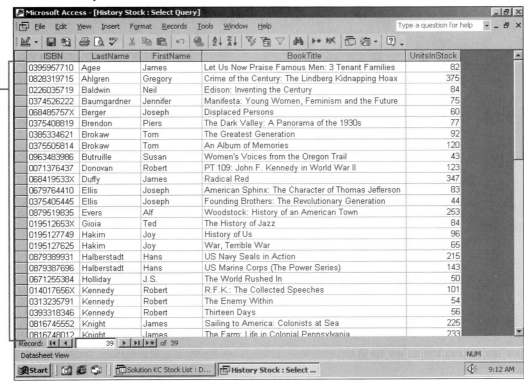

FIGURE F-2: Access table copied into Word document

Table in Word document

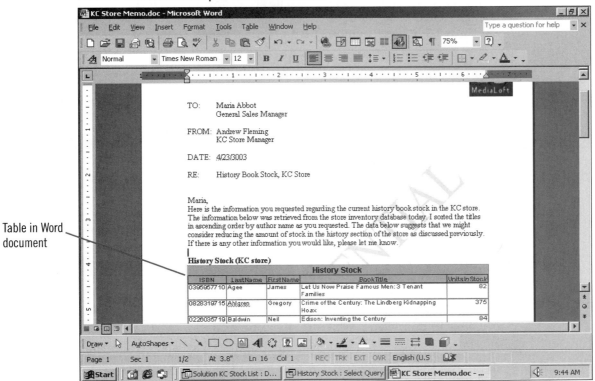

Copying an Access Datasheet to Excel

As you have learned, each Office program allows you to work with information in a unique way. For example, Access enables you to create and store large amounts of data, such as product inventory information or customer records. Excel, on the other hand, enables you to analyze numerical data by calculating totals, filtering data, and graphing data in ways that the other Office programs do not. Maria has requested that Andrew provide her with more information on the history inventory at his store, including a chart that tracks the numbers of history books in stock at the end of each of the last four years. To do this, Andrew will create a query to retrieve the number of units currently in stock. Next, he'll use Excel to analyze the information, and create a chart that explains the overstock trend for history books in his store.

Steps

1. Create a query named **History Stock Analysis** that includes the fields **ISBN**, **Author ID**, **Book Title UnitsInStock**, and **UnitPrice**, sorted in ascending order by **UnitsInStock**, then open the **History Stock Analysis query** in Datasheet view
   The query displays just the fields you need.

2. Select all of the columns in the History Stock Analysis query, then click the **Copy button** on the Access Standard toolbar

3. Start Excel, open the file **INT F-2.xls** from the drive and location where your Project files are stored, then save it as **History Overstock Analysis.xls**
   An Excel worksheet opens, identifying the history units in stock at the end of previous fiscal years.

4. Click the **Sheet2 tab**, rename the sheet tab **2003 Stock**, click **cell A1**, click the **Paste button** on the Excel Standard toolbar, then AutoFit columns as necessary to see all the data
   Compare your screen to Figure F-3. The green error indicators in the upper-left corner of cells indicate that the numbers were pasted into Excel as text instead of numbers. To calculate formulas in Excel, numbers need to be in a numerical format.

5. Convert the data in **columns D** and **E** to **numbers**
   Now you can perform calculations.

6. Calculate the total value of each book in column F, type **TotalValue** in cell F1, then AutoFit column F

7. Calculate the total number of units in stock in **cell D42**, then calculate the total value of all units in stock in **cell F42**

8. Copy the data in **cells D42** and **F42**, then paste the values into **cells B8** and **C8**, respectively, on the History Overstock worksheet
   The calculation results from the 2003 Stock worksheet now appear on the History Overstock worksheet.

9. Create two charts of the data in the History Overstock worksheet, using Figure F-4 as a guide: one showing the units in stock and the other showing the value of the units in stock, for the four years represented in the worksheet
   Compare your results with Figure F-4.

10. Close the History Stock Analysis query data sheet window and the KC Stock List database, then exit Access, *but do not exit Excel*

FIGURE F-3: Results of the Access query copied into Excel

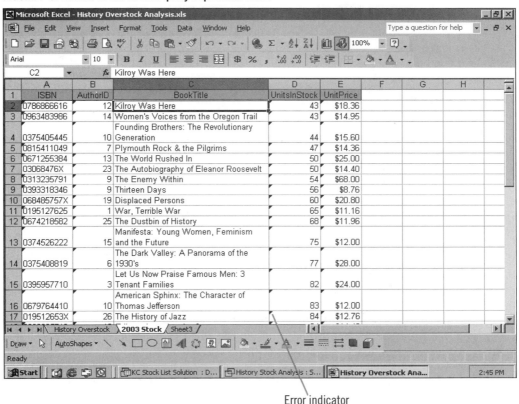

Error indicator

FIGURE F-4: Charts created from data

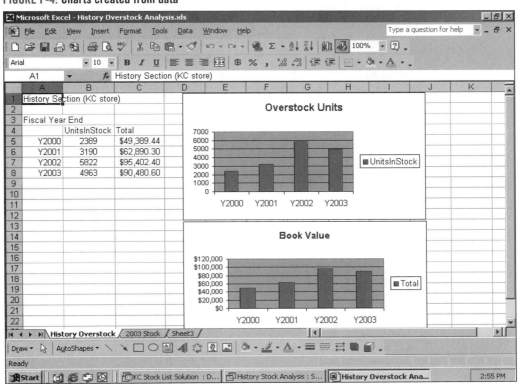

Unit F

Integration

Embedding an Excel Chart into a Word Document

As you have learned, you can embed an entire Excel worksheet in a Word document by using Word's Object command on the Insert menu. You can also embed partial information from an Excel worksheet, such as a chart or specific data, by selecting the information and then copying and pasting it into your Word document. Embedding an Excel chart into a Word document enables you to take advantage of all of Excel's functionality from your Word document, allowing you to create a professional-looking chart. ⬤▬▬ Andrew decides to include his charts showing the overstock at his store in a memo to Maria.

Steps 1234

1. Click the chart containing the data on overstock units, then click the **Copy button** ⬛ on the Standard toolbar

2. Click the **Word program button** on the Windows taskbar, open the file **INT F-3.doc** from the drive and location where your Project Files are stored, then save the document as **KC Store Memo 2.doc**

3. Click in the space directly below **History section unit overstock**, then click the **Paste button** ⬛ on the Standard toolbar
   The chart appears in the document, as shown in Figure F-5. The chart is not embedded at this point because Word gives you the choice of embedding the chart or just inserting a picture of the chart. If you embed the chart as a picture, you will not able to open the chart from Word and edit it in the future.

4. Click the **Paste Options button** ⬛▾ at the bottom of the chart, then click **Excel Chart (entire workbook)**
   The Excel chart is embedded into the document. If you want to edit an Excel chart after you've embedded it, you can double-click the chart to open it. Your Word document will remain open, but Excel's toolbars and menus will appear for you to use. Because the chart is embedded, rather than linked, any changes you make to the chart in Word will not affect the chart in Excel.

5. Embed the chart containing the data on the value of the overstock units from the History Overstock worksheet into the KC Store Memo 2 document below the line **Total overstock value**
   Compare your screen with Figure F-6.

6. Add your name as a footer in your document, then save and print it

7. Close all files, then exit Excel and Word

FIGURE F-5: Chart showing History overstock

Chart from Excel ⟶

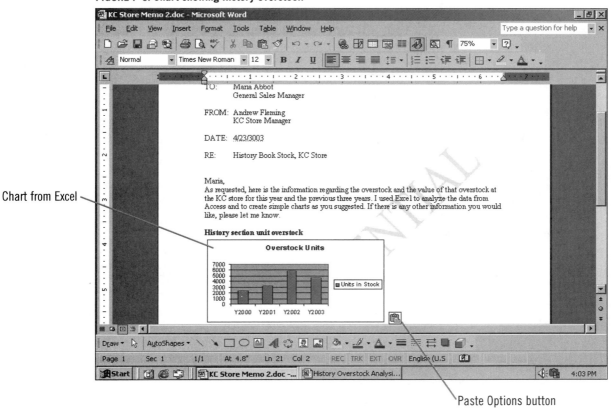

Paste Options button

FIGURE F-6: Word document with embedded Excel charts

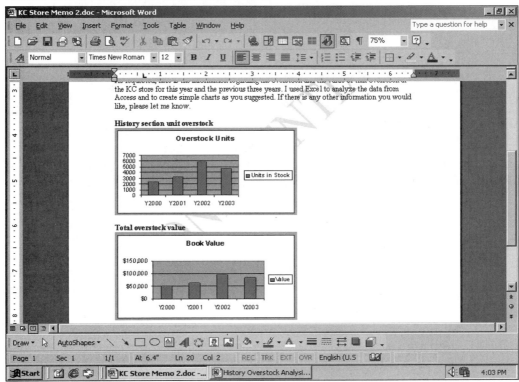

Practice

► Independent Challenge 1

As the new owner of your own flower shop in Spain, Tonia's Flowers, you need to generate a weekly inventory report to help you decide how much new inventory to order. The quickest way to do the inventory report is to create a query in Access, then analyze the data in Excel.

a. Start Access, open the Tonia's Flowers.mdb database from the drive and location where your Project Files are stored, then add at least five new items to the Product Line table.

b. Create a query named In-Stock Items that sorts products in ascending order by the Units On Order field. Make sure your query includes fields that identify the product name, the number of units in stock, the number of units on order, the unit price, and the lead time. Add a criterion that retrieves only those products for which eight or more items are in stock.

c. Copy the results of the In-Stock Items query to a new Excel workbook, then save the workbook as **Stock Report.xls** to the drive and location where your Project files are stored.

d. Calculate the sum of all products in stock, then calculate the value of all the products on order.

e. Include your name on the footer of the worksheet, then save and print the Excel worksheet.

f. Close all open files, then exit Excel and Access.

► Independent Challenge 2

You work for a trade consulting company, XEO Business Systems. You have just been assigned a research project to analyze the latest U.S. government information on retail trade. To complete the project, you will create a query in Access and then use Excel to analyze the data. You will finish the project by embedding the Excel data in a Word document.

a. Open the Access database U.S. Trade Analysis.mdb from the drive and location where your Project Files are stored, then open the Trade by State table.

b. Create a query called Trade by State Query that includes fields from the table that identify the state, industry description, payroll, sales, and sales rank. Sort the query results by the sales rank in ascending order.

c. Copy the query results to a new Excel workbook, then save the workbook as **State Trade Analysis.xls** to the location where your Project files are stored.

d. Use AutoFilter to determine the data for each of the five sales rankings, then create a chart for each sales ranking. Save your changes.

e. Create a Word document named **Top State Trade Analysis.doc**. Include your name in the footer. Enter some basic text describing the data you created in Excel. Insert all five charts in your document.

f. Save and print the Word document. Close all open files, then exit Word, Excel, and Access.

Customizing
Your Presentation

Objectives

- MOUS ► **Understand PowerPoint masters**
- MOUS ► **Format master text**
- MOUS ► **Change master text indents**
- MOUS ► **Adjust text objects**
- MOUS ► **Use advanced drawing tools**
- MOUS ► **Use advanced formatting tools**
- ► **Use the Style Checker**
- MOUS ► **Create a template**

Design features such as text spacing and color are some of the most important qualities of a professional-looking presentation. It is important, however, to make design elements consistent throughout a presentation to hold the reader's attention and to avoid confusion. PowerPoint helps you achieve the look you want by providing ways to customize and enhance your slides, notes pages, and handouts. ✐ Maria Abbott, the general sales manager of MediaLoft, is working on a marketing presentation that she will give later this month. After receiving feedback from her coworkers, she revises her presentation by customizing the format of her slides and enhancing the graphics.

Understanding PowerPoint Masters

Each presentation in PowerPoint uses **Master views** to store information about the design template, including font styles, text placeholder position and size, and color scheme. Design elements that you place in the Slide Master view appear on every slide in the presentation. For example, you could insert a company logo in the upper-right corner of the Slide Master and that logo would then appear on every slide in your presentation. There are three Master views—Slide Master view, Handout Master view, and Notes Master view. Changes made to the slide master are reflected on all the slides, changes made to the notes master are reflected in the Notes Page view, and changes made to the handout master are reflected when you print your presentation using one of the Handout print options. Slide Master view actually has two master slides: one for the slide master and one for the title master. These two masters are called a **slide-title master pair.** Maria wants to make a few changes and add an optional design template to the presentation, so she opens her presentation and examines the Slide Master.

1. **Start PowerPoint, open the presentation PPT E-1 from the drive and folder where your Project Files are stored, then save it as iMedia 5**
   The title slide of the presentation appears.

2. **Click View, point to Master, then click Slide Master**
   The presentation's Slide Master view appears, showing the title master in the slide pane. The slide-title master pair appears as thumbnails to the left of the slide pane. The title master controls the title, subtitle, and footer placeholders for any slide in the presentation with the Title Slide layout. You can add more than one design template to the same presentation.

3. **Click the Slide Design button 🖼 on the Formatting toolbar, click the Compass design template list arrow in the Slide Design task pane under the Available For Use section, then click Add Design**
   There are now two slide-title master pairs to the left of the slide pane indicating that there are two design templates available in this presentation. You can apply a different template for different audiences or situations. You can also use multiple templates in one presentation at the same time.

4. **Click the top slide master thumbnail**
   The slide master for the presentation appears. It contains a **Master title placeholder** and a **Master text placeholder**, as shown in Figure E-1. These placeholders control the format for each title text object and main text object for each slide in the presentation that doesn't have the Title layout. Figure E-2 shows Slide 6 of the presentation. Examine Figures E-1 and E-2 to better understand the relationship between the slide master and the slide.

   - The Master title placeholder, labeled "Title Area for AutoLayouts," indicates the position of the title text object and its font size, style, and color. Compare this to the slide title shown in Figure E-2.
   - The Master text placeholder, labeled "Object Area for AutoLayouts," determines the characteristics of the body text objects on all the slides in the presentation. Notice how the bullet levels in the body text object of Figure E-2 compare to the corresponding bullet levels of the Master text placeholder in Figure E-1.
   - You can resize and move Master title and text placeholders as you would any placeholder in PowerPoint.
   - The Slide Master can contain background objects, such as AutoShapes, clip art, or pictures, that will appear on every slide in the presentation behind the text and objects you place on the slides. In Maria's presentation, the iMedia logo appears on the slide master, so that it shows on every slide in the presentation, except the title slide.

FIGURE E-1: Slide Master

Slide master slide

Title master slide

Additional design template

Thumbtack

Bullet levels

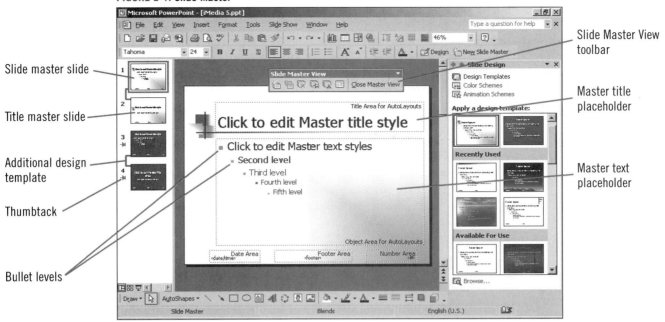

Slide Master View toolbar

Master title placeholder

Master text placeholder

FIGURE E-2: Slide 2 in Normal view

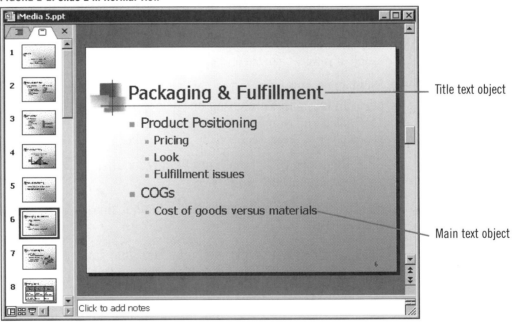

Title text object

Main text object

Restoring the master layout

If a master placeholder is missing or deleted from a master view, you can click the Master Layout button on the master toolbar to reapply the placeholder. Clicking the Master Layout button opens the Master Layout dialog box, as shown in Figure E-3. Click the placeholder check box to reapply the placeholder. Each master view has its own Master Layout dialog box.

FIGURE E-3: Master Layout dialog box

Formatting Master Text

Formatting text in a Master view works the same as it does in other views, but PowerPoint applies the changes you make to the whole presentation. This ensures that you don't use a mixture of fonts and styles throughout the presentation. For example, if your presentation is part of a marketing campaign for a travel tour to the Middle East, you may decide to switch the title text font of the entire presentation from the standard Times New Roman font to a script font. You can change text color, style, size, and bullet type in the master view. When you change a bullet type, you can use a character bullet symbol from a font, a picture bullet from the Clip Gallery, or an image that you scan in. ◢━━ Maria decides to make a few formatting changes to the text of her slide master.

Steps

1. Make sure the slide master is still visible, click **Window** on the menu bar, then click **Arrange All**
   This ensures that your screen will match the figures in this book.

2. Move I anywhere in the first line of text in the Master text placeholder, then click
   Clicking I in a Master view selects the entire line of text. The first line of text could be more prominent.

3. Click the **Bold button** B on the Formatting toolbar, then click the **Shadow button** S on the Formatting toolbar
   The first line of text becomes bold with a shadow. The second-level bullet would be more visible if it were changed and formatted.

4. Right-click anywhere in the second line of text in the Master text placeholder, then click **Bullets and Numbering** on the shortcut menu
   The Bullets and Numbering dialog box opens. Notice that there is also a Numbered tab that you can use to create sequentially numbered or lettered bullets.

5. Click **Customize**, click the **Font list arrow**, then click **Wingdings 2**
   The available bullet choices change.

6. Use the scroll arrows to locate the x symbol shown in Figure E-4, click the **x symbol**, then click **OK**

7. Click the **Color list arrow**, click the **dark blue square** (fourth from the left), click **OK**, then click a blank area of the slide
   A dark blue arrow replaces the third-level bullet.

8. Click the **Normal View button** 🔲, then click the **Slide 2 thumbnail**
   Compare your screen to Figure E-5.

9. Click the **Save button** 💾 on the Standard toolbar to save your changes

FIGURE E-4: Symbol dialog box

Choose this bullet style

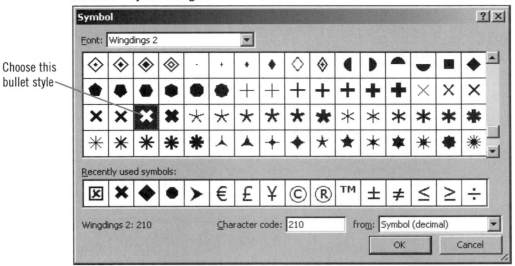

FIGURE E-5: Slide 2 with modified text and bullet styles

First-level text is bold and shadowed

New bullet

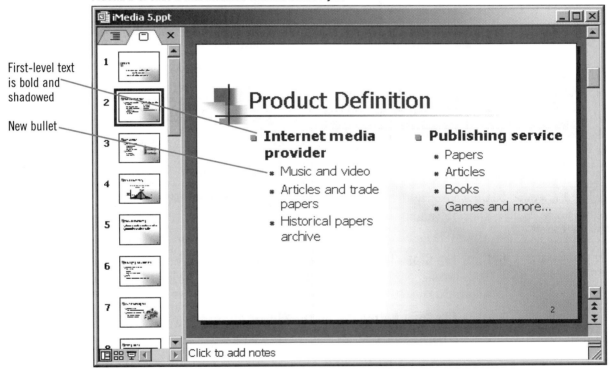

Applying a template from another presentation

When you apply a design template from another presentation, you automatically apply the master layouts, fonts, and colors over the existing presentation's design template. To apply a template from another presentation, open the Slide Design – Design Templates task pane, then click the Browse hyperlink at the bottom of the pane. In the Apply Design Template dialog box, click All PowerPoint Files in the Files of type list box, then use the Look in list arrow to navigate to the presentation whose design you want to apply. (It does not have to be a template.) Click the presentation or template name, then click Apply.

PowerPoint 2002

Changing Master Text Indents

The Master text placeholder in every presentation has five levels of text, called **indent levels**. You can use the horizontal slide ruler to control the space between the bullets and the text or to change the position of the whole indent level. Each indent level is represented by two small triangles called **indent markers** on the ruler that identify the position of each indent level in the Master text placeholder. You can also set tabs on the horizontal ruler by clicking the tab indicator to the left of the horizontal ruler. Table E-1 describes the indent and tab markers on the ruler. Maria decides to change the distance between the bullet symbols and the text in the first two indent levels of her presentation to emphasize the bullets.

1. Press **[Shift]**, then click the **Normal View button**
   Slide Master view appears.

> **Trouble?**
>
> If your rulers are already visible, skip Step 2.

2. Click anywhere in the Master text placeholder to place the insertion point, click **View** on the menu bar, then click **Ruler**
   The rulers and indent markers for the Master text placeholder appear. The indent markers are set so that the first line of text in each level—in this case, the bullet—begins to the left of subsequent lines of text. This is a **hanging indent**.

> **Trouble?**
>
> If you accidentally drag an indent marker into another marker, click the Undo button to restore the indent levels to their original position.

3. Position the pointer over the left indent marker of the first indent level, then drag to the right to the ½" mark
   Compare your screen to Figure E-6.

4. Position the pointer over the left indent marker of the second indent level, then drag to the right to the 1⅛" mark
   See Figure E-7. The rulers take up valuable screen area.

> **Trouble?**
>
> You can add tabs to any level text by clicking on the ruler where you want the tab. Click the tab indicator to the left of the ruler to cycle through the different tab alignment options.

5. Click the right mouse button in a blank area of the slide, then click **Ruler** on the shortcut menu
   The rulers are no longer visible.

6. Click the **Close Master View button** on the Master toolbar
   Slide Master view closes and Slide 2 appears, showing the increased indents in the main text object.

7. Click the **Save button** on the Standard toolbar

Exceptions to the slide master

If you change the format of text on a slide and then apply a different template to the presentation, the slide that you formatted retains the text formatting changes you made. These format changes that differ from the slide master are known as **exceptions**. Exceptions can only be changed on the individual slides where they occur. For example, you might change the font and size of a particular piece of text on a slide to make it stand out and then decide later to add a different template to your presentation. The text you formatted before you applied the template is an exception, and it is unaffected by the new template. Another way to override the slide master is to remove the master graphics on one or more slides. You might want to do this to get a clearer view of your slide text. Click Format on the menu bar, click Background, then click the Omit background graphics from master check box to select it.

FIGURE E-6: Slide Master with first-level, left indent marker moved

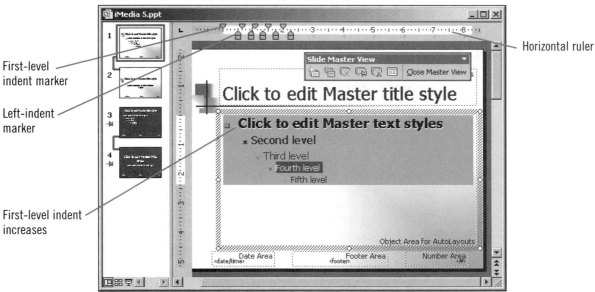

Horizontal ruler

First-level indent marker

Left-indent marker

First-level indent increases

FIGURE E-7: Slide Master with second-level, left indent marker moved

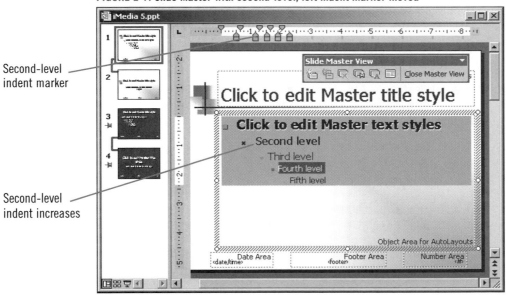

Second-level indent marker

Second-level indent increases

TABLE E-1: Indent and Tab Markers

symbol	name	function
▽	First line indent marker	Controls the position of the first line of text in an indent level
△	Left indent marker	Controls the position of subsequent lines of text in an indent level
▭	Margin marker	Moves both indent markers of an indent level at the same time
⌐	Left-aligned tab	Aligns tab text on the left
⌐	Right-aligned tab	Aligns tab text on the right
⊥	Center-aligned tab	Aligns tab text in the center
⊥	Decimal-aligned tab	Aligns tab text on a decimal point

Adjusting Text Objects

You have complete control over the placement of your text in PowerPoint. With the **text anchor** feature, you can adjust text position within text objects or shapes to achieve the best look. If you want your text to fill more or less of the slide, you can adjust the spacing between lines of text, called **leading** (rhymes with "wedding"). Maria decides to adjust the text position and line spacing of the text object on Slide 5.

Steps

1. Click the **Slide 5 thumbnail** in the Slides tab
   Slide 5 appears.

2. Press **[Shift]**, right-click the **main text object**, then click **Format Placeholder** on the shortcut menu
   The Format AutoShape dialog box opens. The text would look better centered in the text box.

   Trouble?
   If the Format AutoShape dialog box prevents you from seeing the slide, drag it out of the way.

3. Click the **Text Box tab**, click the **Text anchor point list arrow**, click **Middle Centered**, then click **Preview**
   Compare your Format AutoShape dialog box to Figure E-8. The text moves to the middle center of the text object. To make it easier to select, resize the text object.

4. Click the **Resize AutoShape to fit text check box**, then click **Preview**
   The text object shrinks to fit the text. The text object would look better placed more in the center of the slide.

5. Click the **Position tab**, click the **Horizontal down arrow** until **0.79** appears, then click **OK**
   The text object moves to the center of the slide. The bullets are a little too close together.

6. Click **Format** on the menu bar, then click **Line Spacing**
   The Line Spacing dialog box opens.

7. In the After paragraph section, click the **up arrow** four times so that **0.2** appears, click **Preview**, then drag the dialog box out of the way
   The space, or leading, after each paragraph increases. The text is easier to read.

8. In the Line spacing section, click the **up arrow** until **2** appears, then click **Preview**
   Compare your Line Spacing dialog box to Figure E-9. The line spacing between the text lines increases.

9. Click **OK**, then click in a blank area of the slide to deselect the main text object, then save your changes
   Compare your screen to Figure E-10.

Changing margins around text in shapes

You can also use the Text Anchor Point command to change the margins around a text object to form a shape that suits the text better. Right-click the shape, click Format Placeholder, click the Text Box tab, then adjust the Internal margin settings. Click Preview to see your changes before you apply them to the shape.

FIGURE E-8: **Format AutoShape dialog box**

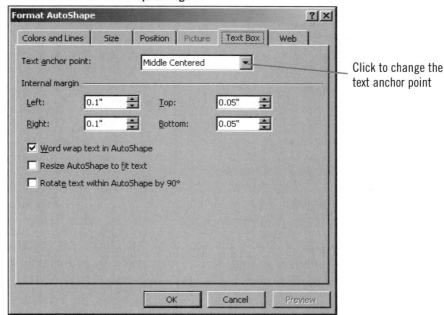

Click to change the
text anchor point

FIGURE E-9: **Line Spacing dialog box**

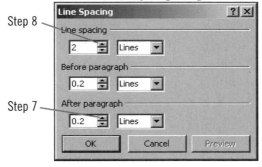

Step 8

Step 7

FIGURE E-10: **Slide showing formatted body text object**

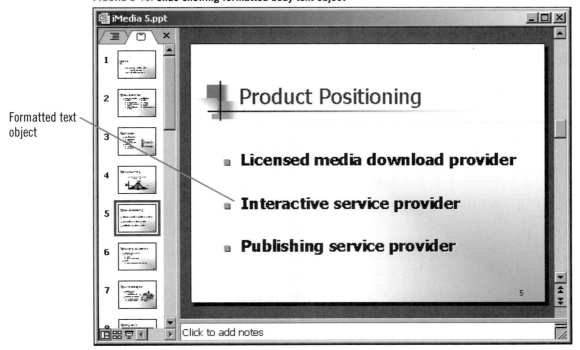

Formatted text
object

Using Advanced Drawing Tools

PowerPoint has a number of powerful drawing tools on the AutoShapes menu to help you draw all types of shapes. For example, the Curve drawing tool allows you to create a freeform curved line, the Arc tool helps you draw smooth, curved lines and pie-shaped wedges, and the Connector line tool allows you to connect AutoShape objects with a line. Once you have drawn a shape, you can format and rearrange it to create the effect you want. Maria uses the Connector line tool to complete the diagram on Slide 11.

Steps

1. Click the **Slide 11 thumbnail**, click the **AutoShapes button** on the Drawing toolbar, point to **Connectors**, then click the **Straight Arrow Connector button**
   The pointer changes to +.

2. Move + to the right side of the **Phase 2 object** until it changes to ⬦ and blue dots appear around the object, then click the **blue dot** on the right side of the Phase 2 object
   See Figure E-11. The blue dots are anchor points for the connector arrow.

Trouble?

If a green box appears at either end of the line, drag the green square until the blue connection point on the object appears.

3. Move the pointer to the left side of the **diamond object**, then, when you see the blue dot inside the pointer, click again to place the right side of the connector arrow
   A red circle appears at either end of the connector arrow, indicating that the arrow connects the two objects.

4. Click the **Line Style button** on the Drawing toolbar, then click the **2¼ pt line style**
   The line style of the arrow connector changes to a thicker weight.

5. Click the **Arrow Style button** on the Drawing toolbar, click **More Arrows**, then click the **Colors and Lines tab**
   The Format AutoShape dialog box opens. The arrow would look better with a more distinct shape.

QuickTip

To change the default attributes of a particular AutoShape, format the AutoShape, select it, click Draw on the Drawing toolbar, then click Set AutoShape Defaults.

6. Under the Arrows section, click the **End size list arrow**, click the **Arrow R Size 8 button** (second button, last row), then click **OK**
   The style of the arrow connector line changes to a more distinct style.

7. Place + over the head of the arrow, drag the connector arrow to the left side of the **Phase 3 object**, then release the mouse button when you see the blue dot on the left side of the Phase 3 object inside the pointer
   The arrow connector now connects the Phase 2 and Phase 3 objects.

8. Click the **Draw button** on the Drawing toolbar, point to **Order**, then click **Send to Back**
   The arrow connector line moves behind the diamond shape.

9. Click in a blank area of the slide, then save the presentation
   Compare your screen to Figure E-12.

FIGURE E-11: Slide showing Connector anchor points

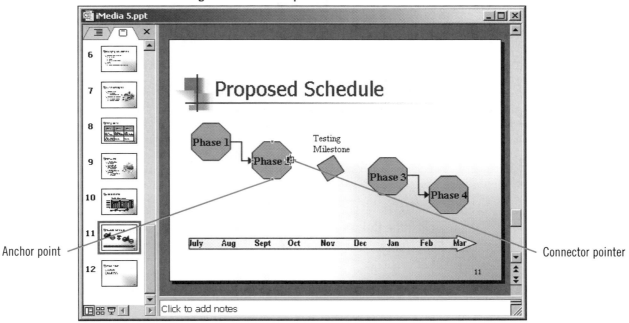

Anchor point

Connector pointer

FIGURE E-12: Slide showing formatted connector arrow

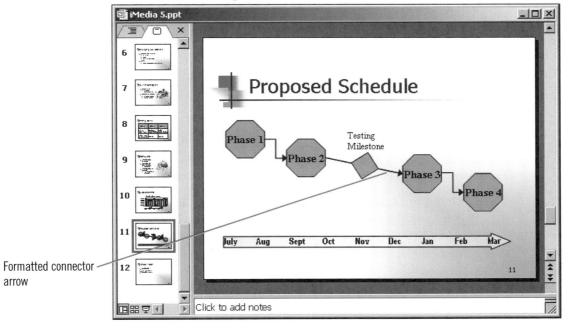

Formatted connector arrow

Drawing a freeform shape

A freeform shape can consist of straight lines, freehand (or curved) lines, or a combination of the two. To draw a freeform shape, click the AutoShapes menu button, point to Lines, then click the Freeform button 🗂. Drag the mouse to draw the desired shape (the cursor changes to a pencil as you draw), then double-click when you are done. To draw a straight line with the Freeform tool, click where you want to begin the line, move the mouse, then double-click to deactivate the Freeform tool. To edit a freeform object, right-click the object, then click Edit Points on the shortcut menu.

Using Advanced Formatting Tools

With PowerPoint's advanced formatting tools, you can change formatting attributes such as fill texture, 3-D effects, and shadow for text and shapes. If you like the attributes of an object, you can use the Format Painter button to pick up the attributes and apply them to another object. ✎ Maria wants to use the advanced formatting tools to enhance the diagram on the slide.

Steps 1 2 3 4

1. Press [Shift], right-click the **Phase 1 object**, click **Format AutoShape** on the shortcut menu, click the **Colors and Lines tab**, click the **Color list arrow** in the Fill section, then click **Fill Effects**
   The Fill Effects dialog box opens.

2. Click the **Texture tab**, click the **Newsprint square** (first square in the top row), click **OK**, then click **OK** again
   The newsprint texture fills the shape.

QuickTip

When you click the 3-D Style button on the Drawing toolbar, you can click one of the 3-D styles on the pop-up menu. The default 3-D style is Style 1, the first style in the first row.

3. Click the **3-D Style button** 🔲 on the Drawing toolbar, then click **3-D Settings**
   The 3-D Settings toolbar appears.

4. Click the **Depth button** 🔲 on the 3-D Settings toolbar, then click **36 pt.**
   A 3-D effect is applied and the depth of the 3-D effect lengthens from the default of 36 points.

5. Click the **Direction button** 🔲 on the 3-D Settings toolbar, click the right effect in the middle row, as shown in Figure E-13, then click the **Close button** ⊠ on the 3-D Settings toolbar
   The 3-D effect changes to the left side of the object.

6. With the Phase 1 object still selected, click the **Font Color list arrow** 🄰 ▾ on the Drawing toolbar, then click the **dark blue square** (labeled Follow Title Text Scheme Color)
   The other four objects would look better if they matched the one you just formatted.

7. Double-click the **Format Painter button** 🖌 on the Standard toolbar, click each of the other four objects, then click 🖌 again to turn off the Format Painter
   Now all the objects on the slide have the same fill effect. When you use the Format Painter tool, it "picks up" the attributes of the object that is selected and copies them to the next object that you click. If you click the Format Painter button only once, it pastes the attributes of the selected object to the next object you select, then turns off automatically. The Phase 3 object is now on top of the arrowhead.

8. Click the **Phase 3 object**, click the **Draw button** on the Drawing toolbar, point to **Order**, click **Send to Back**, click in a blank area of the slide, then save your changes
   Compare your screen to Figure E-14.

9. Press [Home] to move to Slide 1, click the **Slide Show button** 🖳, then press [Spacebar] or click the left mouse button to run through the presentation

FIGURE E-13: Slide showing formatted 3-D object

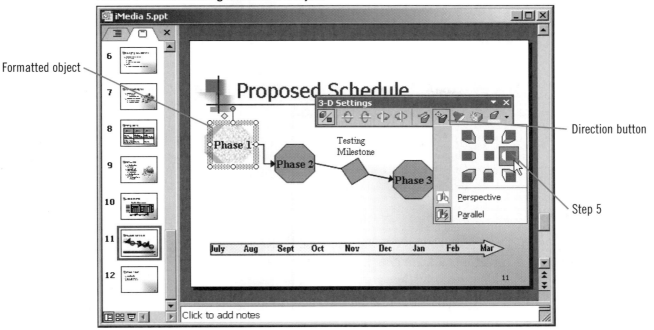

FIGURE E-14: Slide with formatted objects

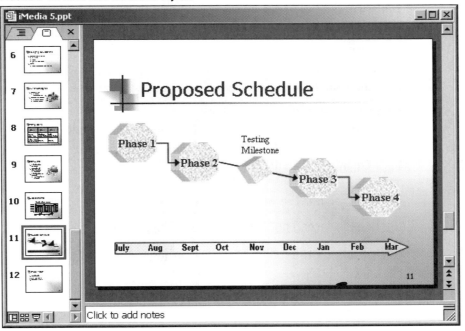

Applying a color scheme to another presentation

If you develop a custom color scheme that you like, you can use the Format Painter tool to apply it to another presentation. To apply a color scheme from one presentation to another, open each presentation in Slide Sorter view, then use the Arrange All command on the Windows menu to arrange the Presentation windows side by side. Select a slide in the presentation with the color scheme you want to copy, double-click the Format Painter button on the Standard toolbar, then click each slide that you want to change in the other presentation.

PowerPoint 2002

Using the Style Checker

To help you correct common design mistakes, the Style Checker feature in PowerPoint reviews your presentation for typical errors such as incorrect font sizes, use of too many fonts, extra words, errors in punctuation, and other readability problems. When you activate the Style Checker, PowerPoint checks your presentation for style inconsistencies and flags potential problem areas with a lightbulb. If you see the lightbulb, click it to see a list of suggested options for handling the problem or improving the presentation. ⬩⬩⬩⬩ Maria knows it's easy to overlook mistakes while preparing a presentation, so she reviews the Style Checker settings, then looks for errors she may have missed.

Steps 1 2 3 4

Trouble?

If a dialog box opens asking if you want to enable the Office Assistant, click Enable Assistant.

1. Click **Tools** on the menu bar, click **Options**, click the **Spelling and Style tab**, then click the **Check style check box**
   Now the Style Checker is activated.

2. Click **Style Options**, click check boxes as necessary so that your screen matches the dialog box shown in Figure E-15

3. Click the **Visual Clarity tab**, click **Defaults**, then review the options
   The Style Checker Options dialog box indicates the current option settings for visual clarity.

4. Click **OK**, then click **OK** again

5. Click the **Slide 12 thumbnail**, click the slide anywhere, then click the **lightbulb** on Slide 12
   The Office Assistant tells you that the text in the title text placeholder should use title case capitalization, in other words, that only the first letter in each word should be uppercase. See Figure E-16. You know this is not a problem.

Trouble?

Read the Style Checker suggestions carefully. Be sure that the Style Checker doesn't make changes that you don't expect. For example, the "Change the text to sentence case" option changes all uppercase letters in bulleted lists to lowercase.

6. Click **OK** in the Office Assistant dialog balloon, go to **Slide 6**, click the slide anywhere, click the **lightbulb** on the slide, then click the **Change the text to sentence case option** in the Help dialog balloon
   The word "positioning" correctly changes so the first letter is lowercase, but the letters in the acronym in the second bullet also change.

7. Change the second bullet to **COGs**, click the lightbulb, then click **OK** in the dialog balloon

8. Click **Tools** on the menu bar, click **Options**, click the **Check style check box**, then click **OK**
   The Style Checker is no longer active.

9. Hide the Office Assistant, if necessary, click the **Slide Sorter View button** ⊞, then add your name in the notes and handouts footer
   Figure E-17 shows the final presentation.

10. Click the **Normal View button** ⊡, save your changes, then print the presentation as handouts (4 per page)

FIGURE E-15: Style Options dialog box

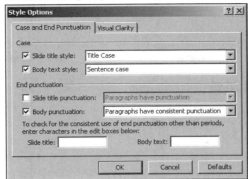

FIGURE E-16: Capitalization tip displayed by the Office Assistant

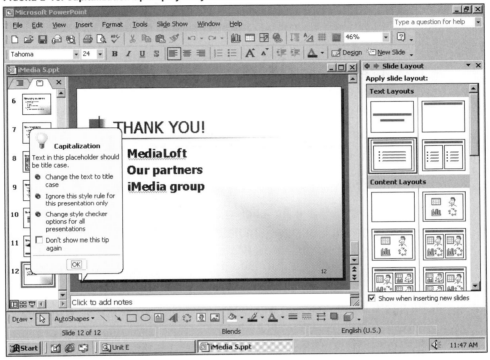

FIGURE E-17: Final presentation in Slide Sorter view

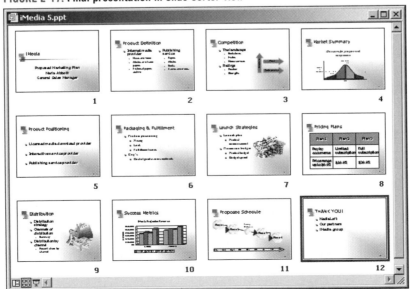

Creating a Template

You are not limited to using the standard templates PowerPoint provides or the ones you find on the Internet. You can create your own template from scratch using a blank presentation, or you can modify any existing PowerPoint template or presentation that you have access to. For example, you might want to use your company's color as a slide background or incorporate your company's logo on the slides of a presentation. If you modify an existing template, you can keep, change, or delete any color, graphic, or font as necessary. When you are finished with your template, you can save it as a special template file in PowerPoint, which adds the .pot extension to the file. You can then use your customized template as a basis for future presentations. ✎ Maria is finished customizing her presentation. Now she wants to insert the new iMedia logo into the presentation and save it as a template for future use.

Steps

1. **Click View, point to Master, then click Slide Master**
   Slide Master view appears.

2. **Click Insert on the menu bar, point to Picture, click From File, locate the logo file PPT E-2 where your Project Files are stored, then click Insert**
   The iMedia logo appears on the slide. The logo needs to be enlarged and positioned on the slide.

3. **Click the bottom-right sizing handle and drag it down ½", then drag the logo to the upper-right corner of the slide**
   Compare your screen with Figure E-18. Adjust the logo as necessary to make it look similar to Figure E-18. You are now ready to save this presentation as a PowerPoint template.

4. **Click File, click Save As, click the Save as type list arrow, click the down scroll arrow, then click Design Template**
   The Save As dialog box opens. Because this is a template, PowerPoint automatically opens the Templates folder on your hard drive as shown in Figure E-19. Templates saved in this folder appear in the Slide Design task pane in PowerPoint.

5. **Navigate to the location where your Project Files are stored, change the filename to iMedia Template, then click Save**
   The presentation is saved as a PowerPoint template to the drive and folder where your Project Files are stored, and it appears in the PowerPoint window. Notice the .pot extension on the filename in the title bar, which identifies this presentation as a template. Because this presentation will be used as a template for other presentations, the slide content is no longer needed.

6. **Click the Slide Sorter View button ▦, click Slide 3, press [Shift], click Slide 12, then press [Delete]**
   Slides 3 through 12 are deleted.

7. **Double-click Slide 2, press [Shift], click each text box, then press [Delete]**
   The content on Slide 2 is deleted.

8. **Go to Slide 1, delete the text in the text boxes, type iMedia Template in the title text placeholder, then save your changes**

9. **Click ▦, click the Zoom button list arrow 100% on the standard toolbar, then click 100%**
   Figure E-20 shows the final template presentation in Slide Sorter view.

10. **Print the template presentation as handouts (2 per page), close the presentation, and exit PowerPoint**

FIGURE E-18: Slide showing new iMedia logo

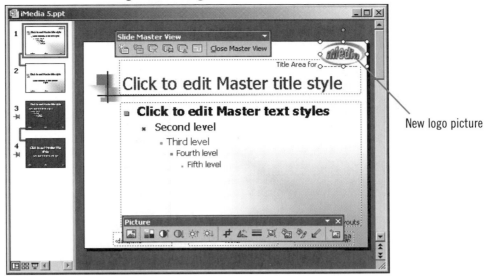

New logo picture

FIGURE E-19: Save As dialog box showing Templates folder

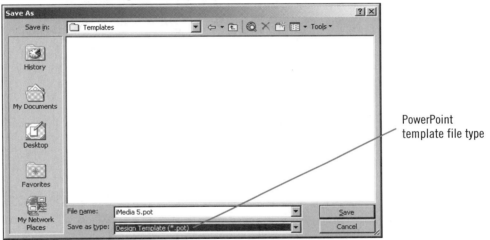

PowerPoint template file type

FIGURE E-20: Completed template presentation in Slide Sorter view

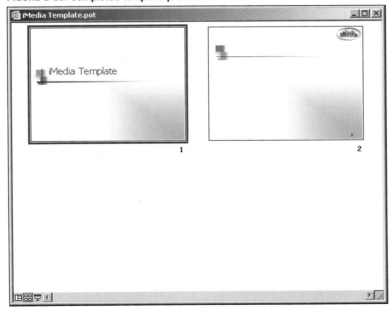

Practice

► Concepts Review

Label each of the elements of the PowerPoint window shown in Figure E-21.

FIGURE E-21

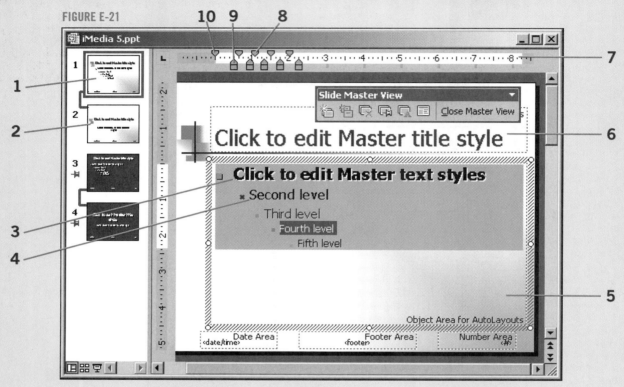

Match each of the terms with the statement that describes its function.

11. **Line spacing**
12. **Indent levels**
13. **Text anchor**
14. **Margin marker**
15. **Master**
16. **Bottom indent marker**

a. The five levels of text in a master text placeholder
b. Moves the whole indent level
c. Controls subsequent lines of text in an indent level
d. A template for all the slides in a presentation
e. Adjusts the distance between text lines
f. Adjusts the position of text in a text object

Select the best answer from the list of choices.

17. A hanging indent is an indent in which the:
a. First line of text begins to the right of subsequent lines of text.
b. First line of text begins to the left of subsequent lines of text.
c. The bullet symbol is to the left of the first line of text.
d. The bullet symbol is to the right of the first line of text.

18. A background item on the title master:
a. Changes all views of your presentation.
b. Is visible on slides with Title Slide layouts.
c. Is a simple way to place an object on every slide of your presentation.
d. Does not affect the slides of your presentation.

19. The Style Checker checks for all of the following except:
a. Case and punctuation.
b. The number of fonts in a presentation.
c. The number of bullets in a presentation.
d. Incorrect color scheme colors.

20. What is leading?
a. Vertical space between lines of text
b. Horizontal space between letters
c. Diagonal space between letters
d. Space between graphics on the slide master

21. In PowerPoint, tabs:
a. Can be aligned on the left, right, or center of a character or on a decimal.
b. Determine the location of margins.
c. Have symbols for top and bottom tabs.
d. Can be only left- or center-aligned.

22. The Format Painter button:
a. Is the feature you use to paint objects in PowerPoint.
b. Allows you to change the type of AutoShape.
c. Picks up and applies formatting attributes from one object or slide to another.
d. Changes the order of AutoShapes on a slide.

▶ Skills Review

1. Format Master text.
a. Start PowerPoint and open the presentation PPT E-3, then save it as **Book Presentation**.
b. Go to Slide 2, switch to Slide Master view, then make the first-level bulleted item in the Master text placeholder bold.
c. Change the bullet symbol of the first-level bullet to a character bullet in Wingdings, the third bullet from the right in the last row.
d. Click the Size up arrow in the Bullets and Numbering dialog box once to 75%.
e. Change the bullet color to the green color (far right color).
f. Take the shadow attribute off the second-level bulleted item and change its font to Arial.
g. Save the presentation.

2. Change Master text indents.

a. Display the rulers.

b. Move the left indent marker of the first-level bullet to ½" and the second-level bullet to 1⅛" as shown in Figure E-22.

c. Hide the rulers, switch to Normal view, then save the presentation.

3. Adjust text objects.

a. Right-click anywhere in the main text object on Slide 2, then click Format Placeholder on the shortcut menu.

b. Click the Text Box tab.

c. Set the text anchor point to Top Centered.

d. Adjust the internal margin on the left and right sides to 0.5 and preview your change.

e. Select the Resize AutoShape to fit text check box, preview it, and click OK.

f. Select the entire text object. (*Hint:* Press [Shift] while clicking the object.)

g. Change the line spacing to 0.75, preview it, then click OK.

h. Move the text object up and to left about ½".

i. Save your changes.

4. Use advanced drawing tools.

a. Go to Slide 4.

b. Use the Elbow Connector to connect the left corner of the Warehouse diamond to the top corner of the MediaLoft Regional Warehouse diamond.

c. Use the Straight Connector to connect the right side of the MediaLoft Regional Warehouse diamond to the left side of the Individual Stores diamond.

d. Use the Elbow Connector to connect the top corner of the Individual Stores diamond to the right corner of the Warehouse diamond.

e. Select all three of the connector lines, make them 3 points wide, then deselect them.

f. Change the arrow style of the connector line connecting the MediaLoft Regional Warehouse diamond to the Individual Stores diamond to the Square Dot, dashed line style. (*Hint*: Click More Arrows from the Arrow Styles button, then click the Dashed list arrow.)

g. Deselect all objects, then save your changes.

5. Use advanced formatting tools.

a. Go to Slide 1.

b. Select the entire text object in the lower-right corner of the slide.

c. Use the Texture tab in the Fill Effects dialog box to apply the Green Marble texture to the object. (*Hint:* Read the description of the selected texture in the box under the textures.)

d. Change the font to 20 pt. Arial.

e. Double-click the Format Painter to pick up the format of the selected text box on the title slide and apply it to each of the diamond objects on Slide 4, then deselect the Format Painter and all objects.

f. Use the 3-D Style button to apply 3-D Style 7 to the objects on Slide 4.

g. Click the 3-D Color list arrow on the 3-D Settings toolbar, then click the dark green color (Follow Background Scheme Color).

h. Deselect all objects, close the 3-D Settings toolbar, then save your changes.

FIGURE E-22

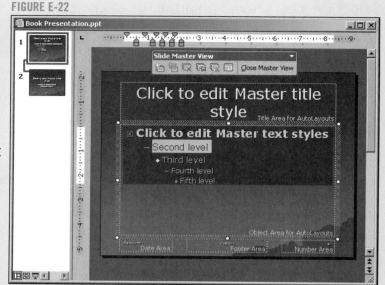

6. Use the Style Checker.

   a. Activate the Style Checker, open the Style Options dialog box, and on the Visual Clarity tab, make sure there is a check mark next to Title text size should be at least, select 48 from the list, then click OK twice.

   b. Go to Slide 1, then click the lightbulb on the title slide. Notice that the title text font is too small based on your adjustment to the style options.

   c. In the Office Assistant dialog balloon, click Change text to be at least 48 point.

   d. Scroll through the presentation clicking the lightbulbs that appear on the screen. Decide whether to accept the Office Assistant's suggestions or to ignore them.

   e. Turn the Style Checker off, then hide the Office Assistant, if necessary.

   f. Add your name to the footer in the slides and notes and handouts, save the presentation, then print the presentation as handouts, 3 slides per page.

7. Create a template.

   a. Open the Save As dialog box, then save the presentation as **MediaLoft Template** where your Project Files are stored.

   b. Delete Slides 3, 4, and 5, delete all the text in the text objects on Slide 2, then delete the clip art on Slide 2.

   c. Type **MediaLoft Template** in the title text object on Slide 1 in place of the current text.

   d. Save the presentation template, then print the presentation as handouts, 2 slides per page.

   e. Close the presentation and exit PowerPoint.

▶ Independent Challenge 1

You are the owner of Premier Catering in Brisbane, Queensland, Australia. You have built your business on private parties, wedding receptions, and special events over the last five years. To expand, you decide to cater to the business community by offering executive meals and business luncheons. Use PowerPoint to develop a presentation that you can use to gain corporate catering accounts.

In this independent challenge, you will create an outline and modify the look of a presentation. You will create your own material to complete the slides of the presentation. Assume the following about Premier Catering:

- Premier Catering has 10 full-time employees and 15 on-call staff.
- Premier Catering handles catering jobs up to 500 people.
- Premier Catering is a full-service catering business providing cost estimates, setup, complete preparation, service personnel, and cleanup.

   a. Open the file PPT E-4, then save it as **Premier**. Add your name to the notes and handout footer.

   b. Switch to the Outline tab and create a presentation outline. Add your name to the notes and handout folder.

   c. Customize your presentation by formatting the Slide Master.

   d. Search PowerPoint clip art and add a koala bear to both the slide master and the title master. Format the clip art as necessary.

   e. Use PowerPoint's advanced drawing and formatting tools to give your presentation a unique look.

   f. Add clip art and format the presentation using PowerPoint's formatting tools.

   g. Switch to the last slide and change the text anchor and line spacing to create the best look.

   h. Review the Style Checker options, then check the style of the presentation.

   i. Create a template from this presentation. Delete all the slides except the first slide and the last slide.

   j. Add two additional title-master pairs to the template.

   k. Name the template **Catering 1** and save it to the location where your Project Files are stored.

   l. Print the slides of your final template.

   m. Close the presentation template and exit PowerPoint.

▶ Independent Challenge 2

You are the finance director at Splat Records in Los Angeles, California. Splat Records specializes in alternative music. As an emerging record company, your business is looking for investment capital to expand its talent base and increase sales. It is your responsibility to develop the outline and basic look for a standard presentation that the president can present to various investors.

In this independent challenge, you will complete an outline and choose a custom background for the presentation. You'll need to create a presentation consisting of at least six slides. Assume the following about Splat Records:

- Splat Records has been in business for eight years.
- Splat Records currently has 22 recording contracts. Splat wants to double that during the next year and a half.
- Splat Records has six superstar recording groups including the groups: RIM and InHand.

a. Open the file PPT E-5, then save it as **Splat**.
b. Enter text into the title and main text placeholders of the slides.
c. Format the Master text placeholder by changing master text indents and bullet styles.
d. Add clip art and format the presentation using PowerPoint's formatting tools.
e. Use advanced drawing and formatting tools to create a unique look.
f. Check the style of the presentation.
g. Add your name to the notes and handouts footer, save the presentation, then print the slides of your final presentation as handouts in pure black and white.
h. Close the presentation and exit PowerPoint.

▶ Independent Challenge 3

You are a computer game designer for GameNet, an interactive game developer. One of your jobs is to develop new interactive game concepts and present the information at a company meeting. Develop a 10- to 15-slide presentation that promotes two of the new interactive games concepts you've developed. Use PowerPoint clip art and shapes to enhance your slides. Use one of PowerPoint's templates, design one of your own, or copy one from another presentation. You can use one of the following, or you can develop your own.

- **Showdown** is an interactive game that puts you in one of six different historical situations, where you are either a US Marshal or a gunman.
- **Spy for US** is an adventure game in which you are a spy for the Axis Powers or the Allies during World War II; assume there are four different situations to choose from for each political side.

Create your own information, but assume the following:

- The product is designed for adults and children ages 13 and up.
- The cost of product development is estimated to be $250,000.
- Development time is four months.

a. Open a new presentation and save it as **Games** to the location where your Project Files are stored.
b. Plan the story line of how the software was developed using five or more slides. Plan the beginning and ending slides. What do you want your audience to know about the product idea?
c. Use clip art and shapes to enhance the presentation. Change the bullet and text formatting in the Master text and title placeholders to fit the subject matter.
d. Use advanced drawing and formatting tools to create a unique look.
e. Add your name to the notes and handouts footer, save the presentation, then print the final slide presentation as handouts in pure black and white.
f. Close the presentation and exit PowerPoint.

Independent Challenge 4

You are the Travel Coordinator for Bandwidth Inc., a large graphic multimedia development company in Seattle, Washington. One of the benefits Bandwidth offers its employees is the option to vacation at a destination planned by the company. Your job is to find a reasonable vacation spot and then negotiate with travel companies for reduced group rates that are charged to Bandwidth employees if they choose to utilize the benefit. Once you negotiate a contract with a travel organization, you create a brief presentation that outlines the vacation benefit packages for the employees.

Plan and create an 8- to 10-slide presentation that details the vacation package for the current year. Develop your own content, but assume the following:

- The vacation package is a 7-day Alaskan cruise or a 7-day Mexican cruise.
- Air travel originates from the Seattle/Tacoma Airport (SeaTac).
- Cruises can be booked on one of two different cruise lines.
- The price is 30% off the listed price based on double occupancy.
- Bandwidth employees can book a cruise anytime during the current year.

You'll need to find the following information on the Web:
- Price and schedule information. (*Hint:* Remember the price you list in the presentation is 30% lower than the listed price you find on the Internet.)
- A list of ships with a brief description of at least one ship from each cruise line.
- Ports of call for one Mexican cruise and one Alaskan cruise.

a. Open a new presentation, and save it as **Bandwidth** to the location where your Project Files are stored.

b. Add your name as the footer on all slides and handouts.

c. Connect to the Internet, then use a search engine to locate Web sites that have information on Mexican and Alaskan cruises. If your search does not produce any results, you might try the following sites:

      www.carnival.com

      www.hollandamerica.com

      www.ncl.com

      www.royalcaribbean.com

      www.celebrity-cruises.com

d. Review at least two Web sites that contain information about Mexican cruises and Alaskan cruises. Print the Home pages of the Web sites you use to gather data for your presentation.

e. Decide on two cruise lines to use in your presentation, then create slides that present the information.

f. Use clip art and shapes to enhance the presentation. Change the bullet and text formatting in the Master text and title placeholders to fit the subject matter.

g. Apply a template to the presentation and customize the slide background appropriately.

h. Use advanced drawing and formatting tools to create a unique look.

i. Use text formatting as necessary to make text visible and help emphasize important points.

j. Spell check the presentation, view the final presentation, save the final version, then print the slides and handouts.

k. Close the presentation and exit PowerPoint.

PowerPoint 2002

▶ **Visual Workshop**

Create two slides that look like the examples in Figures E-23 and E-24. Be sure to use connector lines. Add your name to the handout footer, then save the presentation as **New Products**. Print the Slide view of the presentation. Submit the final presentation output.

FIGURE E-23

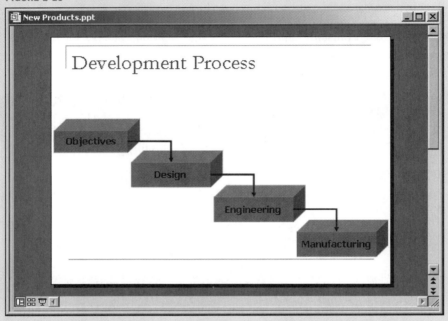

FIGURE E-24

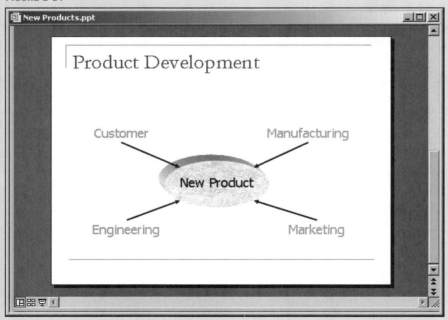

Unit **F**

Enhancing
Charts

Objectives

- ► **Insert data from a file into a datasheet**
- ► **Format a datasheet**
- ► **Change a chart's type**
- ► **Change a chart display**
- ⌐MOUS˥ ► **Work with chart elements**
- ⌐MOUS˥ ► **Animate charts and sounds**
- ⌐MOUS˥ ► **Embed an organizational chart**
- ⌐MOUS˥ ► **Modify an organizational chart**

A PowerPoint presentation is a visual communication tool. A slide that delivers information with a relevant graphic object has a more lasting impact than a slide with plain text. Graphs and charts often communicate information more effectively than words. Microsoft Graph and Microsoft Organization Chart are built-in PowerPoint programs that allow you to easily create and embed charts in your presentation. ✐━ In this unit, Maria Abbott updates the data and enhances the appearance of a Microsoft Graph chart and then creates and formats an organizational chart showing the management structure of the iMedia group.

PowerPoint 2002

Inserting Data from a File into a Datasheet

With Microsoft Graph, you can enter your own data into a datasheet using the keyboard, or you can import existing data from a spreadsheet program like Microsoft Excel. ✐ The accounting department gave Maria updated sales projection information in an Excel file. Maria wants to insert this data into the chart on Slide 11. To do this, she will open Graph and import the data from Excel.

Steps

1. Start PowerPoint, open the presentation **PPT F-1** from the location where your Project Files are stored, then save it as **iMedia 6**

2. Click **View** on the menu bar, click **Task Pane**, click **Window** on the menu bar, then click **Arrange All**

3. Click the **Slide 11 thumbnail**, then double-click the **chart object**
   The data in the datasheet needs to be replaced with the updated data in the Excel worksheet.

4. Click the **first cell** in the datasheet (labeled Dept.)
   This indicates where the imported data will appear in the datasheet.

QuickTip

If you don't see the Import File button on the Standard tool-bar, click a Toolbar Options button ▾, on a toolbar to locate buttons that are not visible on your toolbar.

5. Click the **Import File button** 🖳 on the Graph Standard toolbar
   The Import File dialog box opens.

6. Click the Excel file **PPT F-2** from the location where your Project Files are stored, then click **Open**
   The Import Data Options dialog box opens. Because you want to import the entire sheet and overwrite the existing cells, all the options are correctly marked.

7. Click **OK**
   The chart changes to reflect the new data you inserted into the datasheet. Compare your screen to Figure F-1. Notice the **column headings**, the gray boxes along the edges of the datasheet. The data in column D does not need to be included in the chart.

Trouble?

To include data that you've previously excluded, double-click the control box again.

8. Double-click the **column D column heading**
   The data in column D is grayed out, indicating that it is excluded from the datasheet and will not appear in the chart. See Figure F-2.

9. Click the **Save button** 🖫 on the Graph Standard toolbar

FIGURE F-1: Datasheet showing imported data

Step 5

Column heading

Row heading

New data

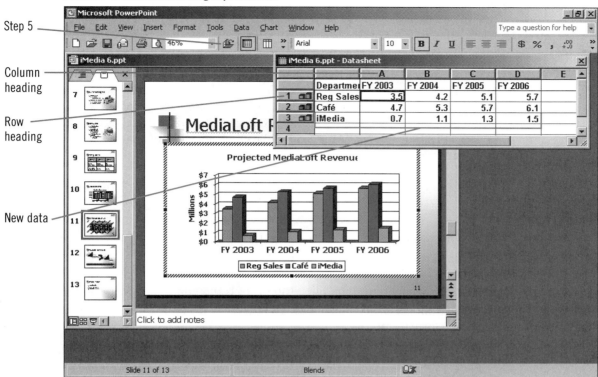

FIGURE F-2: Datasheet showing excluded column

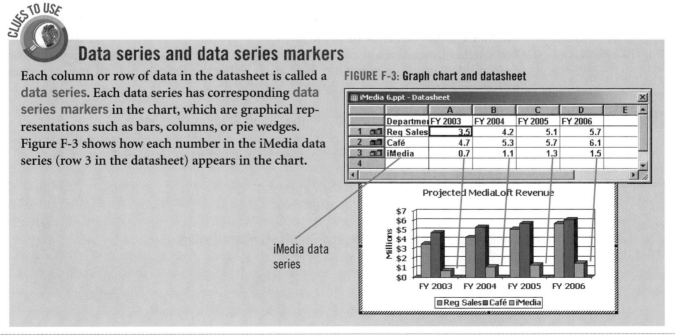

Excluded column

Data series and data series markers

Each column or row of data in the datasheet is called a data series. Each data series has corresponding data series markers in the chart, which are graphical representations such as bars, columns, or pie wedges. Figure F-3 shows how each number in the iMedia data series (row 3 in the datasheet) appears in the chart.

FIGURE F-3: Graph chart and datasheet

iMedia data series

Formatting a Datasheet

Once you've imported the data from another file, it can be helpful to modify and format the datasheet to make your data easier to view and use. With Graph, you can make simple formatting changes to the font, number format, and column size in your datasheet. To format the data in the datasheet, you must first select the data. Maria changes the number format to show the sales numbers correctly, then she changes the chart to show the sales by department rather than by year.

Steps

1. Click cell **A1** in the datasheet, then drag to cell **D3**
All the data in this group of continuous cells, or **range**, is selected.

2. Right-click the selection, then click **Number** on the shortcut menu
The Format Number dialog box opens. The Category list on the left side of the dialog box indicates the format categories.

3. Click **Currency** in the Category list
The Sample box at the top of the dialog box shows you how your data will appear in the selected format. See Figure F-4.

4. Click **OK**
The data in the datasheet and in the chart change to the currency format. The numbers indicate millions of dollars, so the number of digits after the decimal place needs to be adjusted.

QuickTip

To quickly change the number format to Currency, click the Currency Style button $ on the Graph Formatting toolbar.

5. Click **Format** on the menu bar, click **Number**, click the **Decimal places down arrow** once to display **1**, click **OK**, then click anywhere in the datasheet
The datasheet would look better if the columns containing the numbers were not so wide and if the first column were wide enough to accommodate the column head.

QuickTip

To quickly adjust the column width to fit the widest cell of data in a column, double-click the border to the right of the column control box.

6. Drag to select the first cell in each column, click **Format** on the menu bar, click **Column Width**, then click **Best Fit**
The selected column widths automatically resize to fit the widest label in each column. The chart would be more helpful if it showed the sales figures along the vertical axis, in a series by column.

Trouble?

If you don't see the By Column button on the Standard toolbar, click a Toolbar Options button ≫ on a toolbar to locate buttons that are not visible on your toolbar.

7. Click the **By Column button** ▥ on the Graph Standard toolbar
The icons now appear in the column headings in the datasheet to indicate that the fiscal year in the columns is now the legend. Compare your datasheet to Figure F-5.

8. Click the **Close button** ⊠ in the datasheet
The datasheet closes, but Graph is still open.

9. Click the **Save button** ▣ on the Graph Standard toolbar

FIGURE F-4: Format Number dialog box

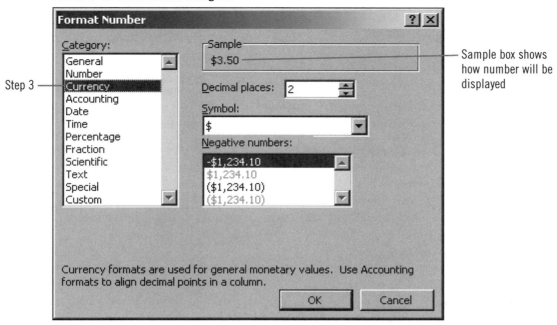

Step 3 ──→ Currency

Sample box shows
how number will be
displayed

FIGURE F-5: Datasheet showing formatted data

Icon indicates
that data is
displayed in a
series by
column

	Department	A FY 2003	B FY 2004	C FY 2005	D FY 2006	E	F
1	Req Sales	$3.5	$4.2	$5.1	$5.7		
2	Café	$4.7	$5.3	$5.7	$6.1		
3	iMedia	$0.7	$1.1	$1.3	$1.5		
4							

iMedia 6.ppt - Datasheet

CLUES TO USE

Formatting datasheets and charts

You can format data in both datasheets and in charts created by Graph. Sometimes it's easier to view the numbers in the datasheet after they have been formatted; other times, you may want to manipulate the numbers after they have been placed into a chart to get a better picture. After you've formatted the data in the datasheet, the formatting changes will be reflected in the chart; however, formatting changes made to the data in the chart will not be reflected in the datasheet.

Changing a Chart's Type

The type of chart you choose depends on the amount of information you have and how it's best depicted. For example, a chart with more than six or seven data series does not fit well in a pie chart. You can change a chart type quickly and easily by using the Chart Type command on the Chart menu. ➤ Maria decides that a bar chart on Slide 11 would communicate the information more clearly than a column chart.

Steps

1. **With Graph still open, click Chart on the menu bar, then click Chart Type**
   The Chart Type dialog box opens, as shown in Figure F-6. The current chart type is a clustered column chart with a 3-D effect.

2. **In the Chart type list, click Bar, then in the Chart sub-type section, make sure that the upper-left sub-type is selected**
   The selected sub-type is a Clustered Bar chart. To see how your data would look in any selected format without closing the dialog box, you can preview it.

3. **Click and hold Press and Hold to View Sample**
   A preview of the chart with your data appears in the area where the sub-types had been listed. This chart would look better if it were 3-D.

4. **Release the mouse button, then click the first sub-type in the second row**
   The box below the sub-type section shows that you have selected a 3-D bar chart with a 3-D visual effect.

5. **Click Press and Hold to View Sample**
   The preview shows a 3-D version of the column chart.

6. **Release the mouse button, then click OK**
   The chart type changes to the 3-D bar chart. Compare your screen with Figure F-7.

7. **Click the Save button 💾 on the Graph Standard toolbar**

FIGURE F-6: Chart Type dialog box

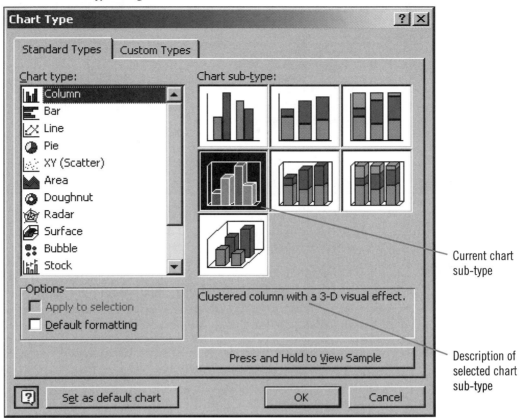

Current chart
sub-type

Description of
selected chart
sub-type

FIGURE F-7: Chart showing new bar chart type

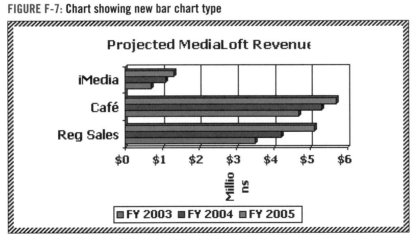

Customized chart types

There are two ways to create customized chart types: you can use PowerPoint custom types or customize your own. To use PowerPoint custom types, click the Custom Types tab in the Chart Type dialog box. You will then see more chart types, such as Floating Bars and the Area Blocks. To define a custom chart, click any chart series element (such as a bar) in the chart window, click Format on the menu bar, then click the selected series to open the Format Chart dialog box. Use the Patterns, Shape, Data Labels, or Options tabs to customize the color, shape, or appearance of the selected element. To reuse the chart type you have created, make it a type in the Chart Type dialog box by clicking the User-defined option button, clicking Add, then assigning a name to it and clicking OK. To use it later, click the name of the type you added.

Changing a Chart Display

Graph provides many advanced formatting options so that you can customize your chart to emphasize the information you think is important. For example, you can add gridlines to a chart, change the color or pattern of data markers, and format the axes. Maria wants to improve the appearance of her chart, so she makes several formatting changes.

1. **With Graph still open, click Chart on the menu bar, then click Chart Options**
   The Chart Options dialog box opens. Gridlines will help separate and clarify the data series markers.

QuickTip

To quickly add major gridlines, click the Category Axis Gridlines button ▦ on the Standard toolbar.

2. **Click the Gridlines tab, and in the Category (X) axis section, click the Major gridlines check box, click the Minor gridlines check box, then click OK**
   Horizontal gridlines appear on the chart. Compare your screen to Figure F-8. Adding minor gridlines increases the number of gridlines in the chart.

Trouble?

If you don't see the Data Table button on the Standard toolbar, click a Toolbar Options button ⊠ on a toolbar to locate buttons that are not visible on your toolbar.

3. **Click the Data Table button ▦ on the Standard toolbar**
   Adding the data table dramatically decreases the size of the chart, so you decide to return to the previous format.

4. **Click ▦ again**
   The chart returns to its previous format. Adding data labels to one of the data series will make the series easier to identify.

Trouble?

If the incorrect formatting dialog box opens, you double-clicked the wrong chart element. Close the dialog box, then double-click the correct chart element.

5. **Double-click one of the FY 2005 data markers in the chart**
   The Format Data Series dialog box opens.

6. **Click the Data Labels tab, click the Value check box to select it, then click OK**
   The FY 2005 values from the datasheet appear on the data markers, as shown in Figure F-9. Changing the way the numbers appear on the horizontal axis will improve the chart's appearance.

7. **Right-click one of the values on the horizontal axis, click Format Axis on the shortcut menu, click the Number tab, click the Decimal places up arrow until 1 appears, then click OK**
   After the Format Axis dialog box closes, the values on the horizontal axis display one decimal point. The labels on the vertical axis would look better if they were oriented at an angle.

8. **Right-click any of the labels on the vertical axis, click Format Axis on the shortcut menu, click the Alignment tab, drag the red diamond under the Orientation section up until the Degrees text box reads 15, then click OK**
   The labels on the vertical axis are oriented at a 15-degree angle. The Value axis title would look better if it were rotated to a horizontal position.

9. **Right-click the Millions axis label, click Format Axis Title on the shortcut menu, click the Alignment tab, drag the red diamond in the Orientation section until the Degrees text box reads 0, then click OK**

10. **Click a blank area of the slide, then save your presentation**
    Compare your screen to Figure F-10.

FIGURE F-8: Chart with new gridlines

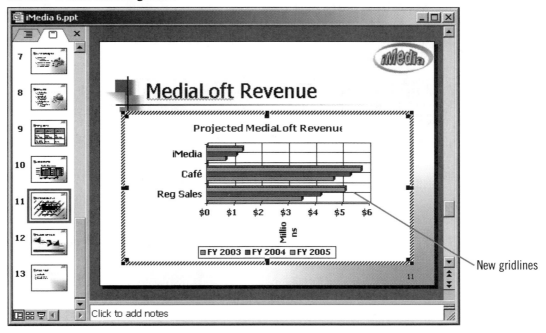

New gridlines

FIGURE F-9: Chart showing data marker labels

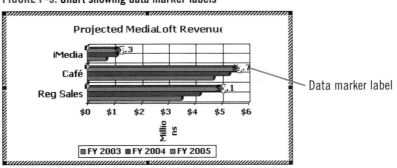

Data marker label

FIGURE F-10: Modified chart

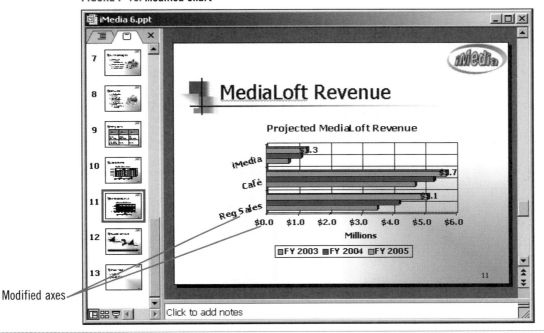

Modified axes

PowerPoint 2002

Working with Chart Elements

Chart elements are objects you can add and format to help highlight certain information in your chart. Chart elements include legends, arrows, shapes or lines, text objects, and chart titles. Maria decides to add a text object and an arrow to draw attention to the strong expected sales in the café in 2005.

Steps

1. Double-click the **Graph chart object**, then click the **Text Box button** 📖 on the Drawing toolbar
   Graph opens and the Drawing toolbar is displayed on the screen. The pointer changes to $+$ when it is positioned in the chart area.

2. Position $+$ above the Café FY 2005 data marker, drag to create a text box, then type **Over Goal**
   If the text object is not where you want it, position the pointer over its edge, then drag to reposition the object. Changing the color and size of the text would make it easier to read.

3. Drag I over the text to select it, click the **Font Size list arrow** 8 ▾ on the Formatting toolbar, then click 20

4. Click the **Font Color list arrow** 🅰 ▾ on the Drawing toolbar, click the Red box, then click a blank area of the chart
   Compare your screen to Figure F-11. An arrow would help connect the new text object to a data marker in the chart.

5. Click the **Arrow button** 🢆 on the Drawing toolbar, position $+$ under the word "Over," then drag an arrow to the end of the Café FY 2005 data marker
   The arrow could be more prominent.

6. Click the **Arrow Style button** ⇄ on the Drawing toolbar, click **More Arrows**, then click the **Color list arrow** in the Line section

7. Click the **Red box**, click the **Weight up arrow** until **2 pt** appears, then click **OK**

8. Click a blank area of the slide, then save your presentation
   Compare your screen to Figure F-12.

FIGURE F-11: Chart showing new text object

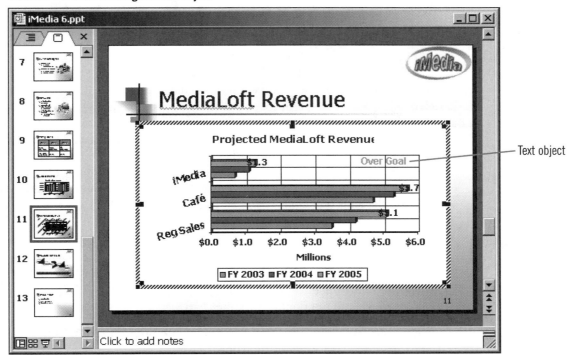

Text object

FIGURE F-12: Chart showing added elements

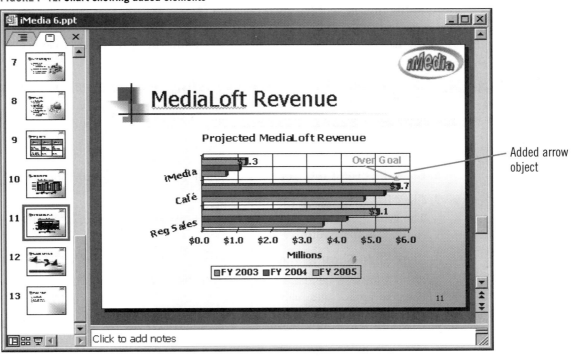

Added arrow
object

Moving and sizing chart elements

To move a chart element, such as an arrow or the legend, you must first select the object to view its resizing handles, then drag the object to its new location. Make sure that the pointer is over the object's border when you drag it, not over a resizing handle. To change the size of a chart element, click the object to view its resizing handles, then drag a resizing handle.

Animating Charts and Sounds

Just as you can animate bullets and graphics on slides, you can animate chart elements. You can have bars appear by series, groups, or individually. You can choose to have the legend and grid animated. You can also control the order and timing of the animations. Sound effects, including applause, a drum roll, a typewriter, and an explosion, can accompany the chart animation. Be sure to choose sounds that are appropriate for your presentation. For example, you would not use the screeching brakes sound in a serious financial presentation. Many presentations are effective with no sound effects to distract from the speaker's message. ✐ Maria decides to animate the elements on her chart and add a sound effect.

Steps

1. **Click the chart once to select it**
   Make sure you do not double-click the chart.

2. **Click Slide Show on the menu bar, then click Custom Animation**
   The Custom Animation task pane opens.

3. **Click Add Effect in the task pane, point to Entrance, click More Effects, click Fade in the Subtle section, then click OK**
   The Fade animation effect is added to the chart, and the chart is added to the Effects list in the task pane as Chart 2. Now you can animate specific chart elements. Compare your screen to Figure F-13.

4. **Click the Chart 2 list arrow in Effects list in the task pane, then click Effect Options**
   The Fade dialog box opens.

5. **Click the Chart Animation tab, click the Group chart list arrow, then click By element in category**

6. **Click the Effect tab, click the Sound list arrow, scroll down the list, then click Push**

7. **Click OK, then watch the slide pane**
   The grid appears first, then each bar appears in each category, accompanied by the Push sound. Compare your screen to Figure F-14.

8. **Click Slide Show at the bottom of the task pane, then click the mouse button as many times as necessary to view the complete chart animation**
   Each bar appears gradually accompanied by the Push sound effect.

9. **When the animation on Slide 11 is finished, press [Esc] to return to Normal view**

10. **Click the Save button 🖫 on the Standard toolbar**

FIGURE F-13: Screen showing Custom Animation task pane

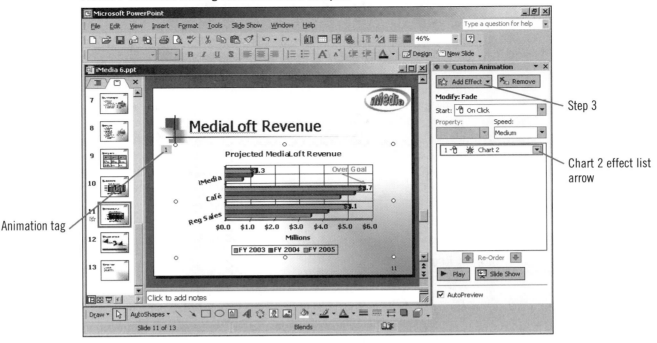

FIGURE F-14: Slide showing animated Graph chart

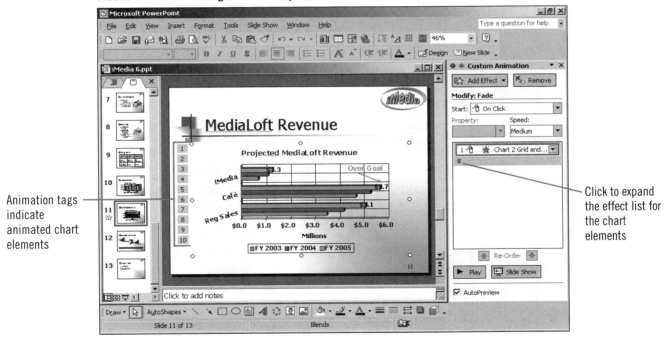

Adding voice narrations

If your computer has a sound card and a microphone, you can record a voice narration that plays with your slide show. To record a voice, click Slide Show on the menu bar, then click Record Narration. If you want the recording to be linked to the presentation, click the Link narrations in check box. If you do not select this option, the recording will be embedded in the presentation. If the Record Narration command is not available, then you do not have the necessary hardware.

Embedding an Organizational Chart

When you need to illustrate a hierarchical structure, such as the organization of a company or group, you can create and embed an organizational chart in your presentation by using the Insert Diagram or Organization Chart button on the Drawing toolbar or by changing the layout of your slide to one of the Content layouts. An organizational chart is made up of a series of connected boxes called **chart boxes** in which you can enter text, such as the names and job titles of people in your organization. Maria is satisfied with her graph and now turns her attention to creating an organizational chart showing the management structure for the iMedia group.

Steps

Trouble?

If the text you type doesn't appear as the slide title, click in the title placeholder, then type it again.

1. Go to **Slide 12**, click the **New Slide button** 🗒 on the Formatting toolbar, then type **iMedia Group**

   A new Slide 13 appears.

2. Click the **Insert Diagram or Organization Chart button** 🗒 on the Drawing toolbar

   The Diagram Gallery dialog box opens. In the Diagram Gallery dialog box, you have the option to insert one of six diagrams. See Table F-1 for information on how to use the different diagrams. The Organization Chart option is selected.

3. Click **OK**

   An organizational chart appears on the slide with the Organization Chart toolbar. See Figure F-15. The default organizational chart contains four blank chart boxes. The chart box at the top of the window is a **Manager chart box** and the three chart boxes below it are **Subordinate chart boxes**. The Manager chart box is selected and ready to accept text.

4. Type **Leilani Ho**, press **[Enter]**, then type **Manager**

   The text is entered into the text box.

5. Click the **left Subordinate chart box**, type **David Dumont**, press **[Enter]**, type **Development**, click the **middle Subordinate chart box**, type **Ann Rodriguez**, press **[Enter]**, type **Marketing**, click the **right Subordinate chart box**, type **John Wen**, press **[Enter]**, then type **Sales**

   Additional chart boxes can be added to the default organizational chart.

6. With the **John Wen chart box** still selected, click the **Insert Shape list arrow** on the Organization Chart toolbar, then click **Coworker**

   A new Coworker chart box is added to the right of the John Wen chart box.

QuickTip

Each chart box you add automatically decreases the size of all the chart boxes and their text so that the entire organizational chart will fit on the slide.

7. Click the **new chart box**, type **Cory Abrahams**, press **[Enter]**, then type **Prod. Development**

8. Click the **Ann Rodriguez chart box**, click the **Insert Shape list arrow** on the Organization Chart toolbar, then click **Subordinate**

   A new Assistant chart box appears under the Ann Rodriguez chart box.

9. Click the **new chart box,** type **Gary Robbins**, press **[Enter]**, then type **Associate**

   The chart would look better moved a little to the left on the slide.

10. Drag the chart by its border to the center of the slide, click a blank area of the slide to deselect the chart, then save your changes

    Compare your screen to Figure F-16.

FIGURE F-15: Default organization chart

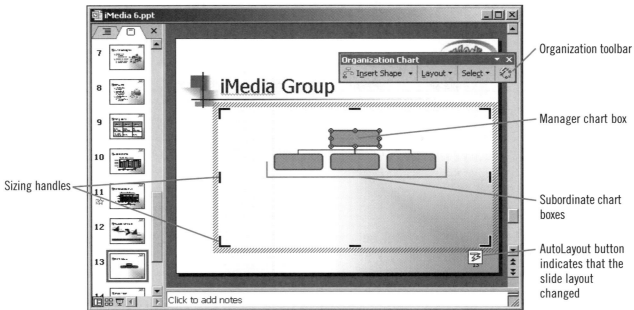

Sizing handles

Organization toolbar

Manager chart box

Subordinate chart boxes

AutoLayout button indicates that the slide layout changed

FIGURE F-16: Organization chart showing new chart boxes

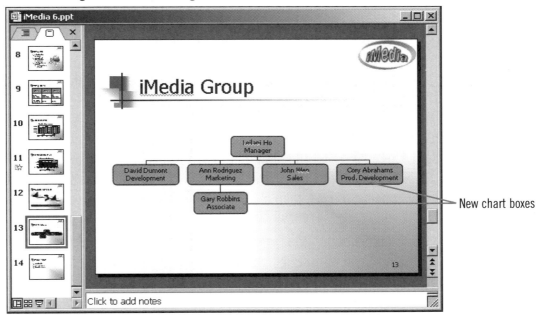

New chart boxes

TABLE F-1: Diagram Gallery dialog box

diagram icon	diagram name	diagram use
	Organization chart	Used to show hierarchical relationships
	Cycle Diagram	Used to show a process with a continuous cycle
	Radial Diagram	Used to show relationships with a core element
	Pyramid Diagram	Used to show foundational relationships
	Venn Diagram	Used to show overlap between elements
	Target Diagram	Used to show steps toward a goal

Modifying an Organizational Chart

After you add all the chart boxes you need for your organizational chart, you can format the chart boxes and connecting lines. Attributes of a chart box that you can format include fill color, line color, line style, font size, color, and type and shadow style. Chart boxes can also be rearranged within the organizational chart as desired. ✎ Maria formats the chart boxes and connecting lines of her organization chart and rearranges a chart box.

Steps

Trouble?

If chart box text overlaps the edge of a chart box, click inside the chart box to expand it.

1. Click the **Leilani Ho chart box**, click the **Select button** on the Organization Chart toolbar, then click **Branch**
   All the chart boxes are selected and ready to be formatted.

2. Click the **Fill Color list arrow** on the Drawing toolbar, then click the **light green color** (the first color cell from the right)
   The fill color of the chart boxes changes to light green.

3. Click the **Font list arrow** on the Formatting toolbar, scroll to the top of the list, click **Arial Black**, then click the **Shadow button** on the Formatting toolbar
   Compare your screen to Figure F-17.

4. Click the **Shadow Style button** on the Drawing toolbar, then click **Shadow Style 4** (last style in the first row)
   A shadow is applied to each chart box. A darker shadow might make the chart boxes stand out more on the slide.

5. Click , click **Shadow Settings** to open the Shadow Settings toolbar, click the **Shadow Color list arrow** , click the **Black color** (labeled Follow Text and Line Schemes Color), then click the **Close button** on the Shadow Settings toolbar
   Thicker connecting lines between the chart boxes would look better.

6. Click **Select** on the Organization Chart toolbar, click **All Connecting Lines**, click the **Line Style button** on the Drawing toolbar, then click **3 pt**
   The connector lines are now thicker. Gary Robbins is actually John Wen's associate.

QuickTip

Only chart boxes at the end of a branch can be moved to another position in the organizational chart.

7. Position the mouse pointer over the edge of the **Gary Robbins chart box** so that it changes to ☝, then drag it on top of the John Wen chart box
   Compare your organizational chart to Figure F-18.

8. Drag the chart to the center of the slide, click the **Slide Show button** to view Slide 13, then press **[Esc]** to end the slide show

9. Click the **Slide Sorter View button**
   Compare your screen to Figure F-19. Slides 11 and 13 are the only slides you modified in this unit.

10. Click the **Normal View button**, add your name as a footer to the notes and handouts, click the **Save button** on the Standard toolbar, then print the presentation as handouts (6 slides per page)

FIGURE F-17: Organization chart showing formatted chart boxes

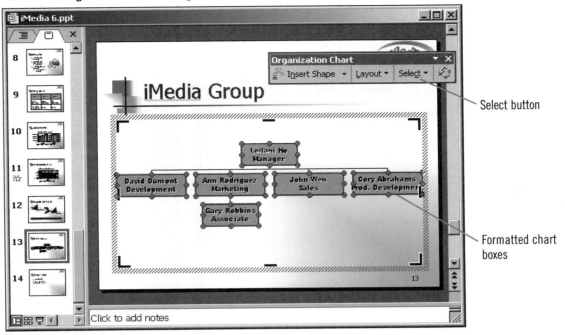

Select button

Formatted chart boxes

FIGURE F-18: Organization chart showing rearranged chart box

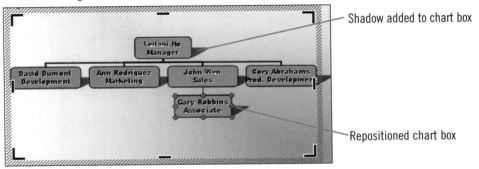

Shadow added to chart box

Repositioned chart box

FIGURE F-19: Final presentation in Slide Sorter view

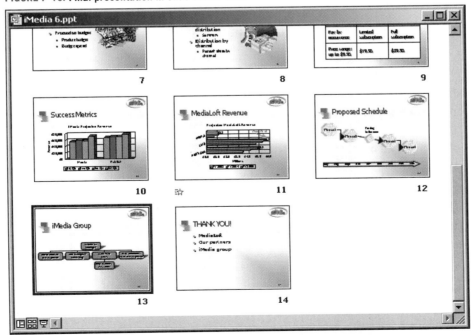

Practice

► Concepts Review

Label each of the elements of the PowerPoint window shown in Figure F-20.

FIGURE F-20

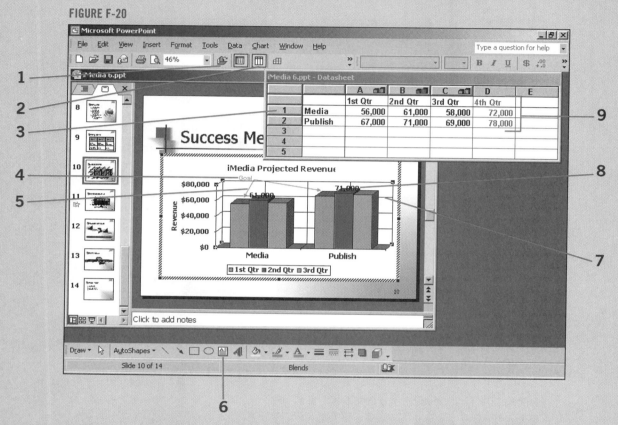

Match each of the terms with the statement that describes its function.

10. A row or column of data in a datasheet
11. A box at the edge of a datasheet, usually with a row number or column letter in it
12. A group of connected cells in a datasheet
13. Graphical representation of a data series
14. Lines that separate and clarify data series markers

a. Data series markers
b. Range
c. Data series
d. Control box
e. Gridlines

Select the best answer from the list of choices.

15. In Graph, clicking a column control box:
   a. Selects all column data markers in a chart.
   b. Selects an entire column of data in the datasheet.
   c. Switches the chart format to 3-D column.
   d. Controls the format of the datasheet.

16. **Which of the following statements about Graph charts is incorrect?**
    a. There are 2-D and 3-D chart types.
    b. You can change the format of data markers.
    c. You can format every element of a chart.
    d. The type of chart you choose does not depend on the data you have.

17. **Which of the following is incorrect about animating charts?**
    a. You can accompany chart animations with a sound.
    b. You can't control the timing of the animation.
    c. You can choose to have chart elements appear in a variety of ways.
    d. You don't need to accompany every animation with a sound.

18. **Based on what you know of organizational charts, which of the following data would best fit in an organizational chart?**
    a. A company's division structure
    b. A company's database mailing list
    c. A company's annual financial numbers
    d. Spreadsheet data

19. **To change a column's width in a datasheet, you can:**
    a. Double-click cell A1 in the datasheet.
    b. Drag the row control box up.
    c. Double-click the column control box border.
    d. Both A and C.

20. **What do chart gridlines help you do?**
    a. Gridlines help you combine data series markers.
    b. Gridlines help you separate and clarify data series markers.
    c. Gridlines help you see chart elements, such as text or lines.
    d. Gridlines help you change the chart type.

21. **Which of the following is false about organization charts?**
    a. You can create an organization chart by clicking the Insert Diagram or Organization Chart button on the Formatting toolbar.
    b. Connecting lines between chart boxes can be formatted.
    c. An assistant chart box cannot be moved.
    d. A chart box and all of its subordinate chart boxes can be moved.

► Skills Review

1. **Insert data from a file into a datasheet.**
    a. Start PowerPoint, open the presentation PPT F-3, then save it as **Royal Publishing** to the drive and location where your Project Files are stored.
    b. On Slide 3, open Microsoft Graph.
    c. Click the upper-left cell in the datasheet, and import Sheet1 of the Excel file PPT F-4 into the Graph datasheet.
    d. Exclude the Mystery row from the chart, then save the chart.

2. **Format a datasheet.**
    a. Select the range of cells from cell A1 to cell E4.
    b. Format the datasheet numbers with Currency format.
    c. Change the format of the datasheet numbers so that they have no decimal places. (*Hint*: Click the Decrease Decimal button on the Standard toolbar twice to do this quickly.)

d. Adjust the column width for all the columns to Best Fit.

e. Change the data so the series are in columns. Compare your datasheet with Figure F-21.

f. Close the datasheet.

g. Save the chart.

FIGURE F-21

		A ⊕	B	C	D	E
	2003 Fiscal Year	Victoria	Waterloo	Paddington	Euston	Liverpool
1	Fiction	$250	$230	$260	$250	$320
2	Non-Fiction	$180	$200	$240	$300	$229
3	Children's	$120	$130	$115	$120	$100
4	Mystery	$130	$150	$110	$90	$140
5						
6						
7						

PPT F-3.ppt - Datasheet

3. **Change a chart's type.**

a. Change the chart type to a clustered 3-D bar chart, preview it, then accept it.

b. Change the chart to a clustered 3-D column chart.

c. Save the chart.

4. **Change a chart display.**

a. Show major gridlines on both the x- and the z-axes.

b. Add a label to the z-axis that reads **Thousands**.

c. Open the Format Axis Title dialog box for the z-axis label and change its orientation to 90 degrees.

d. Save your changes.

5. **Work with chart elements.**

a. Add a text box to add a label pointing to Euston non-fiction sales.

b. Add the text **A record!** to the text box.

c. Change the point size of the text to 22 point and the font to Times New Roman.

d. Change the color of the text to blue.

e. Add a blue arrow pointing from the text box to the appropriate data point.

f. Format the arrow line as 3 point.

g. Compare your chart with Figure F-22 and adjust the text box and arrow positions as necessary.

h. Click a blank area of the slide, then save your changes.

FIGURE F-22

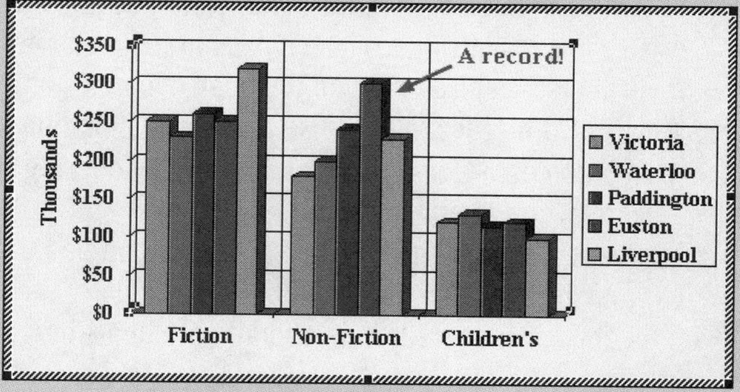

6. **Animate charts and sounds.**

a. Animate the chart with the Entrance Fade effect.

b. Animate the chart elements so they are introduced by series.

c. Add the Arrow sound effect to the animation.

d. In the Custom Animation task pane, click the Speed list arrow and change the speed to Fast.

e. Preview the animation.

f. Check the animation in Slide Show view, then save the presentation.

7. **Embed an organizational chart.**

a. Go to Slide 4.

b. Add an organization chart to the slide.

c. At the top level, type **John Edwards** as **Division Manager**.

d. In the Subordinate chart boxes, type the following names and titles:
   Sarah Wiley, Distribution Manager
   Robert Sarhi, Purchasing Manager
   Evelyn Storey, Circulation Manager

e. Change the fill color for all the chart boxes to a light yellow color.

f. Change the line color for all the chart boxes to a dark purple color, then save your changes.

8. Modify an organizational chart.

   a. Add an assistant chart box to the Sarah Wiley chart box.

   b. Drag the organization chart sizing handles to make the chart as big as possible.

   c. Enter **Michael Raye** as her **Special Assistant**.

   d. Add two Subordinate boxes to the Evelyn Storey chart box, and enter the following:
      Janee Fugishi, Purchase Orders
      Lynn Perry, Financial Assistant

   e. Drag the Janee Fugishi chart box and the Lynn Perry chart box so they are under the Robert Sarhi chart box.

   f. Select the John Edwards chart box and change the font to 16 pt.

   g. Format all the other chart boxes using the formatting characteristics from the John Edwards chart box. (*Hint:* Use the Format Painter button.)

   h. Format the connecting lines to 3 pt.

   i. Go to Slide 1, then run through a slide show in Slide Show view.

   j. Add your name to the notes and handouts footer.

   k. Save your changes, print the presentation as handouts (3 slides per page), then close the presentation and exit PowerPoint.

► Independent Challenge 1

You work for Larsen Concepts, a business consulting company that helps small- and medium-sized businesses organize or restructure themselves to be more efficient and profitable. You are one of six senior consultants who works directly with clients. To prepare for an upcoming meeting with executives at ComSystems, a mobile phone communications company, you create a brief presentation outlining Larsen's typical investigative and reporting techniques, past results versus the competition, and the company's business philosophy.

The following is a sample of the type of work you perform as part of your duties at Larsen: You usually investigate a client's business practices for two weeks and analyze all relevant records. Once the initial investigation stage is complete, you submit a client recommendation report to your boss that describes the known problem areas, the consequences of the problems, the reasons for the problems, the recommended solutions, the anticipated results for each solution, the anticipated cost to the client for each solution, and Larsen's final professional recommendation. After your boss approves the client recommendation report, you prepare a full report for the client. If the client approves the plan, you develop a maintenance schedule (usually one year or less) to make sure the plan is implemented correctly.

   a. Open the file PPT F-5 from the folder where your Project Files are stored, then save it as **Larsen Presentation**.

   b. Think about the results you want to see, the information you need, and how you want to communicate the message. Sketch how you want your presentation to look.

   c. Create charts on Slides 3 and 4 using one of the charts available in the Diagram Gallery. Use the information provided to show the various stages of investigation and reporting.

   d. Create a Graph chart on Slide 5 that shows how Larsen compares with two competitors. For example, you might illustrate the satisfaction level of Larsen clients compared to its competitors' clients. Format the chart to present the information clearly.

   e. Add a concluding slide that includes a graphic.

   f. Format the text on the slides. Modify the master views to achieve the look you want.

   g. Add a template and shaded background to finish the presentation.

h. Spell check and save your presentation.

i. Add your name as a footer to the slides and handouts, print the slides of the presentation, then submit your presentation plan and printouts.

j. Close the presentation and exit PowerPoint.

▶ Independent Challenge 2

This year, you have been selected by your peers to receive a national teaching award for the educational program that you created for disabled children in your home state of Connecticut. In accepting this award, you have the opportunity to give a presentation describing your program's results since its introduction. You will give the presentation at an educator's convention in Washington, D.C.

Plan and create a slide presentation describing your results. Create your own data, but assume the following:

- Over the last four years, 3,548 children in 251 classrooms throughout Connecticut have participated in your program.
- Children enrolled in your program have shown at least a 7% improvement in skills for every year the program has been in effect.
- Children ages 4 through 12 have participated in the program.
- Money to fund the program comes from the National Education Association (NEA) and the State of Connecticut Public School Department. The money goes to each participating school district in the state.
- Funding per child is $2,867 per school year. Funding per child in a regular classroom is $3,950 per year.

a. Think about the results you want to see, the information you need to create the slide presentation, and how your message should be communicated.

b. Create a color slide presentation using a chart from the Diagram Gallery to build some of your slides. Think about how you can effectively show information in a chart.

c. Format the charts using PowerPoint's formatting features.

d. Use clip art, shapes, and a shaded background to enhance the presentation. Change the bullet and text formatting in the Master text and title placeholders to fit the subject matter.

e. Spell check and save the presentation as **Teaching Award**.

f. Add your name as a footer to the slides and handouts, then print the final slide presentation.

g. Close the presentation and exit PowerPoint.

▶ Independent Challenge 3

LabTech Industries is a large company that develops and produces technical medical equipment and machines for operating and emergency rooms throughout the United States. You are the business manager, and one of your assignments is to prepare a presentation for the stockholders on the profitability and efficiency of each division in the company.

Plan and create a slide presentation that shows all the divisions and divisional managers of the company. Also, graphically show how each division performed in relation to its previous year's performance. Create your own content, but assume the following:

- The company has seven divisions: Administration, Accounting, Sales and Marketing, Research and Development, Product Testing, Product Development, and Manufacturing.
- Three divisions increased productivity by at least 15%.
- The presentation will be given in a boardroom using a projector.

a. Think about the results you want to see, the information you need to create the slide presentation, what type of message you want to communicate, and the target audience.

b. Use Outline view to create the content of your presentation.

c. Create a Graph chart, then insert the Excel file PPT F-6 into the datasheet.

d. Create organization charts to help present the information you want to communicate.

e. Use clip art, pictures, or a shaded background to enhance the presentation, and format the content.

f. Save the presentation as **LabTech Industries** to the drive and location where your Project Files are stored.

g. Add your name as a footer to the slides and handouts, then print the final slide presentation.

h. Close the presentation and exit PowerPoint.

Independent Challenge 4

You are a PC game analyst for IGame Resources Inc., a computer game software research company. One of your responsibilities every quarter is to create a brief presentation that identifies the top computer games based on industry and consumer reviews. In your presentation, you include charts that help define the data you compile.

Develop your own content, but assume the following:

- Include five computer games in your presentation.
- Each game has at least two missions.
- Consumer satisfaction of each game is identified on a scale of 1.0 to 10.0.
- There are four categories of games: Adventure, Action, Driving, and Strategy.

You'll need to find the following information on the Web:

- Consumer or industry reviews of five PC computer games.
- A description of each game, including the story line of the game or mission.
- The price of each game.

a. Open a new presentation, and save it as **PC Game Review** where your Project Files are stored.

b. Add your name as the footer on all slides and handouts.

c. Connect to the Internet, then use a search engine to locate Web sites that have information on PC computer games. If your search does not produce any results, you might try the following sites: www.zdnet.com/gamespot, www.gamesdomain.com, or www.gamecenter.com.

d. Review at least two Web sites that contain information about computer games. Print the Home pages of the Web sites you use to gather data for your presentation.

e. Using PowerPoint, create an outline of your presentation. It should contain between eight and 10 slides, including a title slide.

f. Include at least one chart that identifies consumer satisfaction numbers that you develop.

g. Create a diagram or organization chart that briefly explains the story line of one of the games.

h. Create a table that lists the price of each game.

i. Enhance the presentation with clip art or other graphics, an appropriate template and/or background, or other items that improve the look of the presentation.

j. Change the master views, if necessary, to fit your presentation.

k. Spell check and save the presentation.

l. Print the slides of the presentation as handouts (4 slides per page).

m. Close the presentation and exit PowerPoint.

► Visual Workshop

Create two slides that look like the examples in Figures F-23 and F-24. Save the presentation as **Central Industries**. Add your name as a footer on the slides, then save and print the presentation slides.

FIGURE F-23

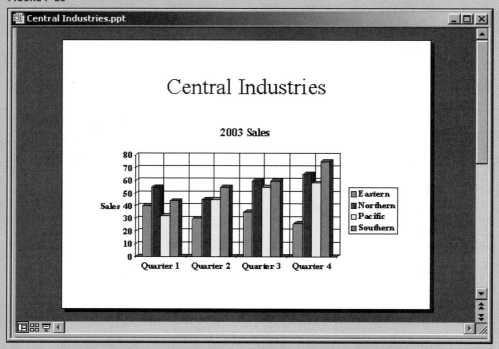

FIGURE F-24

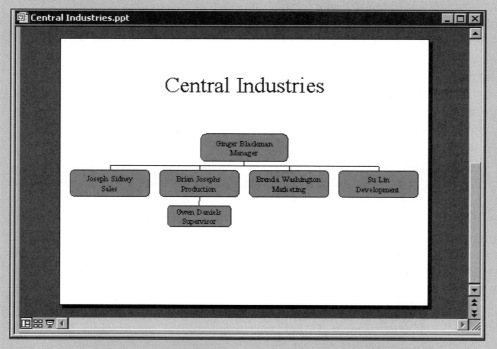

Working

with Embedded and Linked Objects and Hyperlinks

Objectives

- ▶ **Embed a picture**
- ▶ **Insert a Word table**
- ▶ **Embed an Excel chart**
- ▶ **Link an Excel worksheet**
- ▶ **Update a linked Excel worksheet**
- ▶ **Insert an animated GIF file**
- ▶ **Insert a sound**
- ▶ **Insert a hyperlink**

PowerPoint offers many ways to add graphic elements to a presentation. In this unit, you will learn how to embed and link objects. Embedded and linked objects are created in another program and then stored in or linked to the PowerPoint presentation. In this unit, Maria Abbott, MediaLoft's general sales manager, uses embedded and linked objects to create a brief presentation that outlines MediaLoft's video department. She will use the presentation in a proposal she will make to a potential new video supplier.

Embedding a Picture

You can embed more than 20 types of pictures using the Insert Picture command. Frequently, a presentation's color scheme will not match the colors in pictures, especially photographs. In order to make the picture look good in the presentation, you may need to adjust the slide's color scheme, recolor the picture, or change the presentation's template. ◄━━━ Maria wants to embed a photograph in a slide. She will adjust the slide's color scheme to make the photograph look good.

Steps 1234

1. Start PowerPoint, open the presentation **PPT G-1** from the drive and folder where your Project Files are located, save it as **Video Division**, click **View** on the menu bar, click **Task Pane**, click **Window** on the menu bar, then click **Arrange All**

Trouble?

If the Picture toolbar is in the way, move the toolbar to another part of the screen.

2. Click the **Slide 2 thumbnail** in the Slides tab, click the **Insert Picture button** 🖼 on the Drawing toolbar, select the file **PPT G-2** from the drive and location where your Project Files are stored, then click **Insert**

   A picture of a tropical scene appears on the slide and the Picture toolbar opens. The Automatic Layout Options button appears below the picture, which indicates that the slide layout has changed to accommodate the picture. The slide would look fine with the original slide layout.

3. Click the **Automatic Layout Options button** 📝 on the slide, then click **Undo Automatic Layout**

   The picture moves to the middle of the slide and the size of the text in the body text box increases.

4. Resize and drag the picture to match Figure G-1

   A different slide color would provide a better contrast to the picture.

5. Click the **Slide Design button** 📝 on the Formatting toolbar, then click the **Color Schemes link** in the Slide Design task pane

   The Slide Design task pane opens, showing the available color schemes. There are nine standard color schemes from which to choose.

6. Click each **color scheme thumbnail list arrow**, then click **Apply to Selected Slides** to preview the color schemes

   Each color scheme is applied to the presentation. The third color scheme down in the second column fits best with the picture colors.

Trouble?

If you click Apply to All Slides by mistake, click the Undo button 🔄, then repeat Step 7.

7. Click the **green color scheme list arrow** in the third row, second column, then click **Apply to Selected Slides**

   Make sure you do not click Apply to All Slides or click the color scheme box itself, which is the same as applying the scheme to all slides. The color scheme for Slide 2 changes to a green background.

8. Click a blank area of the slide, compare your screen to Figure G-2, then click the **Save button** 🖫 on the Standard toolbar

FIGURE G-1: Slide showing embedded picture

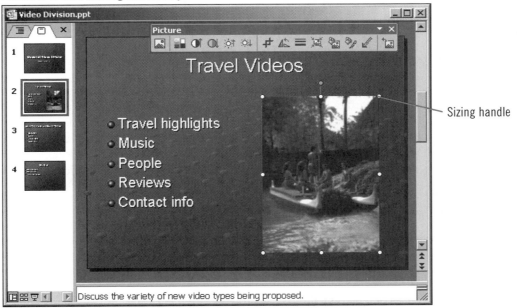

Sizing handle

FIGURE G-2: Slide showing new color scheme

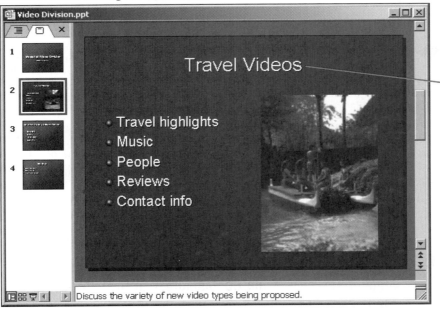

Changed title text color in new color scheme

CLUES TO USE

Creating a photo album

You can use PowerPoint to create a photo album using your favorite pictures. A PowerPoint **photo album** is a presentation set up with specific formats. To create a photo album, click Insert on the menu bar, point to Picture, then click New Photo Album. The Photo Album dialog box opens. Click File/Disk or Scanner/Camera to add pictures to the photo album. To format an existing photo album, click Format on the menu bar, then click Photo Album. You can add pictures to a photo album from your hard drive, digital camera, scanner, or Web camera. As with any presentation, you can customize the layout of a photo album by adding title text to slides, applying frames around the pictures, and applying a design template. You can also format the pictures of the photo album by adding a caption below the pictures, converting the pictures to black and white, rotating the pictures, and changing their brightness and contrast.

Inserting a Word Table

You can easily insert a PowerPoint table in your presentation using the Insert Table button on the Standard toolbar. If you want to format a table using the Table AutoFormat command available in Microsoft Word, you can embed a Microsoft Word table in your PowerPoint slide. With an embedded Word table, you can use formatting features of both Word and PowerPoint to call attention to important information and to make the table visually appealing. ✏️ Maria decides to add a new slide with a table showing the types of videos MediaLoft offers.

Steps

1. Click the **New Slide button** 🗋 on the Formatting toolbar, then click the **Title Only layout** in the Slide Layout task pane
   A new Slide 3 appears.

2. Type **Largest Video Categories**, then click in a blank area of the slide

3. Click **Insert** on the menu bar, click **Object**, scroll down the Object type list box, click **Microsoft Word Document**, then click **OK**
   A blank Word document appears on the slide. The Microsoft Word menu bar and toolbars replace the PowerPoint menu bar and toolbars.

QuickTip

You can also click the Insert Table button 🔲 ▾ on the Standard toolbar to insert a table.

4. Click **Table** on the menu bar, point to **Insert**, click **Table**, click the **Number of columns down arrow** in the Insert Table dialog box until **2** appears, then click **OK**
   A blank table with two rows and two columns appears on the screen. Compare your screen with Figure G-3.

5. Click **Edit** on the menu bar, click **Select All**, click the **Font Size list arrow** 12 ▾ on the Formatting toolbar, click **36**, click in the first cell in the table, enter the data shown in Figure G-4, press **[Tab]** to move from cell to cell, then click in a blank area of the slide outside the table
   After you click the slide, the PowerPoint menus and toolbars return. The table text would be easier to read if it were formatted to make it stand out from the background. Because the table is embedded, you can use Word's AutoFormat feature to do this.

QuickTip

To edit or open an embedded object in your presentation, the object's source program must be available on your computer or network.

6. Double-click the **table** to return to Word, click **Table** on the menu bar, click **Table AutoFormat**, click **Table Contemporary** in the Table styles list, click the **Heading rows check box** to deselect it, then click **Apply**
   This table is a simple list, so it doesn't need special formatting for the first row. The new table format changes the fill of the rows to two different shades of gray.

7. Click **Edit** on the menu bar, click **Select All**, click the **Center button** 🢂 on the Formatting toolbar, then click the **Bold button** **B** on the Formatting toolbar
   The text moves to the center of the cells, increases in size, and becomes bold.

8. Click the **Line Spacing (1) list arrow** 🢂 on the Formatting toolbar, click **3.0**, click the **Outside Border list arrow** 🔲 ▾ on the Formatting toolbar, click the **All Borders button** 🔳, then click in a blank area of the slide
   The spacing between the rows increases and border lines are added to the table.

9. Click on the slide outside the table, then save your work
   Compare your screen to Figure G-4.

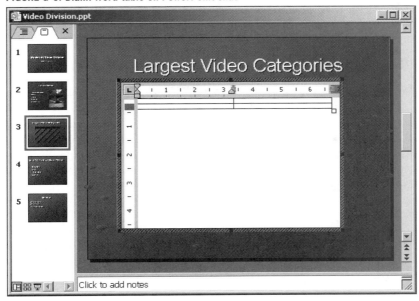

FIGURE G-3: Blank Word table on PowerPoint slide

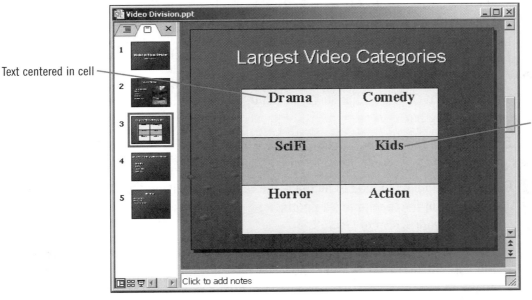

FIGURE G-4: Slide with formatted Word table

Text centered in cell

Table with color and format of Table Contemporary AutoFormat

Exporting a presentation

Sometimes it's helpful to use a word-processing program like Word to create detailed speaker's notes or handouts. You might also want to create a Word document based on the outline of your PowerPoint presentation. To export a presentation to Word, click File on the menu bar, point to Send to, then click Microsoft Word. The Send to Microsoft Word dialog box opens and provides you with a number of document layout options from which to choose. Select a layout, click

OK, and a new Word document opens with your embedded presentation or outline, using the layout you selected. Another way to export just the text of your presentation is to save it as an outline in Rich Text format (.rtf format). You can view RTF documents in any word processing program. To do this, click File on the menu bar, click Save As, click Outline/RTF in the Save as type list box, then click Save.

Embedding an Excel Chart

When a chart is the best way to present information on a slide, you can create a chart using Microsoft Graph from within PowerPoint; however, for large amounts of data, it's easier to create a chart using a spreadsheet program like Excel. Then you can embed the chart file in your PowerPoint presentation and edit it using Excel tools. Excel is the chart file's **source program**, the program in which the file was created. PowerPoint is the **destination program**, the file into which the chart is embedded. ✐ Maria created an Excel chart showing MediaLoft's quarterly video sales. She wants to include this chart in her presentation, so she embeds it in a slide.

Steps

1. Click the **New Slide button** 🔲 on the Formatting toolbar, then click the **Title Only layout** in the Slide Layout task pane
   A new Slide 4 appears.

2. Type **Quarterly Sales** in the title placeholder

3. Click **Insert** on the menu bar, click **Object**, click the **Create from file option button** in the Insert Object dialog box, click **Browse**, locate the file **PPT G-3** in the location where your Project Files are stored, click **OK**, then click **OK** in the Insert Object dialog box
   The chart containing the video data appears on the slide. Because the chart is embedded, you can edit the worksheet using Excel formatting tools. The text labels on the chart are too small to read.

   Trouble?
   If the Chart toolbar appears in the middle of your screen, drag it out of the way.

4. Double-click the **chart** to open Microsoft Excel, right-click the **chart title**, click **Format Chart Title** on the shortcut menu, then click the **Font tab** in the Format Chart Title dialog box

5. Click **28** in the Size list, then click **OK**
   The chart title becomes larger.

   QuickTip
   After you change the first axis, you can select the next object, then press [F4] to repeat the font size increase.

6. Use the same technique to increase the text and labels on the vertical and horizontal **axes** and in the legend to **24 points**
   Compare your screen to Figure G-5.

7. Double-click the **chart background** to the right of the title, click the **Patterns tab** in the Format Chart Area dialog box, click **Fill Effects**, click the **Preset option button**, click the **Preset colors list arrow**, then scroll down and click **Gold**

8. Click the **Diagonal down option button** in the Shading styles section, click **OK**, then click **OK** in the Format Chart Area dialog box
   The chart background becomes a shaded gold color.

9. Click outside the chart to exit Excel, click a blank area of the slide to deselect the object, then save the presentation
   Compare your screen to Figure G-6.

FIGURE G-5: Embedded chart with resized text

Title text increased to 28 points

Formatted axis title

Formatted axes

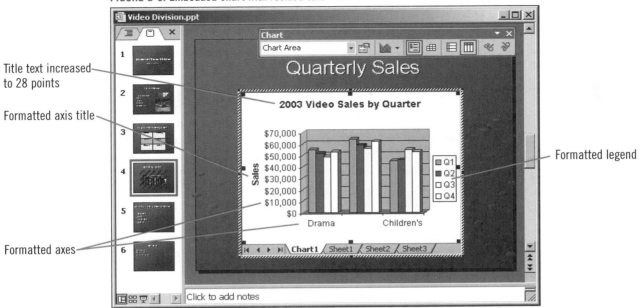

Formatted legend

FIGURE G-6: Embedded chart with gold background

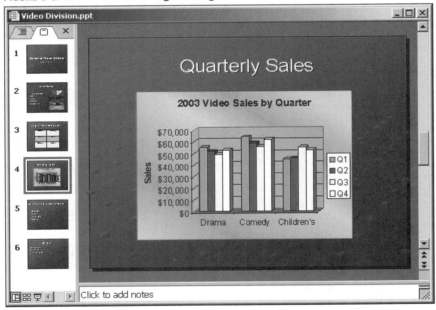

CLUES TO USE

Embedding a worksheet

You can embed all or part of an Excel worksheet into a PowerPoint slide. To embed an entire worksheet, go to the slide where you want to place the worksheet. Click Insert on the menu bar, then click Object. The Insert object dialog box opens. Click the Create from file option button, click Browse, locate and double-click the spreadsheet filename, then click OK. The worksheet is inserted into the slide. Double-click it to edit it using Excel's formatting commands as you did in this lesson. To insert only a portion of a worksheet, open the Excel workbook and copy the cells you want to include in your presentation. Leaving Excel and the source worksheet open, open the PowerPoint presentation, click Edit on the menu bar, then click Paste Special. To paste the cells as a worksheet object that you can edit in Excel, click Microsoft Excel Worksheet Object in the Paste Special dialog box.

Linking an Excel Worksheet

Another way to connect objects like Excel worksheets to your presentation is to establish a **link**, or connection, between the source file and the PowerPoint presentation. Unlike an embedded object, a linked object is stored in its source file, not on the slide, so when you link an object to a PowerPoint slide, a representation (picture) of the object, not the object itself, appears on the slide. Any changes made to the source file of a linked object are automatically reflected in the linked representation in your PowerPoint presentation. Some of the objects that you can link to PowerPoint include movies, Microsoft Excel worksheets, and PowerPoint slides from other presentations. Use linking when you want to be sure your presentation contains the latest information and when you want to include an object, such as an accounting spreadsheet, that may change over time. See Table G-1 for suggestions on when to embed an object and when to link an object. ✐ Maria needs to link an Excel worksheet to her presentation. The worksheet was created by the Accounting Department manager earlier in the year.

Steps

QuickTip

If you plan to do the steps in this unit again, be sure to make and use a copy of the Excel file Video Division Budget.

1. Click the **New Slide button** 🖼 on the Formatting toolbar, click the **Title Only layout** in the Slide Layout task pane, then type **Video Division Budget**
   A new Slide 5 appears.

2. Click **Insert** on the menu bar, click **Object**, click the **Create from file option button**, click **Browse**, locate the file **Video Division Budget** from the location where your Project Files are stored, click **OK**, then click the **Link check box** to select it
   Compare your screen to Figure G-7.

3. Click **OK** in the Insert Object dialog box
   The image of the linked worksheet appears on the slide. The worksheet would be easier to see if it were larger and had a background fill color.

4. With the worksheet still selected, drag the bottom, right sizing handle down to the right about **2"**, drag the bottom, left sizing handle down to the left about **2"**, then position the worksheet vertically in the middle of the slide
   The worksheet should be about as wide as the slide.

5. Click the **Fill Color list arrow** on the Drawing toolbar, click the **Light Blue box** (Follow Accent and Hyperlink Scheme Color), then click a blank area of the slide
   A blue background fill color appears behind the worksheet, as shown in Figure G-8.

6. Click the **Save button** 🖫 on the Standard toolbar, then click the **Close button** ☒ in the presentation title bar
   PowerPoint remains open but the Presentation window closes.

Linking objects using Paste Special

You can also link an object or selected information from another program to PowerPoint by copying and pasting. This technique is useful when you want to link part of a worksheet rather than the entire file. For example, you may want to link a worksheet from a Microsoft Excel workbook that contains both a worksheet and a chart. To link just the worksheet, open the Microsoft Excel workbook file that contains the worksheet, select the worksheet, then copy it to the Clipboard. Leaving Excel and the source worksheet open, open the PowerPoint presentation, click Edit on the menu bar, click Paste Special, click the Paste link option button, then click OK.

FIGURE G-7: Insert Object dialog box ready to link an object

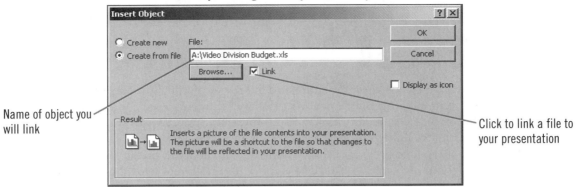

Name of object you will link

Click to link a file to your presentation

FIGURE G-8: Linked worksheet with background fill color

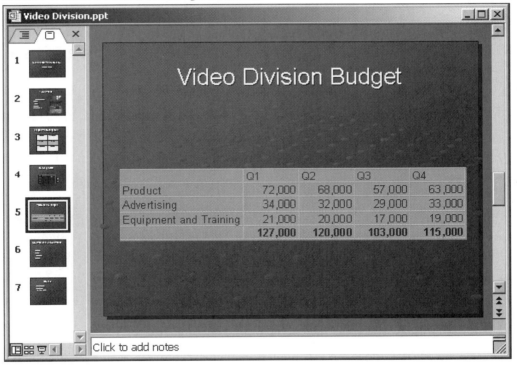

TABLE G-1: Embedding vs. Linking

situation	action
When you are the only user of an object and you want the object to be a part of your presentation	Embed
When you want to access the object in its source application, even if the original file is not available	Embed
When you want to update the object manually while working in PowerPoint	Embed
When you always want the latest information in your object	Link
When the object's source file is shared on a network or when other users have access to the file and can change it	Link
When you want to keep your presentation file size small	Link

Updating a Linked Excel Worksheet

To edit or change the information in a linked object, you must open the object's source program. For example, you must open Microsoft Word to edit a linked Word table, or you must open Microsoft Excel to edit a linked Excel worksheet. You can open the source program by double-clicking the linked object in the PowerPoint slide, as you did with embedded objects, or by starting the source program directly using any method you prefer. When you work in the source program, you can close your PowerPoint presentation or leave it open. ✒ Maria needs to update some of the data in the Excel worksheet and then update the linked object in PowerPoint. She decides to start Excel and the source file to do this.

1. Click the **Start** button on the taskbar, point to **Programs**, then click **Microsoft Excel**
   The Microsoft Excel program opens.

QuickTip

To edit or open a linked object in your presentation, the object's source program and source file must be available on your computer or network.

2. Click the **More workbooks hyperlink** in the New Workbook task pane, select the file **Video Division Budget** from the location where your Project Files are stored, then click **Open**
   The Video Division Budget worksheet opens.

3. Click cell **C2**, type **64000**, click cell **C4**, type **18000**, then press **[Enter]**
   The Q2 total is automatically recalculated and now reads 114,000 instead of 120,000.

4. Click the **Close button** ☒ in the Microsoft Excel program window, then click **Yes** to save the changes
   Microsoft Excel closes and the PowerPoint window opens.

QuickTip

The destination file can remain open when you update links. After you change the source file and switch back to the presentation file, the linked object is updated.

5. Click in the PowerPoint program window to activate it, click the **Open button** 🗁 on the Standard toolbar, locate the file **Video Division**, then click **Open**
   A Microsoft PowerPoint alert box opens, telling you that the Video Division presentation contains links and asking if you want to update them. See Figure G-9. This message appears whether or not you have changed the source file.

6. Click **Update Links**
   The worksheet in the presentation slide is updated.

7. Click **Window** on the menu bar, click **Arrange All**, then click the **Slide 5 thumbnail** in the Slides tab
   Compare your screen to Figure G-10. The linked Excel worksheet shows the new Q2 total, 114,000. The changes you made in Excel were automatically made in this linked copy when you updated the links.

8. Click the **Save button** 🖫 on the Standard toolbar

FIGURE G-9: Alert box to update links

FIGURE G-10: Slide with updated, linked worksheet

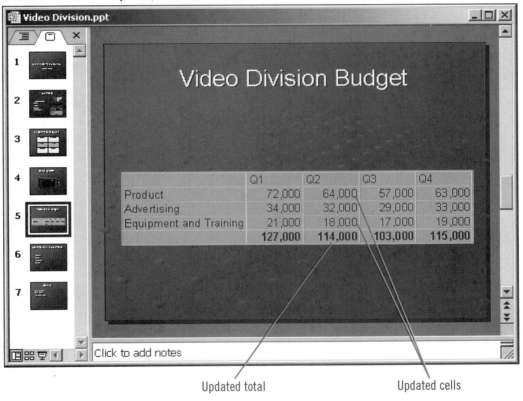

Updated total   Updated cells

CLUES TO USE

Using the Links dialog box

You can use the Links dialog box to update a link, open a linked object's source program, change a linked object's source program, break a link, and determine if links are updated automatically or manually. To open the Links dialog box, click Edit on the menu bar, click Links, then click the link you want. The Links dialog box opens, as shown in Figure G-11. If the Manual option button is selected, the links in the target file will not be updated unless you select the link in this dialog box and click Update Now.

FIGURE G-11: Links dialog box

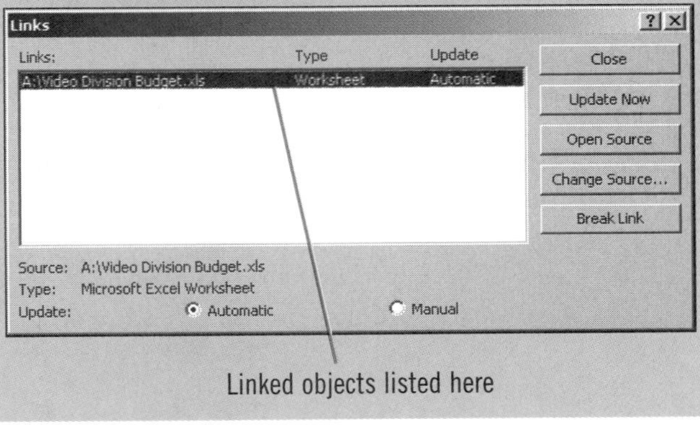

Linked objects listed here

Inserting an Animated GIF file

In your presentations, you may want to use special effects to illustrate a point or capture the attention of your audience. You can do this by inserting an animation or a movie. An **animation** contains multiple images that move or stream together when you run a slide show. Animations are stored as GIF (Graphics Interchange Format) files. PowerPoint comes with a number of animated GIFs, which are stored in the Microsoft Clip Organizer. The Clip Organizer contains various drawings, photographs, clip art, sounds, animated GIFs, and movies that you can insert into your presentation. A **movie** is live action captured in digital format by a movie camera. Maria continues developing her presentation by embedding an animated GIF file in a slide about international videos.

Steps

1. Click the **Slide 6 thumbnail** in the Slides tab

2. Click **Insert** on the menu bar, point to **Movies and Sounds**, then click **Movie from Clip Organizer**
   The Insert Clip Art task pane opens and displays all the animated GIFs available for you to use. If you don't want to view all the animation clips in the Clip Art task pane, you can narrow the results that it displays.

3. Click **Modify** in the Insert Clip Art task pane, drag to select any text in the Search text text box, type **international**, then click **Search**
   All the clips that have an international attribute appear in the Insert Clip Art task pane. The animation clips are at the bottom of the list.

4. Click the **down scroll arrow** until it reaches the bottom, then click the GIF file shown in Figure G-12
   The animated GIF appears on the slide and the Picture toolbar opens. If the colors of an animated GIF don't fit with the color scheme of the presentation, you can format the GIF image.

5. Click the **Automatic Layout button** ☒ on the slide, then click **Undo Automatic Layout**

6. Resize the image so it is approximately the same height as the bulleted list, then drag the image so it's directly across from the text box

7. Click the **Color button** ☒ on the Picture toolbar, then click **Grayscale**
   The animated GIF's colors are changed to shades of gray, which look better with the presentation's color scheme. Compare your screen with Figure G-13. The animation won't begin unless you view it in Slide Show view.

8. Click the **Slide Show button** ☒, watch the animation, then press **[Esc]**

9. Click the **Save button** ☒ on the Standard toolbar

QuickTip

If you do not see the GIF file in Figure G-12, choose a different GIF or ask your instructor or technical support person for help.

QuickTip

An animated GIF file will also play if you publish the presentation as a Web page and view it in a browser such as Internet Explorer or Netscape.

FIGURE G-12: Clip Organizer showing animated GIF files

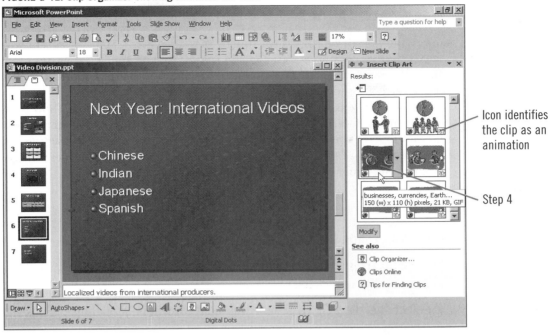

Icon identifies the clip as an animation

Step 4

FIGURE G-13: Animated GIF in slide show view

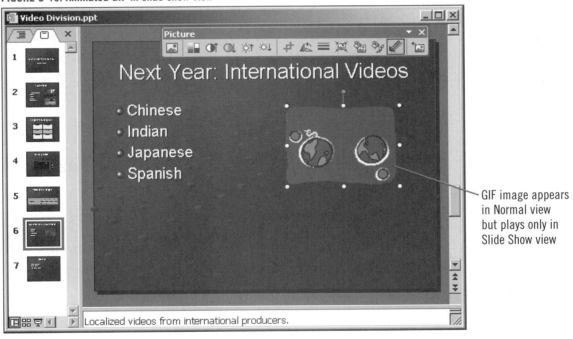

GIF image appears in Normal view but plays only in Slide Show view

CLUES TO USE

Inserting movies

You can insert movies from the Clip Organizer, the Microsoft Design Gallery Live Web site, or from disk files. To insert a movie from a disk, click Insert on the menu bar, point to Movies and Sounds, then click Movie from File. Navigate to the location of the movie you want, then insert it. If you're using the Insert Clip Art task pane, search for the file you want, then insert it. After you insert a movie, you can edit it using the Picture toolbar. You can also open the Custom Animation task pane and apply an effect to the movie. From the Custom Animation task pane, you can indicate whether to continue the slide show or to stop playing the clip.

Inserting a Sound

PowerPoint allows you to embed sounds in your presentation just as you would embed animated GIF files or movies. You can add sounds to your presentation from files on a disk, the Microsoft Clip Organizer, the Internet, or a location on a network. Use sound to enhance the message of a slide. For example, if you are creating a presentation about a raft tour of the Colorado River, you might embed a rushing water sound on a slide showing a photograph of people rafting. If you try to embed a sound that is larger than 100 KB, PowerPoint will automatically link the sound file to your presentation. You can change this setting on the General tab in the Options dialog box. ✎▬▬ Maria embeds the sound of a camera click on Slide 2 of her presentation to enhance the picture on the slide.

Steps

1. Click the **Slide 2 thumbnail** in the Slides tab

2. Click **Insert** on the menu bar, point to **Movies and Sounds**, then click **Sound from File**
   The Insert Sound dialog box opens.

3. Select the file **PPT G-4** from the location where your Project Files are stored, then click **OK**
   A dialog box opens asking if you want the sound to play automatically or if you want it to play only when you click the icon during the slide show.

> **Trouble?**
>
> The sound icon you see may be different from the one illustrated in Figure G-14, depending on your sound card software.

4. Click **Yes** to play the sound automatically
   A small sound icon appears on the slide, as shown in Figure G-14. The icon would be easier to see if it were larger.

5. Click **Format** on the menu bar, click **Picture**, then click the **Size tab**
   The Size tab opens in the Format Picture dialog box.

6. Double-click **100** in the Height text box in the Scale section, type **150**, then click **OK**
   The sound icon enlarges to 150% of its original size.

7. Drag the **sound icon** to the lower-right corner of the Presentation window, then click the slide background to deselect the icon
   Compare your screen to Figure G-15.

> **Trouble?**
>
> If you do not hear a sound, your computer may not have a sound card installed. See your instructor or technical support person for help.

8. Double-click the **sound icon**
   The sound of a camera clicking plays out of your computer's speakers.

9. Click the **Save button** 🖫 on the Standard toolbar

FIGURE G-14: Slide showing small sound icon

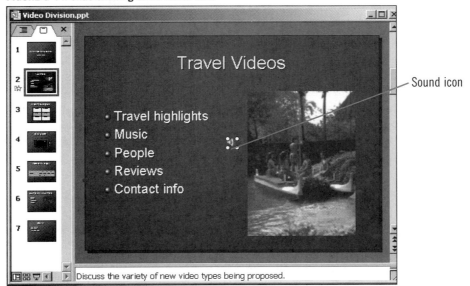

Sound icon

FIGURE G-15: Slide showing repositioned sound icon

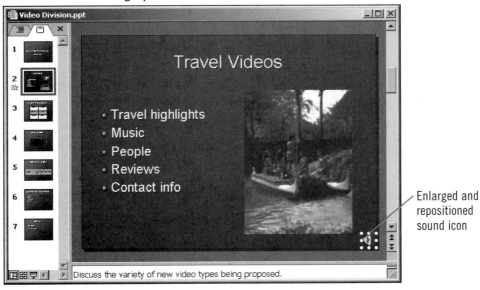

Enlarged and repositioned sound icon

Playing music from a CD

You can play a CD audio track during your slide show. Click Insert on the menu bar, point to Movies and Sounds, then click Play CD Audio Track. The Movie and Sound Options dialog box opens. Select the beginning and ending track number and the timing options you want. See Figure G-16. When you are finished in the Movie and Sound Options dialog box, click OK. A CD icon appears on the slide. You can indicate if you want the CD to play automatically when you move to the slide or only when you click the CD icon during a slide show. The CD must be in the CD-ROM drive before you can play an audio track.

FIGURE G-16: Movie and Sound Options dialog box

Sound Options

Play options
☐ Loop until stopped
☐ Rewind movie when done playing

Play CD audio track

Start:		End:	
Track:	1	Track:	1
At:	00:28	At:	00:56

Total playing time: 00:28
File: [CD Audio]

OK   Cancel

Inserting a Hyperlink

Often you will want to view a document that either won't fit on the slide or is too detailed for your presentation. In these cases, you can insert a **hyperlink**, a specially formatted word, phrase, graphic, or drawn object that you click during your slide show to "jump to," or display, another slide in your current presentation; another PowerPoint presentation; a Word, Excel, or Access file; or an address on the World Wide Web. Inserting a hyperlink is similar to linking because you can change the object in the source program after you click the hyperlink. ✎ Maria decides to add a hyperlink to her presentation to show a recent product review, which is in a Word document.

Steps 1234

1. Click the **Slide 7 thumbnail** in the Slides tab

2. Drag ⍓ across **Video News** to select it, then click the **Insert Hyperlink button** 🔗 on the Standard toolbar, then click **Existing File or Web Page**
   The Insert Hyperlink dialog box opens. Compare your dialog box with Figure G-17. You want to hyperlink to another file.

3. Select the file **PPT G-5** from the location where your Project Files are stored, click **OK**, then click in a blank area of the slide
   Now that you have made "Video News" a hyperlink to the file PPT G-5, the text formatting changes to a blue color, the hyperlink color for this presentation's color scheme, and is underlined. It's important to test any hyperlink you create.

4. Click the **Slide Show button** 🖵, then click the **Video News hyperlink**
   The Word document containing the review appears on the screen, as shown in Figure G-18. The Web toolbar appears below the Formatting toolbar.

5. Click the **Back button** ⬅ on the Web toolbar
   The Reviews slide reappears in Slide Show view. The hyperlink is now light purple, the color for followed hyperlinks in this color scheme, indicating that the hyperlink has been used.

6. Press **[Esc]** to end the slide show, right-click the **Word program button** on the taskbar, click **Close** on the shortcut menu, click the **Slide 1 thumbnail**, click the **Slide Sorter View button** 🔳, click in the **Zoom box** on the Standard toolbar, type **50**, then press **[Enter]**
   The Word program closes. Compare your screen to Figure G-19.

7. Run through the entire slide show, making sure you click the hyperlink on Slide 7

8. Add your name to the notes and handouts footer, click **File** on the menu bar, click **Print**, click the **Print what list arrow**, click **Notes Pages**, then click **OK**

9. Save your changes, close the presentation, then exit PowerPoint

FIGURE G-17: Insert Hyperlink dialog box

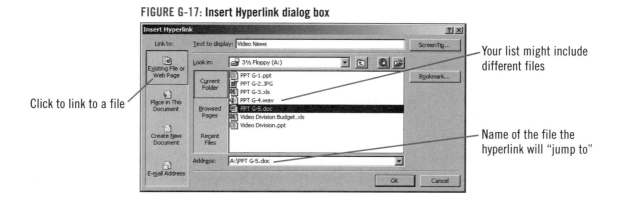

Click to link to a file

Your list might include different files

Name of the file the hyperlink will "jump to"

FIGURE G-18: Linked review in Word document

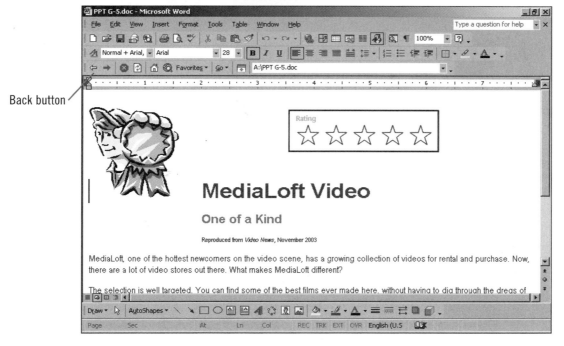

Back button

FIGURE G-19: Final presentation in Slide Sorter view

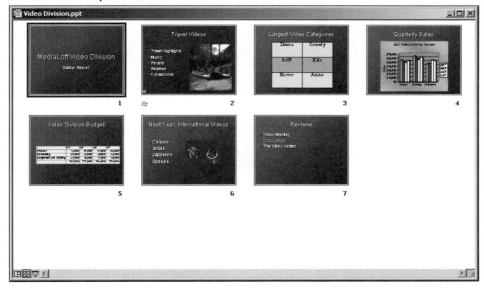

Practice

▶ Concepts Review

Label each of the elements of the PowerPoint window shown in Figure G-20.

FIGURE G-20

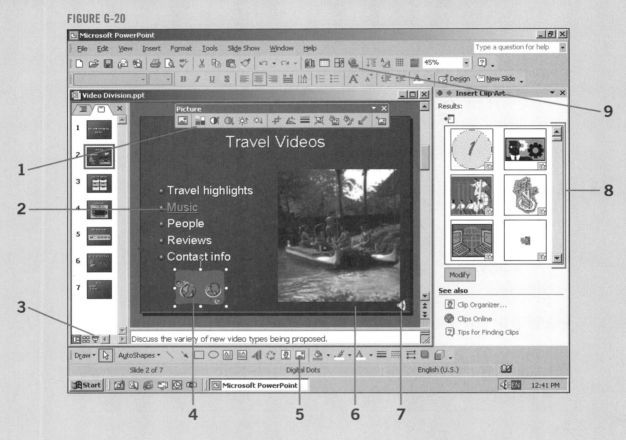

Match each of the terms with the statement that describes its function.

10. **Photo album**
11. **Embedded object**
12. **Link**
13. **Source program**
14. **Hyperlink**
15. **Destination program**
16. **Animation**
17. **Movie**

a. An object created in another program, then stored in PowerPoint
b. The program into which an embedded or linked object is placed
c. A presentation that displays your pictures
d. A word or object you click to view another file
e. The connection between a source file and a PowerPoint presentation
f. The program in which an embedded object is created
g. Live action captured by a movie camera
h. A multiple-imaged graphic that moves

Select the best answer from the list of choices.

18. **Which is true of a hyperlink?**
    a. Hyperlinks can only be used between two PowerPoint presentations.
    b. A hyperlink can be a word, a graphic, or a drawn object.
    c. Clicking a hyperlink closes the current file and opens a new file.
    d. Hyperlinks are used to copy a slide from one presentation to another.
19. **Which statement about embedded objects is false?**
    a. You can format embedded objects in their source program.
    b. Embedded objects are not dependent on a source file.
    c. Embedded objects are not a part of the presentation.
    d. Embedded objects increase your presentation file size more than linked objects do.
20. **Which statement about linked objects is true?**
    a. To edit a linked object, you must open its source file.
    b. A linked object is an independent object embedded directly into a slide.
    c. You can access a linked object even when the source file is not available.
    d. A linked object substantially increases the size of your presentation file.

 Skills Review

1. **Embed a picture.**
    a. Start PowerPoint, open the presentation PPT G-6 from the drive and folder where your Project Files are located, then save it as **Marketing 2003**.
    b. Go to Slide 4 and embed the figure PPT G-7.
    c. Resize the picture so it fits in the blank area of the slide, then use the arrow keys on the keyboard to adjust its position. Save your changes.
2. **Insert a Word table.**
    a. Insert a new slide after Slide 4 with the Title Only slide layout.
    b. Title the slide **Top Cheese Selections**.
    c. Insert a Microsoft Word table that is three columns wide and four rows tall.
    d. Select all the cells, then change the font to 28 point Arial, bold.
    e. Enter the information shown in Table G-2.
    f. Center the information in the cells and increase the line spacing in the bottom row to 2.0 using the Word Formatting toolbar.
    g. Apply the Table Grid 8 AutoFormat, with no special formatting for the last row or last column.
    h. Select the cells in the first row, then change the font to Arial Black.
    i. Exit Word, then center the table below the slide title. Save the presentation.

TABLE G-2

Cow Cheese	Goat Cheese	Ewe Cheese
Abondance	Banon	Ardi-Gasna
Beaufort	Ile-D'yeu	Broccio
Camembert	Sarment	Pigouille

3. **Embed an Excel chart.**
    a. Insert a new slide after Slide 5 using the Blank slide layout.
    b. Embed the chart from the file PPT G-8.
    c. Using Excel tools, enlarge the chart title text to 26 points and the value and category axes to 14 points.
    d. Change the value axis title and legend text to 18 points and reposition the legend so it is at the bottom of the chart (*Hint*: Click the Placement tab in the Format Legend dialog box.)
    e. Resize and reposition the chart so it is centered horizontally and vertically on the slide.
    f. Save your changes.

4. Link an Excel worksheet.

   a. Create a new slide after Slide 6 with the Title Only layout.

   b. Title the slide **Basic P & L**.

   c. Link the spreadsheet file **P & L** from the location where your Project Files are stored.

   d. Resize the object so that it fills the slide width.

   e. Reposition the object so it is centered vertically. (*Hint:* To center it more precisely, hold down [Alt] while you drag, or hold down [Ctrl] while you press the arrow keys.)

   f. Fill the spreadsheet object with light gray (the Follow Accent and Followed Hyperlink Scheme Color).

   g. Save and close the Marketing 2003 presentation.

5. Update a linked Excel worksheet.

   a. Start Excel and open the P & L worksheet.

   b. Replace the value in cell B4 with **95,000**.

   c. In cell D7, enter **1,350,000**.

   d. Close the Excel program after saving your changes.

   e. Open the Marketing 2003 file in PowerPoint, updating the link as you do so.

   f. Go to Slide 7 and view your changes. Save the presentation.

6. Insert an animated GIF file.

   a. Go to Slide 8.

   b. Insert an animated GIF file on the slide. Use the word **email** to search for an appropriate animated GIF.

   c. Resize and reposition the GIF file as necessary.

   d. Preview it in Slide Show view. Save the presentation.

7. Insert a sound.

   a. Go to Slide 2.

   b. Insert the sound file PPT G-9 from the location where your Project Files are stored. Set the sound to play when you click the sound icon.

   c. In the Format Picture dialog box, scale the sound icon to 150% of its original size.

   d. Drag the sound icon to the lower-right corner of the slide.

   e. Test the sound in Slide Show view. Save the presentation.

8. Insert a hyperlink.

   a. Go to Slide 7 in the presentation, then add a new slide with the Title and Text layout.

   b. Title the slide **Reviews**.

   c. In the first line of the main text placeholder, enter **Jeff Sanders, Web Cheese Review** and on the second line enter **Jorge Fonseca, Online Cheese Today**.

   d. Select the entire main text placeholder, and change its font size to 36 points.

   e. Resize the text placeholder to fit the text, then center it on the slide.

   f. Convert the Jeff Sanders bullet into a hyperlink to the file PPT G-10.

   g. Click in the notes pane, then type **The hyperlink links to Jeff's cheese review of the 2003 Camembert**.

   h. Run the slide show and test the hyperlink.

   i. Use the Back button to return to the presentation.

   j. End the slide show.

   k. Exit Word.

   l. Run the spellchecker, view the entire presentation in Slide Show view, and evaluate your presentation. Make any necessary changes.

   m. Add your name as a footer to notes and handouts, print the slides as Notes Pages, save and close the presentation, then exit PowerPoint.

▶ Independent Challenge 1

Quincy Engineering is a mechanical and industrial design company that specializes in designing manufacturing plants in the United States and Canada. As the company financial analyst, you need to investigate and report on a possible contract to design and build a large manufacturing plant in Belize. The board of directors wants to make sure that they can make a minimum profit on the deal. It is your job to provide a recommendation to the board.

Create your own information using the basic presentation provided and assume the following about Quincy Engineering:

- The new manufacturing plant in Belize will be 75,000 square feet in size. The projected cost for Quincy Engineering to design and build the plant in Belize is about $280.00 per square foot based on a four-phase schedule: planning and design, site acquisition and preparation, underground construction, and above-ground construction.
- Factors that helped determine Quincy Engineering's cost to build the plant include: Quincy Engineering payroll for 45 people in Belize for 24 months; materials cost; hiring two Belizean construction companies to construct the plant; and travel expenses.
- Factor in a 1.5 million dollar profit margin for Quincy Engineering above the cost of the building.

a. Open the file PPT G-11, then save it as **Belize Plant**.

b. Think about what results you want to see, what information you will need to create the slide presentation, and how your message should be communicated. In order for your presentation to be complete, it must include the following objects: (i) an embedded Word table; (ii) an embedded Excel chart; and (iii) a sound from the Clip Organizer

c. Use Microsoft Word and PowerPoint to embed objects into your presentation. Use the assumptions listed above to develop information that would be appropriate for a table.

d. Give each slide a title and add main text where appropriate.

e. Make the last slide in the presentation your recommendation to pursue the contract, based on the financial data you present.

f. Add your name as a footer to the notes and handouts, save your changes, then print the final slide presentation as handouts (2 slides per page).

▶ Independent Challenge 2

You are the director of operations at The Franklin Group, a large investment banking company in Texas. Franklin is considering merging with Redding, Inc, a smaller investment company in Arizona, to form the 10th largest financial institution in the United States. As the director of operations, you need to present some financial projections regarding the merger to a special committee formed by Franklin to study the proposed merger.

Create your own information using the basic presentation provided on your Project Disk. Assume the following facts about the merger between Franklin and Redding:

- Franklin earned a $21 million profit last year. Projected profit this year is $28 million. Projected profit next year with the merger with Redding is $34 million. Franklin's operating expenses run approximately $31 million each year. Redding's operating expenses run approximately $18 million each year.
- Redding earned $9 million in profit last year. Projected profit this year is $11 million. Projected profit next year with the merger is $19 million.
- Franklin has a 19% share of the market without Redding. Redding has a 6% share of the market without Franklin. Combined, the companies would have a 25% share of the market.
- With the merger, Franklin would need to cut $7.6 million from its annual operating costs and Redding would need to cut $2 million from its annual operating costs.

a. Open the file PPT G-12 from the drive and folder where your Project Files are located, then save it as **Merger**.

b. Think about what results you want to see, what information you will need to create the slide presentation, and how your message should be communicated. In order for your presentation to be complete, it must include the following objects: (i) an embedded Excel worksheet; (ii) a linked Excel worksheet; (iii) an embedded table, chart, or other object; and (iv) a hyperlink.

c. Use Microsoft Excel to embed a worksheet and link a worksheet to your presentation. Use the preceding assumptions to develop related information that would be appropriate for the worksheets. Use the profit and operating expense figures to create your own revenue figures for one of the worksheets. (Revenue minus operating expenses equals profit.)

d. Hyperlink to the file Redding, Inc. Choose the slide in the presentation where the hyperlink should be placed. You can use existing text or create a drawn or other object to use as the hyperlink.

e. Give each slide a title and add main text where appropriate. Create slides as necessary to make the presentation complete.

f. Add your name as a footer to the notes and the handouts, save your changes, then print the final slide presentation.

▶ Independent Challenge 3

You have just been promoted to the position of sales manager at DWImports, a U.S. company that exports goods and professional services to companies in Japan, South Korea, China, and the Philippines. One of your new responsibilities is to give a presentation at the biannual finance meeting showing how the Sales Department performed during the previous six-month period.

Plan and create a short slide presentation (six to eight slides) that illustrates the Sales Department's performance during the last six months. Identify the existing accounts (by country), then identify the new contracts acquired during the last six months. Create your own content, but assume the following:
- The majority of goods and services being exported are as follows: food products (such as rice, corn, and wheat); agriculture consulting; construction engineering; and industrial designing and engineering.
- The company gained five new accounts in China, South Korea, and the Philippines.
- The Sales Department showed a $6 million profit for the first half of the year.
- Department expenses for the first half of the year were $3.5 million.
- The presentation will be given in a boardroom using a projection machine.

a. Think about what results you want to see, what information you will need to create the slide presentation, and how your message should be communicated. In order for your presentation to be complete, it must include the following objects: (i) an embedded Word table; (ii) an embedded Excel chart; (iii) an embedded picture; and (iv) an animated GIF file or embedded movie.

b. Use the movies provided for you in PowerPoint, or if you have access to another media source, choose another appropriate movie to embed in your presentation.

c. Give each slide a title and add main text points where appropriate.

d. Add a template, background shading, or other enhancing objects to make your presentation look professional.

e. Save the presentation as **Imports** to the drive and folder where your Project Files are stored.

f. Open the Save As dialog box, click the Save As type list arrow, scroll down and click Outline/RTF, change the filename to **Imports RTF**, then click Save.

g. Add your name as a footer to the slides and notes and handouts, save your changes, then print the final slide presentation.

Independent Challenge 4

You are the business manager for LA EduCorp, a large non-profit educational organization in Los Angeles, California. One of your duties is to purchase new and used computer equipment for the organization every three years. LA EduCorp has allotted some money in the budget this year to upgrade some of the computer equipment. Your job is to prepare a brief presentation for the board of directors' next monthly meeting, which outlines the cost of purchasing new and used equipment and selling the old equipment.

Develop your own content, but assume the following:
- 15 computer systems need to be sold.
- The old computers are configured as follows: Pentium, 200 MHz, 32MB RAM, 3GB HDD, 24X CDROM with Sound and 4MB Video, 56K Modem 10/100 3Com Network Card, Windows 95.
- The 15 replacement computer systems are configured as follows: Pentium 600-800MHz, 128MB RAM, 10GB HD, 48X CD-ROM with Sound and 24MB Video, 56K Modem 10/100 3Com Network Card, Windows 98.
- Add $50.00 to the price of each purchased computer for tax and shipping.
- You are allowed to spend up to $900.00 per new computer.

You'll need to find the following information on the Web:
- The average price of the old computer systems that need to be sold.
- The prices of the new computer systems.
- Auction Web sites where the old computers can be sold.

a. Open a new presentation, and save it as **EduCorp** to the drive and folder where your Project Files are located.
b. Add your name as the footer on all slides and handouts.
c. Connect to the Internet, then use a search engine to locate Web sites that have information on used computer systems. If your search does not produce any results, you might try the following sites: www.affordablecomputers.com, www.usedcomputer.com, www.timco-computers.com
d. Think about what results you want to see, what information you will need to create the slide presentation, and how your message should be communicated. Review at least two Web sites that contain information about used computers. Print the pages of the Web sites you use to gather data for your presentation. (Remember to gather information on the old computers as well as the new computers.)
e. In order for your presentation to be complete, it must include the following objects: (i) an embedded Word table; (ii) an embedded Excel worksheet or chart; (iii) a GIF animation or movie; and (iv) a sound.
f. Use the assumptions listed above to develop worksheet and/or table information that describes the configurations and prices of the new computer systems. Categorize the new systems by their speed; for example: 600MHz, 650MHz, and 700MHz.
g. Create an Excel chart or worksheet that describes the difference between the purchase of the new systems and the sale of the old systems.
h. Create a slide that identifies different auction Web sites that you can use to sell the old computers. If your search does not produce any results, you might try the following sites: www.ebay.com, www.ubid.com, www.dealdeal.com
i. Give each slide a title and add main text where appropriate. Create slides as necessary to make the presentation complete.
j. Apply an appropriate slide design. Change the slide design colors as necessary.
k. Spell check the presentation, view the final presentation, save the final version, then print the slides as handouts.
l. Close the presentation, exit PowerPoint, and disconnect from the Internet.

PowerPoint 2002

► Visual Workshop

Create two slides that look like the examples in Figures G-23 and G-24. Save the presentation as **New Classes**. Save and print the slides. Submit the final presentation output.

FIGURE G-21

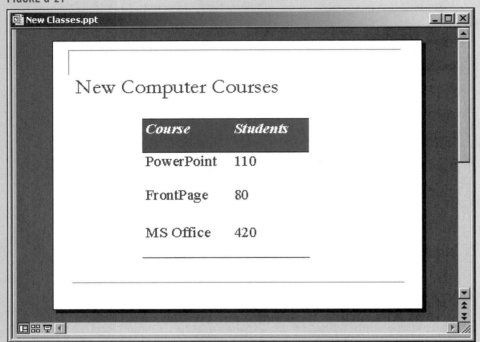

FIGURE G-22

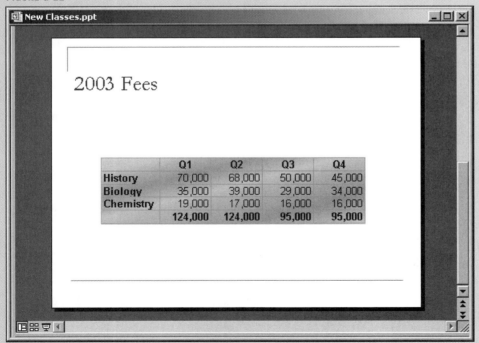

Using
Advanced Features

Objectives

- ▶ **Send a presentation for review**
- ▶ **Combine reviewed presentations**
- ▶ **Set up a slide show**
- ▶ **Create a custom show**
- ▶ **Use the Meeting Minder**
- ▶ **Rehearse slide timings**
- ▶ **Publish a presentation for the Web**
- ▶ **Broadcast a presentation**
- ▶ **Use the Pack and Go Wizard**

After your work on a presentation is complete, you have the option of sending the presentation over the Internet for others to review and send back to you. Reviewers can make changes to the presentation and add their own comments. Once you are finished making changes to your presentation, you need to produce the final output that you will use when you give your presentation. You can print your presentation, display it as a slide show using a computer or projector, publish it to the Web for others to view, or broadcast it live over the Web. ✐ Maria Abbott has finished creating the content of her presentation. She decides to send it out for review, then produce an on-screen slide show, and publish it for viewing on the World Wide Web.

Sending a Presentation for Review

When you finish creating a presentation, it is often helpful to have others look over the content for accuracy and clarity. You can use Microsoft Outlook or any other compatible 32-bit email program to send a presentation out for review. When you send a presentation for review using Outlook, a review request e-mail message is created automatically that includes an attached copy of the presentation file. Reviewers can use any version of PowerPoint to make changes and insert comments on the slides of your presentation. Outlook automatically tracks changes made by multiple reviewers, so you don't have to keep track of which reviewer made which change. Changes to a presentation sent electronically are much easier to track and combine than changes marked on printed copies of the presentation. ✒ Maria uses Outlook to send her presentation to two colleagues for their suggestions and comments.

1. Start PowerPoint, open the presentation **PPT H-1**, then save it as **Video Division Final**

Trouble?

If you don't have access to Microsoft Outlook, read the information in the Clues to Use to send your presentation for review using another method.

2. Click **File** on the menu bar, point to **Send To**, then click **Mail Recipient (for Review)**
A Microsoft Outlook e-mail window opens, as shown in Figure H-1. Notice that the subject line and some basic e-mail text are automatically entered in the Outlook window, and the presentation is attached.

3. Click the **To button**
The Select Names dialog box opens. Use this dialog box to select all the people who you want to review the presentation.

Trouble?

If your name does not appear in the list of names in the Select Names dialog box, ask your instructor or technical support person for help.

4. Click your name in the list of names, click the **To button**, then click **OK**
Your name and e-mail address appear in the To text box in the Outlook window.

5. Click in the Outlook window below the message text, then type **Please return your review this Friday by 3:00.**
The new text appears below the original text. Compare your screen to Figure H-2.

QuickTip

If there are linked files in the presentation you are sending for review, you need to attach the linked files to your e-mail message or change the linked files to embedded objects.

6. Click the **Send button** 🔽 on the Outlook toolbar
Outlook sends the e-mail message with the attached presentation file (or places it in the Outlook Outbox). The Outlook window closes and you are returned to the PowerPoint presentation window. The Reviewing toolbar now appears below the Formatting toolbar, indicating that the presentation has been sent out for review.

7. Start Outlook, send the message if necessary, go to the Inbox window, then click the **Send/Receive button** 🗎 on the Outlook toolbar
The message you just sent to yourself appears in the Inbox window. You may have to wait a short time before the message appears.

8. Click the Outlook **Close button** ☒ on the title bar
Outlook closes and the PowerPoint screen appears.

FIGURE H-1: Outlook window

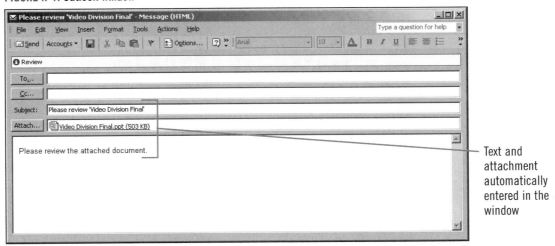

Text and attachment automatically entered in the window

FIGURE H-2: Completed Outlook window

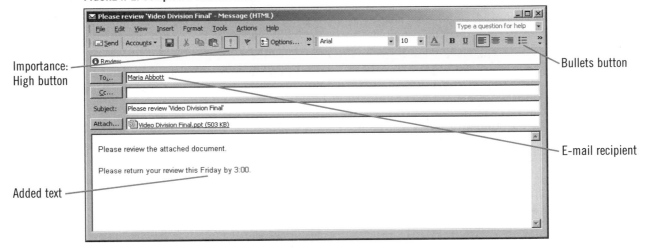

Importance: High button

Added text

Bullets button

E-mail recipient

Other ways to send or route a presentation

If you are not using Outlook as your e-mail program, you can still send a presentation out for review over the Web using another 32-bit e-mail program, as long as it is compatible with Messaging Application Programming Interface (MAPI). You can also use a Microsoft Exchange server, a network server, or a floppy disk. To send a presentation out for review using any of these methods, open the presentation, then use the Save As command to save it with a new name. In the Save As dialog box, click the Save as type list arrow, click Presentation for Review, then click Save. Open your e-mail program, create a new message, attach the presentation file to the message, then send the message.

You can also route the presentation to multiple reviewers in a specific order so they each receive the presentation after another reviewer. To route a presentation, click File on the menu bar, point to Send To, then click Routing Recipient. The Add Routing Slip dialog box opens. Click Address, then add the names of the reviewers from your e-mail address book. Select any other options in the Add Routing Slip dialog box. To send the presentation to the first reviewer, click Route; to close the dialog box without sending the presentation out for review, click Add Slip; to send the presentation out for review at a later time, click File on the menu bar, point to Send To, then click Next Routing Recipient.

Combining Reviewed Presentations

Once a reviewer has completed their review of your presentation and sends it back, you can combine the changes into your original presentation using the Compare and Merge Presentations command. You can apply individual changes, changes by slide, changes by reviewer, changes on the slide master, or changes to the entire presentation. You can continue to combine changes to your original presentation until you have applied all the changes, deleted all the changes markers, saved the presentation, or ended the review. ➤ Maria sent out the Video Division presentation to two of her colleagues. She now wants to combine the two reviewed versions with her original presentation.

Steps

1. Click **Tools** on the menu bar, then click **Compare and Merge Presentations**
   The Choose Files to Merge with Current Presentation dialog box opens.

2. Switch the Look in list to the drive and location where your Project Files are stored, click the file **PPT H-2**, press and hold [Shift], click **PPT H-3**, then click **Merge**
   The two reviewed presentations are merged with your original presentation. The Revisions Pane task pane opens on the right side of the screen. It is divided into two tabs: the List tab and the Gallery tab. The List tab displays individual changes by reviewer for the current slide. The Gallery tab displays a thumbnail of the current slide and shows what the slide would look like if all the suggested changes were made. Each reviewer's changes are identified by a marker of a different color on the slide. If more than one reviewer made a change on the same object, the change is identified by a white color marker.

3. Click the **Slide 3 thumbnail**, then click the top item in the Slide changes section of the Revisions Pane
   The top item on this slide is a comment made by one of the reviewers. A description of the comment appears on the slide next to its corresponding color marker. Since this is a comment, no action on your part is required.

4. Click the next item in the Slide changes section
   See Figure H-3. Alice suggests replacing the word "Largest" in the title with the word "Primary," as shown in Figure H-3. By selecting the All changes to Title 1 check box, you will accept both changes: the word "Largest" will be deleted, and the word "Primary" will be inserted.

5. Click the **All changes to Title 1 check box** in the change description box on the slide, then click the **Next Item button** ⊡ on the Reviewing toolbar
   Slide 4 appears and a change description box with both reviewers' comments opens. The color marker is white, indicating that the marked change contains more than one reviewer's comments.

6. Click the **top check box from Anne Sarri** in the change description box, notice the change in the body text box, then click the **second check box from Anne Sarri**
   Clicking the top check box inserts some words in the body text box; clicking the next check box deletes some words that are no longer necessary. When you click the second check box, the last check box, from Alice Wegeman, also is selected, which indicates that both reviewers had made the same change. Compare your screen to Figure H-4.

7. Click the **End Review button** ⊡ End Review.. on the Reviewing toolbar, read the information in the dialog box, then click **Yes** to end the review
   The Reviewing toolbar and Revisions Pane task pane close and the color markers on the slide are deleted.

8. Save your changes, click **View** on the menu bar, click **Task Pane**, click **Window** on the menu bar, then click **Arrange All**
   Now your screen will match the rest of the figures in this book.

QuickTip
To undo one change or all the changes made on a slide, click the Unapply button ⊡ ▾ on the Reviewing toolbar, then select one of the options.

FIGURE H-3: Figure showing Revisions Pane

Comment color marker

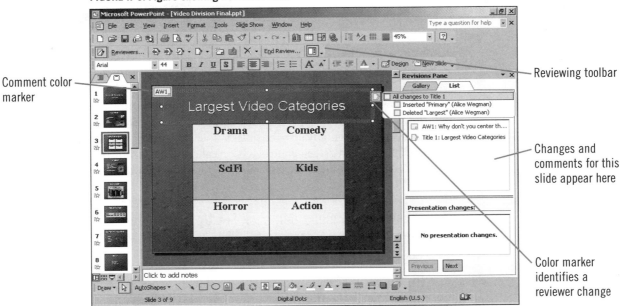

Reviewing toolbar

Changes and comments for this slide appear here

Color marker identifies a reviewer change

FIGURE H-4: Figure showing revised slide

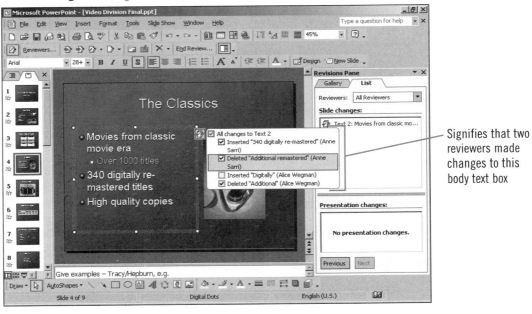

Signifies that two reviewers made changes to this body text box

CLUES TO USE

Reviewing a presentation

To evaluate a presentation someone sends for your review, simply open the presentation in PowerPoint and make your changes. The Reviewing toolbar will automatically open when you open the presentation. When you are finished making changes, save the presentation. Next, click File on the menu bar, point to Send To, then click Original Sender to send the presentation back to its original owner using Outlook. If you want to edit the message in the e-mail before you send the presentation back, you can click the Reply with Changes button on the Reviewing toolbar.

Setting Up a Slide Show

With PowerPoint, you can create a slide show that runs automatically. Viewers can then watch the slide show on a stand-alone computer, called a **kiosk,** at a convention or trade show. You can create a self-running slide show that loops, or runs, through the entire show, without users touching the computer. You can also let viewers advance the slides at their own pace by pressing the spacebar, clicking the mouse, or clicking an on-screen control button called an **action button.** A self-running slide show is also useful when you publish a presentation to the Web for others to view. ✎ Maria prepares the Video Division Final presentation so it can be used at an upcoming trade show.

Steps

1. Click **Slide Show** on the menu bar, click **Set Up Show**, then click the **Browsed at a kiosk (full screen) option button** under Show type
   The Set Up Show dialog box opens.

2. Make sure the **All option button** is selected in the Show slides section, then make sure the **Using timings, if present option button** is selected in the Advance slides section
   This will include all the slides in the presentation and have PowerPoint advance the slides at time intervals you set. Compare your Set Up Show dialog box to Figure H-5.

Trouble?

If you don't see the Slide Transition button on the Standard toolbar, click a Toolbar Options button 〉〉 on a toolbar to locate buttons that are not visible on your toolbar.

3. Click **OK**, click the **Slide Sorter View button** 🀫, then click the **Slide Transition button** 🖼 on the Slide Sorter toolbar
   The Slide Transition task pane opens.

4. In the task pane, click the **Automatically after check box** to select it in the Advance slide section, click the **Automatically after up arrow** until **00:08** appears, click **Apply to All Slides**, click **Slide Show**, view the show, let it start again, then press **[Esc]**
   PowerPoint advances the slides automatically at eight-second intervals, or faster if someone clicks the mouse or presses [Spacebar]. There may be times when you want users to advance slides by themselves. You can do this by inserting a button that is actually a hyperlink for the user to click to jump to the next slide.

5. Click **Slide Show** on the menu bar, click **Set Up Show**, in the Advance slides section, click the **Manually option button**, then click **OK**

6. Double-click **Slide 1** to view it in Normal view, click **Slide Show** on the menu bar, point to **Action Buttons**, click the **Action Button: Forward or Next button** ▷, then drag the pointer to draw a button in the lower-left corner of Slide 1
   A new action button appears on the bottom of the slide and the Action Settings dialog box opens, as shown in Figure H-6.

7. Make sure the **Hyperlink to option button** is selected, click the **Hyperlink to list arrow**, click **Next Slide** if necessary, then click **OK**
   Compare your screen to Figure H-7.

8. With the action button selected, press **[Ctrl][C]** to copy it, click the **Next Slide button** 🢃, press **[Ctrl][V]** to paste the button on Slide 2, repeat for each slide that follows, then return to **Slide 1**

QuickTip

You must be in Slide Show view to use the hyperlink buttons.

9. View the slide show, clicking the **action buttons** to move from slide to slide, press **[Esc]** to end the slide show once you've viewed it all the way through, then save your changes
   Make sure you wait for the animated objects to appear on the slides before you click the action buttons.

FIGURE H-5: Set Up Show dialog box

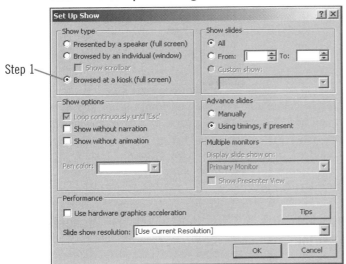

Step 1

FIGURE H-6: Action Settings dialog box

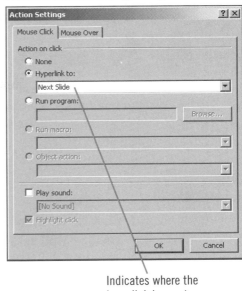

Indicates where the
hyperlink jumps to

FIGURE H-7: Slide 1 with action button to the next slide

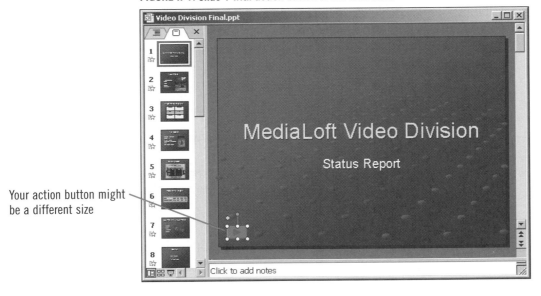

Your action button might
be a different size

CLUES TO USE

Hiding a slide during a slide show

During a slide show, you can hide slides you don't want the audience to see. Hidden slides are not deleted from the presentation; they just don't appear during a slide show. The easiest way to hide a slide is to right-click the slide thumbnail in Normal view or Slide Sorter view, then click Hide Slide. When a slide is hidden, its slide number has a hide symbol—a gray box with a line through it—over it. To unhide the slide, right-click the slide thumbnail, then click Hide Slide. You can display a hidden slide during a slide show by right-clicking the slide prior to the hidden slide, pointing to By Title, then clicking the title of the hidden slide.

Creating a Custom Show

Often when you create a slide show, you need to create a custom version of it for a different audience or purpose. For example, you might create a 20-minute presentation about a new product to show to potential customers who will be interested in the product features and benefits. Then you could create a five-minute version of that same show for an open house for potential investors, selecting only appropriate slides from the longer show. ✐ Maria wants to use a reduced version of the slide show in a marketing presentation, so she creates a custom slide show containing only the slides relating to the video product line.

Steps

1. Click **Slide Show** on the menu bar, click **Set Up Show**, click the **Presented by a speaker (full screen) option button**, then click **OK**
   This turns off the kiosk setting.

2. Click **Slide Show** on the menu bar, click **Custom Shows**, then click **New** in the Custom Shows dialog box
   The Define Custom Show dialog box opens with the slides that are in your current presentation in the Slides in presentation list box.

3. Press and hold [Ctrl], click **2. Travel Videos**, **4. The Classics**, **7. Next Year: International Videos**, and **8. Reviews**, then click **Add**
   The four selected slides move to the Slides in custom show list box, indicating that they will be included in the new presentation. See Figure H-8.

4. Click **4. Reviews** in the Slides in custom show list, then click the **Slide Order up arrow button** three times to move it to the top of the list
   You can arrange the slides in any order in your custom show.

5. Drag to select the existing text in the Slide show name text box, type **Marketing Presentation**, then click **OK**
   The Custom Shows dialog box lists your custom presentation. The custom show is not saved as a separate slide show on your disk even though you assigned it a new name, so to show a custom slide show, you must first open the show you used to create it. You then open the custom show from the Custom Shows dialog box.

6. Click **Show**, view the slide show, clicking the **action buttons** to move from slide to slide, then press **[Esc]** to end the custom show after you view the International Videos slide
   The slides appear in the new order: Slide 8, 2, 4, then 7. Because the slide show is not set up to loop continuously, clicking the action button on the International Videos slide doesn't do anything. You return to the presentation in Normal view. You can also run a custom show from within the presentation slide show.

7. Press **[Ctrl][Home]**, click the **Slide Show button** 🖵, watch the text animation, right-click anywhere on the screen, point to **Go**, point to **Custom Show**, then click **Marketing Presentation**, as shown in Figure H-9

8. Use the **action buttons** to move from slide to slide in the custom show, then press **[Esc]** after viewing the International Videos slide

9. Save your changes, click **File** on the menu bar, click **Print**, click the **Custom Show option button**, make sure **Marketing Presentation** is listed in the list box, click the **Print what list arrow**, select **Handouts, 3 slides per page**, then click **OK**

FIGURE H-8: **Define Custom Show dialog box**

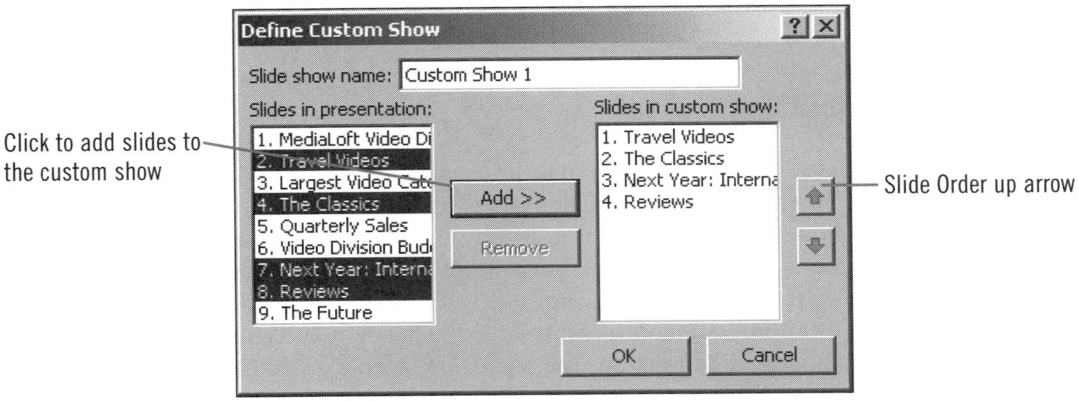

Click to add slides to the custom show →

Slide Order up arrow

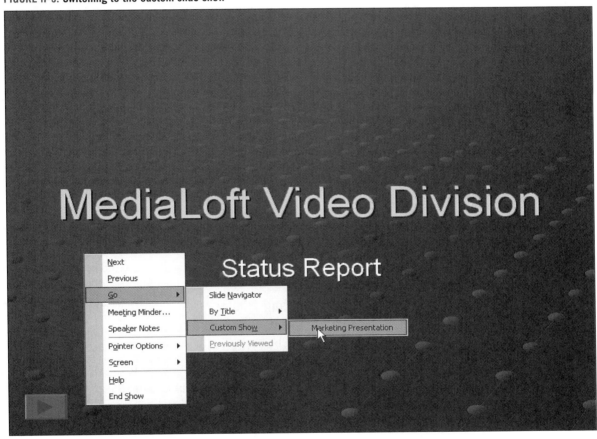

FIGURE H-9: **Switching to the custom slide show**

Using action buttons to hyperlink to a custom slide show

You can use action buttons to switch from the "parent" show to the custom show. Click Slide Show on the menu bar, point to Action Buttons, then choose any action button. Drag the pointer to draw a button on the slide, then, in the Action Settings dialog box, select Custom Show in the Hyperlink to list box. Select the name of the custom show to which you want to hyperlink, then click OK. When you run the show, click the hyperlink button you created to run the custom show.

Using the Meeting Minder

Occasionally, it's helpful to assign tasks or take notes as you present a slide show to make sure people follow up on meeting items. PowerPoint makes this task easy with the Meeting Minder. The Meeting Minder is a dialog box you use in Slide Show view to enter information related to the slides in your presentation. The action items you enter are automatically added to a new slide at the end of your presentation. You can export the action items to a Microsoft Word document to edit them or to make them part of another document. ✐ Maria practices adding action items with the Meeting Minder so she'll know how to use it when she actually runs the presentation.

1. Click the **Slide 5 thumbnail** in the Slides tab
   Slide 5 appears.

2. Click the **Slide Show button** 🖳, wait for the chart to appear, right-click the slide, click **Meeting Minder** on the shortcut menu, then click the **Action Items tab**
   The Meeting Minder dialog box opens.

QuickTip

The Assigned To text box can accept a maximum of 15 characters, including spaces.

3. Type **Compile detailed figures for Q1 Children's sales**, press **[Tab]**, type **Jodi** in the Assigned To text box, press **[Tab]**, then type **8/14/03** to replace today's date in the Due Date text box, compare your screen to Figure H-10, then click **Add**
   The action item you entered appears in the list box on the Action Items tab. If you were to enter any more action items, they would be added to this list.

4. Click **OK**
   The Meeting Minder dialog box closes and the action items are added as a new slide at the end of the presentation.

5. Right-click the slide, point to **Go** on the shortcut menu, point to **By Title**, then click **10 Action Items**
   The new Action Items slide appears with the action item you entered in the Meeting Minder. See Figure H-11.

6. Right-click the slide, click **Meeting Minder** on the shortcut menu, click the **Action Items tab**, click the item in the list, then click **Export**
   The Meeting Minder Export dialog box opens.

7. Click the **Post action items to Microsoft Outlook check box** to deselect it, make sure that the **Send meeting minutes and action items to Microsoft Word check box** is selected, then click **Export Now**
   Microsoft Word starts and opens a new Word document containing your Meeting Minder action items. See Figure H-12. Word assigns a temporary filename that begins with PPT to the document. You can edit and print this document just as you would any Word document.

8. Add your name as the first line in the document, click the **Print button** 🖨 on the Word Standard toolbar, click **File** on the menu bar, click **Save As**, save the document as **Video Division Action Items** to the location where you store your Project Files, then click the **Close button** in the Word program window
   Word saves the action items list in **Rich Text Format (RTF)**, a file format that is readable by other word processors. Your PowerPoint presentation reappears in Slide Show view.

9. Click **OK** in the Meeting Minder dialog box, click the left mouse button twice to end the slide show, then save your changes

FIGURE H-10: Meeting Minder dialog box

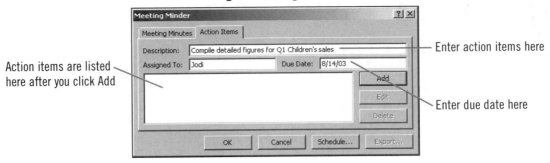

Action items are listed here after you click Add

Enter action items here

Enter due date here

FIGURE H-11: New Action Items slide at the end of the presentation

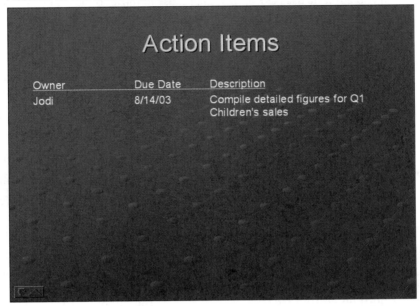

FIGURE H-12: Action items after exporting to Microsoft Word

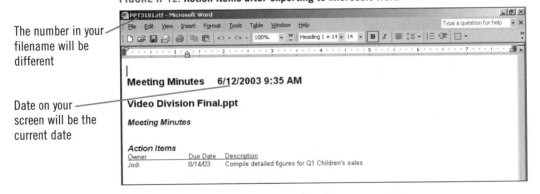

The number in your filename will be different

Date on your screen will be the current date

CLUES TO USE

Keeping track of meeting minutes and speaker notes

You can use the Meeting Minder to keep a record of meeting minutes you type during the slide show. Right-click any slide in Slide Show view, click Meeting Minder, click the Meeting Minutes tab, then type notes in the text box. You can export the meeting minutes to Microsoft Word in the same way you export action items. You can also create speaker notes during a slide show. Right-click any slide in Slide Show view, click Speaker Notes on the shortcut menu, then type any items you want to remember. They will automatically be transferred to the Speaker Notes section of that slide.

Rehearsing Slide Timings

Whether you are creating a self-running slide show or you're planning to talk about the slides as they appear, you should rehearse the **slide timings**, the amount of time each slide stays on the screen. If you assign slide timings to your slides without actually running through the presentation, you will probably discover that the timings do not allow enough time for each slide or point in your presentation. To set accurate slide timings, use the PowerPoint Rehearse Timings feature. As you run through your slide show, the Rehearsal toolbar shows you how long the slide stays on the screen. When enough time has passed, click the mouse to move to the next slide. 🖋 Maria rehearses the slide timings.

Steps

1. Click the **Slide Sorter View button** 🔡, then click **Slide 1**
   Before you continue through the steps of the lesson, you may first want to read the steps and comments in this lesson so you are aware of what happens during a slide show rehearsal.

2. Click the **Rehearse Timings button** 🖳 on the Slide Sorter toolbar
   Slide Show view opens, and Slide 1 appears. The Rehearsal toolbar appears in the upper-left corner of the screen, as shown in Figure H-13.

   Trouble?
   Make sure you wait until the animations are finished on each slide before clicking the Next button.

3. When you feel an appropriate amount of time has passed for the presenter to speak and for the audience to view the slide, click the **Next button** ➡ on the Rehearsal toolbar or click your mouse anywhere on the screen
   Slide 2 appears.

4. Click ➡ at an appropriate interval after Slide 2 appears, then click ➡ after viewing Slide 3

   QuickTip
   If too much time has elapsed, click the Repeat button 🔙 on the Rehearsal toolbar to restart the timer for that slide. You can also set the time for each slide by typing it in the Elapsed Time text box.

5. Continue setting timings for the rest of the slides in the presentation
   Be sure to leave enough time to present the contents of each slide thoroughly. At the end of the slide rehearsal, a Microsoft PowerPoint message box opens asking if you want to save the slide timings. If you save the timings, the next time you run the slide show, the slides will appear automatically at the intervals you specified during the rehearsal.

6. Click **Yes** to save the timings
   Slide Sorter view appears showing the new slide timings, as shown in Figure H-14. Your timings will be different. When you run the slide show, it will run by itself, using the timings you rehearsed. The rehearsed timings override any previous timings you set.

   QuickTip
   To move to the next slide before your rehearsed slide timing has elapsed, click the slide to advance to the next slide.

7. Click the **Slide Show button** 🖳, then view the presentation with your timings

8. Save your changes, click **File** on the menu bar, click **Print**, click the **All option button**, click the **Print what list arrow**, click **Handouts, 4 slides per page**, click the Include comment pages check box, then click **OK**
   The presentation is printed, including the comment made by a reviewer on Slide 3.

FIGURE H-13: Rehearsal toolbar in Slide Show view

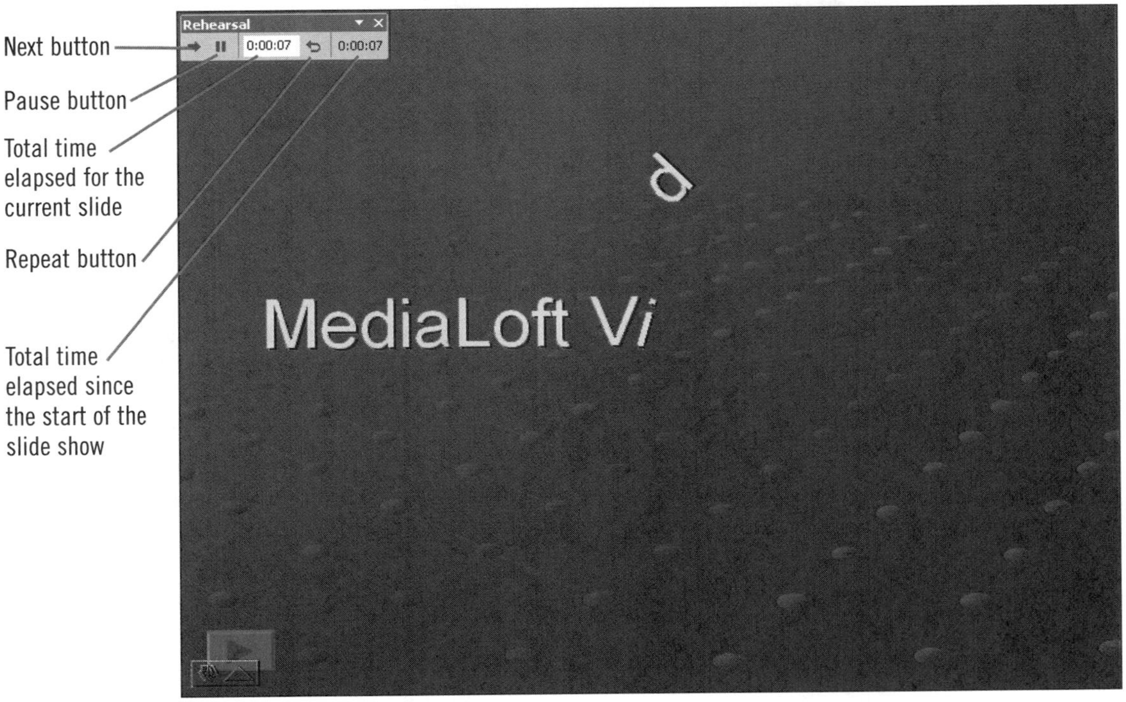

Next button

Pause button

Total time elapsed for the current slide

Repeat button

Total time elapsed since the start of the slide show

MediaLoft Vi

FIGURE H-14: Final presentation in Slide Sorter view showing new slide timings

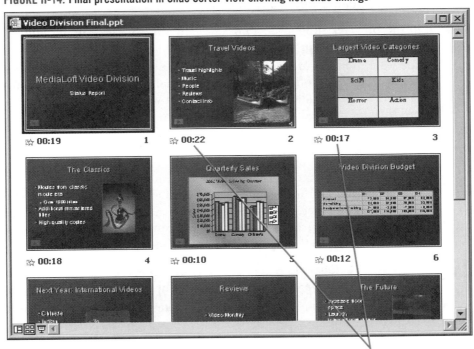

Slide timings you rehearsed (your times will be different)

PowerPoint 2002

Publishing a Presentation for the Web

You can use PowerPoint to create presentations for viewing on the Web by saving the file in Hypertext Markup Language (HTML) format. To save the entire file in its current version, click Save as Web Page from the File menu, then click Save in the dialog box that opens. Others can then view (but not change) the presentation over the Web. If you want to customize the version that you are saving as a Web page (for example, if you wanted to save only the custom show, or if you wanted to make adjustments to how the presentation will look as a Web page), use the Publish command. ⬧⬧⬧ Maria wants to create a version of her Video Division Final presentation that can be viewed on the MediaLoft intranet page. She does not want to include the financial information on Slides 5 and 6, so she uses the Publish feature to publish the custom show she created earlier.

1. Click **File** on the menu bar, click **Save as Web Page**, click the **Save in list arrow**, then select the drive and location where your Project Files are stored
   The Save As dialog box opens.

2. Make sure the filename in the File name text box is selected, then type **videofnl**

3. Click **Publish**
   The Publish as Web Page dialog box opens.

4. Click the **Custom Show option button** in the Publish what? section, then click the **Display speaker notes check box** to deselect it

5. In the Browser support section, click the **All browsers listed above (creates larger files) option button**
   You want to make sure most browsers can view the HTML file you publish. At the bottom of the dialog box, notice that the default filename for the HTML file you are creating is the same as the presentation filename, and that it will be saved to the same folder in which the presentation is stored. Compare your screen to Figure H-15.

6. Click the **Open published Web page in browser check box** to select it, then click **Publish**
   PowerPoint creates a copy of your presentation in HTML format and opens the published presentation in your default Internet browser similar to Figure H-16, which shows the presentation in Internet Explorer 5. Your original presentation remains open on the screen. There is also a folder named videofnl_files that contains necessary supporting files for the HTML file. The list of slide titles on the left are hyperlinks to each slide.

7. Click the **Previous Slide** ⬧ and **Next Slide** ⬧ buttons at the bottom of the screen or the **slide title hyperlinks** on the left side of the screen to view the presentation slides
   Because each slide in this presentation has an action button, you can also click them to advance the slides.

8. Close your browser window, save the PowerPoint presentation, then close the presentation

FIGURE H-15: Publish as Web Page dialog box

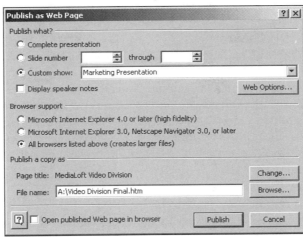

FIGURE H-16: Custom show from Video Division presentation in Internet Explorer

Browser menu and toolbars

Slide titles appear as hyperlinks in the browser

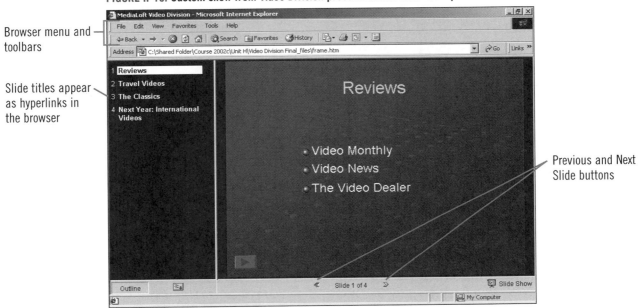

Previous and Next Slide buttons

CLUES TO USE

Online meetings

If you are on a network, you can use Windows NetMeeting and PowerPoint to host or participate in meetings over an intranet or the Web. As the host of a meeting, you can share a presentation in real time with others who may be located in another office in your building or across the country. If you are the host of a meeting, you are required to have NetMeeting (a program automatically installed with Office), the shared document, and its application installed on your computer. As a participant in a meeting, all you are required to have installed on your computer is NetMeeting. As the host, you can schedule a meeting by clicking Tools on the menu bar, pointing to Online Collaboration, then clicking Schedule Meeting. Follow the steps in the dialog boxes to send an e-mail message to the person you are inviting to the meeting. To start an unscheduled online meeting from within the presentation you want to share, click Tools on the menu bar, point to Online Collaboration, then click Meet Now. Follow the steps in the dialog boxes to call participants to the meeting. If the participants accept your meeting invitation, the Online Meeting toolbar opens and the meeting begins.

PowerPoint 2002

Broadcasting a Presentation

You can use PowerPoint as a communication tool to broadcast the presentation over an intranet or the Web. You can start an unscheduled broadcast at any time, or use NetMeeting to schedule a broadcast to take place at a specific date and time. If you want your presentation broadcast available for on-demand viewing, you can record and save it to a network server where others can access the broadcast and replay it at their convenience.  In this lesson, Maria learns the basics of broadcasting a presentation.

▶ Set up a presentation broadcast

Using PowerPoint's broadcasting feature, you can set up a presentation broadcast for a small group of up to 10 computers that are all on the same intranet or have access to the Web. As the presenter, you will need PowerPoint 2002, Microsoft Internet Explorer 5.1 or later, Microsoft Outlook 2002, or another e-mail program, a shared computer or server, and a connected video camera and microphone if you want to broadcast live video and audio. To broadcast a presentation to more than 10 computers at one time, you'll need to have access to a Windows Media Server or a third-party Windows Media Server provider.

▶ Schedule a presentation broadcast

To give the members of your audience plenty of time to prepare for a presentation broadcast, you can schedule the broadcast for a specific date and time. To schedule a broadcast, open the presentation that you want to broadcast, click **Slide Show** on the menu bar, point to **Online Broadcast**, then click **Schedule a Live Broadcast**. In the Schedule Presentation Broadcast dialog box, click **Settings** to open the Broadcast Settings dialog box. Indicate your audio, video, and display preferences. Use the File Location section to enter your server or shared computer information. See Figure H-17. If you will be using a Windows Media Server or including audience feedback, click the **Advanced tab**, then enter the necessary information. Click **OK**, then click **Schedule**. A dialog box similar to an e-mail message box opens. Add participants' e-mail addresses to the To text box, change other settings in the dialog box as necessary, then click the Send button on the toolbar.

▶ Begin a presentation broadcast

When you are ready to begin your presentation broadcast, you start by clicking **Slide Show** on the menu bar, pointing to **Online Broadcast**, then clicking **Start Live Broadcast Now**. If Outlook is your e-mail program, a message dialog box opens telling you that a program is trying to access your e-mail addresses; click **Yes** to continue. The Live Presentation Broadcast dialog box opens and lists the available presentations ready for broadcast. Select the **presentation** you want to broadcast, then click **Broadcast**.

- If the broadcast has been previously scheduled and you are using a microphone or camera in your broadcast, the Broadcast Presentation dialog box opens. Complete the testing of the equipment, then click Start. The presentation broadcast begins.

- If the broadcast is unscheduled, the Live Presentation Broadcast dialog box opens similar to Figure H-18. Click Settings, select the appropriate preferences for this broadcast, then click OK. Click Invite Audience and let the people you want to attend know that you are broadcasting. When you are ready to start the broadcast, click Start. If you are using audio and video, complete the testing of the equipment, then click Start.

▶ View a presentation broadcast

The easiest way to participate in an online broadcast is to open the e-mail message that contains the broadcast invitation and click the URL for the broadcast. The lobby page of the online broadcast appears in your browser. At the scheduled broadcast time, the presentation appears on your screen. During the meeting, you are able to send e-mail messages to the presenter. Figure H-19 shows how your screen might look if you were participating in an online broadcast.

FIGURE H-17: Broadcast Settings dialog box

Indicate your display preferences in this section

Enter server or shared file location here

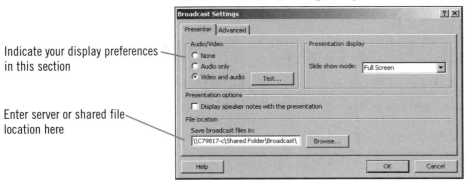

FIGURE H-18: Live Presentation Broadcast dialog box

Click to open the Broadcast Settings dialog box

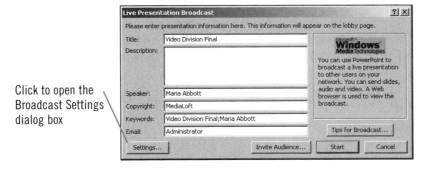

FIGURE H-19: Presentation broadcast in Internet Explorer

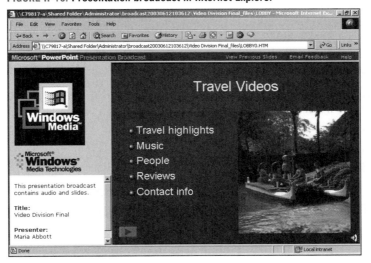

Record and save a broadcast

If you don't want to broadcast your presentation live, you can record it and save it to a network server where others can access it at any time. Open the presentation you want to broadcast, click Slide Show on the menu bar, point to Online Broadcast, then click Record and Save a Broadcast. The Record Presentation Broadcast dialog box opens. Change the information as necessary. Click Settings, change any of the video, audio, and display preferences, then identify the server or shared computer where the broadcast files will be stored. Click Record, complete the equipment testing, then click Start. Record your broadcast. When you want others to view the recorded broadcast, you will need to send an e-mail and identify the link to the starting page of the broadcast. To view the broadcast, the audience member clicks Replay Broadcast on the start page of the presentation.

PowerPoint 2002

Using the Pack and Go Wizard

Occasionally you need to present your slide show using another computer. To transport everything (including your presentation, embedded objects, linked objects, and fonts) to the new computer, you use the Pack and Go Wizard. The Pack and Go Wizard compresses and packages all the necessary files that you'll need to take a presentation on the road. You can also package the PowerPoint Viewer with the presentation. **PowerPoint Viewer** is a program that allows you to view a slide show even if PowerPoint is not installed on the computer. Maria packages the Video Division Final presentation using the Pack and Go Wizard so she can present it at an off-site meeting at a conference center.

Steps

1. Open the file **Video Division Offsite**, click **File** on the menu bar, click **Save As**, click the **Save in list arrow**, navigate to the folder where your Project Files are stored, then click the **Create New Folder button** 📁 in the dialog box toolbar
   The New Folder dialog box opens.

2. Type **PackNGo** in the Name text box, then click **OK**
   The Save in list box changes to the new PackNGo folder. You will save your packaged presentation in this new folder.

3. Click the **Save as type list arrow**, then click **PowerPoint 97-2002 & 95 Presentation**
   Now save the file with a new name.

4. Change the filename in the File name list box to **Video Division Offsite Packed Version**, click **Save**, then click **Yes** in the warning box
   If your original presentation is on your hard disk, you can place the packaged version directly on a floppy disk. If the presentation is too big for one disk, PowerPoint lets you save across multiple floppy disks.

5. Click **File** on the menu bar, click **Pack and Go**, read the screen, then click **Next**
   The Pick files to pack screen opens, as shown in Figure H-20. You indicate here which presentation you would like to package.

6. Make sure the **Active presentation check box** is selected, then click **Next**
   The Choose destination screen opens.

7. Click the **Choose destination option button**, click **Browse**, locate and click the **PackNGo folder** you created, then click **Select**
   See Figure H-21.

8. Click **Next,** click the **Embed TrueType fonts check box** to select it, then click **Next**
   The Links screen opens. There aren't any links in this version of the presentation. The Viewer screen opens. To package the PowerPoint Viewer with your presentation, it needs to be installed on your computer. If the PowerPoint Viewer is not installed on your computer, the Viewer screen displays information on how to download and install the latest PowerPoint Viewer from the Microsoft Office Web site.

9. Make sure the **Don't include the Viewer option button** is selected, click **Next**, read the Finish screen, then click **Finish**
   The Pack and Go Wizard packages the Video Division Offsite presentation. Now you can show this presentation on any computer that has PowerPoint installed.

10. Close the presentation, exit PowerPoint, then delete the PackNGo folder and its contents from the hard drive

FIGURE H-20: Pick files to pack screen in the Pack and Go Wizard

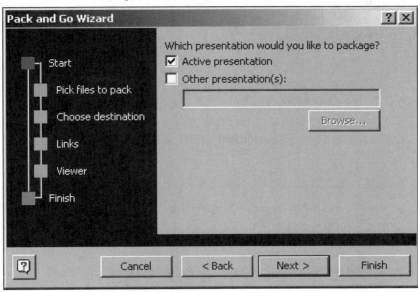

FIGURE H-21: Choose destination screen in the Pack and Go Wizard

CLUES TO USE

Using the Microsoft PowerPoint Viewer

The Microsoft PowerPoint Viewer is a program used to show a presentation on a computer that doesn't have PowerPoint installed. The PowerPoint Viewer is a free program distributed by Microsoft from the Office Web site. You can include the PowerPoint Viewer with your presentation by choosing the Viewer for Microsoft Windows in the Pack and Go Wizard. To view a presentation slide show using the PowerPoint Viewer, open the PowerPoint Viewer dialog box by double-clicking the Ppview32 icon. From the Microsoft PowerPoint Viewer dialog box, you can run a slide show, set Viewer options, and print a presentation. To show a packaged presentation using the PowerPoint Viewer, you must first unpackage the presentation. Locate the folder that contains the packaged presentation, then double-click the pngsetup icon. Extract the presentation to a folder. A message dialog box appears asking if you want to run a slide show; click Yes.

Practice

► Concepts Review

Label each of the elements of the PowerPoint window shown in Figure H-22.

FIGURE H-22

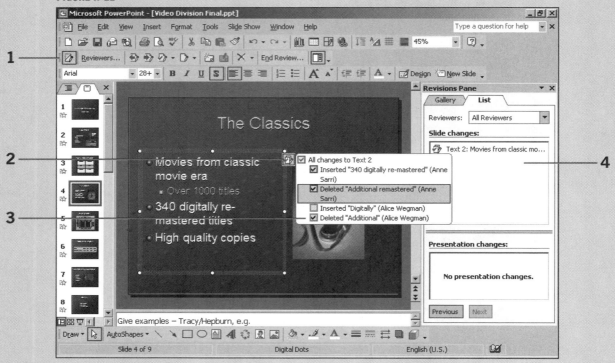

Match each of the terms with the statement that describes its function.

5. A presentation created from selected slides in a presentation
6. An on-screen control button
7. A stand-alone computer that runs a slide show
8. A dialog box that lets you keep track of meeting minutes and action items during a slide show
9. A feature that packages a presentation to take it to another computer

a. Action button
b. Kiosk
c. Custom show
d. Pack and Go Wizard
e. Meeting Minder

Select the best answer from the list of choices.

10. Which method could you use to send a presentation out for review?
   a. Microsoft Outlook
   b. Any 32-bit e-mail program compatible with MAPI
   c. A floppy disk
   d. Any of the above answers

11. Which of the following statements is true about rehearsing your slide timings?
   a. Rehearsing the slides in your presentation gives each slide the same slide timing.
   b. During a rehearsal, you have no way of knowing how long the slide stays on the screen.
   c. If you give your slides random slide timings, you may not have enough time to adequately view each slide.
   d. If you rehearse your presentation, someone on another computer can set the slide timings.

▶ Skills Review

1. **Send a presentation for review.**
   a. Open the presentation PPT H-4 and save it as **KC Series Proposal**.
   b. Send the presentation to yourself for review.
   c. Open Outlook, then make sure the e-mail message was received, then close Outlook.

2. **Combine reviewed presentations.**
   a. Compare and merge the presentation PPT H-5 to KC Series Proposal.
   b. Read but do not accept any comments, then accept all other suggested changes from the reviewer.
   c. End the review, then save your changes.

3. **Set up a slide show.**
   a. Set up a slide show that will be browsed at a kiosk, using slide timings.
   b. Set the slides to appear every three seconds.
   c. Run the slide show all the way through once, then stop it.
   d. Set the slide show to run manually, presented by a speaker.
   e. Put a Forward or Next action button, linked to the next slide, in the lower-right corner of Slide 1.
   f. Copy the action button, then paste it onto all of the slides except the last one.
   g. Move to Slide 2 and place an Action Button: Back or Previous in the lower-left corner. Have it link to the previous slide. Resize the button so it is the same size as the button you created in Step e, and place it at the bottom of the slide, approximately one inch from the left side.
   h. Copy the Back button, then paste it on all of the slides except the first one.
   i. Run through the slide show from Slide 1 using the action buttons you inserted. Move forward and backward through the presentation, watching the animation effects as they appear.
   j. When you have finished viewing the slide show, save your changes.

4. **Create a custom show.**
   a. Create a custom show called **New Series Format** which includes Slides 3, 4, 5, 6, and 7.
   b. Move the two performance slides above the lecture slides.
   c. View the show from within the Custom Shows dialog box, using the action buttons to move among the slides and waiting for the graphics animations. Press [Esc] to end the slide show after viewing the Financing Lectures slide.
   d. Move to Slide 1, begin the slide show, then, when Slide 1 appears, go to the Custom Show.
   e. View the custom slide show, then return to slide view and save your changes.

5. **Use the Meeting Minder.**
   a. Run the slide show beginning at Slide 2, then open the Meeting Minder.
   b. Display the Meeting Minutes tab and enter the following items, pressing [Enter] after each one:
      Work with community liaison committee.
      Do research on literary/cultural profile.
   c. Display the Action Items tab.
   d. Enter an action item with the description 1. **Speak to Marketing for their ideas**. Assign the task to yourself, then change the Due Date to one week from today's date.
   e. Add the note to the Action Items list, click OK, then click [Esc].
   f. Add a Forward or Next action button to Slide 9, and a Back or Previous action button to Slide 10.
   g. In Slide Show view, go through the presentation until the Action Items slide appears.
   h. Open the Meeting Minder, then export the meeting minutes and action items to Word. (Do not post the action items to Outlook.)
   i. Add your name as the first line of the Word document. Save the Microsoft Word document as **ML Action**, print the document, then exit Word.
   j. Close the Meeting Minder dialog box and end the slide show.

6. Rehearse slide timings.

   a. Open the Rehearsal toolbar, set new slide timings, then save your new timings and review them.

   b. Add your name as a footer on notes and handouts, then save your changes.

   c. Print your New Series Format custom show without animations as handouts, 6 slides per page.

   d. Print all the slides in the presentation as handouts, 6 slides per page.

7. Publish a presentation for the Web.

   a. Publish the entire KC Series Proposal presentation for the World Wide Web as **kcpropsl**. Make the page title "Kansas City Series Proposal." Do not include speaker notes, and make it viewable using all browsers listed.

   b. Open the HTML file in your browser and navigate through the presentation.

   c. Close your browser, then close the presentation and PowerPoint.

8. Use the Pack and Go Wizard.

   a. Create a new folder on your hard drive and name it **PackNGo2**.

   b. Save the presentation in the PackNGo2 folder you created, naming it **KC Series Proposal Packed**.

   c. Open the Pack and Go Wizard and specify that you want to pack the active presentation.

   d. For the destination, navigate to the PackNGo2 folder on your hard drive.

   e. Indicate that you want to Embed TrueType Fonts, then don't include the Viewer for Microsoft Windows.

   f. Close the KC Series Proposal presentation, then delete the PackNGo2 folder.

▶ Independent Challenge 1

You work for Pacific Tours, an international tour company that provides specialty tours to destinations in the Pacific Ocean region. You have to develop presentations that the sales force can use to highlight different tours at conferences and meetings. In this challenge, you will use some of PowerPoint's advanced slide show features such as slide builds and interactive settings to finish the presentation you started. Create at least two additional slides for the basic presentation provided on your Project Disk using your own information. Assume that Pacific Tours has a special (20% off regular price) on tours to Bora Bora and Tahiti during the spring of 2004. Also assume that Pacific Tours best-selling tour packages are to the major islands of the Pacific: the Philippines, Japan, Australia, and New Zealand.

   a. Open the file PPT H-6, then save it as **South Pacific** to the drive and folder where your Project Files are located.

   b. Merge the file PPT H-7 to the South Pacific file. Accept all the suggested changes.

   c. Use the assumptions provided to help you develop additional content for your presentation. Use pictures, movies, and sounds provided on the Office CD-ROM or from other media sources to complete your presentation.

   d. Animate the entire chart object so that it dissolves in and have an appropriate sound effect play as it appears.

   e. Create a custom version of the show that can be shown at a trade show kiosk.

   f. Rehearse slide timings.

   g. Use the Meeting Minder to create action items that could result from your presentation. Export the minutes and action items to Word. Add your name as the first line in the document. Save the document as **SP Action Items**, then print it.

   h. Add your name as a footer on all notes and handouts. Print the final slide presentation and all related documents in the format of your choice.

▶ Independent Challenge 2

You work for WorldWide Travel Services, a travel service company. WorldWide Travel is a subsidiary of Globus Inc. Every year in October, WorldWide Travel needs to report to Globus Inc on the past year's activity. Create your own information using the basic presentation provided in the Project File. Assume the following:

- WorldWide purchased major routes from Canada to Asia and the Far East from Canadian AirTours.
- WorldWide's operating expenses run $8 million per quarter.

- Twelve new tour packages to Eastern Europe were created this year. Two of the new tours are The Great Wall Tour and The Trans-Siberian Rail Tour.
- WorldWide hired 35 new employees during the year.

a. Open the file PPT H-8, then save it as **WorldWide**.

b. Use the assumptions provided to help you develop additional content for your presentation. Use pictures, movies, or sounds provided on the Office CD-ROM or from other media sources to complete your presentation.

c. Animate the chart object so it enters from the bottom and have an appropriate sound effect play as it appears.

d. Rehearse slide timings.

e. Create a custom version of your show to run continuously at a conference kiosk, using the timings that you rehearsed.

f. Create a custom version of the show for a specific audience of your choice.

g. Publish the presentation in HTML format, save it as **wrldwide**, then preview it in your browser.

h. Print the final slide presentation and all related documents in the format of your choice.

▶ Independent Challenge 3

You are the assistant director of operations at Pacific Fleet Inc, an international marine shipping company based in San Francisco, California. Pacific Fleet handles 65% of all the trade between Asia, the Middle East, and the West Coast of the United States. You need to give a quarterly presentation to the company's operations committee which outlines the type and amount of trade Pacific Fleet handled during the previous quarter. Plan and create a 10- to 15-slide presentation that details the type of goods Pacific Fleet carried, how much was carried, which companies (foreign and domestic) purchased goods, which companies (foreign and domestic) sold goods, and how much revenue Pacific Fleet earned. You also need to identify the time it took to deliver the goods to their destinations and the delivery cost. Create your own content, but assume the following:

- Pacific Fleet hauled cars and trucks from Tokyo to San Francisco during the last quarter. A car carrier ship can hold 184 cars or 166 pickup trucks.
- Pacific Fleet hauled large tractor equipment and parts made by Caterpillar Tractor and John Deere Tractor from the United States. One ship went to Brazil and one went to Kuwait.
- Typical household goods carried by Pacific Fleet include electronic equipment, appliances, toys, and furniture.
- The cost of hauling goods by ship is $3,380 per ton. Pacific Fleet owns five cargo ships that can operate simultaneously. All five ships were in operation during the last quarter.
- Pacific Fleet hauled a total of 980,000 tons during the last quarter.

a. Create a new presentation, then save it as **Pacific Report Q1**.

b. Use clip art or shapes to enhance your presentation.

c. Use the assumptions provided to help you develop the content for your presentation. Use movies and sounds provided on the Office CD-ROM or from other media sources to complete your presentation.

d. Use Word and Excel to embed or link objects into your presentation. Use the preceding assumptions to develop related information that would be appropriate for a table or worksheet.

e. Set transitions and animations, and rehearse slide timings.

f. Publish your presentation in HTML format, then preview the new version using your browser.

g. Review the lesson on broadcasting, then broadcast your presentation.

h. Print the final slide presentation and all related documents in the format of your choice.

 Independent Challenge 4

You are the sales manager for Music International, an international music distributor of South American music located in Brasilia, Brazil. This year, a large music festival, which showcases different musical groups and styles from all over Central and South America. This year, the festival is being held in Brasilia, and your boss wants you to create a presentation that highlights the variety of musical groups and styles distributed by Music International. There is wide international appeal for South and Central American music, especially in Europe and Asia. The music festival attracts thousands of artists, presenters, recording company representatives, promoters, and fans every year.

a. Open a new presentation, and save it as **Music Pres**.

b. Add your name as the footer on all slides and handouts.

c. Connect to the Internet, then use a search engine to locate Web sites that have information on South American music. You'll need to find the names of at least five South American musical groups. If your search does not produce any results, you might try the following site: www.half.com.

d. Think about what results you want to see, what information you need to create the slide presentation, and how your message should be communicated. Print the pages of the Web sites you use to gather data for your presentation.

e. In order for your presentation to be complete, it must include the following objects: (i) an embedded Word table; (ii) a GIF animation or movie; and (iii) a sound.

f. Title each slide and add main text where appropriate. Create more slides to make the presentation complete.

g. Apply an appropriate slide design. Change the slide design colors as necessary.

h. Create a custom show that focuses on the interest in South American music in Europe and Asia.

i. Spell check the presentation, view the final presentation, save the final version, then print the slides and handouts.

j. Publish the presentation for the Web as **music**, then view the presentation using your Internet browser.

k. Close the presentation, exit PowerPoint, then disconnect from the Internet.

▶ Visual Workshop

Create the slide shown in Figure H-23. Save the presentation as **Sierra Tours**. The clip art is in the Clip Organizer. Set transitions, animations, and slide timings. Insert forward and backward action buttons for this slide. Create a title slide and a third slide with appropriate information. Print the presentation as handouts, 3 slides per page.

FIGURE H-23

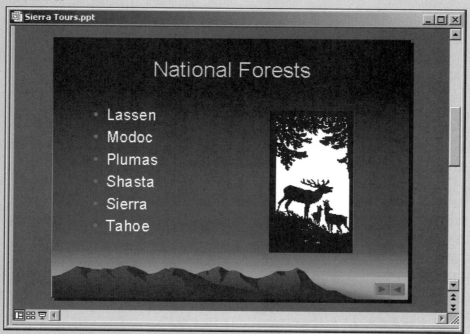

Integrating

Word, Excel, Access, and PowerPoint

Objectives

- ► **Create a PowerPoint presentation from a Word outline**
- ► **Embed a Word table and Excel worksheet into a presentation**
- ► **Insert Access data into an Excel worksheet**
- ► **Analyze Access data in Excel**
- ► **Insert Excel data in a Word document**
- ► **Import Excel data into a PowerPoint presentation**

With Microsoft Office, you can create professional-looking, integrated PowerPoint presentations using not only PowerPoint's built-in tools, but also the formatting and data analysis tools available in Word, Excel, and Access. Because PowerPoint is a part of Microsoft Office, you can exchange files or data easily between PowerPoint and Word, Excel, and Access. ✐ Maria Abbott, MediaLoft's general sales manager, needs to prepare a store evaluation presentation using information she has compiled for the Kansas City store. You will help Maria develop her PowerPoint presentation using information from Word, Excel, and Access.

Creating a PowerPoint Presentation from a Word Outline

When you want to use content from an existing Word document in a PowerPoint presentation, you can simply send the information to PowerPoint using the Send To command from Word. This approach can save you a lot of time because you need not retype or copy the information into PowerPoint. If the Word document is formatted with styles, each level 1 heading becomes a title for an individual slide, and all headings below each level 1 heading become subtitles or bulleted lists. Even if you don't have an existing Word document, you might prefer to create presentation outlines in Word and then send the outline to PowerPoint. In this lesson, Maria uses a Word outline to create a PowerPoint presentation. She then applies a design template to the entire presentation.

Steps

1. Open Word, then open the document **INT G-1.doc** from the drive and location where your Project Files are stored
   A Word document opens.

2. Click **File** on the menu bar, point to **Send To**, then click **Microsoft PowerPoint**
   A new PowerPoint presentation opens, displaying the text from the Word document.

3. Save the new presentation as **KC Store Evaluation.ppt**

4. Click the **Outline tab**, then examine the slides
   Compare your screen with Figure G-1.

5. Click the **Slides tab**, open the Slide Layout task pane, then modify the layout of your slides appropriately
   You may need to change a slide's layout, for example, so that the slide can accommodate a picture or chart.

QuickTip

If you don't find a suitable PowerPoint design template, create one or modify an existing template. If you modify a template, make sure that you rename the template and save it as a presentation template to the location where your Project Files are stored.

6. Click the **Slide Design button** ✎, then select a **design template** of your choice
   As you look through the design templates, keep in mind that the template you choose may affect where large objects, such as charts and tables, appear on your slides. Figure G-2 shows a slide with a template applied.

7. Save your changes, click the **Word program button** on the Windows taskbar, close the file INT G-1.doc, *but do not exit Word*

FIGURE G-1: Word outline inserted into presentation

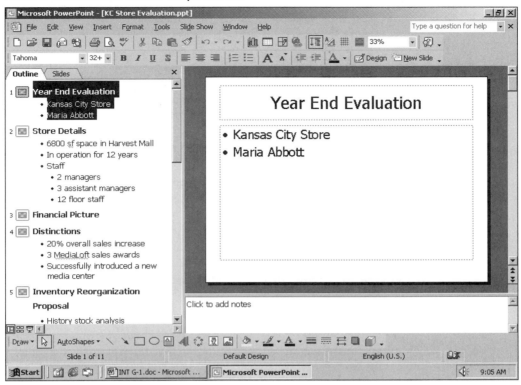

FIGURE G-2: Presentation with new design template

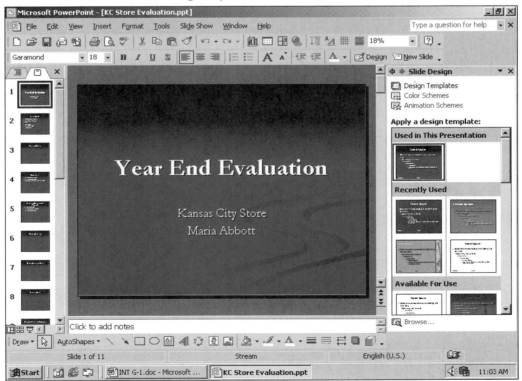

Unit G
Integration

Embedding a Word Table and Excel Worksheet into a Presentation

After changing the design of your slides, you can add objects and change formatting as needed. When you insert content or an outline from another source, such as a Word document, the text or data may not fit the slide design or have the appropriate appearance. Therefore, you may need to change the slide layout or the content on the slide to achieve the desired look. At this stage, you can also decide whether to add data from other programs, such as Excel, to help communicate your message. Maria continues working on her presentation by embedding an object on the Slide Master, and then embedding an Excel worksheet and a Word table.

1. In Word, open the document **INT G-2.doc** from the drive and location where your Project Files are stored
The Word document identifies the overstocked inventory by store in a table.

2. Select the table, then click the **Copy button** 📑 on the Standard toolbar

3. Click the **PowerPoint program button** on the Windows taskbar, click the **Slide 9 thumbnail** in the Slides tab, click **Edit** on the menu bar, then click **Paste Special**
The Paste Special dialog box opens. The Paste Special command allows you to paste the Word table into PowerPoint as an embedded object. Since it's an embedded object, you can double-click the table to open it up in Word to edit or format the content.

4. Click **Microsoft Word Document Object** in the list, then click **OK**
The table is embedded in the slide.

5. Resize the table appropriately, then center it on the slide
Your slide should look similar to Figure G-3.

6. Start Excel, then open the file **INT G-3.xls** from the drive and location where you store your Project Files
The History Overstock worksheet opens.

7. Select the range A3:C8, click 📑, switch to Slide 8 of the PowerPoint presentation, then use the **Paste Special** command to embed the partial worksheet

8. Resize the worksheet, format it using PowerPoint's formatting commands, then save your presentation
Your slide might look similar to Figure G-4.

9. Close both the INT G-3.xls workbook and the INT G-2.doc document

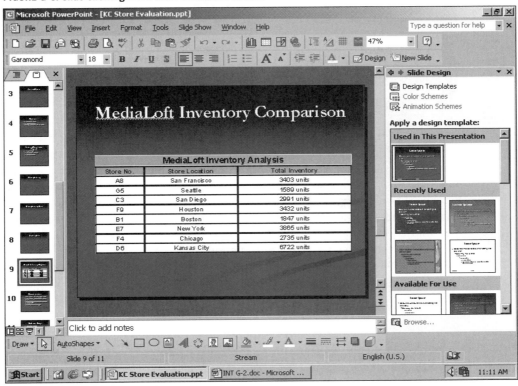

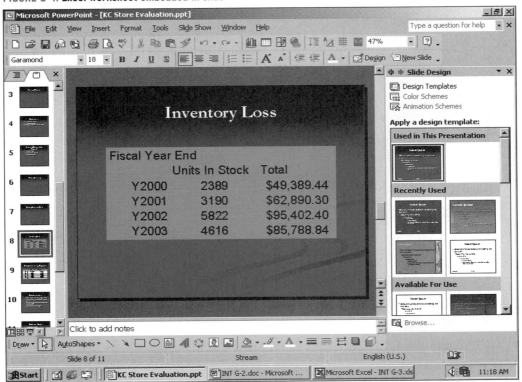

Unit G Integration

Inserting Access Data into an Excel Worksheet

You can import data from an existing Access database into a PowerPoint presentation. To get just the information needed, you retrieve and organize the data in Access, export the information into Excel for analysis and formatting, and finally import the information into the PowerPoint presentation. In this lesson, you'll create a select query in Access and export the data into a new Excel workbook. To emphasize the inventory problem at the Kansas City store, Maria decides to incorporate data from Access into her presentation. To get the appropriate information, Maria first creates a select query in Access, then exports the results of the query to an Excel worksheet so she can analyze the information.

Steps 1 2 3 4

1. Open the Access database **KC Stock List-IG.mdb** from the drive and location where you store your Project Files

2. Create a query named **History Inventory** using the following fields: **AuthorID**, **BookTitle**, **ISBN**, **UnitsInStock**, and **UnitPrice**
   You might want to review the table in Datasheet view.

3. In Datasheet view, sort the results of the query in ascending order by AuthorID, then save the results
   Compare your screen with Figure G-5.

4. Analyze the History Inventory query with Excel
   An Excel worksheet and workbook, named History Inventory opens, displaying the data from the Access query.

5. Save the Excel workbook as **History Inventory List** to the drive and location where your Project Files are stored
   Your screen should look similar to Figure G-6.

6. Save and close KC Stock List database, then close Access

FIGURE G-5: History Inventory query in Datasheet view

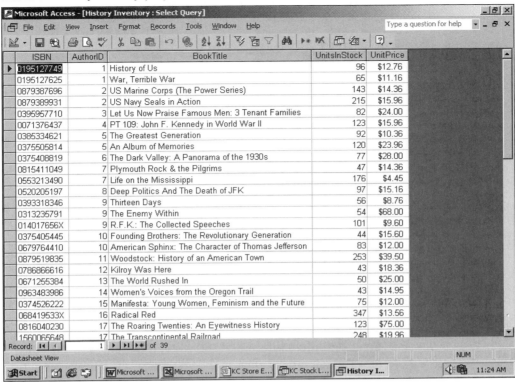

FIGURE G-6: Excel worksheet showing imported Access data

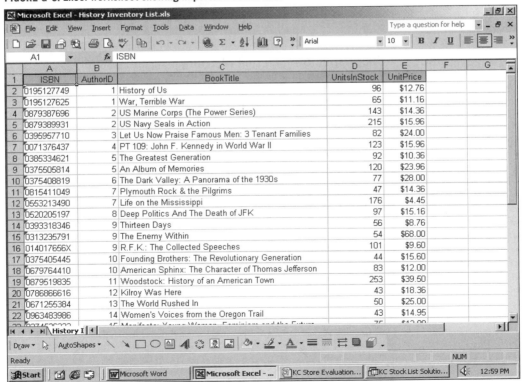

Analyzing Access Data in Excel

When you import data from an Access database into an Excel workbook it may need to be modified for others to understand it. Using Excel's analyzing and organizing features, you can format the data, filter the data, and perform calculations. Importing Access data into Excel can be very helpful when you want to use the Access data in a PowerPoint presentation. In this lesson, Maria hides a column of data that it is not necessary to view, calculates new data, filters and copies data to new worksheets, and then embeds data into her PowerPoint presentation.

1. Hide the Book Title column, then add two columns to the worksheet, titled **Total** and **35%**
   The worksheet should have a total of six columns containing data.

2. Calculate each book's total value in the Total column, then calculate a 35% increase for each book in the 35% column
   Use Excel formulas to calculate all of these figures. 40 rows of data won't fit on a slide, so you will need to divide the data in half so you can embed it into the PowerPoint presentation.

3. Create a new worksheet titled **Top 20**, filter the top 20 items in the Total column, then copy and paste the filtered data and the column headings to the Top 20 worksheet
   Be sure to copy the column headings in the first row of the History Inventory worksheet to the new worksheet.

4. Create a new worksheet titled **Bottom 19**, filter the bottom 19 items in the Total column on the History Inventory worksheet, then copy and paste the filtered data and the column headings to the Bottom 19 worksheet
   Figure G-7 shows how the second new worksheet might look.

5. Copy the data in the Top 20 worksheet, click the **PowerPoint program button** on the Windows taskbar, click the **Slide 6 thumbnail** in the Slides tab, click **Edit** on the menu bar, click **Paste Special**, then link the worksheet to the slide
   The data from the worksheet is linked to the PowerPoint presentation.

6. Follow the same procedure to link the data in the Bottom 19 worksheet to Slide 7 of the presentation

7. Format the linked worksheet objects using PowerPoint's formatting commands, to make them easier to view, then save your work
   Figure G-8 shows a formatted linked object.

FIGURE G-7: Excel worksheet showing filtered data

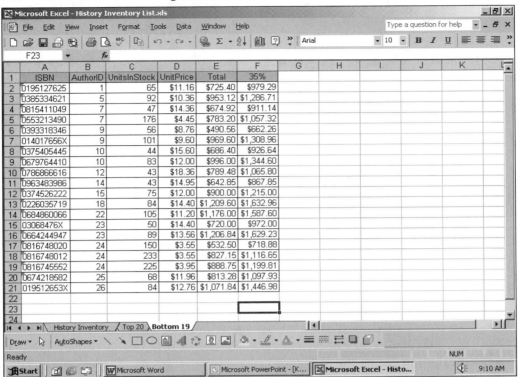

FIGURE G-8: PowerPoint slide showing linked worksheet

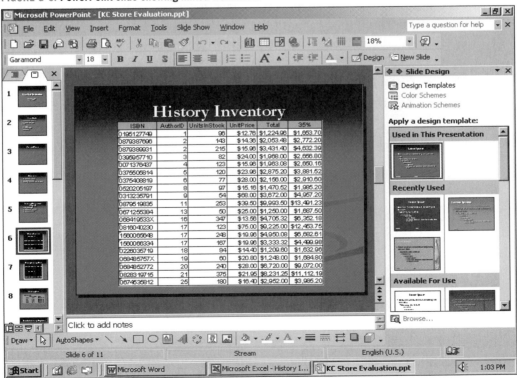

Unit G

Integration

Inserting Excel Data in a Word Document

Trying to explain Excel data in a Word document can be difficult, especially when there are complex calculations involved. A visual object, such as a worksheet or a chart, can really enhance the message of a document and make all the difference in communicating the correct information. ✏️ Maria needs to send her boss, the VP of sales, a memo regarding the inventory data from the Kansas City store. She decides to insert the Excel worksheet directly into her Word document.

Steps 1 2 3 4

1. Click the **Excel program button** on the Windows taskbar, then click the **History Inventory tab**
   The History Inventory worksheet appears.

2. Calculate the total sum for column F in cell F42, calculate the sum total for column G in cell G42, then format both cells using the **Bold button** 🅱 on the Formatting toolbar

3. Unhide the BookTitle column, select the data in the worksheet, then click the **Copy button** 📋 on the Standard toolbar
   The data in the worksheet is selected.

4. Open the Word document **INT G-4.doc** from the drive and location where you store your Project Files, then save it as **Memo to VP**
   The Word document opens.

5. Place the insertion point in the space between the paragraphs, then click the **Paste button** 📋 on the Standard toolbar
   The data from Excel is inserted in the Word document, as shown in Figure G-9. The table needs to be modified to fit in the Word document.

6. Delete the AuthorID and the UnitPrice columns, then adjust the width of the BookTitle column so that the book titles fits on one line
   Compare your screen to Figure G-10.

7. Format the table using Word formatting commands

8. Include your name in the footer of the document, then save and print the document

FIGURE G-9: Data from worksheet pasted in Word document

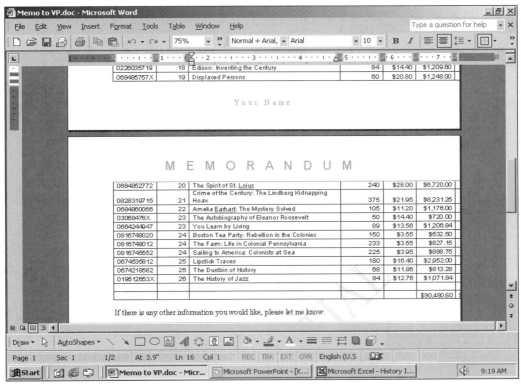

FIGURE G-10: Formatted table in Word document

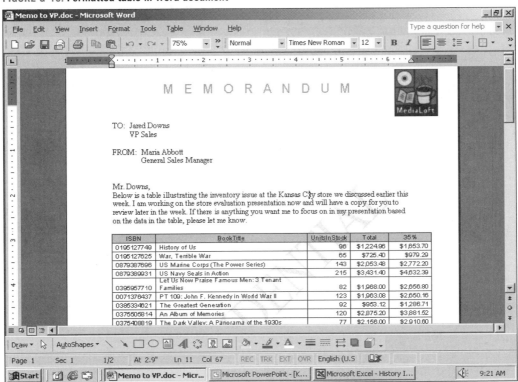

Importing Excel Data into a PowerPoint Presentation

An easy way to create a chart in PowerPoint is to import existing data from Excel using Microsoft Graph. Once you import data into Microsoft Graph and create a chart for your presentation, you don't need to use Excel to change or modify the chart. ✎━━ Maria finishes her work by importing data from Excel into Microsoft Graph and then embedding the chart in a new slide. She evaluates the presentation to verify that it's organized and complete, then creates handouts using Word.

Steps 1 2 3 4

1. Click the **PowerPoint program button** on the Windows taskbar, click the **Slide 3 thumbnail** in the Slides tab, then click the **Insert Chart button** 📊 on the Standard toolbar
   A new chart appears on the slide with default data.

2. Clear the default data in the datasheet, click the first cell in the datasheet, click the **Import File button** 📈, locate the Excel workbook **INT G-5.xls** from the drive and location where your Project Files are stored, then click **Open**
   The Import Data options dialog box opens.

3. Click the **Range option button**, type **A1:D5**, then click **OK**
   The data from the workbook appears in the datasheet.

4. Format the Graph datasheet and chart as needed
   Experiment with the chart's type and 3-D view to determine the best format. Figure G-11 shows an example of how your chart might look.

5. Review the presentation, then make changes as necessary
   You might use clip art, drawn objects, photographs, animated movies, digital movies, or sound to enhance your presentation. Remember, however, that movies and photographs greatly increase the presentation's file size. If necessary, change an object's appearance to better fit with the slide color scheme or slide design. Make sure that the content of the presentation flows logically and is complete. You may need to add or remove some content to complete the presentation.

6. Finish the presentation by checking for spelling errors, then set custom animations, slide timings, and interactive settings for the presentation slides
   Figure G-12 shows an example of how your presentation might look.

7. Send the presentation to Word to create linked handouts, then save the document as **KC Pres Handouts**
   Use the Send To command on the File menu in PowerPoint to create a link between your presentation and a Word document.

8. Include your name on the slides and notes and handouts, save and print the presentation and the handouts, then close all open programs
   You may need two disks to save the entire presentation.

FIGURE G-11: Microsoft Graph datasheet showing imported Excel data

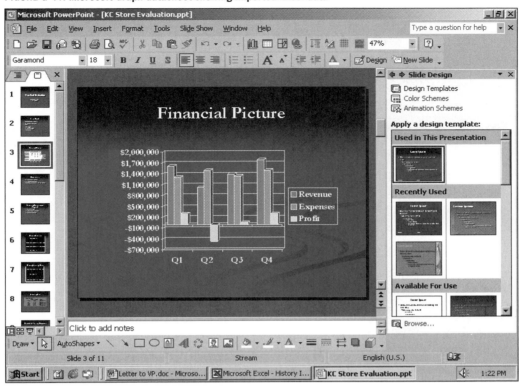

FIGURE G-12: Final presentation

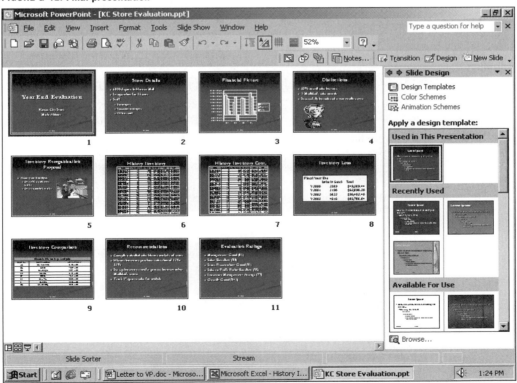

▶ Independent Challenge 1

As a marketing analyst at Davis Press, a publishing company, you have been asked to research a marketing strategy for a new sports magazine that will compete with periodicals such as *Sports Illustrated*. You decide to use PowerPoint to develop a presentation to illustrate your research findings and marketing recommendations.

To help you complete this independent challenge, a partially completed Word document is provided. You will complete the Word outline and then use it as the outline for a new PowerPoint presentation. Assume the following information to be true as you work on the outline and create the presentation:

- The name of the new magazine is *AllSports*.
- Currently, only three magazines have some of the features that the new *AllSports* magazine will offer.
- *AllSports* should appeal to both men and women aged 25–50.
- *AllSports* should include articles on major sports, such as football, baseball, and basketball, as well as sports such as gymnastics, tennis, and fishing.
- The magazine will focus on sports analysis and the people behind the sports.

a. Open the Word document INT G-6.doc from the drive and location where your Project Files are stored, then save it as **AllSports Outline**.

b. Review the partially completed Word document, then replace the italicized text with your own content.

c. Add information to the Word outline that strengthens your presentation.

d. Create a presentation using your completed Word outline, then save it as **AllSports Magazine**. Consider what kind of results you want and how you need to adjust the text in PowerPoint.

e. Preview the presentation and plan the design of each slide. Change the slide layout, if necessary.

f. Apply a template or a shaded background. Customize an existing presentation template or create one of your own.

g. Add or create objects to enhance the slides in your presentation. Analyze each slide to see whether an object might enhance the impact of the text on that slide.

h. Open the Word document INT G-7.doc from the location where you store your Project Files, then save it as **AllSports Table**.

i. Use your own information to add one or more magazine examples and two more categories to the table.

j. Format the table, then embed it into your presentation. Your presentation may look similar to Figure G-13.

k. Spell check the presentation, then set slide show animations and transitions to the slides of your presentation.

l. Include your name as a footer on slides and notes and handouts in the final presentation, then save and print your presentation slides. Close PowerPoint and Word.

FIGURE G-13

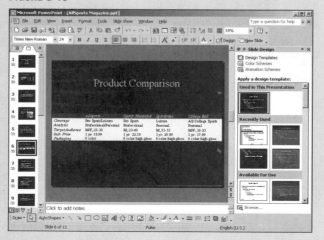

▶ Independent Challenge 2

You are the controller for Health & Goodness Inc. (H&G), a distributor of dried foods. Vomar Ltd., an international food wholesaler located in Madrid, Spain, is purchasing H&G. You need to give a detailed presentation to the chief financial officer at Vomar on the revenue generated by all of H&G's clients during the last quarter. The information you present will help determine the relevant issues regarding the sale.

In this independent challenge, you will analyze an Excel worksheet, then embed the charts that you create into a PowerPoint presentation. Your presentation should be at least 10 slides long. Use the Excel worksheet provided to help complete your presentation.

a. Open the Excel worksheet INT G-8 from the drive and location where your Project Files are stored, then save it as **H&G Sale**.

b. Review the partially completed Excel worksheet. You'll need to create a separate chart for each client.

c. Create an analysis of the data on a separate worksheet that shows the total value for each product.

d. Create similar analyses of the worksheet data that enable you to design charts showing each client's total product revenue as well as the total revenue from all clients.

e. Format each chart appropriately using Excel's formatting tools.

f. Open a new PowerPoint presentation, then save it as **H&G Financial Review**.

g. You may want to use the AutoContent Wizard to help with the basic content of your presentation. Consider the results you want to see in PowerPoint and how you might design the slides of the presentation. Remember, this slide show is primarily a financial presentation showing revenue figures taken from Excel worksheets.

h. Preview the presentation and plan the design of each slide. Change the slide layout, if necessary. If you used the AutoContent Wizard in Step g, change the sample text.

i. Apply a template or shaded background, if necessary. Customize an existing presentation template or create one of your own.

j. Switch to Excel and embed each chart in a different slide for your presentation. Figure G-14 shows an example of an embedded Excel chart in the presentation.

k. Add or create objects to enhance the slides of your presentation as necessary. Analyze each slide to see whether an object might enhance the impact of the text on that slide.

l. Spell check the presentation, include your name as a footer on the slides and notes and handouts, then save your changes.

m. Print your final presentation slides, then close PowerPoint and Excel.

FIGURE G-14

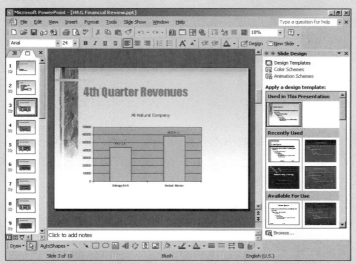

Independent Challenge 3

One of your jobs at XEO Business Systems, a trade consulting company, is to research government census data and then present your findings. You have already compiled much of the information you need; now you need to focus on creating a presentation using your research information. To complete the project, you will download information from the Internet, then create an Excel chart. You will finish the project by creating a PowerPoint presentation, then embedding six Excel charts into the presentation.

a. Connect to the Internet, then use a search engine to locate Web sites that have information on the 2000 census population figures for the states of California, Florida, New York, Pennsylvania, and Texas. If your search does not produce any results, you might try the following link: www.census.gov.

b. Identify the total population for each state.

c. Open the Excel workbook INT G-9 from the drive and location where your Project Files are stored, then save it as **Census 2000**. The workbook identifies the top five retail sales producing states in the United States. The charts in the workbook identify the top five sales categories for each of these states.

d. Create a new worksheet called **Population**, enter the information you retrieved from the Internet, then create a chart.

e. Create a new presentation called **Trade Data**, then enter information that summarizes the data in the Census 2000 workbook.

f. Embed all six charts from the Census 2000 workbook as pictures, using the Paste Special command into your presentation.

g. Format the Excel charts in PowerPoint if needed, then add concluding text to the last slide in the presentation. Include appropriate information to reinforce the message of the presentation.

h. Add an appropriate design template, customize the color scheme, and adjust the placeholders on the master views as necessary.

i. Set slide transitions, slide timings, and custom animations as necessary. Include your name as a footer on the slides and notes and handouts in the presentation.

j. Spell check, save, and print your presentation slides and the Population worksheet.

Getting
Started with Publisher 2002

Objectives

► **Define desktop publishing software**
► **Start Publisher and view the Publisher window**
► **Create a publication using an existing design**
► **Replace text in text boxes**
► **Format text**
► **Resize and move objects**
► **Insert a picture**
► **Save, preview, and print a publication**
► **Close a publication and exit Publisher**

Microsoft Publisher 2002 is a desktop publishing program that helps you transform your ideas into visually appealing publications and Web sites for your business, organization, or home. In this unit, you will learn how to use one of Publisher's existing designs to create a publication that includes text and graphics. Then, you will save and print your publication before closing it and exiting Publisher. ✎ Karen Rosen is the director of human resources at MediaLoft, a nationwide chain of bookstore cafés that sells books, CDs, and videos. Karen is planning the MediaLoft company picnic for the San Francisco–based employees. She uses Publisher to create a flyer announcing the event.

Publisher 2002

Defining Desktop Publishing Software

A **desktop publishing program** lets you integrate text, pictures, drawings, tables, and charts in one document using your personal computer. A document created in Publisher is called a **publication**. You can design a publication from scratch, or you can start with one of Publisher's existing designs and customize it to your needs. Figure A-1 shows three publications created using Publisher's premade designs.  Karen wants the flyer announcing the MediaLoft company picnic to be informative and eye-catching. She decides to create it using one of Publisher's designs. Figure A-2 shows the original design that Karen annotated to show how she will customize it to create the flyer. Karen reviews Publisher's features.

Details

► **Create professionally designed publications**

Publisher includes more than 1,000 premade designs for creating newsletters, flyers, calendars, and many other types of publications. The premade designs include sample text and graphics, a sample layout, and sample color palettes that look great together. You can create publications quickly and easily by starting with a premade design and replacing the text and graphics to suit your needs and tastes. Karen plans on using the Company Picnic flyer design to create the MediaLoft Company picnic flyer.

► **Create a set of publications with a common design**

Publisher includes more than 40 **design sets**, groups of sample publications with the same design theme. You could use a design set to ensure a consistent look for all the printed materials for your company.

► **Change your publication's color scheme**

Publisher includes more than 50 preset color schemes that you can apply to the publications you create using one of Publisher's existing designs. Each color scheme contains five colors that work well together. Karen plans on using the Parrot color scheme in the flyer.

► **Insert text and graphics created in other applications and insert clip art**

You can insert files created in other programs into your publications. You can insert text from a Word file into a company newsletter. You can insert photos, scanned images, or images drawn using Publisher or another drawing program. The Media Gallery, included with Publisher and all Microsoft Office applications, contains thousands of pictures, sounds, and motion clips that you can also add to your publications.

► **Arrange text and graphics easily**

All elements of a publication are **objects**—boxes that contain text or frames that contain graphics that you can easily move, flip, resize, overlap, or color to control the overall appearance of a publication.

► **Choose from preset font schemes and format text easily**

Fonts play a very important role in setting the mood and conveying the message of a publication. A **font** is the typeface or design of a set of characters, such as letters and numbers. Publisher includes 25 **font schemes**, or sets of fonts that look good together. You can also use Publisher's text-formatting features to enhance fonts by adding characteristics such as bold and italics. Karen chooses the Economy font scheme, because it has a casual and fun look.

► **Print publications on your own printer or prepare a publication for commercial printing**

Publisher's commercial printing technology supports process color, spot color and black and white printing, the four major color models (RGB, HSL, CMYK, and PANTONE), and automatic and manual color trapping.

► **Publish to the Web**

You can create professional-looking Web sites using one of Publisher's Web site premade designs. Publisher includes hundreds of Web page backgrounds and animated GIF files. You can also convert an existing publication to a Web page.

FIGURE A-1: Sample Publisher publications

Placeholder text replaced with your text

Placeholder graphic replaced with clip art

FIGURE A-2: Karen's notes for modifying the flyer

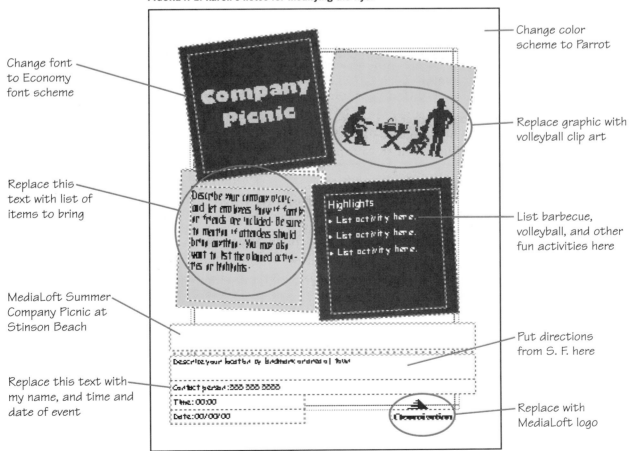

Change font to Economy font scheme

Replace this text with list of items to bring

MediaLoft Summer Company Picnic at Stinson Beach

Replace this text with my name, and time and date of event

Change color scheme to Parrot

Replace graphic with volleyball clip art

List barbecue, volleyball, and other fun activities here

Put directions from S. F. here

Replace with MediaLoft logo

Publisher 2002

Starting Publisher and Viewing the Publisher Window

You start Publisher just as you start any other Windows application—by using the Start menu. When you start Publisher, you see that the screen is divided into two panes. The left pane is called the **task pane**, which is a window that provides the most commonly used commands. Using the task pane, you can create a publication either from scratch or by choosing a premade design and customizing it to meet your needs. The task pane displays different options based on the task you are performing. The right pane, called the **Publications Gallery**, displays thumbnails of existing designs from which you can choose if you don't want to start from scratch. Karen starts Publisher, starts a new blank publication, and takes a look at the important elements of the program.

1. Click the **Start button** ⊞Start on the taskbar, point to **Programs**, then click **Microsoft Publisher**

   Publisher opens. You can see that the screen is divided into two panes, as shown in Figure A-3. The Publication Gallery, on the right side of the screen shows **thumbnails** or small representations, of the Quick Publications, the Publication Type currently selected in the task pane on the left.

2. Click **Blank Publication** in the New section of the task pane

   The task pane and the Publications Gallery close, and a blank one-page publication appears in the publication window, as shown in Figure A-4. The Publisher window displays the following elements:

► The **title bar** contains the name of your publication and the program name. Until you save a publication and give it a name, the temporary name is Publication1. The title bar also contains the Minimize, Restore, and Close buttons.

► The **menu bar** lists the names of menus that contain Publisher commands. Clicking a menu name displays a list of related commands from which you can choose.

► Four **toolbars** appear by default when you start Publisher. The **Standard toolbar** includes buttons for the most commonly used commands, such as opening, saving, or printing a publication. The **Formatting toolbar** contains buttons for the most frequently used formatting commands, such as those for changing the font, and formatting and aligning text. The **Objects toolbar** includes buttons for selecting and creating text boxes, shapes, and picture frames, as well as buttons for working with other types of objects. The **Connect Frames toolbar** gives you options for connecting overflow text from one part of your publication to another.

► The **publication window** includes the **publication page** or pages and a **desktop workspace** for storing text and graphics prior to placing them in your publication.

► The **vertical and horizontal rulers** help you to position, size, and align text and graphics precisely in your publications.

► The **vertical and horizontal scroll bars** work like scroll bars in any Windows program—you use them to display different parts of your publication in the publication window.

► The **status bar**, located below the publication window, displays the position and size of the selected object in a publication and shows the current page. You can use the **Page Navigation buttons** to jump to a specific page in your publication. You can use the **Object Position indicator** to precisely position an object containing text or graphics, and the **Object Size indicator** to accurately gauge the size of an object.

FIGURE A-3: Publisher opening screen with task pane open

New Publication task pane

Click to hide Publication Gallery

Click to open a blank presentation

Ask a Question box

Publication Gallery displays thumbnails of Quick Publications designs

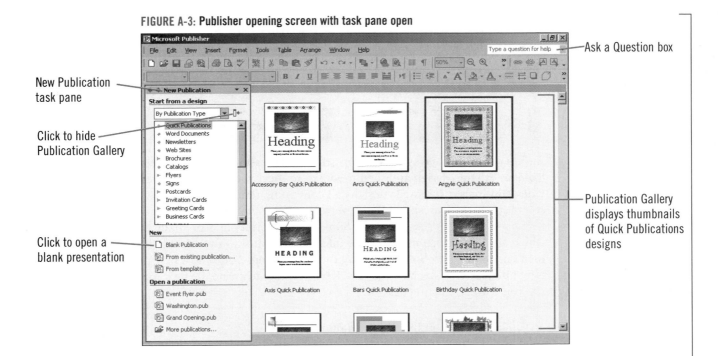

FIGURE A-4: Blank one-page publication

Title bar

Standard toolbar

Objects toolbar

Publication window

Vertical ruler

Status bar

Menu bar

Connect Frames toolbar

Formatting toolbar

Horizontal ruler

Desktop workspace

Publication page

Scroll bars

Page Navigation button

Object Position indicator

Object Size indicator

TABLE A-1: Task pane options available when starting a new publication

area of task pane	options available
Start from a design	Click a publication type from the list, then click a design in the Publication Gallery
New	Start a blank publication from scratch, from an existing publication, or from a template
Open a publication	Open a publication that has been recently opened by clicking its name on the list or click More publications to find a publication on your computer

Publisher 2002

Creating a Publication Using an Existing Design

Although you can always start from scratch, the easiest way to create a publication is to start from an existing design and then modify it to meet your needs and preferences. Publisher provides hundreds of premade designs all containing sample layouts, font schemes, graphics, and colors schemes. You can use the New by Design or the New by Publication Type options in the task pane to access these designs. Some of the objects in a premade design contain **wizards**, which ask you questions about the information you want to include in your publication, and then customize the object according to your answers. You start a new publication by using the New Publication task pane. Karen decides to create the flyer for the company picnic by starting with an existing design.

1. Click **File** on the menu bar, then click **New**
   The task pane opens, displaying options for creating a new publication.

Trouble?

If you don't see any thumbnails click the Show Publication Gallery button ⬚ next to the By Publication Type list arrow.

2. Click **Flyers** in the By Publication Type list at the top of the task pane, then click **Event** in the expanded list of flyer types
   The Publication Gallery displays thumbnails of Event Flyers, as shown in Figure A-5.

3. Click the **Company Picnic Flyer** in the Publications Gallery
   The Company Picnic flyer appears in the publication window. The task pane now displays options for modifying the layout of the flyer.

Trouble?

If a Publisher dialog box opens asking you to enter information about yourself, click OK, then click Cancel in the Personal Information dialog box that appears.

4. Click **Publication Designs** in the task pane
   The Publications Designs task pane displays flyers with the Company Picnic flyer design selected. You can apply a new design at this point by clicking to any one of the designs listed.

5. Click **Color Schemes** in the task pane
   The Apply a color scheme list appears in the task pane. Each color scheme includes five colors that work well together. Trout is the color scheme selected by default for the Company Picnic flyer design.

6. Scroll through the alphabetical list of color schemes, then click **Parrot**
   The Parrot color scheme is applied to the flyer in the publication window.

7. Click **Font Schemes** in the task pane
   A list of named font schemes appears in the task pane, showing 25 predefined sets of fonts that work well together. Font schemes make it possible to change the look of your publication quickly, assigning all text that are major fonts to one style, and all text that are in a minor font to another, ensuring that fonts will be applied consistently throughout your publication.

QuickTip

If you don't like the choice of color scheme or font scheme, you can click the Undo button on the toolbar, then click Undo Color Scheme or Undo Font Scheme.

8. Scroll down the list of font schemes, then click **Economy**
   The new font scheme that includes the Franklin Gothic Demi font and Times New Roman bold is applied to the company picnic flyer. Compare your screen to Figure A-6.

9. Click the task pane **Close button**
   The task pane closes, and the publication window expands to give you more room to work.

FIGURE A-5: Event flyers displayed in Publication Gallery

New Publication task pane

Types of publications listed here

Click to open blank presentation

Click to open a saved publication

Publication Gallery displays thumbnails of event flyers

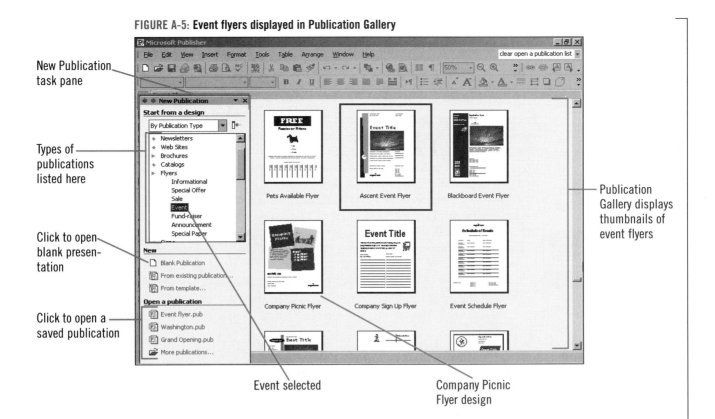

Event selected

Company Picnic Flyer design

FIGURE A-6: Company Picnic flyer with Parrot Color scheme and Economy font scheme

Font Schemes task pane

Click to choose a color scheme

Click to choose Economy font scheme

Logo may differ

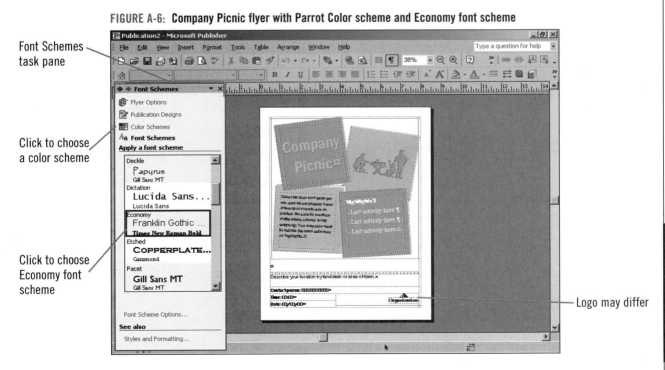

Publisher 2002

Replacing Text in Text Boxes

In Publisher, every element in a publication is contained in a frame. A **frame** is an object that contains text or graphics. A **text box** is a frame that holds text. Before you type in a Publisher publication, you must first create a text box to hold text. Once you create a text box, you can type text directly into it, or you can insert text from a Word document file into it. To enter text in a text box, first you must select it. When you click a text box to select it, **handles** (small circles) appear around its edges. To insert text from a Word document right-click the text box, then use the Change text from file command on the shortcut menu that appears. ✏️ Karen is ready to replace the placeholder text in the flyer with her own text. She types some of the text directly into the text boxes and inserts text describing the company picnic from a Word file she created last week.

Steps 1 2 3 4

1. Click in the center of the **Highlights text box** to select the List Activity placeholder text
   The bulleted placeholder items are selected and handles appear around the text box, indicating that the box itself is also selected. You use the white round handles to resize and move the text box.

2. Press **[F9]**
   Pressing [F9] zooms in on the selected section of your publication, making it easier to see your work in detail. The [F9] key is a **toggle key**—press it once to zoom in, then press it again to zoom back out.

3. Type **Beach Barbecue**, press **[Enter]**, type **Volleyball**, press **[Enter]**, type **Swimming**, press **[Enter]**, then type **Fun in the Sun!**

4. Select the text in the **rectangular text box** below the Highlights text box, then type **MediaLoft Summer Company Picnic at Stinson Beach!**
   The text you typed replaces the placeholder text and takes on the default formatting for the text box.

5. Click in the **Describe your location text box** to select the placeholder text in the frame, then type **Directions: Route 101 North to Highway 1. Take Stinson Beach exit—23 miles north of San Francisco**

6. Select **555 555 5555**, type **your name**, press **[Spacebar]** then type **x5140**

7. Select **00:00**, type **11 AM to dusk**, select **00/00/00**, then type **July 28**
   If you are writing long stories, it's sometimes easier to create the document in Word then insert the file into a text frame in Publisher.

8. Right-click in the blue **Describe your company picnic frame**, point to **Change Text** on the shortcut menu, then click **Text File**
   The Insert Text dialog box opens. You need to locate and then select the file you plan to insert.

9. Click the **Look in list arrow** in the Insert Text dialog box, locate the drive and folder where your Project Files are stored, click the file **PB A-1**, as shown in Figure A-7, then click **OK**
   The placeholder text is replaced with the text from the Word file. Notice that the font of the imported text is in the Economy font scheme.

10. Press **[F9]** to zoom out, if necessary
    Compare your flyer with Figure A-8.

FIGURE A-7: **Insert Text dialog box**

Location of Project Files (yours may be different)

File PB A-1

Click OK to insert the text file

FIGURE A-8: **Company Picnic flyer with placeholder text replaced**

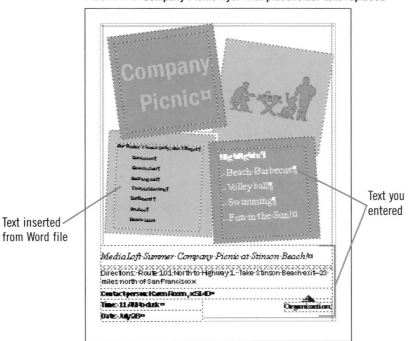

Text you entered

Text inserted from Word file

CLUES TO USE

Creating text boxes

If you need additional text boxes in your publication, or if you are creating a publication from scratch, you can create a new text box easily. To create a text box, click the Text Box button 🖼 on the Objects toolbar. The pointer changes to a crosshair pointer ✛. Position the pointer where you want one corner of the text frame to appear, press and hold the mouse button, then drag diagonally to create a rectangular frame, as shown in Figure A-9. Release the mouse button when the text box is the size and shape that you want. Then you can enter text in the text box by clicking in the frame and typing or inserting a Word file.

FIGURE A-9: **Creating a text box**

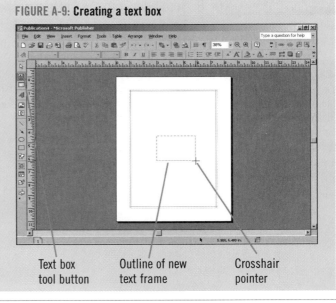

Text box tool button

Outline of new text frame

Crosshair pointer

Formatting Text

Once you enter text in your publication, you can select it and then apply formatting to enhance its appearance. You can format text using the Formatting toolbar, which includes buttons for boldfacing, italicizing, and underlining text, and for changing text alignment and text color. You can easily change the font style and the **font size**, the physical size of the characters measured in points, using the Font Size list arrow on the Formatting toolbar. Another formatting feature is AutoFit. **AutoFit** automatically sizes text to fit it in a text box. ✎ Karen formats the text to make the flyer more attractive and readable. She uses the AutoFit feature to resize text, she changes the font in other text boxes from Times Roman to Franklin Gothic Demi, then she removes bold formatting.

Steps

1. Click in the Highlights text box, press **[F9]** to zoom in, select the word **Highlights**, click **Format** on the menu bar, click **AutoFit Text**, then click **Best Fit**
   All the text in the Highlights text box is now bigger, as shown in Figure A-10. The font and font size of the selected text are displayed on the Formatting toolbar. The font is Franklin Gothic Demi and the font size is 26.7.

2. Press **[F9]** then click in the **For Friday's beach party text box**

3. Press **[Ctrl][A]** to select all the text in the text box, press **[F9]** to zoom in then click the **Font list arrow** on the Formatting Toolbar
   The names of the fonts in the Font list are formatted in the font they represent, making it easier for you to choose among them.

4. Scroll the list of fonts, then click **Franklin Gothic Demi Cond** on the Font drop-down list, as shown in Figure A-11
   The selected text changes to Franklin Gothic Demi Condensed.

5. Click in the Highlights text box, select the bulleted items, click the **Font list arrow**, click **Franklin Gothic Demi**, click the **Font Color list arrow** ▲▾ then click **the black square**
   The bullets now appear in black in Franklin Gothic Demi. The Font Color button now shows the color black, indicating that you can click it to apply black formatting to selected text.

6. Scroll down to the bottom of the publication, select **your name, x5140**, then click the **Bold button** Ⓑ on the Formatting toolbar
   The selected text is now not boldface.

7. Select **11 AM to Dusk**, click Ⓑ, select **July 28**, then click Ⓑ
   The flyer is looking good. The fonts are consistent, and bold is now used to highlight just the headings at the bottom of the flyer.

FIGURE A-10: Autofitting text in a frame

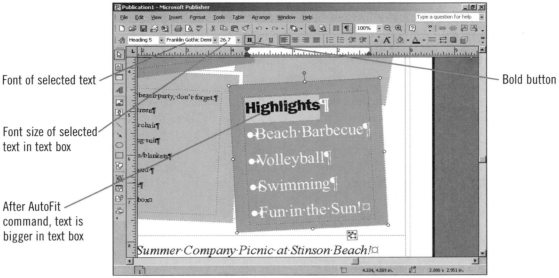

Font of selected text

Font size of selected text in text box

After AutoFit command, text is bigger in text box

Bold button

FIGURE A-11: Choosing a font

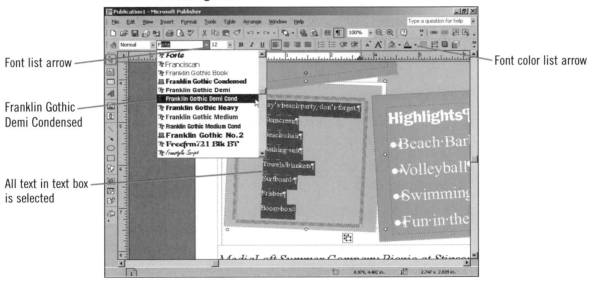

Font list arrow

Franklin Gothic Demi Condensed

All text in text box is selected

Font color list arrow

Spell checking your publication

Before you finalize a publication, you should check it for spelling errors. To have Publisher check for spelling errors in your publication, click Tools on the menu bar, point to Spelling, then click Spelling. In the Check Spelling dialog box, shown in Figure A-12, you can choose to ignore or change the words Publisher identifies as misspelled. You can also add a word to the dictionary. To check the spelling in every text box in your publication, make sure the Check all stories check box is selected in the Check Spelling dialog box.

FIGURE A-12: Check Spelling dialog box

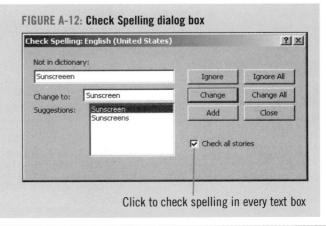

Click to check spelling in every text box

Resizing and Moving Objects

In the course of creating a publication, you might find it necessary to resize or move objects. For example, you might want to make a text box smaller because there is too much white space, or you might want to move a picture closer to its caption. To move or resize an object you must first select it. To resize an object, you drag a handle. To move an object you click anywhere on the object (except on a handle) and drag it to a new location. ✐ Karen resizes the text boxes at the bottom of the flyer to align their right edges. She also decides to move the picture frame up and to the right so that it doesn't overlap the blue text box.

Steps

1. Click the **Directions text box** to select it
   Handles appear around the edges of the text box.

2. Position the pointer over the middle-right handle
   When you position the pointer over a handle, a Resize pointer appears. Depending on the handle, the pointer will be either a horizontal, vertical, or diagonal resize pointer. See Table A-2 for a list of common pointer shapes. The rulers can be used as guides to precisely align objects as you resize and move them. A line will move along the ruler as you move the object, to guide your placement.

Trouble?

If the rulers do not appear, click View on the menu bar, then click Rulers.

3. Drag the **middle-right handle** left to the 6" mark on the horizontal ruler, as shown in Figure A-13
   The text automatically wraps to fill the resized text box area.

4. Select the **Contact person text box**, then drag the **middle-right handle** to the 6" mark on the horizontal ruler

5. Resize the **Time** and **Date frames** to align their right edge with the 6" mark on the horizontal ruler and the Contact and Directions text boxes

QuickTip

To change the length and width of a frame at the same time, drag a corner handle. To keep the center of the frame in the same location, press [Ctrl] as you drag.

6. Scroll to the top of the flyer and position the pointer over the **picnic graphic** in the blue frame
   The pointer changes to the Move pointer 🖫. You use this pointer to move any Publisher object.

7. Click and drag the **picnic graphic** up and to the right slightly until it doesn't touch the other blue frame, then release the mouse button
   You actually dragged two objects at once. This is because the frame and the graphic are grouped together, as indicated by the Ungroup objects button 🔳 located just below the blue frame. The handles still surround the blue frame, with a green rotation handle at the top. You can adjust the angle of any object by dragging the rotation handle.

QuickTip

If you make a mistake, click the Undo button 🔄 on the Standard toolbar.

8. Drag the rotation handle of the picnic frame to the right ¼", then press **[F9]** to zoom out and see the entire publication
   The blue picture frame is now more sharply angled. Compare your screen to Figure A-14.

FIGURE A-13: **Resizing an object**

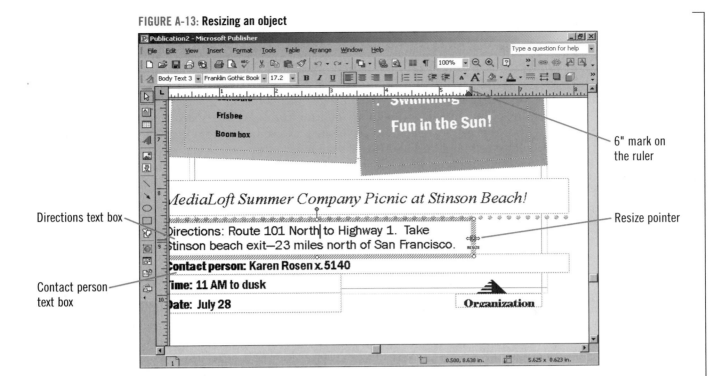

6" mark on the ruler

Directions text box

Resize pointer

Contact person text box

FIGURE A-14: **Moving and rotating object**

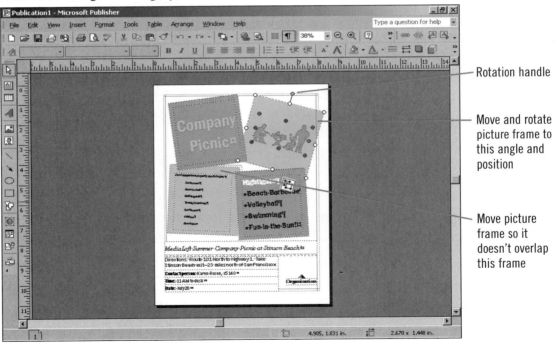

Rotation handle

Move and rotate picture frame to this angle and position

Move picture frame so it doesn't overlap this frame

TABLE A-2: **Common Pointer Shapes**

pointer shape	use to	pointer shape	use to
	Resize an object in the direction of the arrows	+	Draw a frame
	Move an object to a new location		Crop an object
	Drag selected text to a new location		Insert overflow text
	Rotate an object		

Inserting a Picture

Publications usually include both text and graphics. With Publisher, you can insert many types of graphic images into your publications, including clip art, images created in other applications (such as a logo or a chart), scanned images, or photographs taken with a digital camera. The Microsoft **Clip Organizer** is a library of art, pictures, sounds, video clips, and animations that all Office applications share. You can easily preview images from the Clip Organizer and insert them into your publications. Also, you can insert other images that are stored on a disk directly into your publication. Karen replaces the placeholder clip art in the flyer with an image of a volleyball in motion from the Clip Organizer. She also replaces the placeholder logo with the MediaLoft logo.

Steps

1. Click **View** on the menu bar, then click **Task Pane**
   The task pane opens.

   > **Trouble?**
   > If the Add Clips to gallery dialog box appears asking if you would like to catalog all your media files, click Later.

2. Click the blue frame containing the picnic graphic, click the **picnic graphic** to select it, right-click the **picnic graphic**, point to **Change Picture**, then click **Clip Art**
   The Insert Clip Art task pane opens.

3. Click in the **Search text box**, type **volleyball**, then click **Search**
   The Results window in the task pane appears, and images relating to volleyball appear. It may take a minute or two to display all the images.

   > **Trouble?**
   > If you don't see the image shown in Figure A-15, click another image.

4. Click the first **volleyball image** in the Results window
   The volleyball image replaces the picnic table image on the flyer, as shown in Figure A-15. Your search results may be different.

5. Click the **logo placeholder** in the lower-right corner of the flyer, then click the **Wizard button** beneath the logo placeholder
   The Logo Designs task pane opens. You can use these options to create a new logo or to modify an existing one.

6. Click **Logo Options** in the task pane, click **Inserted picture**, then click **Choose picture**
   The Insert Picture dialog box opens.

7. Click the **Look in list arrow**, locate the drive and folder where your Project Files are stored, click **PB A-2**, wait for the preview of the image to appear, then click **Insert**
   The MediaLoft logo replaces the placeholder in the flyer.

8. Close the task pane

9. Press **[F9]** to zoom in on the logo if necessary, drag the **upper-left handle** to resize the logo picture frame until it reaches 6" on the horizontal ruler and 8½" on the vertical ruler, as shown in Figure A-16, then release the mouse button
   Congratulations, you have successfully completed the flyer!

FIGURE A-15: Clip Art search results

Click to insert this image in flyer

Results of search for volleyball images. Your results might be different

Volleyball image replaces picnic image in frame

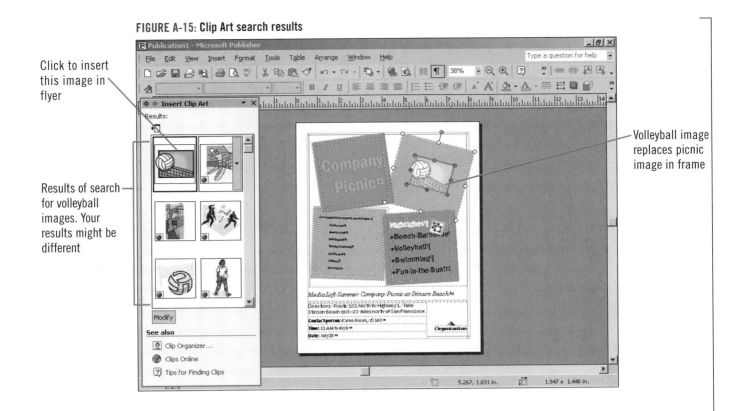

FIGURE A-16: Resizing MediaLoft's logo

Logo sized to 8½" mark on vertical ruler

Resize pointer

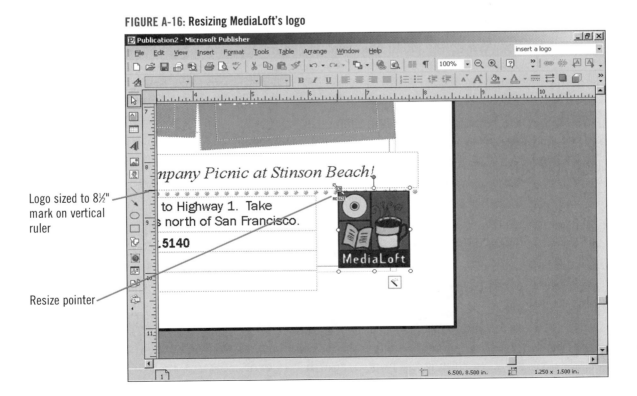

Saving, Previewing, and Printing a Publication

You need to save your work in order to store it permanently on a disk. You should save your work every 10 to 15 minutes, after any significant changes that you don't want to lose, and before you print your publication. By default, Publisher automatically saves your work every 10 minutes, so you can take advantage of the AutoRecover feature if you lose power or if you have a system problem. To save a file for the first time, you can use the Save or Save As command, or click the Save button on the Standard toolbar. After you've named the file, you must save any new changes to the publication. Once you have saved a publication, you can print it using the Print command. It's a good idea to proofread your publication before you print so that you can catch and fix any mistakes. Karen saves the flyer, checks it for mistakes, then prints it so she can distribute it to the MediaLoft employees.

QuickTip
After you've saved your publication for the first time, click the Save button 🖫 on the Standard toolbar to quickly save changes to your publication.

1. Click **File** on the menu bar, then click **Save**
   The Save As dialog box opens.

2. Click the **Save in list arrow**, locate the drive and folder where your Project Files are stored, type **Picnic** in the File name text box, compare your dialog box with Figure A-17, then click **Save**

3. Click **No** in the alert box that opens asking if you want to add the MediaLoft logo to your personal information set

4. Click **View** on the menu bar, point to **Zoom**, then click **Whole Page**
   The zoom level adjusts so that the whole page fits in the publication window. When you change the zoom level, you can select a specific zoom percentage, or a specific view. You can also click the Zoom list arrow on the Standard toolbar to change the zoom level.

QuickTip
Press [Ctrl][P] to quickly access the Print dialog box. Click the Print button 🖨 on the Standard toolbar to print the publication with the current settings.

5. Click **File** on the menu bar, then click **Print**
   The Print dialog box opens, as shown in Figure A-18.

6. Make sure the number of copies is **1**, then click **OK**
   Your publication prints in color if you have a color printer, or in black and white if you don't have a color printer. Figure A-19 shows a copy of the completed flyer.

Using the Pack and Go Wizard

When you want to take your publication to another computer or to a commercial printing service, you can use the Pack and Go Wizard to assemble and compress all the files necessary for viewing and printing your publication in a different location. Packing your publication (that is, including the fonts and graphics that you used in your publication) ensures that it will look the same on another computer as it does on yours. If you're packing your publication to disks, Publisher automatically compresses and splits the files so they fit on multiple disks and includes a program to unpack the files on other computers. To use the Pack and Go Wizard, click File on the menu bar, point to Pack and Go, then click Take to Another Computer or Take to a Commercial Printing Service. Read the Wizard screens and make your selections, click Next after each choice, then click Finish when you have answered all of the Wizard's questions.

FIGURE A-17: **Save As dialog box**

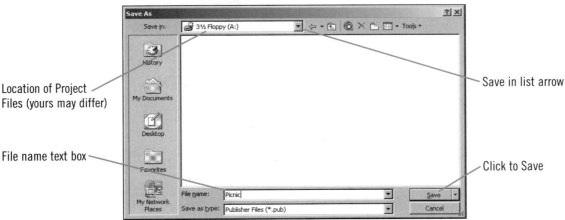

Location of Project
Files (yours may differ)

Save in list arrow

File name text box

Click to Save

FIGURE A-18: **Print dialog box**

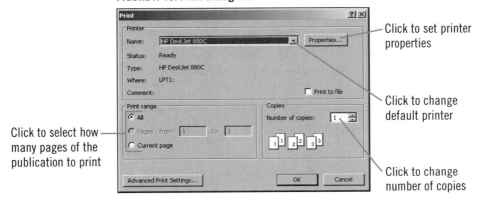

Click to set printer
properties

Click to change
default printer

Click to select how
many pages of the
publication to print

Click to change
number of copies

FIGURE A-19: **Completed publication**

Closing a Publication and Exiting Publisher

Publisher 2002

When you are finished working on a publication, you need to close it. You close a publication by using the Close command on the File menu. When you are finished working with Publisher, you can exit the program by using the Exit command on the File menu. ✐ Karen closes the flyer and exits Publisher.

Steps

1. Click **File** on the menu bar, then click **Close**, as shown in Figure A-21

2. If an alert box appears asking if you want to save changes before closing, click **Yes** to save your changes

   The flyer closes and a new, blank publication appears in the Publisher window. You can create a new publication or open an existing publication. If you are finished working with Publisher, you can exit the program.

3. Click **File** on the menu bar, then click **Exit**, as shown in Figure A-22

   The program closes; Publisher is no longer running.

Getting Help

Publisher includes an extensive Help system that you can use to learn about features and commands. You can get help while working with Publisher by using the Office Assistant, by using the Help menu, or by typing a question in the Ask a Question box. The Office Assistant, shown in Figure A-20, is an animated character that gives context-appropriate tips while you work. To get Help from the Office Assistant, simply click the Office Assistant, then type your question. This unit assumes that the Office Assistant is hidden. If the Office Assistant appears on your screen, you can hide it by right-clicking the character then clicking Hide on the shortcut menu. If you've hidden the Office Assistant, press [F1] to have it reappear, and ask for help. If you've turned off the Office Assistant, you can click Help on the menu bar then click Microsoft Publisher Help. To access Help online, click Help on the menu bar, then click Office on the Web. You must be able to connect to the Internet to access the Web site.

FIGURE A-20: **Office Assistant**

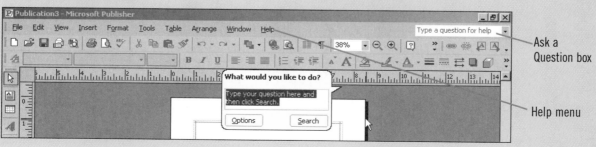

Ask a Question box

Help menu

FIGURE A-21: Closing a publication

File menu ——

Click to close a
publication ——

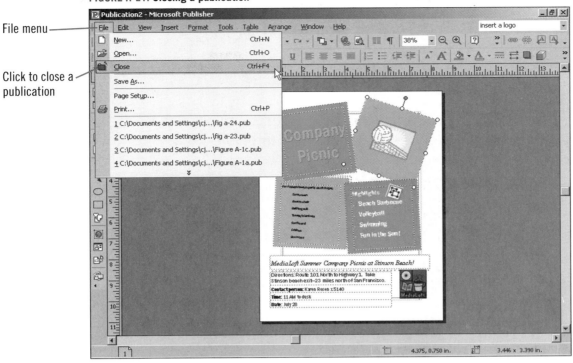

FIGURE A-22: Exiting Publisher

Click to close
publication and
exit Publisher at
the same time

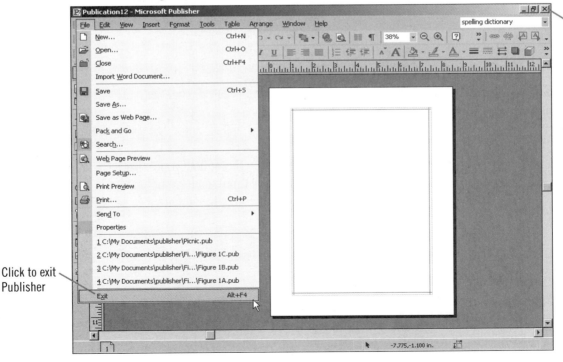

Click to exit
Publisher ——

Practice

► Concepts Review

Label each element of the Publisher window shown in Figure A-23.

FIGURE A-23

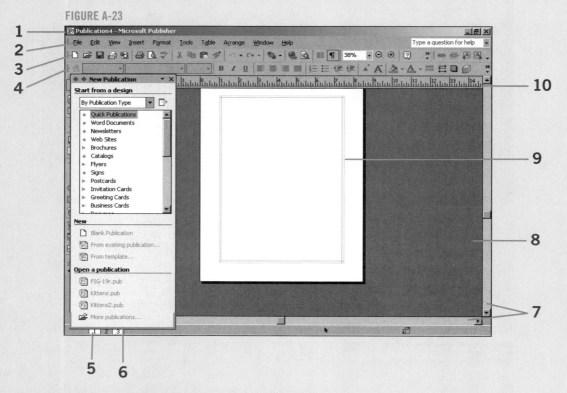

Match each term with the statement that describes it.

11. **Clip Organizer**
12. **Color scheme**
13. **Handles**
14. **Text box**
15. **Font scheme**

a. Object that contains the words in the publication, and can be moved or resized

b. Library of art, pictures, sounds, video, and animations that all Office programs share

c. Preset colors used consistently throughout a publication

d. Preset fonts used consistently throughout a publication

e. Circles that appear around a frame to indicate it is selected

► Skills Review

1. **Start Publisher and view the Publisher window.**
   a. Start Publisher and open a blank publication.
   b. Identify as many parts of the publication window as you can without referring to the unit material.

2. **Create a publication using an existing design.**
   a. Start a new publication.
   b. In the task pane, select the Apartment for Rent Flyer from the Sale Flyers category.

   c. Change the color scheme to Tropics.

   d. Change the font scheme to Facet, which includes the font Gil Sans MT.

3. Replace text in text boxes.

   a. Close the task pane, zoom as needed, then type 6/1/03 for the Available date.

   b. Select the Amount of rent text box, then type the following information, pressing [Enter] after each bullet except the last:

     $1,000/month, 12-month lease, $2,000 deposit required, 2 bedrooms, 2 bathrooms, View of ocean, Access to boat dock, Nonsmokers only, 10-minute walk to shopping.

   c. Select the Describe your location text box, then insert into the text box the text file PB A-3.

   d. Select the text in the Contact person frame, and replace the text with **Call your name for more information: (978) 555-1000.**

   e. Select one of the tear-off Name text boxes at the bottom of the flyer, then type your name and the phone number (978) 555-1000. (*Hint*: Click a text box to select it, then start typing.)

   f. Click another tear-off Name text box to update all the other text boxes with your name and phone number.

4. Format text.

   a. Select the first tear-off Your Name text box, then press [Ctrl][A] to select all of the text in the frame.

   b. Bold the text in that text box, then click another Your Name text box to format all the other text boxes.

   c. Italicize the text in the Available frame. (*Hint*: Scroll if necessary to locate the frame.)

   d. Reduce the font size of the text in the $1,000/month text box to 14 points. (*Hint*: Click the Decrease Font Size button on the Formatting toolbar.)

   e. Change the text color of the Call your name text box to red. (*Hint*: Use the Font Color button on the Formatting toolbar to choose another color in the scheme.)

   f. Select the Located in text box, press [Ctrl][A], then format the text to AutoFit, best fit.

5. Resize and move objects.

   a. Drag the right-middle resizing handle of the Located in frame to the 4¼" mark on the horizontal ruler.

   b. Select the Call Your Name text box, drag the middle-left resizing handle to the 4¼" mark on the horizontal ruler.

   c. Drag the Call Your Name text box up to the 7" mark on the vertical ruler to position it next to the Located in text box.

   d. Select the Located in text box and drag the lower-middle resizing handle down to the 8" mark on the vertical ruler. The text automatically resizes because you set it to AutoFit.

   e. Press [F9] to zoom back out and see more of your publication.

6. Insert a picture.

   a. Double-click the house picture frame at the top of the flyer to open the Insert Clip Art task pane. (If a dialog box opens asking if you want to catalog your media files, click Later. If the Format AutoShape dialog box opens, you clicked the graphic. Close the dialog box and try again.)

   b. Type apartment in the Search box, click Search, then insert one of the images in the Results box.

   c. Close the Insert Clip Art task pane, then resize the image if necessary.

7. Save, preview, and print a publication.

   a. Save the publication as Apartment to the drive and folder where your Project Files are located.

   b. Switch to Whole Page view to proof your publication and make any last-minute changes.

   c. Save your changes, then print your publication.

8. Close a publication and exit Publisher.

   a. Close the publication, then exit Publisher.

▶ Independent Challenge 1

Your cat has just had kittens and you would like to place them in good homes. You decide to use a Publisher template to create a flyer to post at the local veterinary clinic.

a. Start Publisher, use the New from Existing Publication task pane and select the Pets Available Flyer from the Sale Flyers category.

b. Using Figure A-24 as a guide, replace the placeholder text and format that text. Use the Wildflower color scheme.

c. Replace the Describe text frame with the text file PB A-4.

d. Replace the placeholder kitten graphic with a cat of your choosing from the Media Gallery and size the image appropriately.

e. Replace the name Trey with Your Name in the Please call text box and in the tear-off Kittens frames.

f. Save the publication as **Kittens**.

g. Proof the flyer for mistakes, print and close the publication, then exit Publisher.

FIGURE A-24

▶ Independent Challenge 2

You've volunteered to create a home page for your son's elementary school's Web site.

a. Start Publisher, then choose the School Web Site design from the Web Sites category in the New Publication task pane.

b. Choose Sunrise as the color scheme, and Galley as the font scheme.

c. Replace the placeholder text with the text in Table A-3. (*Hint*: Click No in the Autoflow dialog box.)

d. Increase the size of the Vision text box by dragging the lower-middle resizing handle to the 8½" mark on the vertical ruler. Autofit the text.

e. Delete the empty text box at the bottom of the page under the School address frame. Increase the size of the school address frame by dragging the bottom edge of the frame to the 13" mark on the vertical ruler.

f. Apply bold formatting to Vision and Mission, and change the text color to Red. (*Hint*: Use the Font Color button.)

g. Delete the placeholder logo.

h. Save the publication as **Washington**.

i. Proof your publication, print and close the publication, then exit Publisher.

TABLE A-3

placeholder text frame	replace with
Home Page Title	**Washington Elementary School**
Your home page….	Text File PB A-5 (Click No to have Publisher fit the text.)
Your business tag line here	**Making Education Count!** (*Hint*: Resize frame so that text fits.)
Frame below "To contact us"	*Your Name* **Washington Elementary School** **23 School Street** **Waverly, WA 98722**

Independent Challenge 3

Create a calendar for next month using a Publisher template.

a. Start Publisher, click the Calendar category, then select a full-page calendar template from the New Publication task pane.

b. On the Calendar options task pane, choose the monthly option and change the date range from the beginning of next month to the end of next month. Do not include a schedule of events.

c. Choose a color and font scheme of your choice.

d. Replace the placeholder text with text of your own, making sure to include your name somewhere on the calendar. Format the text appropriately, and customize the logo if a logo placeholder is part of the template. Replace any clip art with appropriate images.

e. Save the publication as **Calendar**. Click No if asked to save the logo to the Primary Business personal information set.

f. Proofread and spell check your publication, print and close the publication, then exit Publisher.

Independent Challenge 4

You own a small travel agency and have put together a five-day tour package to London. You plan to create a brochure providing information to prospective tour guests about the package. To complete the flyer, you will first need to do some research on the Internet about London.

a. Use a search engine site such as Google (www.google.com) or AltaVista (www.altavista.com) and research the following information:

1. Name and street address of 5-star hotel
2. Name of art museum, with specific exhibit mentioned
3. Name of another museum that is not art-related
4. Shopping at <insert names of two shopping districts or stores>
5. One nightlife activity (such as a cabaret, disco, or comedy club) providing the name of the locale
6. Sightseeing activity of your choosing.

When you've gathered all your information, you are ready to create the flyer. To create the flyer:

b. Start Publisher. In the New Publication task pane, select the 3 Picture Product Flyer in the Sale Flyers category.

c. Replace the Product Title Placeholder text with **5 Days in London**. Replace the text in the Product Heading text box with **Theatre, museums, and more!**

d. In the text box directly below Theatre, museums, and more! replace the placeholder text with file PB A-6. Click No in the autoflow dialog box, then resize the text box so the text fits. Change the font to Franklin Gothic Book 12 point.

e. In the List feature here frame, replace the placeholder bullets with six bullets of your own, providing information on the items you researched. Use step A as a guide for creating the bullets.

f. Replace the three placeholder graphics on the flyer with clip art images from the Clip Organizer.

g. Include a logo at the bottom of the flyer for Cultural Excursions, Inc., using the Font Focus logo.

h. In the Contact person frame, replace the placeholder text with **Call Your Name for pricing and reservations**. Add a phone number.

i. Save the flyer as **London**.

j. Check the spelling, print and close the publication, then exit Publisher.

Publisher 2002

▶ Visual Workshop

Create the flyer shown in Figure A-25 using the Ascent Event design in the Event Flyer category. Use the Field color scheme and the Verbatim font scheme. Replace the placeholder photo and graphics with the clip art shown. (*Hint*: Open the Insert Clip Art task pane, then search for **Fish**. If the images shown are not available, choose other ones.) Drag the green rotation handle to rotate the fish in the green and black rectangles 90 degrees to the right. To create the logo, click the Logo Wizard button to open the Logo Designs task pane, then choose the Open Oval design. (*Hint*: To add the fish graphic to the logo at the bottom of the page, right-click the graphic placeholder, click Change Picture, click Clip Art to open the Insert Clip Art task pane, then type **fish** in the Search text box.) Add your name to the Call frame. Autofit the text in every frame except the Date, Time, and Call Your Name frames. Save the publication as **Grand Opening** in the drive and folder where your Project Files are stored, then print a copy.

FIGURE A-25

Working
with Text and Graphics

Objectives

▶ Plan a publication
▶ Create columns of text
▶ Work with overflow text
▶ Use guides
▶ Create picture captions
▶ Create headers and footers
▶ Insert and format WordArt
▶ Wrap text around objects
▶ Layer and group objects

Publisher provides you with a wide array of tools to help you work with text and graphics. In this unit, you will learn how to create a newsletter. You will place text in columns and learn how to manage text that doesn't all fit in one text box. Then, you will insert a caption for a picture and learn how to wrap text around that and other objects. You will learn how to insert headers and footers that appear on every page of your publication. You will also create and format WordArt and learn about layering and grouping objects. ✎ Karen Rosen produces a quarterly newsletter called *LoftLife* for MediaLoft employees. Karen starts by planning the content of the newsletter. Then, she uses the skills covered in this unit to create it.

Planning a Publication

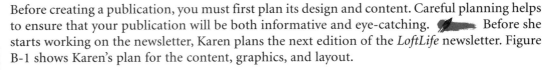

Before creating a publication, you must first plan its design and content. Careful planning helps to ensure that your publication will be both informative and eye-catching. Before she starts working on the newsletter, Karen plans the next edition of the *LoftLife* newsletter. Figure B-1 shows Karen's plan for the content, graphics, and layout.

► What layout to use

Choosing the layout is the first decision you need to make in planning a multipage publication. Either you can use one of the many sample designs that Publisher provides and customize it to meet your needs, or you can start from scratch. No matter which option you choose, you need to decide up front how many columns of text the publication will have, as well how many pages, it will be. You also need to decide how you want it to look when printed. For example, will the pages be folded or printed back to back? Karen uses the same newsletter design for each issue of *LoftLife* so that all issues have the same look and feel. For this issue, Karen decides to change the layout of the inside pages of the newsletter from three columns to two. As in the last issue, the pages will not be folded but will be printed back to back.

► What text to include and how to present it

Once you've chosen your layout, you then need to decide on your content. Write a list of all the articles you plan on including, like the one Karen created in the first column of Figure B-1. Then decide how you want to present your content. In a publication you can present text in two ways—either as a story or as a table. A **story**, also called an article, is comprised of text and is meant to be read from beginning to end. A **table** contains text or numbers in columns and rows. Use tables to organize information so that it is easy to read at a glance, such as the table of contents. Karen lists all the stories the *LoftLife* Editorial board picked for this issue.

► Where to place your text

Next, you have to plan where to place each story and table in the publication. Sometimes, all the text for a particular story won't fit in one text box, and needs to continue into another text box in a different part of the publication. This type of text is called **overflow text**. In the plan in Figure B-1, Karen notes that she needs to use overflow text for the Common Review Date story on page 1; she plans to continue it on page 4.

► What pictures and captions to include

Once you've settled on your stories, it's time to plan for graphics. A **picture caption** is a description that appears adjacent to a picture. When you add a picture or any object to your publication, you can choose to have Publisher wrap the text around that object or around the object's frame. **Wrapping** means that the text flows around the object rather than over it. Karen plans to wrap text around graphics for four stories in the newsletter.

► What content should appear on every page

A **header** is information that appears at the top of every page in your publication. A **footer** is information that appears at the bottom of every page in your publication. Karen will put the Volume and Issue number in the header of the newsletter, and will add a footer containing page numbers. She will specify not to show the header and footer on page 1.

► What special effects to include

Publisher gives you many tools to create special effects. For example, you can add **WordArt**—text that Publisher treats as a graphic. You can also add a pull quote or sidebar. A **pull quote** is a quotation from an article that is pulled out and treated like a graphic. A **sidebar** is text that is set apart from the major text but in some way relates to that text. You can also create unique effects by layering objects on top of each other to add depth and dimension to your publication. Figure B-2 shows the first page of the completed newsletter.

FIGURE B-1: Karen's content, layout, and graphics plan for the March issue of *LoftLife*

Stories for March issue →

Requires overflow text →

Stories	Page	Contributor	Graphics
A Word from Our President	1	Leilani Ho	Insert pull-quote and wrap text around it; add Success graphic at end
Common Review Date	1, 4	Me	
Loftlife Needs You (sidebar)	1	Me	
Vision Service Plan	2	Jim Fernandez	Wrap text around Owl picture
401K Notes	2	John Kim	
Employee Advisory Resource	2	Me	Wrap text around EAR WordArt
Slaves to Fashion	3	Elizabeth Reed	Wrap text around pull quote between columns
They Asked for What?	4	Elizabeth Reed	

FIGURE B-2: Printout of page 1 of the completed newsletter

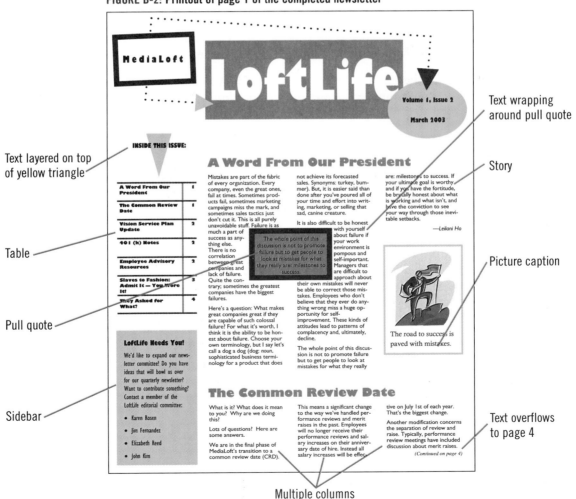

Text layered on top of yellow triangle

Table

Pull quote

Sidebar

Text wrapping around pull quote

Story

Picture caption

Text overflows to page 4

Multiple columns

Creating Columns of Text

Formatting text in columns can make text easier to read, and more visually appealing. To create columns, either you can choose a Publisher design that includes columns, or you can format text into columns using the options on the Newsletter Options task pane. Karen has been working on the newsletter for a few days. She used a Publisher sample design to create the newsletter, and then she replaced the placeholder text and graphics with the content for *LoftLife*. Today, she plans to finish the newsletter. She begins by opening the partially completed publication and changing the column format on the inside pages from three columns to two.

Steps

1. Start Publisher, then click the **More publications** link in the New Publication task pane
   The Open Publication dialog box opens.

2. Click the **Look in list arrow**, locate the drive and folder where your Project Files are stored, click **LoftLife.pub**, then click **Open**
   The newsletter opens with the first page displayed. Some graphic images are in the workspace below, which you will use later in the unit. The Mobile newsletter sample design with a three-column format was used to create the publication. The Page Navigation buttons indicate that the publication has four pages. The Newsletter Options task pane is open, with the two-sided printing and Customer Address/None options selected. You stick with these default options.

QuickTip

The task pane can be moved on the screen by dragging its title bar.

3. Click the **Page 2 Page Navigation button** on the status bar, click the **Zoom list arrow** on the Standard toolbar, then click **Whole Page**
   Pages 2 and 3 appear in the Publication window, as shown in Figure B-3. Pages 2 and 3 are a **two-page spread**. These are pages that will face each other when the publication is printed.

4. Click **Page Content** in the Newsletter Options task pane, then make sure **Left inside page** appears in the Select a page to modify text box
   See Figure B-4. The options on the task pane will apply to the left page because you have selected the Left inside page as the page to modify.

QuickTip

You can apply column formatting changes quickly to the current page or to all pages of your publication. Position the pointer on the selected Columns on Left Page icon in the task pane, click the down arrow to open a shortcut menu, then click Apply to all pages, or Apply to this page.

5. In the Columns on Left Page section in the task pane, click **2**
   Publisher reformats the left inside page with two columns. At this point, you could continue to change the content by choosing from the options under Content for Left Page in the task pane, but you are happy with the selected option of three stories. You see that Page 3 still has three columns, and looks odd next to the reformatted page 2.

6. Click the **Select a page to modify list arrow** in the Page Content task pane, click **Right inside page**, then click **2** in the Columns on Right Page section
   Page 3 now has two columns.

7. Close the task pane to view more of your workspace
   With the task pane closed, you can now see more of the newsletter. You can also see that there are graphic images in the workspace. You will add these to the newsletter later in the unit.

8. Save your changes to the newsletter

FIGURE B-3: Pages 2 and 3 of the newsletter

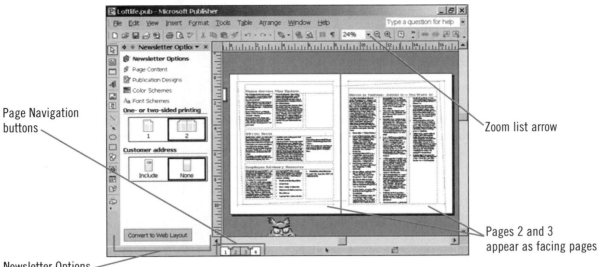

Page Navigation buttons

Zoom list arrow

Pages 2 and 3 appear as facing pages

Newsletter Options task pane

FIGURE B-4: Changing the number of columns with the Page Content task pane

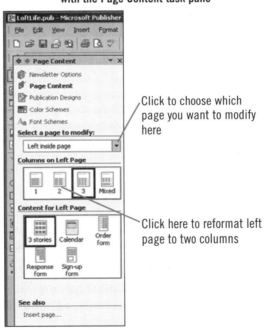

Click to choose which page you want to modify here

Click here to reformat left page to two columns

Creating columns in existing text boxes

You can also change the number of columns of text in existing text boxes. Sometimes it is easier to read narrower columns. For example, you could turn one wide column of text into two or three more readable columns. To create columns in an existing text box, right-click the text box, then click Format Text Box from the shortcut menu. Click the Text Box tab, click Columns to open the Columns dialog box, then specify the number of columns and the amount of spacing between the columns, as shown in Figure B-5.

FIGURE B-5: Columns dialog box

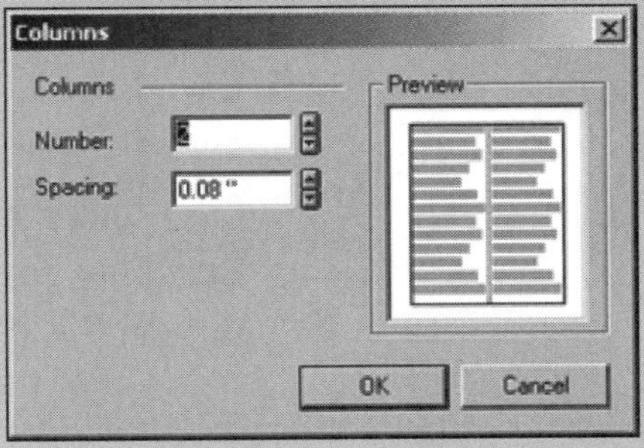

Working with Overflow Text

Sometimes there isn't enough room in a text box to hold all of the text for a particular story. When this happens, a Text in Overflow icon appears at the bottom of the text box to indicate that not all text in the story is visible. To display all the text, you either must enlarge the text box or continue the story in another text box in the publication. To continue a story in another text box, you connect that text box to the overflowing text box, and then "pour" the overflow text into the next text box. See Table B-1 for a description of the different text flow icons. Karen asked one of her colleagues to write a 500-word article for the newsletter on MediaLoft's new annual review policy. She plans to begin this story on page 1 and continue it on page 4. Karen receives the article as a Word file and imports it into the newsletter.

QuickTip

Click [====→] to select the next frame.

1. Click the **Page 1 Page Navigation button**, click the **first column text box** beneath the headline "The Common Review Date" to select it, then press **[F9]**
   The Go to Next Frame icon [====→] indicates that the selected frame is linked to the text box in the next column, as shown in Figure B-6. These text boxes are **connected**.

2. Click **Insert** on the menu bar, click **Text File** to open the Insert Text dialog box, click the **Look in list arrow** to locate the drive and folder where your Project Files are stored, click **PB B-1.doc**, then click **OK**
   The text from the Word document automatically pours into the three connected text boxes on page 1, but there's too much text to fit in the three boxes, so a message appears asking if you want to use autoflow. When you use **Autoflow**, Publisher automatically flows text from one existing empty text box to the next, asking for confirmation before it flows into each text box.

3. Click **No**
   The Text in Overflow icon appears at the bottom of the text box.

4. Click the **Create Text Box Link button** on the Connect Frames toolbar
   The pointer changes to a pitcher. When you place the pointer over a text box that doesn't include the current story, the pitcher changes to. When you click an empty text box with the pitcher pointer, the overflow text flows into that text box.

QuickTip

You can press [Ctrl][G], enter a page number, then click OK to move to another page in your publication.

5. Click the **Page 4 Page Navigation button**, then click the **first column text box** under the headline "The Common Review Date (continued)"
   Again, the text does not entirely fit in the text box, as shown in Figure B-7.

6. Click, click the **second column text box**, click then click the **third column text box**

QuickTip

If you add pages to a publication, Continued on page numbers are automatically updated.

7. Go to **page 1**, right-click the **third column text box** of the story, click **Format Text Box** on the shortcut menu, then click the **Text Box tab**
   See Figure B-8. **Continued notices** provide a roadmap. If a story continues on another page, these cues help the reader find the rest of the story.

8. Click the **Include "Continued on page..." check box** to select it, then click **OK**
   Publisher adds the text "(Continued on page 4)" to the bottom of the text box.

9. Go to **page 4**, right-click the **first column text box** of the story, click **Format Text Box**, click the **Text Box tab**, click the **Include "Continued from page..." checkbox** to select it, click **OK**, then save your work

FIGURE B-6: **Two connected text boxes**

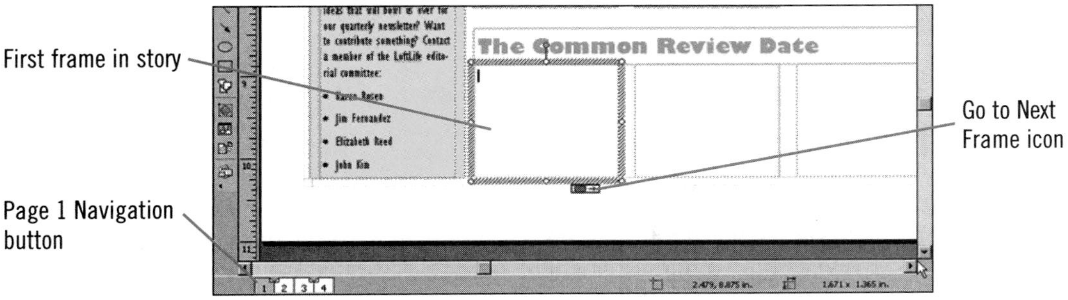

First frame in story

Page 1 Navigation button

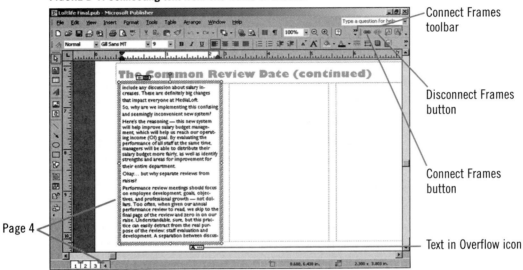

Go to Next Frame icon

FIGURE B-7: **Connecting text from one frame to another**

Connect Frames toolbar

Disconnect Frames button

Connect Frames button

Page 4

Text in Overflow icon

FIGURE B-8: **Format Text Box dialog box with Text Box tab displayed**

Click to add Continued on page 4 message to page 1

Click to add Continued from page 1 message to page 4

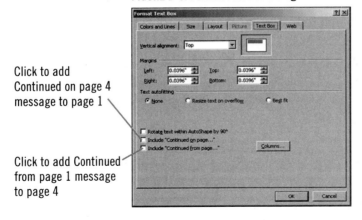

TABLE B-1: **Text Flow icons**

text flow icon	description
 ⬅	Indicates that text box is connected to another text box and that text flows from that text box to this one. Click to quickly move to the previous frame.
 ➡	Indicates that text box is connected to another text box and that text flows to that text box. Click to quickly move to the next frame.
 A	Indicates that text box is not connected to another text box and that there is more text that does not fit in the text frame.

Using Guides

When you are working with columns, it can be helpful to use layout and ruler guides. **Layout guides** are nonprinting lines that help you to align text, pictures, and other objects into columns and rows so that your publication will have a consistent look across all pages. Layout guides appear on every page of your publication and are represented by blue and pink dotted lines on the screen. **Ruler guides** are similar to layout guides but appear only on a single page. Use ruler guides whenever you need a little extra help aligning an object on a page. Ruler guides are represented by green dotted lines on the screen. ✎ Karen notices that the column containing the table of contents and sidebar on page 1 is not the same width as the other columns on the page. Setting vertical layout guides will help her to fix this. She inserts a ruler guide to help position a picture.

Steps 1234

1. Go to **page 1**, click the **Zoom list arrow**, click **Whole Page**, click **Arrange** on the menu bar, then click **Layout Guides**

   The Layout Guides dialog box opens, as shown in Figure B-9. Use this dialog box to adjust the margin guides and grid guides. The margin guides appear in pink on screen and outline the **margin**, or perimeter, of the page. The grid guides appear in blue on screen and provide a perimeter for each column on the page.

2. Click the **Columns up arrow** to display 4 in the Number of Columns text box

   The Preview shows blue grid guides dividing the page into four columns.

3. Click **OK**

   Layout guides appear on the newsletter.

4. Select the **table of contents table frame**, then press **[F9]** to zoom in on that frame, as shown in Figure B-10

   If you carefully position the pointer over a sizing handle on the vertical border of a column in the table, the pointer ↔ and a ScreenTip that says "Table Frame" appear, allowing you to adjust the width of the column. If you place the pointer on a sizing handle on the horizontal border the ↕ pointer appears to allow you to adjust the height of the row.

5. Point to the **sizing handle on the right border** of the table, drag ↔ to the left to align the right edge of the table frame with the blue grid guide, then click outside the frame to check your work

   The table of contents table frame is now the same width as the grid guide.

6. Scroll down and click the **yellow sidebar LoftLife Needs You! text box**, drag the **middle-right handle** to the left to align with the blue grid guide, then click outside the text box to check your work

   Both frames in the first column have been resized.

7. Scroll up to view the "A Word From…" story, click **Arrange** on the menu bar, point to **Ruler Guides**, then click **Add Horizontal Ruler Guide**

   A green horizontal line appears on the page.

8. Place the pointer over the green line, press and hold **[Shift]** so the pointer changes to the Adjust pointer ↕ click and drag ↕ to align with the 5½" mark on the vertical ruler, then release **[Shift]**

   The ruler guide is now set as shown in Figure B-11. You will use this newly created ruler guide in the next lesson.

9. Save your changes

FIGURE B-9: Layout Guides dialog box

Margin Guides section

Number of Columns

Number of Rows

Grid Guides section

Preview guides

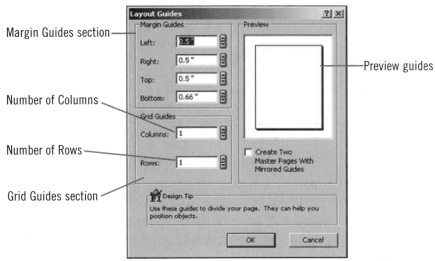

FIGURE B-10: Table of contents table frame

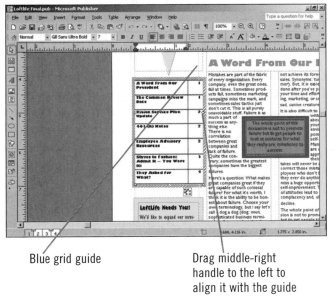

Blue grid guide

Drag middle-right handle to the left to align it with the guide

FIGURE B-11: Setting a ruler guide

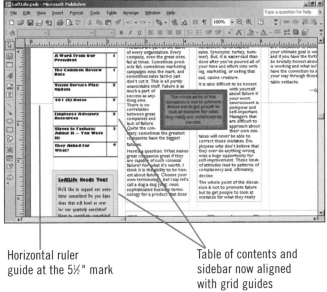

Horizontal ruler guide at the 5½" mark

Table of contents and sidebar now aligned with grid guides

Aligning objects

You can align objects with guides by hand or you can have Publisher align them for you. To align an object by hand, simply drag or resize the object using the mouse. The Object Position and Object Size indicators in the status bar can help you to place objects exactly. You can also use Publisher's Snap to and Nudge features to help you align objects precisely to guides. To turn on the Snap to feature, enable one or more of the Snap to commands on the Arrange menu. Snap to Ruler Marks snaps an object to the closest ruler mark, Snap to Guides automatically snaps an object to the closest layout guide, and Snap to Objects snaps an object to the closest object. Publisher's Nudge feature allows you to move or "nudge" an object one small increment at a time. To nudge an object, select the object, click Arrange on the menu bar, click Nudge, then click Up, Down, Left, or Right. You can also nudge an object by pressing and holding [Alt] while pressing one of the arrow keys.

Creating Picture Captions

A **picture caption** is text that describes or elaborates on a picture. Captions can be located above, below, or next to a picture. You can create a picture caption by typing text in a text box that you create, or you can use Publisher's Design Gallery to choose one of the picture caption designs. The design collection includes objects such as picture captions, logos, and calendars. The designs are organized by category and design type. You can also create and save your own objects in the Design Gallery. ▰▰▰ Karen would like to add an inspirational piece of clip art at the bottom of the president's article on page 1. She does this by using one of Publisher's preset picture captions in the Design Gallery and choosing an appropriate piece of clip art.

Steps 1 2 3 4

1. On page 1, select the **first column text box** below the "A Word From Our President" text box, then press **[F9]** to zoom in on the article, if necessary

2. Click the **Design Gallery Object button** 🖼 on the Objects toolbar
   The Microsoft Publisher Design Gallery opens, as shown in Figure B-12. Each of the three tabs has a list of categories or design sets. The Categories list in the left pane shows the large variety of types of predesigned objects you can use to enhance your publications. The right pane shows thumbnails of the selected category you can insert in the publication.

3. On the Objects by Category tab, click **Picture Captions** in the Categories list, click the **Thin Frame Picture Caption**, then click **Insert Object**
   The object, an image with "Caption describing picture or graphic" text appears on top of the article.

4. Scroll to view the bottom of the third column of that story, then drag the **object** using the Move Pointer 🖮 so that the upper-left handle of the object is positioned at the intersection of the ruler guide and the layout guide, as shown in Figure B-13

5. Drag the **lower-right handle** up and to the left using the Resize Pointer 🖱 to resize the frame so that it is aligned with the bottom of the column at the 7⅞" mark on the vertical ruler and the right layout guide
   The Design Gallery provides a placeholder graphic as well as placeholder caption text. You can change it at any time.

Trouble?
If a dialog box opens asking if you want to catalog all the images on your hard drive for the Media Gallery, click Later.

6. Click the **picture of the coffee cup,** handles appear around the picture when it is selected, right click the **picture**, point to **Change Picture** on the shortcut menu, then click **Clip Art**
   The Insert Clip Art Task pane opens.

7. Type **success** in the Search text text box, click **Search**, then scroll down the results to display the **picture of a man holding a flag on a mountain top**, as shown in Figure B-14
   The Insert Clip Art task pane displays the results of your search. If you click the right side of any image a menu appears with various options for working with the image in the Clip Organizer.

Trouble?
If you don't see this picture click another image.

8. Click the **picture of a man holding a flag on a mountain top** to insert it, click the **placeholder caption text** to select it, type **The road to success is paved with mistakes.**, then click outside the object
   The placeholder picture and caption are replaced with a relevant image and text.

9. Close the Clip Art task pane, then save your changes

FIGURE B-12: Microsoft Publisher Design Gallery

Objects by Category tab

Categories of Publisher-designed objects

Your Objects tab

Objects by Design tab

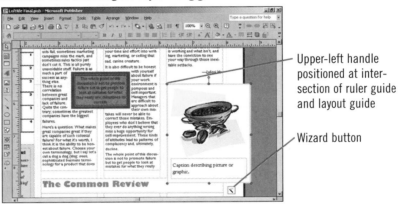

Picture Captions

Click to insert object

FIGURE B-13: Positioning the object using guides

Upper-left handle positioned at intersection of ruler guide and layout guide

Wizard button

FIGURE B-14: Inserting Clip Art using the task pane

Search results for "success"

Click to insert this image into the newsletter

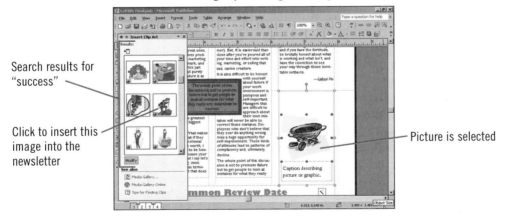

Picture is selected

Publisher 2002

CLUES TO USE

Adding your own objects to the Design Gallery

You can add your own objects to the Design Gallery for use in future publications. For example, if you design your own pull quote that you intend to use in every edition of an annual publication, you would want to add this to the Design Gallery. Select the object you want to save, click Insert on the menu bar, and then click Add Selection to Design Gallery. In the Add Object dialog box, type a name for the object and type or choose a category, then click OK. This object will then appear on the Your Objects tab. To delete an object from the Your Objects tab of the Design Gallery, right-click the object, click Delete This Object on the shortcut menu, then click Yes to confirm the deletion.

Creating Headers and Footers

A **header** is information that appears on the top of every page of a publication, such as the name of the publication. A **footer** is information that appears on the bottom of every page of a publication, such as a page number. When you create a header or footer in Publisher, you use the Header and Footer command on the View menu. When you choose the Header and Footer command, Publisher opens the **master page**, also known as the **background**, which is a layer that appears behind every page in a publication. The **foreground** sits on top of the background and consists of the objects that appear on a specific page of a publication. Karen adds a header and a footer to her newsletter. She does not want them to appear on page 1.

1. Click **View** on the menu bar, click **Header and Footer**, then press **[F9]** to zoom out
   The background right master page appears, showing an empty text box at the top of the page for a header and one at the bottom for a footer. The Header and Footer toolbar is also open. At the moment, the page navigation buttons show an "R," indicating that there is only one master page, which by default is the right-hand one. Because this publication has two-page spreads, you need both a right and a left master page, which will be mirror images of each other.

2. Click **Arrange** on the menu bar, click **Layout Guides**, click the **Create Two Master Pages With Mirrored Guides** check box, then click **OK**
   Before entering text in the header text box, you need to make sure that both header text boxes and both footer text boxes are correctly aligned with the blue layout guides.

3. If necessary, drag header text box and each footer text box to the position shown in Figure B-15

4. Click in the **left page Header text box**, press **[F9]** to zoom in, type **VOLUME 1 ISSUE 2**, then click the **Align Right button** on the Formatting toolbar

5. Scroll over to the right page, click in the **right page Header text box**, then type **VOLUME 1 ISSUE 2**
   The right header text is left-aligned by default. Compare your publication with Figure B-16.

6. Click the **Show Header/Footer button** on the Header and Footer toolbar to move the insertion point to the right-page footer, type **Page**, press **[Spacebar]**, click the **Insert Page Number button** on the Header and Footer toolbar, then click
   A yellow box appears, explaining that Publisher will automatically insert a page number. The page number will be right-aligned in the footer on the right page.

7. Select **Page #**, click the **Copy button** on the Standard toolbar, scroll over to the left page, click in the **footer text box**, then click the **Paste button**
   The footer text from the right page is copied to the left footer. See Figure B-17.

8. Press **[Ctrl][M]**, then use the Page Navigation buttons to view all pages of your publication
   You can see both headers and footers on each page.

9. Go to page 1, click **View** on the menu bar, then click **Ignore Master Page**
   The header and footer no longer appear on page 1 but still appear on pages 2–4.

FIGURE B-15: **Left and right master pages**

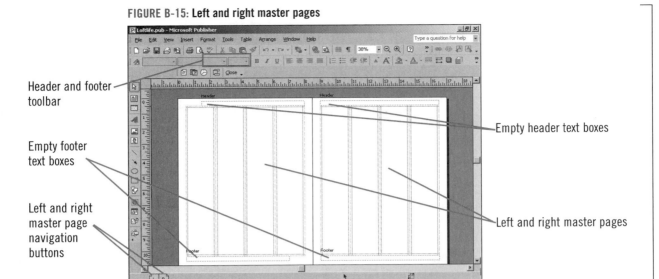

Header and footer toolbar

Empty footer text boxes

Left and right master page navigation buttons

Empty header text boxes

Left and right master pages

FIGURE B-16: **Completed headers**

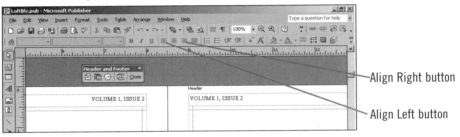

Align Right button

Align Left button

FIGURE B-17: **Completed left page footer**

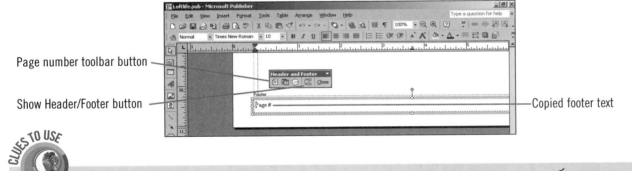

Page number toolbar button

Show Header/Footer button

Copied footer text

CLUES TO USE

Working with text styles

A text style is a set of formatting characteristics that you can quickly apply to text on a paragraph-by-paragraph basis. A style contains all text formatting information: font and font size, font color, alignment, indents, character and line spacing, tabs, and special formatting, such as numbered lists. Publisher includes preset styles that you can apply, or you can import text styles from other publications or define your own styles. To apply a text style, select the text you want to format, click the Style list arrow on the Formatting toolbar, as shown in Figure B-18, and then choose from the list of styles. To modify a style or create a new style, use the Styles and Formatting command on the

Formatting menu to open the Styles and Formatting task pane.

FIGURE B-18: **Publisher preset styles**

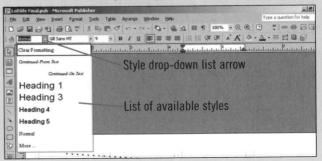

Style drop-down list arrow

List of available styles

Publisher 2002

Inserting and Formatting WordArt

WordArt is text that Publisher treats as a graphic. You click the Insert Word Art button on the Objects toolbar to choose one of the preset designs, you enter the text that you want to create as art, then you use the many formatting options available on the WordArt toolbar to curve, stretch, and twist the text. WordArt is a fun way to add color and style to your publications. The Employee Advisory Resource article is all text with no graphics. Karen decides to create WordArt out of the letters EAR to make the article more appealing to read.

Steps

1. Go to **page 2**, scroll so that the Employee Advisory Resource story is in view, then click in the **desktop workspace** so that no frames are selected in the newsletter

2. Click the **Insert WordArt button** 📐 on the Objects toolbar
   The WordArt Gallery dialog box opens, displaying 30 preset styles for WordArt.

3. Click the **blue curved design in the fourth row**, as shown in Figure B-19, then click **OK**
   The Edit WordArt dialog box opens. This is where you enter the text and specify the font, the font size, and whether the text is bold or italic.

4. Type **EAR** in the text box, click the **Font list arrow**, click **Ravie**, click the **Size list arrow**, click **40**, then click **OK**
   The WordArt appears selected on your publication, and the WordArt toolbar is open. You can use this toolbar to make additional formatting changes to the WordArt. First you need to position the WordArt in the Employee Advisory Resource story.

5. Drag the **EAR** WordArt until it is positioned between the two columns of text in the middle of the Employee Advisory Resource story
   Notice that the text in the story automatically wraps around the WordArt. Wrapping is explored in the next lesson.

6. Click the **Format WordArt button** 🎨 on the WordArt toolbar
   The Format WordArt dialog box opens, as shown in Figure B-20. You can use this dialog box to change the lines, borders, colors, size, and layout of your WordArt.

7. Click the **Fill Color list arrow** on the Colors and Lines tab, click **the yellow square**, click the **Line Color list arrow**, click **the red square**, click the **Line Dashed list arrow**, click the **Square Dot pattern**, then click **OK**
   The EAR WordArt now appears with the formatting changes you made.

8. Click the **WordArt Shape button** 🅰 on the WordArt toolbar, then click the **Can Up shape** in the third row, third column
   The EAR WordArt now appears with a new shape. You can always drag a handle on the selected WordArt to change the existing shape if you want.

9. Close the Word Art toolbar, then save your changes to the newsletter
   The WordArt you created looks great! See Figure B-21.

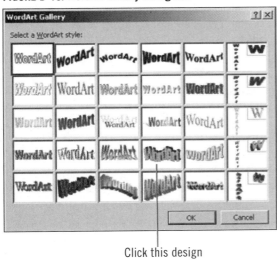

Click this design

Figure B-20: Format WordArt dialog box

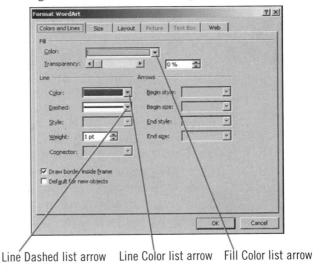

Line Dashed list arrow   Line Color list arrow   Fill Color list arrow

FIGURE B-21: Completed WordArt

Newly created WordArt

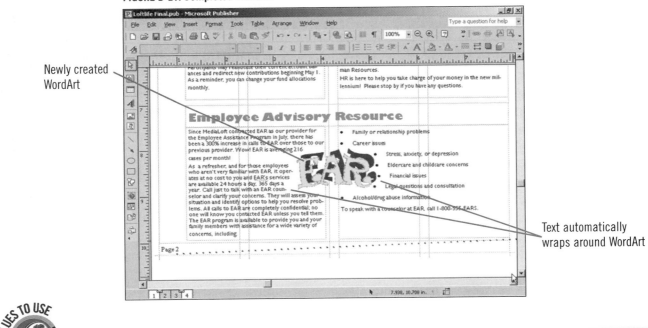

Text automatically wraps around WordArt

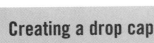

Creating a drop cap

A **drop cap** is a specially formatted first letter of the first word of a paragraph. Usually, a drop cap is in a much larger font size than the paragraph text itself, and sometimes the drop cap is formatted in a different font. To create a drop cap, click anywhere in the paragraph where you want the drop cap to appear, click Format on the menu bar, click Drop Cap, click one of the available drop cap styles in the Drop Cap dialog box, shown in Figure B-22, then click OK. You can also use the options on the Custom Drop Cap tab to create your own drop cap style.

FIGURE B-22: Drop Cap dialog box

Use the Custom Drop Cap tab to design your own drop-cap style

Select a Drop cap style

Preview the Drop cap style

Click to remove Drop cap

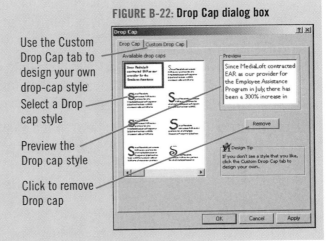

Publisher 2002

Wrapping Text Around Objects

To help make your stories more visually interesting, Publisher gives you the ability to wrap text around any object. **Wrapping** means that the text flows around the object rather than on top of or behind it. You can wrap text around pictures or around other text, such as pull quotes. A **pull quote** is a quotation from a story that is pulled out into its own frame and treated like a graphic. You can choose to wrap text around an object's frame or around the object itself. ✍ Karen is ready to add graphics to her stories on page 2 and 3. She collected graphics and placed them on the workspace. She plans to place an owl graphic in the Vision Service story on page 2, and will insert a pull quote into the Fashion story on page 3. She will wrap text around both objects.

Steps 1 2 3 4

1. Go to page **2**, zoom out to view the whole page if necessary
   You can store clip art in the desktop workspace for use in the publication.

2. Drag the **owl clip art** located at the bottom of your desktop workspace so that it is centered in between the two columns of text in the "Vision Service Plan Update" story, click **Arrange** on the menu bar, point to **Order**, then click **Bring to Front**
   The text in the article automatically wraps around the square-shaped frame containing the owl.

3. Click **Arrange** on the menu bar, point to **Text Wrapping**, then click **Tight**
   The text now wraps tightly around the contours of the owl's body.

4. Click **Insert** on the menu bar, click **Design Gallery Object**, then click **Pull Quotes** in the Categories list
   The Design Gallery opens, with the Objects by Category tab and Pull Quotes selected, as shown in Figure B-23.

5. Scroll down the Pull Quotes in the right pane, click the **Mobile Pull Quote** design, then click **Insert Object**
   The pull quote frame with placeholder text is now positioned in the middle of the two-page spread, between page 2 and 3.

6. Drag the **Pull Quote frame** to the "Slaves to Fashion" story so that it is centered between the two columns at the 4" mark on the vertical ruler
   Notice that the text automatically wraps around the pull quote frame.

7. Zoom in on the lower-right corner of page 3, drag to select the last bulleted item in the second column, beginning with In junior high…, including Paul Roudenko, then click the **Copy button** 🖼 on the Standard toolbar
   Text can be copied from one text box or frame to another.

8. Scroll to view the Pull quote box, click to select the **placeholder text**, then click the **Paste button** 🖼 on the Standard toolbar
   The quote from Paul Roudenko is pulled out and highlighted in the pull quote on the page.

9. Select all the text in the pull quote, click the **Font list arrow** on the Formatting toolbar, click **Times New Roman**, click the **Size list arrow**, click **10**, click the **Italic button** 𝐼 on the Formatting toolbar, then save your changes
   Compare your publication with Figure B-24.

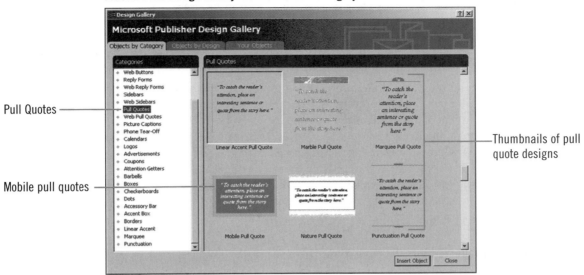

Pull Quotes

Mobile pull quotes

Thumbnails of pull quote designs

FIGURE B-24: Wrapping text around clip art and pull quotes

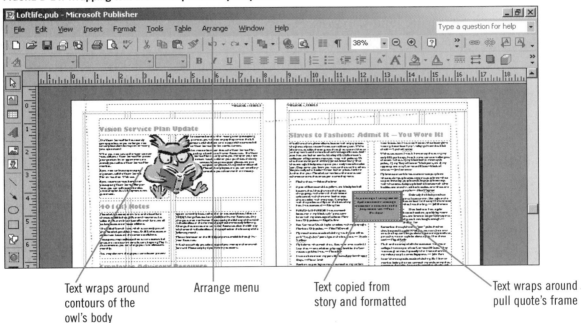

Text wraps around contours of the owl's body

Arrange menu

Text copied from story and formatted

Text wraps around pull quote's frame

Publisher 2002

CLUES TO USE

Rotating and flipping objects

You can create interesting effects in a publication by rotating or flipping text and objects. When you rotate an object, you change its angle in degrees relative to a baseline. For example, text that is rotated 90 degrees appears vertically rather than horizontally. To rotate an object in 90-degree increments, select the object, click Arrange on the menu bar, point to Rotate of Flip, then click the option you want. To rotate an object by dragging it, select the object, then point to the green rotation handle at the top of the frame. Drag the mouse in the direction you want to rotate. To rotate the object in 15-degree increments using the dragging method, press and hold [Shift] while dragging the rotation handle.

Layering and Grouping Objects

You can layer two or more objects on top of each other in a publication to create an interesting visual effect. When you layer objects, they appear on the page in the order you placed them, as if you had placed different pieces of paper on top of one another. You can change the layer order by using the Bring to Front, Send to Back, Bring Forward, or Send Backward commands. When you are happy with the arrangement of your layered objects, you can **group** them so you can work with the objects as a single object. Grouping objects allows you to move and resize the group rather than each object individually, saving time. ◆ Karen wants to improve the look of the MediaLoft contact information on page 4 of *LoftLife*. She decides to layer the logo on top of several different rectangle shapes to make it more attractive.

Steps

QuickTip

Autoshapes provide you with a wide variety of shapes, connectors, callouts, and arrows. To access them click the AutoShapes button on the Objects toolbar.

1. Go to **page 4**, then zoom in on the upper-left corner of the page and the desktop workspace to the left of the page
   The MediaLoft logo is positioned above the yellow box, and an autoshape graphic with a blue border is seen in the desktop workspace. An **autoshape** is a predesigned shape provided with Publisher that you can use in your publications.

2. Select the **blue-bordered rectangle** in the desktop workspace, then drag it to the publication page so that the upper-left corner is positioned at the 1" marks on both the horizontal and vertical rulers
   Compare your screen to Figure B-25.

Trouble?

Be sure to select the entire yellow rectangle and not one of the text boxes that appears on top of the rectangle. If you send the wrong frame to the back, click the Undo button on the Standard toolbar and repeat the step.

3. Click the **top-left corner of the yellow rectangle** to select it, click **Arrange** on the menu bar, point to **Order**, then click **Send to Back**
   The yellow rectangle is now positioned behind the blue-bordered rectangle. Once you perform an Order operation, an order button will appear on the Standard toolbar with a list arrow.

4. Click the **logo**, click the **Bring to Front button** on the Standard toolbar, then drag the logo down so that it is centered in the blue-bordered rectangle
   The logo is now on top of the blue-edged rectangle, which is on top of the yellow rectangle.

5. Click the **logo**, press and hold [Shift], then click the **blue-bordered rectangle**
   Notice that both of the frames are selected and the Group Objects button appears in the lower-right corner of the selection box. Clicking this button groups all the selected objects into one single object.

6. Click the **Group Objects button**
   The objects are now all grouped and you can move, resize, or format them as a whole, as shown in Figure B-26. The Group Objects button has changed to an Ungroup Objects button now that the selected object is a group. You can click this button to ungroup the objects and work with them individually.

7. Select **Tel: (415) 555-2398** in the yellow rectangle, type **your name**, press [Enter], type **Editor**, then save your changes to the newsletter

8. Click the **Spell check button** on the Standard toolbar, check all the stories in the publication, correct any misspelled words, save any changes, then print the newsletter

9. Compare your newsletter to Figure B-27

FIGURE B-25: Working with three layers

Bring to Front button

Logo

Blue-bordered rectangle

Yellow rectangle

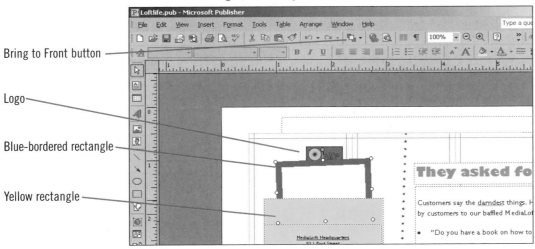

FIGURE B-26: Grouping objects

Both objects are selected as a group

Ungroup Objects button

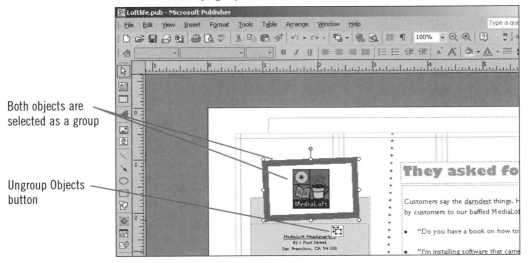

FIGURE B-27: Completed newsletter

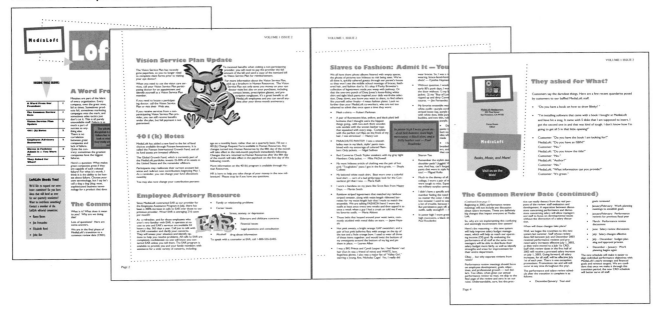

Practice

▶ Concepts Review

Label each element of the publication shown in Figure B-28.

FIGURE B-28

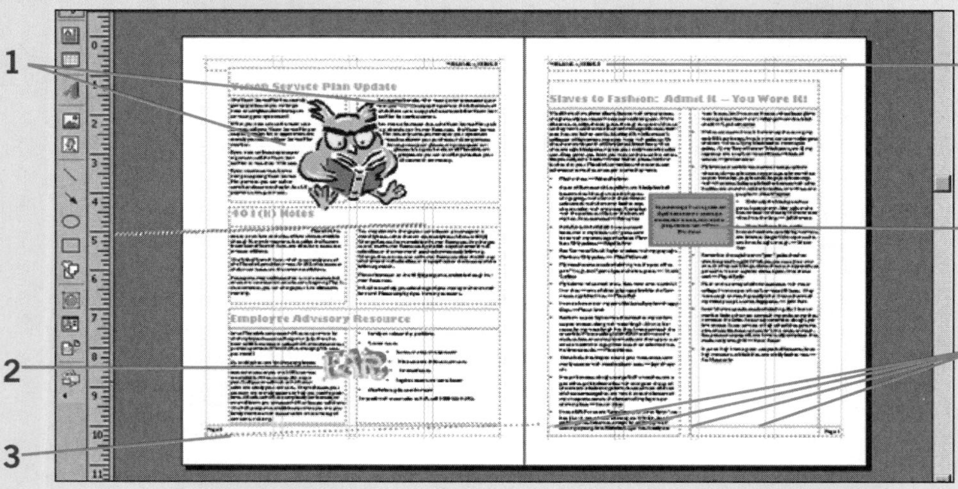

Match each term with the statement that best describes it.

7. **Ruler guides**
8. **Foreground**
9. **Autoflow**
10. **Send to Back**
11. **Story**
12. **Layout guides**
13. **Master page**
14. **Header**

a. Also called an article, is comprised of text and meant to be read from top to bottom
b. Feature that flows text from one text box to another
c. The layer where you place objects that you want to appear on every page
d. The layer where you place objects that you want to appear on individual pages
e. Command used to send an object behind of a stack of objects
f. Nonprinting lines that can assist you in aligning objects on individual pages
g. Information that appears at the top of every page of a publication
h. Nonprinting lines that can assist you in aligning objects on all pages

▶ Skills Review

1. **Create columns of text.**
   a. Start Publisher, open the file Rental.pub, then go to page 2 of the publication.
   b. Right-click the text box beneath the heading "Why Rent a Computer", then change the number of columns in this text box to **2**, with **.14"** of space in between then close the Format Text Box dialog box.

2. **Work with overflow text.**
   a. Select the empty text box in the second panel on page 2, insert the file PB B-2.doc into it, then click No when asked if you want to use autoflow.
   b. Connect the text box containing PB B-2 to the empty text box in the third panel on page 2, then insert the overflow text into this connected text box.
   c. Connect the text box in the third column of page 2 to the blue text box in the first column of page 1.
   d. Go to page 2. Insert a Continued on notice at the end of the text box in the third panel on page 2, then insert a Continued from notice at the beginning of the text box in the first panel on page 1.

3. Use guides.

   a. Create layout guides for three columns.

   b. In the first panel on page 2, increase the width of the text box containing the double columns of text so that both sides of the text box are aligned with the blue layout guides.

   c. Drag the bottom middle handle of the text box up to the 5 ½" mark on the vertical ruler.

4. Create picture captions.

   a. In the Why Rent a Computer? panel, insert a picture caption below the text box. Choose the Box Picture design.

   b. Resize and move the picture so that its top edge is just below the text, and its bottom edge is at the 8" mark on the vertical ruler.

   c. Replace the placeholder graphic with a picture of a computer from the Insert Clip Art task pane, then replace the placeholder caption text with **Why buy when you can rent?**

   d. Change the font of the picture caption to 9 pt Rockwell Condensed.

5. Create headers and footers.

   a. Insert a header at the top of the first column that contains this text: **Visit us at www.qcrental.com!**

   b. Insert a footer at the bottom of the first column that contains this text: **Call Quality Computer today at (314) 555-1000!**

   c. Verify that the footer and header text is left-aligned, format the footer and header text in Rockwell 10 point italic, then close the Header and Footer toolbar.

6. Insert and format WordArt.

   a. Go to page 1, then open the WordArt Gallery.

   b. Choose the WordArt Style that is in the second row, fifth column of the WordArt Gallery.

   c. Type **the computer experts** in the text box, and choose Bodoni MT Black 20 point bold for the font.

   d. Position the WordArt frame so that it is centered in the middle panel with the top of the WordArt frame at the 1" mark on the vertical ruler.

   e. Format the WordArt with the Wave 1 shape (third row, fifth column), change the fill color to orange and the line color to dark blue, then close the WordArt toolbar.

7. Wrap text around objects.

   a. Go to page 1, select the computer clip art from the bottom of the first column and move it up into the paragraph of text, so its top edge is at the 3" mark on the vertical ruler and its left edge is flush against the text box. Choose the square text wrapping option.

   b. Go to the story in the first panel of page 2, then insert a pull quote using the Arcs Pull Quote design.

   c. Position the pull quote frame so that it is centered between the two columns of text in the first panel, with the top edge at the 3" mark on the vertical ruler.

   d. Replace the placeholder text with **As soon as you buy a system, it is outdated.** Resize the pull quote frame by dragging the bottom-middle handle up to the 4" mark on the vertical ruler, then format the text in Rockwell 9 point italic.

8. Layer and group objects.

   a. In the workspace to the right of the brochure, create the Quality Computer logo by assembling the Quality Computer, Inc. text with the red rectangle, the dot pattern, the black square, and the black-bordered shape. Use the logo at the top of page 1 as a model, using the red rectangle in place of the blue.

   b. Use the Order buttons as necessary to complete this task. When the logo is assembled correctly, group the items and move the logo to just above the address on page 2.

c. Go to page 1, then create a text box at the 5" mark on the vertical ruler of the middle panel, that is approximately 1/2" high and spanning the width of the column, then type your name in the text box and format the font as 14 pt Rockwell. Center-align the text.

d. Proofread and spell check all stories, save your changes, print and close the publication, then exit Publisher.

 # Independent Challenge 1

You are a travel agent with Escape Travel. You are in charge of creating a brochure on vacations to Nova Scotia. Several colleagues have e-mailed you marketing text to include in the brochure. You started your brochure a few days ago and now need to add the finishing touches.

a. Start Publisher, open the file Nova Scotia.pub, then add layout guides for three columns.

b. On page 2, insert the Project File PB B-3.doc into the two empty columns. Do not use autoflow.

c. Insert a picture caption under Nova Scotia in the third column of page 1. Choose a picture frame that you like and change the placeholder text to **Get away today!** Format the caption text in 14 point Franklin Gothic Demi. Replace the picture with a map of Nova Scotia from the Insert Clip Art task pane.

d. Insert a right-aligned footer with the text **Call Escape Travel at (207) 555-1234 for more information**, then create a left-aligned header that contains your name.

e. Create WordArt in the second column on page 1 with the text **Nova Scotia**. Format the WordArt with any shape, font, and colors that you choose, then proofread, spell check, save, and print the publication.

 # Independent Challenge 2

You are the development director for the Wolf Pond Arts Academy. You have partially completed a brochure announcing the annual fundraiser. You need to finish placing objects and formatting it.

a. Start Publisher, and open the file **Fundraiser.pub**.

b. In the third panel on page 1, replace the text <name> in the 2 text boxes with **Wolf Pond Arts Academy**.

c. In the leftmost panel on page 1, replace the text Back panel heading with **Live Onstage**. In the text box below this heading, insert two pieces of clip art that illustrate the paragraph text. Resize the graphics to appropriate sizes, and specify the text wrapping of your choice.

d. In the first panel on page 2, insert PB B-4.doc in the text box below "Our annual fundraising gala!" increase the size of the text box by aligning the right edge with the layout guide, then format the text into two columns.

e. Insert any pull quote centered between the two columns of text. Use the Carla Davis quote from the paragraph, and format the text in Times New Roman 9 point italic. Reduce the size of the pull quote box to 1" tall by 1" wide.

f. Create WordArt for **WPAA**, and insert it in the space above the address on the second panel of page 1.

g. In the top text box in the middle panel on page 1, replace the text <designer> with your name, proofread, spell check, save, print and close the publication.

Independent Challenge 3

You've written a few pages of text outlining methods for improving food access in your community. Now, you want to print and distribute what you've written as a pamphlet, as four pages on a folded sheet of paper.

a. Start Publisher, open a new blank publication, then save the publication as **Food Recovery**.

b. Click File on the menu bar, open the Page Setup dialog box, choose Booklet in the Publication type list box, choose Portrait for the Orientation, click OK, then click Yes in the dialog box that asks if you want to automatically insert pages.

c. On page 1 of the publication, insert a text box that aligns with the left, right, and bottom layout guides, and begins at the 5" mark on the vertical ruler.

d. Add text boxes to pages 2, 3, and 4 that occupy all the space within the blue layout guides.

e. Connect the text box from page 1 to page 2, connect the text box from page 2 to page 3, and then connect the text box from page 3 to page 4.

f. Insert the text from the file PB B-5.doc, beginning in the text box on page 1. Click No if asked about Autoflow. Pour the text to all four pages.

g. Add a text box to the top of page 1, and enter an appropriate title, along with your name as the author.

h. Format the first letter of the first paragraph of the essay as a drop cap. (*Hint:* See clues on page B-15.)

i Create a pull quote of your own choice on page 2 or 3 of the publication.

j. Proofread and spell check, save the publication, print, close it, then exit Publisher.

 # Independent Challenge 4

You own a small bed and breakfast in a city of your choice, anywhere in the world. You decide to create a brochure to attract visitors to your inn. You first need to do some research on the Internet about your chosen city.

a. Log on to the Internet, go to a search engine site such as AltaVista (www.altavista.com) and research the following information to include in your brochure:

- The name, address, and phone number of the bed and breakfast in your chosen city.
- The price per night for a single and double room, using the local currency.
- A description of the hotel with a picture.
- Photos or pictures of the city or country in which your Inn is located.
- 3 short articles about your hotel and the interesting tourist attractions that are nearby, written by you, based on your research. You should write these articles using Microsoft Word, then save them with the filenames specified in the table below.

story title	story description	word count	save as file
Welcome to <City>	Describe the city, providing brief overview of key facts	100	City.doc
About the Inn	Describe the inn, it's offerings and amenities	100	Inn.doc.
What to do in <City>	Describe the key tourist attractions in your chosen city	100	Attractions.doc.

b. Open a new publication and choose the Borders Informational brochure from the New Publications task pane.

c. Type the name of your Bed and Breakfast in the top text box on the third panel of page 1. [If your name or another name appears as the Business Name in this panel, replace that with the name of your Bed and Breakfast.]

d. Replace the text in the Product/Services Information with a short phrase that summarizes the experience you want your guests to have (such as **A home away from home**).

e. Replace the placeholder photo in the third column of page 1 with a picture of an inn.

f. In the bottom text box in the third column of page 1, replace the placeholder phone number with the Inn's phone number. Insert the Inn's address in the text box above the phone number.

g. On page 2, Replace the "Main Inside Heading" placeholder text with the heading **Welcome to < your city>**, then replace the story placeholder text with the file City.doc that you created.

h. Replace the first Secondary Heading in column 2 of page 2 with the text **About Our Inn**, then replace the placeholder story text with your file Inn.doc.

i. Replace the second Secondary Heading with the title **What to do in <your city>**, then replace the placeholder story text under the heading with your file Attractions.doc.

j. On page 1, replace the placeholder text for the Back Panel Heading with **Why Not Book Now?**, then replace the story placeholder text with the file PB B-6.doc. Insert the rate information for your inn into the story.

k. Replace all the placeholder photos with images relating to your city or inn.

l. On the Second column of page 1, delete the placeholder logo, if necessary, then insert the name, address, and phone number of the inn in the empty text box at the bottom of the page.

m. Save your publication as Inn Brochure.pub, then spell check, print and close the publication.

▶ Visual Workshop

Create the advertisement for the play shown in Figure B-29. Use the Floating Oval Event Flyer Wizard. Replace the placeholder clip art with the image of Romeo and Juliet, which is available in the Clip Art task pane. Group the four text boxes containing date, time, location, and contact information, and then move them into the position shown. Insert your name in the Contact text box. In the black rectangle at the bottom of the page, insert a text box with two columns and insert the text file PB B-7.doc. (Hint: click inside the text box, press [Ctrl][A] to select all the text, then change the font color to white.) Insert a pull quote, choosing the Frames pull quote design from the Design Gallery. To create the WordArt shown, choose the Wave 1 shape. Save your publication with the name Play flyer.pub.

FIGURE B-29

Publisher 2002

Creating
a Web Publication

Objectives

- ► **Understand and plan Web publications**
- ► **Create a new Web publication**
- ► **Format a Web publication**
- ► **Modify a Web form**
- ► **Add form controls**
- ► **Preview a Web publication**
- ► **Convert a Web publication to a Web site**
- ► **Convert a print publication to a Web site**

Publisher 2002 lets you quickly and easily create Web pages. You can start with a premade design and customize it to your needs. Publisher provides many tools that facilitate the development of Web pages. You can also convert an existing publication to a layout suitable for the Web. Karen Rosen produces a quarterly newsletter called *LoftLife* for MediaLoft employees. She will use one of the Web site designs available from the New Publication task pane to create a two-page *LoftLife* Web site for the company intranet. She will also convert the most recent issue to a Web layout.

Publisher 2002

Understanding and Planning Web Publications

The **World Wide Web,** or simply the **Web,** is a collection of electronic documents available to people around the world through the **Internet,** a global computer network. **Web pages** are the documents that make up the Web. A group of associated Web pages is known as a **Web site.** Anyone with Internet access can create Web pages and Web sites and add them to the network. **Web browsers** are the software that allow anyone to view Web sites. All Web pages are written in a common programming language called **Hypertext Markup Language (HTML).** With Publisher, you can create a **Web publication**—a publication that you later convert to either a Web page or a Web site—without needing to know HTML. You can use the Publisher skills you already possess to design and create the content, and then let Publisher create the HTML code for you. Figure C-1 shows how a Web page created with Publisher looks in a browser.  Karen plans which features she will add to her Web site. Figure C-2 shows a sketch of her plan.

► A **hyperlink,** or simply a **link,** is specially formatted text or a graphic that a user can click to open an associated Web page. Links serve as the foundation of the Web. Almost all pages on the Web are connected to each other through a series of links because each Web page can contain many links to different Web sites. Karen will place a welcome paragraph on the home page that describes the features of *LoftLife Online,* and Karen will add a link to the Feedback Form on page 2.

► Much like their paper counterparts, a **Web form** can include areas for text input, such as name and address, and provide an easy way for a user to submit information. Unlike their paper counterparts, Web forms also can offer boxes that users click to submit information via the Web. Many organizations that do business online allow users to select products or services using a Web form. Karen will add a Feedback Form to *LoftLife Online,* where users can answer the Question of the Month and provide comments on the latest issue.

► When your Web site has multiple pages, it's important to provide users with an easy and consistent method of navigating between them. A **navigation bar** provides a set of links to the most important pages in a Web site, displayed in the same location on each page. When you create a Web publication using the New Publication task pane, Publisher can automatically create one or more navigation bars on the main pages and update them as you add or delete pages. Karen will have navigation bars at the top and bottom of both pages, making it easier for viewers to jump quickly to where they want to go.

FIGURE C-1: Web page created using Publisher

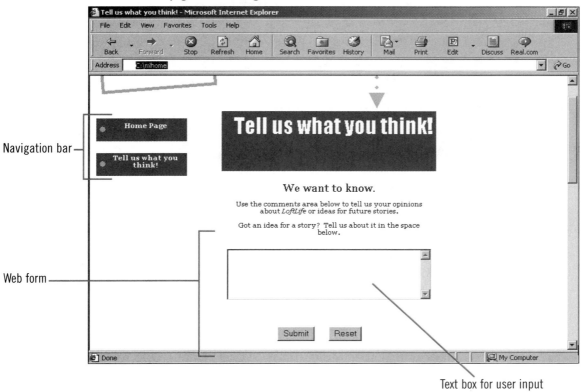

Navigation bar

Web form

Text box for user input

FIGURE C-2: Karen's sketch of the *LoftLife Online* Web site

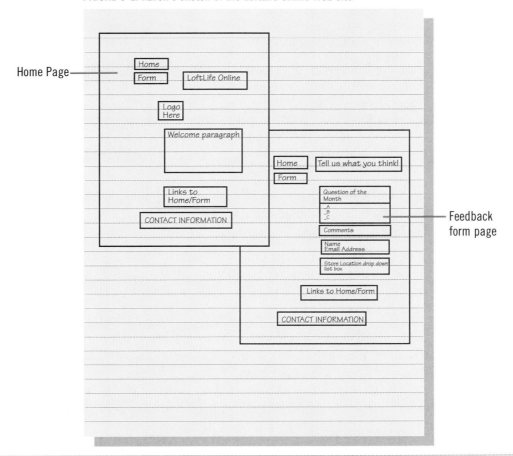

Home Page

Feedback form page

Creating a New Web Publication

You can use one of the Web site designs on the New Publication task pane to create a single Web page, or a Web site containing several pages. In either case, the first page you create is known as the **home page**. A home page is the introductory page of a Web site, which usually gives an overview of the site's contents and provides easy access to other pages in the Web site. If you want to create a Web presence but have little information to publicize, you may be able to fit all the information on a single Web page, which stands alone as your home page. The MediaLoft Web site will eventually have many pages to include links to past issues of *LoftLife*. For now, though, Karen creates two pages—the home page and a feedback form using the New Publication task pane.

1. Start Publisher, if the new Publication task page is not open, click **File** on the menu bar, then click **New**
   The New Publication task pane opens.

2. Click **Web Sites** in the By Publication Type list
   The Publication Gallery displays sample home page layouts, as shown in Figure C-3.

Trouble?

If a dialog box asks you to enter information about yourself in the wizard, click OK, then click Cancel.

3. Scroll down the Publication Gallery, then click the **Mobile Web Site** design
   The Publication Gallery closes, and a new publication opens in the workspace with the Mobile Web site design. The Web Site Options task pane displays options for adding a navigation bar and a form. The navigation bar will contain links to all the pages in the Web site.

4. Verify that the **Multiple icon** is selected in the Navigation bar section of the task pane
   Clicking multiple places a navigation bar at the top (Vertical navigation bar) and the bottom (Horizontal navigation bar) of every page of your site, making it easy for users to view different parts of the site quickly.

5. Click the **Response form icon** in the Form section of the task pane
   Forms are Web page elements that allow users to input information, such as their name, address, and credit card number to place an order. There are three types of forms shown in the task pane. You want to include a response form so that MediaLoft employees can easily provide feedback about *LoftLife*. The Web site will have only two pages. If you want to add more pages you can click Insert page at the bottom of the task pane and add up to six different kinds of pages to the site. See Table C-1 for the different kinds of pages Publisher allows you to add.

6. Click **Color Schemes** in the Web Site Options task pane, then click **Wildflower** from the Apply a color scheme list
   The home page colors have changed, and now the bars are red.

7. Click **Font Schemes** in the Color Schemes task pane, click **Impact** in the Apply a font scheme list, then close the task pane
   Publisher reformats the Web page so that the placeholder text fonts are Impact and Georgia. See Figure C-4.

Trouble?

If a dialog box opens asking if you want to save the modified logo, click No.

8. Click the **Save button** on the Standard toolbar, type **loftweb** in the file name text box, click the **Save in list arrow**, locate the drive and the folder where your Project Files are stored, then click **Save**
   The file is saved in Publisher publication format with a .pub file extension; later, you will convert it to HTML format, the format for displaying documents on the Web.

9. Close the task pane

FIGURE C-3: Web site designs in Publication Gallery

Web Sites category selected

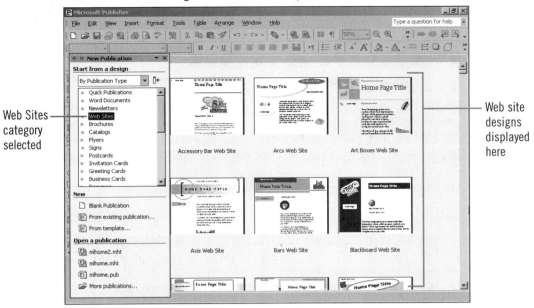

Web site designs displayed here

FIGURE C-4: New home page with Wildflower color scheme and Impact font scheme

Vertical navigation bar

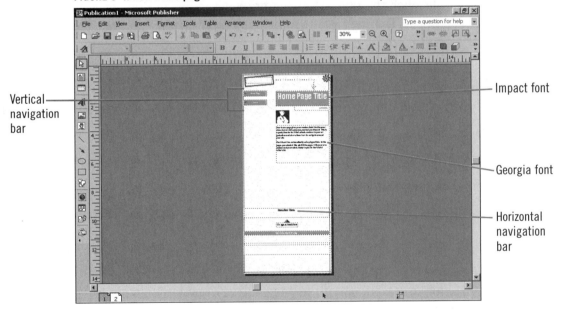

Impact font

Georgia font

Horizontal navigation bar

TABLE C-1: Types of Web pages you can create using the insert pages command from the task pane

web page type	useful for
Story	Organization's history, report of recent event, open letter
Calendar	List of upcoming important dates/events
Event	Information about an upcoming event
Special offer	Details of a sale or discount
Price list	Costs and descriptions of available products or services
Related links	Descriptions and links for other relevant Web sites

Publisher 2002

Formatting a Web Publication

After you create a Web publication using a design from the task pane, you need to personalize the contents and adjust the formatting to your needs. In addition to the standard formatting options available for all publications, Publisher offers several tools specifically for use in Web publications. Table C-2 shows these special toolbar buttons and explains how to use them. Karen starts customizing her Web publication by changing the default home page text and graphics.

Steps 1 2 3 4

Trouble?

The placeholder text may differ if the Personal Information dialog box has been completed for your installation of Publisher.

1. Zoom in as necessary, triple-click in the **blue rectangle frame** in the top-left corner of the page to select the **Business Name placeholder text**, then type **MediaLoft**

2. Click in the **Home Page Title frame** to select the placeholder text, then type **LoftLife Online**

3. Select the text **Your business tag line here.** in the frame below LoftLife Online, then type **What's up in the 'Loft?**

4. Right-click the **clip art** of the graduate, point to **Change Picture**, click **From File**, select **PB C-1.jpg** from the drive and folder where your Project Files are stored, then click **Insert**
   The MediaLoft logo now appears in the picture frame.

Trouble?

If a dialog box opens asking if you want to install the file converter, click Yes, then follow the onscreen instructions.

5. Right-click the first paragraph of text, point to **Change Text**, click **Text File**, select the **PB C-2.doc** from the drive and folder where your Project Files are stored, then click **OK**
   The new text now appears in the text box. Compare your screen with Figure C-5.

6. Select the text **Feedback Form** in the second paragraph you inserted, then click the **Insert Hyperlink button** on the Standard toolbar
   The Insert Hyperlink dialog box opens.

7. Click the **Place in This Document icon**, click **Page 2. Form** in the Select a place in this document list, then click **OK**
   The text "Feedback Form" now appears underlined and in color, indicating that it is now a link that viewers can click to open the page that contains the feedback form.

Trouble?

If the text boxes differ, it's because your personal information has been set up. Use Figure C-6 as a guide to delete one text box, add text and resize the text box below the red box.

8. Scroll to the bottom of the page, click the **pyramid image** to select the **Organization logo**, press **[Del]**, click the **Primary Business Address text box frame** at the bottom of the page, press **[Del]**, click the text box with phone numbers below **To Contact Us:**, drag the lower-middle sizing handle to the 13-inch mark on the vertical ruler, then type the contact information and format the text for MediaLoft as shown in Figure C-6

9. Save the publication

FIGURE C-5: Top section of home page completed

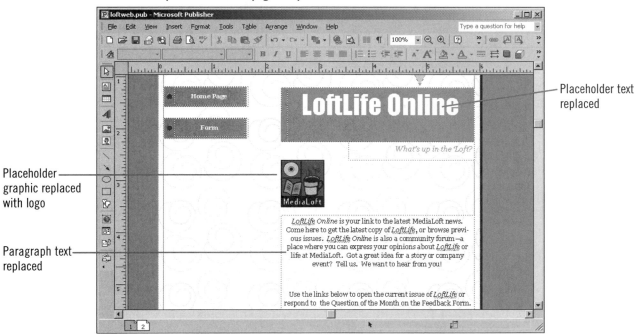

Placeholder text replaced

Placeholder graphic replaced with logo

Paragraph text replaced

FIGURE C-6: *LoftLife* contact information

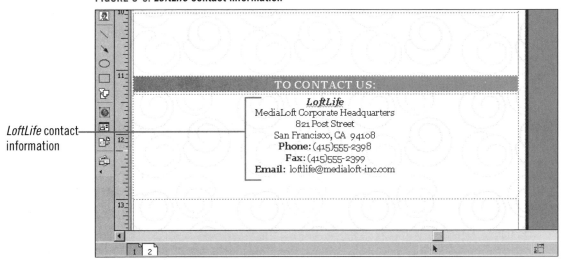

LoftLife contact information

TABLE C-2: Web Page Formatting Options

option	button	description
Hot Spot Tool		Formats a single graphic with links to multiple Web pages
Form Control		Inserts a form field for user input, such as a text box or check box
HTML Code Fragment		Allows advanced users to add additional HTML code to a specific part of a publication
Insert Hyperlink		Adds a hyperlink to the selected object
Web Page Preview		Opens the current Web page using your system's default Web browser

Publisher 2002

Modifying a Web Form

Including a form in a Web page is a great way to encourage users to interact with your organization. With forms you can collect valuable information, such as customer names and addresses, or feedback on a product. The response form that Karen selected in the Web Options task pane contains four placeholder questions, a comments text area, and user contact information text boxes. ◀▬▬ Karen wants to customize the response form provided through the task pane by changing the form headings and modifying one of the questions. She deletes the other three questions and rearranges the remaining objects.

Steps 1 2 3 4

1. Click the **Page 2 navigation button** then zoom in on the top of the page

   The publication's second page contains the feedback form you selected in the Web Page Options task pane. Notice that several of the text fields reflect formatting changes that you made to corresponding fields on the home page.

2. Click **Form Page Title**, type **Tell us what you think!**, click **General Response Form Title**, type **We want to know.**, click **Briefly describe your desired feedback**, then type **Answer the question below and use the comments area to tell us your opinions about** *LoftLife***.**

   Compare your screen with Figure C-7.

3. Click **First Question**, type **Which job perk is most important to you?**, click **Answer A**, type **Flextime**, click **Answer B**, type **Free beverages**, click **Answer C**, then type **Telecommuting policy**

   The question and three choices are complete. You can select multiple objects by dragging the mouse diagonally to create a rectangular shape around the objects. This is called dragging a selection rectangle.

4. Drag a selection rectangle around the **Third Question and its three answers** and the **Fourth Question and its three answers** to select all eight objects, then press **[Delete]**

   You deleted two of the placeholder questions and answer options.

5. Drag a selection rectangle around the **Second Question and its three answers**, then press **[Delete]**

   One question remains on the form.

6. Drag a selection rectangle around the **Comments label** and the **Comments multiline text box** to select both objects, then drag them up until they are just below Telecommuting policy

   Compare your screen with Figure C-8.

7. Save your changes

Trouble?

Be sure to include all parts of each object when dragging a selection rectangle. If your selection box doesn't include all the desired objects or you select too many objects, press [Esc] and try again.

FIGURE C-7: Form Page with new heading text

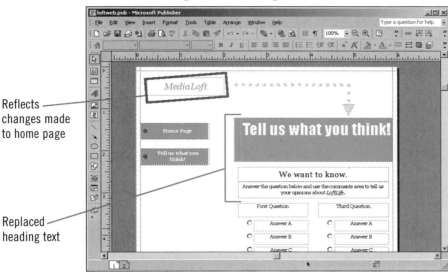

Reflects changes made to home page

Replaced heading text

FIGURE C-8: Form page with modified question and comments fields moved

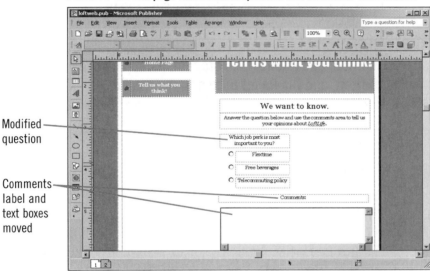

Modified question

Comments label and text boxes moved

Adding multimedia components to a Web publication

In addition to including text and graphics in your Web sites, Publisher allows you to add multimedia elements to make the site more eye-catching and to make more information available to your viewers. The Web Site Options task pane lets you select a background fill, as well as sound, for your site, which plays on the user's browser when the page opens. To insert and format a sound, click Background Fill and sound on the Web Site Options task pane, click Background sound to open the Web Options dialog box, then type a sound file location in the Background sound file name text box. You can choose to have the sound loop continuously or play as many times as you specify.

You can add simple animation to a site by inserting an animated GIF. GIF is a standard format for dis-

playing images on Web pages. An animated GIF is a short animation encoded in the same format, which plays repeatedly when it opens in a browser. The Web site you converted the newsletter to contained an animated wheel at the top of the home page. To add GIFs to your Web publication, click Insert on the menu bar, point to Picture, click From File, then type the name and location of the .gif file you want to add. Some .gif files are available in the Clip Organizer.

You can also add video and other objects by selecting Object on the Insert menu, clicking the Create from File option button, then specifying the object's location in the dialog box.

Adding Form Controls

Each item in a form, such as a text box or a check box, is known as a **form control**. HTML allows Web pages to use seven different types of form controls to collect information from users, as shown in Table C-3. Each control is usually associated with a text box, which can display a label or question, or provide guidance to the user about the type of information to be collected.

Karen customizes the Feedback Form further by modifying the contact information form controls and labels. She deletes some of the default controls and labels to make it less cluttered, and leaves the controls and labels for a name and an e-mail address. She also adds a drop-down list for users to provide their store location.

Steps

1. Scroll down as necessary, click the **Address:** label for the first single-line text box, then type **Name:**

2. Click the **City single-line text box control**, then press **[Del]**
   Selecting the text box control also selects the corresponding text box label because the two objects are grouped.

3. Delete the text box controls and corresponding text labels for **State/Prov.**, **Country**, **Zip/Post. Code**, and **Phone**, then drag the **Name** and **E-mail controls and label**, the **Submit button**, and the **Reset button** to the positions shown in Figure C-9
   You deleted and rearranged the controls to better meet your needs.

4. Click the **Form Control button** 🖳 on the Objects toolbar, then click **List Box**
   A list box appears showing three items.

5. Drag the **lower middle resizing handle** of the list box up so that only Item One appears, then drag the **list box** to just below the E-mail: text box control
   You modified the list box to show only one item at a time.

6. Double-click the **list box**, make sure **Item One** is selected in the Appearance section of the List Box Properties dialog box, click **Modify**, type **Boston** in the Item text box, click the **Not Selected option button**, then click **OK**

7. Click **Item Two**, click **Modify**, type **Chicago**, click **OK**, click **Item Three**, click **Modify**, type **Houston**, then click **OK**
   The List Box Properties dialog box shows three items: Boston, Chicago, and Houston.

8. Click **Add**, type **Kansas City** in the Item text box, click **OK**, click **Add**, type **New York**, click **OK**, click **Add**, type **San Diego**, click **OK**, click **Add**, type **San Francisco**, click **OK**, click **Add**, type **Seattle**, click **OK**, then click **OK**
   The list box displays the text "Boston." MediaLoft employees who use this form will be able to click the arrow next to the text and select the city where they work.

QuickTip

Click the label, press and hold [Shift], click the text box control then click the Group objects button 🗗 then move them together as a group.

9. Click the **Text Box button** 🖹 on the Objects toolbar, drag to create a text box to the left of the list box you just created that is the same size as the E-mail label above, then type **Store:**
   The list box now has a Store label next to it. Compare your screen with Figure C-10.

10. Double-click the **Submit button**, click **Form Properties**, click the **Save the data in a file on my Web server option button**, click **OK** twice, then save your publication
    All data entered by users will be stored in a file on the MediaLoft Web server.

FIGURE C-9: **Form page with deleted and moved controls and labels**

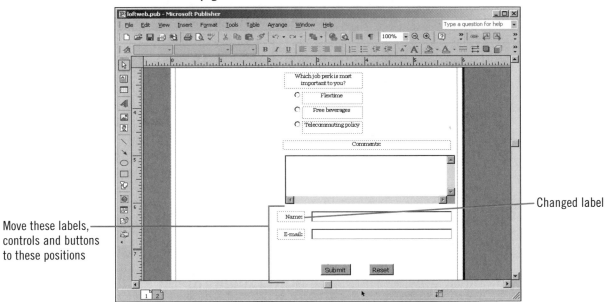

Move these labels, controls and buttons to these positions

Changed label

FIGURE C-10: **Completed form**

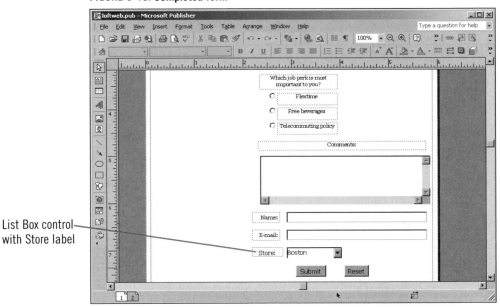

List Box control with Store label

TABLE C-3: **Web Page Form Controls**

control name	uses
Single-line Text Box	Short input, such as a name or e-mail address
Multi-line Text Box	Longer input, such as comments
Check Box	A question or option that the user can select, such as not being added to a mailing list
Option Button	A list of choices, of which the user should pick a limited number
List Box	A drop-down menu providing a list of choices
Submit Button	A command button, used to submit information entered in the form
Reset Button	A command button, used to clear information from a form

Previewing a Web Publication

Creating and editing your Web publication in Publisher gives you an idea of the appearance of your final Web site. However, whenever you develop a Web site, it's best to look at the publication in a Web browser before actually turning it into a Web site and making it available on a network. Because some aspects of the publication can appear differently in a browser, Publisher provides a tool that lets you preview the publication in a Web browser to ensure that it appears the way you want. Upon review, you can make changes to the publication, if necessary, before publishing it on a network. ◆ Karen previews *LoftLife Online* in her browser and makes final adjustments.

Steps

1. Click the **Web Page Preview button** 🔍 on the Standard toolbar, click the **Web site option button** (if it is not already selected), then click **OK**
   Publisher creates a temporary version of your Web site in HTML and opens the file in your Web browser, as shown in Figure C-11.

2. Scroll down the home page to view the entire contents, click **Tell us what you think!** on the navigation bar to open the second page, then scroll to view all the contents of page 2
   You notice that you need to delete the placeholder logo on page 2 and adjust the size of some of the text boxes containing the information on page 2. Both pages contain large gaps between the elements at the top and the bottom.

3. Click the **loftweb.pub-Microsoft Publisher program button** on the taskbar, click the **page 2 Navigation button**, drag the right-middle sizing handle on the question text box to the right so that the question fits on one line, delete the **placeholder logo**, then resize the contact information text box so that all the information is visible

4. Click the **page 1 Navigation button** of the publication, click the **Zoom list arrow** on the Standard toolbar, then click **Whole Page**
   You can now view the whole page.

5. Drag a selection rectangle to select all the objects at the bottom of the page, as shown in Figure C-12, then drag the selected items up so that the top of the selected section lines up at the 7-inch mark on the vertical ruler
   The entire contents of the home page are now closer to the top of the page.

6. Click the **page 2 Navigation button**, drag a selection rectangle to select all the objects at the bottom of the page, then drag the selected items up to that they begin approximately at the 8-inch mark on the vertical ruler

7. Save your publication, click **NO** if asked to save the modified logo, click the **Web Page Preview button** 🔍, click the **Web Site option button**, then click **OK**
   The home page appears with all the elements consolidated, as shown in Figure C-13.

8. Test the links on the navigation bar to view the second page, then click the link to return to the home page

FIGURE C-11: **Preview of home page in browser**

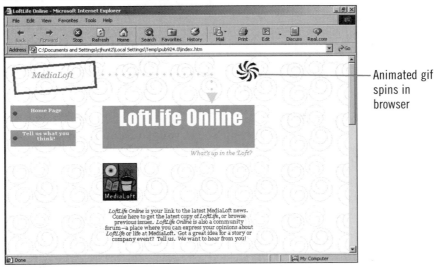

Animated gif
spins in
browser

FIGURE C-12: **Selected objects at the bottom of the home page**

Objects selected using
selection rectangle

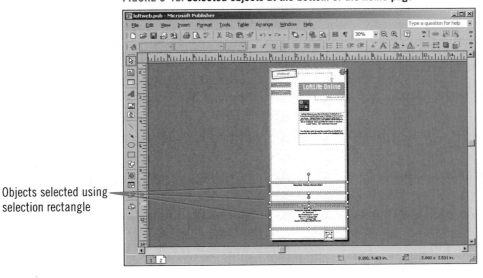

FIGURE C-13: **Preview of home page with lower objects moved up**

Lower objects now
closer to top of page

Converting a Web Publication to a Web Site

In your work on the Web site so far, you have edited and saved the publication in the Publisher file format (which has the file extension .pub). When you are satisfied with the publication's appearance and layout, you need to convert the publication to HTML format (which has the file extension .htm). The HTML document you produce can then be published on a network (either the Internet or an intranet) and displayed by Web browsers. ✎▬▬ Karen is satisfied with the preview of her Web site in the Web browser and is ready to convert the publication to an HTML document.

1. If necessary, click the **loftweb.pub Microsoft Publisher program button** on the taskbar to open the Publisher window containing *LoftLife Online*

2. Click **File** on the menu bar, then click **Save As Web Page**
   The Save as dialog box opens, as shown in Figure C-14.

> **Trouble?**
> Be sure to select the drive and folder where your Project Files are stored.

3. Click the **Create New Folder button** 🗁, type **loft_on** in the Name text box, click **OK**, then click **Save**
   This creates a separate folder just for this Web site so that all the files, including the graphics for the top and bottom page borders, are grouped together. The Save as Web Page dialog box displays a status indicator as Publisher saves the publication in HTML format.

4. Click **File** on the menu bar, click **Close**, start Internet Explorer (or your default browser), click **File** on the Internet Explorer menu bar, click **Open**, click **Browse**, open the **loft_on folder** where you saved the .HTML file, click **loftweb.htm**, click **Open**, then click **OK**
   The *LoftLine Online* Web page, now saved as an HTML file, appears in your default Web browser.

5. Click the **Tell us what you think! link** on the navigation bar
   The second page of the Web site opens, as shown in Figure C-15.

6. Type *your name* in the Name text box control, click **File** on the menu bar, click **Print**, click **Print**, click the **Home Page link** on the navigation bar, click **File** on the menu bar, click **Print**, then click **Print**
   You printed both the home page and the form page of your Web site.

7. Click **File** on the Internet Explorer menu bar, then click **Close**
   You exited the browser but Publisher is still running.

FIGURE C-14: Save As dialog box

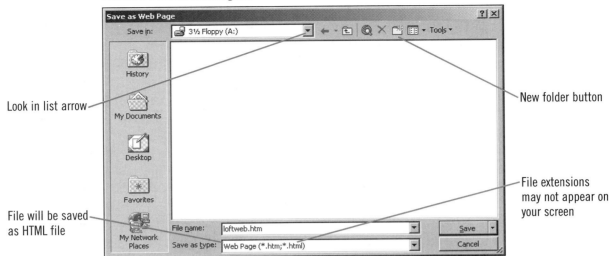

Look in list arrow

New folder button

File extensions may not appear on your screen

File will be saved as HTML file

FIGURE C-15: Feedback form page in Web browser

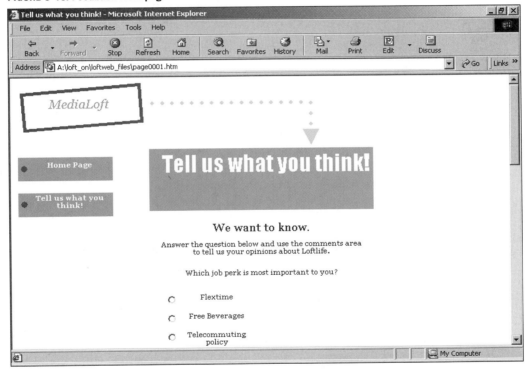

Formatting Web publications for different audiences

When you create a Web page, you want to make it available to the largest possible audience. Publisher allows you to create Web pages for Internet Explorer 4.0 or later, or Netscape Navigator 4.0 or later. If your site is going to be viewed on a corporate intranet, where all users have Internet Explorer 5.5, you might want to optimize your site and include features that can only be viewed with this version of the browser. However, if your site is being viewed on the Internet by a wide range of users, you will want to make sure that you optimize the site for an earlier browser version. To optimize your site for a specific browser click Tools on the menu bar, click Options, then click Web Options. Click the browsers tab, click the browser for which you want to optimize your site in the Target Browsers list, then click OK.

Converting a Print Publication to a Web Site

When you create a Web site from scratch, you format the text, preview it using the Web Page Preview button, make adjustments as necessary, and then save it as a Web page. You can use this same process to convert print publications such as flyers and newsletters into Web pages. Karen wants to start making the *LoftLife* newsletter available on the MediaLoft intranet. She starts by converting a recent issue to a Web publication.

Steps

1. **Click File on the menu bar, click Open, open the file PB C-3.pub from the drive and folder where your Project Files are stored**
   The first page of *LoftLife* appears in the workspace.

2. **Click View on the menu bar, then click Task Pane to open the Newsletter Options task pane if it is not already open**
   The Newsletter Options task pane opens.

3. **Click Convert to Web Layout at the bottom of the Newsletter Options task pane**
   The newsletter appears in Web format in the workspace as a 10-page publication, and the Web Site Options task pane displays options for formatting the Web site. See Figure C-16.

4. **Close the task pane, then use the Zoom feature and the page navigation buttons to explore the Web publication pages**
   In order to lay out existing publications as Web sites, you must decide the order of the stories and the relation of the elements in a publication. Because the newsletter is a long and fairly complex publication, Publisher automatically puts each story on its own page, regardless of how much room it needs. You need to adjust the Web site's layout so that it makes sense. Notice that each page containing a story includes placeholder pull quotes and graphics. Notice, too, that the pages need a lot of adjusting. Text boxes are spilling off the page and overlapping with each other. You need to spend considerable time finalizing the layout using Publisher skills. You can also add hyperlinks to lead users from page to page throughout a story. However, using the Convert to Web layout feature gives you a good head start in getting the project done.

5. **Click File on the menu bar, click Close, then click No**
   Karen realizes she has a lot of work to do to convert the newsletter to a Web site. She plans on sketching out a plan for how the site will be structured. When her plan is complete, she will go back and use her Publisher skills to format the pages and link them so that viewers can find the information they need.

6. **Exit Publisher**

FIGURE C-16: *LoftLife* issue converted to Web publication

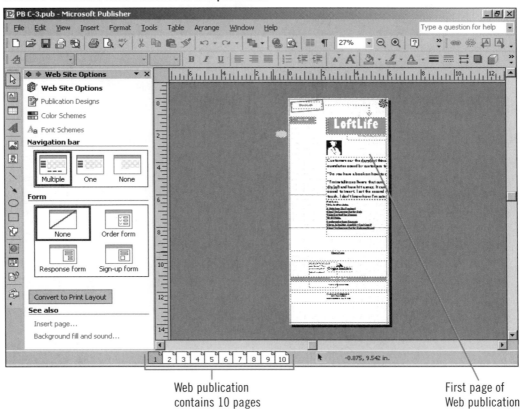

Web publication
contains 10 pages

First page of
Web publication

Publishing a Web site

If you want to make your Web site available to all users of the Internet, you need to publish it, or store your Web site files on a Web server known as a host. A Web server is always connected to the Web, making your pages available to anyone with Web access. If you already have an account with a commercial Internet Service Provider (ISP) or a school, room for your Web site on the Web server may be included with the account. Additionally, several Internet companies offer free space for Web pages on their servers; in exchange, they place an advertisement on each page in your Web site. All Web servers impose limits on the amount of data you can store; be sure to check these limits before publishing your Web site. A graphics-heavy site can quickly mushroom in size, so it is important to place graphics sparingly in your Web if your allotted space is small. There are many ways to publish your Web site. If you are using Microsoft Windows ME or Windows 98, you can use the Microsoft Web Publishing Wizard. To start the Wizard, click Start on the Start menu, click Programs, click Accessories, click Internet Tools, then click Web Publishing Wizard. Answer the questions posed to you by the Wizard to publish your site to the Web.

Practice

► Concepts Review

Label each item marked in Figure C-17.

FIGURE C-17

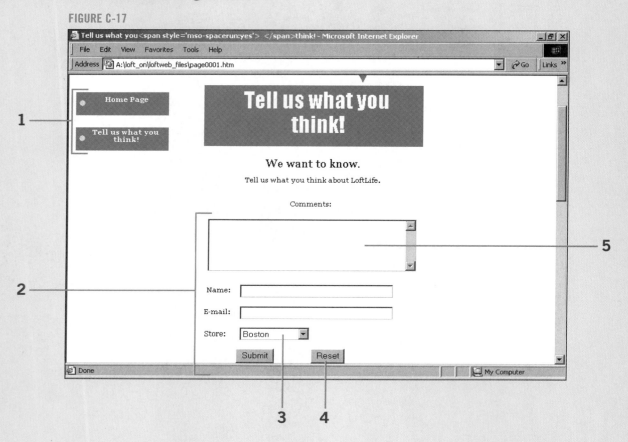

Match each item with its definition.

6. HTML
7. Web form
8. browser
9. home page
10. navigation bar
11. Web site

a. A means for users of a Web page to enter and submit information
b. The introductory page of a Web site
c. Special software for viewing Web pages and Web sites
d. The programming language in which all Web pages are created
e. Area on a Web page that provides links to the most important pages in a Web site, in the same location on each page
f. A group of associated Web pages

Select the best answer from the list of choices.

12. Which Web page control would most commonly be found in a form?

 a. Image box

 b. Link

 c. Navigation bar

 d. Check box

13. Which is not true about Web pages and Web sites?

 a. They can be created and added to the network by anyone with Internet access.

 b. They can be created only by using software designed exclusively for that purpose.

 c. They can be viewed with special software called Web browsers.

 d. They are written in a common programming language called Hypertext Markup Language (HTML).

14. If you want a user to open a Web page by clicking on text or graphics, you insert a(n):

 a. Hyperlink.

 b. User input field.

 c. Form control.

 d. HTML code fragment.

15. You can create a Web publication from a print publication by:

 a. Using the Save As Web Page command.

 b. Selecting the Page Setup command.

 c. Using the Web Publishing Wizard.

 d. Using the Convert to Web layout command.

▶ Skills Review

1. Create a new Web publication.

 a. Start Publisher, then, if necessary, open the New Publication task pane.

 b. In the By Publication Type list in the task pane, click Web Sites, then click the Spotlight Web Site design in the Publication Gallery.

 c. In the Web Site Options task pane, verify that Multiple is selected in the Navigation bar area.

 d. In the Form section, click Sign-up form.

 e. Choose the Prairie Color Scheme.

 f. Choose the Facet Font Scheme, then close the task pane.

2. Format a Web publication.

 a. Zoom in on the top of the Web page, click the image of the pagoda at the top of the page, right-click, point to Change Picture, click From File, select the file PB C-4.jpg from the drive and folder where your Project Files are located, then click Insert.

 b. Replace the graphic of a dragon with a clip art image of your choice relating to sports, and size it appropriately.

 c. Select the text Home Page Title, then type **MediaLoft Recreation**.

 d. Select the text Your business tag line here placeholder text below MediaLoft Recreation, then type **And you thought your job was fun!**

 e. Delete the pyramid placeholder logo and graphic at the bottom of the page.

 f. Right-click the paragraph placeholder text, point to Change Text, click Text File, then insert the file PB C-5.doc from the drive and folder where your Project Files are located. Click No in the Autoflow alert window, then drag the bottom of the text frame down until all text is visible and the Text in Overflow icon disappears.

 g. Select the text "sign-up form" in the last line of the paragraph before Boston, then click the Insert Hyperlink button on the Standard toolbar.

h. Click the Place in This Document option, click Page 2, Form, then click OK.

i. Scroll to the bottom of the page, then type the following information in the two adjacent text boxes below:
To contact us:

MediaLoft, Inc. Your name 821 Post Street San Francisco, CA 94108	Phone: 415-555-2398 Fax: 415-555-2399 Email: Recreation@medialoft-inc.com

j. Resize the text box as necessary to make the text fit, then save your publication as **recsite** to the drive and folder where your Project Files are stored. Do not save the logo.

3. Modify a Web form.

a. Open page 2 of the publication and zoom in on the top of the page.

b. Select the text Form Page Title, then type **Event Registration**.

c. Replace Sign-up Form Title with **Sign up today for your store's event!**

d. Drag a selection rectangle to select all the controls and text labels from the Sign up for: label through the Total: control, then press [Delete].

e. Select and delete the text labels and controls for Country, Zip/Post. code, and Phone, delete all the labels and controls from Method of Payment through Exp. Date, then scroll down and delete the pyramid place-holder graphic.

f. Replace the text in the label "Address" with **Event**, then replace the label text "State/Prov." with **Number of Guests**.

g. Drag the E-mail: control and label up until it is just below the City: control and label.

h. Drag the Submit and Reset buttons up so they are positioned just below the E-mail control.

4. Add form controls.

a. Click the City: label and text box, click the Ungroup Objects button, select only the City text box, then press [Delete].

b. Click the Form Control button, click List Box, drag to create a one-line list box in the space formerly occupied by the City text box, then double-click the list box you inserted.

c. Make sure Item One is selected in the Appearance section, click Modify, replace the text in the Item text box with **Boston**, click the Not Selected option button, then click OK.

d. Replace the Item text with **Chicago** for Item Two, and with **Houston** for Item Three.

e. Click Add, type **Kansas City** in the Item text box, click OK, create four new items with the text **New York**, **San Diego**, **San Francisco**, and **Seattle**, then click OK to close the List Box Properties dialog box.

f. Double-click the Submit button, click Form Properties, click the Save the data in a file on my Web server option button, click OK, click OK, then save your changes.

5. Preview a Web publication.

a. Click the Web Page Preview button, verify that the Web site option button is selected.

b. Scroll down your home page to view the entire contents, click Event Registration on the navigation bar to open the second page, then scroll to view all the page's contents.

c. Click the Publisher Program Button on the taskbar, go to page 2.

d. Drag a selection rectangle to select all objects from the Name label to the Reset button, then drag them up to just below "Sign up today for your store's event!"

e. Click the Page 1 navigation button, drag to select the MediaLoft Address at the bottom of the page, click the Copy button on the Standard toolbar, click the Page 2 navigation button, select the contact information in the text box at the bottom of the page, click the Paste Button on the Standard toolbar, then drag the lower middle sizing handle of the text box down so that all the contact information is visible.

f. Drag a selection rectangle to select the Home Page and Event Registration links and the contact information text boxes, then drag them up to just below the Submit and Reset buttons.

g. Save your changes, click the Web Page Preview button, verify that the Web site option button is selected, click OK, and review your changes.

h. Close the browser window.

6. **Convert a Web publication to a Web site.**

a. Click the Publisher program button on the taskbar if it is not open to view the recsite publication.

b. Click File on the menu bar, then click Save As Web Page.

c. Locate the drive and folder where your Project Files are stored, click the Create New Folder button, type **mediarec** as the new folder name, click OK, then click Save.

d. Open your default Web browser. Click File on the menu bar, click Open, open the mediarec folder, double-click the file recsite.htm, then click OK.

e. Click the Event Registration button on the navigation bar.

f. Type your name in the Name field, click the Print button on the browser toolbar. Click the home Page link, then print that page.

g. Close the Browser window.

h. Close the recsite.htm file, but keep Publisher open.

7. **Convert a print publication to a Web site.**

a. Open the file PB C-6.pub from the drive and folder where your Project Files are stored.

b. In the Brochure Options task pane, click Convert to Web layout.

c. In the Web options task pane, verify that the Multiple icon in the navigation bar section is selected, then click None in the Form section.

d. Starting on page 1, use your Publisher skills to arrange the text and graphics on the pages appropriately, resizing, moving and arranging text and graphics as necessary. Replace placeholder graphics with appropriate pieces of clip art.

e. In an appropriate place on the home page, type **Designed by** *Your Name*, then save the file as a Web page with the name **fund.htm** in a folder called **fund** to the drive and folder where your Project Files are stored.

f. Open the pages in your browser, test the links, then print the pages from the browser.

g. Close your browser, then exit Publisher, do not save the publication.

► **Independent Challenge 1**

You have been hired by a local café to advertise their Saturday Karaoke Night series. You have decided to create a Web page describing the series that the café can publish on their ISP's (Internet Service Provider's) Web server. You start by creating a Web publication.

a. Start Publisher, then create a new Web publication using the Radial Web Site design.

b. Choose Multiple navigation bars, then insert a sign-up form on the second page.

c. Choose a Color Scheme and Font Scheme that appeals to you.

d. Replace the text Home Page Title with **Sing at Java Jerry's Café!**, delete the business tag line placeholder, replace the main paragraph text with the contents of the file PB C-7.doc, and do not use AutoFlow. Expand the text box so you can see all the text,

e. Delete the placeholder logo near the bottom of the page and replace the graphic with an appropriate piece of clip art.

f. Scroll to the bottom of the page, and insert the following text in the text box below To contact us:

Your Name, Karaoke Coordinator
Phone: 415-555-5232
E-mail: javajerryscafe@isp-services.com
98 Danvers Street
San Francisco, CA 94114

g. Save the publication with the name **karaoke**.

Publisher 2002

h. Open page 2 of the publication, replace the text Form Page Title with **Karaoke Night Registration**, replace the Sign-Up Form Title text with **Sing at Java Jerry's!**, delete all the labels and controls from Sign up for through Total, then delete all the labels and controls from Method of Payment through Exp. date: and the placeholder logo.

i. Just below the E-mail label, insert a text box for a label, then type **Song style** in it to create a song style label.

j. Insert a list box to the right of the Song style label that contains the following items **Country**, **R&B**, **Pop**, **Showtunes**, **Hip Hop**, and **Other**, resize the list box so that only the first item is showing.

k. Drag the remaining controls and labels up to fill in the empty space on the page, double-click the Submit button, click the Save the data in a file on my Web server option button, click OK, then save your publication.

l. Preview your page in a Web browser, then make any necessary formatting adjustments in Publisher, save your publication as a Web page named **karaoke.htm** in a folder called **karaoke** in the drive and folder where your Project Files are stored.

m. Print the pages, close your browser, close the publication, then exit Publisher.

► Independent Challenge 2

You are the human resources director for Jasmine Herbal Harvest, a producer of herbal products. You are conducting a contest for your sales force, offering prizes for the best success story relating to your line of herbal products. You will post the information about the contest on your company intranet.

a. Start Publisher. Create a Web site using one of the Web site designs in the New Publication task pane.

b. Add multiple navigation bars and a response form.

c. Choose a color and font scheme that you like, and replace any graphics with appropriate ones.

d. Insert the following text on your home page, replacing the placeholder text as appropriate:
   Jasmine Herbal Harvest, Inc., 2230 Red Rock Way, Sedona, Arizona 86336, (520) 555-9010

e. Type your name somewhere on the home page, and delete the placeholder logos on both pages.

f. On the home page, replace the paragraph text with the file PB C-8.doc. Don't use Autoflow and be sure you can view all the text in the text box.

g. Create a link from "Contest Form" at the end of the paragraph to the Contest form on page 2.

h. On page 2, replace the placeholder Form headings with the following:

Form Heading Placeholder	Replace with:
Form Page Title	Success Story Contest
General Response Form Title	Win a Caribbean Cruise for two!
Briefly describe your desired feedback	Describe the best success story you've heard from a customer about Jasmine Herbal Harvest products.

i. Delete all the placeholder questions, and the comments label, then drag the text box control up to close up the empty space.

j. Modify the remaining placeholder controls and labels so that the form contains only an E-mail label and text box and Submit and Reset buttons. Create a list box below the E-mail text box with four items as follows: **North**, **South**, **East**, **West**, then add a label with the text **Sales Territory**.

k. Drag all the remaining elements up to close up the space. Delete the placeholder logo.

l. Double-click the Submit button, click the save data in a file on my Web server option button, then click OK.

m. Preview your Publication in a browser using the Web Page Preview button, then make necessary changes. Save the publication as a Web page called **jasmine.htm**, in a new folder called **jasmine** in the drive and folder where your Project Files are stored.

n. View the pages in your browser, print both pages, close the browser, then exit Publisher.

Independent Challenge 3

Create a Web site about yourself using your Publisher Web site creation skills.

a. Start by planning the information you want to include in your site. Remember that you can include several pages in your site, so you should plan on breaking the information up logically into separate Web pages. Make a list of information you want your site to contain, and create an outline of the site showing what information will appear on each page.

b. Start Publisher, choose a Web Site design from the New Publication task pane, then select the options you want to use for your Web site. In addition to your home page, include at least one Story page, and one Form page. You may include other pages if you want.

c. Replace the placeholder text and graphics on your Web site with graphics that are appropriate for you. If you need to add additional pages, click Insert page on the Web Site Options task pane. Publisher inserts a new page after the currently selected page.

d. Save your publication with the name **myweb.pub**.

e. Preview your Publication in a browser using the Web Page Preview button, make necessary changes, then use the Save As Web Page command to save the file as myweb.htm to a new folder called **mywebpg**.

f. View the pages in a browser, print the pages, close the browser, close the file, then exit Publisher. Do not save the modified logo.

 Independent Challenge 4

There are many organizations that help people worldwide. Pick a cause that is important to you that works in the global community. It could be a health issue, a political cause, or a charitable organization. Create a Web site about this topic.

a. Log on to the Internet, go to a search engine site such as AltaVista, (www.altavista.com), and research your chosen topic. Be sure to find out how organizations work around the world to help and support this cause.

b. To create the Web site, choose a Web site design, color scheme, and font scheme that appeal to you, and appropriate graphics. Your site should have at least three pages, including a home page, a Response Form page, and a Related Links page. On the home page, include a paragraph written by you that provides an overview of the topic. Insert links from the paragraph to the Related Links page and the Response Form page.

c. On the Related Links page, insert at least five links to other Web sites that relate to your topic.

d. On the Response Form page, include at least one survey question for your viewers to answer relating to your cause.

e. Type your name somewhere on the Web page, use the Web page preview button to preview your work, then make any necessary adjustments in Publisher. Save your publication as **mycause.pub**, then save it as a Web page named **mycause.htm** in a folder called **my_cause**.

f. View the page in Publisher, view the page in your default browser. Print your pages.

g. Exit Publisher.

► Visual Workshop

Use Publisher to create the Web page shown in Figure C-18. Use the Bars Web design, the Trout color scheme, and the Industrial font scheme. Move the coffee cup graphic to the position shown in the figure, then import the paragraph text from the file PB C-9.doc. Format the paragraph text in Franklin Gothic Book 11 point. Resize the text box so that the paragraph fits as shown. Create the controls shown using the Web form control button. Add the E-mail label. Type your name in the E-mail text box on the page, save the publication as **inn_site.pub**, then save it as a Web page called **innsite.htm** in a new folder titled **inn**. View the publication in your default browser then print it. Close the browser, then exit Publisher.

FIGURE C-18

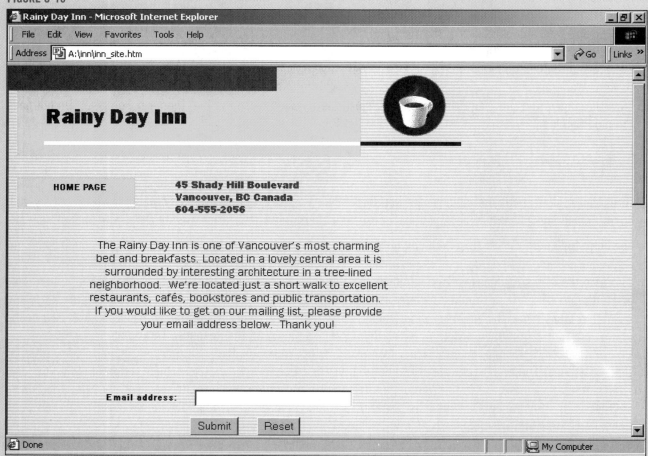

FrontPage 2002

Getting
Started with FrontPage

Objectives

- ► **Define Web authoring tools**
- ► **Start FrontPage and view the FrontPage window**
- ► **Create a Web page from a template**
- ► **Insert images and change background color**
- ► **Enter text**
- ► **Format text**
- ► **Format paragraphs**
- ► **Save and view a Web page**

The World Wide Web is an important means of communication for organizations and individuals alike. Almost every business needs to have a presence on the Web to provide customers with information about their company and their products. FrontPage 2002 is an easy-to-use and powerful Web authoring tool that makes it easy to create professional-looking Web pages. Helen Redwing works in the Information Systems Department at MediaLoft, a nationwide chain of bookstore cafés that sells books, CDs and videos. The company recently decided to establish a presence on the Web, and Helen was chosen to design the MediaLoft Web site. You will work with Helen as she learns to use FrontPage to create the company's Web pages.

Defining Web Authoring Tools

Microsoft FrontPage 2002 is a Web authoring tool that lets you design, administer, and publish Web pages to create Web sites. A **Web page** is a document that can be viewed on the World Wide Web through a **browser**—software designed to display Web pages. A **Web site** is a group of related Web pages. A Web site can be hosted on a Web server or on a local computer. A **Web server** is a computer that is always connected to the Internet. It runs software that makes Web pages available to anyone with access to the World Wide Web. Most Web sites have a **home page**, which is the main page of a Web site and usually contains hyperlinks to other pages on the site. A **hyperlink** is text or a graphic that you click to go to another location—either on the same site or another site. In FrontPage, a Web site is called a **web**. Helen plans to begin the project by creating MediaLoft's home page. Before she begins, she reviews the key advantages of using FrontPage to create the Web site.

The advantages of using FrontPage include being able to:

► **Create impressive Web pages without programming**

All Web pages are written in a standard language called **Hypertext Markup Language (HTML)**, which uses special codes to mark how different parts of the page should appear. Rather than requiring you to learn these codes, FrontPage shows the page as it would appear in the browser and inserts the codes for you. FrontPage lets you set up a Web page simply by typing text and inserting objects, such as images or link bars, in the document window. A **link bar** is a set of hyperlinks used for navigating a Web site.

► **Use templates and wizards to speed site creation**

FrontPage comes with dozens of ready-made templates and wizards that you can use to jump-start your Web sites. A **template** is a set of predesigned formats for text and graphics that you can use as a basis for a new page or site. Figure A-1 shows a template before modifications. Figure A-2 shows a Web page that was created by modifying the template shown in Figure A-1. A **wizard** is an interactive program that presents you with a series of dialog boxes in which you must choose options or answer questions, resulting in a finished Web page.

► **Administer Web sites easily**

FrontPage includes easy-to-use tools for administering Web sites. For instance, FrontPage lets you view and manage the relationships between multiple pages in a Web site. You can also check internal and external hyperlinks, or view a report showing an overview of your Web site's vital statistics such as which pages are visited most frequently by viewers, or which pages take the longest time to download.

► **Use formatting tools to enhance the look of your Web site**

FrontPage provides you with an arsenal of tools to help you create visually appealing Web sites. You can change the color of the background or fonts, insert your own image from a file or from the Clip Organizer, or create textual special effects.

► **Apply a common look and feel across a Web site**

FrontPage comes with dozens of professionally designed themes. A **theme** is a way to apply graphics, colors, and fonts across a Web site, or part of a Web site, to create a consistent, visually appealing site.

► **Use FrontPage with other Microsoft Office applications**

FrontPage is part of the Microsoft Office XP suite, and therefore shares many of its features, including a similar interface and the ability to copy content easily between applications. FrontPage also shares the Clip Organizer and the Spell Checker.

FIGURE A-1: Web page template in its original condition before customization

Placeholder graphics

Placeholder text

Table borders are visible

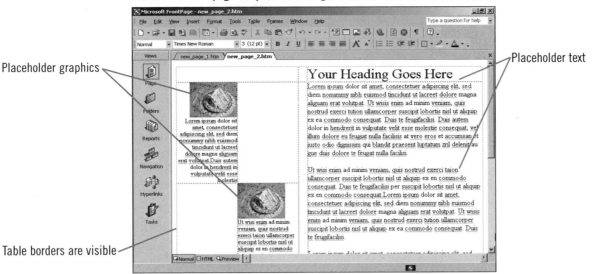

FIGURE A-2: Web site created by modifying a template

Placeholder text replaced and formatted

Clip art replaced placeholder graphics

Text formatted to wrap around graphic

Hyperlinks

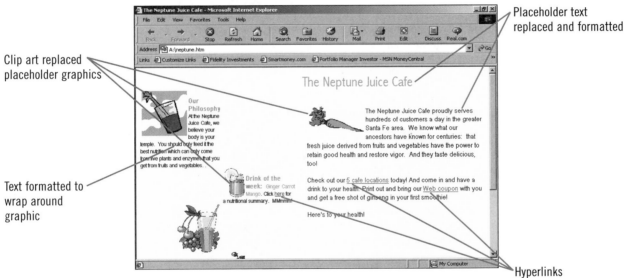

CLUES TO USE

Keys to an effective Web page

As you plan your Web page, keep in mind these three key qualities for making it effective:

1. **Focus.** Your Web page should have a clear purpose and you should avoid adding distracting elements to the page. Two of the most common goals for Web pages are marketing products and making information available. Focus helps to make a page effective in achieving its goal and makes it easy for viewers to use.

2. **Visual appeal.** Formatting is critical in making your page one that people enjoy viewing, rather than just tolerating. Plan how you will use colors for the background and for text, select a few fonts, and design graphics to create a unified look and feel. To create

a really effective page, it can be worth the time and expense to create graphics and color schemes that fit both your image and the information on the page you are creating. If design is not one of your strengths, take advantage of the themes provided with FrontPage.

3. **Simplicity.** Although adding visual effects helps to create an interesting page, it's just as important not to overdo it. Colors and fonts are most effective when used in moderation. Keep the page's content simple. Limit your information to the amount that fits on a single screen, so users can see all the information without scrolling.

FrontPage 2002

Starting FrontPage and Viewing the FrontPage Window

To start FrontPage, you use the Start button on the taskbar. If you are using a computer that is connected to a network you might need to follow a slightly different procedure. ✎ Helen begins the project by starting FrontPage and familiarizing herself with the main elements of the program window.

Steps

1. **Click the Start button** 🏁 Start **on the taskbar, then point to Programs**
   The Programs menu opens, displaying a list of programs installed on your computer. Compare your screen to Figure A-3.

Trouble?

If a dialog box opens asking if you want to make FrontPage your default editor, click No.

2. **Click Microsoft FrontPage**
   The FrontPage program window opens with a blank new page in the Web page window. The New Page or Web task pane is on the right side of the window. The **task pane** gives you access to the most commonly used commands; FrontPage has several task panes that help you with the task you are performing. The New Page or Web task pane displays commands for opening an existing page or web, or creating a new page or web.

Details

Refer to Figure A-4 to review the following elements:

► The **title bar** at the top of the window indicates the program name and contains the window sizing buttons. You can type in a question about FrontPage in the **Ask a Question box**. After you press [Enter], the Help system provides a list of topics in response to your query.

► The **menu bar** shows the names of FrontPage menus. When you click a menu name on the menu bar, FrontPage provides a short list of related commands. If you want to see an expanded list, you can wait a few seconds, or you can double-click the menu name, or click the down arrows at the bottom of the menu to see the full menu.

► The **toolbars** contain buttons for commonly used FrontPage commands. The **Standard toolbar** contains buttons for commonly used commands. The **Formatting toolbar** makes it easy to change the appearance of text and other elements in a Web page.

► The **Views bar** on the left side of the screen lets you choose the way you want to view your Web page. Currently, the Page button is selected and a blank page appears in the Page View window. The **Page View window** is the area of the screen where you create, view, and edit your page. Review Table A-1 for a description of the other buttons on the Views bar.

► The three buttons at the bottom of the Page View window allow you to change the way a Web page appears in the Page View window. Use the **Normal pane** for all your Web page creating and editing tasks. The Normal pane shows basic formatting and lets you add, delete, and modify Web page elements. The **HTML pane** reveals the underlying HTML code that creates the current page in a Web browser. If you are familiar with HTML, you can use this pane to edit a page's code directly. The **Preview pane** shows most page elements as they would appear in a Web browser, but does not allow you to make changes to the Web page. Whereas the Normal pane represents some elements with placeholder icons that don't reflect their appearance in a browser, the Preview pane shows all but the most complex Web page elements.

► The **Status bar** contains information about the current view, including helpful hints on the activity you are currently performing, and the approximate download time of the current Web page.

FIGURE A-3: Programs menu

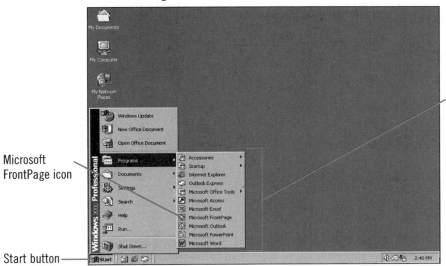

Microsoft
FrontPage icon

Programs submenu,
your items may differ

Start button

FIGURE A-4: FrontPage program window

Title bar
Menu bar
Standard
toolbar
Formatting
toolbar

Ask a
question box

View bar

Task pane

New blank page
open in Normal
pane in Page View

Normal
pane
button

Status bar

HTML pane button   Preview pane button

Estimated time to download

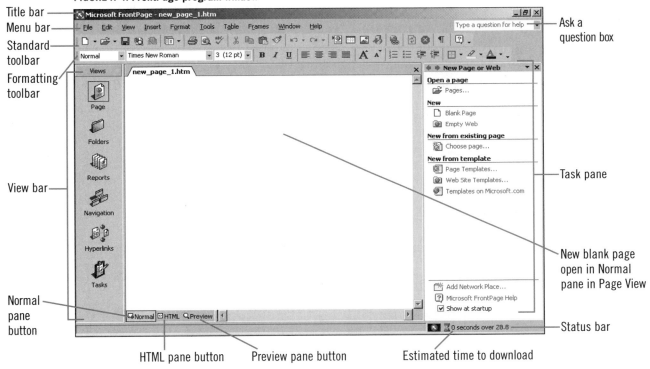

TABLE A-1: Views bar buttons

button	name	allows you to
	Page	view, create, and edit a Web page
	Folders	view your Web site at a directory level and organize your folders
	Reports	check information about your Web site, such as how many links are broken, which pages are slow to load, and other details
	Navigation	create and edit the overall structure of your Web site by dragging pictorial representations of each page
	Hyperlinks	view a visual map of the hyperlinks in your Web site and edit them
	Tasks	prioritize and keep track of tasks necessary to create and maintain a Web site

Creating a Web Page from a Template

The easiest way to create a Web page is to start from a template. The main benefit to using a template is that the underlying structure of the page is already set up for you. All you need to do is replace the placeholder text and graphics with your own, and modify the existing structure to suit your needs. When you open a template, you can see that the underlying structure uses a table, much like a table you create in Microsoft Word. A table allows you to organize your page elements, such as a graphic and text, so that they appear side by side in a browser. You open a template by clicking the Page Templates link on the New Page or Web task pane. ✎ Helen plans to include a short paragraph about MediaLoft and the MediaLoft logo on the home page. She decides to use a Page template to get started.

Trouble?

To open the task pane, click **View** on the menu bar, then click Task Pane.

1. Click **File** on the menu bar, click **Close** to close the blank page, if one is open, then click **Page Templates** in the New from template area in the **New Page or Web** task pane
   The Page Templates dialog box opens with the General tab displayed.

2. Click the **Narrow, Left-aligned Body template** in the second row
   A preview of the template appears in the lower-right corner of the dialog box, as shown in Figure A-5.

3. Click **OK**
   The Page Templates dialog box closes and a new page appears in the Normal pane of the Page View window with placeholder text and graphics, as shown in Figure A-6. The temporary name of the new page, new_page_1.htm, appears in the Page View page tab and also in the title bar.

FIGURE A-5: Page Templates dialog box

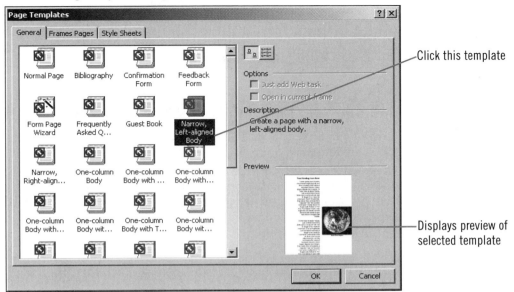

Click this template

Displays preview of selected template

FIGURE A-6: New Web page with placeholder text and graphics

Temporary name appears here

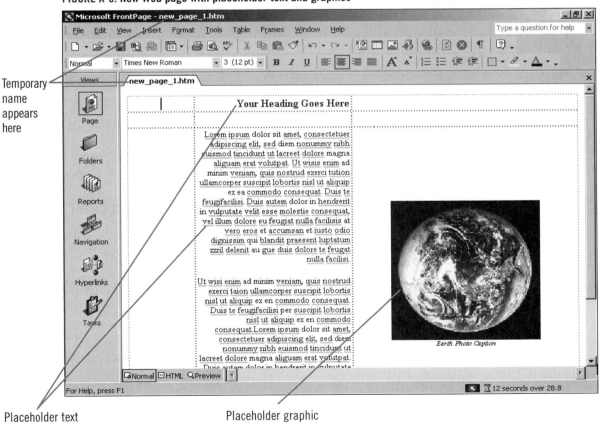

Placeholder text

Placeholder graphic

Inserting Images and Changing Background Color

A graphic can serve as a focal point around which to build a Web page. A well-designed image, such as a photograph, corporate logo, or simple drawing, can help create a mood or convey a message. You can insert your own images or use clip art from the **Clip Organizer**, a library of images that comes with Microsoft Office that you access from the task pane. You can also change the color of the background. Helen wants to replace the photo of the earth with the MediaLoft logo, and add an image from the Clip Organizer. She also plans to use one of the logo's colors as the background color for the page.

Trouble?

If the Pictures toolbar doesn't open, click on the Standard toolbar. If the Drawing toolbar opens, close it.

1. Click the **photo of the earth** to select it, click the **Insert Picture From File button** on the Pictures toolbar that opened

   The Picture dialog box opens.

2. Click the **Look in list arrow**, locate the drive and folder where your Project Files are stored, click **fpa-1.jpg**, then click **Insert**

   The MediaLoft logo appears in the cell of the table where the earth image used to be, as shown in Figure A-7. The Status bar indicates that it will take 10 seconds for a user with a 28K modem to download this page.

QuickTip

If a dialog box opens asking if you would like the Clip Organizer to catalog the contents of your hard disk, click Later.

3. Position the insertion point to the left of the first word in the placeholder paragraph text in the second column, click **Insert** on the menu bar, point to **Picture**, then click **Clip Art**

   The Insert Clip Art task pane opens.

4. Select any text that may be in the Search text text box in the Search For area, type **books** in the Search text text box, then click **Search**

   A list of results appears in the task pane as **thumbnails**, or small representations, of each image. If you are connected to the Internet, your search results will display the images available on the Web.

Trouble?

If you don't get results shown in the figure, select any appropriate image.

5. Scroll down the list of results, then click **the image of the open book** that has a ScreenTip that tells you it is 100 (w) × 100 (h) pixels, as shown in Figure A-8, then click the **task pane close button**

6. Click the **clip-art image** to select it, double-click **Format** on the menu bar, click **Position** to open the Position dialog box, click **Left** in the Wrapping style area, then click **OK**

   The paragraph text now wraps around the image. **Wrapping** means that text flows around an object rather than through it.

7. Position the mouse pointer on the lower-right corner of the clip art until it changes to a ↖, then drag it up and to the left so that the clipart is approximately 1" square

   The image is now smaller, and the paragraph text rewraps around it.

8. Double-click **Format** on the menu bar, click **Background** to open the Page Properties dialog box, click the **Background list arrow** in the Colors area, then click **More Colors**

   The More Colors dialog box opens.

9. Click the **second cell** in the top row of the color sampler to display the value Hex={33,66,99}, click **OK** to close the More Colors dialog box, then click **OK** to close the Page Properties dialog box

   The blue color that matches the logo replaces the default white background. See Figure A-9.

FIGURE A-7: New page with MediaLoft logo inserted

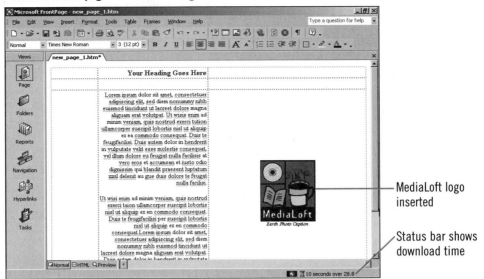

MediaLoft logo inserted

Status bar shows download time

FIGURE A-8: Insert Clip Art task pane with book image selected

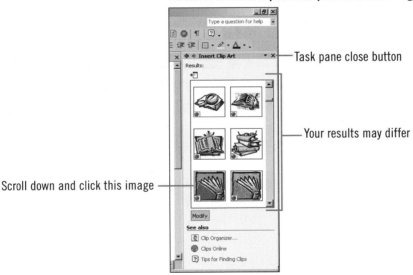

Task pane close button

Your results may differ

Scroll down and click this image

FIGURE A-9: Web page with blue background color

Text wraps around clip art

Blue background matches logo color

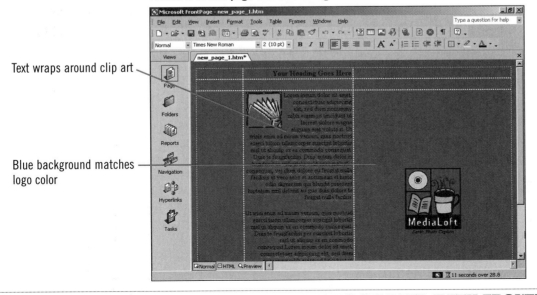

Entering Text

When you create a Web site, there's no question that you will need to incorporate text into it. However, keep in mind that large blocks of text can diminish the effectiveness of your Web site and cause a viewer to lose interest and go elsewhere. It's a good idea to keep your blocks of text small and your headings short. FrontPage allows you to enter and edit text just as you would in a word processor such as Microsoft Word. ▰▰▰ Helen plans to modify the page further by replacing the placeholder text with appropriate headings and text. She plans to insert text describing a typical visitor's experience at a MediaLoft store, and will import this text from a file.

Steps

1. At the top of the page, select the text **Your Heading Goes Here**, then type **A Dream Come True**

2. Drag to select all the placeholder text in the third row of the middle column of the table

QuickTip

Select only the text in the middle column; if you select anything else, click anywhere to deselect it and try again.

3. Click **Insert** on the menu bar, then click **File**
   The Select File dialog box opens.

4. Click the **Look in list arrow** locate the drive and folder where your Project Files are stored, click the **Files of type list arrow**, click **Text files**, click **FP A-2.txt**, click **Open**, click the **Normal paragraphs option button** in the Convert Text dialog box, then click **OK**
   A paragraph of text from a text file is imported onto the page, as shown in Figure A-10.

Trouble?

If the font size for the inserted text is 2 (10), select the inserted text, click the font size list arrow, then click 3 (12)

5. Press **[Tab]** twice
   A new row is added to the bottom of the table and the insertion point is now in the first column of the new row.

6. Press **[Tab]** to move the insertion point to the middle cell of the bottom row, then type **Well, wake up. You're at MediaLoft.**
   The new text is in the middle column, and has the same formatting attributes of the text paragraph in the cell above.

7. Press **[Tab]** to move the insertion point to the far right cell of the bottom row, then type **Books. Music. Coffee.**

8. Double-click **Insert** on the menu bar, click **Break**, verify that the **Normal line break option button** is selected in the Break dialog box, click **OK**, then type **It's all right here.**
   Although pressing [Enter] after a line inserts a space between paragraphs, you can insert a break to move the subsequent text to a new line without a blank line between the lines.

9. Place the pointer over the vertical table border dividing the second and third columns, when the pointer changes to ↔, drag the border to the right edge of the letter **M** in the MediaLoft logo, then release the mouse button
   The table still fills the page; however, the right column has narrowed, and the middle column has widened.

10. Drag to select the text **Earth Photo Caption** under the MediaLoft logo, then press **[Delete]**
   Compare your screen to Figure A-11.

FIGURE A-10: Web page containing imported text file

New heading text ——

Inserted Text file ——

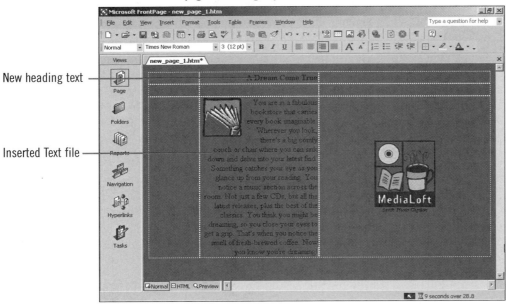

FIGURE A-11: MediaLoft Home page with all text entered and column widths adjusted

Additional table row inserted ——

Column width adjusted ——

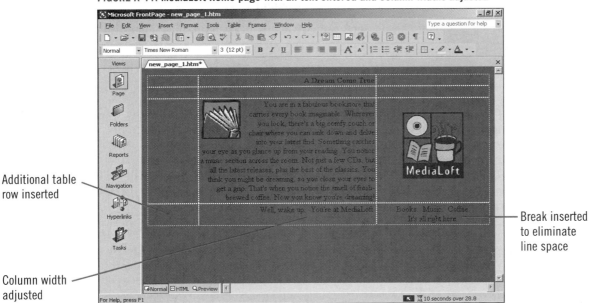

—— Break inserted to eliminate line space

Table formatting options

You can adjust many aspects of tables in your Web page by using the Table Properties dialog box. To open the Table Properties dialog box, right-click the table that you want to customize, then click Table Properties on the shortcut menu. You can apply colors to table borders by choosing a color from the Borders Color list box. To give your table a colored background different from the rest of the page, click the Color list arrow in the Background area then choose a color you want. To use a graphic file as the table background, check the Use background picture check box, then click the Browse button to select a graphic file. You can also adjust space between cells. To do this, use the up and down arrows to adjust the settings in the Cell spacing boxes in the Layout area. Setting the cell spacing value to 0 creates borders composed of single thin lines, while setting it to a higher number enhances the default 3D effect.

Formatting Text

FrontPage includes tools that allow you to format Web page text easily. In addition to changing the font and font size of text, FrontPage allows you to apply font styles, such as bold and italic, and to change text color. You can use the Format Painter button to copy the formatting attributes of one portion of text and apply it to another. Now that Helen has added all the text to her page, she wants to apply different fonts, font styles, and colors to individual selections.

Steps

1. Drag to select the heading text **A Dream Come True**, click the **Font list arrow** on the Formatting toolbar, then click **Franklin Gothic Medium Cond** on the Font list, as shown in Figure A-12

   The heading text now appears in Franklin Gothic Medium Condensed. The text is still selected.

2. Click the **Format Painter button** on the Standard toolbar, then click to select the text in the fourth row, second column

   The text "Well, Wake up. You're at MediaLoft" now appears in the same font as the main heading and also has bold formatting applied to it.

   Trouble?

   If California FB is not available, choose another font.

3. Drag to select the **paragraph text** in the middle column, click the **Font list arrow** on the Formatting toolbar, then click **Californian FB**

   The text is formatted in the Californian FB font and is still selected.

4. Position the mouse pointer on the top table border above A Dream Come True until the pointer changes to a ↓, click to select all the text in the column, click the **Font Color list arrow** ▲▾ on the Formatting toolbar, then click **More Colors**

   The More Colors dialog box opens, as shown in Figure A-13.

5. Click the **yellow color** in the fourth row from the bottom to display Value Hex-{FF,FF,66}, click **OK**, then click anywhere to deselect the text

   The light yellow color matches one of the logo colors and makes the text stand out more clearly against the dark blue background.

6. Select the text in the bottom-middle cell, then click the **Bold button** **B** on the Formatting toolbar

   The text now appears without bold formatting.

7. Select both lines of text in the bottom-right cell, click the **Font list arrow**, click **Franklin Gothic Medium Cond**, click the **Font Size list arrow**, then click **4 (14 pt)**

8. Click the **Font Color list arrow** ▲▾, click **More colors**, click the **orange color** in the third row from the bottom to display Value Hex={FF,CC,00}, click **OK** then click anywhere to deselect the text

   Compare your screen to Figure A-14.

FIGURE A-12: Font list box with Franklin Gothic Medium Condensed selected

Font list arrow

Font color button

Click this font

Format painter button

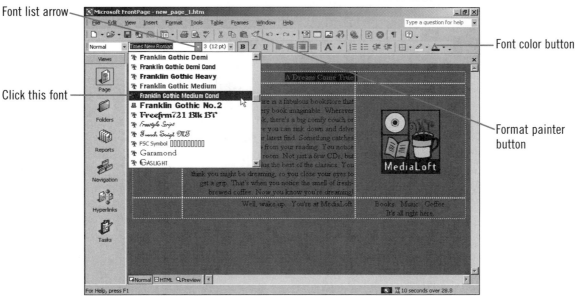

FIGURE A-13: More Colors dialog box

Click this yellow cell for the middle column text color

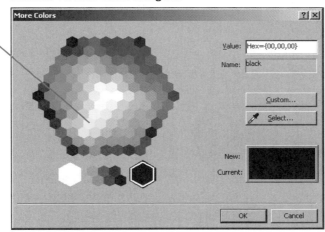

FIGURE A-14: Web page with formatted text

Reformatted yellow text

Reformatted orange text

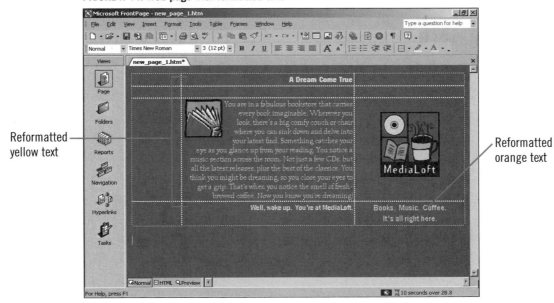

Formatting Paragraphs

In addition to applying formats to selected passages of text, FrontPage allows you to change the way each paragraph appears on a Web page. For instance, you can change a paragraph's alignment, indentation, or line spacing. **Alignment** determines whether a paragraph is lined up on its left or right edge, or is centered between the two. **Indentation** means the distance between the left or right edges of the paragraph text and any adjacent objects. Table A-2 shows the alignment and indentation buttons available in FrontPage, with an example or explanation of what they do. For the finishing touches on the MediaLoft home page, Helen wants to change the alignment of the headings and the paragraph text. She also wants to increase the line spacing of the paragraph text to make it more readable.

Steps

1. Click anywhere in the top cell in the second column, then click the **Center button** ▦ on the Formatting toolbar
   The text is **center aligned**, meaning that it is evenly placed between the right and left edges of the cell.

2. Click anywhere in the bottom cell in the second column, then click the **Center button** ▦
   This text is now also centered in its cell.

> **Trouble?**
>
> If Medialoft does not go to a second line, drag the column border between columns two and three to the left until it does.

3. With the insertion point still in the bottom middle cell, click the **Increase Indent button** ▦ twice on the Formatting toolbar
   The paragraph text is now indented. Because all the text no longer fits on one line, the word MediaLoft moves down to the next line. Compare your screen with Figure A-15.

4. Click anywhere in the cell containing the paragraph text, then click the **Align Left button** ▦ on the Formatting toolbar

5. Click **Format** on the menu bar, then click **Paragraph**
   The Paragraph dialog box opens, showing the Indents and Spacing tab.

6. Click the **Line spacing list arrow**, click **1.5 lines**, then click **OK**
   The paragraph appears with more space between each line.

7. Click the **Preview pane button** at the bottom of the Page View window
   The Preview pane now displays the Web page as it would appear in a browser. The table is no longer visible because it was only used to set up the page. Compare your screen to Figure A-16.

FIGURE A-15: Reformatted paragraph after adjusting alignment

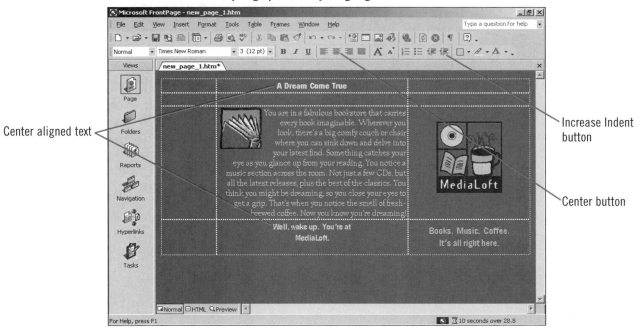

Center aligned text

Increase Indent button

Center button

FIGURE A-16: Web page with paragraph formatting completed in the Preview pane

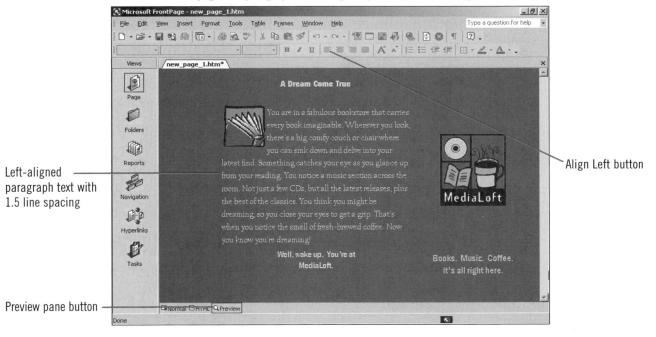

Left-aligned paragraph text with 1.5 line spacing

Align Left button

Preview pane button

TABLE A-2: Paragraph alignment buttons

button	name	example/explanation
	Align Left	You're at MediaLoft.
	Center	You're at MediaLoft.
	Align Right	You're at MediaLoft.
	Decrease Indent	Makes paragraph indentation smaller, in 0.5 in. increments
	Increase Indent	Makes paragraph indentation larger, in 0.5 in. increments

Saving and Viewing a Web Page

When you're satisfied with the way your page looks in Page View, you will need to save your page to a permanent location on a disk. To ensure that you have no problems transferring your Web page to a Web server, you should always save your files using the standard 8.3 filenaming convention; that is, with a maximum of eight alpha-numeric characters followed by a period and a three-letter extension. Do not use capital letters or spaces. When you save the Web page, FrontPage opens a dialog box showing a list of embedded files that are part of the page, such as graphics, sound files, or animations. You have the option to specify where to save these files so that FrontPage knows where they are when you open the page again. You can either save your page to an existing web if it is going to be one page of a Web site that you have already started, or you can save it as a separate file. Once you save the Web page, you can then use the Preview in Browser button to see what the page will look like to viewers on the Web. If something doesn't look right in the browser, you can then switch back to Page View and make necessary adjustments. You cannot make any changes to the page in Preview in Browser mode. ◆━━ Now that she has the MediaLoft home page set up, Helen decides to save the page she created as a file to a disk. She then uses the Preview in Browser button to see what the page will look like on the Web.

1. Click the **Save button** 🖫 on the Standard toolbar

   The Save As dialog box opens.

2. Click the **Save in list arrow**, then navigate to the drive and folder where your Project Files are stored

3. Type **ml_home** in the File name text box then click **Save**

   The Save Embedded Files dialog box appears, as shown in Figure A-17, showing a list of associated files that are part of the Web page you are saving, giving you options for how you want to save them.

4. Click **OK**

   The dialog box closes and the file name ml_home.htm now appears in the tab at the top of the Page View window, and also in the title bar. By default, FrontPage saved your page with an .htm extension.

5. Click the **Preview in Browser button** 🖳 on the Standard toolbar

   Your default browser opens with the ml_home file displayed in the address bar, as shown in Figure A-18. The title of the page, which is taken from the first row of the table, is in the title bar. If Helen is not pleased with the way it looks, she can switch back to FrontPage and continue making modifications.

6. Click the **Close button** on the browser window

   The browser window closes, and the FrontPage window with the Preview pane is now visible.

7. Click the **Normal pane button**, click in the cell in the last row, third column, press **[Tab]**, then type **Designed by: your name** in the first column of the fifth row

8. Click the **Save button** 🖫, click **File** on the menu bar, click **Print**, click **OK**, click **File** on the menu bar, then click **Close**

   The ml_home Web page closes.

9. Click **File** on the menu bar, then click **Exit**

   FrontPage closes.

FIGURE A-17: Save Embedded Files dialog box

Clip art file ——

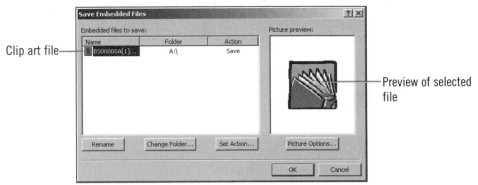

—— Preview of selected file

FIGURE A-18: MediaLoft Home page in browser window

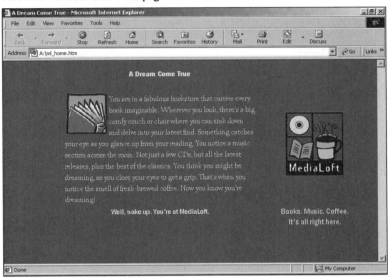

Getting Help

FrontPage includes an extensive Help system that you can use to learn about features and commands. To get immediate help while working in FrontPage, type a question in the Ask a Question box on the far right of the Menu bar. Doing so brings up a list of topics in the Help system, as shown in Figure A-19, any of which you can click to learn more about a given topic. You can also get help by using the Office Assistant, using the Help menu, or by visiting the Microsoft Web site, which includes tutorials. The Office Assistant is an animated character that gives context-appropriate tips while you work. To get Help from the Office Assistant, simply click the Office Assistant, then type your question. If the Office Assistant appears on your screen, you can hide it by right-clicking the character, then clicking Hide on the shortcut menu. If you've hidden the Office Assistant, press [F1] to have it reappear, then ask for help. If you've turned off the Office Assistant, you can click Help on the menu bar, then click Show the Office Assistant to make it reappear. To access Help online, click Help on the menu bar, then click Office on the Web. You must be able to connect to the Internet to access the Web site.

FIGURE A-19: Help topics displayed after using Ask a Question box

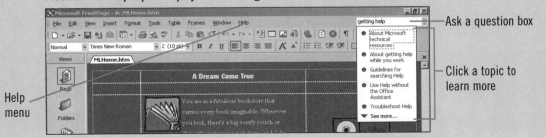

Help menu

—— Ask a question box

—— Click a topic to learn more

Practice

► Concepts Review

Label each of the elements of the FrontPage window shown in Figure A-20.

FIGURE A-20

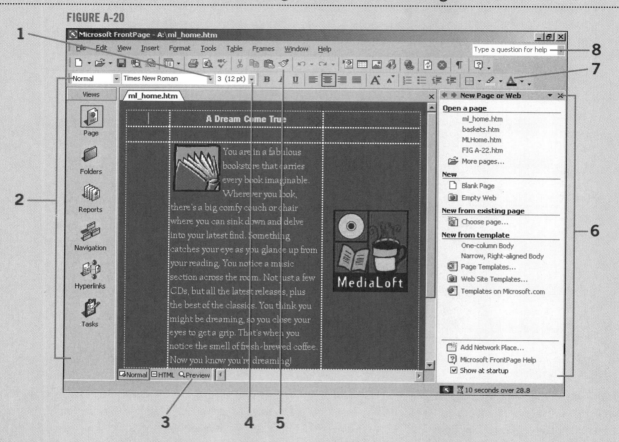

Match the following buttons with the descriptions of their functions.

9.
10.
11.
12.
13.

a. Aligns text in the center of two margins
b. Copies the formatting of one piece of text to another
c. Applies a new color to the selected text
d. Opens the current Web page in the default browser
e. Increases the indent of a paragraph by 0.5 inches

Select the best answer from the list of choices.

14. The standard language for writing Web pages is:
- **a.** HTTP.
- **b.** Visual Basic.
- **c.** HTML.
- **d.** C.

15. The view you use to create a Web page in FrontPage is:
- **a.** Page View.
- **b.** Folders View.
- **c.** Navigation View.
- **d.** Hyperlinks View.

16. The Normal pane in FrontPage shows:
- **a.** The basic components of the current Web page.
- **b.** A Web page as it would appear in a browser.
- **c.** Only the graphic files of a page.
- **d.** The underlying Web page code.

17. The Preview pane in FrontPage shows:
- **a.** The basic components of the current Web page.
- **b.** The underlying Web page code.
- **c.** Only the graphic files of a page.
- **d.** A Web page as it would appear in a browser.

18. A quick way to apply consistent graphics, color, and fonts across a Web site is called a:
- **a.** Template.
- **b.** Thumbnail.
- **c.** Wizard.
- **d.** Theme.

▶ Skills Review

1. Start FrontPage and view the FrontPage window.
- **a.** Start FrontPage.
- **b.** Identify as many parts of the FrontPage window as you can without referring to the unit material.

2. Create a Web page from a template.
- **a.** Close the open blank new_page_1.htm page, click View on the menu bar, click Task Pane to open the New Page or Web task pane if it is not already open, then click the Page Templates link in the New from template area.
- **b.** Click the Narrow Right-Aligned Body template then click OK.

3. Insert images and change background color.
- **a.** Click the placeholder photograph, click Insert on the menu bar, point to Picture, then click Clip Art. (If a dialog box opens asking if you want to catalog your image files, click Later.)
- **b.** In the Insert Clip Art task pane, type **fitness** in the Search box, click Search, click a graphic that you think will positively portray a fitness club's image, then close the task pane.
- **c.** Click Format on the menu bar, click Background, make sure the Background tab is selected in the Page Properties dialog box, click the Colors Background list arrow, click More Colors, click the yellow hexagon Value Hex={FF,FF,99}, then view the background as yellow.

4. Enter text.

a. Replace the heading placeholder text with **Emerson Fitness Center**.

b. Select all three placeholder paragraphs below the heading, click Insert on the menu bar, click File, locate the drive and folder where your Project Files are stored, click the Files of type list arrow, click Text files, open the file FP A-3.txt, click the Normal paragraphs option button in the Convert Text dialog box, then click OK.

c. Replace the caption under the clip art image you inserted with an appropriate description.

d. Increase the size of the column containing the paragraph text by dragging the left border of the column to the left about 2 inches.

5. Format text.

a. Select the heading Emerson Fitness Center, change the font to Franklin Gothic Medium Cond, with a Font size of 5 (18 pt).

b. With the heading text still selected, change the Font color to red.

c. Format the subheadings Tennis Center, Aquatics Center, and Fitness Center in a red font, Franklin Gothic Medium Condensed 4 (14 pt). (*Hint*: If you double-click the Format Painter button, you can use it over and over until you press [ESC].)

d. Format the paragraph text in Arial Narrow 3 (12 pt), keeping the color black.

e. Format the caption text you inserted in Times New Roman 2 (10 pt) italic.

6. Format paragraphs.

a. Center-align the cell containing the Emerson Fitness Center heading text.

b. Select all of the paragraph text and subheadings in the third row, click Format on the menu bar, click Paragraph, type **20** in the Before text box and **20** in the After text box in the Indentation area, then click OK.

c. Center-align the caption text under the clip art.

7. Save and view a Web page

a. Insert a new row at the bottom of the table, click in the middle cell of this new row, type **Designed by your name**, then center align this text.

b. Click the Save button on the Standard toolbar, click the Save in list arrow, navigate to where your Project Files are stored, save your Web page with the name **fitness.htm**, and save the embedded clip art file.

c. Click the Preview in Browser button on the Standard toolbar and compare your screen with Figure A-21.

d. Close the browser, print the page, then exit FrontPage.

FIGURE A-21

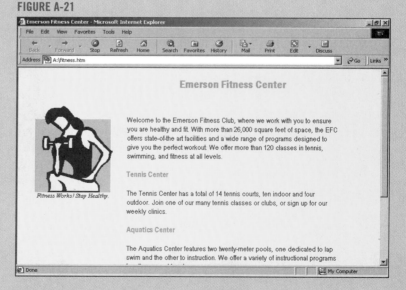

Independent Challenge 1

Ruby Williams is starting up a business creating and selling personalized gift baskets containing food and specialty items. Because such a business started in a storefront would be limited by the size of the customer base in the local area, she plans instead to market and sell her baskets on the Internet. She believes this strategy will not only give her access to a larger market, but will also reduce her costs by eliminating the rent expense. She decides to create her own Web pages.

a. Start FrontPage, then use the New Page or Web task pane to create a new page using the One-column body template.

b. Replace the text Your Heading Goes Here with **Ruby's Basketworld**.

c. Format Ruby's Basketworld in 18-pt Garamond font, change the color of the text to navy blue, then apply bold formatting to it.

d. Click in the empty cell below Ruby's Basketworld, click the Insert Picture From File button on the Picture toolbar, then select the file fpa-4.jpg from the folder where your Project Files are stored.

e. Drag the left edge of the third column to the left so that it is flush with the photograph.

f. Use the Format Background dialog box to change the background color to a light blue shade.

g. Delete the paragraph placeholder text, then double-click the bottom edge of the table so that the bottom row is narrowed.

h. Click in the bottom-middle cell of the table, click Table on the menu bar, point to Table Properties, click Cell, click the Color list arrow in the Background area, click the red square, then click OK.

i. In the red cell, insert the file FP A-5.txt from the drive and folder where your Project Files are stored as normal paragraphs.

j. Format the paragraph to insert **20** pixels of indentation before text and **20** pixels of indentation after text.

k. In the cell to the left of the paragraph text, type the following items, pressing [Enter] after each one so that each item is on a line by itself: **Birthday, Holiday, Get Well, Friendship, Romantic, Thanks.** Apply bold formatting to each of the items.

l. In the cell to the right of the red cell, type **Create a custom basket**, then apply bold formatting to it.

m. Select all of the text in the bottom row of the table, then change the font to High Tower Text.

n. Add another row to the bottom of the table, then type your name in the bottom-right cell.

o. Save the Web page as **baskets.htm** in the drive and folder where your Project Files are stored; preview the Web page in a browser.

p. Use the Print command on the File menu to print the page.

q. Close the browser, then exit FrontPage.

Independent Challenge 2

You and your friend recently graduated from cooking school and have started your own catering company, called What's For Dinner? Your business focuses on the busy working professional who has no time to cook and wants to pick up a home-cooked meal on the way home from work. You also offer delivery. Create a home page for your new company.

    a. Start FrontPage, then choose a page template that you like from the New Page or Web task pane.

    b. Replace any placeholder graphics with one or more pieces of appropriate clip art.

    c. Choose and apply a background color to the page that matches the colors in the graphic(s) you inserted.

    d. Replace the heading text and placeholder text with the company name and a paragraph describing your services, format it as necessary using different fonts, font sizes, font styles, or font colors, then align the paragraphs as appropriate.

    e. Type your name somewhere on the page, then save the page as **dinner.htm.**

    f. Preview the page in your browser, then return to FrontPage to adjust the layout if necessary.

    g. Print the page.

    h. Close the browser, then exit FrontPage.

Independent Challenge 3

Create a personal home page about yourself, using the skills you learned in this unit.

a. Start FrontPage, then choose a page template from the New Page or Web task pane and customize it with fonts, colors, and a background color that you feel describes you.

b. You can include any information about yourself that you care to share, including any of the following: your favorite hobbies or sports, topics that you are interested in, photos of yourself or your family, quotes that are meaningful to you, your philosophy of life, your favorite places.

c. Replace any placeholder graphics with appropriate clip art or photographs of your own.

d. Be creative and have fun! Be sure to put your name on your finished page. Save your page as **my_page.htm**.

e. Close the browser, print the page, then exit FrontPage.

Independent Challenge 4

Pick a city anywhere in the world that you are interested in visiting. Create a Web page about that city using the skills you learned in this unit.

a. You will first need to do some research on your chosen city. Log on to the Internet, go to a search engine site, such as AltaVista (www.altavista.com), and find out the following information to include in your page: (1) historical information, (2) sightseeing attractions, (3) performing arts events, (4) sporting or cultural events (if any).

b. Choose a page template from the New Page or Web task pane that appeals to you.

c. Replace any placeholder graphics with appropriate clip art or images downloaded from the Web.

d. Replace any placeholder text with text written by you from your research. Include sections on historical information, sightseeing attractions, performing arts events, and sporting or cultural events. You can type the information directly into your Web page, or create a text file in another program and insert it into the page.

e. Choose a background color and fonts that convey a message about your city.

f. Be sure to put your name somewhere on your page. Save your page with the name **my_city.htm**.

g. Close the browser, print the page, then exit FrontPage.

► Visual Workshop

Use FrontPage to create the Web page shown in Figure A-22. Use the page template One-column Body with Contents on Right to create the page. Format the heading text in Arial Black 6(24-pt). For the paragraph text, insert the text file FP A-6.txt as normal paragraphs from the drive and folder where your Project Files are stored. Format the paragraph text in Tahoma 3(12-pt). Format the text in the right column as Arial 3(12-pt). Insert the images shown or similar ones from the Clip Organizer. (*Hint*: in the Clip Art task pane, type **groceries** in the Search box.) Type your name somewhere on the page, then save the page as **redwgn.htm** with the embedded images in the folder where your Project Files are stored. Print the page and view it in a browser.

FIGURE A-22

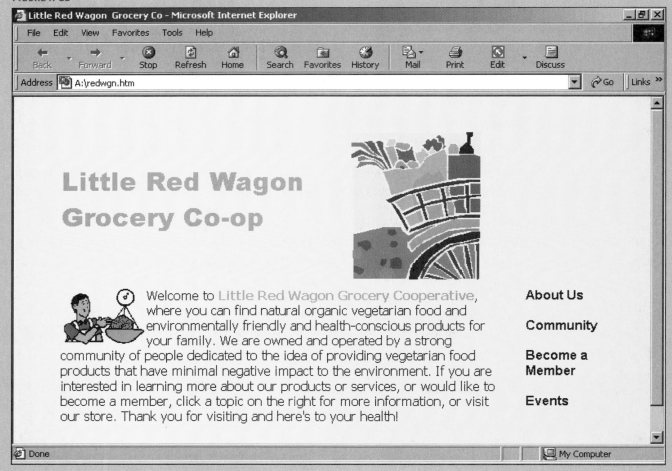

Creating
a Web Site

Objectives

► **Plan a Web site**
► **Create a new Web site**
► **Set up a navigation structure**
► **Add link bars**
► **Insert hyperlinks and bookmarks**
► **Format hyperlinks**
► **Add special effects**
► **Use site reports**

You can easily use FrontPage to create a **Web site**, a group of related Web pages. FrontPage includes wizards and templates to help you create a Web site by importing premade pages, by using a template, or from scratch. You can use FrontPage to set up a navigation structure and have FrontPage automatically insert links to all the pages in that structure. You can also add your own hyperlinks and add special effects. Once the pages look the way you want them to, you can use the site management tools to identify and troubleshoot problems before making your site available on the World Wide Web. After redesigning the home page for Medialoft, Helen Redwing uses FrontPage to create additional Web pages, describing the company's products and stores. She uses FrontPage to join the pages together into a Web site and create hyperlinks among them.

Planning a Web Site

Web site design, like Web page creation, benefits from thoughtful planning. A plan can help ensure that you are meeting your goals in creating the site and can serve as a guide that helps you avoid omission or duplication of elements. Even though it is possible to modify or add ideas at any time in the development, a good plan provides a solid foundation on which to develop your Web site. Helen uses the following guidelines to plan and create the MediaLoft Web site:

▶ Define a clear purpose

You need to define your goals. What information will you make available on your site? Why would a viewer visit and what kind of experience do you want them to have while at the site? Helen will describe a typical store experience on the home page. She will tell viewers about MediaLoft products, the locations of stores, store events, and the benefits of having a MediaLoft Club Card.

▶ Create a Web hierarchy

Web sites are composed of multiple Web pages. You want to be sure that people who use your Web site can easily access the information they want. A **Web hierarchy** is a visual representation of the structure of your Web site. Planning the structure is an important part of Web site design. For example, certain Web pages should be accessible, through hyperlinks, from the home page. Other pages in the Web site may not be accessible from the home page, but from other pages in the site. Identifying the Web hierarchy helps you visualize the project by illustrating the relationships among the Web pages. Helen decides how to break up the information she wants to include into separate pages and then draws a site hierarchy, as shown in Figure B-1.

▶ Create and format the Web pages

Once you have a structure for your Web site, you can create the component pages. In addition to creating several individual pages, you can use FrontPage's templates and automated wizards to create and format a group of Web pages. Helen creates each of her Web pages individually and uses a wizard to join them together as a **web**, or a group of pages that FrontPage treats as a single Web site.

▶ Establish relationships

Once you are happy with the content and design of your pages, you then need to create relationships between your pages. The most common way to relate the pages in a Web site is to create hyperlinks among them. The Web site creation tools in FrontPage allow you to add hyperlinks automatically by specifying the pages that a Web page should contain links to. This tool also automatically updates the hyperlinks when you add pages to your Web, or change or delete the associated pages.

▶ Test and verify the function and appearance

Before you make your completed Web site available on the Web, you should confirm that all the links and components work the way you intend. Generally, giving your Web site a final check includes viewing the pages in a browser, clicking each hyperlink to be sure it opens the intended page, and making sure the other components of the page appear and work correctly. FrontPage contains reporting tools that simplify the checking process. This summary provides an easy way to identify any problems with your Web site, which you can then fix before making it available.

▶ Publish the site

After you complete your Web site, the final step is to **publish** it, or make it available on the World Wide Web. This step involves copying all the Web files, including Web pages, graphics, and any other components, to a computer with a permanent connection to the Internet, known as a **Web server**. Helen plans to use FrontPage to specify the location of her Web site files and the address of her Web server, and then to publish the MediaLoft Web site.

FIGURE B-1: MediaLoft Web site hierarchy

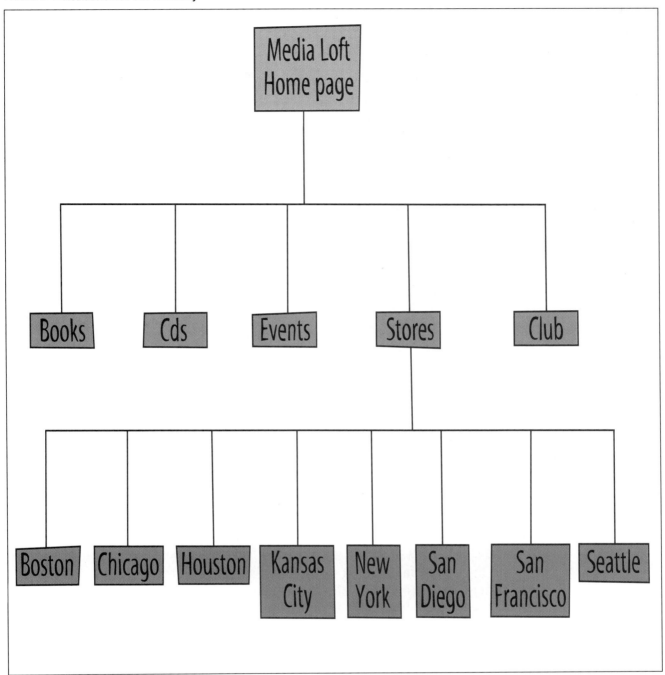

Using Subwebs

In addition to grouping Web pages together as a Web site, FrontPage allows you to subdivide the pages in a Web site into smaller groupings, known as subwebs. Grouping some pages into a subweb can allow you to make changes easily to the properties for those pages, while leaving the other pages in the Web site with the default properties. Because you can set Web pages to be accessible only to certain people or groups using an internal network, structuring a site with subwebs provides an easy way to designate which pages are available to which users.

Unit B

FrontPage 2002

Creating a New Web Site

When you create an individual Web page, it is saved as a single file, with the extension .htm or .html. Any associated files, such as graphics, are located in separate files. When you create a Web site in FrontPage, however, it groups all the Web pages, graphics, and other files into a named object, called a **Web**. All the files associated with a Web are located in a single folder on disk. When you open a Web, you specify the folder, rather than a particular file, to open. You can create a new Web in FrontPage either by importing existing files or by creating a group of new Web pages based on a template or wizard. Helen designed her own unique format for the MediaLoft Web pages and used FrontPage to create each one individually. Now she uses the Import Web Wizard to associate the Web pages, graphics, and other files into a FrontPage Web.

Trouble?

If a message box opens asking if you want to make FrontPage your default HTML editor, click No.

1. Start FrontPage, click **File** on the menu bar, then click **Close** to close new_page_1.htm.

2. If the New Page or Web task pane is not open, click **File** on the menu bar, point to **New**, then click **Page or Web**
   The New Page or Web task pane has several options for creating a new Page.

3. Click **Web Site Templates** in the New from template section
   The Web Site Templates dialog box opens showing several wizards and templates. The icons indicate whether it's a template or wizard that can help you create a Web site.

QuickTip

If you plan to create the Web in a location other than on a floppy disk, create a folder called mloftweb, then enter the path to that location in the Specify the location of the new web box. A Web should be in its own folder.

4. Click **Import Web Wizard** on the Web Sites tab, click **Browse**, specify the location where you want to save the new web, click **Open**, place the insertion point to the right of the slash in the Specify the location of the new web text box, then type **mloftweb**
   Your Web Site Templates dialog box should look similar to Figure B-2.

5. Click **OK**
   The Create New Web status window appears while the Wizard sets up the Web folder. The Import Web Wizard – Choose Source dialog box opens, as shown in Figure B-3.

6. Click the **From a source directory of files on a local computer or network option button**, click **Browse**, locate the drive and folder where your Project Files are stored, click the **Lesson folder**, click **Open**, then click **Next**
   The Import Web Wizard-Edit File List dialog box opens, showing all the files that Helen used to create the individual Web pages. These include graphic files and the htm files.

Trouble?

If you get a Server Busy error message, click Switch to, to correct the problem.

7. Click **Next**, then click **Finish**
   FrontPage imports all the files from the Lesson folder into the new Web. When the Wizard has finished importing all the files, you'll see the location and name of the new Web in the title bar.

8. Click the **Folders button** on the Views bar
   The Folder List and Contents pane appear, as shown in Figure B-4. In the Folder List you can see the mloftweb folder with two subfolders named _private and images. FrontPage automatically creates these two subfolders every time you create a new Web, to help you organize your files. You can use the _private folder to limit access to certain files, and the image folder to store all your graphics. At the moment, these subfolders are empty. The Contents pane displays all the files you just imported.

FIGURE B-2: Web Site Templates dialog box

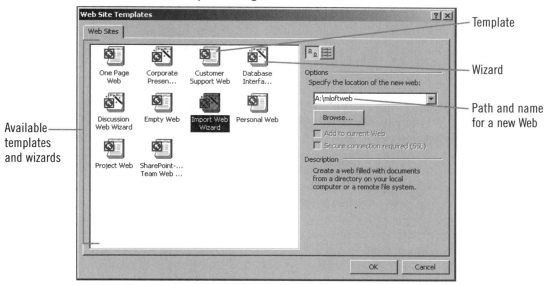

Template

Wizard

Path and name
for a new Web

Available
templates
and wizards

FIGURE B-3: Import Web Wizard - Choose Source dialog box

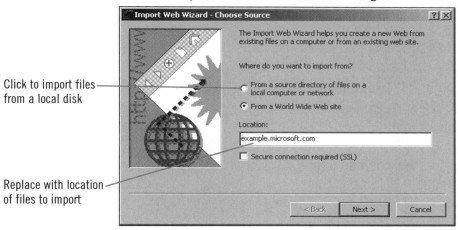

Click to import files
from a local disk

Replace with location
of files to import

FIGURE B-4: Folders View

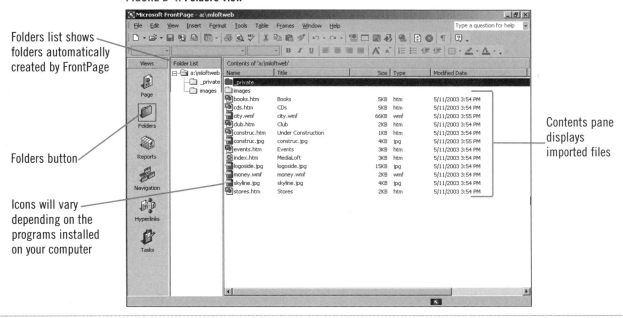

Folders list shows
folders automatically
created by FrontPage

Folders button

Icons will vary
depending on the
programs installed
on your computer

Contents pane
displays
imported files

Setting up a Navigation Structure

Once you've imported a collection of individual Web pages into a Web, it's a good idea to set up its navigation structure. You can use Navigation view to create a **Web hierarchy**, or a visual map of how your pages will relate to each other. In FrontPage, pages relationships are defined as one of three types: a parent page, a child page, or a peer page. A **parent page** is in an upper level of the hierarchy and has pages below linked to it. For instance, a home page is a parent page. A **child page** is at a lower level in the hierarchy and is linked to a parent page. A **peer page** is a page that shares a common parent with another page. Once you've set up a navigation structure, you can instruct FrontPage to use this hierarchy to automatically insert links throughout the Web. Helen uses Navigation View to set up the Web hierarchy she sketched in her original plan. Because she has no Store pages created yet, she will create an Under Construction page that will be linked from the Stores page.

Trouble?

If you do not see the Navigation toolbar just above the Folder List, click View on the menu bar, point to Toolbars, then click Navigation. If you don't see the Folder List, click View on the menu bar, then click Folders List.

Trouble?

If you position an icon correctly, simply drag it to the correct position shown in the figure.

QuickTip

To rename an icon, right click the icon, click Rename on the shortcut menu, type the new name, then press [Enter].

QuickTip

You can rearrange your hierarchy by dragging the page icon in the Navigation pane to a different location.

1. Click the **Navigation button** on the Views bar

   FrontPage switches to Navigation view, as shown in Figure B-5. At the moment, you only see the MediaLoft home page icon, which is the file named index.htm, in the Navigation pane. Because index.htm is the standard name for a Web site's home page, the file index.htm that you imported into your Web, mloftweb, is identified as the MediaLoft home page and automatically appears in the Navigation pane.

2. Drag the file **books.htm** from the Folder List into the Navigation pane, positioning it just below the MediaLoft icon

   A line connects the two icons indicating their relationship, as shown in Figure B-6. The home page is the parent page to the Books page, and the Books page is the child page to the home page.

3. Drag the file **cds.htm** from the Folder List into the Navigation pane, positioning it to the right of the Books icon

   The CDs and Books pages are now peer pages on the same level of the hierarchy.

4. Drag the file **stores.htm**, positioning it to the right of the CDs icon

5. Drag the file **events.htm**, positioning it to the right of the Stores icon

6. Drag the file **club.htm**, positioning it to the right of the Events icon

7. Drag the file **construc.htm**, so that it is positioned below the Stores icon

   Figure B-7 shows the relationships among these seven files. The under cons... icon is the child page to the Stores page, and is also a **placeholder page**, or a page that tells viewers that the Web site is incomplete.

8. Double-click the **MediaLoft icon** to open the home page in Page View, click the **Navigation button** in the Views bar, then double-click the **Books icon**

   Now both the MediaLoft home page and the Books page are open in Normal Page View, and you can switch between them by clicking the page tabs.

9. Click the **Navigation button** in the Views bar, then repeat Step 8 to open the remaining 5 pages

FIGURE B-5: Navigation view showing only MediaLoft home page

Navigation toolbar

Index.htm is the MediaLoft home page

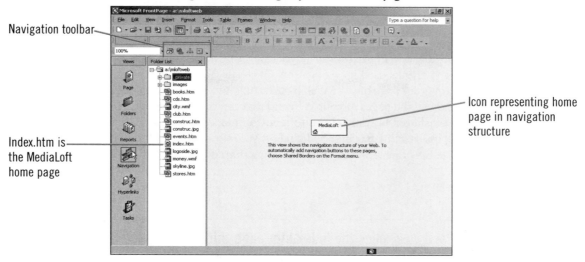

Icon representing home page in navigation structure

FIGURE B-6: Hierarchical relationship between home page and books page

Your icons may look different

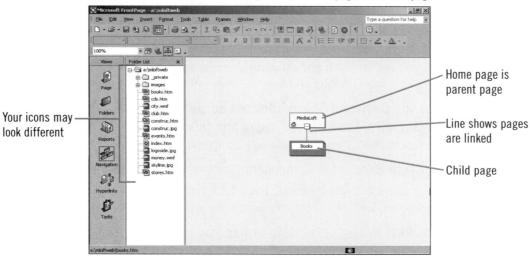

Home page is parent page

Line shows pages are linked

Child page

FIGURE B-7: Navigational structure for MediaLoft Web site

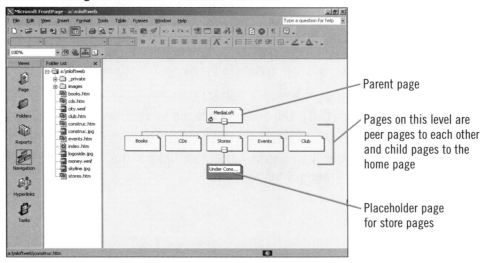

Parent page

Pages on this level are peer pages to each other and child pages to the home page

Placeholder page for store pages

Adding Link Bars

Once you set up a hierarchical relationship among your pages using Navigation view, you can automatically add hyperlinks to all your pages by adding link bars to your Web site. A **link bar** is a set of hyperlinks used for navigating a Web site. You can set up a link bar to appear in the same format on every page of your Web by inserting it in a shared border. A **shared border** is a bar that appears on all the pages in your Web and that can contain text, graphics, or other objects. You can position a shared border on the top, bottom, left, or right side of a Web page. ▰▰▰ Helen wants to insert a link bar in the MediaLoft Web site so users see the same set of hyperlinks on each Web page they open. She starts by adding a shared border to all the pages in the Web.

Steps

1. In Page view, click the **index.htm page tab** to display the MediaLoft home page
   The home page appears in Normal Page view.

2. Press **[Ctrl][End]** to move the insertion point to the end of the page, click **Format** on the menu bar, then click **Shared Borders**
   The Shared Borders dialog box opens, as shown in Figure B-8.

Trouble?

If necessary, scroll to the bottom of the page to see the text in the shared border.

3. Make sure the **All pages option button** is selected, click the **Bottom check box** to check it, then click **OK**
   A shared border containing placeholder text appears at the bottom of the index.htm home page. The shared border will appear at the bottom of every page in the site.

4. Click the **Comment Shared Bottom Border** placeholder text in the shared border to select it, click **Insert** on the menu bar, then click **Web Component**
   The Insert Web Component dialog box opens, as shown in Figure B-9.

5. Click **Link Bars** in the Component type list, click **Bar based on navigation structure** in the Choose a bar type list, then click **Next**
   The Choose a bar style list box displays the styles you can choose from for your link bar.

6. Click **Next** to accept the default **Use Page's Theme**, then click **Finish** to accept the horizontal orientation option
   The Link Bar Properties dialog box opens, with the General tab displayed.

QuickTip

You can change the order of the links in a navigation bar throughout the Web by changing their order in Navigation View.

7. Click the **Child pages under Home option button** in the Hyperlinks to add to page section, click the **Home page check box**, click **OK**, then close the folder list if it is still open
   The link bar now appears in the shared border, as shown in Figure B-10. In a navigation bar, the order of hyperlinks for files located on the same hierarchy level is determined by their order from left to right in the navigation structure.

8. Position the mouse pointer over the Books link until it changes to a 🖥️, press and hold **[Ctrl]**, the pointer changes to 👆, then click to follow the hyperlink
   The Books page opens, confirming that the hyperlink in the link bar you created works.

9. Repeat Step 8 to test the other links in the link bar, then click the **Save button** 💾 on the Standard toolbar

FIGURE B-8: Shared Borders dialog box

Click to insert the shared border on every page of your Web

Click to position the shared border at the bottom of the pages

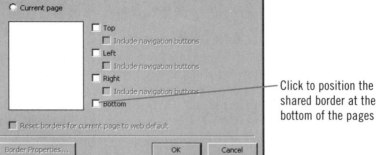

FIGURE B-9: Insert Web Component dialog box

Click to insert link bar in shared border

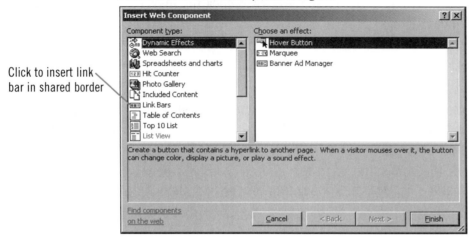

FIGURE B-10: Home page with link bar inserted in shared border

Link bar based on navigational structure

Shared border

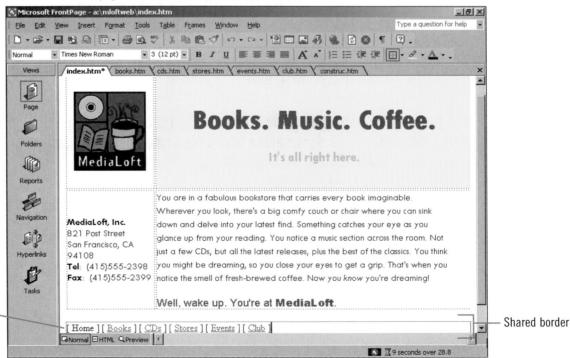

Inserting Hyperlinks and Bookmarks

Although it's convenient to insert link bars to help viewers navigate a site, you will sometimes want to insert hyperlinks manually. You can do this easily using the Insert Hyperlink button on the Standard toolbar. You can insert hyperlinks in text or images, and they can be used to jump to another part of the Web site or to external places, such as other Web sites. Also, you might want viewers to be able to jump from one place to another on the same Web page. Rather than forcing the viewer to scroll down to see another part of the page, you can insert a **bookmark**, or a hyperlink that takes viewers to another location on the same page. Helen wants to insert hyperlinks and bookmarks to make the site easier to navigate.

Steps 1 2 3 4

1. Click the **index.htm page tab** to open the MediaLoft home page, select the word **book** in the first line of paragraph text, then click the **Insert Hyperlink button** 🔗 on the Standard toolbar
   The Insert Hyperlink dialog box opens, displaying a list of pages in the current Web.

2. Click **books.htm (open)** in the list, click **OK,** then click anywhere outside the selection area
   The word "books" now appears underlined in blue, showing that it is a hyperlink.

3. Select the words **music section** in the fourth sentence of paragraph text, click 🔗, click **cds.htm (open)** in the list, click **OK**, then click anywhere outside the selection area
   Compare your screen to Figure B-11.

4. Click the **books.htm page tab** to open the Books page, click the **MediaLoft logo** to select it, click 🔗, click **index.htm (open)** from the list, then click **OK**
   The MediaLoft logo on the Books page is now a hyperlink. When you click it, the home page will open.

5. Repeat Step 4 to insert a hyperlink from the MediaLoft logo on the CDs, Stores, Events and Clubs pages, linking back to the home page

6. Click the **books.htm page tab** to display the Books at MediaLoft page, select the text **Best-Selling Books for September** in the blue box, click **Insert** on the menu bar, click **Bookmark**, click **OK,** then click outside the selection
   A white dotted line appears below the text Best-Selling Books for September, indicating that this is a bookmark.

7. Select the words **Best Sellers** in the second sentence of the paragraph, click 🔗, click **Bookmark**, click **Best-Selling Books for September** in the Select Place in Document dialog box, click **OK**, then click **OK** again
   Compare your screen to Figure B-12.

8. Click the **cds.htm page tab**, create a bookmark for **Best-Selling CDS for September**, then insert a hyperlink from **Best Selling CDs** in the second sentence of the paragraph to the bookmark **Best-Selling CDs for September**

9. Test all the hyperlinks and bookmarks you inserted, then click the **Save button** 💾

FIGURE B-11: MediaLoft home page with hyperlinks to books and CDs pages

Index.htm page tab

Hyperlink to books page

Hyperlink to CDs page

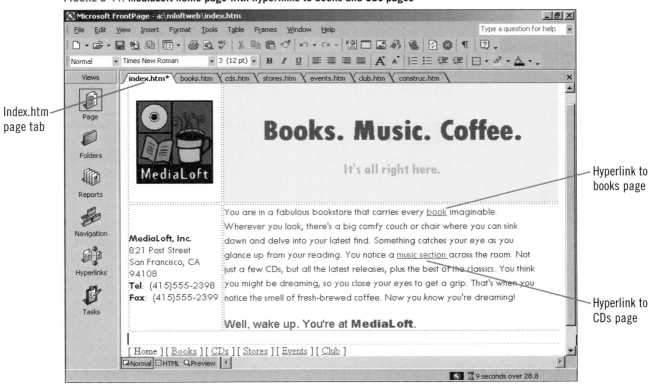

FIGURE B-12: Books page with bookmark and hyperlink to bookmark

Hyperlink to bookmark

Dotted white underline indicates bookmark

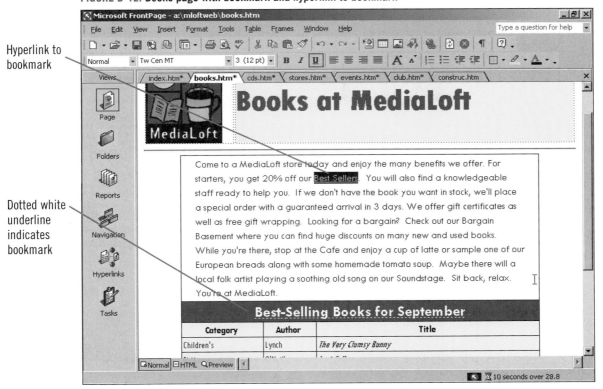

Formatting Hyperlinks

Hyperlinked text appears differently from other text on your Web page. By default, hyperlinked text that has not been selected is blue and underlined (**unvisited**). This text changes to another color when it is clicked and currently selected (**active**), and to yet a third color when its associated link has already been followed (**visited**). When you add hyperlinks to text on your Web pages, you might need to change these three colors to ensure that the text is readable, works well with your Web color scheme, and contrasts well with your page's background. ✎ Helen decides to change the color of her hyperlinks to match her color scheme.

Steps

1. Click the **index.htm page tab** to display the MediaLoft home page

2. Click **Format** on the menu bar, then click **Background**
   The Page Properties dialog box opens with the Background tab selected, as shown in Figure B-13.

If the Document's colors contain no blue square, click More Colors, click the second cell in the top row, then click OK.

3. Click the **Hyperlink list arrow**, then click the **blue square** RGB (33,66,99) in the Document's colors section
   Unvisited hyperlinks will now appear in blue, matching the other blue text on the screen.

If the Document's colors contain no orange square, click More Colors, click the orange cell RGB (FF, 99,33) fifth from the left in the third row from the bottom, then click OK.

4. Click the **Visited hyperlink list arrow** in the Colors area, then click the **orange square** RGB (FF,99,33) in the Document's colors section
   Hyperlinked text whose links have already been visited will match the orange color used for other text on the Web page. There is no need to change the red color for Active hyperlink because it stands out from the other colors on the page, making it clear to users that the browser is in the process of opening the selected hyperlink.

5. Click **OK**, then click the **Save button** 🖫 on the Standard toolbar
   The two hyperlinks in the paragraph text appear in the blue color.

6. Click the **Preview in Browser button** 🔲 on the Standard toolbar
   Your default browser opens, showing the MediaLoft home page.

The formatting you specified will only be applied to the links on the home page. To specify similar formatting on the other pages, open the page you want, click Format on the menu bar, click Background, then choose the settings you want in the Colors area.

7. Click the **book hyperlink** in the first line of paragraph text to open the Books page, then click the **MediaLoft logo** to go back to the home page
   The book hyperlink now appears in orange, indicating that you have visited it. See Figure B-14.

8. Close your browser, click in the blank line above the links bar, type **your name**, then click 🖫 to save your changes to the index.htm page

9. Save your changes to all the other pages by clicking each page tab then clicking 🖫

FIGURE B-13: **Page Properties dialog box with Background tab displayed**

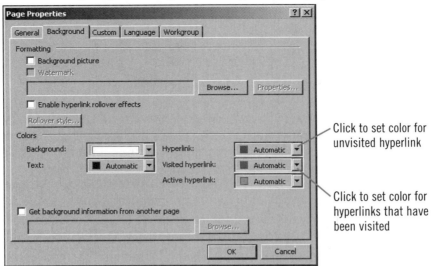

Click to set color for unvisited hyperlink

Click to set color for hyperlinks that have been visited

FIGURE B-14: **Hyperlinks on the home page with blue and orange colors applied**

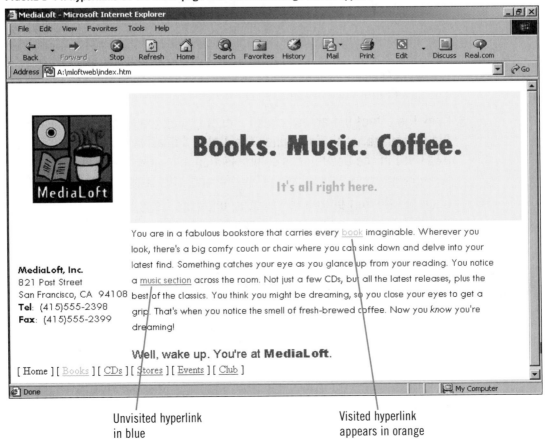

Unvisited hyperlink in blue

Visited hyperlink appears in orange

Adding Special Effects

FrontPage comes with built-in components to help you jazz up your Web site. For instance, you can insert a moving **marquee** across your page, containing a message to your viewers. You can insert **hover buttons**, which are specially formatted buttons containing a text label that change their appearance when a viewer moves the mouse pointer over them. A hover button can perform a Web page activity, such as submitting the information in a form, or it can serve as a hyperlink to open another Web page. These and other features are available in the Insert Web Component dialog box. ✎ Helen decides to liven up her site by adding a marquee to the home page and hover buttons for the store locations on the Stores page.

Steps

Trouble?

If Marquee appears dimmed, click Tools on the menu bar, click Page Options, click the Compatibility tab, select Microsoft Internet Explorer only in the Browsers list box, then select 4.0 browsers and later in the Browser versions list box.

1. Click the **index.htm page tab**, select the text **Books. Music. Coffee.**, click the **Web Component button** 🔲 on the Standard toolbar, verify that **Dynamic Effects** is selected in the Component type list, click **Marquee** in the Choose an effect list box, then click **Finish**
   The Marquee Properties dialog box opens, with the selected text highlighted in the Text text box.

2. Click **OK,** click the **Save button** 🖫, then click the **Preview pane button**
   The marquee scrolls from right to left across the top. See Figure B-15.

3. Click the **Normal pane button**, click the **stores.htm page tab**, click in the empty cell below Check out sales…, then click 🔲

4. Verify that **Dynamic Effects** are selected and **Hover button**, then click **Finish**.
   The Hover Button Properties dialog box opens.

5. Type **Boston** in the Button text text box, click in the **Link to text box**, type **construc.htm**, click the **Button color list arrow**, then click the **Blue square** RGB (33,66,99) in the Document's colors section
   The hover button will be linked to construct.htm, the placeholder file.

6. Click the **Effect list arrow**, click **Color fill**, click the **Effect color list arrow**, click the **Black square**, click **Font**, click the **Color list arrow**, click the **Yellow square** RGB (FF,FF,99) in the Document's colors section, click **OK**, then click **OK** again
   Boston appears as yellow text in a blue square in the table.

7. Click the **Boston button** to select it, click the **Copy button** 🔳 , click to the right of the button, click **Insert** on the menu bar, click **Break**, click **OK** to insert a normal line break, then click the **Paste button** 🔳
   A copy of the button is below the original one with all the properties of the original.

QuickTip

Once the button is copied to the Clipboard, press [Ctrl] V to paste the new buttons. Press [Shift][Enter] to insert a line break.

8. Double-click the **lower button**, type **Chicago** in the Button text text box, click **OK**, then click to the right of the new button
   Rather than creating and formatting new buttons from scratch, Helen copies the first button and simply changes the label so that all subsequent buttons have the same properties.

9. Repeat Steps 7 and 8 to create six more buttons for **Houston, Kansas City, New York, San Diego, San Francisco,** and **Seattle**, click the **Save button** 🖫, click the **Preview pane button**, then move the mouse pointer over the hover buttons
   Compare your screen with Figure B-16.

FIGURE B-15: Home page with scrolling marquee

Save button

Marquee scrolling
across screen

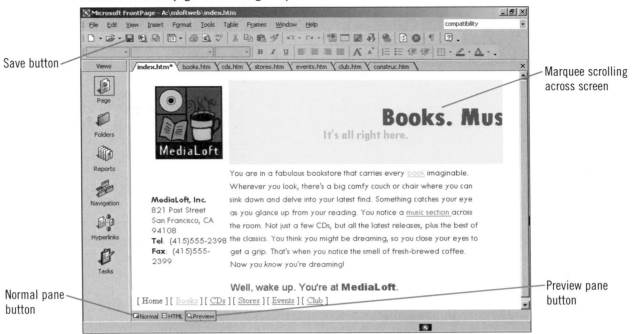

Normal pane
button

Preview pane
button

FIGURE B-16: Stores page in the Preview pane with inserted hover buttons

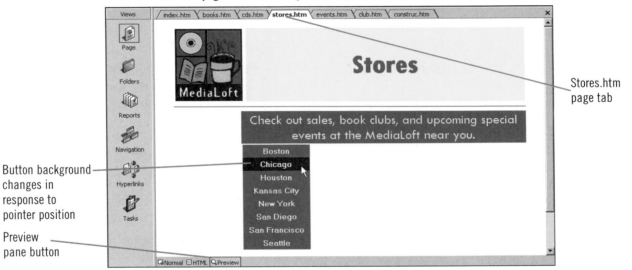

Stores.htm
page tab

Button background
changes in
response to
pointer position

Preview
pane button

CLUES TO USE

Browser compatibility

Some Web page features, such as marquees and hover buttons, can be viewed only by later versions of certain Web browsers. Marquees, for instance cannot be viewed in some versions of Netscape Navigator. If reaching the widest possible audience is a priority, you can adjust FrontPage settings to make newer technologies unavailable for the current Web. Click Tools on the menu bar, click Page Options, then click the Compatibility tab in the Page Options dialog box. You can choose to keep your Web compatible with specific browser brands and versions, servers, and technologies.

Using Site Reports

Before making your Web site available to the rest of the world, it's a good idea to check for errors and problems that users might encounter. Often, this process requires manually verifying links and using the site as your intended audience might, in order to discover hidden glitches. The Site Summary pane in Reports View provides a comprehensive list of management-related items to help you correct any problems in your site. You can also use Hyperlinks view to make sure you've set up all the links you want. And you can use the Tasks view to keep track of tasks that need to be completed. Before showing the MediaLoft site to her team members and publishing it, Helen uses FrontPage's site management tools to check for errors, review all the links, and keep track of additional tasks that need to be done.

Steps

Trouble?

If the Reports pane does not read "Site Summary" along the top, click the Reports list arrow on the Reporting toolbar, then click Site Summary on the list.

1. **Click the Normal pane button, then click the Reports button on the Views bar**
   The Site Summary report appears in the Reports pane, along with the Reporting toolbar, as shown in Figure B-17. The list summarizes 15 reports about the current Web and describes each report.

2. **Click Unlinked files in the Name column**
   The Unlinked Files report opens.

3. **Click skyline.jpg in the Name column, press [Delete], then click Yes**
   You delete this file because you do not need it for the MediaLoft Web site.

4. **Click the Reports list arrow on the Reporting toolbar, then click Site Summary**
   The Count value for Unlinked files changes because you deleted a file.

5. **Click the Hyperlinks button on the Views Bar, then click index.htm in the Folder List**
   FrontPage switches to Hyperlinks view, as shown in Figure B-18. You can see the MediaLoft home page icon in the center, with arrows pointing to it and away from it. The arrows pointing to it show the links to the home page from the other pages. The arrows pointing away from it show the links from the home page to the other pages. There are multiple instances of icons on the left because each page has two links back to MediaLoft; one on the link bar and one on the MediaLoft icon. When you view a Web page in Page view, you can't easily tell to which page a hyperlink refers. Hyperlinks View is helpful in verifying that none of the links on a page refers to nonexistent pages and that a page contains the number of links you intended.

6. **Click Edit on the menu bar, point to Tasks, then click Add Task**
   The New Task dialog box opens.

7. **Type Create Store pages, if your name doesn't already appear in the Assigned to text box, click the Assigned to list arrow, type your name, click in the Description text box, type Call meeting with store directors to review guidelines for store pages, then click OK**

8. **Click the Navigation button on the Views bar, double-click the MediaLoft icon to open the index.htm page, then click the Print button** 🖨
   You have to print each page individually.

9. **Print the remaining pages, save your changes, then exit FrontPage**

Reports list arrow

Reporting toolbar

Report names

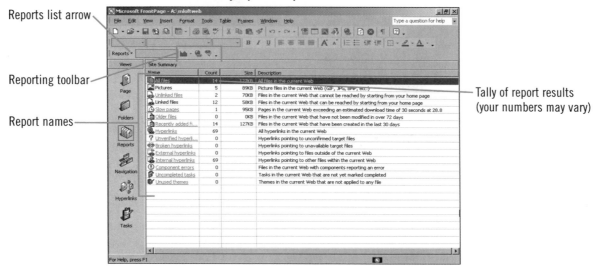

Tally of report results
(your numbers may vary)

Links to MediaLoft
home page from
other pages

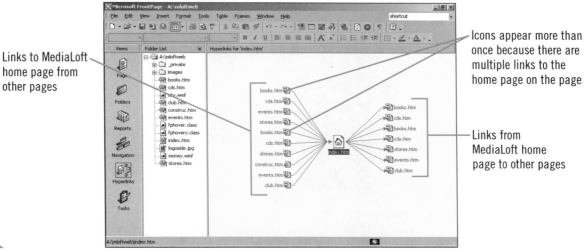

Icons appear more than
once because there are
multiple links to the
home page on the page

Links from
MediaLoft home
page to other pages

Publishing a Web site

The final step in producing a Web site is to make it available to World Wide Web users, completing a process known as publishing. When you publish your Web site, you copy all of its files—including Web pages and graphics—from your local disk drive to a Web server. A Web server, or Web presence provider, is always connected to the Web, making your pages available to anyone with Web access. If you already have an account with a commercial Internet Service Provider (ISP) or a school, room for your Web site on the Web server may be included with the account. Additionally, several Internet companies offer free space for Web pages on their servers; in exchange, they place an advertisement on each page in your Web site. All Web servers impose limits on the amount of data you can store; be sure to check these limits before publishing your Web site. A graphics-heavy site can quickly mushroom in size, so it is important to place graphics sparingly in your Web if your allotted space is small.

To Publish your Web site using FrontPage, click File on the menu bar, then click Publish Web. In the Publish Destination dialog box, enter the destination of your server, then click OK. In the Publish Web dialog box, verify that all your files are included in the list, then click Publish. If you are using Microsoft Windows ME or Windows 98, you can use the Microsoft Web Publishing Wizard. To start the Wizard, click Start on the Start menu, click Programs, click Accessories, click Internet Tools, then click Web Publishing Wizard. Answer the questions posed to you by the Wizard to publish your site to the Web.

Practice

► Concepts Review

Label each element of the Web page shown in Figure B-19.

FIGURE B-19

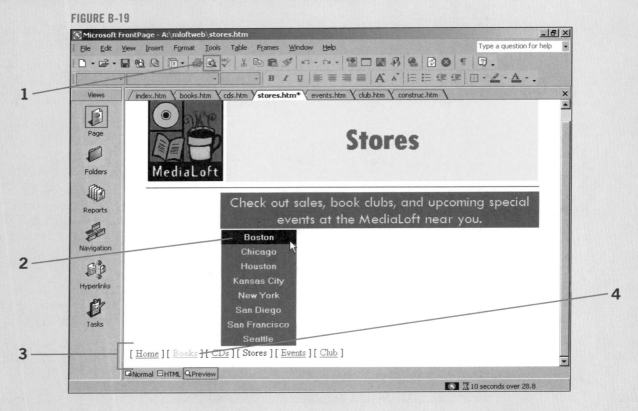

Match each of the terms with the statement that describes it.

5. Shared border
6. Child page
7. Bookmark
8. Link bar
9. Web
10. Peer page
11. Placeholder page

a. In a Web hierarchy, a page that shares a common parent page with another page
b. In FrontPage, a named object containing all the files for a Web site
c. A bar containing elements that appear on all the pages of your Web site
d. A temporary page explaining that the Web page is incomplete
e. In a Web hierarchy, a page that is linked to a parent page
f. A set of links to other Web pages on your site
g. A location in a file to which you can insert a hyperlink

Select the best answer from the list of choices.

12. **Which view do you use to set up a Web hierarchy?**
    a. Page View
    b. Navigation View
    c. Reports View
    d. Hyperlinks View

13. **If you are creating a Web site based on pages you have already created, you can use the _____ to join them together into a Web.**
    a. Corporate Presence Wizard
    b. Import Web Wizard
    c. Database Interface Wizard
    d. Template Gallery

14. **One of the last tasks you should perform before you make your completed Web site available on the Web is to:**
    a. Create relationships among the pages of your Web site.
    b. Publish your Web site.
    c. Verify that all the links and components work the way you intend.
    d. Look at other Web sites.

15. **Which of the following buttons do you click to insert a Marquee?**
    a.
    b.
    c.
    d.

16. **If you want your viewers to be able to link to a location on the same page, you can insert a:**
    a. Bookmark.
    b. Shared border.
    c. Web component.
    d. Link bar.

17. **You can add a hyperlink to text or a graphic by clicking which button?**
    a.
    b.
    c.
    d.

18. **An example of a graphic button that can open another Web page is:**
    a. A marquee.
    b. Hyperlinked text.
    c. A link bar.
    d. A hover button.

19. **Which view do you use to identify work items that need to be completed?**
    a. Reports View
    b. Tasks View
    c. Folders View
    d. Hyperlinks View

▶ Skills Review

1. **Create a new Web site.**
   a. Start FrontPage.
   b. Click Web Site Templates in the New Page or Web task pane, then click Import Web Wizard.
   c. Click in the Specify location of the new web list box in the Options section to select the text, type **a:\sfmlweb**, then click OK. (*Note*: if you plan to save your web to an empty folder on your hard drive, type the correct path to the folder you want to save to followed by **sfmlweb**.)
   d. Click the From a source directory of files on a local computer or network option button, click the Browse button, locate the drive and folder where your Project Files are stored, click the Skills Review folder, click Open, then click Next.
   e. Click Next to select all the files in the folder, then click Finish.
   f. Click the Folders button on the Views bar to see the list of imported files.

2. **Set up a navigation structure.**
   a. Click the Navigation button on the Views bar.
   b. Drag the file sfevents.htm from the folder list into the Navigation pane, just below the "MediaLoft S…" icon.

c. Drag the file direct.htm from the folder list into the Navigation pane, so it is positioned to the right of the Events icon.

d. Drag the file café.htm from the folder list into the Navigation pane, so it is positioned to the right of the Directions icon.

e. Drag the file construc.htm from the folder list into the Navigation pane so it is positioned below the Café icon.

f. Double-click the MediaLoft icon to open it in Page view, click to the right of "Sun: 10 am-8 pm", press [Enter], then type your name.

g. Go back to Navigation view and double-click the Events, Directions, Café, and the Under Construction icons to open each page in Page view.

3. **Add link bars.**

a. Click the index.htm page tab to display the MediaLoft San Francisco home page.

b. Press [Ctrl][End] to move the insertion point to the end of the page, click Format on the menu bar, then click Shared Borders.

c. Click the All pages option button if it is not selected, then click the Bottom check box, then click OK.

d. Click the text in the shared border to select it, then click the Web Component button.

e. Click Link Bars in the Component type list box, click Bar based on navigation structure in the Choose a bar type list box, click Next, then click Next again to accept the default bar style, choose the horizontal orientation if it is not selected, and then click Finish.

f. In the Link Bar Properties dialog box, click the Child Pages under Home option button, click the Home page check box, then click OK.

g. Save your changes, then check each of the hyperlinks on the link bar by pressing [Ctrl] as you click each one.

4. **Insert hyperlinks and bookmarks.**

a. Click the index.htm page tab to display the MediaLoft San Francisco home page, select the text **November events** near the bottom of the paragraph text, then insert a hyperlink to the sfevents.htm page.

b. Go to the sfevents.htm page, then insert a hyperlink from the MediaLoft logo to the index.htm page.

c. Open the direct.htm page, then insert a hyperlink from the MediaLoft logo to the index.htm page.

d. Open the café.htm page, then insert a hyperlink from the MediaLoft logo to the index.htm page.

e. Open the sfevents.htm page, select the heading text November Events in the middle of the page, click Insert on the menu bar, click Bookmark, then click OK.

f. Select the text "November Events" at the bottom of the paragraph text, then insert a hyperlink to the November Events bookmark.

g. Save your changes, click the Preview pane button, then test the hyperlinks you just inserted.

5. **Format hyperlinks.**

a. Click the Normal pane button, go to the index.htm page, click Format on the menu bar, then click Background.

b. Click the Hyperlink list arrow, then click the orange cell in the Document's colors section.

c. Click the Visited hyperlink list arrow, then click the blue cell in the Document's colors section.

d. Format the hyperlinks on the Events, Directions, and Café pages to match the Index page so that the hyperlink is orange and the visited hyperlink is blue.

e. Save your changes, then click the Preview pane button and test the links on each page to make sure they are applied.

6. **Add special effects.**

a. Click the Normal pane button, then click the index.htm page tab to display the MediaLoft San Francisco home page.

b. Select the text **Relax. You're at MediaLoft**, then insert a Marquee containing this selected text.

c. In the Marquee Properties dialog box, click the Left direction option button if it is not selected, accept the default settings for speed, click the Alternate option button in the Behavior section, then click OK.

d. Click the cafe.htm page tab to display the Café page.

e. Double-click the word Coffee in the bottom cell, press [Ctrl][C] to copy the selected text, click the Web Component button, click Hover button, then click Finish.

f. In the Button text text box, press [Ctrl][V] to paste the selected text, click in the Link to text box, type **construc.htm**, click the Button color list arrow, then click the light yellow square in the Document's colors section.

g. Verify that Effect is set to Glow, click the Effect color list arrow, then click the orange square in the Document's colors section.

h. Click the Font button, click the Color list arrow, then click the black color in the Document's colors section.

i. Click the Font style list arrow, verify that the style is Bold, click the Size up arrow twice to change the value in the Font text box to 16, then click OK twice.

j. Create hover buttons for Tea, Bread, and Soup that have the same formatting attributes as the Coffee button. Be sure to insert a line break after each button. (*Hint*: Copy the Coffee button, change the text as needed, then delete the existing Tea, Bread, and Soup text labels.)

k. Save the Web, click the Preview in Browser button, move the mouse pointer over the hover buttons, click each one to make sure it works, then close your browser.

7. Use site reports.

a. Click the FrontPage program button on the taskbar if necessary to return to the FrontPage window.

b. Click the Reports button on the Views bar.

c. Click Unlinked files in the Name column.

d. Click statue.jpg in the Name column, press [Delete], then click Yes.

e. Click the Reports list arrow on the Reporting toolbar, then click Site Summary.

f. Click the Hyperlinks button on the Views bar, then click index.htm in the Folder List.

g. Check the links to the remaining Web pages in the Web: construc.htm, events.htm, direct.htm, and café.htm.

h. Click Edit on the menu bar, point to Tasks, click Add Task, create a task named "Create Café Pages," assign it to your name, then type the following description: "Create pages for each of the café menu items."

i. Save your changes.

j. Print each page of the Web.

k. Exit FrontPage.

► Independent Challenge 1

Ruby Williams recently created several Web pages to help market and provide Information about her personalized gift baskets. Now she wants to link all the pages together as a Web site.

a. Start FrontPage, then click Web Site Templates in the New Page or Web task pane.

b. Click in the specify location of the new web list box in the Options section to select the text, type **a:\baskets**, then click OK. (*Note:* if you plan to save your Web to an empty folder on your hard drive, type the correct path to the folder you want to save to followed by **baskets**.)

c. Click Import Web Wizard, then click OK.

d. Click the From a source directory of files on a local computer or network option button, click the Browse button, select the IC1 folder in the drive and folder where you Project Files are stored, click Open, then click Next.

e. Click Next to select all the files in the list, then click Finish.

f. Click the Navigation button on the Views bar, then drag the file ingred.htm from the folder list into the Navigation pane, just below the Ruby's Bask… icon.

g. Drag the file orderfrm.htm, positioning it to the right of the Basket Com… icon.

h. Double-click the Ruby's Bask… icon in the Navigation pane.

i. Insert a shared border at the bottom of the home page that appears at the bottom of all the pages.
j. Insert a link bar in the shared border that is based on the navigation structure. Choose the horizontal orientation and the Use this Page's theme option, and specify that it contain links to the child pages under the home page.
k. Click to the right of the phone number, press [Enter], then type your name.
l. Save your changes, then click the Preview pane button and check your links.
m. Print the Web, then exit Front Page.

► Independent Challenge 2

Jose Gomez works in the Marketing Department of Half Moon Grocers, a distributor of organic and natural foods. His current project is to create a Web site for the company. He has heard that FrontPage 2002 includes wizards that can automatically create the layout for an entire Web site. He creates a sample Web with a wizard to learn more about creating Web sites.

a. Start FrontPage; in the New Page or Web Task pane, click Web Page Templates, then click Corporate Presence Wizard.
b. Select the Corporate Presence Wizard to create a new Web site from scratch. if you plan to save your Web to an empty folder on your hard drive, type the correct path to the folder you want to save to followed by the Web name **halfmoon**, then click OK. (If you are completing these exercises using floppy disks, use a blank formatted disk and type **A:\halfmoon** as the Web name.)
c. Read the information in the wizard dialog box, click Next, click check boxes if necessary so that only Home (required), Products/Services, and Feedback Form are checked, then click Next.
d. Click check boxes so that only Introduction and Contact Information are selected, click Next, specify that the text box values are **3** for Products and **0** for services, then click Next.
e. Click check boxes if necessary so that only Product image is selected, click Next, click check boxes if necessary so that only Full Name and E-mail Address are selected, click Next, make sure the Yes option button is selected, then click Next.
f. Select only Your company's logo to appear at the top of each page, and only Links to your main pages and Date page was last modified to appear at the bottom of each page, click Next, click the No option button, then click Next.
g. Enter the following corporate information in the next two dialog boxes:

Company name: Half Moon Grocers
One-word version: Half Moon
Address: 1 Joshua Street, Atlanta, Georgia 30349
Phone: 404-555-8733
Fax: 404-555-8734
Webmaster: webmaster@half-moon-inc.com
Info: info@half-moon-inc.com

h. Click Next, click the Choose Web Theme button, click Capsules on the list, make sure only the Active Graphics box is checked, click OK, click Next, then click Finish.
i. When FrontPage finishes creating the Web, use Navigation view to open the home page. Click at the end of the first paragraph, press [Enter] then type your name.
j. Use Navigation view to explore the pages. Many pages have placeholder text for you to replace with information about the company and its products.
k. Make any changes you think are necessary.
l. When you are finished reviewing the Web, save the Web, print the pages, then exit FrontPage.

Independent Challenge 3

Create a Web site about yourself using the FrontPage skills you learned in this unit.

a. Start FrontPage, then create a new Web using the Personal Web template available in the Web Site Templates dialog box. Save the Web in a new empty folder. Name the Web **myweb**. (If you are completing these exercises using floppy disks, use a blank formatted disk.)

b. Choose a theme for your Web. To choose a theme, click Format on the menu bar, click Theme, then choose a design that appeals to you.

c. Replace any text with text of your own that describes you: your hobbies or interests, your family, your likes and dislikes. Feel free to change the titles of the template pages to different ones that are more appropriate for you.

d. Replace any placeholder graphics with appropriate clip art or photographs of your own. Insert hyperlinks to your favorite Web sites.

e. Include a marquee.

f. Check the hyperlinks in Hyperlinks View, save your Web, print the Web, then exit FrontPage.

 Independent Challenge 4

You and your friends or family (pick one) are planning a reunion. It is up to you to pick the reason for your reunion and who is going. On this reunion, you will travel on a cruise ship that will stop at three destinations of your choosing. You have been put in charge of creating a Web site to communicate the details of this trip.

a. Start by creating a sketch of your Web hierarchy. The hierarchy should include a home page, and at least five child pages. Three of the child pages should focus on the three destinations you have chosen, providing information that would be interesting and appropriate for travelers. Include a fourth child page on what to bring, and a fifth describing the type of ship you will be traveling on.

b. Log on to the Internet, go to a search engine site such as AltaVista (www.altavista.com) or Google (www.google.com) and search for cruises. Find out the following information to include on each of the destination pages: the name of the cruise ship and the cruise line, the port that you will be leaving from and the rate information, three ports that you will be stopping at. You should also research cruise ships and appropriate items to bring so that you can provide information for your Cruise Ship and What to Bring pages. Create each page of your Web site in FrontPage using a template of your choice from the Web page template dialog box. Replace any placeholder graphics with appropriate clip art or photographs downloaded from the Web.

c. When you have created all your Web pages, use the Import Web Wizard to import them into a Web called **mycruise**.

d. Use Navigation view to set up the navigation structure for the site based on the Web hierarchy that you sketched.

e. Insert a Shared Border at the bottom of each page, then insert a Link Bar in the Shared Border based on the Navigation structure.

f. Insert any other appropriate hyperlinks or bookmarks, then format them appropriately.

g. Insert a marquee on the home page, and insert at least one hover button somewhere in the site.

h. Type your name somewhere on the home page.

i. Click the Tasks button on the Views bar to create a task to remind you to research the menu on the ship and cabin accommodations.

j. Use Reports View and Hyperlinks View to troubleshoot any problems, then save your Web.

k. Print the Web, then exit FrontPage.

► Visual Workshop

Use FrontPage to create the Web site shown in Figure B-20. Use the Import Web Wizard to create a new Web called **crabshak** and save it to the new folder. Import the files from the Visual Workshop folder to create the Web. In Navigation view, set up the navigation structure with four child pages linked to the Uncle Bobby home page. Format the text as shown. Insert the link bar shown into a shared border. Insert the other hyperlinks shown, linking to the appropriate pages. Format the hyperlinks on all pages so that the visited hyperlinks appear in red, and unvisited hyperlinks appear in black. Create a marquee out of the heading "The best darn crabs you've ever tasted!" Create the hover buttons shown, choosing red as the button color, Color fill as the effect, and black as the Effect color. Type your name below the phone number. Test the Web, print all the pages, then save it.

FIGURE B-20

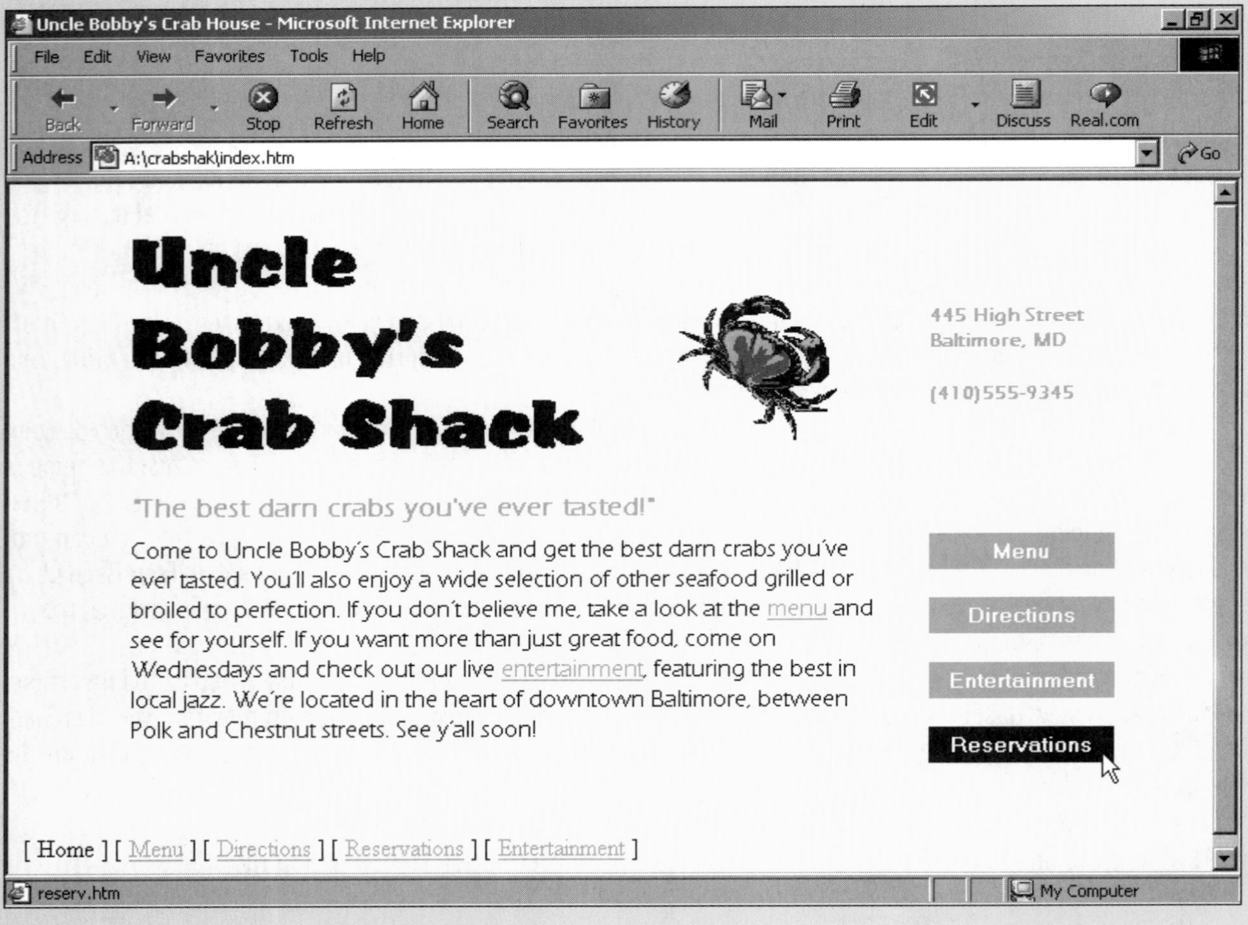

Project Files List

Read the following information carefully!

It is very important to organize and keep track of the files you need for this book.

1. Find out from your instructor the location of the Project Files you need and the location where you will store your files.

- To complete many of the units in this book, you need to use Project Files. Your instructor will either provide you with a copy of the Project Files or ask you to make your own copy.

- If you need to make a copy of the Project Files, you will need to copy a set of files from a file server, stand-alone computer, or the Web to the drive and folder where you will be storing your Project Files.

- Your instructor will tell you which computer, drive letter, and folders contain the files you need, and where you will store your files.

- You can also download the files by going to www.course.com. See the inside back cover of the book for instructions on how to download your files.

2. Copy and organize your Project Files.

Floppy disk users

- If you are using floppy disks to store your Project Files, the list on the following pages shows which files you'll need to copy onto your disk(s).

- Unless noted in the Project Files List, you will need one formatted, high-density disk for each unit. For each unit you are assigned, copy the files listed in the **Project File Supplied column** onto one disk.

- Make sure you label each disk clearly with the unit name (e.g., Word Unit E).

- When working through the unit, save all your files to this disk.

Users storing files in other locations

- If you are using a zip drive, network folder, hard drive, or other storage device, use the Project Files List to organize your files.

- Create a subfolder for each unit in the location where you are storing your files, and name it according to the unit title (e.g., Word Unit E).

- For each unit you are assigned, copy the files listed in the **Project File Supplied column** into that unit's folder.

- Store the files you modify or create for each unit in the unit folder.

3. Find and keep track of your Project Files and completed files.

- Use the **Project File Supplied column** to make sure you have the files you need before starting the unit or exercise indicated in the **Unit and Location column**.

- Use the **Student Saves File As column** to find out the filename you use when saving your changes to a Project File that was provided.

- Use the **Student Creates File column** to find out the filename you use when saving a file you create new for the exercise.

Office Unit B

Note: In Access, you do not save the database files with a different name. It is a good practice to make a backup copy of the files before you use them, in case you need to go back and repeat any of the exercises. Because some of the files in this unit are large, you will need to organize the files onto 4 floppy disks if you are completing all the exercises. Copy the files as outlined above, then label each disk clearly (e.g., Office Unit B Disk1.)

DISK 1

Unit and Location	Project File Supplied	Student Saves File As	Student Creates File
Visual Workshop—Word	Office B-1.doc	MediaLoft Update Memo.doc	
Visual Workshop—Excel	Office B-2.xls	MediaLoft Retreat Budget.xls	
Visual Workshop—Access	Office B-3.mdb		
Visual Workshop—PowerPoint	Office B-4.ppt	MediaLoft Retreat Presentation.ppt	

DISK 2

Independent Challenge 1	Office B-5.doc	HD Multi-Page Letter.doc	
Independent Challenge 2	Office B-6.xls	London Demographics.xls	
Independent Challenge 3	Office B-7.mdb		
Independent Challenge 4	Office B-8.ppt	Office XP Programs.ppt	

DISK 3

Independent Challenge 5	Office B-9.doc Office B-10.mdb Office B-11.ppt Office B-12.xls	Blood Drive Events.doc Blood Drive Promotion.ppt Blood Donation Statistics.xls Previous Donor Query.xls (exported query from Office B-10 file.)	

DISK 4

Independent Challenge 6	Office B-13.mdb Office B-14.doc Office B-15.ppt Office B-16.doc (imported into Roswell Presentation file.) Office B-17.xls	Office B-13.mdb Roswell Mailing Letter.doc Roswell Presentation.ppt Roswell Special Event.xls Attending Club Members.rtf (published query in Word) Merged Roswell Letters.doc (merged document)	

Word Unit E

Lessons			Boston Ad Budget.doc
Skills Review			Mutual Funds.doc
Independent Challenge 1	WD E-1.doc	40K Relay.doc	
Independent Challenge 2			Business Cards.doc
Independent Challenge 3	WD E-2.doc	Ad Dimensions.doc	
Independent Challenge 4			My Resume.doc
Visual Workshop			March 2003.doc

Unit and Location	Project File Supplied	Student Saves File As	Student Creates File
Word Unit F			
Lessons	WD F-1.doc Mloft.jpg	Ad Tips.doc	
	WD F-2.doc	Age and Gender.doc	Genre Sales.doc
Skills Review	WD F-3.doc Farm.jpg	Farm Flyer.doc	
			Realty Sales.doc
Independent Challenge 1			Letterhead.doc
Independent Challenge 2	Vacation.jpg		GoTropper Ad.doc
Independent Challenge 3			Bookmarks.doc
Independent Challenge 4	WD F-4.doc	Copyright Info.doc	
Visual Workshop	WD F-5.doc Surfing.jpg		Surf Safe.doc
Word Unit G			

If you are saving your solution files to a floppy disk, then the files for the Lessons, Skills Review, each Independent Challenge, and the Visual Workshop must be stored on separate disks. Copy the files you need for the exercise you are completing onto one disk, and label it clearly (e.g. Word Unit G Lessons).

Unit and Location	Project File Supplied	Student Saves File As	Student Creates File
Lessons	mloft.jpg WD G-1.doc	swfevent.htm	swfhome.htm
Skills Review	WD G-2.doc reader.gif WD G-3.doc	whattodo.htm	literacy.htm
Independent Challenge 1	WD G-4.doc rwolf.jpg jackson.jpg		longwalk.htm
Independent Challenge 2	WD G-5.doc	Products and Prices.htm	default.htm Monet's Garden Home.htm
Independent Challenge 3	WD G-6.doc WD G-7.doc WD G-8.doc WD G-9.doc	tri_home.htm tri_view.htm tri_get.htm tri_athl.htm	
Independent Challenge 4			my_web.htm
Visual Workshop	rest.jpg bridge.jpg studlamp.jpg		azulhome.htm azulexhb.htm

Unit and Location	Project File Supplied	Student Saves File As	Student Creates File
Word Unit H			
Lessons	WD H-1.doc	Coffee Letter Main.doc	
			New Coffee Club Data.mdb
			Coffee Letter Merge.doc
			Coffee Labels Main.doc
			US Coffee Labels Zip Code Merge.doc
	WD H-2.mdb		
Skills Review			Donor Labels Main.doc
			Donor Thank You Main.doc
			Donor Data.mdb
			Donor Thank You Merge.doc
			NH Donor Labels Merge.doc
Independent Challenge 1	WD H-3.doc	Member Letter Main.doc	
	WD H-4.mdb		
			Member Letter Merge.doc
Independent Challenge 2			Employee Data.mdb
			Business Cards Main.doc
			Business Cards Merge.doc
Independent Challenge 3			Softball Team Data.mdb
			Softball Roster Merge.doc
			Softball Labels Merge.doc
Independent Challenge 4			5160 Labels Memo.doc
Visual Workshop			Party Data.mdb
			Party Card Main.doc
			Party Card Merge.doc
Excel Unit E			
Lessons	EX E-1.xls	Company Data.xls	
Skills Review	EX E-2.xls	Manager Bonuses.xls	
Independent Challenge 1	EX E-3.xls	Mike's Sales.xls	
Independent Challenge 2	EX E-4.xls	Fly Away Sales.xls	
Independent Challenge 3			Custom Fit Loan Options.xls
Independent Challenge 4			IRA Rates.xls
Visual Workshop			Car Payment Calculator.xls

Unit and Location	Project File Supplied	Student Saves File As	Student Creates File
Excel Unit F			
Lessons	EX F-1.xls Pay Rate Classifications.xls	Timecard Summary.xls timesum.htm	Student creates hyperlink to this file from Timecard Summary.xls Student creates from Timecard Summary file
Skills Review	EX F-2.xls Expense Details.xls	San Francisco Budget.xls sfbudget.htm	Student creates hyperlink to this file from San Francisco budget file Student creates from San Francisco Budget file
Independent Challenge 1			Software Sales Summary.xls
Independent Challenge 2	EX F-3.xls	Update to Check Register.xls	
Independent Challenge 3		 phone.htm	Monthly Long Distance.xls Next Door.xls Phonebill.xlw Workspace file student creates from Monthly Long Distance.xls and Next Door.xls.) Student creates from Monthly Long Distance file Monthly Long Distance-4.xls
Independent Challenge 4		 cameras.htm	Camera Research.xls Student creates from Camera Research file
Visual Workshop		Martinez Agency.xls martinez.htm	
Excel Unit G			
Lessons			My Excel Macros.xls
Skills Review			Macros.xls
Independent Challenge 1			Excel Utility Macros.xls
Independent Challenge 2			Header and Footer Stamp.xls
Independent Challenge 3			Computers Inc Macro.xls
Independent Challenge 4	EX G-1.xls		Office Supplies.xls
Visual Workshop			File Utility Macros.xls
Excel Unit H			
Lessons	EX H-1.xls	New Customer List.xls	
Skills Review			MediaLoft New York Employee List.xls
Independent Challenge 1			Personalize IT.xls
Independent Challenge 2	EX H-2.xls	Television Shows of the Past.xls	
Independent Challenge 3	EX H-3.xls	Best Films.xls	
Independent Challenge 4			MP3 Titles.xls
Visual Workshop			Famous Jazz Performers.xls

Unit and Location	Project File Supplied	Student Saves File As	Student Creates File
Integration Unit E			
Lessons	INT E-1.doc INT E-2.xls INT E-3.xls Q3 Expenditures Worksheet.xls	Advertising Report.doc Q3 Ad Costs.xls	
Independent Challenge 1	INT E-4.doc INT E-5.xls	Lysander Budget Memo.doc Lysander Budget.xls	
Independent Challenge 2			Computer Budget.xls Computer Memo.doc
Access Unit E			
Note: In Access, you do not save the database files with a different name. It is a good practice to make a backup copy of the files before you use them, in case you need to go back and repeat any of the exercises.			
Lessons	Training-E.mdb		
Skills Review			Membership-E.mdb
Independent Challenge 1			Music Store-E.mdb
Independent Challenge 2			
Independent Challenge 3			
Independent Challenge 4	Baltic-E.mdb		
Visual Workshop	Training-E.mdb		
Access Unit F			
Lessons	Training-F.mdb		
Skills Review	Membership-F.mdb		
Independent Challenge 1	Music Store-F.mdb		
Independent Challenge 2	Music Store-F.mdb		
Independent Challenge 3	Music Store-F.mdb		
Independent Challenge 4	Baltic-F.mdb		
Visual Workshop	Training-F.mdb		
Access Unit G			
Lessons	Training-G.mdb		
Skills Review	Membership-G.mdb		
Independent Challenge 1	Music Store-G.mdb		
Independent Challenge 2	Music Store-G.mdb		
Independent Challenge 3	Music Store-G.mdb		
Independent Challenge 4			
Visual Workshop	Training-G.mdb		

Unit and Location	Project File Supplied	Student Saves File As	Student Creates File

Access Unit H

*Because the files created in this unit are large, you will need to organize the files onto three floppy disks if you are using floppies and completing all the exercises. Copy the files as outlined above, and label each disk clearly (e.g., Access Unit H Disk 1).

DISK 1

Lessons			Accounting.mdb
	Training-H.mdb		
	Deptcodes.xls		EmployeeData.xls
			edata.html
			einfo.htm
Visual Workshop	Training-H.mdb		

DISK 2

Skills Review			Contacts.mdb
	Membership-H.mdb		
	Prospects.xls		zip.htm
			list-yi.html (yi for your initials)

DISK 3

Independent Challenge 1	Music Store-H.mdb		
Independent Challenge 2	Music Store-H.mdb		
Independent Challenge 3	Music Store-H.mdb		school.htm
Independent Challenge 4			

Integration Unit F

*Because the files created in this unit are large, you will need to organize the files onto 2 floppy disks if you are completing all the exercises. Copy the files as outlined below, and label each disk clearly (e.g., Integration Unit F Disk 1).

DISK 1

Lessons	KC Stock List.mdb	KC Store Memo.doc	
	INT F-1.doc	History Overstock Analysis.xls	
	INT F-2.xls	KC Store Memo 2.doc	
	INT F-3.doc		

DISK 2

Independent Challenge 1	Tonia's Flowers.mdb		
			Stock Report.xls
Independent Challenge 2	U.S. Trade Analysis.mdb		
			State Trade Analysis.xls
			Top State Trade Analysis.doc

Unit and Location	Project File Supplied	Student Saves File As	Student Creates File
PowerPoint Unit E			
Lessons	PPT E-1.ppt PPT E-2.tif	iMedia5.ppt	
			iMedia Template.pot
Skills Review	PPT E-3.ppt	Book Presentation.pot	
			MediaLoft Template.pot
Independent Challenge 1	PPT E-4.ppt	Premier.ppt	
			Catering 1.pot
Independent Challenge 2	PPT E-5.ppt	Splat.ppt	
Independent Challenge 3			Games.ppt
Independent Challenge 4			Bandwidth.ppt
Visual Workshop			New Products.ppt
PowerPoint Unit F			
Lessons	PPT F-1.ppt PPT F-2.xls	iMedia 6.ppt	
Skills Review	PPT F-3.ppt PPT F-4.xls	Royal Publishing.ppt	
Independent Challenge 1	PPT F-5.ppt	Larsen Presentation.ppt	
Independent Challenge 2			Teaching Award.ppt
Independent Challenge 3	PPT F-6.xls		LabTech Industries.ppt
Independent Challenge 4			PC Game Review.ppt
Visual Workshop			Central.ppt
PowerPoint Unit G*			

*Because the files created in this unit can be very large, depending on the elements you insert into each presentation, you will need to organize the files onto 7 floppy disks if you are completing all the exercises. Copy the files as outlined above, and label each disk clearly (e.g., PowerPoint Unit G Disk 1).

Unit and Location	Project File Supplied	Student Saves File As	Student Creates File
DISK 1			
Lessons	PPT G-1.ppt PPT G-2.jpg PPT G-3.xls Video Division Budget.xls PPT G-4.wav PPT G-5.doc	Video Division.ppt	
DISK 2			
Skills Review	PPT G-6.ppt PPT G-7.jpg PPT G-8.xls P & L.xls PPT G-9.wav PPT G-10.doc	Marketing 2003.ppt	

Unit and Location	Project File Supplied	Student Saves File As	Student Creates File
DISK 3			
Independent Challenge 1	PPT G-11.ppt	Belize Plant.ppt	
DISK 4			
Independent Challenge 2	PPT G-12.ppt Redding, Inc.ppt	Merger.ppt	
DISK 5			
Independent Challenge 3			Imports.ppt Imports RTF.rtf
DISK 6			
Independent Challenge 4			EduCorp.ppt
DISK 7			
Visual Workshop			New Classes.ppt

PowerPoint Unit H*

*Because the project files used in the lessons are very large, you will need to have access to a hard disk to complete the lessons. The final solution files for the lessons, except for the HTML file and its associated folder, can then be copied onto a floppy disk (Disk 1). The HTML file and its associated folder also can be copied onto a floppy disk (Disk 2). If you complete all of the exercises, you will need to organize these files onto separate floppy disks as well. Copy the files as outlined above, and label each disk clearly (e.g., PowerPoint Unit H Disk 1).

HARD DISK and DISKS 1 and 2

Unit and Location	Project File Supplied	Student Saves File As	Student Creates File
DISK 1			
Lessons	PPT H-1.ppt PPT H-2.ppt PPT H-3.ppt	Video Division Final.ppt	
DISK 2			
			Video Division Action Items.doc Videofnl.htm
DISK 1			
	Video Division Offsite.ppt	Video Division Offsite Packed Version.ppt	
DISK 3			
Skills Review	PPT H-4.ppt PPT H-5.ppt	KC Series Proposal.ppt	
			ML Action.doc kcpropsl.htm KC Series Proposal Packed Version.ppt

Unit and Location	Project File Supplied	Student Saves File As	Student Creates File
DISK 4			
Independent Challenge 1	PPT H-6.ppt PPT H-7.ppt	South Pacific.ppt	
			SP Action Items.doc
Independent Challenge 2	PPT H-8.ppt	WorldWide.ppt	
			wrldweb.htm
Independent Challenge 3			Pacific Report Q1.ppt pacrepq1.htm
Independent Challenge 4			Music Pres.ppt musicweb.htm
Visual Workshop			Sierra Tours.ppt
Integration Unit G			

*Because the files created in this unit are large, you will need to organize the files onto 2 floppy disks if you are completing all the exercises. Copy the files as outlined above, and label each disk clearly (e.g., Integration Unit G Disk 2).

Unit and Location	Project File Supplied	Student Saves File As	Student Creates File
DISK 1			
Lessons	INT G-1.doc INT G-2.doc INT G-3.xls KC Stock List.mdb INT G-4.doc INT G-5.xls	KC Store Evaluation.ppt Letter to VP.doc	
			KC Pres Handouts.doc
DISK 2			
Independent Challenge 1	INT G-6.doc	AllSports Outline.doc	AllSports Magazine.ppt
	INT G-7.doc	AllSports Table.doc	
Independent Challenge 2	INT G-8.xls	H&G Sales.xls	
			H&G Financial Review.ppt
Independent Challenge 3	INT G-9.xls	Census 2000.xls	
			Trade Data.ppt
Publisher Unit A			
Lessons	PB A-1.doc PB A-2.jpg		Picnic.pub
Skills Review	PB A-3.doc		Apartment.pub
Independent Challenge 1	PB A-4.doc		Kittens.pub
Independent Challenge 2	PB A-5.doc		Washington.pub
Independent Challenge 3			Calendar.pub
Independent Challenge 4	PB A-6.doc		London.pub
Visual Workshop			Grand Opening.pub

Publisher Unit B*

*Because the files created in this unit are large, you cannot open and then save the files with a new name to the same floppy disk. You will need to make backup copies of your Project Files before beginning this unit. Because the files created in this unit are large, if you are using floppy disks, you will need to organize the files for this unit onto seven floppy disks if you are using floppies. Copy the files as outlined below, and label each disk clearly (e.g., Publisher Unit B Disk 1).

DISK 1

Unit and Location	Project File Supplied	Student Saves File As	Student Creates File
Lessons	Loftlife.pub PB B-1.doc	Loftlife.pub	

DISK 2

Unit and Location	Project File Supplied	Student Saves File As	Student Creates File
Skills Review	Rental.pub PB B-2.doc	Rental.pub	
Independent Challenge 1	Nova Scotia.pub PB B-3.doc	Nova Scotia.pub	
Independent Challenge 2	Fundraiser.pub PB B-4.doc	Fundraiser.pub	
Independent Challenge 3	PB B-5.doc		Food Recovery.pub
Independent Challenge 4	PB B-6.doc		Inn Brochure.pub City.doc Inn.doc Attractions.doc
Visual Workshop	PB B-7.doc		Play flyer.pub

Publisher Unit C*

*Because the files created in this unit are large, if you are using floppy disks, you will need to organize the files for this unit onto seven floppy disks if you are using floppies. Copy the files as outlined below, and label each disk clearly (e.g., Publisher Unit C Disk 1).

Disk 1

Unit and Location	Project File Supplied	Student Saves File As	Student Creates File
Lessons	PB C-1.jpg PB C-2.doc PB C-3.pub		loftweb.htm loftweb.pub

Disk 2

Unit and Location	Project File Supplied	Student Saves File As	Student Creates File
Skills Review	PB C-4.jpg PB C-5.doc PB C-6.pub		Folder: mediarec recsite.pub recsite.htm Folder: fund fund.htm

Disk 3

Unit and Location	Project File Supplied	Student Saves File As	Student Creates File
Independent Challenge 1	PB C-7.doc		karaoke.pub Folder: karaoke karaoke.htm

Disk 4

Unit and Location	Project File Supplied	Student Saves File As	Student Creates File
Independent Challenge 2	PB C-8.doc		Folder: jasmine jasmine.htm

Disk 5

Independent Challenge 3			myweb.pub folder: mywebpg myweb.htm

Disk 6

Independent Challenge 4			mycause.pub folder: my_cause mycause.htm

Disk 7

Visual Workshop	PB C-9.doc		innsite.pub folder: inn innsite.htm

FrontPage Unit A

Lessons	fpa-1.jpg FP A-2.txt		ml_home.htm
Skills Review	FP A-3.txt		fitness.htm
Independent Challenge 1	fpa-4.jpg FP A-5.txt		baskets.htm
Independent Challenge 2			dinner.htm
Independent Challenge 3			my_page.htm
Independent Challenge 4			my_city.htm
Visual Workshop	FP A-6.txt		redwgn.htm

FrontPage Unit B

Because of the way FrontPage organizes files and webs, in order to complete the lessons and exercises in this unit, you need to have the files organized in separate folders as indicated below.

Lessons

Lesson folder	books.htm cds.htm city.wmf club.htm construc.htm events.htm index.htm logoside.jpg money.wmf skyline.jpg stores.htm		mloftweb

Unit and Location	Project File Supplied	Student Saves File As	Student Creates File
Skills Review			
Skills Review folder	café.htm construc.htm construc.jpg direct.htm index.htm logo.jpg sfevents.htm statue.jpg trolley.wmf		**sfmlweb**
Independent Challenge 1			
IC1 folder	baskets.jpg index.htm ingred.htm orderfrm.htm		**baskets**
Independent Challenge 2			**halfmoon**
Independent Challenge 3			**myweb**
Independent Challenge 4			**mycruise**
Visual Workshop			
Visual Workshop folder	construc.jpg crab.wmf direct.htm entertn.htm index.htm menu.htm reserv.htm		**crabshak**

Microsoft Word 2002 MOUS Certification Core Objectives

Below is a list of the Microsoft Office User Specialist program objectives for the Core Word 2002 skills, showing where each MOUS objective is covered in the Lessons and Practice. This table lists the Core MOUS certification skills covered in the units in this book (Units E-H). The Core skills with page references to Units A-D are covered in *Microsoft Office^xp-Illustrated Introductory*. When used in a sequence, these two books cover all the Core objectives and are approved courseware for preparation for the Word 2002 Core MOUS exam. For more information on which Illustrated titles meet MOUS certification, please see the inside cover of this book.

MOUS Standardized Coding Number	Activity	Lesson page where skill is covered	Location in lesson where skill is covered	Practice
W2002-1	**Inserting and Modifying Text**			
W2002-1-1	Insert, modify and move text and symbols	WORD B-4	Steps 1-8	Skills Review
		WORD B-5	Clues to Use	Independent Challenges 1-4
		WORD B-6	Steps 1-7	Visual Workshop
		WORD B-7	Clues to Use	
		WORD B-8	Steps 1-8	
		WORD B-9	Clues	
		WORD B-10	Steps 1-9	
		WORD B-11	Clues	
		WORD B-14	Steps 1-9	
		WORD B-15	Clues to Use	
		WORD D-12	Steps 2-3	Skills Review
				Independent Challenges 2, 3
W2002-1-2	Apply and modify text formats	WORD C-2	Steps 2-9	Skills Review
		WORD C-3	Clues to Use	Independent Challenges 1-3
		WORD C-4	Steps 1-9	Visual Workshop
		WORD C-5	Clues to Use	
W2002-1-3	Correct spelling and grammar usage	WORD B-12	Steps 1-9	Skills Review
				Independent Challenges 1-4
				Visual Workshop
W2002-1-4	Apply font and text effects	WORD C-4	Steps 1-9	Skills Review
		WORD C-5	Clues to use	Independent Challenges 1-3
		WORD C-16	Clues to Use	Visual Workshop
W2002-1-5	Enter and format Date and Time	WORD D-8	Clues to Use	Skills Review
		WORD D-10	Steps 2-3, Quick Tip Clues to Use	Independent Challenge 3
		WORD D-11		
W2002-1-6	Apply character styles	WORD C-3	Clues to Use	Independent Challenge 3
		WORD C-7	Clues to Use	
W2002-2	**Creating and Modifying Paragraphs**			
W2002-2-1	Modify paragraph formats	WORD C-6	Steps 1-9	Skills Review
		WORD C-7	Clues to Use	Independent Challenges 1-3
		WORD C-8	Steps 1-9	Visual Workshop
		WORD C-9	Clues to Use	
		WORD C-10	Steps 1-9	
		WORD C-12	Steps 1-6, Table	
		WORD C-16	Steps 1-8	
W2002-2-2	Set and modify tabs	WORD C-10	Steps 1-9	Skills Review
				Independent Challenges 1-3

MOUS Standardized Coding Number	Activity	Lesson page where skill is covered	Location in lesson where skill is covered	Practice
W2002-2-3	Apply bullet, outline, and numbering format to paragraphs	WORD C-14 WORD C-15	Steps 1-8 Clues to Use	Skills Review Independent Challenges 1-3
W2002-2-4	Apply paragraph styles	WORD C-7	Clues to Use	Independent Challenge 3
W2002-3	**Formatting Documents**			
W2002-3-1	Create and modify a header and footer	WORD D-10 WORD D-11 WORD D-12	Steps 1-7, Quick Tips Table Steps 1-8 Steps 1-9	Skills Review Independent Challenges 1-4
W2002-3-2	Apply and modify column settings	WORD D-4 WORD D-5 WORD D-6 WORD D-14	Steps 4-5 Clues to Use Clues to Use Steps 1-8, Quick Tip	Skills Review Independent Challenges 1, 2 Visual Workshop
W2002-3-3	Modify document layout and Page Setup options	WORD D-2 WORD D-3 WORD D-4 WORD D-5 WORD D-6 WORD D-7 WORD D-8	Steps 1-6 Clues to Use Steps 1-6, Quick Tip Clues to Use Steps 1-5, Clues to Use Table Steps 1-6, Quick Tip	Skills Review Independent Challenges 1-4 Visual Workshop
W2002-3-4	Create and modify tables	WORD C-11 WORD E-2 WORD E-3 WORD E-4 WORD E-5 WORD E-6 WORD E-10 WORD E-14 WORD E-15 WORD E-16 WORD E-17	Clues to Use Steps 1-8 Clues to Use Steps 1-9 Clues to Use Steps 1-8 Steps 1-9 Steps 1-5 Clues to Use Steps 3-9 Clues to Use	Skills Review Independent Challenges 1-4 Visual Workshop
W2002-3-5	Preview and Print documents, envelopes, and labels	WORD A-12 WORD H-14 WORD H-16 WORD H-17	Steps 1-4, 6-7 Steps 1-6 Steps 1-10 Clues to Use	Skills Review Independent Challenges 1-4 Visual Workshop Skills Review Independent Challenges 1-3 Visual Workshop
W2002-4	**Managing Documents**			
W2002-4-1	Manage files and folders for documents	WORD B-3	Clues to Use	Independent Challenge 2
W2002-4-2	Create documents using templates	WORD B-16	Steps 1-9	Skills Review Independent Challenge 3 Visual Workshop
W2002-4-3	Save documents using different names and file formats	WORD A-10 WORD A-11 WORD B-2 WORD B-3	Steps 1-5 Table Steps 5-6 Clues to Use	Skills Review Independent Challenges 1-4 Visual Workshop Skills Review Independent Challenges 1-4 Visual Workshop

MOUS Standardized Coding Number	Activity	Lesson page where skill is covered	Location in lesson where skill is covered	Practice
W2002-5	**Working with Graphics**			
W2002-5-1	Insert images and graphics	WORD D-16	Steps 1-8	Skills Review Independent Challenges 1, 2 Visual Workshop
		WORD F-2	Steps 1-8	Skills Review
		WORD F-3	Clues to Use	Independent Challenges 1-4
		WORD F-4	Steps 1-6, Table	Visual Workshop
		WORD F-5	Clues to Use	
		WORD F-6	Steps 1-8	
		WORD F-8	Steps 1-10	
		WORD F-10	Steps 1-8	
		WORD F-12	Steps 1-8	
		WORD F-13	Clues to Use	
		WORD F-14	Steps 1-8	
W2002-5-2	Create and modify diagrams and charts	WORD F-16	Steps 1-10	Skills Review
		WORD F-17	Clues to Use	
W2002-6	**Workgroup Collaboration**			
W2002-6-1	Compare and Merge documents	WORD H-2	Details	Skills Review
		WORD H-3	Clues to Use	Independent Challenges 1-3
		WORD H-4	Steps 1-7	Visual Workshop
		WORD H-5	Clues to Use	
		WORD H-6	Steps 1-8	
		WORD H-7	Clues to Use	
		WORD H-8	Steps 1-8	
		WORD H-10	Steps 1-9	
		WORD H-11	Clues to Use	
		WORD H-12	Steps 1-9	
		WORD H-13	Table	
		WORD H-17	Clues to Use	
W2002-6-2	Insert, view, and edit comments	WORD G-14	Clues to Use	Independent Challenge 2
W2002-6-3	Convert documents into web pages	WORD G-2	Steps 7-10	Skills Review
		WORD G-3	Clues to Use	Independent Challenges 1-4
		WORD G-4	Steps 1-10	Visual Workshop
		WORD G-5	Clues to Use	
		WORD G-6	Steps 1-9	
		WORD G-7	Clues to Use	
		WORD G-8	Steps 1-6	
		WORD G-9	Clues to Use	
		WORD G-10	Steps 1-3	
		WORD G-11	Clues to Use	
		WORD G-12	Steps 1-9	
		WORD G-13	Clues to Use	
		WORD G-14	Steps 1-6, Clues to Use	
		WORD G-16	Steps 1-10	
		WORD G-17	Clues to Use	

Microsoft Excel 2002 Core MOUS Certification Objectives

Below is a list of the Microsoft Office User Specialist program objectives for the Core Excel 2002 skills, showing where each MOUS objective is covered in the Lessons and Practice. This table lists the Core MOUS Certification skills covered in the units in this book (Units E-H). The Core skills with page references to Units A-D are covered in *Microsoft Office xp-Illustrated Introductory.* When used in a sequence, these two books cover all the Core objectives and are approved courseware for preparation for the Excel 2002 Core MOUS Exam. For more information on which Illustrated titles meet MOUS certification, please see the inside front cover.

MOUS Standardized Coding Number	Activity	Lesson page where skill is covered	Location in lesson where skill is covered	Practice
Ex2002-1	**Working with Cells and Cell Data**			
Ex2002-1-1	Insert, delete and move cells	EXCEL B-19	Clues to Use	Skills Review
		EXCEL C-6	Step 6	Skills Review, Independent Challenge 4
		EXCEL B-12	Step 7	Skills Review
Ex2002-1-2	Enter and edit cell data including text, numbers, and formulas	EXCEL A-10	Steps 1-7 Step 2 Tip	Skills Review, Independent Challenges 2-4
		EXCEL B-4	Steps 2-9	Skills Review
		EXCEL B-6	Steps 1-6	Skills Review, Independent Challenges 1-4
		EXCEL B-8	Steps 1-5 Clues to Use	Skills Review, Independent Challenges 1-4
		EXCEL B-10	Steps 2-9	Skills Review, Independent Challenge 2
		EXCEL C-2	Steps 2-7	Skills Review, Independent Challenges 1-4
		EXCEL C-3	Clues to Use	Skills Review, Independent Challenges 1-4
		EXCEL E-2	Steps 3-5	Skills Review, Independent Challenges 1, 3, 4
		EXCEL E-8	Steps 1-3	Skills Review, Independent Challenges 1, 3
Ex2002-1-3	Check spelling	EXCEL C-16	Steps 1-5	Skills Review, Independent Challenges 1-4
Ex2002-1-4	Find and replace cell data and formats	EXCEL F-15	Clues to Use	Independent Challenge 2
		EXCEL E-2	Step 2	Skills Review
Ex2002-1-5	Work with a subset of data by filtering lists	EXCEL H-5	Clues to Use	Independent Challenge 4
Ex2002-2	**Managing Workbooks**			
Ex2002-2-1	Manage workbook files and folders	EXCEL A-8	Steps 1-3 Step 4 Tip	Skills Review
Ex2002-2-2	Create workbooks using templates	EXCEL A-9	Clues to Use	Independent Challenge 3
Ex2002-2-3	Save workbooks using different names and file formats	EXCEL A-8	Step 4 Tip	Skills Review
		EXCEL A-8	Steps 4-5	Skills Review, Independent Challenges 1-4
		EXCEL F-16	Steps 1-5; Step 1 Tip	Skills Review, Independent Challenges 3-4

MOUS Standardized Coding Number	Activity	Lesson page where skill is covered	Location in lesson where skill is covered	Practice
Ex2002-3	**Formatting and Printing Worksheets**			
Ex2002-3-1	Apply and modify cell formats	EXCEL C-2	Steps 2-7	Skills Review, Independent Challenges 1-4
		EXCEL C-3	Clues to Use	Skills Review
		EXCEL C-4	Steps 2-5	Skills Review, Independent Challenge 2, Visual Workshop
		EXCEL C-6	Steps 1-7	Skills Review, Independent Challenges 1-4, Visual Workshop
		EXCEL C-12	Steps 1-8	Skills Review, Independent Challenges 1, 4, Visual Workshop
		EXCEL C-14	Steps 2-5	Skills Review, Independent Challenges 1, 2, 4, Visual Workshop
Ex2002-3-2	Modify row and column settings	EXCEL C-10	Steps 1-6	Skills Review, Independent Challenges 1, 2
		EXCEL F-2	Steps 1-6	Skills Review
		EXCEL F-8	Steps 1-4	Skills Review
		EXCEL F-9	Table	Skills Review
Ex2002-3-3	Modify row and column formats	EXCEL C-6	Steps 6-7	Skills Review, Independent Challenges 2-4
		EXCEL C-7	Table	Skills Review
		EXCEL C-8	Steps 1-7	Skills Review, Independent Challenges 1-3
		EXCEL C-9	Clues to Use	Independent Challenge 3
Ex2002-3-4	Apply styles	EXCEL E-4	Step 4	Skills Review, Independent Challenge 2
Ex2002-3-5	Use automated tools to format worksheets	EXCEL C-7	Clues to Use	Independent Challenges 3, 4
Ex2002-3-6	Modify Page Setup options for worksheets	EXCEL C-16	Step 8	Independent Challenge 2
		EXCEL D-16	Step 4	Skills Review
		EXCEL E-16	Intro, Step 5 tip, Step 6	Skills Review, Independent Challenges 1, 3, 4,
		EXCEL E-16	Tip Step 7	Independent Challenge 2
		EXCEL E-17	Clues to Use	Independent Challenge 2
		EXCEL F-5	Clues to Use	Skills Review, Independent Challenges 1-4, Visual Workshop
		EXCEL H-16	Step 2	Independent Challenge 2
		EXCEL H-17	Clues to Use	Independent Challenge 4
Ex2002-3-7	Preview and print worksheets and workbooks	EXCEL H-16	Step 2 Tip	Independent Challenge 2
		EXCEL H-17	Clues to Use	Skills Review, Independent Challenge 2

MOUS Standardized Coding Number	Activity	Lesson page where skill is covered	Location in lesson where skill is covered	Practice
Ex2002-4	**Modifying Workbooks**			
Ex2002-4-1	Insert and delete worksheets	EXCEL F-4	Step 1	Skills Review, Independent Challenge 3
		EXCEL F-4	Step 3	Skills Review, Independent Challenge 2
Ex2002-4-2	Modify worksheet names and positions	EXCEL A-12	Step 7	Skills Review
		EXCEL A-12	Step 3 Tip, 5-6	Skills Review, Independent Challenge 3
Ex2002-4-3	Use 3-D references	EXCEL F-6	Step 3-5	Skills Review, Independent Challenges 1-3
Ex2002-5	**Creating and Revising Formulas**			
Ex2002-5-1	Create and revise formulas	EXCEL B-6	Steps 1-6	Skills Review, Independent Challenges 1, 2, 4, Visual Workshop
		EXCEL B-8	Steps 1-5, Clues to Use	Skills Review, Independent Challenges 1, 2, 4, Visual Workshop
		EXCEL B-10	Steps 4-6	Skills Review, Independent Challenge 2
		EXCEL B-14	All	Skills Review, Independent Challenges 1, 4
		EXCEL B-16	Steps 1-6	Skills Review, Independent Challenges 1, 4, Visual Workshop
		EXCEL B-18	Steps 4-7	Skills Review, Independent Challenges 1, 4, Visual Workshop
		EXCEL E-2	Steps 3-5	Skills Review, Independent Challenges 1,2
		EXCEL E-12	Steps 1-3	Skills Review
Ex2002-5-2	Use statistical, date and time, financial, and logical functions in formulas	EXCEL B-10	Steps 1-4, 6	Independent Challenge 2
		EXCEL B-11	Clues to Use	Skills Review
		EXCEL E-2	Steps 3-5	Skills Review
		EXCEL E-8	Steps 1-2	Skills Review, Independent Challenge 1
		EXCEL E-10	Steps 1-4	Skills Review
		EXCEL E-12	Steps 1-8	Skills Review, Independent Challenge 4
		EXCEL E-14	Steps 1-3	Skills Review, Independent Challenge 3, Visual Workshop
		EXCEL E-15	Clues to Use	Independent Challenge 4
Ex2002-6	**Creating and Modifying Graphics**			
Ex2002-6-1	Create, modify, position and print charts	EXCEL D-4	Steps 2-7	Skills Review, Independent Challenges 1-4
		EXCEL D-6	Steps 3-8	Skills Review, Visual Workshop
		EXCEL D-8	Steps 3-6	Skills Review, Independent Challenges 1-4
		EXCEL D-10	Steps 1-6	Skills Review, Independent Challenges 1-4
		EXCEL D-12	Steps 1-8	Skills Review, Independent Challenges 1, 3
		EXCEL D-14	Steps 1-8	Skills Review, Independent Challenges 2, 3, Visual Workshop
		EXCEL D-16	Steps 2-7	Skills Review, Independent Challenges 1-4, Visual Workshop
		EXCEL D-17	Clues to Use	

MOUS Standardized Coding Number	Activity	Lesson page where skill is covered	Location in lesson where skill is covered	Practice
Ex2002-6-2	Create, modify and position graphics	EXCEL C-5 EXCEL D-14	Clues to Use Steps 1-8	Independent Challenge 3 Skills Review, Independent Challenges 2, 3, Visual Workshop
Ex2002-7	**Workgroup Collaboration**			
Ex2002-7-1	Convert worksheets into Web pages	EXCEL F-16	Steps 1-8	Skills Review, Independent Challenge 4, Visual Workshop
Ex2002-7-2	Create hyperlinks	EXCEL F-14 EXCEL F-14	Steps 3-7 Clues to Use	Skills Review, Independent Challenges 3, 4, Visual Workshop Skills Review, Independent Challenge 3
Ex2002-7-3	View and edit comments	EXCEL C-11 EXCEL F-17	Clues to Use Clues to Use	Skills Review Skills Review

Microsoft Access 2002 MOUS Certification Core Objectives

Below is a list of the Microsoft Office User Specialist program objectives for the Core Access 2002 skills, showing where each MOUS objective is covered in the Lessons and Practice. This table lists the Core MOUS Certification skills covered in the units in this book (Units E-H). The Core skills with page references to Units A-D are covered in *Microsoft Office*^{xp}*-Illustrated Introductory*. When used in a sequence, these two books cover all the Core objectives and are approved courseware for preparation for the Access 2002 Core MOUS Exam. For more information on which Illustrated titles meet MOUS certification, please see the inside cover of this book.

MOUS Standardized Coding Number	Activity	Lesson page where skill is covered	Location in lesson where skill is covered	Practice
AC2002-1	**Creating and Using Databases**			
AC2002-1-1	Create Access databases	ACCESS B-4	Steps 1-2	Skills Review
				Independent Challenges 1, 3
		ACCESS H-2	Steps 1-6	Skills Review
AC2002-1-2	Open database objects in multiple views	ACCESS A-4	Table A-2	Skills Review
		ACCESS A-10	Step 1	Independent Challenges 2, 3
		ACCESS A-16	Step 1	Visual Workshop
		ACCESS B-6	Step 7	Units B, C, D, F:
		ACCESS B-16	Steps 5, 7	Skills Review
		ACCESS C-6	Steps 1, 7	Independent Challenges 1, 2, 3
		ACCESS D-6	Steps 1, 7	Visual Workshop
		ACCESS F-4	Step 6	
		ACCESS F-16	Steps 2, 7	
		ACCESS H-12	Step 4	Skills Review
				Independent Challenges 1, 2, 3, 4
				Visual Workshop
AC2002-1-3	Move among records	ACCESS A-10	Steps 1-6	Skills Review
		ACCESS A-11	Table A-4	Independent Challenges 2, 3
				Visual Workshop
		ACCESS C-4	Steps 5-6	Skills Review
		ACCESS C-12	Steps 5-7	Independent Challenges 1, 2, 3, 4
AC2002-1-4	Format datasheets	ACCESS B-8	Steps 3-5	Skills Review
				Independent Challenges 2, 3
AC2002-2	**Creating and Modifying Tables**			
AC2002-2-1	Create and modify tables	ACCESS B-2	Clues to Use	Skills Review
		ACCESS B-3	Table B-1	Independent Challenges 1, 3
		ACCESS B-4	Steps 3-7	
		ACCESS B-6	Steps 1-6	
		ACCESS B-7	Clues to Use	
		ACCESS E-6	Steps 2-7	Skills Review
				Independent Challenge 1
				Visual Workshop
AC2002-2-2	Add a pre-defined input mask to a field	ACCESS E-8	Step 5	Skills Review
		ACCESS E-12	Step 5	
AC2002-2-3	Create Lookup fields	ACCESS E-4	Detail 5	Skills Review
		ACCESS E-5	Table E-2	
		ACCESS E-18	Steps 1-8	

MOUS Standardized Coding Number	Activity	Lesson page where skill is covered	Location in lesson where skill is covered	Practice
AC2002-2-4	Modify field properties	ACCESS B-6 ACCESS B-7	Steps 2-6 Clues to Use	Skills Review Independent Challenge 1, 4
		ACCESS E-6 ACCESS E-8 ACCESS E-9 ACCESS E-10 ACCESS E-11 ACCESS E-12 ACCESS E-13	Steps 2-7 Steps 1-6 Table E-3 Steps 1-4 Table E-4 Steps 1-5 Steps 1-3	Skills Review Independent Challenges 1, 4 Visual Workshop
AC2002-3	**Creating and Modifying Queries**			
AC2002-3-1	Create and modify Select queries	ACCESS B-16 ACCESS B-18	Steps 1-7 Steps 1-8	Skills Review Independent Challenges 2, 3 Visual Workshop
		ACCESS F-2 ACCESS F-4 ACCESS F-6 ACCESS F-7 ACCESS F-8 ACCESS F-9	Steps 2-6 Steps 1-3 Steps 1-5 Table F-1 Steps 1-4 Clues to Use	Skills Review Independent Challenges 1, 2, 3, 4 Visual Workshop
AC2002-3-2	Add calculated fields to Select queries	ACCESS F-10	Steps 2-6	Skills Review
AC2002-4	**Creating and Modifying Forms**			
AC2002-4-1	Create and display forms	ACCESS C-4 ACCESS C-5 ACCESS C-5	Steps 2-4 Table C-2 Clues to Use	Skills Review Independent Challenges 1, 2, 3, 4 Visual Workshop
		ACCESS G-4 ACCESS G-5	Steps 2-6 Table G-1	
AC2002-4-2	Modify form properties	ACCESS C-2 ACCESS C-6 ACCESS C-7 ACCESS C-8 ACCESS C-9 ACCESS C-10 ACCESS C-12 ACCESS C-13 ACCESS C-16	Table C-1 Steps 1-6 Table C-3 Steps 1-6 Table C-4 Steps 1-7 Steps 2-4 Table C-5 Steps 1-5	Skills Review Independent Challenges 1, 2, 3 Visual Workshop
		ACCESS G-8 ACCESS G-10 ACCESS G-12 ACCESS G-14 ACCESS G-15 ACCESS G-16	Steps 1-7 Steps 1-7 Steps 1-8 Steps 1-7 Table G-3 Steps 1-8	Skills Review Independent Challenges 1, 2, 3, 4 Visual Workshop
AC2002-5	**Viewing and Organizing Information**			
AC2002-5-1	Enter, edit, and delete records	ACCESS A-12 ACCESS A-14 ACCESS A-15	Steps 2-5 Steps 1-9 Table A-5	Skills Review Independent Challenge 3 Visual Workshop
		ACCESS B-16	Step 4	Skills Review Independent Challenges 1, 2, 3, 4 Visual Workshop
		ACCESS C-12 ACCESS C-14 ACCESS C-16	Steps 1, 5-7 Steps 1-5 Step 6	Skills Review Independent Challenges 1, 2, 3, 4 Visual Workshop

MOUS Standardized Coding Number	Activity	Lesson page where skill is covered	Location in lesson where skill is covered	Practice
AC2002-5-2	Create queries	ACCESS B-16 ACCESS B-18 ACCESS B-19	Steps 1-8 Steps 1-7 Clues to Use	Skills Review Independent Challenges 2, 3 Visual Workshop
		ACCESS F-2 ACCESS F-4 ACCESS F-6 ACCESS F-7 ACCESS F-8 ACCESS F-9 ACCESS F-12 ACCESS F-13 ACCESS F-14	Steps 2-6 Steps 1-3 Steps 1-5 Table F-1 Steps 1-4 Clues to Use Steps 1-6 Table F-4 Steps 1-7	Skills Review Independent Challenges 1, 2, 3, 4 Visual Workshop
AC2002-5-3	Sort records	ACCESS B-11 ACCESS B-12 ACCESS B-13 ACCESS B-18	Table B-2 Steps 1-3 Clues to Use Step 4	Skills Review Independent Challenges 2, 3 Visual Workshop
		ACCESS C-4	Step 5	Skills Review Independent Challenge 2
		ACCESS F-4	Steps 1-3	Skills Review Independent Challenges 1, 2, 3
AC2002-5-4	Filter records	ACCESS B-11 ACCESS B-14 ACCESS B-17	Table B-2 Steps 1-5 Table B-4	Skills Review Independent Challenge 2
		ACCESS C-4 ACCESS C-14	Step 7 Steps 6-8	Skills Review Independent Challenge 3
AC2002-6	**Defining Relationships**			
AC2002-6-1	Create one-to-many relationships	ACCESS E-2 ACCESS E-4 ACCESS E-16	Details 1-3 Details 1-4 Steps 1-5	Skills Review Independent Challenge 1
AC2002-6-2	Enforce referential integrity	ACCESS E-16 ACCESS E-17	Steps 3-4 Clues to Use	Skills Review Independent Challenge 1
AC2002-7	**Producing Reports**			
AC2002-7-1	Create and format reports	ACCESS D-3 ACCESS D-4 ACCESS D-14 ACCESS D-15 ACCESS D-16	Table D-1 Steps 2-6 Steps 1-6 Table D-3 Steps 1-7	Skills Review Independent Challenges 1, 2, 3, 4 Visual Workshop
		ACCESS H-6 ACCESS H-8 ACCESS H-10	Steps 1-8 Steps 1-7 Steps 1-8	Skills Review Independent Challenges 1, 2 Visual Workshop
AC2002-7-2	Add calculated controls to reports	ACCESS D-6 ACCESS D-10	Steps 4-6 Steps 1-3	Skills Review Independent Challenge 2 Visual Workshop
AC2002-7-3	Preview and print reports	ACCESS D-8 ACCESS D-14	Steps 3-5 Steps 6-7	Skills Review Independent Challenges 1, 2, 3, 4 Visual Workshop
AC2002-8	**Integrating with Other Applications**			
AC2002-8-1	Import data to Access	ACCESS H-4 ACCESS H-5	Steps 1-6 Table H-1	Skills Review
AC2002-8-2	Export data from Access	ACCESS H-14 ACCESS H-15	Steps 1, 5 Table H-2	Skills Review
AC2002-8-3	Create a simple data access page	ACCESS H-12	Steps 1-6	Skills Review Independent Challenge 3

Microsoft PowerPoint 2002
MOUS Certification Objectives

Below is a list of the Microsoft Office User Specialist program objectives for the Comprehensive PowerPoint 2002 skills, showing where each MOUS objective is covered in the Lessons and Practice. Units E-H are covered in this book, and Units A-D are included in *Microsoft Office*^{xp}*-Illustrated Introductory*. When used in a sequence, these two titles cover all the Certification Objectives for the PowerPoint 2002 Comprehensive MOUS exam. For more information on which Illustrated titles meet MOUS certification, please see the inside cover of this book.

MOUS Standardized Coding Number	Activity	Lesson page where skill is covered	Location in lesson where skill is covered	Practice
PP2002-1	**Creating Presentations**			
PP2002-1-1	Create presentations (manually and using automated tools)	POWERPOINT A-8	Steps 1-9	Skills Review Independent Challenges 2, 3 Visual Workshop
		POWERPOINT B-3	Clues to Use	Skills Review
		POWERPOINT B-4	Steps 1-10	Independent Challenges 1-4
		POWERPOINT B-12	Steps 1-5 QuickTip Step 2	Visual Workshop
		POWERPOINT B-13	Clues to Use	
		POWERPOINT E-16	Steps 4-8	Skills Review Independent Challenge 1
PP2002-1-2	Add slides to and delete slides from presentations	POWERPOINT B-6	Steps 1-3	Skills Review
		POWERPOINT B-8	Steps 2-6	Independent Challenges 1-4 Visual Workshop
		POWERPOINT C-14	Step 6	Skills Review Independent Challenges 2-4
		POWERPOINT E-16	Step 7	Skills Review Independent Challenge 1
PP2002-1-3	Modify headers and footers in the Slide Master	POWERPOINT B-10	Steps 1-9	Skills Review Independent Challenges 1-4 Visual Workshop
		POWERPOINT E-2	Step 4 and bulleted list	
PP2002-2	**Inserting and Modifying Text**			
PP2002-2-1	Import text from Word	POWERPOINT C-14	Steps 1-3	Skills Review Independent Challenge 2
PP2002-2-2	Insert, format, and modify text	POWERPOINT B-4	Steps 2-9	Skills Review
		POWERPOINT B-6	Steps 4-9	Independent Challenges 1-4
		POWERPOINT B-8	Steps 3-6	Visual Workshop
		POWERPOINT B-14	Steps 1-4	
		POWERPOINT C-10	Steps 2-8	Skills Review
		POWERPOINT C-12	Steps 1-10	Independent Challenges 2-4 Visual Workshop

MOUS Standardized Coding Number	Activity	Lesson page where skill is covered	Location in lesson where skill is covered	Practice
PP2002-3	**Inserting and Modifying Visual Elements**			
PP2002-3-1	Add tables, charts, clip art, and bitmap images to slides	POWERPOINT D-2	Steps 3-5 Clues to Use	Skills Review Independent Challenges 1-4 Visual Workshop
		POWERPOINT D-4	Steps 1-9 Clues to Use	
		POWERPOINT D-6	Steps 2-3	
		POWERPOINT D-12	Steps 1-4	
		POWERPOINT G-2	Step 2-7	Skills Review
PP2002-3-2	Customize slide backgrounds	POWERPOINT C-16	Steps 1-8	Skills Review Independent Challenges 2-4
		POWERPOINT D-4	Steps 2-3 Clues to Use	Skills Review Independent Challenge 2
		POWERPOINT E-16	Steps 2-3	
PP2002-3-3	Add OfficeArt elements to slides	POWERPOINT C-4	Steps 4-8	Skills Review
		POWERPOINT C-6	Steps 1-9	Independent Challenges 2-4 Visual Workshop
		POWERPOINT E-10	Steps 1-9 Clues to Use	Skills Review Independent Challenges 1-4
		POWERPOINT E-12	Steps 1-8	Visual Workshop
		POWERPOINT F-10	Steps 6-8	Skills Review
		POWERPOINT F-14	Steps 2-10	Independent Challenges 1, 3, 4
		POWERPOINT F-16	Steps 1-8	Visual Workshop
PP2002-3-4	Apply custom formats to tables	POWERPOINT D-12	Steps 5-9	Skills Review Independent Challenges 1, 3, 4
		POWERPOINT G-4	Steps 3-8	Skills Review Independent Challenges 1-4 Visual Workshop
PP2002-4	**Modifying Presentation Formats**			
PP2002-4-1	Apply formats to presentations	POWERPOINT B-6	Steps 2-3	Skills Review
		POWERPOINT B-7	Table	Independent Challenge 1-4
		POWERPOINT B-12	Steps 1-5 QuickTip Step 5	Visual Workshop
		POWERPOINT C-4	Steps 2-3	Skills Review Independent Challenges 2, 4
		POWERPOINT D-4	Step 3-4	Skills Review
		POWERPOINT D-6	Steps 1-2	Independent Challenges 1-4
		POWERPOINT E-2	Step 3-4	Skills Review
		POWERPOINT E-6	Clues to Use	Independent Challenges 1, 4
		POWERPOINT E-8	Steps 2-9	
		POWERPOINT E-13	Clues to Use	
		POWERPOINT E-14	Step 6	
PP2002-4-2	Apply animation schemes	POWERPOINT D-18	Steps 1-7	Skills Review Independent Challenges 1-3
		POWERPOINT F-12	Steps 1-9	Skills Review
PP2002-4-3	Apply slide transitions	POWERPOINT D-16	Steps 1-6	Skills Review Independent Challenges 1-3

MOUS Standardized Coding Number	Activity	Lesson page where skill is covered	Location in lesson where skill is covered	Practice
PP2002-4-4	Customize slide formats	POWERPOINT B-6 POWERPOINT B-7 POWERPOINT B-12	Steps 2-3 Table Steps 1-5	Skills Review Independent Challenges 1-4 Visual Workshop
		POWERPOINT C-4	Steps 2-3	Skills Review Independent Challenges 2, 4
		POWERPOINT D-4 POWERPOINT D-6	Steps 3-4 Steps 1-2	Skills Review Independent Challenges 1-4
		POWERPOINT E-2 POWERPOINT E-4 POWERPOINT E-6 POWERPOINT E-8 POWERPOINT E-13 POWERPOINT E-14	Step 3 Steps 2-7 Clues to Use Steps 2-9 Clues to Use Step 6	Skills Review Independent Challenges 1-4
PP2002-4-5	Customize slide templates	POWERPOINT B-12	Steps 1-5 QuickTip Step 2 Clues to Use	Skills Review Independent Challenge 1 Visual Workshop
		POWERPOINT C-16	Steps 1-8	Skills Review Independent Challenge 2-4
		POWERPOINT E-16	Steps 1-8	Skills Review Independent Challenge 1
PP2002-4-6	Manage a Slide Master	POWERPOINT E-2	Steps 3-4 QuickTip Step 4	Independent Challenge 1
PP2002-4-7	Rehearse timing	POWERPOINT H-12	Steps 1-7	Skills Review Independent Challenge 1, 2, 3
PP2002-4-8	Rearrange slides	POWERPOINT B-8 POWERPOINT B-16	Steps 8-9 Steps 2-3	Skills Review Independent Challenges 1-4
		POWERPOINT H-8	Step 4	Skills Review Independent Challenges 1, 2
PP2002-4-9	Modify slide layout	POWERPOINT B-6 POWERPOINT B-7	Steps 2-3 Table	Skills Review Independent Challenges 1-4 Visual Workshop
		POWERPOINT C-4	Steps 2-3	
		POWERPOINT D-4 POWERPOINT D-6	Steps 3-4 Steps 1-2	Skills Review Independent Challenges 1-4
		POWERPOINT E-6 POWERPOINT E-8 POWERPOINT E-14	Clues to Use Steps 2-9 Step 6	Independent Challenges 1, 4
PP2002-4-10	Add links to a presentation	POWERPOINT G-16	Steps 2-6	Skills Review Independent Challenge 2
PP2002-5	**Printing Presentations**			
PP2002-5-1	Preview and print slides, outlines, handouts, and speaker notes	POWERPOINT A-16	Steps 1-7	Skills Review Independent Challenge 2, 3 Visual Workshop
		POWERPOINT B-11 POWERPOINT B-14	Clues to Use Step 5 QuickTip	Skills Review
		POWERPOINT G-16	Step 8	Skills Review
		POWERPOINT H-4	Step 9	Skills Review

MOUS Standardized Coding Number	Activity	Lesson page where skill is covered	Location in lesson where skill is covered	Practice
PP2002-6	**Working with Data from Other Sources**			
PP2002-6-1	Import Excel charts to slides	POWERPOINT G-6 POWERPOINT G-7 POWERPOINT G-8	Steps 1-9 Clues to Use Steps 1-5 Table Clues to Use	Skills Review Independent Challenges 1-4
PP2002-6-2	Add sound and video to slides	POWERPOINT D-16	Step 5	Independent Challenges 1-3
		POWERPOINT G-12 POWERPOINT G-13 POWERPOINT G-14 POWERPOINT G-15	Steps 2-7 Clues to Use Steps 2-8 Clues to Use	Skills Review Independent Challenges 1, 3
PP2002-6-3	Insert Word tables on slides	POWERPOINT G-4	Steps 3-9	Skills Review Independent Challenges 1-4 Visual Workshop
PP2002-6-4	Export a presentation as an outline	POWERPOINT G-5	Clues to Use	Independent Challenge 3
PP2002-7	**Managing and Delivering Presentations**			
PP2002-7-1	Set up slide shows	POWERPOINT H-6 POWERPOINT H-8	Steps 1-10 Steps 1-8	Skills Review Independent Challenges 1, 2, 4
PP2002-7-2	Deliver presentations	POWERPOINT A-10	Steps 6-7	Skills Review Independent Challenge 2
		POWERPOINT B-16	Steps 1-4 Details	Skills Review Independent Challenges 1-4
		POWERPOINT D-14 POWERPOINT D-16 POWERPOINT D-18	Steps 1-9 Steps 1-6 Steps 1-7	Skills Review Independent Challenges 1-4
		POWERPOINT H-6 POWERPOINT H-8 POWERPOINT H-12	Steps 1-10 Steps 1-8 Steps 1-7 QuickTip Step 7	Skills Review Independent Challenges 1-4
PP2002-7-3	Manage files and folders for presentations	POWERPOINT H-18	Steps 1-2	Skills Review
PP2002-7-4	Work with embedded fonts	POWERPOINT A-13	Clues to Use	Skills Review
		POWERPOINT H-18	Steps 1-9	Skills Review
PP2002-7-5	Publish presentations to the Web	POWERPOINT H-14	Steps 1-2 QuickTip Step 1	Skills Review Independent Challenge 2-4
PP2002-7-6	Use Pack and Go	POWERPOINT H-18	Steps 1-9	Skills Review
PP2002-8	**Workgroup Collaboration**			
PP2002-8-1	Set up a review cycle	POWERPOINT H-2	Steps 2-8 Clues to Use	Skills Review
PP2002-8-2	Review presentation comments	POWERPOINT H-4	Steps 1-7	Skills Review Independent Challenge 1
PP2002-8-3	Schedule and deliver presentation broadcasts	POWERPOINT H-16	Details 1-4	Independent Challenge 3
PP2002-8-4	Publish presentations to the Web	POWERPOINT H-14 POWERPOINT H-16	Steps 1-6 QuickTip Step 1 Details 1-2	Skills Review Independent Challenge 2-4

Office XP

Glossary

3-D references A reference that uses values on other sheets or workbooks, effectively creating another dimension to a workbook.

Absolute link A hyperlink that contains a fixed Web page address.

Absolute reference A cell reference that contains a dollar sign before the column letter and/or row number to indicate the absolute, or fixed, contents of specific cells. For example, the formula $A$1+$B$1 calculates only the sum of these specific cells no matter where the formula is copied in the workbook.

Action button An object on a screen that you click to perform an activity, such as advancing to the next slide.

Active cell A selected cell in a Graph datasheet or an Excel worksheet; the current location of the cell pointer.

ActiveX control A control that follows ActiveX standards.

ActiveX standards Programming standards developed by Microsoft to allow developers to more easily share software components and functionality across multiple applications.

Address See *Cell address.*

Adjustment handle A small yellow diamond that changes the appearance of an object's most prominent feature.

Aggregate function A special function used in a summary query that calculates information about a group of records rather than a new field of information about each record such as Sum, Avg, and Count.

Align To place objects' edges or centers on the same plane.

Alignment Determines whether a paragraph lines up on its left or right edge, or is centered between the two; you can align left, align right, or center text, cell contents, and graphical objects.

Alignment (Access) Commands used in Form or Report Design View to either left-, center-, or right-align a value within its control, or to align the top, bottom, right, or left edge of the control with respect to other controls.

Anchored The state of a floating graphic that will move with a paragraph if the paragraph is moved; an anchor symbol appears with the floating graphic when formatting marks are displayed.

AND criteria Criteria placed in the same row of the query design grid. All criteria on the same row must be true for a record to appear on the resulting datasheet.

AND query A query that contains AND criteria (two or more criteria present on the same row of the query design grid. Both criteria must be true for the record to appear on the resulting datasheet).

Animated GIF File format used to display animations in Web pages.

Animation A graphic such as a .gif (Graphics Interchange Format) file that moves (like a cartoon) when you run the slide show.

Animation scheme A set of predefined visual effects for a slide transition, title text, and bullet text of the slides in a PowerPoint presentation.

Annotate A freehand drawing on the screen made by using the Annotation tool. You can annotate only in Slide Show view.

Application See *Program.*

Area chart A line chart in which each area is given a solid color or pattern to emphasize the relationship between the pieces of charted information.

Argument Information that a function uses to create the final answer. In an expression, multiple arguments are separated by commas. All of the arguments are enclosed in parentheses; for example, =SUM(A1:B1).

Argument ToolTip A yellow box that appears as you build a function; shows function elements, which you can click to display online help for each one.

Arithmetic operator Plus (+), minus (−), multiply (*), divide (/), or exponentiation (^) character used in a mathematical calculation.

Ascending order Lists data alphabetically or sequentially (from A to Z, 0 to 9, or earliest to latest).

Ask a Question box The list box at the right end of the menu bar in which you can type or select questions for the Help system.

Attribute The styling features such as bold, italics, and underlining that can be applied to cell contents.

AutoComplete A feature that automatically completes entries based on other entries in the same column, or suggests text to insert.

AutoContent Wizard A wizard that helps you get a presentation started by supplying a sample outline and a design template.

AutoCorrect A feature that automatically detects and corrects typing errors, minor spelling errors, and capitalization, and inserts certain typographical symbols as you type.

AutoFill A feature that creates a series of text entries or numbers when a range is selected using the fill handle.

AutoFit A feature that automatically adjusts the width of a column to accommodate its widest entry when the boundary to the right of the column selector is double-clicked. Also, a formatting feature that automatically sizes text to fit in a frame.

Autoflow A feature that automatically flows text from one existing empty text frame to the next, asking for confirmation before it flows to the next frame.

AutoFormat (Access) Predefined format that you can apply to a form or report to set the background picture, font, color, and alignment formatting choices.

AutoFormat (Excel) Preset schemes that can be applied to format a range instantly. Excel comes with 16 AutoFormats that include colors, fonts, and numeric formatting.

AutoNumber A field data type in which Access enters a sequential integer for each record added into the datasheet. Numbers cannot be reused even if the record is deleted.

AutoReport A tool used to quickly create a new report based on the selected table or query.

Autoshapes Drawing objects, such as rectangles, ovals, triangles, lines, block arrows, stars, banners, lightning bolts, hearts, and suns, that you create using the tools on the Drawing toolbar.

AutoSum A feature that automatically creates totals using the SUM function when you click the AutoSum button.

AutoText A feature that stores frequently used text and graphics so they can be easily inserted into a document.

Background The area behind the text and graphics on a slide.

Background Layer that appears behind every page in a publication where you put objects such as headers that you want repeated on each page.

Background color The color applied to the background of a cell.

Backup An up-to-date copy of data files.

Bar chart A chart that shows information as a series of horizontal bars.

Bitmap graphic A graphic that is composed of a series of small dots called "pixels."

.bmp The abbreviation for the bitmap graphics file format.

Body text Subpoints or bullet points on a slide under the slide title.

Boilerplate text Text that appears in every version of a merged document.

Bold Formatting applied to text to make it thicker and darker.

Bookmark A hyperlink that takes viewers to another location on the same page.

Border Lines that can be added above, below, or to the sides of paragraphs, text, cells, an area of a worksheet, or a selected object; you can change its color or line style.

Bound control A control used in either a form or report to display data from the underlying record source; also used to edit and enter new data in a form.

Bound image control A bound control used to show OLE data such as a picture on a form or report.

Browser Software such as Microsoft Internet Explorer used to find, download, view, and use Web pages.

Bullet A small graphic symbol, usually a round or square dot, often used to identify items in a list.

Calculated control A control that uses information from existing controls to calculate new data such as subtotals, dates, or page numbers; used in either a form or report.

Calculated field A field created in Query Design View that results from an expression of existing fields, Access functions, and arithmetic operators. For example the entry Profit: [RetailPrice]-[WholesalePrice] in the field cell of the query design grid creates a calculated field called Profit that is the difference between the values in the RetailPrice and WholesalePrice fields.

Calculation A new value that is created by entering an expression in a text box on a form or report.

Calendar control An ActiveX control that shows the current date selected on a small calendar. You can use this control to find or display a date in the past or future.

Cancel button The X in the Formula bar; it removes information from the formula bar and restores the previous cell entry.

Caption A field property used to override the technical field name with an easy-to-read caption entry when the field name appears on datasheets, forms, and reports.

Caption property A field property used to override the technical field name with an easy-to-read caption when the field name appears on datasheets, forms, and reports.

Category axis On a PivotChart, the horizontal axis. Also called the x-axis.

Cell The intersection of a column and row in a worksheet, datasheet, or table.

Cell address The location of a cell expressed by the column and row coordinates; the cell address of the cell in column A, row 1, is A1.

Cell pointer A highlighted rectangle around a cell that indicates the active cell.

Cell reference Identifies a cell's position in a table. Each cell reference contains a letter (A, B, C, and so on) to identify its column and a number (1, 2, 3, and so on) to identify its row. Cell references in worksheets can be used in formulas and are relative or absolute.

Center Alignment in which an item is centered between the margins.

Character spacing Formatting that changes the width or scale of characters, expands or condenses the amount of space between characters, raises or lowers characters relative to the line of text, and adjusts kerning (the space between standard combinations of letters).

Character style A named set of character format settings that can be applied to text to format it all at once.

Chart A graphical representation of information from a datasheet or worksheet. Types include 2-D and 3-D column, bar, pie, area, and line charts.

Chart boxes In Organization Chart, the placeholders for text. The placeholders can contain names and positions in an organization's structure.

Chart Field List A list of the fields in the underlying record source for a PivotChart.

Chart sheet A separate sheet that contains only a chart linked to worksheet data.

Chart title The name assigned to a chart.

Chart Wizard A series of dialog boxes that helps you create or modify a chart.

Check box Bound control used to display "yes" or "no" answers for a field. If the box is "checked" it indicates "yes" information in a form or report.

Child page A page in a web hierarchy that is at a lower level and is linked to a parent page.

Circular reference A formula that refers to its own cell location.

Clear A command on the Edit menu used to erase a cell's contents, formatting, or both.

Click and Type pointer A pointer used to move the insertion point and automatically apply the paragraph formatting necessary to insert text at that location in the document.

Clip art A collection of graphic images that can be inserted into documents, presentations, Web pages, spreadsheets, and other Office files.

Clip art Predesigned graphic images you can insert in any document or presentation to enhance its appearance.

Clipboard A temporary storage area for cut or copied items that are available for pasting. See *Office Clipboard*.

Clipboard task pane A task pane that shows the contents of the Office Clipboard; contains options for copying and pasting items.

Clip Organizer A library of art, pictures, sounds, video clips, and animations that all Office applications share.

Close A command that closes the file so you can no longer work with it, but keeps the program open so that you can continue to work on other files.

Collapse button A button that looks like a "minus sign" to the left of a record displayed in a datasheet that when clicked, collapses the subdatasheet that is displayed.

Color scheme (PowerPoint) The eight coordinated colors that make up a PowerPoint presentation; a color scheme assigns colors for text, lines, objects, and background. You can change the color scheme on any presentation at any time.

Color scheme (Publisher) A named set of five colors that can be applied consistently throughout a publication. There are 66 professionally selected color schemes provided in Publisher.

Column break A break that forces text following the break to begin at the top of the next column.

Column chart The default chart type in Excel, which displays information as a series of vertical columns.

Column heading The gray box containing the letter above the column.

Combo box A bound control used to display a list of possible entries for a field in which you can also type an entry from the keyboard. It is a "combination" of the list box and text box controls.

Command button An unbound control used to provide an easy way to initiate an action or run a macro.

Compacting Rearranging the data and objects on the storage medium so space formerly occupied by deleted objects is eliminated. Compacting a database doesn't change the data, but reduces the overall size of the database.

Comparison operators Characters such as > and < that allow you to find or filter data based on specific criteria.

Complex formula An equation that uses more than one type of arithmetic operator.

Conditional formatting Formatting that is based on specified criteria. For example, a text box may be conditionally formatted to display its value in red if the value is a negative number. Or, a cell's format that is based on the cell's value or the outcome of a formula.

Connected text box A text box whose text flows either from or to another text box.

Consolidate To combine values on multiple worksheets and show the result on another worksheet.

Continued notice A phrase that identifies where the overflow text continues from or continues to.

Control Any element on a form or report such as a label, text box, line, or combo box. Controls can be bound, unbound, or calculated.

Control boxes Gray boxes along the top of a datasheet that contain the row and column identifiers.

Control menu box A box in the upper-left corner of a window used to resize or close a window.

Control Source The most important property of a bound control on a form or report because it determines which field the bound control will display.

Copy To place a copy of an item on the Clipboard without removing it from a document.

Criteria The entry that determines which records are displayed when finding or filtering records in a datasheet or form, or when building a query.

Crop To hide part of a picture or object using the Cropping tool.

Crosstab query A query that presents data in a crosstabular layout (fields are used for both column and row headings), similar to PivotTables in other database and spreadsheet products.

Crosstab Query Wizard A wizard used to create crosstab queries that helps identify which fields will be used for row and column headings, and which fields will be summarized within the datasheet.

Crosstab row A row in the query design grid used to specify the column and row headings and values for the crosstab query.

Currency A field data type used for monetary values.

Current record box *See* specific record box.

Current record symbol A black triangle symbol that appears in the record selector box to the left of the record that has the focus in either a datasheet or a form.

Cut To remove an item from a file and place it on the Clipboard.

Cut and paste To move text or graphics using the Cut and Paste commands.

Data The unique information you enter into the fields of the records.

Data access page *See* page.

Database An organized collection of related information. In Excel, a database is called a list.

Database software Software used to manage data that can be organized into lists of things such as customers, products, vendors, employees, projects, or sales.

Database window The window that includes common elements such as the Access title bar, menu bar, and toolbar.

Database Wizard An Access wizard that creates a sample database file for a general purpose such as inventory control, event tracking, or expenses. The objects created by the Database Wizard can be used and modified.

Data entry area The unlocked portion of a worksheet where users are able to enter and change data.

Data field   A category of information, such as last name, first name, street address, city, or postal code.

Data form   In an Excel list (or database), a dialog box that displays one record at a time.

Data label   Information that identifies the data in a column or row in a datasheet.

Data Marker   A graphical representation of a data point, such as a bar or column.

Data point   Individual piece of data plotted in a chart.

Data record   A complete set of related information for a person or an item, such as a person's name and address.

Data series   A column or row in a datasheet that is converted into a graphic and shown as a chart.

Data series marker   A graphical representation of a data series, such as a bar or column.

Data source   In a mail merge, the file with the unique data for individual people or items.

Data type   A required property for each field that defines the type of data that can be entered in each field. Valid data types include AutoNumber, Text, Number, Currency, Date/Time, OLE Object, and Memo.

Datasheet   The component of a chart that contains the numerical data displayed in a chart.

Datasheet View   A view that lists the records of the object in a datasheet. Table, query, and most form objects have a Datasheet View.

Date function   Access function that returns today's date.

Date/Time   A field data type used for date and time data.

Decimal Places   A field property that determines the number of digits that should be displayed to the right of the decimal point (for Number or Currency fields).

Default Value   A field property that provides a default value, automatically entered for a given field when a new record is created.

Delete   To permanently remove an item from a file.

Descending order   Lists data in reverse alphabetical or sequential order (Z to A, 9 to 0, or latest to earliest).

Design Gallery   A collection of Publisher-designed objects such as logos, calendars, sidebars, Web page components, and other design elements that you can use to enhance your publications.

Design grid   *See* query design grid.

Design Set   A group of sample designs provided by Publisher applied to a broad range of publication types including business cards, letterhead, and fax cover sheets to ensure a consistent and professional look.

Design templates   Predesigned slide designs with formatting and color schemes that you can apply to an open presentation.

Design View   A view in which the structure of the object can be manipulated. Every Access object has a Design View.

Desktop publishing program   A program for creating publications containing text and graphics.

Desktop workspace   The area around the publication page you can use to store text and graphics prior to placing them in a publication.

Destination file   The file into which you paste, link, or embed data from another file.

Destination program   The program used to create the destination file.

Detail   A section of the form or report that contains the controls that are printed for each record in the underlying query or table.

Detail section The section of a form or report that contains the controls that are printed for each record in the underlying query or table.

Dialog box A window that opens when a program needs more information to carry out a command.

Display Control A field property that determines how a Yes/No field appears in Datasheet View and Form View.

Display When A control property that determines whether the control will appear only on the screen, only when printed, or at all times.

Document The electronic file you create using Word.

Document window The workspace in the program window that displays the current document.

Drawing canvas A workspace for creating your own graphics.

Drawing toolbar A toolbar that contains buttons that let you create lines, shapes, and special effects.

Drop area A position on a PivotChart or PivotTable where you can drag and place a field. Drop areas on a PivotTable include the Filter Field, Row Field, Column Field, and Totals or Detail Field. Drop areas on a PivotChart include the Filter Field, Category Field, Series Field, and Data Field.

Drop cap A specially formatted first letter of the first word of a paragraph.

Dummy column/row Blank column or row included at the end of a range that enables a formula to adjust when columns or rows are added or deleted.

Dynamic page breaks In a larger workbook, horizontal or vertical dashed lines that represent the place where pages print separately. They also adjust automatically when you insert or delete rows or columns, or change column widths or row heights.

Dynamic Web page A Web page automatically updated with the latest changes to the database each time it is opened. Web pages created by the page object are dynamic.

Edit A change made to the contents of a cell or worksheet.

Edit mode The mode in which Access assumes you are trying to edit a particular field, so keystrokes such as [Ctrl][End], [Ctrl][Home], [←], and [→] move the insertion point within the field.

Edit record symbol A pencil-like symbol that appears in the record selector box to the left of the record that is currently being edited in either a datasheet or a form.

Electronic spreadsheet A computer program that performs calculations on data and organizes information into worksheets. A worksheet is divided into columns and rows, which form individual cells.

Embed To paste an object into a file while maintaining a connection to the source file; you can edit an embedded object in the destination file by double-clicking it to open the source program.

Embedded object An object that is created in one application and copied to another. Embedded objects remain connected to the original program file in which they were created for easy editing.

Enabled Control property that determines whether the control can have the focus in Form View.

Enter button The check mark in the formula bar used to confirm an entry.

Expand button A button that looks like a "plus sign" to the left of a record displayed in datasheet view that when clicked, will show related records in a subdatasheet.

Exploding pie slice A slice of a pie chart that has been pulled away from the whole pie to add emphasis.

Exporting A process to quickly convert data from access to another file format such as an Excel workbook, a Word document, or a static Web page.

Expression A combination of values, functions, and operators that calculates to a single value. Access expressions start with an equal sign and are placed in a text box in either Form Design View or Report Design View.

External reference indicator The exclamation point (!) used in a formula to indicate that a referenced cell is outside the active sheet.

Field (Access) The smallest piece of information in a database such as the customer's name, city, or phone number.

Field (Excel) In a list (an Excel database), a column that describes a characteristic about records, such as first name or city.

Field (Word) A code that serves as a placeholder for data that changes in a document, such as a page number.

Field list A list of the available fields in the table or query that it represents.

Field name The name of the data field.

Field names (Access) The names given to each field in Table Design or Table Datasheet View.

Field property *See* properties.

Field selector button The button to the left of a field in Table Design View that indicates which field is currently selected.

Field Size A field property that determines the largest number that can be entered in a field (for Number or Currency fields) or the number of characters that can be entered in a field (for Text fields).

File An electronic collection of information that has a unique name, distinguishing it from other files.

File format A file type, such as .wmf or .gif.

Filename The name given to a document when it is saved.

Fill color The cell background color.

Fill Down A command that duplicates the contents of the selected cells in the range selected below the cell pointer.

Fill handle A small square in the lower-right corner of the active cell used to copy cell contents.

Fill Right A command that duplicates the contents of the selected cells in the range selected to the right of the cell pointer.

Filter A program built into the Office suite that converts data from one program into a format that can be read by another program.

Filter (Acess) A temporary view of a subset of records. A filter can be saved as a query object if you wish to apply the same filter later without recreating it.

Filter window A window that appears when you click the Filter By Form button when viewing data in a datasheet or in a form window. The Filter window allows you to define the filter criteria.

Filtering In mail merge, pulls out records that meet specific criteria and includes only those records in the merge.

Find A command used to locate information the user specifies.

Find Duplicates Query Wizard A wizard used to create a query that determines whether a table contains duplicate values in one or more fields.

Find & Replace A command used to find one set of information and replace it with new information.

Find Unmatched Query Wizard A wizard used to create a query that finds records in one table that doesn't have related records in another table.

First line indent A type of indent in which the first line of a paragraph is indented more than the subsequent lines.

Fit (print option) An option that automatically adjusts a preview to display all pages in a report.

Floating graphic A graphic to which a text wrapping style has been applied which makes the graphic independent of text and able to be moved anywhere on a page.

Floating toolbar A toolbar within its own window, not anchored along an edge of the workspace.

Focus The property that indicates which field would be edited if you were to start typing.

Folder A subdivision of a disk that works like a filing system to help you organize files.

Folders View The view in FrontPage that lets you view your Web site at a directory level and organize your folders.

Font The typeface or design of a set of characters (letters, numbers, symbols, and punctuation marks).

Font effects Font formatting that applies special effects to text, such as shadow, outline, small caps, or superscript.

Font scheme A named set of two fonts, a major font and a minor font, that are applied consistently throughout a publication.

Font size The physical size of characters measured in units called points (pts).

Footer Information that prints at the bottom of each printed page; on the screen, a footer is visible only in Print Preview. To add a footer, use the Header and Footer command on the View menu.

Foreground The layer that sits on top of the background layer and consists of the objects that appear on a specific page of a publication.

Foreign key field In a one-to-many relationship between two tables, the foreign key field is the field in the "many" table that links the table to the primary key field in the "one" table.

Form An Access object that provides an easy-to-use data entry screen that generally shows only one record at a time.

Format Field property that controls how information will be displayed and printed.

Format The appearance of text and numbers, including color, font, attributes, borders, and shading. See also *Number format*.

Format Painter A feature used to copy the formatting applied to one set of text or in one cell to another.

Formatting toolbar A toolbar that contains buttons for frequently used formatting commands.

Form control An item in a form that's used for gathering information from a user, such as a text box, list box, command button, or check box.

Form Design toolbar The toolbar that appears when working in Form Design View with buttons that help you modify a form's controls.

Form Design View The view of a form in which you add, delete, and modify the form's properties, sections, and controls.

Form Footer A section that appears at the bottom of screen in Form View for each record, but prints only once at the end of all records when the form is printed.

Form Header A section that appears at the top of the screen in Form View for each record, but prints only once at the top of all records when the form is printed.

Form Wizard An Access wizard that helps you create a form.

Format Painter A feature used to copy the format settings applied to text, cell contents or a control, to other text, cell contents or controls.

Formatting marks Nonprinting characters that appear on-screen to indicate the ends of paragraphs, tabs, and other formatting elements.

Formatting toolbar A toolbar that contains buttons for frequently used formatting commands.

Formula A set of instructions used to perform numeric calculations (adding, multiplying, averaging, etc.).

Formula bar The area below the menu bar and above the Excel workspace where you enter and edit data in a worksheet cell. The formula bar becomes active when you start typing or editing cell data. It includes the Enter button and the Cancel button.

Formula prefix An arithmetic symbol, such as the equal sign (=), used to start a formula.

Frame An object that contains text or graphics and that can be moved or resized.

Frame (FrontPage) A section of a Web page window in which a separate Web page can be displayed.

Freeze To keep columns or rows in place so they remain visible while other parts of the worksheet are viewed.

Function A special, predefined formula that provides a shortcut for a commonly used calculation; for example, AVERAGE.

Function Wizard A feature that provides assistance in entering the arguments for a selected function.

.gif The abbreviation for the graphic interchange format; the standard format for displaying images on Web pages.

Graphic *See* image.

Grid Evenly spaced horizontal and vertical lines that appear on a slide when it is being created but not when it is shown or printed.

Gridlines Horizontal and/or vertical lines within a chart that make the chart easier to read.

Group To combine multiple objects into a single object so you can easily move and resize them as a unit.

Group Footer A section of the report that contains controls that print once at the end of each group of records.

Group Header A section of the report that contains controls that print once at the beginning of each group of records.

Grouping To sort records in a particular order plus provide a section before and after each group of records.

Grouping controls Allows you to identify several controls as a group to quickly and easily apply the same formatting properties to them.

Grouping records In a report, to sort records based on the contents of a field, plus provide a group header section that precedes the group of records as well as a group footer section that follows the group of records.

Gutter Extra margin space left for a binding at the top or left side of a document.

Handles Small circles that appear around a selected object that you can drag to resize or rotate the selected object.

Handout master The master view for printing handouts.

Hanging indent A type of indent in which the second and subsequent lines of a paragraph are indented more than the first.

Hard page break A page break inserted to force the text following the break to begin at the top of the next page.

Header Text or graphics that appears at the top of every page in a document, document section, worksheet, report, or publication.

Help system A utility that gives you immediate access to definitions, steps, explanations, and useful tips.

Hide To make rows, columns, formulas, or sheets invisible to workbook users.

Hide Duplicates Control property that when set to "Yes," hides duplicate values for the same field from record to record in the Detail section.

Highlighting Transparent color that can be applied to text to call attention to it.

Home page The first page that a visitor to a Web site usually sees. The home page usually links to other pages in the Web site, and other pages link back to it.

Horizontal ruler A ruler that appears at the top of the document window in Print Layout, Normal, and Web Layout view.

Host A location where you can store the files for a Web site.

Hover button Specially designed button that is a hyperlink. It contains a text label and the appearance of the text or background has special effects that change when the user moves the pointer over it.

HTML HyperText Markup Language, a set of codes inserted into a text file that browser software such as Internet Explorer can use to determine the way text, hyperlinks, images, and other elements appear on a Web page.

HTML (Hypertext Markup Language) The programming language used to describe how each element of a Web page should appear when viewed with a browser.

HTML pane The pane in the Page View window that displays the underlying HTML code that creates a page in a Web browser; if you are familiar with HTML code, you can edit a page's code directly in this pane.

Hyperlink An object or link (a filename, word, phrase, or graphic) that, when clicked, "jumps to" another location in the current file or opens another PowerPoint presentation, a Word, Excel, or Access file, or an address on the World Wide Web.

Hyperlink (Access) A field data type that stores World Wide Web addresses. A hyperlink can also be a control on a form that when clicked, opens another database object, external file, or external Web page.

Hyperlinks View The view in FrontPage that lets you view a visual map of the hyperlinks in your Web site and edit them.

HyperText Markup Language *See* HTML.

I-beam pointer The Ⅰ pointer, used to move the insertion point and select text.

Image A nontextual piece of information such as a picture, piece of clip art, drawn object, or graph. Because images are graphical (not numbers or letters), they are sometimes referred to as graphical images.

Importing A process to quickly convert data from an external source, such as Excel or another database application, into an Access database.

Indent The space between the edge of a line of text or a paragraph and the margin.

Indent levels Text levels in the master text placeholder. Each level is indented a certain amount from the left margin, and you control their placement by dragging indent markers on the ruler.

Indent markers Small triangles on the horizontal ruler that indicate the indent settings for the selected text.

Indentation The distance between the left and right edges of the text and any adjacent elements.

Inline graphic A graphic that is part of a line of text.

Input Information that produces desired results, or output, in a worksheet.

Input Mask A field property that controls the type of data that can be entered into a field and also provides a visual guide as the data is entered.

Insertion point A blinking vertical line that indicates where entries or edits will appear when you type.

Insertion point The blinking vertical line that appears in the formula bar or in a cell during editing in Excel.

Integration The ability to use data created in one Office program in a file created in another Office program.

Internet A system of connected computers and computer networks located around the world by telephone lines, cables, satellites, and other telecommunications media.

Intranet An internal computer network that is used by a group of people, such as employees in a company's office.

Is Not Null Criterion that finds all records in which any entry has been made in the field.

Is Null Criterion that finds all records in which no entry has been made in the field.

Italic Formatting applied to text to make the characters slanted.

Junction table A table created for the purpose of establishing separate one-to-many relationships to two tables that have a many-to-many relationship.

Justify Alignment in which an item is flush with both the left and right margins.

Keyboard shortcut A combination of keys or a function key that can be pressed to perform a command.

Key field *See* primary key field.

Key field combination Two or more fields that as a group contains unique information for each record.

Key field symbol In Table Design View, the symbol that appears as a miniature key in the field indicator box to the left of the field name. It identifies the field that contains unique information for each record.

Keyword A representative word on which the Help system can search to find information on your area of interest.

Kiosk A freestanding computer used to display information, usually in a public area.

Label Descriptive text or other information that identifies the rows and columns of a worksheet. Labels are not included in calculations.

Label (Acess) An unbound control that displays static text on forms and reports.

Label prefix A character, such as the apostrophe, that identifies an entry as a label and controls the way it appears in the cell.

Label Wizard A report-generation tool that helps you create mailing labels.

Landscape orientation Page orientation in which the page is wider than it is tall.

Layout The general arrangement in which a form will display the fields in the underlying recordset. Layout types include Columnar, Tabular, Datasheet, Chart, and PivotTable. Columnar is most popular for a form, and Datasheet is most popular for a subform.

Layout guides Nonprinting lines that appear in every page of your publication to help you to align text, pictures, and other objects into columns and rows so that your publication will have a consistent look across all pages.

Leading The spacing between lines of text in a text object.

Left-align Alignment in which the item is flush with the left margin.

Left function Access function that returns a specified number of characters starting with the left side of a value in a Text field.

Left indent A type of indent in which the left edge of a paragraph is moved in from the left margin.

Legend A key explaining how information is represented by colors or patterns in a chart.

Len function Access function that returns the count of the number of characters in a given field.

Like operator An Access comparison operator that allows queries to find records that match criteria that include a wildcard character.

Line chart A graph of data that is mapped by a series of lines. Line charts show changes in data or categories of data over time and can be used to document trends.

Line control An unbound control used to draw lines on a form or report that divide it into logical groupings.

Line spacing The amount of space between lines of text.

Link A "live" connection between a source file and its representation in a destination file; when one is updated, the other is updated automatically. Can also refer to a hyperlink (see also *Hyperlink*).

Link bar A set of hyperlinks used for navigating a Web site.

Link Child Fields A subform property that determines which field will serve as the "many" link between the subform and main form.

Link Master Fields A subform property that determines which field will serve as the "one" link between the main form and the subform.

Linked table A table created in another database product or application such as Excel, that is stored outside an Access database, but which can still be used within an Access database.

Linking The dynamic referencing of data in other workbooks, so that when data in the other workbooks is changed, the references in the current workbook are automatically updated.

List The Excel term for a database, an organized collection of related information.

List box A bound control that displays a list of possible choices for the user. Used mainly on forms.

Lock To secure a row, column, or sheet so that data therein cannot be changed.

Locked A control property that specifies whether you can edit data in a control in Form View.

Logical test The first part of an IF function; if the logical test is true, then the second part of the function is applied, and if it is false, then the third part of the function is applied. In the function IF (Balance>1000, Balance*0.05,0), 5% of the balance is calculated if the balance exceeds $1,000.

Lookup A reference table or list of values used to populate the values of a field.

Lookup field A field that has lookup properties. Lookup properties are used to create a drop-down list of values to populate the field.

Lookup Wizard A wizard used in Table Design View that allows one field to "lookup" values from another table or entered list. For example, you might use the Lookup Wizard to specify that the CustomerNumber field in the Sales table display the CustomerName field entry from the Customers table.

Macro A set of instructions, or code, that performs tasks in the order you specify.

Main document In a mail merge, the document into which you are merging the data source.

Main form A form that contains a subform control.

Main text placeholder A reserved box on a slide for the main text points.

Many-to-many relationship The relationship between two tables in an Access database in which one record of one table relates to many records in the other table and vice versa. You cannot directly create a many-to-many relationship between two tables in Access. To relate two tables with such a relationship, you must establish a third table called a junction table that creates separate one-to-many relationships with the two original tables.

Margin The blank area between the edge of the text and the edge of a page.

Marquee A text message that moves across a Web page when displayed in a browser; you determine the direction, speed, behaviors, and repetition of the movement.

Master page The page where you place any object that you want to repeat on every page of a publication.

Master text placeholder The placeholder on the Slide Master that controls the formatting and placement of the Main text placeholder on each slide. If you modify the Master text placeholder, each Main text placeholder is affected in the entire presentation.

Master title placeholder The placeholder on the Slide Master that controls the formatting and placement of the Title placeholder on each slide. If you modify the Master title placeholder, each Title placeholder is affected in the entire presentation.

Master view A specific view in a presentation that stores information about font styles, text placeholders, and color scheme. There are three master views: Slide Master view, Handout Master view, and Notes Master view.

Memo A field data type used for lengthy text such as comments or notes. It can hold up to 64,000 characters of information.

Menu bar A bar beneath the title bar that lists the menus that contain the program's commands.

Merge Combining data from one file with data from another file to create a new file.

Merge cells To combine adjacent cells into a single larger cell.

Merge field A placeholder that you insert in the main document to indicate where the data from each record should be inserted when you perform the merge.

Microsoft Graph The program that creates a datasheet and chart to graphically depict numerical information.

Mirror margins Margins used in documents with facing pages, where the inside and outside margins are mirror images of each other.

Mixed reference A formula containing both a relative and absolute reference.

Mode indicator A box located at the lower-left corner of the status bar that informs you of a program's status. For example, when Excel is performing a task, the word "Wait" appears.

Module (Access) An Access object that stores Visual Basic programming code.

Module (Excel) A program container attached to a workbook that holds a macro.

Mouse pointer A symbol that indicates the current location of the mouse on the desktop. The mouse pointer changes its shape to indicate what you can do next; for example, when you insert data, select a range, position a chart, change the size of a window or a column, or select a topic in Help.

Movie Live action captured in digital format.

Moving border The dashed line that appears around a cell or range that is copied to the Clipboard.

Multitask The ability to open several programs and files at once and then to switch back and forth among them.

Name box The left-most area in the formula bar that shows the cell reference or name of the active cell. For example, A1 refers to cell A1 of the active worksheet. You can also display a list of names in a workbook using the Name list arrow.

Name property Property of a text box that gives the text box a meaningful name.

Named range A range of cells given a meaningful name; it retains its name when moved and can be referenced in a formula.

Navigation bar The bar that provides a set of links to other Web pages that are part of a Web site.

Navigation buttons Buttons in the lower-left corner of a datasheet or form that allow you to quickly navigate between the records in the underlying object as well as add a new record.

Navigation mode A mode in which Access assumes that you are trying to move between the fields and records of the datasheet (rather than edit a specific field's contents), so keystrokes such as [Ctrl][Home] and [Ctrl][End] move you to the first and last field of the datasheet.

Navigation View The view in FrontPage that lets you create and edit the overall structure of your Web site by dragging pictorial representations of each page.

Negative indent A type of indent in which the left edge of a paragraph is moved to the left of the left margin.

New Document task pane A task pane that contains shortcuts for opening documents and for creating new documents.

New Workbook task pane A task pane that lets you quickly open new or existing workbooks.

Normal view (PowerPoint) A presentation view that divides the presentation window into Outline, Slide, and Notes panes.

Normal view (Word) A view that shows a document without margins, headers and footers, or graphics.

Normal pane The pane in Page view window that provides the best workspace to add, delete, and modify Web page elements as you create and edit Web pages, by providing a graphical representation of each element.

Notes master The master view for Notes Page view.

Notes Page view A presentation view that displays a reduced image of the current slide above a large text box where you can type notes.

Notes pane The area in Normal view that shows speaker notes for the current slide; also in Notes Page view, the area below the slide image that contains speaker notes.

Nudge Feature that allows you to move an object one small increment at a time.

Null The state of "nothingness" in a field. Any entry such as 0 in a numeric field or a space in a text field is not null. It is common to search for empty fields by using the Null criteria in a filter or query. Is Not Null criteria finds all records where there is an entry of any kind.

Number A field data type used for numeric information used in calculations, such as quantities.

Number format A format applied to values to express numeric concepts, such as currency, date, and percentage.

Object A chart, graphic image, or other item that can be moved and resized and that contains handles when selected.

Object An item in a document that can be manipulated. Objects are drawn lines and shapes, text, clip art, imported pictures, and embedded objects.

Object (Access) A table, query, form, report, page, macro, or module in Access.

Objects bar In the opening database window, the toolbar that presents the seven Access objects and groups.

Object list box In Form Design view and Report Design view, this box is located on the Formatting (Form/Report) toolbar and displays the name or caption for the currently selected control.

Object Position indicator An indicator on the status bar used to precisely position an object.

Object Size indicator An indicator on the status bar used to accurately gauge the size of an object.

Office Assistant An animated character that appears to offer tips, answer questions, and provide access to the program's Help system.

Office Assistant tip A hint, indicated by the appearance of an onscreen light bulb, about the current action you are performing.

Office Clipboard A temporary storage area shared by all Office programs that can be used to cut, copy and paste multiple items within and between Office programs. The Office Clipboard can hold up to 24 items collected from any Office program. See also *System Clipboard*.

OLE Object A field data type that stores pointers that tie files created in other programs to a record such as pictures, sound clips, or spreadsheets.

One-to-many line The line that appears in the Relationships window that shows which field is duplicated between two tables to serve as the linking field. The one-to-many line displays a "1" next to the field that serves as the "one" side of the relationship and an infinity symbol next to the field that serves as the "many" side of the relationship when referential integrity is specified for the relationship. Also called one-to-many join line.

One-to-many relationship The relationship between two tables in an Access database in which a common field links the tables together. The linking field is called the primary key field in the "one" table of the relationship and the foreign key field in the "many" table of the relationship.

Open A command that retrieves a file and displays it on the screen.

Operators Symbols such as add (+), subtract (−), multiply (*), and divide (/) used in an expression.

Option button A bound control used to display a limited list of mutually exclusive choices for a field such as "female" or "male" for a gender field in a form or report.

Option group A bound control placed on a form that is used to group together several option buttons that provide a limited number of values for a field.

Option Group Wizard An Access wizard that guides the process of developing an option group with option buttons.

Option Value Property for each option button within an option group that identifies what value will be placed in the field when that option button is clicked.

OR criteria Criteria placed on different rows of the query design grid. A record will appear in the resulting datasheet if it is true for any single row.

OR query A query that contains OR criteria (two or more criteria present on different rows in the query design grid). A record will appear on the resulting datasheet if it is true for either criteria.

Order of precedence The order in parts of a formula are calculated: (1) exponents, (2) multiplication and division, and (3) addition and subtraction.

Organization chart A diagram of connected boxes that shows reporting structure in a company or organization.

Orphan record A record in a "many" table that doesn't have a linking field entry in the "one" table. Orphan records can be avoided by using referential integrity.

Outline tab The area in Normal view that displays your presentation text in the form of an outline, without graphics.

Outline view A view that shows the headings of a document organized as an outline.

Output The end result of a worksheet.

Overflow text Text that won't fit in a text frame.

Overtype mode A feature that allows you to overwrite existing text as you type.

Pack and Go Wizard A wizard that lets you package your publication to take to another computer or to a commercial printing service.

Page An Access object that creates Web pages from Access objects as well as provides Web page connectivity features to an Access database. Also called Data Access Page.

Page Design View A view that allows you to modify the structure of a data access page.

Page Footer A section of a form or report that contains controls that print once at the bottom of each page.

Page Header A section of a form or report that contains controls that print once at the top of each page. On the first page of the report, the Page Header section prints below the Report Header section.

Page Navigation buttons The buttons at the bottom of the publication window that are used to jump to a specific page in your publication.

Page View A view that allows you to see how your dynamic Web page will appear when opened in Internet Explorer.

Page View window The area of the FrontPage screen where you create, view and edit your page.

Pane (FrontPage) A feature used in FrontPage that lets you change the way a Web page appears in the Page View window; there are three panes, Normal, HTML, and Preview.

Pane (PowerPoint) A section of the PowerPoint window, such as the Slide or Notes pane.

Panes (Excel) Sections into which you can divide a worksheet when you want to work on separate parts of the worksheet at the same time; one pane freezes, or remains in place, while you scroll in another pane until you see the desired information.

Paragraph spacing The amount of space between paragraphs.

Paragraph style A named set of paragraph and character format settings that can be applied to a paragraph to format it all at once.

Parameter query A query that displays a dialog box prompting you for criteria each time you run it.

Parent/Child relationship (Acess) The relationship between the main form and subform. The main form acts as the parent, displaying the information about the "one" side of a one-to-many relationship between the forms. The subform acts as the "child" displaying as many records as exist in the "many" side of the one-to-many relationship.

Parent page A page that is at a higher level of a Web hierarchy and has pages below it in the hierarchy linked to it.

Paste A command that copies information on the Clipboard to a new location.

Paste Function A series of dialog boxes that helps you build functions; it lists and describes all Excel functions.

Paste Options Button A button that appears after an item is pasted; click its list arrow to select options including keeping source formatting, or matching destination formatting.

Peer page A page that is at an equal level to another in a Web hierarchy, and shares a common parent with that page.

Personal Macro Workbook A place to store commonly used macros that are available to all workbooks.

Photo album A type of presentation that displays photographs.

Picture caption Text that appears next to, above, or below a picture to describe or elaborate on the picture.

Pie chart A circular chart that represents data as slices of a pie. A pie chart is useful for showing the relationship of parts to a whole; pie slices can be extracted for emphasis. See also *Exploding pie slice*.

PivotChart A graphical presentation of the data in a PivotTable.

PivotChart View The view in which you build a PivotChart.

PivotTable An organization of data that groups and summarizes records according to a field that serves as a row heading, and another field that serves as a column heading.

PivotTable View The view in which you build a PivotTable.

Pixel One pixel is the measurement of one picture element on the screen.

Placeholder A dashed line box where you place text or objects.

Placeholder page A Web page that explains that the Web page is incomplete and provides instructions on how to return to the active Web site; allows a Web designer to structure and format a Web site before all Web pages are ready.

Plot area The area inside the horizontal and vertical chart axes.

PMT function Access function that returns the monthly payment for a loan.

Point A unit of measure used for fonts and row height. One inch equals 72 points, or a point is equal to $\frac{1}{72}$ of an inch.

Pointing method Specifying formula cell references by selecting the desired cell with the mouse instead of typing

Office XP

its cell reference; it eliminates typing errors. Also known as Pointing.

Portrait orientation Page orientation in which the page is taller than it is wide.

PowerPoint Viewer A special program designed to run a PowerPoint slide show on any compatible computer that does not have PowerPoint installed.

PowerPoint window A window that contains the running PowerPoint application. The PowerPoint window includes the PowerPoint menus, toolbars, and Presentation window.

Precedence Algebraic rules used to determine the order of calculations in a formula with more than one operator.

Presentation software A software program used to organize and present information.

Presentation window The area where you work and view your presentation. You type text and work with objects in the Presentation window.

Preview pane The pane in the Page View window that opens a FrontPage Web page as it will appear in a Web browser; you cannot make changes to the page in this view.

Primary key field A field that contains unique information for each record. A primary key field cannot contain a null entry.

Primary sort field In a query grid, the left-most field that includes sort criteria. It determines the order in which the records will appear and can be specified "ascending" or "descending."

Print Layout view A view that shows a document as it will look on a printed page.

Print Preview A command you can use to view a file as it will look when printed.

Print title In a list that spans more than one page, the field names that print at the top of every printed page.

Program Task-oriented software (such as Excel or Word) that enables you to perform a certain type of task such as data calculation or word processing.

Program Code Program instructions used to create a macro.

Programs menu The Windows Start menu that lists all available programs on your computer.

Properties Characteristics that further define the field (if field properties), control (if control properties), section (if section properties), or object (if object properties).

Property sheet A window that displays an exhaustive list of properties for the chosen control, section, or object within the Form Design View or Report Design View.

Publication A file created in Publisher.

Publication Gallery A pane that displays thumbnails of Publisher ready-made designs for the selected category in the New Publication task pane.

Publication page A visual representation of your publication that appears in the publication window.

Publication window The area that includes the workspace for the publication page or pages and a desktop workspace for storing text and graphics prior to placing them in your publication.

Publish To post Web pages on an intranet or the Web so people can access them using a Web browser.

Publish Excel data Place a workbook or worksheet on a network or the Web.

Pull quote A quotation from a story that is pulled out and treated like a graphic.

Query An Access object which provides a spreadsheet-like view of the data similar to tables. It may provide the user with a subset of fields and/or records from one or more tables. Queries are created when the user has a "question" about the data in the database.

Query design grid The bottom pane of the Query Design View window in which you specify the fields, sort order, and limiting criteria for the query.

Query Design View The window in which you develop queries by specifying the fields, sort order, and limiting criteria that determine which fields and records are displayed in the resulting datasheet.

Range A selected group of adjacent cells.

Range finder A feature that outlines an equation's arguments in blue and green.

Range format A format applied to a selected range in a worksheet.

Record A group of related fields, such as all demographic information for one customer.

Recordset The value of the Record Source property.

Record selector box The small square to the left of a record in a datasheet that marks the current record or the edit record symbol when the record has the focus or is being edited.

Record Source In a form or report, the property that determines which table or query object contains the fields and records that the form or report will display. It is the most important property of the form or report object. A bound control on a form or report also has a Record Source property. In this case, the Record Source property identifies the field to which the control is bound.

Rectangle control An unbound control used to draw rectangles on the form that divide the other form controls into logical groupings.

Referential integrity Ensures that no orphan records are entered or created in the database by making sure that the "one" side of a linking relationship (CustomerNumber in a Customer table) is entered before that same value can be entered in the "many" side of the relationship (CustomerNumber in a Sales table).

Relational database A database in which more than one table, such as the customer, sales, and inventory tables, can share information. The term "relational database" comes from the fact that the tables are linked or "related" with a common field of information. An Access database is relational.

Relative cell reference A type of cell reference used to indicate a relative position in the worksheet. It allows you to copy and move formulas from one area to another of the same dimensions. Excel automatically changes the column and row numbers to reflect the new position. Also known as Relative reference.

Relative link A hyperlink that gives another Web page's address in relation to the current page.

Replace A command used to find one set of criteria and replace it with new information.

Report An Access object that creates a professional printout of data that may contain such enhancements as headers, footers, and calculations on groups of records.

Report Design View View of a report in which you add, delete, and edit the report's properties, sections, and controls.

Report Footer On a report, a section that contains controls that print once at the end of the last page of the report.

Report Header On a report, a section that contains controls that print once at the top of the first page of the report.

Report Wizard An Access wizard that helps you create a report.

Reports View The view in FrontPage that lets you check information about your Web site such as how many links are broken, which pages are slow to load, and other details.

Required A field property that determines if an entry is required for a field.

Resize bar The bar that separates the upper and lower panes in Query Design View. You drag the resize bar up or down to provide more room for one of the panes.

Reset usage data An option that allows adapted toolbars and menus to be returned to their default settings.

Office XP

Right-align Alignment in which an item is flush with the right margin.

Right function Access function that returns a specified number of characters starting with the right side of a value in a Text field.

Right indent A type of indent in which the right edge of a paragraph is moved in from the right margin.

Rollover effect The font effect that occurs when the user moves the pointer over a link or hover button; used to highlight the user's current position for emphasis.

Rotate handle A green circular handle at the top of a selected object that you can drag to, rotate the selected object upside-down, sideways, or to any angle in between.

Row heading The gray box containing the row number to the left of the row.

Row height The vertical dimension of a cell.

Row selector The small square to the left of a field in Table Design View.

Row Source A field Lookup property that provides values for the drop-down lookup list for that field.

Rulers Vertical and horizontal bars in the publication window marked in inches, centimeters, picas, or points that help you position text and graphics in your publications.

Ruler guides Nonprinting lines that appear on a single page of your publication that help you align text, pictures, and other objects into columns and rows.

Run a macro Test or execute a macro.

Sans-serif font A font that does not have serifs, the small strokes at the ends of the characters. Arial is a sans-serif font.

Save To store a file permanently on a disk or to overwrite the copy of a file that is stored on a disk with the changes made to the file.

Save As Command used to save a file for the first time or to create a new file with a different filename, leaving the original file intact.

Scale To change the size of a graphic to a specific percentage of its original size.

ScreenTip A label that appears on the screen to identify a button or to provide information about a feature.

Scroll To use the scroll bars or arrow keys to display different parts of a file.

Scroll arrows The arrows at the ends of the scroll bars that are clicked to scroll a file one line at a time.

Scroll bars Bars at the right and bottom edges of the window used to view different parts of your file not currently visible in the window.

Scroll box The box in the scroll bars that can be dragged to scroll a document.

Secondary sort field In a query grid, the second field from the left that includes sort criteria. It determines the order in which the records will appear if there is a "tie" on the primary sort field. (For example, the primary sort field might be the State field. If two records both contained the data "IA" in that field, the secondary sort field, which might be the City field, would determine the order of the IA records in the resulting datasheet.)

Section (Acess) A location of a form or report that contains controls. The section in which a control is placed determines where and how often the control prints.

Section (Word) A portion of a document that is separated from the rest of the document by section breaks.

Section break A formatting mark inserted to divide a document into sections.

Select To click or highlight an item in order to perform some action on it.

Selection box A slanted line border that appears around a text object or placeholder, indicating that it is ready to accept text.

Select query The most common type of query that retrieves data from one or more linked tables and displays the results in a datasheet.

Selection handles Small boxes or circles that appear around a selected object that are used for moving and resizing the object.

Series of labels Preprogrammed series, such as days of the week and months of the year. They are formed by typing the first word of the series, then dragging the fill handle to the desired cell.

Serif font A font that has small strokes (called serifs) at the ends of the characters. Times New Roman and Palatino are serif fonts.

Shading A background color or pattern that can be applied to text, tables, or graphics.

Shared border A bar that appears on all the pages in a web that can contain text, graphics, or other hyperlinks to other Web pages.

Sheet A term used for a worksheet.

Sheet tab A description at the bottom of each worksheet that identifies it in a workbook. In an open workbook, move to a worksheet by clicking its sheet tab. Also known as Worksheet tab.

Sheet tab scrolling buttons Buttons that enable you to move among sheets within a workbook.

Shortcut key See *Keyboard shortcut*.

Sidebar Text that is set apart from the major text but in some way relates to that text.

Simple Query Wizard A wizard used to create a select query.

Sizing handles Small squares at each corner of a selected control in Access. Dragging a handle resizes the control. Also known as handles.

Sizing handles Shapes that appear on the sides and corners of a graphic when it is selected.

Slide indicator box A small box that appears when you drag the vertical scroll box in Slide and Notes Page view identifying which slide you are on.

Slide layout This determines how all of the elements on a slide are arranged, including text and content placeholders.

Slide Master A template for all slides in a presentation except the title slides. Text and design elements you place on the slide master appear on every slide of the presentation. See also *Title Master*, *Notes Master*, and *Handout Master*.

Slide-master title pair The title master and the slide master slides in Slide Master view.

Slide pane The area of Normal view that contains the current slide.

Slide Show view A view that shows a presentation as and electronic slide show.

Slide Sorter view A view that displays a thumbnail of all slides in the order in which they appear in your presentation; used to rearrange slides and add special effects.

Slides tab The area in Normal View that displays the slides of your presentation as small thumbnails.

Slide timings The amount of time a slide is visible on the screen during a slide show. You can assign specific slide timings to each slide, or use the PowerPoint Rehearse Timings feature to simulate the amount of time you will need to display each slide in a slide show.

Slide transition The special effect that moves one slide off the screen and the next slide on the screen during a slide show. Each slide can have its own transition effect.

Smart tag A purple dotted line that appears under text that Word identifies as a date, name, address, or place.

Smart Tag Actions button The button that appears when you point to a smart tag.

Soft page break A page break that is inserted automatically at the bottom of a page.

Sort keys Criteria on which a sort, or a reordering of data, is based.

Sorting (Acess) Reordering records in either ascending or descending order based on the values of a particular field.

Sorting (Word) In mail merge, determines the order in which records are merged.

Source file The file from which you copy the data you are going to paste, link, or embed in the destination file.

Source program The program in which a file was created.

Specific record box Part of a box in the lower-left corner in Datasheet view and Form view of the Navigation buttons that indicates the current record number. You can click in the specific record box, then type a record number to quickly move to that record. Also called the current record box or record number box.

Spelling check A command that attempts to match all text in a worksheet with the words in the dictionary.

Spreadsheet control An ActiveX control that provides similar functionality.

Standard toolbar The toolbar containing the buttons that perform some of the most frequently used commands such as saving or printing a file.

Start To open a software program so you can use it.

Static Web page Web pages created by exporting a query or report to HTML from an Access database are static because they never change after they are created.

Status bar (Acess) The bar at the bottom of the Access window that provides informational messages and other status information (such as whether the Num Lock is active or not).

Status bar (Excel) The bar at the bottom of the Excel window that provides information about various keys, commands, and processes.

Status bar (FrontPage) The bar at the bottom of the program window that provides information about the estimated time to download the current page in addition to other information about the current window or view.

Status bar (PowerPoint) The bar at the bottom of the PowerPoint window that contains messages about what you are doing and seeing in PowerPoint, such as the current slide number or a description of a command or button.

Status bar (Publisher) The bar at the bottom of the publication window that indicates the current page, and the position and size of the selected object in a publication.

Status bar (Word) The bar at the bottom of the Word window that shows the vertical position, section, and page number of the insertion point, the total number of pages in a document, and the on/off status of several Word features.

Story A single article that is contained in either one text box or a series of connected text boxes.

Structured query language *See* SQL.

Structured Query Language (SQL) A standard programming language for selecting and manipulating data stored in a relational database.

Style A named collection of character and paragraph formats that are stored together and can be applied to text to format it quickly.

Subdatasheet A datasheet that shows related records in the "many" table. It appears when the user clicks a record's expand button.

Subform A form placed within a form that shows related records from another table or query. A subform generally displays many records at a time in a datasheet arrangement.

Subscript A font effect in which text is formatted in a smaller font size and placed below the line of text.

Subweb A Web site that is nested inside another Web site; subwebs allow you to make changes easily to the properties for the pages within a subweb while leaving the other pages in the Web site with the default properties.

SUM The most frequently used function, this adds columns or rows of cells.

Summary query A query used to calculate and display information about records grouped together.

Superscript A font effect in which text is formatted in a smaller font size and placed above the line of text.

Symbols Special characters that can be inserted into a document using the Symbol command.

Syntax The technical rules that govern a language or program.

System Clipboard A clipboard that stores only the last item cut or copied from a document.

Tab See *Tab stop*.

Tab control An unbound control used to create a three-dimensional aspect to a form so that other controls can be organized and shown in Form View by clicking the "tabs."

Tab leaders Lines that appear in front of tabbed text.

Tab order The sequence in which the controls on the form receive the focus when the user presses [Tab] or [Enter] in Form view.

Tab stop A location on the horizontal ruler that indicates where to align text.

Table Information that appears in columns and rows for quick reference and analysis. Also, a grid made up of rows and columns of cells that you can fill with text and graphics.

Table Datasheet toolbar The toolbar that appears when you are viewing a table's datasheet.

Table Design View The view in which you can add, delete, or modify fields and their associated properties.

Table Wizard An interactive tool used to create a new table from a list of sample tables and sample fields.

Tags HTML codes that describe how the elements of a Web page should appear when viewed with a Web browser.

Target The file that a hyperlink displays when you click it.

Task pane A window that gives you access to commonly used commands, and changes based on the task you are performing.

Tasks View The view in FrontPage that lets you prioritize and keep track of tasks necessary to create and maintain a Web site.

Template A model for a publication that contains formatting specifications for text, fonts, and colors that can be used as a basis for a new publication.

Template A file saved with a special format that lets you open a new file based on an existing file's design and/or content and modify it for your own purposes.

Text (Acess) A field data type that allows text information or combinations of text and numbers such as a street address. By default, it is 50 characters. The maximum length of a text field is 255 characters.

Text anchor The location in a text object that determines the location of the text within the placeholder.

Text annotations Labels added to a chart to draw attention to a particular area.

Text box (Access) A common control used on forms and reports to display data bound to an underlying field. A text box can also show calculated controls such as subtotals and dates.

Text box A container that you can fill with text and graphics.

Text color The color applied to text in a cell or on a chart.

Text flow icon An icon that appears in a text box to indicate whether the text in the text box flows to another text box, or whether it fits in the text box.

Text label   A text box you create using the Text Box button, where the text does not automatically wrap inside the box.

Text placeholder   A box with a dashed-line border and text that you replace with your own text.

Text style   A set of formatting characteristics that you can quickly apply to text on a paragraph-by-paragraph basis.

Theme   A set of complementary design elements that you can apply to Web pages, e-mail messages, and other documents that are viewed on-screen.

Thumbnail   A small image of a slide. Thumbnails are found on the Slides tab and in Slide Sorter view.

Tick marks   Notations of a scale of measure on a chart axis.

Timing   See *slide timings*.

Title   The first line or heading on a slide.

Title bar   The bar at the top of the program window that indicates the program name and the name of the current file.

Title Master   A template for all title slides in a presentation. Text and design elements you place on the Title Master appear on all slides in the presentation that use the title slide layout.

Title placeholder   A box on a slide reserved for the title of a presentation or slide.

Title slide   The first slide in your presentation.

Toggle button   A bound control used to indicate "yes" or "no" answers for a field. If the button is "pressed" it displays "yes" information.

Toggle button   A button that turns a feature on and off.

Toggle key   A key that switches between two options – press once to turn the option on, press again to turn it off.

Toolbar   A bar that contains buttons that you can click to perform commands.

Toolbar Options button   A button you click on a toolbar to view toolbar buttons not currently visible.

Toolbox toolbar   The toolbar that has common controls that you can add to a report or form when working in Report Design View or Form Design View.

Truncate   To shorten the display of cell information because a cell is too wide.

Two-page spread   Pages that will face each other when the publication is printed.

Unbound control   A control that does not change from record to record and exists only to clarify or enhance the appearance of the form, such as labels, lines, and clip art.

Unbound image control   An unbound control that is used to display clip art and that doesn't change as you navigate from record to record on a form or report.

Undo   To reverse a change by using the Undo button or command.

Unvisited link   A hyperlink that has not yet been followed by a particular viewer.

URL (Uniform Resource Locator)   A Web address.

Validation Rule   A field property that helps eliminate unreasonable entries by establishing criteria for an entry before it is accepted into the database.

Validation Text   A field property that determines what message will appear if a user attempts to make a field entry that does not pass the validation rule for that field.

Value axis   Also known as the y-axis in a 2-dimensional chart, this area often contains numerical values that help you interpret the size of chart elements.

Value axis   On a PivotChart, the vertical axis. Also called the y-axis.

Values Numbers, formulas, or functions used in calculations.

Vertical alignment The position of text in a document relative to the top and bottom margins.

Vertical ruler A ruler that appears on the left side of the document window in Print Layout view.

View (Excel) A set of display and/or print settings that you can name and save for access at another time. You can save multiple views of a worksheet.

View (PowerPoint) A way of displaying a presentation, such as Normal view, Notes Page view, Slide Sorter view, and Slide Show view.

View (Word) A way of displaying a document in the document window; each view provides features useful for editing and formatting different types of documents.

View buttons Buttons on the horizontal scroll bar that are used to change views.

View buttons The buttons at the bottom of the Outline tab and the Slides tab that you click to switch among views.

Views bar A bar that contains buttons for displaying the different views of the open FrontPage Web page in the Page view window, such as the navigational structure of a Web site or the hyperlinks associated with a particular page.

Visited link A hyperlink that has been followed by a viewer.

Web A named component of a Web site containing a group of Web pages, graphics, and other files.

Web browser A software program used to access and display Web pages.

Web forms Forms that provide an easy way for a user to submit information via the Web.

Web hierarchy A visual representation of the structure of your Web site.

Web Layout view A view that shows a document as it will look when viewed with a Web browser.

Web page A document that can be stored on a computer called a Web server and viewed on the World Wide Web or on an intranet using a browser.

Web page A file saved in HTML format that can be viewed using a Web browser.

Web publication A group of associated Web pages.

Web server A computer with a permanent connection to the Internet; it runs Web server software and it makes Web pages available to anyone with Web access.

Web site A group of associated Web pages that are linked together with hyperlinks.

What-if analysis A decision-making feature in which data is changed and formulas based on it are automatically recalculated.

Wildcard Character A special symbol you use in defining search criteria. The most common types of wildcards are the question mark (?), which stands for any single character, and the asterisk (*), which represents any group of characters.

Window A rectangular area of the screen where you view and work on the open file.

Wizard An interactive series of dialog boxes that guides you through a task.

.wmf The abbreviation for the Windows metafile file format, which is the format of much clip art.

WordArt A drawing object that contains text formatted with special shapes, patterns, and orientations.

Word processing box A text box you create using the Text Box button, where the text automatically wraps inside the box.

Word processing program A software program that includes tools for entering, editing, and formatting text and graphics.

World Wide Web (WWW) A collection of electronic documents available to people around the world via the Internet, commonly referred to as the Web.

Word wrap A feature that automatically moves the insertion point to the next line as you type.

Workbook A collection of related worksheets contained within a single file.

Worksheet An electronic spreadsheet containing 256 columns by 65,536 rows.

Worksheet menu bar The toolbar at the top of the Excel screen.

Worksheet tab See *Sheet tab*.

Workspace A group of workbooks that can be opened in one step.

World Wide Web (Web) A structure of documents, called pages, connected by hyperlinks over a large computer network called the Internet.

Wrapping The flow of text around an object rather than over it or behind it.

X-axis The horizontal axis in a chart; because it often shows data categories, such as months, it is also called the category axis.

X-axis label A label describing a chart's x-axis.

Y-axis The vertical axis in a chart; because it often shows numerical values in a 2 dimensional chart, it is also called the value axis.

Y-axis label A label describing the y-axis of a chart.

Yes/No A field data type that stores only one of two values, "Yes" or "No."

Zoom A feature that enables you to focus on a larger or smaller part of the worksheet in Print Preview.

Zoom pointers Mouse pointers displayed in Print Preview that allow you to change the zoom magnification of a printout.

Index

Index

embedding
 editing embedded objects, POWERPOINT G-4
 Excel charts. *See* embedding charts
 Excel worksheets. *See* embedding worksheets
 linking versus, POWERPOINT G-9
 opening embedded objects, POWERPOINT G-4
 pictures, POWERPOINT G-2–3
 Word tables into presentations, INTEGRATION G-4–5
embedding charts
 Excel charts in presentations, POWERPOINT G-6–7
 Excel charts into Word documents, INTEGRATION F-6–7
embedding worksheets
 in presentations, INTEGRATION G-4–5
 in slides, POWERPOINT G-7
 in Word documents, INTEGRATION E-4–5
Enabled property, ACCESS G-13
entering. *See also* inserting
 calculated fields, ACCESS F-10, ACCESS F-11
 formulas, EXCEL E-3
 text in Web pages, FRONTPAGE A-10–11
 values, EXCEL E-3
equal to operator (=), EXCEL E-11
Eraser button, WORD E-17
error correction, spelling errors, PUBLISHER A-11
Excel 2002
 analyzing Access data in Excel, INTEGRATION G-8–9
 copying Access datasheets to, INTEGRATION F-4–5
 embedding charts in presentations, POWERPOINT G-6–7
 embedding charts in Word documents, INTEGRATION F-6–7
 embedding worksheets in presentations, INTEGRATION G-4–5
 embedding worksheets in slides, POWERPOINT G-7
 embedding worksheets in Word documents, INTEGRATION E-4–5
 exporting data, ACCESS H-15
 importing data, ACCESS H-5
 importing Excel data into PowerPoint presentations, INTEGRATION G-12–13
 inserting Access data into worksheets, INTEGRATION G-6–7
 inserting Excel data in Word documents, INTEGRATION G-10–11
 inserting hyperlinks to Excel files in Word documents, INTEGRATION E-6–7
 linking charts to Word documents, INTEGRATION E-2–3
 linking worksheets to presentations, POWERPOINT G-8–9
 task reference, OFFICE XP B-7–9
 updating linked worksheets, POWERPOINT G-10–11
 visual workshop, OFFICE XP B-10
exceptions to slide master, POWERPOINT E-6
Exchange, importing data, ACCESS H-5
excluded data, importing data from files into datasheets, POWERPOINT F-2, POWERPOINT F-3
exiting Publisher, PUBLISHER A-18, PUBLISHER A-19
expand button, ACCESS E-16, ACCESS E-17
exponentiation operator (^), ACCESS F-11
exporting data, ACCESS H-14–15
exporting presentations, POWERPOINT G-5
expressions, ACCESS F-10

▶F

field(s)
 adding to query designs, ACCESS F-2
 calculated, ACCESS F-10–11
 Currency, defining, ACCESS E-10–11
 foreign key, ACCESS E-2
 key. *See* key field(s)
 lists. *See* fields in lists
 Lookup, ACCESS E-4, ACCESS E-5, ACCESS E-18, ACCESS E-19
 multiple, sorting queries on, ACCESS F-4–5
 Number, defining, ACCESS E-10–11
 primary key, ACCESS E-2, ACCESS E-4, ACCESS E-5
field properties, ACCESS E-8–9
 validation, ACCESS E-14–15
fields in lists, EXCEL H-2
 multiple, sorting on, EXCEL H-14–15
 names, EXCEL H-4, EXCEL H-5
 single, sorting on, EXCEL H-12–13
Field Size property, Number and Currency fields, ACCESS E-11
file properties in workbooks, changing, EXCEL F-9
filtering lists using AutoFilter, EXCEL H-5
Find and Replace dialog box, EXCEL H-8, EXCEL H-9
Find Duplicates Query Wizard, ACCESS F-15
finding
 records in lists, EXCEL H-8–9
 worksheet data and formats, EXCEL F-15
Find Unmatched Query Wizard, ACCESS F-15
First function, ACCESS F-13
first line indent marker, POWERPOINT E-7
fixed-width text files
 exporting data, ACCESS H-15
 importing data, ACCESS H-5
flipping objects, PUBLISHER B-17
Folders button, Views bar, FRONTPAGE A-5
Folders view, FRONTPAGE B-4, FRONTPAGE B-5
fonts, PUBLISHER A-1
 limiting number, PUBLISHER A-10
 selecting, PUBLISHER A-10, PUBLISHER A-11
font schemes, PUBLISHER A-1
 imported files, PUBLISHER A-8
font size, PUBLISHER A-10
footers, PUBLISHER B-2, PUBLISHER B-12, PUBLISHER B-13
 worksheets, EXCEL F-5
foreground, PUBLISHER B-12
foreign key field, ACCESS E-2
form(s), ACCESS G-1
 ActiveX controls, ACCESS G-16–17
 combo boxes, ACCESS G-10–11
 command buttons, ACCESS G-14–15
 layouts, ACCESS G-4, ACCESS G-5
 linking to subforms, ACCESS G-7
 main, ACCESS G-2
 option groups, ACCESS G-12–13
 relationship to subforms, ACCESS G-2–3
 subforms. *See* subform(s)
 Web. *See* Web forms
format(s)
 custom. *See* custom formats
 finding in worksheets, EXCEL F-15
Format AutoShape dialog box, POWERPOINT E-8, POWERPOINT E-9

Format Cells dialog box, EXCEL F-8, EXCEL F-9
Format Number dialog box, POWERPOINT F-4, POWERPOINT F-5
Format Painter, ACCESS H-10, ACCESS H-11
Format Painter tool, POWERPOINT E-13
Format property
 Date/Time fields, ACCESS E-12
 Text fields, ACCESS E-9
Format Text dialog box, PUBLISHER B-6, PUBLISHER B-7
formatting
 blank tables, WORD E-3
 calculated fields, ACCESS F-10, ACCESS F-11
 charts, POWERPOINT F-5
 columns, PUBLISHER B-4
 conditional, in reports, ACCESS H-6–7
 datasheets, POWERPOINT F-4–5
 organizational charts, POWERPOINT F-16–17
 paragraphs, FRONTPAGE A-14–15
 reports, ACCESS H-10–11
 tables, FRONTPAGE A-11
 text. *See* formatting text
 Web publications, PUBLISHER C-6
formatting text, PUBLISHER A-10–11
 Master views, POWERPOINT E-4–5
 Web pages, FRONTPAGE A-12–13
formatting tool(s), POWERPOINT E-12–13
Formatting toolbar, FRONTPAGE A-4, FRONTPAGE A-5, PUBLISHER A-4, PUBLISHER A-5
Format WordArt dialog box, PUBLISHER B-14, PUBLISHER B-15
form control(s), PUBLISHER C-10–11
Form Control button, PUBLISHER C-7
Form Design View, ActiveX controls, ACCESS G-16, ACCESS G-17
Form Footer section, ACCESS G-14, ACCESS G-15
Form Header section, ACCESS G-14, ACCESS G-15
formula(s), EXCEL E-1, WORD E-12, WORD E-13
 conditional, building with IF function, EXCEL E-10–11
 displaying and printing contents, EXCEL E-16–17
 entering, EXCEL E-3
 hiding/unhiding, EXCEL F-9
 names, EXCEL E-4–5
Formula dialog box, WORD E-12, WORD E-13
Form Wizard, creating subforms, ACCESS G-4–5
frames, PUBLISHER A-8
 autofitting text, PUBLISHER A-10, PUBLISHER A-11
Freeform button, POWERPOINT E-11
freezing columns and rows, EXCEL F-2
FrontPage 2002
 advantages, FRONTPAGE A-2
 starting, FRONTPAGE A-4, FRONTPAGE A-5
functions, ACCESS F-10, EXCEL E-1
 aggregate, ACCESS F-12, ACCESS F-13
 with several operators, EXCEL E-2
 statistical, EXCEL E-12–13
future value, calculating, EXCEL E-15
FV function, EXCEL E-15

▶G

GIF (Graphics Interchange Format) files, inserting, POWERPOINT G-12–13
Graph. *See also* chart(s)
 importing Excel data into PowerPoint presentations, INTEGRATION G-12–13
graphics. *See* images

Index

Index

Index

worksheet(s)
    copying, EXCEL F-4
    deleting from workbooks, EXCEL F-4, EXCEL F-5
    deleting records in lists using, EXCEL H-11
    discussion comments, EXCEL F-17
    embedding. *See* embedding worksheets
    footers, EXCEL F-5
    headers, EXCEL F-5
    hiding/unhiding, EXCEL F-8, EXCEL F-9
    inserting in workbooks, EXCEL F-4, EXCEL F-5
    large, navigating, EXCEL F-14
    multiple, previewing and printing, EXCEL F-4
    multiple, printing, EXCEL H-16
    page breaks and page numbering, EXCEL F-12–13
    printing parts, EXCEL H-16, EXCEL H-17
    protecting areas, EXCEL F-8–9
    rows. *See* worksheet rows
    saving. *See* saving worksheets
worksheet rows
    freezing, EXCEL F-2, EXCEL F-3
    hiding/unhiding, EXCEL F-9
workspaces, EXCEL F-11
World Wide Web (Web), PUBLISHER C-1, PUBLISHER C-3.
    See also Web *entries*
wrapping text around objects, PUBLISHER B-2,
    PUBLISHER B-16–17

▶**X**

XML documents
    exporting data, ACCESS H-15
    importing data, ACCESS H-5

▶**Y**

Yes/No fields, defining, ACCESS E-12

▶**Z**

zeros, EXCEL H-2, EXCEL H-4
Zoom dialog box, ACCESS F-10